Programming and Problem Solving with C++

Programming and Problem Solving with C++

NELL DALE
University of Texas, Austin

CHIP WEEMS
University of Massachusetts, Amherst

MARK HEADINGTON
University of Wisconsin–La Crosse

Jones and Bartlett Publishers

Sudbury, Massachusetts

Boston   London   Singapore

Editorial, Sales, and Customer Service Offices
Jones and Bartlett Publishers
40 Tall Pine Drive
Sudbury, MA 01776
(508) 443-5000
(800) 832-0034
info@jbpub.com
http://www.jbpub.com

Jones and Bartlett Publishers International
Barb House, Barb Mews
London W6 7PA
UK

Trademark Acknowledgments: Turbo C++ and Borland C++ are registered trademarks of Borland International, Inc.

p. 18 (top), Courtesy of IBM; p. 18 (middle left), Courtesy of Hewlett-Packard; p. 18 (middle right), Courtesy of IBM; p. 18 (bottom left), Courtesy of IBM; p. 18 (bottom right), Courtesy of IBM; p. 19 (top left), Courtesy of IBM; p. 19 (top right), Courtesy of IBM; p. 19 (bottom left), Courtesy of Hewlett-Packard; p. 19 (bottom right), Courtesy of IBM; p. 23, Courtesy of Digital Equipment Corporation; p. 24 (top), Courtesy of IBM; p. 24 (bottom left), Courtesy of IBM; p.24 (bottom right), Courtesy of Apple Computer Inc.; p. 25, Courtesy of IBM; p. 26 (top left), Courtesy of IBM; p. 26 (top right), Sun Microsystems, Inc.; p. 26 (bottom), © Thinking Machines Corporation; p. 78, David Libby; p. 146, Courtesy of BASF; p. 198, Topham/The Image Works; p. 330, The Bettmann Archive; p. 406, Culver Pictures; p. 434, Courtesy of Beech Aircraft Corporation; p. 466, Courtesy of U.S. Navy.

Library of Congress Catalog Card Number: 94-74301

ISBN 0-7637-0292-7

Printed in the United States of America

00 99 98 97 96   10 9 8 7 6 5 4 3

To you, and to all of our other students for whom it was begun and without whom it would never have been completed.

   N. D.   C. W.   M. H.

To the memory of my parents, Rog and Anne, who fostered in me a lifelong love of reading and learning.

   M. H.

Programming and Problem Solving with C++ Program Disk

Jones and Bartlett Publishers offers free to students and instructors a program disk with all the complete programs found in *Programming and Problem Solving with C++*. The program disk is available through the Jones and Bartlett World Wide Web site on the Internet.*

Download Instructions

1. Connect to the Jones and Bartlett student diskette home page **(http://www.jbpub.com/disks/)**.

2. Choose *Programming and Problem Solving with C++*.

3. Follow the instructions for downloading and saving the *Programming and Problem Solving with C++* data disk.

4. If you need assistance downloading a Jones and Bartlett student diskette, please send e-mail to help@jbpub.com.

*Downloading the *Programming and Problem Solving with C++* program disk via the Jones and Bartlett home page requires access to the Internet and a World Wide Web browser such as Netscape Navigator or Microsoft Internet Explorer. Instructors at schools without Internet access may call 1-800-832-0034 and request a copy of the program disk. Jones and Bartlett grants adopters of *Programming and Problem Solving with C++* the right to duplicate copies of the program disk or to store the files on any stand-alone computer or network.

PREFACE

C and C++ are seeing explosive growth, not only in industry but also in academia. Many colleges and universities are adopting these languages in the CS1 and CS2 courses. Multitudes of C and C++ books are on the market, but most are written for experienced programmers and concentrate almost exclusively on language features. In contrast, *Programming and Problem Solving with C++* is geared specifically to the first course in computer science fundamentals, with content and organization guided by the ACM recommended curriculum for CS1 (October 1984) and the following knowledge units from the ACM/IEEE Computing Curricula 1991 recommendations for a C101 course: AL1–AL4, AL6, NU1, PL3–PL5, and SE1–SE5.

The Pascal version of this book has been widely accepted as a model for textbooks for the ACM-recommended curriculum for CS1 and the first section of the AP exam in computer science. *Programming and Problem Solving with C++* continues to reflect our view of the future direction of computer science education—more rigor, more theory, greater use of abstraction, and the earlier application of software engineering principles.

Our experience has shown that topics once considered too advanced can be taught in the first course. For example, we address metalanguages explicitly as the formal means of specifying programming language syntax. We introduce Big-O notation early and use it to compare algorithms in later chapters. We present finite state machines as one model for designing certain algorithms. We discuss modular design in terms of abstract steps, concrete steps, functional equivalence, and functional cohesion. Preconditions and postconditions are used in the context of the algorithm walk-through, in the development of testing strategies, and as interface documentation for user-written functions. Loop invariants are used in program code examples to document the semantics of loops. The discussion of function interface design includes encapsulation, control abstraction, and communication complexity. Data abstraction and abstract data types are explained in conjunction with the C++ class mechanism, forming a natural lead-in to object-oriented programming.

In this book, we continue our commitment to presenting the material in a way that is precise yet accessible to the student. The chapters contain many exercises and examples that have been compiled and tested thoroughly. Every chapter concludes with one or more complete case studies. These case studies appear after the chapter discussion, which is interrupted only by short examples.

The Use of C++

Some educators reject the C and C++ languages as too permissive and too conducive to writing cryptic, unreadable programs. Our experience does not support this view, *provided that the use of language features is modeled appropriately.* That C and C++ permit a terse, compact programming style cannot be labeled simply as "good" or "bad." Almost any programming language can be used to write in a style that is too terse and clever to be easily understood. C and C++ may indeed be used in this manner more often than are other languages, but we have found that, with careful instruction in software engineering, students can learn to use these languages to produce clear, readable code. Many of our colleagues who have switched to C++ in the introductory courses—and model a programming style that is straightforward, disciplined, and free of intricate language features—report that students find it no more difficult to learn C++ than Pascal.

Our choice of C++ over C was a very easy one. C++ enforces stronger type checking than C does. C++ all but eliminates the need for preprocessor macros. C++ provides reference types, with the result that parameter passage by reference does not require a premature exposure to pointers as in C. C++ stream I/O is simpler for students to use than the printf and scanf functions. C++ provides linguistic support for data abstraction, information hiding, and object-oriented programming. And, of course, learning the fundamental features of C++ in the first course eliminates a transition from C to C++ in subsequent course work.

It must be emphasized that, although we use C++ as a vehicle for teaching computer science concepts, the book is not a language manual and does not attempt to cover all of C++. One example is our omission of the C++ template mechanism. At the time of this writing, some compiler vendors' implementations of templates were not entirely stable, were not standardized, or were absent. Other language features—operator overloading, default parameters, and mechanisms for advanced forms of inheritance, to name a few—are omitted in an effort not to overwhelm the beginning student with too much too fast.

Object-Oriented Programming

Currently, there are diverse opinions about when to introduce the topic of object-oriented programming (OOP). Some educators advocate an immersion in OOP from the very beginning, whereas others (for whom this book is intended) favor a more heterogeneous approach in which both structured design and object-oriented design are presented as design tools.

Among schools adopting OOP from the start, the literature discloses mixed results. And what some advocates refer to as OOP might more properly be called *OBP*—object-based programming. OBP entails the use of existing, externally supplied C++ classes, *as-is*. Although OBP is useful in allowing the student to construct programs with "interesting" (for example, graphical) objects, true OOP requires much more: design and implementation of abstract data types (ADTs), the analysis and design of inheritance hierarchies, and the use of polymorphism in the form of run-time binding of operations to objects.

The chapter organization of *Programming and Problem Solving with C++* reflects a transitional approach to OOP. Although we provide an early preview of object-oriented design (Chapter 4), we delay a focused discussion until Chapter 16. The sequence of topics in Chapters 1 through 15 mirrors our belief that OOP is best understood after a firm grounding in algorithm design, control abstraction, and data abstraction. As one reviewer of the book manuscript, who was originally critical of the delayed introduction to OOP, stated in a subsequent review, "The logical flow of the chapters is excellent. In the earlier review, I commented on the late introduction to OOP. I now (having nearly completed teaching a CS1 with C++) believe that is a good strategy."

Synopsis

Chapter 1 is designed to create a comfortable rapport between students and the subject. Because many students now enter the introductory course with some prior exposure to computers, Chapter 1 moves rather quickly into meaty topics. It includes a section on problem-solving techniques and applies them immediately in a case study. By the end of Chapter 1, students have a basic knowledge of what computers are, what programming is, and the techniques used in problem solving.

Because Chapter 2 is the student's first look at syntax, we include a section on metalanguages, which describes both BNF and syntax diagrams. Our experience is that students miss many of the subtleties of language syntax when it is presented by the traditional syntax diagrams. More generally, beginners have trouble translating from a metalanguage to programming language constructs when the metalanguage is formulated much differently from the programming language. Thus, Chapter 2 also introduces the syntax template—a metalanguage every bit as rigorous as the syntax diagram but one that closely resembles C++ constructs.

The goal of Chapters 2 and 3 is to bring students to the point where they can design a simple program independently. In fact, students should be able to do so after reading Chapter 2. Because there are so many concepts and rules to learn before even the simplest program may be written, the chapter concludes with a streamlined discussion of program entry, correction, and execution. Students then can reinforce the new concepts by trying them on the computer. Chapter 3 fleshes out the rudiments of C++ with more complex expressions, function calls, and output. Unlike many books that detail *all* of the C++ data types and *all* of the C++ operators at once, these two chapters focus only on the `int`, `float`, and `char` types and the basic arithmetic operators. Details of the other data types and the more elaborate C++ operators are postponed until Chapter 10.

The top-down and object-oriented design methodologies are a major focus of Chapter 4, and the discussion is written with a healthy degree of formalism. This early in the book, the treatment of object-oriented design is necessarily more superficial than that of top-down design. However, students gain the perspective that there are two—not one—design methodologies in widespread use and that each serves a specific purpose. Chapter 4 also covers input and file I/O. The early introduction of files permits the assignment of programming problems that require the use of sample data files.

Students learn to recognize functions in Chapters 1 and 2, and they learn to use standard library functions in Chapter 3. Chapter 4 reinforces the basic concepts of function calls, parameter passing, and function libraries. Chapter 4 also relates functions to the implementation of modular designs and begins the discussion of interface design that is essential to writing proper functions.

Chapter 5 begins with Boolean data, but its main purpose is to introduce the concept of flow of control. Selection, using If-Then and If-Then-Else structures, is used to demonstrate the distinction between physical ordering of statements and logical ordering. We also develop the concept of nested control structures. Chapter 5 concludes with a lengthy Testing and Debugging section that expands on the modular design discussion by introducing preconditions and postconditions. The algorithm walk-through and code walk-through are introduced as means of preventing errors, and the execution trace is used to find errors that made it into the code. We also cover data validation and testing strategies extensively in this section.

Chapter 6 is devoted to looping structures. We introduce all of the structures using the syntax of the While statement. Rather than confuse students with multiple syntactical structures, our approach is to teach the concepts of looping using only the While statement. However, because many instructors have told us that they prefer to show students the syntax for all of C++'s loops at once, the discussion of For and Do-While statements in Chapter 9 can be covered optionally after Chapter 6.

We first introduce students to the basic loop control strategies and common looping operations. We then describe how to design loops using a checklist of seven questions. The checklist leads naturally to a discussion of the loop invariant as a means of validating a loop design. Because of the introduction of preconditions and postconditions in Chapter 5, we can now cover the loop invariant at a higher level. Chapter 6 also introduces the topics of Big-O notation and finite state machines.

By Chapter 7, the students are already comfortable with breaking problems into modules and using library functions, and they are ready to master the complexity of writing their own functions. Chapter 7 focuses on parameter passage by value and covers flow of control in function calls, formal and actual parameters, local variables, and interface design. The last topic includes preconditions and postconditions in the interface documentation, control abstraction, encapsulation, and physical versus conceptual hiding of an implementation. Chapter 8 expands the discussion to include reference parameters, scope and lifetime, stubs and drivers, and more on interface design, including side effects.

Chapter 9 covers the remaining "ice cream and cake" control structures in C++ (Switch, Do-While, and For), along with the Break and Continue statements. We describe the practice of placing a loop invariant as a comment within the loop, and program examples throughout the remainder of the book contain loop invariants as part of the internal documentation. Chapter 9 forms a natural ending point for the first quarter of a two-quarter introductory course sequence.

Chapter 10 begins a transition between the control structures orientation of the first half of the book and the abstract data type orientation of the second half. We examine the built-in simple data types in terms of the set of values that variables or constants of that type can contain and the allowable operations on values of that type. We introduce more C++ operators, and discuss the problems of floating point representation and precision at length. User-defined simple types, user-written header files, and type coercion are among the other topics covered in this chapter.

We introduce the array data type in Chapter 11. Arrays can be a big conceptual hurdle for students: a variable to access another variable? Three case studies and numerous small examples assist students in making the jump successfully. Three typical types of array processing (subarray processing, parallel arrays, and indices with semantic content) and patterns of array access (randomly, sequentially, and as a single object) are covered.

Chapter 12 gives students more experience with array processing and introduces the list, informally, as an abstract data type. Algorithms that are commonly applied to lists are developed and coded as general-purpose C++ functions. We describe strings and string-handling routines. A case study applies several of the functions written in the first part of the chapter to strings to demonstrate the general applicability of the functions. We use Big-O notation to compare the various searching and sorting algorithms developed in the chapter.

Multidimensional arrays are introduced in Chapter 13, and records (structs) are presented in Chapter 14 along with a discussion on how to choose an appropriate data structure. In this discussion, we introduce the concept of data abstraction as a prelude to the material in Chapter 15.

In Chapter 15, we give a precise definition to the notion of an ADT, emphasizing the separation of specification from implementation. The C++ class mechanism is introduced as a programming language representation of an ADT. The concepts of encapsulation, information hiding, and public and private class members are stressed. We describe separate compilation of program files, and students learn the technique of placing a class's declaration and implementation into two separate files: the specification (.h) file and the implementation file.

Chapter 16 extends the concepts of data abstraction and C++ classes to an exploration of object-oriented software development. Object-oriented design, introduced briefly in Chapter 4, is revisited in greater depth. Students learn to distinguish between inheritance and composition relationships during the design phase, and C++ derived classes are used to implement inheritance. This chapter also introduces C++ virtual functions, which support polymorphism in the form of run-time binding of operations to objects.

Chapter 17 examines pointer and reference types. We present pointers as a way of making programs more efficient and of allowing the run-time allocation of program data. The coverage of dynamic data structures continues in Chapter 18, in which linked lists, linked-list algorithms, and alternative representations of linked lists are presented.

Chapter 19 deals with recursion. There is no consensus as to the best place to introduce this subject. We believe that it is better to wait until at least the second semester to cover this topic. However, we have included recursion for those instructors who have requested it. Although Chapter 19 is the last chapter, we divide the examples into two parts: those that require only simple data types and those that require structured data types. Instructors can cover the first part after Chapter 8. The second part contains examples from simple arrays to dynamic linked lists. These examples could be used individually after the appropriate chapter (for example, simple arrays after Chapter 11) or as a unit after Chapter 18.

Additional Features

Goals   Each chapter begins with a list of learning objectives for the student. These goals are reinforced and tested in the end-of-chapter exercises.

Special Sections   Five kinds of features are set off from the main text. Theoretical Foundations sections present material related to the fundamental theory behind various branches of computer science. Software Engineering Tips discuss methods of making programs more reliable, robust, or efficient. Matters of Style address stylistic issues in the coding of programs. Background Information sections explore side issues that enhance the student's general knowledge of computer science. May We Introduce sections contain biographies of computing pioneers such as Blaise Pascal, Ada Lovelace, and Grace Murray Hopper.

Problem-Solving Case Studies   Problem solving is best demonstrated through case studies. In each case study we present a problem and use problem-solving techniques to develop a manual solution. Next, we expand the solution to an algorithm, using structured design and/or object-oriented design, and then we code the algorithm in C++. We show sample test data and output and follow up with a discussion of what is involved in thoroughly testing the program.

Testing and Debugging Following the case studies in each chapter, this section considers in depth the implications of the chapter material with regard to thorough testing of programs. The section concludes with a list of testing and debugging hints.

Quick Checks At the end of each chapter are questions that test the student's recall of major points associated with the chapter goals. Upon reading each question, the student immediately should know the answer, which he or she can then verify by glancing at the answers at the end of the section. The page number on which the concept is discussed appears at the end of each question so that the student can review the material in the event of an incorrect response.

Exam Preparation Exercises These questions help the student prepare for tests. The questions usually have objective answers and are designed to be answerable with a few minutes of work. Answers to selected questions are given in the back of the book, and the remaining questions are answered in the *Instructor's Guide*.

Programming Warm-Up Exercises This section provides the student with experience in writing C++ code fragments or functions. The student can practice the syntactic constructs in each chapter without the burden of writing a complete program. Solutions to selected questions from each chapter appear in the back of the book; the remaining solutions may be found in the *Instructor's Guide*.

Programming Problems These exercises, drawn from a wide range of disciplines, require the student to design solutions and write complete programs.

Case Study Follow-Up These questions require the student to analyze or modify the case studies in the chapter. The exercises afford experience in reading and understanding the documentation and code for existing programs.

Supplements

Instructor's Guide with Test Item File Prepared by the authors, the *Instructor's Guide* features chapter-by-chapter teaching notes, answers to the balance of the exercises, an extensive collection of transparency masters drawn from figures and program code in the text, and a compilation of exam questions. The *Instructor's Guide* is available on request from D. C. Heath.

Computerized Testing Disk Also available on request from the publisher is an electronic version of the exam questions in the *Instructor's Guide*, distributed in both IBM PC and Macintosh formats.

Program Disk Packaged with this book is a 3½-inch disk containing the source code for all the programs in the text.

Acknowledgments

We would like to thank the many individuals who have helped us in the preparation of this text. We are indebted to the members of the faculties of the Computer Science Departments at the University of Texas at Austin, the University of Massachusetts at Amherst, and the University of Wisconsin–La Crosse.

We extend special thanks to Jeff Brumfield for developing the syntax template metalanguage and allowing us to use it in the text.

For their many helpful suggestions, we thank the lecturers, teaching assistants, consultants, and student proctors who run the courses for which this book was written, and the students themselves.

We are grateful to the following people who took the time to review our manuscript: James Abele, Arkansas Tech University; Don Bailes, East Tennessee State University; Lee A. Becker, Worcester Polytechnic Institute; Eric Braude, Boston University; Ken W. Collier, Northern Arizona University; Ed C. Epp, University of Portland; Bill Grosky, Wayne State University; R. James Guild, California Lutheran University; Bob Hale, Deakin University, Australia; Robert Kline, West Chester University; Mark D. LeBlanc, Wheaton College; Tony L. McRae, Collin County Community College; M. Dee Medley, Augusta College; James C. Miller, Bradley University; Ned Okie, Radford University; David Ranum, Luther College; Larry F. Sells, Oklahoma City University; David B. Teague, Western Carolina University; F. Layne Wallace, University of North Florida; William L. Ziegler, State University of New York, Binghamton.

We also thank the many people at D. C. Heath who contributed so much, especially Karen Jolie, Heather Monahan, Andrea Cava, Randall Adams, Dave Serbun, Walter Cunningham, and Andra Stein.

Anyone who has ever written a book—or is related to someone who has—can appreciate the amount of time involved in such a project. To our families—all the Dale clan and the extended Dale family (too numerous to name); to Lisa, Charlie, and Abby; to Anne, Brady, and Kari—thanks for your tremendous support and indulgence.

N. D.
C. W.
M. H.

BRIEF CONTENTS

CONTENTS

Programming and
Problem Solving
with C++

1

Overview of Programming and Problem Solving

GOALS

- To understand what a computer program is.
- To be able to list the basic stages involved in writing a computer program.
- To understand what an algorithm is.
- To learn what a high-level programming language is.
- To be able to describe what a compiler is and what it does.
- To understand the compilation and execution processes.
- To learn the history of the C++ programming language.
- To learn what the major components of a computer are and how they work together.
- To be able to distinguish between hardware and software.
- To be able to choose an appropriate problem-solving method for developing an algorithmic solution to a problem.

Overview of Programming

> **com•put•er** \kəm-'pyüt-ər\ *n. often attrib* (1646): one that computes; *specif:* a programmable electronic device that can store, retrieve, and process data[*]

What a brief definition for something that has, in just a few decades, changed the way of life in industrialized societies! Computers touch all areas of our lives: paying bills, driving cars, using the telephone, shopping. In fact, it would be easier to list those areas of our lives that are *not* affected by computers.

It is sad that a device that does so much good is so often maligned and feared. How many times have you heard someone say, "I'm sorry, our computer fouled things up" or, "I just don't understand computers; they're too complicated for me"? The very fact that you are reading this book, however, means that you are ready to set aside prejudice and learn about computers. But be forewarned: This book is not just about computers in the abstract. This is a text to teach you how to program computers.

What Is Programming?

Much of human behavior and thought is characterized by logical sequences. Since infancy, you have been learning how to act, how to do things. And you have learned to expect certain behavior from other people.

A lot of what you do every day you do automatically. Fortunately, it is not necessary for you to consciously think of every step involved in a process as simple as turning a page by hand:

1. Lift hand.
2. Move hand to right side of book.
3. Grasp top right corner of page.
4. Move hand from right to left until page is positioned so that you can read what is on the other side.
5. Let go of page.

Think how many neurons must fire and how many muscles must respond, all in a certain order or sequence, to move your arm and hand. Yet you do it unconsciously.

---

[*]By permission. From *Merriam-Webster's Collegiate Dictionary,* Tenth Edition © 1994 by Merriam-Webster Inc.

Much of what you do unconsciously you once had to learn. Watch how a baby concentrates on putting one foot before the other while learning to walk. Then watch a group of three-year-olds playing tag.

On a broader scale, mathematics never could have been developed without logical sequences of steps for solving problems and proving theorems. Mass production never would have worked without operations taking place in a certain order. Our whole civilization is based on the order of things and actions.

We create order, both consciously and unconsciously, through a process we call **programming.** This book is concerned with the programming of one of our tools, the **computer.**

Programming   Planning, scheduling, or performing a task or an event.

Computer   A programmable device that can store, retrieve, and process data.

Computer Programming   The process of planning a sequence of steps for a computer to follow.

Just as a concert program lists the actions the players perform, a **computer program** lists the steps the computer performs. From now on, when we use the words *programming* and *program*, we mean *computer programming* and *computer program*.

Computer Program   A list of instructions to be performed by a computer.

The computer allows us to do tasks more efficiently, quickly, and accurately than we could by hand—if we could do them by hand at all. In order to use this powerful tool, we must specify what we want done and the order in which we want it done. We do this through programming.

How Do We Write a Program?

To write a sequence of instructions for a computer to follow, we must go through a two-phase process: *problem solving* and *implementation* (see Figure 1-1).

Problem-Solving Phase

1. *Analysis and Specification.*   Understand (define) the problem and what the solution must do.

2. *General Solution (Algorithm).*   Develop a logical sequence of steps to be used to solve the problem.
3. *Verify.*   Follow the steps exactly to see if the solution really does solve the problem.

Implementation Phase

1. *Concrete Solution (Program).*   Translate the algorithm into a programming language.
2. *Test.*   Have the computer follow the instructions. Then manually check the results. If you find errors, analyze the program and the algorithm to determine the source of the errors, and then make corrections.

Once a program has been written, it enters a third phase: maintenance.

Maintenance Phase

1. *Use.*   Use the program.
2. *Maintain.*   Modify the program to meet changing requirements or to correct any errors that show up in using it.

Each time the program is modified, it is necessary to repeat the problem-solving and implementation phases for those aspects of the program that change. Together, the problem-solving, implementation, and maintenance phases constitute the program's *life cycle.*

A computer is not intelligent. It cannot analyze a problem and come up with a solution. The programmer must analyze the problem, arrive at the solution, and then communicate it to the computer. What's the advantage of using a computer if it can't solve problems? Once we have a solution for a problem and have prepared a version of it for the computer, the computer can repeat the solution very quickly and consistently, again and again. The computer frees people from repetitive and boring tasks.

The programmer begins the programming process by analyzing the problem and developing a general solution called an **algorithm.** Understanding and analyzing a problem take up much more time than Figure 1-1 implies. They are the heart of the programming process.

Algorithm   A step-by-step procedure for solving a problem in a finite amount of time.

If our definitions of a computer program and an algorithm look similar, it is because all programs are implementations of algorithms. A program is simply an algorithm that has been written for a computer.

An algorithm is a verbal or written description of a logical sequence of actions. We use algorithms every day. Recipes, instructions, and directions are all examples of algorithms that are not programs.

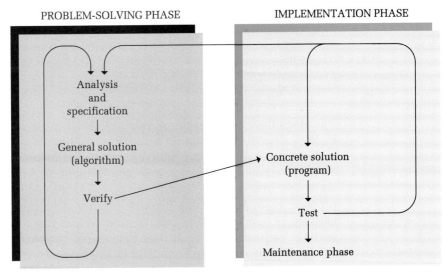

PROBLEM-SOLVING PHASE   IMPLEMENTATION PHASE

When you start your car, you follow a step-by-step procedure. The algorithm might look something like this:

1. Insert the key.
2. Make sure the transmission is in Park (or Neutral).
3. Depress the gas pedal.
4. Turn the key to the start position.
5. If the engine starts within six seconds, release the key to the ignition position.
6. If the engine doesn't start in six seconds, release the key, wait ten seconds, and repeat steps 3 through 6, but not more than five times.
7. If the car doesn't start, call the garage.

Without the phrase "but not more than five times" in step 6, you could be trying to start the car forever. Why? Because if something is wrong with the car, repeating steps 3 through 6 over and over again will not start it. This kind of never-ending situation is called an infinite loop. If we leave the phrase "but not more than five times" out of step 6, the procedure does not fit our definition of an algorithm. An algorithm must terminate in a finite amount of time for all possible conditions.

Suppose a programmer needs an algorithm to determine an employee's weekly wages. The algorithm reflects what would be done by hand:

1. Look up the employee's pay rate.
2. Determine the number of hours worked during the week.
3. If the number of hours worked is less than or equal to 40, multiply the number of hours by the pay rate to calculate regular wages.

4. If the number of hours worked is greater than 40, multiply 40 by the pay rate to calculate regular wages, and then multiply the difference between the number of hours worked and 40 by one and a half times the pay rate to calculate overtime wages.
5. Add the regular wages to the overtime wages (if any) to determine total wages for the week.

The steps the computer follows are often the same steps you would use to do the calculations by hand.

After developing a general solution, the programmer tests the algorithm, "walking through" each step mentally or manually. If the algorithm doesn't work, the programmer repeats the problem-solving process, analyzing the problem again and coming up with another algorithm. Often the second algorithm is just a variation of the first. When the programmer is satisfied with the algorithm, he or she translates it into a **programming language.** We use the C++ programming language in this book.

Programming Language   A set of rules, symbols, and special words used to construct a program.

A programming language is a simplified form of English (with math symbols) that adheres to a strict set of grammatical rules. English is far too complicated a language for today's computers to follow. Programming languages, because they limit vocabulary, are much simpler.

Although a programming language is simple in form, it is not always easy to use. Try giving someone directions to the nearest airport using a vocabulary of no more than 45 words, and you'll begin to see the problem. Programming forces you to write very simple, exact instructions.

Translating an algorithm into a programming language is called *coding* the algorithm. The product of that translation—the program—is tested by running (*executing*) it on the computer. If the program fails to produce the desired results, the programmer must *debug* it—that is, determine what is wrong and then modify the program, or even the algorithm, to fix it. The combination of coding and testing an algorithm is called *implementation*.

There is no single way to implement an algorithm. For example, an algorithm can be translated into more than one programming language. Each translation produces a different implementation. Even when they translate an algorithm into the same programming language, different people are likely to come up with different implementations (see Figure 1-2). Why? Because every programming language allows the programmer some flexibility in how an algorithm is translated. Given this flexibility, people adopt their own *styles* in writing programs, just as they do in writing short stories or es-

One Algorithm Can
Have Many
Different
Implementations

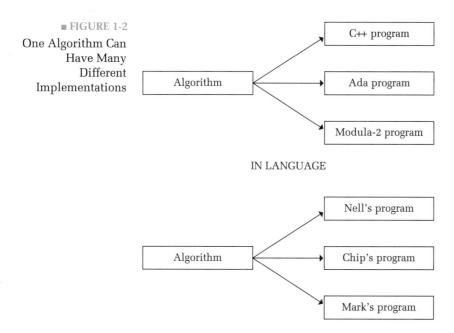

IN LANGUAGE

IN PERSONAL PROGRAMMING STYLE

says. Once you have some programming experience, you develop a style of your own. Throughout this book, we offer tips on good programming style.

Some people try to speed up the programming process by going directly from the problem definition to coding the program (see Figure 1-3). A short-cut here is very tempting and at first seems to save a lot of time. However, for many reasons that will become obvious to you as you read this book, this kind of shortcut actually takes *more* time and effort. Developing a general solution before you write a program helps you manage the problem, keep your thoughts straight, and avoid mistakes. If you don't take the time at the beginning to think out and polish your algorithm, you'll spend a lot of extra time debugging and revising your program. So think first and code later! The sooner you start coding, the longer it takes to write a program that works.

In addition to solving the problem, implementing the algorithm, and maintaining the program, **documentation** is an important part of the programming process. Documentation includes written explanations of the problem being solved and the organization of the solution; comments embedded within the program itself; and user manuals that describe how to use the program. Most programs are worked on by many different people over a long period of time. Each of those people must be able to read and understand your code.

■ FIGURE 1-3

Programming
Shortcut?

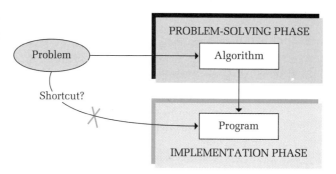

After you write a program, you must give the computer the information or data necessary to solve the problem. **Information** is any knowledge that can be communicated, including abstract ideas and concepts. **Data** are information in a form the computer can use—for example, numbers and letters.

Information   Any knowledge that can be communicated.
Data   Information that has been put into a form a computer can use.

Documentation   The written text and comments that make a program easier for others to understand, use, and modify.

THEORETICAL FOUNDATIONS

Data Representation

In a computer, data are represented electronically by pulses of electricity. Electric circuits, in their simplest form, are either on or off. Usually a circuit that is on is represented by the number 1; a circuit that is off is represented by the number 0. Any kind of data can be represented by combinations of enough 1s and 0s. We simply have to choose which combination represents each piece of data we are using. For example, we could arbitrarily choose the pattern 1101000110 to represent the name *C++*.

Data represented by 1s and 0s is in *binary form*. The binary (base-2) number system uses only 1s and 0s to represent numbers. (The decimal [base-10] number system uses the digits 0 through 9.) The word *bit* (short for <u>bi</u>nary dig<u>it</u>) often is used to refer to a single 1 or 0. So the pattern 1101000110 has 10 bits. A binary number with 10 bits can represent 2^{10} (1024) different patterns. A *byte* is a group of 8 bits; it can represent 2^8 (256) patterns. Inside the computer, each character (such as the letter *A*, the letter *g*, or a question mark) is usually represented by a byte. Four bits, or half of a byte, is called a *nibble* or *nybble*—a name that was originally proposed with tongue in cheek but is now standard terminology. Groups of 16, 32, and 64 bits are generally referred to as *words* (although the terms *short word* and *long word* are sometimes used to refer to 16-bit and 64-bit groups, respectively).

The process of assigning bit patterns to pieces of data is called *coding*—the same name we give to the process of translating an algorithm into a programming language. In the early days of computers, programming meant translating an algorithm into patterns of 1s and 0s because the only language the first computers could work with was binary in form.

Binary coding schemes can be used to represent both the instructions that the computer follows and the data that it uses. For example, 16 bits can represent the decimal integers from 0 to $2^{16} - 1$ (65535). More complicated coding schemes are necessary to represent negative numbers, real numbers, and numbers in scientific notation. Characters also can be represented by bit combinations. In one coding scheme, 01001101 represents *M* and 01101101 represents *m*.

The patterns of bits that represent data and instructions vary from one computer to another. Even on the same computer, different programming languages can use different binary representations for the same data. A single programming language may even use the same pattern of bits to represent different things in different contexts. (People do this too. The four letters that represent the word *tack* have different meanings depending on whether you are talking about upholstery, sailing, sewing, paint, or horseback riding.) The point is that patterns of bits by themselves are meaningless. It is the way in which the patterns are used that gives them their meaning.

Fortunately, we no longer have to work with binary coding schemes. Today the process of coding is usually just a matter of writing down the data in letters, numbers, and symbols. The computer automatically converts these letters, numbers, and symbols into binary form. Still, as you work with computers, you will continually run into numbers that are related to powers of 2—numbers like 256, 32768, and 65536—reminders that the binary number system is lurking somewhere nearby.

 ## What Is a Programming Language?

In the computer, all data, whatever its form, is stored and used in binary codes, strings of 1s and 0s. When computers were first developed, the only programming language available was the primitive instruction set built into each machine—the **machine language,** or *machine code*.

Machine Language   The language, made up of binary-coded instructions, that is used directly by the computer.

Even though most computers perform the same kinds of operations, their designers choose different sets of binary codes for each instruction. So the machine code for one computer is not the same as for another.

When programmers used machine language for programming, they had to enter the binary codes for the various instructions, a tedious process that was prone to error. Moreover, their programs were difficult to read and modify. In time, **assembly languages** were developed to make the programmer's job easier.

Assembly Language   A low-level programming language in which a mnemonic is used to represent each of the machine language instructions for a particular computer.

Instructions in an assembly language are in an easy-to-remember form called a *mnemonic* (pronounced "ni-'män-ik"). Typical instructions for addition and subtraction might look like this:

Assembly Language	*Machine Language*
ADD	100101
SUB	010011

Although assembly language was easier for humans to work with, the computer could not directly execute the instructions. So a program called an **assembler** was written to translate the instructions written in assembly language into machine code.

Assembler   A program that translates an assembly language program into machine code.

The assembler was a step in the right direction, but programmers still were forced to think in terms of individual machine instructions. Eventually, computer scientists developed high-level programming languages. These

■ FIGURE 1-4

Levels of
Abstraction

Human thought

Natural language (English, French, German, etc.)

High-level language (C++, FORTRAN, COBOL, etc.)

Low-level language (assembly language)

Machine code (computer)

languages are easier to use than assembly languages or machine code be-cause they are closer to English and other natural languages (see Figure 1-4).

A program called a **compiler** translates programs written in certain high-level languages (C++, Pascal, FORTRAN, COBOL, Modula-2, and Ada, for example) into machine language. If you write a program in a high-level lan-guage, you can run it on any computer that has the appropriate compiler. This is possible because most high-level languages are *standardized*, which means that an official description of the language exists.[*]

Compiler   A program that translates a high-level language into machine code.

---

[*]Some programming languages—LISP, Prolog, and many versions of BASIC, for example—are translated into machine language by an *interpreter* rather than a compiler. The difference be-tween a compiler and an interpreter is outside the scope of this textbook, which focuses only on compiled languages.

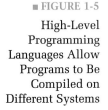

■ FIGURE 1-5

High-Level
Programming
Languages Allow
Programs to Be
Compiled on
Different Systems

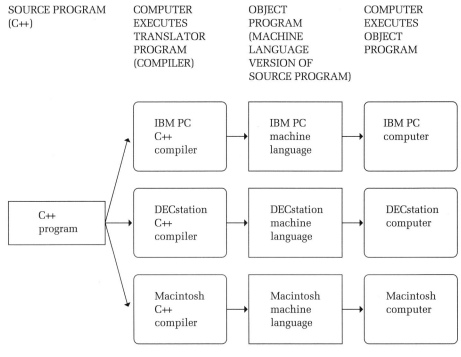

SOURCE PROGRAM (C++) COMPUTER EXECUTES TRANSLATOR PROGRAM (COMPILER) OBJECT PROGRAM (MACHINE LANGUAGE VERSION OF SOURCE PROGRAM) COMPUTER EXECUTES OBJECT PROGRAM

A program in a high-level language is called a **source program.** To the compiler, a source program is just input data. It translates the source program into a machine language program called an **object program** (see Figure 1-5). Some compilers also output a listing—a copy of the program with error messages and other information inserted.

Source Program   A program written in a high-level programming language.
Object Program   The machine language version of a source program.

A benefit of standardized high-level languages is that they allow you to write *portable* (or *machine-independent*) code. As Figure 1-5 emphasizes, a single C++ program can be run on different machines, whereas a program written in assembly language or machine language is not portable from one computer to another. Because each computer has its own machine language, a machine language program written for computer A will not run on computer B.

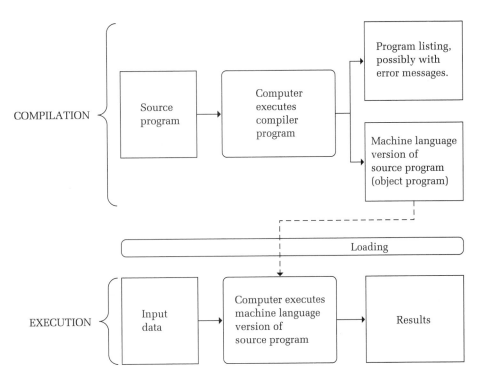

It is important to understand that *compilation* and *execution* are two distinct processes. During compilation, the computer runs the compiler program. During execution, the object program is loaded into the computer's memory unit, replacing the compiler program. The computer then runs the object program, doing whatever the program instructs it to do (see Figure 1-6).

The instructions in a programming language reflect the operations a computer can perform:

- A computer can transfer data from one place to another.
- A computer can input data from an input device (a keyboard, for example) and output data to an output device (a screen, for example).
- A computer can store data into and retrieve data from its memory and secondary storage (parts of a computer that we discuss in the next section).
- A computer can compare two data values for equality or inequality.
- A computer can perform arithmetic operations (addition and subtraction, for example) very quickly.

Programming languages require that we use certain structures to express algorithms as programs. There are four basic ways of structuring statements (instructions) in C++ and other languages: sequentially, conditionally, repetitively, and with subprograms (see Figure 1-7). A *sequence* is a series of statements that are executed one after another. *Selection*, the conditional structure, executes different statements depending on certain conditions. The repetitive structure, the *loop*, repeats statements while certain conditions are met. And the *subprogram* allows us to structure a program by breaking it into smaller units.

Assume you're driving a car. Going down a straight stretch of road is like following a *sequence* of instructions. When you come to a fork in the road, you must decide which way to go and then take one or the other branch of the fork. This is what the computer does when it encounters a *selection* (sometimes called a *branch* or *decision*) in a program. Sometimes you have to go around the block several times to find a place to park. The computer does the same sort of thing when it encounters a *loop* in a program.

A *subprogram* is a process that consists of multiple steps. Every day, for example, you follow a procedure to get from home to work. It makes sense, then, for someone to give you directions to a meeting by saying, "Go to the office, then go four blocks west," without listing all the steps you have to take to get to the office. Subprograms allow us to write parts of our programs separately and then assemble them into final form. They can greatly simplify the task of writing large programs.

 # What Is a Computer?

You can learn a programming language, how to write programs, and how to run (execute) these programs without knowing much about computers. But if you know something about the parts of a computer, you can better understand the effect of each instruction in a programming language.

There are six basic components in most computers: the memory unit, the arithmetic/logic unit, the control unit, input devices, output devices, and auxiliary storage devices. Figure 1-8 is a stylized diagram of the basic components of a computer.

The **memory unit** is an ordered sequence of storage cells, each capable of holding a piece of data. It is like an old-fashioned post office with pigeon-holes for mail. Each memory cell has a distinct address to which we refer in order to store information into it or retrieve information from it. These storage cells are called *memory cells*, or *memory locations*.* The memory unit holds data (input data or the product of computation) and instructions (programs), as shown in Figure 1-9.

___

*The memory unit is also referred to as RAM, an acronym for **r**andom **a**ccess **m**emory (because we can access any location at random).

■ FIGURE 1-7   Basic Structures of Programming Languages

SEQUENCE

Statement → Statement → Statement → • • •

SELECTION   (also called *branch* or *decision*)

IF condition THEN statement1 ELSE statement2

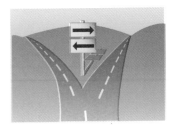

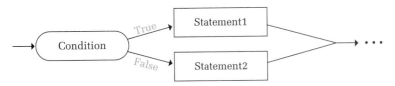

Condition —True→ Statement1
Condition —False→ Statement2
→ • • •

LOOP   (also called *repetition* or *iteration*)

WHILE condition DO statement1

Condition —False→ • • •
Condition —True→ Statement1

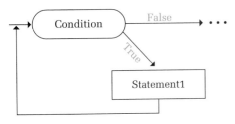

SUBPROGRAM (also called *procedure*, *function*, or *subroutine*)

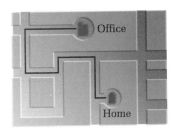

SUBPROGRAM1 → • • •

SUBPROGRAM1
a meaningful collection
of any of the above

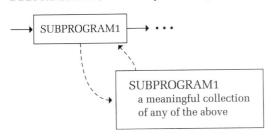

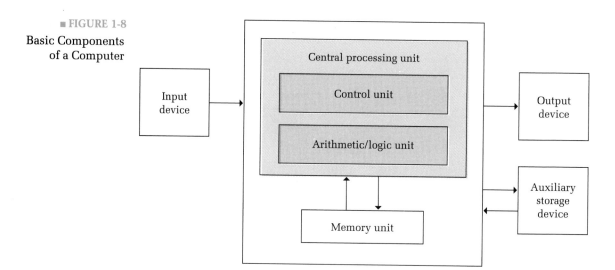

Memory Unit   Internal data storage in a computer.

The part of the computer that follows instructions is called the **central processing unit (CPU)**. The CPU usually has two components. The **arithmetic/logic unit (ALU)** performs arithmetic operations (addition, subtraction, multiplication, and division) and logical operations (comparing two values). The **control unit** controls the actions of the other components so that program instructions are executed in the correct order.

Central Processing Unit (CPU)   The part of the computer that executes the instructions (program) stored in memory; made up of the arithmetic/logic unit and the control unit.

Arithmetic/Logic Unit (ALU)   The component of the central processing unit that performs arithmetic and logical operations.

Control Unit   The component of the central processing unit that controls the actions of the other components so that instructions (the program) are executed in the correct sequence.

For us to use computers, we must have some way of getting data into and out of them. **Input/Output (I/O) devices** accept data to be processed (input)

■ FIGURE 1-9

Memory

MEMORY

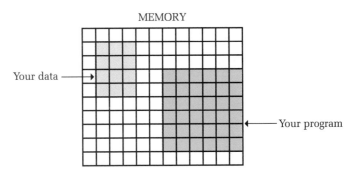

Your data ⟶

Your program

and present data that have been processed (output). A keyboard is a common input device. Another is a *mouse*, a "pointing" device. A video display is a common output device, as are printers and liquid crystal display (LCD) screens.

Input/Output (I/O) Devices   The parts of the computer that accept data to be processed (input) and present the results of that processing (output).

For the most part, computers simply move and combine data in memory. The differences among various computers basically involve the size of their memories and the speed with which data can be recalled, the efficiency with which data can be moved or combined, and limitations on I/O devices.

When a program is executing, the computer proceeds through a series of steps, the *fetch-execute cycle*:

1. The control unit retrieves (*fetches*) the next coded instruction from memory.
2. The instruction is translated into control signals.
3. The control signals tell the appropriate unit (arithmetic/logic unit, memory, I/O device) to perform (*execute*) the instruction.
4. The sequence repeats from step 1.

Computers can have a wide variety of **peripheral devices** (see Figure 1-10). An **auxiliary storage device,** or *secondary storage device*, holds coded data for the computer until we actually want to use the data. Instead of inputting data every time, we can input it once and have the computer store it onto an auxiliary storage device. Whenever we need to use the data, we tell the computer to transfer the data from the auxiliary storage device to its memory. An auxiliary storage device therefore serves as both an input and an output device. Typical auxiliary storage devices are magnetic tape

■ FIGURE 1-10
Peripheral Devices

Keyboard

Scanner

3.5" Disk Drive

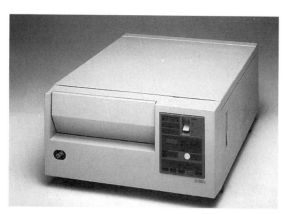

Magnetic Tape Drive

Plotter

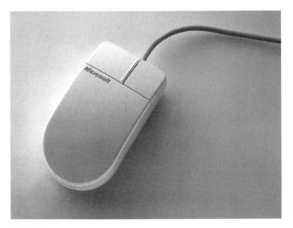

PC Mouse

Monitor

Laser Printer

CD-ROM Drive

drives and disk drives. A *magnetic tape drive* is like a tape recorder. A *disk drive* is a cross between a compact disk player and a tape recorder. It uses a thin disk made out of magnetic material. A read/write head (similar to the record/playback head in a tape recorder) travels across the spinning disk, retrieving or recording data.

Together, all of these physical components are known as **hardware.** The programs that allow the hardware to operate are called **software.** Hardware usually is fixed in design; software is easily changed. In fact, the ease with which software can be manipulated is what makes the computer such a versatile, powerful tool.

Peripheral Device   An input, output, or auxiliary storage device attached to a computer.

Auxiliary Storage Device   A device that stores data in encoded form outside the computer's main memory.

Hardware   The physical components of a computer.

Software   Computer programs; the set of all programs available on a computer.

In addition to the programs that we write or purchase, there are programs in the computer that are designed to simplify the user/computer **interface,** making it easier for us to use the machine. The interface between user and computer is a set of I/O devices—for example, a keyboard and a screen—that allows the user to communicate with the computer. We work with the keyboard and the screen on our side of the interface boundary; wires attached to the keyboard and the screen carry the electronic pulses that the computer works with on its side of the interface boundary. At the boundary itself is a mechanism that translates information for the two sides.

Interface   A connecting link at a shared boundary that allows independent systems to meet and act on or communicate with each other.

When we communicate directly with the computer through a keyboard and a screen, we are using an **interactive system.** Interactive systems allow direct entry of programs and data and provide immediate feedback to the user. In contrast, *batch systems* require that all data be entered before a program is run and provide feedback only after a program has been executed. In this text we focus on interactive systems, although in Chapter 4 we discuss file-oriented programs, which share certain similarities with batch systems.

The set of programs that simplifies the user/computer interface and improves the efficiency of processing is called *system software*. It includes the compiler as well as the operating system and the editor (see Figure 1-11). The **operating system** manages all of the computer's resources. It can input programs, call the compiler, execute object programs, and carry out any other system commands. The **editor** is an interactive program used to create and modify source programs or data.

Interactive System A system that allows direct communication between user and computer.

Operating System A set of programs that manages all of the computer's resources.

Editor An interactive program used to create and modify source programs or data.

*B*ACKGROUND INFORMATION

The Origins of C++

In the late 1960s and early 1970s, Dennis Ritchie created the C programming language at AT&T Bell Labs. At the time, a group of people within Bell Labs were designing the UNIX operating system. Initially, UNIX was written in assembly language as was the custom for almost all system software in those days. To escape the difficulties of programming in assembly language, Ritchie invented C as a system programming language. C combines the low-level features of an assembly language with the ease of use and portability of a high-level language. UNIX was reprogrammed so that approximately 90 percent was written in C, and the remainder in assembly language.

People often wonder where the cryptic name C came from. In the 1960s a programming language named BCPL (Basic Combined Programming Language) had a small but loyal following, primarily in Europe. From BCPL, another language arose with its name abbreviated to B. For his language, Dennis Ritchie adopted features from the B language and decided that the successor to B naturally should be named C. So the progression was from BCPL to B to C.

In 1985 Bjarne Stroustrup, also of Bell Labs, invented the C++ programming language. To the C language he added features for data abstraction and object-oriented programming (topics we discuss much later in this book). Instead of naming the language D, the Bell Labs group named it C++ in a humorous vein. As we see later, ++ signifies the *increment* operation in the C and C++ languages. Given a variable x, the expression x++ means to increment (add one to) the current value of x. Therefore, the name C++ suggests an enhanced ("incremented") version of the C language.

Although C originally was intended as a system programming language, both C and C++ are widely used today in business, industry, and personal computing. C++ is powerful and versatile, embodying a wide range of programming concepts. In this book you will learn a substantial portion of the language, but C++ incorporates sophisticated features that go well beyond the scope of an introductory programming course.

■ FIGURE 1-11

User/Computer
Interface

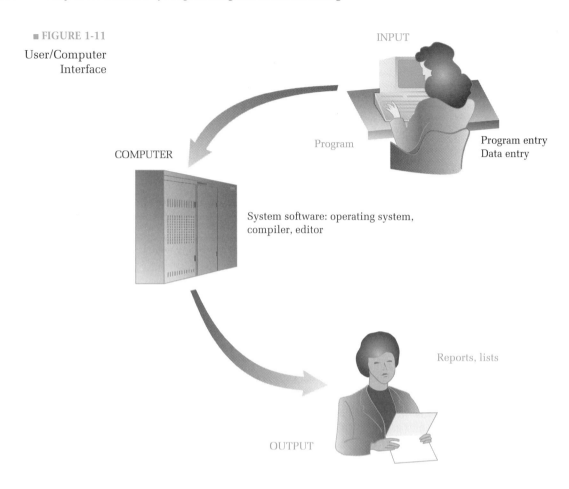

INPUT

Program entry
Data entry

Program

COMPUTER

System software: operating system,
compiler, editor

Reports, lists

OUTPUT

 Problem-Solving Techniques

You solve problems every day, often unaware of the process you are going through. In a learning environment, you usually are given most of the information you need: a clear statement of the problem, the necessary input, and the required output. In real life, the process is not always so simple. You often have to define the problem yourself and then decide what information you have to work with and what the results should be.

After you understand and analyze a problem, you must come up with a solution—an algorithm. Earlier we defined an algorithm as a step-by-step procedure for solving a problem in a finite amount of time. Although you work with algorithms all the time, most of your experience with them is in the context of *following* them. You follow a recipe, play a game, assemble a toy, take medicine. In the problem-solving phase of computer programming,

BACKGROUND INFORMATION

Micros, Minis, and Mainframes

There are many different sizes and kinds of computers. *Mainframes* are very large (they can fill a room!) and very fast. A typical mainframe computer consists of several cabinets full of electronic components. Inside those cabinets are the memory unit, the central processing unit, and input/output units. It's easy to spot the various peripheral devices: Separate cabinets contain the disk drives and tape drives. Other units are obviously printers and terminals (monitors with keyboards). It is common to be able to connect dozens, even hundreds, of terminals to a single mainframe.

At the other end of the spectrum are *microcomputers* or *personal computers (PCs)*. These are so small that they fit comfortably on top of a desk. Because of their size, it can be difficult to spot the individual parts inside personal computers. Many PCs are just a single box with a screen, a keyboard, and sometimes a mouse. You have to open up the case to see the central processing unit, which is usually just an electronic component called an integrated circuit chip.

Personal computers rarely have tape drives; most operate with disk drives and printers. The disk drives for personal computers typically hold much less data than those used with mainframes. Similarly, the printers that are attached to personal computers typically are much slower than those used with mainframes.

Between mainframes and personal computers are *minicomputers*. These intermediate-sized computer systems are less expensive than mainframes and more powerful than personal computers. Minicomputers are sometimes set up for use primarily by one person at a time, in a form called a *workstation*. A typical workstation looks very much like a PC. In fact, as PCs have grown more powerful and workstations have become more compact, the distinction between them has begun to fade.

One last type of computer that we should mention is the *supercomputer*, the most powerful class of computer in existence. Supercomputers typically are designed to perform scientific and engineering calculations on immense sets of data with great speed. They are very expensive and so are not in widespread use.

Mainframe Computer

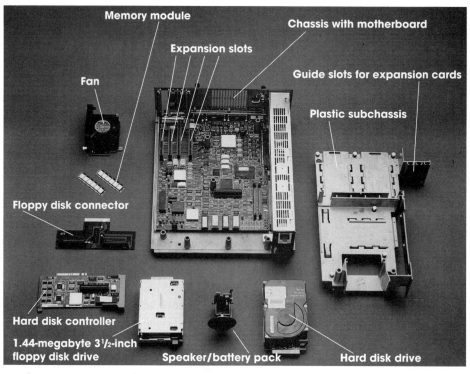

Inside a PC, system unit broken down

Personal Computer, IBM

Personal Computer, Macintosh

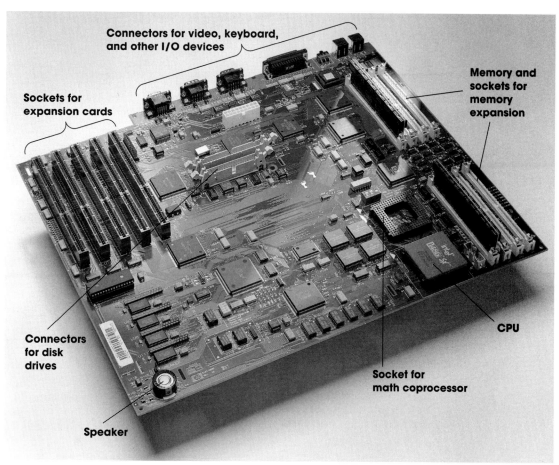

Connectors for video, keyboard, and other I/O devices

Sockets for expansion cards

Memory and sockets for memory expansion

CPU

Connectors for disk drives

Socket for math coprocessor

Speaker

Inside a PC, close-up of a system board

Notebook Computer

Workstation

Supercomputer

you will be *designing* algorithms, not following them. This means you will have to be conscious of the strategies you use to solve problems in order to apply them to programming problems.

Ask Questions

If you are given a task orally, you ask questions—When? Why? Where?—until you understand exactly what you have to do. If your instructions are written, you might put question marks in the margin, underline a word or a sentence, or in some other way indicate that the task is not clear. Your ques-

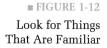

Look for Things
That Are Familiar

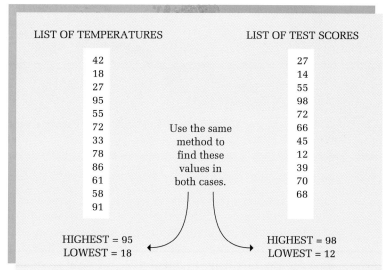

tions may be answered by a later paragraph, or you might have to discuss them with the person who gave you the task.

These are some of the questions you will be asking in the context of programming:

• What do I have to work with—that is, what are my data?
• What do the data look like?
• How much data is there?
• How will I know when I have processed all the data?
• What should my output look like?
• How many times is the process going to be repeated?
• What special error conditions might come up?

Look for Things That Are Familiar

Never reinvent the wheel. If a solution exists, use it. If you've solved the same or a similar problem before, just repeat your solution. People are good at recognizing similar situations. We don't have to learn how to go to the store to buy milk, then to buy eggs, then to buy candy. We know that going to the store is always the same; only what we buy is different.

In programming, you will see certain problems again and again in different guises. A good programmer immediately recognizes a subtask he or she has solved before and plugs in the solution. For example, finding the daily high and low temperatures is really the same problem as finding the highest and lowest grades on a test. You want the largest and smallest values in a set of numbers (see Figure 1-12).

■ FIGURE 1-13

Analogy

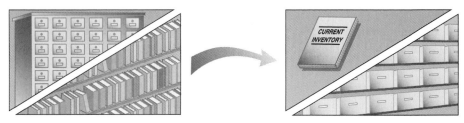

A library catalog system can give insight into how to organize a parts inventory.

Solve by Analogy

Often a problem reminds you of a similar problem you have seen before. You may find solving the problem at hand easier if you remember how you solved the other problem. In other words, draw an analogy between the two problems. For example, a solution to a perspective projection problem from an art class might help you figure out how to compute the distance to a landmark when you are on a cross-country hike. As you work your way through the new problem, you come across things that are different than they were in the old problem, but usually these are just details that you can deal with one at a time.

Analogy is really just a broader application of the strategy of looking for things that are familiar. When you are trying to find an algorithm for solving a problem, don't limit yourself to computer-oriented solutions. Step back and try to get a larger view of the problem. Don't worry if your analogy doesn't match perfectly—the only reason for starting with an analogy is that it gives you a place to start (see Figure 1-13). The best programmers are people who have broad experience solving all kinds of problems.

Means-Ends Analysis

Often the beginning state and the ending state are given; the problem is to define a set of actions that can be used to get from one to the other. Suppose you want to go from Boston, Massachusetts, to Austin, Texas. You know the beginning state (you are in the city of Boston) and the ending state (you want to be in the city of Austin). The problem is how to get from one to the other.

In this example, you have lots of choices. You can fly, walk, hitchhike, ride a bike, or whatever. The method you choose depends on your circumstances. If you're in a hurry, you'll probably decide to fly.

Once you've narrowed down the set of actions, you have to work out the details. It may help to establish intermediate goals that are easier to meet than the overall goal. Let's say there is a really cheap, direct flight to Austin out of Newark, New Jersey. You might decide to divide the trip into legs: Boston to Newark and then Newark to Austin. Your intermediate goal is to

Start: Boston	**Means:** *Fly,* walk, hitchhike, bike,
Goal: Austin	drive, sail, bus
Start: Boston	**Revised Means:** Fly to Chicago and then Austin;
Goal: Austin	*fly to Newark and then Austin;* fly to Atlanta and
	then Austin
Start: Boston	**Means to Intermediate Goal:** *Commuter flight,* walk,
Intermediate Goal: Newark	hitchhike, bike, drive, sail, bus
Goal: Austin	

Solution: Take commuter flight to Newark and then catch cheap flight to Austin

get from Boston to Newark. Now you only have to examine the means of meeting that intermediate goal (see Figure 1-14).

The overall strategy of means-ends analysis is to define the ends and then to analyze your means of getting between them. The process translates easily to computer programming. You begin by writing down what the input is and what the output should be. Then you consider the actions a computer can perform and choose a sequence of actions that can transform the data into the results.

Divide and Conquer

We often break up large problems into smaller units that are easier to handle. Cleaning the whole house may seem overwhelming; cleaning the rooms one at a time seems much more manageable. The same principle applies to programming. We break up a large problem into smaller pieces that we can solve individually (see Figure 1-15). In fact, the top-down methodology and the object-oriented methodology, which we describe in Chapter 4, are based on the principle of divide and conquer.

The Building-Block Approach

Another way of attacking a large problem is to see if there are any existing solutions for smaller pieces of the problem. It may be possible to put some of these solutions together end to end to solve most of the big problem. This strategy is just a combination of the look-for-familiar-things and divide-and-conquer approaches. You look at the big problem and see that it can be divided into smaller problems for which solutions already exist. Solving the big problem is just a matter of putting the existing solutions together, like mortaring together blocks to form a wall (see Figure 1-16).

■ FIGURE 1-15

Divide and Conquer

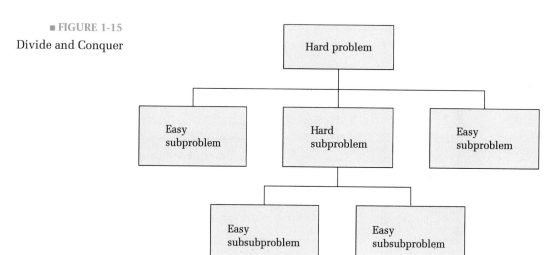

Merging Solutions

Another way to combine existing solutions is to merge them on a step-by-step basis. For example, to compute the average of a list of values, we must both sum and count the values. If we already have separate solutions for summing values and for counting values, we can combine them. But if we first do the summing and then do the counting, we have to read the list twice. We can save steps if we merge these two solutions: read a value and then add it to the running total and add 1 to our count before going on to the next value. Whenever the solutions to subproblems duplicate steps, think about merging them instead of joining them end to end.

Mental Blocks: The Fear of Starting

Writers are all too familiar with the experience of staring at a blank page, not knowing where to begin. Programmers have the same difficulty when they first tackle a big problem. They look at the problem and it seems overwhelming.

Remember that you always have a place to begin solving any problem: Write it down on paper in your own words so that you understand it. Once you begin to try to paraphrase the problem, you can focus on each of the subparts individually instead of trying to tackle the entire problem at once. This process gives you a clearer picture of the overall problem. It helps you see pieces of the problem that look familiar or that are analogous to other problems you have solved. And it pinpoints areas where something is unclear, where you need more information.

As you write down a problem, you tend to group things together into small, understandable chunks, which may be natural places to split the problem up—to divide and conquer. Your description of the problem may

■ FIGURE 1-16   Building-Block Approach

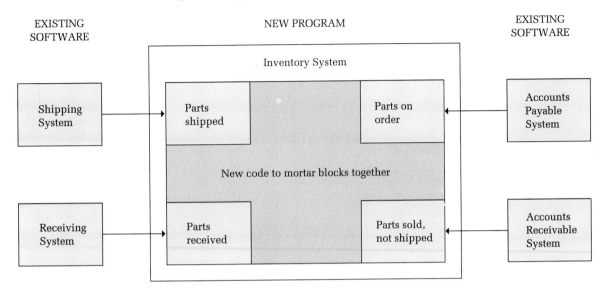

collect all of the information about data and results into one place for easy reference. Then you can see the beginning and ending states necessary for means-ends analysis.

Most mental blocks are caused by not really understanding the problem. Rewriting the problem in your own words is a good way to focus on the subparts of the problem, one at a time, and to understand what is required for a solution.

Algorithmic Problem Solving

Coming up with a step-by-step procedure for solving a particular problem is not always cut-and-dried. In fact, it is usually a trial-and-error process requiring several attempts and refinements. We test each attempt to see if it really solves the problem. If it does, fine. If it doesn't, we try again. You typically use a combination of all of the techniques we've described to solve any nontrivial problem.

Remember that the computer can only do certain things (see p. 13). Your primary concern, then, is how to make the computer transform, manipulate, calculate, or process the input data to produce the desired output. If you keep in mind the allowable instructions in your programming language, you won't design an algorithm that is difficult or impossible to code.

In the case study below, we develop a program for calculating employees' weekly wages. It typifies the thought processes involved in writing an algorithm and coding it as a program, and it shows you what a complete C++ program looks like.

PROBLEM-SOLVING *CASE STUDY*

An Algorithm for a Company Payroll

Problem: A small company needs an interactive program (the payroll clerk will input the data) to figure its weekly payroll. The input data and each employee's wages should be saved in a secondary storage file, and the total wages for the week should be displayed on the screen so that the payroll clerk can transfer the appropriate amount into the payroll account.

Discussion: At first glance, this seems like a simple problem. But if you think about how you would do it by hand, you see that you need to ask questions about the specifics of the process: What employee data is input? How are wages computed? In what file should the results be stored? How does the clerk indicate that all of the data has been entered?

- The data for each employee include an employee identification number, the employee's hourly pay rate, and the hours worked that week.
- Wages equal the employee's pay rate times the number of hours worked up to 40 hours. If an employee worked more than 40 hours, wages equal the employee's pay rate times 40 hours, plus one and a half times the employee's regular pay rate times the number of hours worked above 40.
- The results should be stored in a file called `payFile`.
- There is no employee number 0, so the clerk can indicate the end of the data by entering a 0 when asked for an employee number.

Let's apply the *divide-and-conquer* approach to this problem. There are three obvious steps in almost any problem of this type:

1. Get the data.
2. Compute the results.
3. Output the results.

First we need to get the data. (By *get*, we mean *read* or *input* the data.) We need three pieces of data for each employee: employee identification number, hourly pay rate, and number of hours worked. So that the clerk will know when to enter each value, we must have the computer output a message that indicates when it is ready to accept each of the values (this is called a *prompting message*, or a *prompt*). Therefore, to input the data, we take these steps:

Prompt the user for the employee number (put a message on the screen)
Read the employee number
Prompt the user for the employee's hourly pay rate
Read the pay rate
Prompt the user for the number of hours worked
Read the number of hours worked

The next step is to compute the wages. Let's apply *means-ends analysis*. Our starting point is the set of data values that was input; our desired ending, the payroll for the week. We know that if there is no overtime, wages are simply the pay rate times the number of hours worked. If the number of hours worked is greater than 40, however, wages are 40 times the pay rate, plus the number of overtime hours times one and a half times the pay rate. The number of overtime hours is computed by subtracting 40 from the total number of hours worked. To figure the wages, we take the following steps:

If hours worked is greater than 40.0, then
    wages = (40.0 × pay rate) + (hours worked − 40.0) × 1.5 × pay rate
otherwise
    wages = hours worked × pay rate

The last step, outputting the results, is simply a matter of having the computer write the employee number, the pay rate, the number of hours worked, and the wages onto `payFile`:

Write the employee number, pay rate, hours worked, and wages onto payFile.

There are two things we've overlooked. First, we must repeat this process for each employee, and second, we must compute the total wages for the week. Let's use the *building-block approach* to combine our three main steps (getting the data, computing the wages, and outputting the results) with a structure that repeats the steps for each employee as long as the employee number is not 0. When the employee number is 0, this structure will skip to the end of the algorithm. Next we'll insert a step just after the wages are computed that adds them to a running total.

Finally, we must take care of a couple of housekeeping chores. Before we start processing, we must prepare the output file to receive the results and set the running total to zero. At the end of the algorithm, we must tell the computer to stop processing.

What follows is the complete algorithm. Calculating the wages is written as a separate subalgorithm that is defined below the main algorithm. Notice that the algorithm is simply a very precise description of the same steps you would follow to do this process by hand.

Main Algorithm
Prepare to write a list of the employees' wages (open file payFile)
Set the total payroll to zero
Prompt the user for the employee number (put a message on the screen)
Read the employee number

As long as the employee number is not 0, repeat the following steps:
   Prompt the user for the employee's hourly pay rate
   Read the pay rate
   Prompt the user for the number of hours worked
   Read the number of hours worked
   Perform the subalgorithm for calculating pay (below)
   Add the employee's wages to the total payroll
   Write the employee number, pay rate, hours worked, and wages onto the list
     (file payFile)
   Prompt the user for the employee number
   Read the employee number
When an employee number equal to 0 is read, continue with the following steps:
   Write the total company payroll on the screen
   Stop

Subalgorithm for Calculating Pay

If hours worked is greater than 40.0, then
   wages = (40.0 × pay rate) + (hours worked − 40.0) × 1.5 × pay rate
otherwise
   wages = hours worked × pay rate

Before we implement this algorithm, we should test it. Case Study Follow-Up Exercise 2 asks you to carry out this test.

What follows is the C++ program for this algorithm. It's here to give you an idea of what you'll be learning. If you've had no previous exposure to programming, you probably won't understand most of the program. Don't worry; you will soon. In fact, throughout this book as we introduce new constructs, we refer you back to the Payroll program. One more thing: The remarks following the symbols // are called comments. They are here to help you understand the program; the compiler ignores them. Words enclosed by the symbols /* and */ also are comments and are ignored by the compiler.

```
//******************************************************************
// Payroll program
// This program computes each employee's wages and
// the total company payroll
//******************************************************************
#include <iostream.h>
#include <fstream.h>      // For file I/O

void CalcPay( float, float, float& );
```

```cpp
const float MAX_HOURS = 40.0;    // Maximum normal work hours
const float OVERTIME = 1.5;      // Overtime pay rate factor

int main()
{
    float     payRate;      // Employee's pay rate
    float     hours;        // Hours worked
    float     wages;        // Wages earned
    float     total;        // Total company payroll
    int       empNum;       // Employee ID number
    ofstream payFile;       // Company payroll file

    payFile.open("payfile.dat");              // Open the output file
    total = 0.0;                              // Initialize total
    cout << "Enter employee number: ";        // Prompt
    cin >> empNum;                            // Read employee ID no.
    while (empNum != 0)                       // While employee number
    {                                         //    isn't zero
        cout << "Enter pay rate: ";           // Prompt
        cin >> payRate;                       // Read hourly pay rate
        cout << "Enter hours worked: ";       // Prompt
        cin >> hours;                         // Read hours worked
        CalcPay(payRate, hours, wages);       // Compute wages
        total = total + wages;                // Add wages to total
        payFile << empNum << payRate          // Put results into file
                << hours << wages;
        cout << "Enter employee number: ";    // Prompt
        cin >> empNum;                        // Read ID number
    }
    cout << "Total payroll is "               // Print total payroll
         << total << endl;                    //    on screen
    return 0;                                 // Indicate successful
}                                             //    completion

//*****************************************************************

void CalcPay( /* in */  float   payRate,      // Employee's pay rate
              /* in */  float   hours,        // Hours worked
              /* out */ float&  wages )       // Wages earned

// CalcPay computes wages from the employee's pay rate
// and the hours worked, taking overtime into account

{
    if (hours > MAX_HOURS)                    // Is there overtime?
        wages = (MAX_HOURS * payRate) +       // Yes
                (hours - MAX_HOURS) * payRate * OVERTIME;
    else
        wages = hours * payRate;              // No
}
```

Summary

We think nothing of turning on the television and sitting down to watch it. It's a communication tool we use to enhance our lives. Computers are becoming as common as televisions, just a normal part of our lives. And like televisions, computers are based on complex principles but are designed for easy use.

Computers are dumb; they must be told what to do. A true computer error is extremely rare (usually due to a component malfunction or an electrical fault). Because we tell the computer what to do, most errors in computer-generated output are really human errors.

Computer programming is the process of planning a sequence of steps for a computer to follow. It involves a problem-solving phase and an implementation phase. After analyzing a problem, we develop and test a general solution (algorithm). This general solution becomes a concrete solution—our program—when we write it in a high-level programming language. The sequence of instructions that makes up our program is then compiled into machine code, the language the computer uses. After correcting any errors or "bugs" that show up during testing, our program is ready to use.

Data and instructions are represented as binary numbers (numbers consisting of just 1s and 0s) in electronic computers. The process of converting data and instructions into a form usable by the computer is called coding.

A programming language reflects the range of operations a computer can perform. The basic control structures in a programming language—sequence, selection, loop, and subprogram—are based on these fundamental operations. In this text, you will learn to write programs in the high-level programming language called C++.

Computers are composed of six basic parts: the memory unit, the arithmetic/logic unit, the control unit, input and output devices, and auxiliary storage devices. The arithmetic/logic unit and control unit together are called the central processing unit. The physical parts of the computer are called hardware. The programs that are executed by the computer are called software.

System software is a set of programs designed to simplify the user/computer interface. It includes the compiler, the operating system, and the editor.

We've said that problem solving is an integral part of the programming process. Although you may have little experience programming computers, you have lots of experience solving problems. The key is to stop and think about the strategies you use to solve problems, and then to use those strategies to devise workable algorithms. Among those strategies are asking questions, looking for things that are familiar, solving by analogy, applying means-ends analysis, dividing the problem into subproblems, using existing solutions to small problems to solve a larger problem, merging solutions, and paraphrasing the problem in order to overcome a mental block.

The computer is widely used today in science, engineering, business, government, and the arts. Learning to program in C++ can help you use this powerful tool effectively.

QUICK CHECK

The Quick Check is intended to help you decide if you've met the goals set forth at the beginning of each chapter. If you understand the material in the chapter, the answer to each question should be fairly obvious. After reading a question, check your response against the answers listed at the end of the Quick Check. If you don't know an answer or don't understand the answer that's provided, turn to the page(s) listed at the end of the question to review the material.

1. What is a computer program? (p. 3)
2. What are the three phases in a program's life cycle? (p. 3)
3. Is an algorithm the same as a program? (p. 4)
4. What is a programming language? (p. 6)
5. True or False: Creating documentation is an important part of the programming process. (p. 8)
6. What are the advantages of using a high-level programming language? (p. 11)
7. What does a compiler do? (p. 11)
8. What part does the object program play in the compilation and execution processes? (p. 12)
9. Name the four basic ways of structuring statements in C++ and other languages. (p. 15)
10. What are the six basic components of a computer? (p. 16)
11. What is the difference between hardware and software? (p. 19)
12. What is the divide-and-conquer approach? (p. 29)

Answers   1. A computer program is a sequence of instructions performed by a computer. 2. The three phases of a program's life cycle are problem solving, implementation, and maintenance.   3. No. All programs are algorithms, but not all algorithms are programs.   4. A set of rules, symbols, and special words used to construct a program.   5. True. The written text and comments make a program easier for others to understand, use, modify, and maintain.   6. A high-level programming language is easier to use than an assembly language or a machine language. And programs written in a high-level language can be run on many different computers. 7. The compiler translates a program written in a high-level language into machine language. 8. The object program is the machine language version of a program. It is created by a compiler. The object program is what is loaded into the computer's memory and executed.   9. Sequence, selection, loop, and subprogram.   10. The basic components of a computer are the memory unit, arithmetic/logic unit, control unit, input and output devices, and auxiliary storage devices.   11. Hardware is the physical components of the computer; software is the collection of programs that run on the computer.   12. The divide-and-conquer approach is a problem-solving technique that breaks a large problem into smaller, simpler subproblems.

EXAM PREPARATION EXERCISES

1. Explain why the following series of steps is not an algorithm, then rewrite the series so it is.

   Shampooing
   (1) Rinse.
   (2) Lather.
   (3) Repeat.

2. Describe the input and output files used by a compiler.

3. In the following recipe for chocolate pound cake, identify the steps that are branches (selection) and loops, and the steps that are references to subalgorithms outside the algorithm.

   Preheat the oven to 350 degrees
   Line the bottom of a 9-inch tube pan with wax paper
   Sift 2¾ c flour, ¾ t cream of tartar, ½ t baking soda, 1½ t salt, and 1¾ c sugar into
     a large bowl
   Add 1 c shortening to the bowl
   If using butter, margarine, or lard, then
     add ⅔ c milk to the bowl,
   else
     (for other shortenings) add 1 c minus 2 T of milk to the bowl
   Add 1 t vanilla to the mixture in the bowl
   If mixing with a spoon, then
     see the instructions in the introduction to the chapter on cakes,
   else
     (for electric mixers) beat the contents of the bowl for 2 minutes at medium
     speed, scraping the bowl and beaters as needed
   Add 3 eggs plus 1 extra egg yolk to the bowl
   Melt 3 squares of unsweetened chocolate and add to the mixture in the bowl
   Beat the mixture for 1 minute at medium speed
   Pour the batter into the tube pan
   Put the pan into the oven and bake for 1 hour and 10 minutes
   Perform the test for doneness described in the introduction to the chapter on
     cakes
   Repeat the test once each minute until the cake is done
   Remove the pan from the oven and allow the cake to cool for 2 hours
   Follow the instructions for removing the cake from the pan, given in the
     introduction to the chapter on cakes
   Sprinkle powdered sugar over the cracks on top of the cake just before serving

4. Put a check next to each item below that is a peripheral device.
    _____ a. Disk drive
    _____ b. Arithmetic/logic unit
    _____ c. Magnetic tape drive
    _____ d. Printer
    _____ e. CD-ROM drive
    _____ f. Memory
    _____ g. Auxiliary storage device
    _____ h. Control unit
    _____ i. Terminal
    _____ j. Mouse
5. Next to each item below, indicate whether it is hardware (H) or software (S).
    _____ a. Disk drive
    _____ b. Memory
    _____ c. Compiler
    _____ d. Arithmetic/logic unit
    _____ e. Editor
    _____ f. Operating system
    _____ g. Object program
    _____ h. Terminal
    _____ i. Central processing unit
6. Means-ends analysis is a problem-solving strategy.
    a. What are three things you must know in order to apply means-ends analysis to a problem?
    b. What is one way of combining this technique with the divide-and-conquer strategy?
7. Show how you would use the divide-and-conquer approach to solve the problem of finding a job.

PROGRAMMING WARM-UP EXERCISES

1. Write an algorithm for driving from where you live to the nearest airport that has regularly scheduled flights. Restrict yourself to a vocabulary of 48 words plus numbers and place names. You must select the appropriate set of words for this task. An example of a vocabulary is given in Appendix A, the list of reserved words (words with special meaning) in the C++ programming language. Notice that there are just 48 words in that list. The purpose of this exercise is to give you practice writing simple, exact instructions in an equally small vocabulary.
2. Write an algorithm for making a peanut butter and jelly sandwich, using a vocabulary of just 48 words (you choose the words). Assume that all of the ingredients are in the refrigerator and that the necessary tools are in a drawer under the kitchen counter. The instructions must be very simple and exact because the person making the sandwich has no knowledge of food preparation and takes every word literally.
3. In Exercise 1 above, identify the sequential, conditional, repetitive, and subprogram steps.

CASE STUDY FOLLOW-UP

1. Using Figure 1-15 as a guide, construct a divide-and-conquer diagram of the Problem-Solving Case Study, An Algorithm for a Company Payroll.
2. Use the following data set to test the payroll algorithm presented on pages 33–34. Follow each step of the algorithm just as it is written, as if you were a computer. Then check your results by hand to be sure that the algorithm is correct.

ID Number	Pay Rate	Hours Worked
327	8.30	48
201	6.60	40
29	12.50	40
166	9.25	51
254	7.00	32
0		

2

C++ Syntax and Semantics, and the Program Development Process

GOALS

- To understand how a C++ program is composed of one or more subprograms (functions).
- To be able to read syntax templates in order to understand the formal rules governing C++ programs.
- To be able to create and recognize legal C++ identifiers.
- To be able to declare variables of type int, float, and char.
- To be able to declare named constants.
- To be able to distinguish reserved words in C++ from user-defined identifiers.
- To be able to assign values to variables.
- To be able to construct simple arithmetic expressions made up of constants, variables, and arithmetic operators.
- To be able to evaluate simple arithmetic expressions.
- To be able to construct a statement that writes to an output stream.
- To be able to determine what a given output statement will print.
- To be able to use comments to clarify your programs.
- To be able to construct simple C++ programs.
- To learn the steps involved in entering a program and getting it to run correctly.

The Elements of C++ Programs

Programmers develop solutions to problems using a programming language. In this chapter, we start looking at the rules and symbols that make up the C++ programming language. We also review the steps required to create a program and make it work on a computer.

C++ Program Structure

In Chapter 1, we talked about the four basic structures for expressing actions in a programming language: sequence, selection, loop, and subprogram. We said that subprograms allow us to write parts of our program separately and then assemble them into final form. In C++, all subprograms are referred to as **functions**, and a C++ program is a collection of one or more functions.

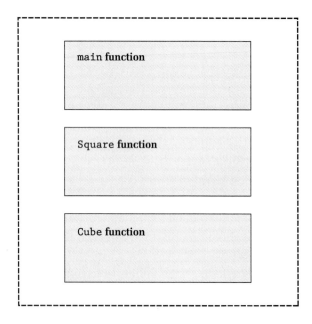

Each function performs some particular task, and collectively they all cooperate to solve the entire problem.

Function   A subprogram in C++.

Every C++ program must have a function named `main`. Execution of the program always begins with the `main` function. You can think of `main` as the master and the other functions as the servants. When `main` wants the function `Square` to perform a task, `main` *calls* (or *invokes*) `Square`. When the `Square` function completes execution of its statements, it obediently returns control to the master, `main`, so the master can continue executing.

Let's look at an example of a C++ program with three functions: `main`, `Square`, and `Cube`. Don't be too concerned with the details in the program—just observe its overall look and structure.

```cpp
#include <iostream.h>

int Square( int );
int Cube( int );

int main()
{
    cout << "The square of 27 is " << Square(27) << endl;
    cout << "and the cube of 27 is " << Cube(27) << endl;
    return 0;
}

int Square( int n )
{
    return n * n;
}

int Cube( int n )
{
    return n * n * n;
}
```

In each of the three functions, the left brace ({) and right brace (}) mark the beginning and end of the statements to be executed. Statements appearing between the braces are known as the *body* of the function.

Execution of a program always begins with the first statement of the `main` function. In our program, the first statement is

```cpp
cout << "The square of 27 is " << Square(27) << endl;
```

This is an output statement that causes information to be printed on the computer's display screen. You will learn how to construct output statements like this later in the chapter. Briefly, this statement prints two items. The first is the message

```
The square of 27 is
```

The second item to be printed is the value obtained by calling (invoking) the `Square` function, with the value 27 as the number to be squared. As the servant, the `Square` function performs its task of squaring the number and sending the computed result (729) back to its *caller*, the `main` function. Now `main` can continue executing by printing the value 729 and proceeding to its next statement.

In a similar fashion, the second statement in `main` prints the message

```
and the cube of 27 is
```

and then invokes the `Cube` function and prints the result, 19683. The complete output produced by executing this program is, therefore,

```
The square of 27 is 729
and the cube of 27 is 19683
```

Both `Square` and `Cube` are examples of *value-returning functions*. A value-returning function returns a single value to its caller. The word `int` at the beginning of the first line of the `Square` function

```
int Square( int n )
```

states that the function returns an integer value.

Now look at the `main` function again. You'll see that the first line of the function is

```
int main()
```

The word `int` indicates that `main` is a value-returning function that should return an integer value. And it does. After printing the square and cube of 27, `main` executes the statement

```
return 0;
```

to return the value 0 to its caller. But who calls the `main` function? The answer is: the computer's operating system.

When you work with C++ programs, the operating system is considered to be the caller of the `main` function. The operating system expects `main` to return a value when `main` finishes executing. By convention, a return value of 0 means everything went OK. A return value of anything else (typically 1, 2, ...) means something went wrong. Later in this book we look at situations in which you might want to return a value other than 0 from `main`. For the time being, we'll always conclude the execution of `main` by returning the value 0.

We have looked only briefly at the overall picture of what a C++ program looks like—a collection of one or more functions, including `main`. And we have mentioned what is special about the `main` function—it is a required function, execution begins there, and it returns a value to the operating system. Now it's time to begin looking at the details of the C++ language.

Syntax and Semantics

A programming language is a set of rules, symbols, and special words used to construct a program. There are rules for both **syntax** (grammar) and **semantics** (meaning).

Syntax   The formal rules governing how valid instructions are written in a programming language.

Semantics   The set of rules that determines the meaning of instructions written in a programming language.

Syntax is a formal set of rules that defines exactly what combinations of letters, numbers, and symbols can be used in a programming language. There is no room for ambiguity in the syntax of a programming language because the computer can't think; it doesn't "know what we mean." To avoid ambiguity, syntax rules themselves must be written in a very simple, precise, formal language called a **metalanguage.**

Metalanguage   A language that is used to write the syntax rules for another language.

Learning to read a metalanguage is like learning to read the notations used in the rules of a sport. Once you understand the notations, you can read the rule book. It's true that many people learn a sport simply by watching others play, but what they learn is usually just enough to allow them to take part in casual games. You could learn C++ by following the examples in this book, but a serious programmer, like a serious athlete, must take the time to read and understand the rules.

Syntax rules are the blueprints we use to "build" instructions in a program. They allow us to take the elements of a programming language—the basic building blocks of the language—and assemble them into *constructs*, syntactically correct structures. If our program violates any of the rules of the language—by misspelling a crucial word or leaving out an important comma, for instance—the program is said to have *syntax errors* and cannot compile correctly until we fix them.

THEORETICAL FOUNDATIONS

Metalanguages

Metalanguage is the word *language* with the prefix *meta*, which means "beyond" or "more comprehensive." A metalanguage is a language that goes beyond a normal language by allowing us to speak precisely about that language. It is a language for talking about languages.

One of the oldest computer-oriented metalanguages is the *Backus-Naur Form (BNF)*, which is named for John Backus and Peter Naur, who developed it in 1960. BNF syntax definitions are written out using letters, numbers, and special symbols. For example, a decimal (base-10) integer number in C++ must be at least one digit, it may or may not be more than one digit, and the first digit must be nonzero. The BNF definition of a decimal integer number in C++ is

```
<DecimalInteger> ::= <NonzeroDigit> | <NonzeroDigit> <DigitSequence>
<NonzeroDigit> ::= 1 | 2 | 3 | 4 | 5 | 6 | 7 | 8 | 9
<DigitSequence> ::= <Digit> | <Digit> <DigitSequence>
<Digit> ::= 0 | <NonzeroDigit>
```

where the symbol ::= is read "is defined as," the symbol | means "or," the symbols < and > are used to enclose words called *nonterminal symbols* (symbols that still need to be defined), and everything else is called a *terminal symbol*.

The first line of the definition reads: "A decimal integer is defined as a nonzero digit or a nonzero digit followed by a digit sequence." This line contains nonterminal symbols that must be defined. In the second line, the nonterminal symbol NonzeroDigit is defined as any one of the numeric characters 1 through 9, all of which are terminal symbols. The third line defines the nonterminal symbol DigitSequence as either a Digit or a Digit followed by another DigitSequence. The self-reference in the definition is a roundabout way of saying that a digit sequence can be a sequence of one or more digits. In the last line, Digit is defined as any one of the numeric characters 0 through 9.

BNF is an extremely simple language, but that simplicity leads to syntax definitions that can be long and difficult to read. An alternative metalanguage, the *syntax diagram*, is easier to follow. It uses arrows to indicate how symbols can be combined. Here are the syntax diagrams that define a decimal integer, a nonzero digit, and a digit in C++:

DecimalInteger

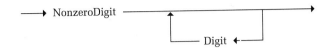

NonzeroDigit

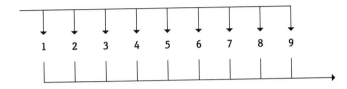

Digit

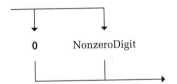

To read the diagrams, start at the left and follow the arrows. When you come to a branch, take any one of the branch paths. A **boldface** word is a terminal symbol, and words not in boldface are nonterminal symbols.

The first diagram shows that a decimal integer consists of a nonzero digit followed, optionally, by one or more digits. The second diagram defines the nonterminal symbol NonzeroDigit to be any one of the positive numeric characters. The third diagram defines Digit to be either 0 or one of the nonzero digits. Using BNF, each nonterminal symbol must be defined separately. Here, we have eliminated the BNF nonterminal symbol DigitSequence by using an arrow in the first syntax diagram to allow a sequence of consecutive digits.

Syntax diagrams are easier to interpret than BNF definitions, but they still can be difficult to read. In this text, we introduce another metalanguage, called a *syntax template*. Syntax templates show at a glance the form a C++ construct takes.

One final note: Metalanguages only show how to write instructions that the compiler can translate. They do not define what those instructions do (their semantics). Formal languages for defining the semantics of a programming language exist, but they are beyond the scope of this text. Throughout this book, we describe the semantics of C++ in English.

Syntax Templates

In this book, we write the syntax rules for C++ using a metalanguage called a *syntax template*. A syntax template is a generic example of the C++ construct being defined. Graphic conventions show which portions are optional and which can be repeated. A **boldface** word or symbol is a literal word or symbol in the C++ language. A non-boldface word can be replaced by another template.

Let's look at an example. This template defines a decimal integer in C++:

The shading indicates the part of the definition that is optional. The three dots (. . .) mean that the preceding symbol or shaded block can be repeated. So a decimal integer in C++ must begin with a nonzero digit and is optionally followed by one or more digits.

Remember that a word not in boldface type can be replaced with another template. These are the templates for NonzeroDigit and Digit:

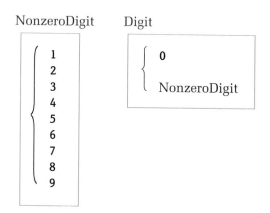

A brace indicates a list of items from which any one can be chosen. So a nonzero digit can be any one of the numeric characters 1 through 9, and a digit can be either the character 0 or a nonzero digit.

Now let's look at the syntax template for the C++ main function:

MainFunction

```
int main()
{
     Statement
       .
       .
       .
}
```

The `main` function begins with the word `int`, followed by the word `main` and then left and right parentheses. This first line of the function is the *heading*. After the heading, the left brace signals the start of the statements in the function (its body). The shading and the three dots indicate that the function body consists of zero or more statements. (In this diagram we have placed the three dots vertically to suggest that statements usually are arranged vertically, one above the next.) Finally, the right brace indicates the end of the function.

In principle, the syntax template allows the function body to have no statements at all. In practice, however, the body should include a `return` statement because the word `int` in the function heading states that `main` returns an integer value. Thus, the shortest C++ program is

```
int main()
{
    return 0;
}
```

As you might guess, this program does absolutely nothing useful when executed!

As we introduce C++ language constructs throughout the book, we use syntax templates to display the proper syntax. In Appendix D, you will find these syntax templates gathered into one central location.

When you finish this chapter, you will know enough about the syntax and semantics of statements in C++ to write programs that perform calculations and print the results. But before we can talk about writing statements, we first must look at how names are written in C++ and at some of the elements of a program.

Naming Program Elements: Identifiers

Identifiers are used in C++ to name things. Identifiers are made up of letters (A–Z, a–z), digits (0–9), and the underscore character (_), but must begin with a letter or underscore.

Identifier   A name associated with a function or data object and used to refer to that function or data object.

Remember that an identifier *must* start with a letter or underscore:

Identifier

LetterOrUnderscore   LetterOrDigitOrUnderscore   . . .

(Identifiers beginning with an underscore have special meanings in some C++ systems, so it is best to begin an identifier with a letter.)
Here are some examples of valid identifiers:

```
sum_of_squares   J9   box_22A   GetData   Bin3D4   count
```

And here are some examples of invalid identifiers and the reasons why they are invalid:

Invalid Identifier	Explanation
40Hours	Identifiers cannot begin with a digit.
Get Data	Blanks are not allowed in identifiers.
box-22	The hyphen (–) is a math symbol (minus) in C++.
cost_in_$	Special symbols such as $ are not allowed.
int	The word int is predefined in the C++ language.

The last identifier in the table, int, is an example of a **reserved word**. Reserved words are words that have specific uses in C++; you cannot use them as programmer-defined identifiers. Appendix A lists all of the reserved words in C++.

Reserved Word   A word that has special meaning in C++; it cannot be used as a programmer-defined identifier.

The Payroll program in Chapter 1 uses the programmer-defined identifiers listed below. (Most of the other identifiers in the program are C++ reserved words.) Notice that we chose the names to convey how the identifiers are used.

Identifier	How It Is Used
MAX_HOURS	Maximum normal work hours
OVERTIME	Overtime pay rate factor
payRate	An employee's hourly pay rate
hours	The number of hours an employee worked
wages	An employee's weekly wages
total	The sum of weekly wages for all employees (total company payroll)
empNum	An employee's identification number
payFile	The output file (where the employee's number, pay rate, hours, and wages are written)
CalcPay	A function for computing an employee's wages

MATTERS OF STYLE

Using Meaningful, Readable Identifiers

The names we use to refer to things in our programs are totally meaningless to the computer. The computer behaves in the same way whether we call the value 3.14159265, pi, or cake, as long as we always call it the same thing. However, it is much easier for somebody to figure out how a program works if the names we choose for elements actually tell something about them. Whenever you have to make up a name for something in a program, try to pick one that will be meaningful to a person reading the program.

C++ is a *case-sensitive* language. Uppercase letters are different from lowercase letters. The identifiers

PRINTTOPPORTION   printtopportion   pRiNtToPpOrTiOn   PrintTopPortion

are four distinct names and are not interchangeable in any way. As you can see, the last of these forms is the easiest to read. In this book, we use combinations of uppercase letters, lowercase letters, and underscores in identifiers. We explain our conventions for choosing between uppercase and lowercase as we proceed through this chapter.

Now that we've seen how to write identifiers, we look at some of the things that C++ allows us to name.

Data and Data Types

A computer program operates on data (stored internally in memory, stored externally on disk or tape, or input from a keyboard, text scanner, or electrical sensor) and produces output. In C++ each piece of data must be of a specific **data type**. The data type determines how the data is represented in the computer and the kinds of processing the computer can perform on it.

Data Type A specific set of data values along with a set of operations on those values.

Some types of data are used so frequently that C++ defines them for us. Also, programmers may define their own data types. We use the standard (built-in) data types until Chapter 10, where we show you how to define your own.

Overview of C++ Data Types The C++ built-in data types are organized into simple types, structured types, and address types (see Figure 2-1).

Do not feel overwhelmed by the quantity of data types shown in this figure. This chapter introduces you to the simple types only. The structured types and address types come much later in the book. First we look at the integral types (those used to represent integers), and then we consider the floating types (used to represent real numbers containing decimal points).

■ FIGURE 2-1   C++ Data Types

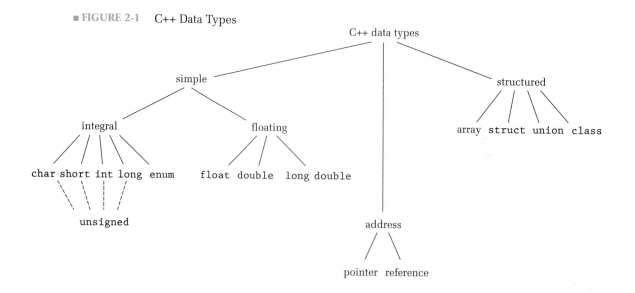

BACKGROUND INFORMATION

Data Storage

Where does a program get the data it needs to operate? Data is stored in the computer's memory. Remember that memory is divided into a large number of separate locations or cells, each of which can hold a piece of data. Each memory location has a unique address that we refer to when we store or retrieve data. We can visualize memory as a set of post office boxes, with the box numbers as the addresses used to designate particular locations.

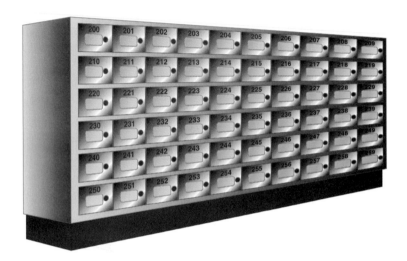

Of course, the actual "address" of each location in memory is a binary number in a machine language code. In C++ we use identifiers to name memory locations, then the compiler translates them for us. This is one of the advantages of a high-level programming language: It frees us from having to keep track of the actual memory locations in which our data and instructions are stored.

Integral Types   The data types char, short, int, and long are known as integral types because they refer to integer values—whole numbers with no fractional part. (We postpone talking about the fifth integral type—enum—until Chapter 10.)

In C++ the simplest form of integer value is a sequence of one or more digits:

22   16   1   498   0   4600

Commas are not allowed.

   In most cases, a minus sign preceding an integer value makes the integer negative:

-378   -912

The exception is when you explicitly add the reserved word unsigned to the data type name:

unsigned int

An unsigned integer value is assumed to be only positive or zero. It is only for very specialized, advanced problems that you will need to use unsigned types. We rarely use unsigned in this book.

   The data types char, short, int, and long are intended to represent different sizes of integers, from smaller (fewer bits) to larger (more bits).

char memory cell   ▭

short memory cell   ▭

int memory cell   ▭

long memory cell   ▭

The sizes are machine dependent (that is, they may vary from machine to machine). In general, the more bits there are in the memory cell, the larger the integer value that can be stored.

   int is by far the most common data type for manipulating integer data. In the Payroll program, the identifier for the employee number, empNum, is of data type int. You nearly always use int for manipulating integer values, but sometimes you have to use long if your program requires values larger than the maximum int value. (On many personal computers, the range of int values is from -32768 through +32767. On larger machines, ints often range from -2147483648 through +2147483647.) If your program tries to compute a value larger than your machine's maximum value, the result is *integer overflow*. Some machines give you an error message when overflow occurs, but others don't. We talk more about overflow in later chapters.

   One caution about integer values in C++: A value beginning with a zero is taken to be an octal (base-8) number instead of a decimal (base-10) number. If you write

015

the C++ compiler takes this to mean the decimal number 13. If you aren't familiar with the octal number system, don't worry about why an octal 15 is the same as a decimal 13. The important thing to remember is not to start a decimal integer value with a zero (unless you want the number 0, which is the same in both octal and decimal). In Chapter 10, we discuss the various integral types in more detail.

More About the `char` Type   We have seen that `char` is the "smallest" data type for representing integer values. A `char` value occupies less memory space than an `int` value, so programmers sometimes use the `char` data type to save memory in programs that use small integer values. But there is another, far more important use of the `char` type: to describe data consisting of one alphanumeric character—a letter, a digit, or a special symbol:

'A'   'a'   '8'   '2'   '+'   '-'   '$'   '?'   '*'   ' '

Each machine uses a particular *character set*, the set of alphanumeric characters it can represent. (See Appendix E for some sample character sets.) Notice that each character is enclosed in single quotes (apostrophes). The C++ compiler needs the quotes to differentiate between the character data '8' and the integer value 8 because the two are stored differently inside the machine. Notice also that the blank, ' ', is a valid character.

You wouldn't want to add the character 'A' to the character 'B' or subtract the character '3' from the character '8', but you might want to compare character values. Each character set has a *collating sequence*, a predefined ordering of all the characters. Although this sequence varies from one character set to another, 'A' always compares less than 'B', 'B' less than 'C', and so forth. And '1' compares less than '2', '2' less than '3', and so on. None of the identifiers in the Payroll program is of type `char`.

Floating Point Types   Floating point types (or floating types), the second major category of simple types in C++, are used to represent real numbers. Floating point numbers have an integer part and a fractional part, with a decimal point in between. Either the integer part or the fractional part, but not both, may be missing. Here are some examples:

18.0   127.54   0.57   4.   193145.8523   .8

Starting 0.57 with a 0 does not make it an octal number. It is only with integer values that a leading 0 indicates an octal number.

Just as the integral types in C++ come in different sizes (`char`, `short`, `int`, and `long`), so do the floating point types. In increasing order of size, the floating point types are `float`, `double` (meaning double precision), and `long` double. Each larger size gives us a wider range of values and more precision (the number of significant digits in the number), but at the expense of more memory space to hold the number.

Floating point values also can have an exponent, as in scientific notation. (In scientific notation, a number is written as a value multiplied by 10 to some power.) Instead of writing 3.504×10^{12}, in C++ we write 3.504E12. The E means exponent of base 10. The number preceding the letter E doesn't need to include a decimal point. Here are some examples of floating point numbers in scientific notation:

1.74536E-12   3.652442E4   7E20

Most programs don't need the double and long double types. The float type usually provides sufficient precision and range of values for floating point numbers. Even personal computers provide float values with a precision of six or seven significant digits and a maximum value of about 3.4E+38. In the Payroll program, the identifiers MAX_HOURS, OVERTIME, payRate, hours, wages, and total are all of type float because they are identifiers for data items that may have fractional parts.

We talk more about floating point numbers in Chapter 10. But there is one more thing you should know about them now. Computers cannot always represent floating point numbers exactly. You learned in Chapter 1 that the computer stores all data in binary (base-2) form. Many floating point values can only be approximated in the binary number system. Don't be surprised if your program prints out the number 4.8 as 4.7999998. In most cases, slight inaccuracies in the rightmost fractional digits are to be expected and are not the result of programmer error.

Naming Elements: Declarations

Identifiers can be used to name both constants and variables. In other words, an identifier can be the name of a memory location whose contents are not allowed to change or it can be the name of a memory location whose contents do change.

How do we tell the computer what an identifier represents? By using a **declaration,** a statement that associates a name (an identifier) with a description of an element in a C++ program (just as a dictionary definition associates a name with a description of the thing being named). In a declaration, we name an identifier and what it represents. For example, the Payroll program uses the declaration

int empNum;

to announce that empNum is the name of a variable whose contents are of type int. When we declare a variable, the compiler picks a location in memory to be associated with the identifier. We don't have to know the actual address of the memory location because the computer automatically keeps track of it for us.

Declaration   A statement that associates an identifier with a data object, a function, or a data type so that the programmer can refer to that item by name.

Suppose that when we mailed a letter, we just had to put a name on it and the post office would look up the address. Of course, everybody in the world would have to have a different name; otherwise the post office wouldn't be able to figure out whose address was whose. The same is true in C++. Each identifier can represent just one thing (except under special circumstances, which we talk about in Chapters 7 and 8). Every identifier you use in a program must be different from all others.

Constants and variables are collectively called *data objects*. Both data objects and the actual instructions in a program are stored in various memory locations. You have seen that a group of instructions—a function—can be given a name. Later on, you'll see that a name also can be associated with a programmer-defined data type, a data type that is not predefined in the C++ language.

In C++ you must declare every identifier before it is used. This allows the compiler to verify that the use of the identifier is consistent with what it was declared to be. If you declare an identifier to be a constant and later try to change its value, the compiler detects this inconsistency and issues an error message.

There is a different form of declaration statement for each kind of data object, function, or data type in C++. The forms of declaration for variables and constants are introduced here; others are covered in later chapters.

Variables   A program operates on data. Data is stored in memory. While a program is executing, different values may be stored in the same memory location at different times. This kind of memory location is called a **variable,** and its contents are the *variable value*. The symbolic name that we associate with a memory location is the *variable name* or *variable identifier* (see Figure 2-2). In practice, we often refer to the variable name as the *variable*.

Variable   A location in memory, referenced by an identifier, in which a data value that can be changed is stored.

■ FIGURE 2-2

Variable

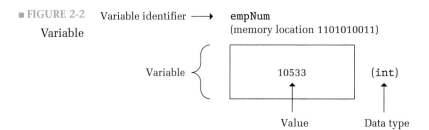

Variable identifier ⟶   empNum
(memory location 1101010011)

Declaring a variable means specifying both its name and its data type. This tells the compiler to associate a name with a memory location whose contents are of a specific type (for example, int, float, or char). The following statement declares empNum to be a variable of type int:

```
int empNum;
```

In C++ a variable can contain only data values of the type specified in its declaration. Because of the above declaration, the variable empNum can contain *only* int values. If the C++ compiler comes across an instruction that tries to store a float value into empNum, it generates extra instructions to convert the float value to an int. In Chapter 3, we examine how these conversions take place.

Here's the syntax template for a variable declaration:

VariableDeclaration

DataType Identifier , Identifier ... ;

where DataType is the name of a data type such as int, float, or char. Notice that a declaration always ends with a semicolon.

From the syntax template, you can see that it is possible to declare several variables in one statement:

```
int studentCount, maxScore, sumOfScores;
```

Here, all three variables are declared to be int variables. Our preference, though, is to declare each variable with a separate statement:

```
int studentCount;
int maxScore;
int sumOfScores;
```

With this form it is easier, when modifying a program, to add new variables to the list or delete ones you no longer want.

Declaring each variable with a separate statement also allows you to attach comments to the right of each declaration, as we do in the Payroll program:

```
float payRate;      // Employee's pay rate
float hours;        // Hours worked
float wages;        // Wages earned
float total;        // Total company payroll
int   empNum;       // Employee ID number
```

These declarations tell the compiler to set up locations in memory for four float variables—payRate, hours, wages, and total—and to set up one location for an int variable named empNum. The comments explain to the reader what each variable represents.

Now that we've seen how to declare variables in C++, let's look at how to declare constants.

Constants   All numbers—integer and floating point—are constants. So are single characters (enclosed in single quotes) and sequences of characters, or *strings* (enclosed in double quotes).

```
16   32.3   'A'   "Howdy boys"
```

In C++ as in mathematics, a constant is something whose value never changes.

We use numeric constants as part of arithmetic expressions (as you will see later in this chapter). For example, we can write a statement that adds the constants 5 and 6 and places the result into a variable named sum. When we use the actual value of a constant in a program, we are using a **literal value** (or *literal*).

Literal Value   Any constant value written in a program.

Notice that a char literal can have only one character within single quotes ('), whereas a string literal can have many characters and must be enclosed within double quotes ("). The use of quotes lets us differentiate between char or string literals and identifiers. "amount" (in double quotes) is the character string made up of the letters *a, m, o, u, n,* and *t* in that order. On the other hand, amount (without the quotes) is an identifier, perhaps the name of a variable.

Although character and string literals are put in quotes, literal integers and floating point numbers are not, because there is no chance of confusing them with identifiers. Why? Because identifiers must start with a letter or underscore, and numbers must start with a digit.

An alternative to the literal constant is the **named constant** (or **symbolic constant**), which is introduced in a declaration statement. A named constant is just another way of representing a literal value. Instead of using the literal value in an instruction, we give it a name in a declaration statement, then use that name in the instruction. For example, we can write an instruction that multiplies the literal values 3.14159 and 4.5. Or we can define a constant in a declaration statement for each of those values, and then use the constant names in the instruction. For example, we can use either

3.14159×4.5 or $PI \times RADIUS$

but the latter is more descriptive.

Named Constant   A location in memory, referenced by an identifier, where a data value that cannot be changed is stored.

It may seem easier to use the literal value of a constant than to give the constant a name and then refer to it by that name. But, in fact, named constants make a program easier to read because they make the meaning of literal constants clearer. And named constants also make it easier to change a program later on.

This is the syntax template for a constant declaration:

ConstantDeclaration

> **const** DataType Identifier = LiteralValue **;**

Notice that the reserved word `const` begins the declaration, and an equal sign (=) appears between the identifier and the literal value.

These are valid constant declarations:

```
const char   BLANK = ' ';
const float  PI = 3.14159;
const float  INTEREST_RATE = 0.12;
const float  TAX_RATE = 0.001;
const int    MAX = 20;
```

Many C++ programmers capitalize the entire identifier of a named constant and separate the English words with an underscore. The idea is to let the reader quickly distinguish between variable names and constant names in the middle of a program.

SOFTWARE ENGINEERING TIP

Using Named Constants

It's a good idea to use named constants instead of literals. In addition to making your program more readable, it can make it easier to modify. Suppose you wrote a program last year to compute taxes. In several places you used the literal 0.05, which was the sales tax rate at the time. Now the rate has gone up to 0.06. To change your program, you have to locate every literal 0.05 and change it to 0.06. And if 0.05 is used for some other reason—to compute deductions, for example—you have to look at each place where it is used, figure out what it is used for, and then decide whether it needs to be changed.

The process is much simpler if you use a named constant. Instead of using a literal constant, suppose you had declared a named constant, TAX_RATE, with a value of 0.05. To change your program, you would simply change the declaration, setting TAX_RATE equal to 0.06. This one modification changes all of the tax rate computations without affecting the other places where 0.05 is used.

C++ allows us to declare constants with different names but the same value. If a value has different meanings in different parts of a program, it makes sense to declare and use a constant with an appropriate name for each meaning.

Named constants also are reliable; they protect us from mistakes. If you mistype the name PI as PO, the C++ compiler will tell you that the name PO has not been declared. On the other hand, even though we recognize that the number 3.14149 is a mistyped version of pi (3.14159), the number is perfectly acceptable to the compiler. It won't warn us that anything is wrong.

It's a good idea to add comments to constant declarations as well as variable declarations. In the Payroll program we describe in comments what each constant represents:

```
const float MAX_HOURS = 40.0;      // Maximum normal work hours
const float OVERTIME = 1.5;        // Overtime pay rate factor
```

MATTERS OF STYLE

Capitalization of Identifiers

Programmers often use capitalization as a quick, visual clue to what an identifier represents. Different programmers adopt different conventions for using uppercase letters and lowercase letters. Some people use only lowercase letters, separating the English words in an identifier with the underscore character:

```
pay_rate    emp_num   pay_file
```

The convention we use in this book is the following:

- For identifiers representing variables, we begin with a lowercase letter and capitalize each successive English word.

```
lengthInYards    sumOfSquares    hours
```

- Names of programmer-written functions and programmer-defined data types (which we discuss later in the book) are capitalized the same as variable names except that they begin with capital letters.

```
CalcPay(payRate, hours, wages)    Cube(27)    MyDataType
```

Capitalizing the first letter allows a person reading the program to tell at a glance that an identifier represents a function name or data type rather than a variable. However, we cannot use this capitalization convention everywhere. C++ expects every program to have a function named main—all in lowercase letters—so we cannot name it Main. Nor can we use Int for the built-in data type int. C++ reserved words use all lowercase letters.

- For identifiers representing named constants, we capitalize every letter and use underscores to separate the English words.

```
UPPER_LIMIT    PI    MAX_LENGTH
```

This convention, widely used by C++ programmers, is an immediate signal that UPPER_LIMIT is a named constant and not a variable, a function, or a data type.

These conventions are only that—conventions. C++ does not require this particular style of capitalizing identifiers. You may wish to capitalize in a different fashion. But whatever you use, it is essential that you use a consistent style throughout your program. A person reading your program will be confused or misled if you use a random style of capitalization.

Taking Action: Executable Statements

Up to this point we've looked at ways of declaring data objects in a program. Now we turn our attention to ways of acting, or performing operations, on data.

Assignment   The value of a variable is changed through an **assignment statement.** For example,

```
quizScore = 10;
```

assigns the value 10 to the variable `quizScore` (stores the value 10 into the memory location called `quizScore`).

Assignment Statement   A statement that stores the value of an expression into a variable.

Here's the syntax template for an assignment statement:

AssignmentStatement

> Variable = Expression **;**

The semantics (meaning) of the assignment operator (=) is "store"; the value of the expression is *stored* into the variable. Any previous value in the variable is destroyed and replaced by the value of the expression.

Only one variable can be on the left-hand side of an assignment statement. An assignment statement is *not* like a math equation ($x + y = z + 4$);

the expression (what is on the right-hand side of the assignment operator) is evaluated, and that value is stored into the single variable on the left of the assignment operator. A variable keeps its assigned value until another statement stores a new value into it.

Given the declarations

```
int   num;
int   alpha;
float rate;
char  ch;
```

we can make the following assignments:

Variable	Expression
alpha =	2856;
rate =	0.36;
ch =	'B';
num =	alpha;

However, the following assignment is not valid:

```
ch = "Hello";
```

A char variable can hold only one character. For the time being, the only thing we do with strings is print them out as messages:

```
cout << "Hello";
```

Expressions are made up of constants, variables, and operators. The following are all valid expressions:

```
alpha + 2    rate - 6.0    4 - alpha    rate    alpha * num
```

The operators allowed in an expression depend on the data types of the constants and variables in the expression. The *arithmetic operators* are

+	Unary plus
-	Unary minus
+	Addition
-	Subtraction
*	Multiplication
/	{ Floating point division (floating point result)
	{ Integer division (no fractional part)
%	Modulus (remainder from integer division)

The first two operators are **unary operators**—they take just one operand. The remaining five are **binary operators**, taking two operands. Unary plus and minus are used as follows:

```
-54    +259.65    -rate
```

You almost never use the unary plus. Without any sign, a numeric constant is assumed to be positive anyway.

Unary Operator An operator that has just one operand.
Binary Operator An operator that has two operands.

You may not be familiar with integer division and modulus (%). Let's look at them more closely. Note that % is used only with integers. When you divide one integer by another, you get an integer quotient and a remainder. Integer division gives only the integer quotient, and % gives only the remainder. (If either operand is negative, the result may vary from one C++ compiler to another.)

$$\begin{array}{r} 3 \\ 2\overline{)6} \\ 6 \\ \hline 0 \end{array} \leftarrow 6 / 2 \qquad \begin{array}{r} 3 \\ 2\overline{)7} \\ 6 \\ \hline 1 \end{array} \leftarrow 7 / 2$$

$$\leftarrow 6 \% 2 \qquad \qquad \leftarrow 7 \% 2$$

In contrast, floating point division yields a floating point result. The expression

```
7.0 / 2.0
```

yields the value 3.5.

Here are some expressions using arithmetic operators and their values:

Expression	Value
3 + 6	9
3.4 - 6.1	−2.7
2 * 3	6
8 / 2	4
8.0 / 2.0	4.0
8 / 8	1
8 / 9	0
8 / 7	1
8 % 8	0
8 % 9	8
8 % 7	1
0 % 7	0
5 % 2.3	error (both operands must be integers)

Be careful with division and modulus. The expressions 7.0 / 0.0, 7 / 0, and 7 % 0 all produce errors. The computer cannot divide by zero.

Because variables are allowed in expressions, the following are valid assignments:

```
alpha = num + 6;
alpha = num / 2;
num = alpha * 2;
num = 6 % alpha;
alpha = alpha + 1;
num = num + alpha;
```

Notice that the same variable can appear on both sides of the assignment operator. In the case of

```
num = num + alpha;
```

the value in num and the value in alpha are added together, then the sum of the two values is stored into num, replacing the previous value stored there. This example shows the difference between mathematical equality and assignment. The mathematical equality

$$num = num + alpha$$

is true only when alpha equals zero. The assignment statement

```
num = num + alpha;
```

is valid for *any* value of alpha.

In the examples of expressions so far, we have been careful not to mix integer and floating point values in the same expression. When mixed-type expressions occur, the compiler applies certain rules for converting operands from one type to another. In the next chapter, we discuss those rules.

Increment and Decrement   In addition to the arithmetic operators, C++ provides *increment* and *decrement operators*:

++   Increment
--   Decrement

These are unary operators that take a single variable name as an operand. For integer and floating point operands, the effect is to add 1 to (or subtract 1 from) the operand. If num currently contains the value 8, the statement

```
num++;
```

causes num to contain 9. You can achieve the same effect by writing the assignment statement

```
num = num + 1;
```

but C++ programmers typically prefer the increment operator.

The ++ and -- operators can be either *prefix operators*

```
++num;
```

or *postfix operators*

```
num++;
```

Both of these statements behave in exactly the same way; they add 1 to whatever is in num. The choice between the two is a matter of personal preference.

C++ allows the use of ++ and -- in the middle of a larger expression:

```
alpha = num++ * 3;
```

In this case, the postfix form of ++ gives a different result from the prefix form. In Chapter 10, we explain the ++ and -- operators in detail. In the meantime, you should use them only to increment or decrement a variable as a separate, stand-alone statement:

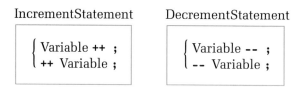

IncrementStatement   DecrementStatement

$$\left\{ \begin{array}{l} \text{Variable ++ ;} \\ \text{++ Variable ;} \end{array} \right. \qquad \left\{ \begin{array}{l} \text{Variable -- ;} \\ \text{-- Variable ;} \end{array} \right.$$

Output   Have you ever asked someone, "Do you know what time it is?" only to have the person smile smugly, say, "Yes, I do," and walk away? This is like the situation that currently exists between you and the computer. You now know enough C++ syntax to tell the computer to perform simple calculations, but the computer won't give you the answers until you tell it to write them out.

In C++ we write out the results of calculations by using a special variable named cout (pronounced "see-out") along with the *insertion operator* (<<):

```
cout << "Hello";
```

This statement displays the characters Hello on the *standard output device,* usually the video display screen.

The variable cout is predefined in C++ systems to denote an *output stream.* You can think of an output stream as an endless sequence of characters going to an output device. In the case of cout, the output stream goes to the standard output device.

The insertion operator << (often pronounced as "put to") takes two operands. Its left-hand operand is a stream expression (in the simplest case, just a stream variable such as cout). Its right-hand operand is either an expression of simple type or a string:

```
cout << "The answer is ";
cout << 3 * num;
```

The insertion operator converts its right-hand operand to a sequence of characters and inserts them into (or, more precisely, appends them to) the output stream. Notice how the << points in the direction the data are going—

from the expression or string written on the right *to* the output stream on the left.

You can use the << operator several times in a single output statement. Each occurrence appends the next data item to the output stream. For example, we can write the preceding two output statements as

```
cout << "The answer is " << 3 * num;
```

If num contains the value 5, both versions produce the same output:

```
The answer is 15
```

The output statement has the following form, where ExprOrString stands for either an expression of simple type or a string constant:

OutputStatement

> **cout** << ExprOrString **<<** ExprOrString ... ;

The following output statements yield the output shown. These examples assume that the variable i contains the value 2, and j contains 6.

Statement	What Is Printed (□ means blank)
`cout << i;`	2
`cout << "i = " << i;`	i□=□2
`cout << "Sum = " << i + j;`	Sum□=□8
`cout << "ERROR MESSAGE";`	ERROR□MESSAGE
`cout << "Error=" << i;`	Error=2
`cout << "j:" << j << "i:" << i;`	j:6i:2
`cout << "j:" << j << ' ' << "i:" << i;`	j:6□i:2

An output statement prints string constants exactly as they appear within quotes. To let the computer know that you want to print a string constant—not a named constant or variable—you must use double quotes to enclose the string. If you don't put quotes around a string, you'll probably get an error message (like "UNDECLARED IDENTIFIER") from the C++ compiler. If you want to print a string that includes a double quote, you must type a backslash (\) character and a double quote, with no space between them, in the string. For example, to print the string

```
Al "Butch" Jones
```

the output statement looks like this:

```
cout << "Al \"Butch\" Jones";
```

   To conclude this introductory look at C++ output, we should mention how to terminate an output line. Normally, successive output statements cause the output to continue along the same line of the display screen. The sequence

```
cout << "Hi";
cout << "there";
```

writes the following to the screen, all on the same line:

```
Hithere
```

To print the two words on separate lines, we can do this:

```
cout << "Hi" << endl;
cout << "there" << endl;
```

The output from these statements is

```
Hi
there
```

The identifier endl (meaning "end line") doesn't fit the pattern in the syntax template we gave. It is neither an expression of simple type nor a string constant. It is a special C++ feature called a *manipulator*. We discuss manipulators in the next chapter. For now, the important thing to note is that endl lets you finish an output line and go on to the next line whenever you wish.

Beyond Minimalism: Adding Comments to a Program

All you need to create a working program is the correct combination of declarations and executable statements. The compiler ignores comments, but they are of enormous help to anyone who must read the program. Comments can appear anywhere in a program.

C++ comments come in two forms. The first is any sequence of characters enclosed by the /* */ pair. The compiler ignores anything within the pair. Here's an example:

```
float fuelLoad;    /* The amount of fuel, entered in pounds */
```

The second, and more common, form begins with two slashes (//) and extends to the end of that line of the program:

```
float fuelLoad;    // The amount of fuel, entered in pounds
```

The compiler ignores anything after the two slashes.

It is good programming style to write fully commented programs. A comment should appear at the beginning of a program to explain what the program does:

```
// This program computes the weight and balance of a Beechcraft
// Starship-1 airplane, given the amount of fuel, number of
// passengers, and weight of luggage in fore and aft storage.
// It assumes that there are two pilots and a standard complement
// of equipment, and that passengers weigh 170 pounds each
```

Another good place for comments is in constant and variable declarations, where the comments explain how each identifier is used. In addition, comments should introduce each major step in a long program and should explain anything that is unusual or difficult to read (for example, a lengthy formula).

It is important to make your comments concise and to arrange them in the program so that they are easy to see and it is clear what they refer to. If comments are too long or crowd the statements of the program, they make the program more difficult to read—just the opposite of what you intended!

Program Construction

We have looked at basic elements of C++ programs: identifiers, declarations, variables, constants, expressions, statements, and comments. Now let's see how to collect these elements into a program. As you saw earlier, C++ programs are made up of functions, one of which must be named main. A program also can have declarations that lie outside of any function. The syntax template for a program looks like this:

Program

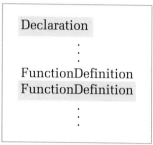

A function definition consists of the function heading and its body, which is delimited by left and right braces:

FunctionDefinition

```
Heading
{
        Statement
        :
        :
}
```

Here's an example of a program with just one function, the `main` function:

```
//********************************************************************
// FreezeBoil program
// This program computes the midpoint between
// the freezing and boiling points of water
//********************************************************************
#include <iostream.h>

const float FREEZE_PT = 32.0;    // Freezing point of water
const float BOIL_PT = 212.0;     // Boiling point of water

int main()
{
    float avgTemp;                       // Holds the result of averaging
                                         //    FREEZE_PT and BOIL_PT

    cout << "Water freezes at " << FREEZE_PT << endl;
    cout << " and boils at " << BOIL_PT << " degrees." << endl;

    avgTemp = FREEZE_PT + BOIL_PT;
    avgTemp = avgTemp / 2.0;
```

```
    cout << "Halfway between is ";
    cout << avgTemp << " degrees." << endl;

    return 0;
}
```

The program begins with a comment that explains what the program does. Immediately after the comment, the line

```
#include <iostream.h>
```

instructs the C++ system to insert the contents of a file named `iostream.h` into our program. This file contains information that C++ requires to output values to a stream such as `cout`. We'll consider exactly what is done by this `#include` line a little later.

Next comes a declaration section where we define the constants `FREEZE_PT` and `BOIL_PT`. Comments explain how each identifier is used. The rest of the program is the function definition for our `main` function. The first line is the function heading: the reserved word `int`, the name of the function, and then opening and closing parentheses. (The parentheses inform the compiler that `main` is the name of a function, not a variable or named constant.) The body of the function includes a declaration of the variable `avgTemp` and then a list of executable statements. The compiler translates these executable statements into machine language instructions. During the execution phase of the program, these are the instructions that are executed.

Our `main` function finishes by returning zero as the function value:

```
return 0;
```

Remember that `main` returns an integer value to the operating system when it completes execution. This integer value is called the *exit status*. On most computer systems, you return an exit status of zero to indicate successful completion of the program; otherwise, you return a nonzero value.

Notice how we use spacing in the FreezeBoil program to make it easy for someone to read. We use blank lines to separate statements into related groups, and we indent the entire body of the `main` function. The compiler doesn't require us to format the program this way; we do so only to make it more readable. We have more to say in the next chapter about formatting a program.

Blocks (Compound Statements)

The body of a function is an example of a *block* (or *compound statement*). This is the syntax template for a block:

Block

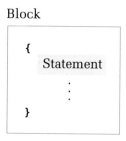

A block is just a sequence of zero or more statements enclosed (delimited) by a { } pair. Now we can redefine a function definition as a heading followed by a block:

FunctionDefinition

> Heading
> Block

In later chapters when we learn how to write functions other than `main`, we'll define the syntax of Heading in detail. In the case of the `main` function, Heading is simply

```
int main()
```

Here is the syntax template for a statement, limited to the C++ statements discussed in this chapter:

Statement

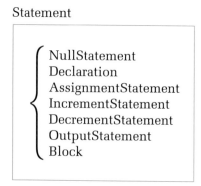

A statement can be empty (the *null statement*). The null statement is just a semicolon (;) and looks like this:

```
;
```

It does absolutely nothing at execution time; execution just proceeds to the next statement. It is not used often.

As the syntax template shows, a statement also can be a declaration, an executable statement, or even a block. The latter means that you can use an entire block wherever a single statement is allowed. In later chapters where we introduce the syntax for branching and looping structures, you'll see that this fact is very important.

We use blocks often, especially as parts of other statements. Leaving out a { } pair can dramatically change the meaning as well as the execution of a program. This is why we always indent the statements inside a block—the indentation makes a block easy to spot in a long, complicated program.

Notice in the syntax templates for the block and the statement that there is no mention of semicolons. Yet the FreezeBoil program contains many semicolons. If you look back at the templates for constant declaration, variable declaration, assignment statement, and output statement, you can see that a semicolon is required at the end of each kind of statement. However, the syntax template for the block shows no semicolon after the right brace. The rule for using semicolons in C++, then, is quite simple: Terminate each statement *except* a compound statement (block) with a semicolon.

One more thing about blocks and statements: According to the syntax template for a statement, a declaration is officially considered to be a statement. A declaration, therefore, can appear wherever an executable statement can. In a block, we can mix declarations and executable statements if we wish:

```
{
    int i;
    i = 35;
    cout << i;
    float x;
    x = 14.8;
    cout << x;
}
```

It's far more common, though, for programmers to group the declarations together before the start of the executable statements:

```
{
    int i;
    float x;

    i = 35;
    cout << i;
    x = 14.8;
    cout << x;
}
```

The C++ Preprocessor

Imagine that you are the C++ compiler. You are presented with the following program. You are to check it for syntax errors and, if there are no syntax errors, you are to translate it into machine language code.

```
//**********************************
// This program prints Happy Birthday
//**********************************

int main()
{
    cout << "Happy Birthday" << endl;
    return 0;
}
```

You, the compiler, recognize the identifier `int` as a C++ reserved word and the identifier `main` as the name of a required function. But what about the identifiers `cout` and `endl`? The programmer has not declared them as variables or named constants, and they are not reserved words. You have no choice but to issue an error message and give up.

The way to fix this program is to insert a line near the top that says

```
#include <iostream.h>
```

just as we did in the FreezeBoil program (as well as in the sample program at the beginning of this chapter and the Payroll program of Chapter 1).

The line says to insert the contents of a file named `iostream.h` into the program. This file contains declarations of `cout`, `endl`, and other items needed to perform stream input and output. The `#include` line is not handled by the C++ compiler but by a program known as the *preprocessor*.

The preprocessor concept is fundamental to C++. The preprocessor is a program that acts as a filter during the compilation phase. Your source program passes through the preprocessor on its way to the compiler (see Figure 2.3).

A line beginning with a pound sign (#) is not considered to be a C++ language statement (and thus is not terminated by a semicolon). It is called a *preprocessor directive*. The preprocessor expands an `#include` directive by physically inserting the contents of the named file into your source program. Files that appear in an `#include` directive usually have a file name ending in `.h`, meaning *header file*. Header files contain constant, variable, and function declarations needed by a program.

■ FIGURE 2-3   C++ Preprocessor

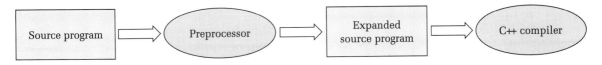

In the directive

```
#include <iostream.h>
```

the angle brackets < > are required. They tell the preprocessor to look for the file in the standard *include directory*—a location in the computer system that contains all the header files that are available to C++ programmers. In Chapter 3, you will see examples of including header files other than `iostream.h`.

Program Entry, Correction, and Execution

Once you have the program on paper, how do you get it into the machine? The most common way is to enter it on the keyboard of a computer or terminal. In this section, we examine the program entry process in general. You should consult the manual for your specific computer to learn the details.

Entering a Program

The first step in entering a program is to get the computer's attention. With a personal computer, this usually means turning it on and possibly inserting a disk.

Larger computers (mainframes) are left running all the time. You must *log on* to a mainframe to get its attention. This means entering a user name and a password. The password system protects information that you've stored in the computer from being tampered with or destroyed by someone else.

Once the computer is ready to accept your commands, you tell it that you want to enter a program by typing a command that tells it to run the editor. As we discussed in Chapter 1, the editor allows you to create and modify programs by entering information into an area of the computer's secondary storage called a **file**.

File   A named area in secondary storage that is used to hold a collection of data; the collection of data itself.

A file in a computer system is like a file folder in a filing cabinet. It is a collection of information that has a name associated with it. You usually choose the name for the file when you create it with the editor. From that point on, you refer to the file by the name you've given it.

There are so many different types of editors, each with different features, that we can't begin to describe them all here. But we can describe some of their general characteristics. (Again, consult the manual for your computer to learn the details of the editor you'll be using.)

The basic unit of information in an editor is a display screen full of characters. The editor lets you change anything that you see on the screen. Most computer keyboards have a special group of keys called *cursor keys*. (The *cursor* is the mark on the screen that indicates the point where you are typing.) The cursor keys are a set of arrows that point up, down, right, and left (see Figure 2-4). Each time you press one of them, the cursor moves one line up or down, or one character right or left. You can use these keys to move the cursor to any point on the screen. The keyboard also may contain command keys that let you look at other parts of the file, delete characters or lines, insert new lines, and so on.

When you create a new file, the editor clears the screen to show you that the file is empty. Then you enter your program, using the cursor and command keys to go back and make corrections as necessary. Figure 2-5 shows an example of an editor's display screen.

Compiling and Running a Program

Once your program is stored in a file, you compile it by issuing a command to run the C++ compiler. The compiler translates the program, then stores the machine language version into a file. On some systems, the compiler also creates and stores a listing into another file. A *listing* is a copy of the

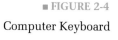

■ FIGURE 2-4

Computer Keyboard

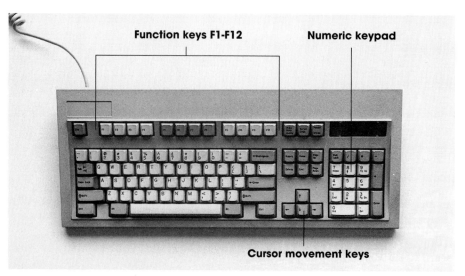

■ FIGURE 2-5   Display Screen for Screen Editor

```
 ≡  File   Edit   Search   Run   Compile   Debug   Project   Options    Window   Help
┌─[■]══════════════════════════PAYROLL.CPP ═══════════════════════ 2 ═[↕]═┐
│ //***************************************************************        │
│ //  Payroll program                                             ■       │
│ //  This program computes each employee's wages and                     │
│ //  the total company payroll                                           │
│ //***************************************************************        │
│ #include <iostream.h>                                                   │
│ #include <fstream.h>        // For file I/O                             │
│                                                                         │
│ void CalcPay( float, float, float& );                                   │
│                                                                         │
│ const float MAX_HOURS = 40.0;    // Maximum normal work hours           │
│ const float OVERTIME = 1.5;      // Overtime pay rate factor            │
│                                                                         │
│ int main()                                                              │
│ (                                                                       │
│     float    payRate;        // Employee's pay rate                     │
│     float    hours;          // Hours worked                            │
│     float    wages;          // Wages earned                            │
│     float    total;          // Total company payroll                   │
│     int      empNum;         // Employee ID number                      │
└══════ 1:1═══════[■                                                      │
```
F1 Help   F2 Save   F3 Open   Alt-F9 Compile   F9 Make   F10 Menu

source program with messages from the compiler inserted into it. Usually the messages indicate errors in the program that are preventing the compiler from completing the translation. Other systems just display the first error in the program and automatically bring up the editor with the cursor positioned at that point.

If the compiler finds errors in your program (syntax errors), you have to determine their cause, go back to the editor and fix them, and then run the compiler again. Once your program compiles without errors, you can run (execute) it.

Some systems automatically run a program when it compiles successfully. On other systems, you have to type a separate command to run the program. Still other systems require that you specify an extra step called *linking* between compiling and running a program. Whatever series of commands your system uses, the result is the same: Your program is loaded into memory and executed by the computer.

Even though a program runs, it still may have errors in its design. The computer does exactly what you tell it to do, even if that's not what you wanted it to do. If your program doesn't do what it should (a *logic error*), you have to go back to the algorithm and fix it, and then go to the editor and fix the program. Finally, you compile and run the program again. This *debugging* process is repeated until the program does what it is supposed to do (see Figure 2-6).

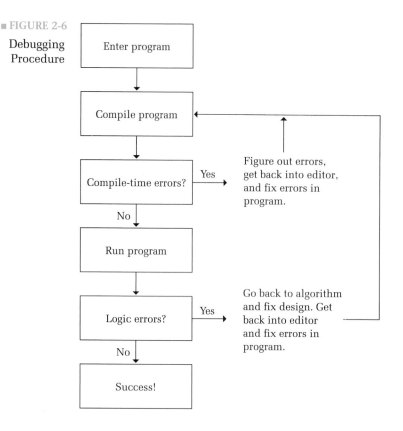

■ FIGURE 2-6

Debugging Procedure

SOFTWARE ENGINEERING TIP

Understanding Before Changing

When you are in the middle of getting a program to run and you come across an error, it's tempting to start changing parts of the program to try to make it work. *Don't!* You'll nearly always make things worse. It's essential that you understand what is causing the error and that you carefully think through the solution. The only thing you should try is running the program with different input data to determine the pattern of the unexpected behavior.

There is no magic trick—inserting an extra semicolon or right brace, for example—that can automatically fix a program. If the compiler tells you that a semicolon or a right brace is missing, you have to examine the program in light of the syntax rules and determine precisely what the problem is. Perhaps you accidentally typed a colon instead of a semicolon. Or maybe there's an extra left brace.

A good rule of thumb is: If the source of a problem isn't immediately obvious, leave the computer and go somewhere where you can quietly look over a printed copy of the program. Studies show that people who do all of their debugging away from the computer actually get their programs to work in less time *and in the end produce better programs* than those who continue to work on the machine—more proof that there is still no mechanical substitute for human thought.*

---

*Basili, V. R., Selby, R. W., "Comparing the Effectiveness of Software Testing Strategies," *IEEE Trans. on Software Engineering*, Vol. SE-13, No. 12, pp. 1278–1296, Dec. 1987.

Finishing Up

On larger computer systems, once you finish working on your program, you have to *log off* by typing a command. This frees up the terminal so that someone else can use it. It also prevents someone from walking up to the terminal after you leave and tampering with your files.

On a personal computer, when you're done working, you save your files, then remove any disks that you've inserted. Turning off the power wipes out what's in the computer's memory, but your files are stored safely on the disks. The next time you use the computer, you simply reinsert the disks and the computer is able to recall the files from them. (If the PC is in a lab where it gets frequent use by many people, you'll probably be asked to leave the computer on in order to save wear and tear on the machine.)

Be sure to read the manual for your particular system and editor before you enter your first program. Don't panic if you have trouble at first—almost everyone does. It becomes much easier with practice.

P ROBLEM-SOLVING CASE STUDY

Mileage

Problem: Write a program to calculate the miles per gallon a car gets on a trip, given the amounts in gallons of the fillups and the starting and ending mileage. The starting mileage was 67308.0; the ending mileage, 68750.5. During the trip, the car was filled up four times. The four amounts were 11.7, 14.3, 12.2, and 8.5 gallons. Assume that the tank was full initially and that the last fillup was at the end of the trip.

Output: The quantities on which the calculations are based and the computed miles per gallon, all appropriately labeled.

Discussion: If you calculated this by hand, you would add up the gallon amounts, then divide the sum into the mileage traveled. The mileage traveled is, of course, just the ending mileage minus the starting mileage. This is essentially the algorithm we use in the program. Let's make all of the numeric quantities named constants, so that it is easier to change the program later. Here is the algorithmic solution:

```
AMT1 = 11.7
AMT2 = 14.3
AMT3 = 12.2
AMT4 = 8.5
START_MILES = 67308.0
END_MILES = 68750.5
Set mpg = (END_MILES – START_MILES) / (AMT1 + AMT2 + AMT3 + AMT4)
Write the fillup amounts
Write the starting mileage
Write the ending mileage
Write the mileage per gallon
```

From the algorithm we can create tables of constants and variables that help us write the declarations in the program.

Constants

Name	Value	Description
AMT1	11.7	Number of gallons for fillup 1
AMT2	14.3	Number of gallons for fillup 2
AMT3	12.2	Number of gallons for fillup 3
AMT4	8.5	Number of gallons for fillup 4
START_MILES	67308.0	Starting mileage
END_MILES	68750.5	Ending mileage

Variables

Name	Data Type	Description
mpg	float	Computed miles per gallon

PROBLEM-SOLVING CASE STUDY cont'd.

Now we're ready to write the program. Let's call it Mileage. We can take the declarations from the tables and create the executable statements from the algorithm. We must add comments and be sure to label the output.

Here is the program:

```cpp
//*****************************************************************
// Mileage program
// This program computes miles per gallon given four amounts
// for gallons used, and starting and ending mileage
//*****************************************************************
#include <iostream.h>

const float AMT1 = 11.7;            // Number of gallons for fillup 1
const float AMT2 = 14.3;            // Number of gallons for fillup 2
const float AMT3 = 12.2;            // Number of gallons for fillup 3
const float AMT4 = 8.5;             // Number of gallons for fillup 4
const float START_MILES = 67308.0; // Starting mileage
const float END_MILES = 68750.5;   // Ending mileage

int main()
{
    float mpg;         // Computed miles per gallon

    mpg = (END_MILES - START_MILES) / (AMT1 + AMT2 + AMT3 + AMT4);

    cout << "For the gallon amounts " << endl;
    cout << AMT1 << ' ' << AMT2 << ' '
         << AMT3 << ' ' << AMT4 << endl;
    cout << "and a starting mileage of " << START_MILES << endl;
    cout << "and an ending mileage of " << END_MILES << endl;
    cout << "the mileage per gallon is " << mpg << endl;
    return 0;
}
```

The output from this program is

```
For the gallon amounts
11.7 14.3 12.2 8.5
and a starting mileage of 67308
and an ending mileage of 68750.5
the mileage per gallon is 30.888651
```

As the output of START_MILES shows, C++ does not display a decimal point and 0 when a floating point value is a whole number. Also, different versions of C++ may display either fewer or more decimal places (digits to the right of the decimal point) than the output shown here. In the next chapter, we discuss how the programmer can control the appearance of floating point numbers in the output.

TESTING AND DEBUGGING HINTS

1. Every identifier that isn't a C++ reserved word must be declared. If you use a name that hasn't been declared—either by your own declaration statements or by including a header file—you get an error message.
2. C++ is a case-sensitive language. Two identifiers that are capitalized differently are treated as two different identifiers. The word `main` and all C++ reserved words use only lowercase letters.
3. An `int` constant other than 0 should not start with a zero. If it starts with zero, it is an octal (base-8) number.
4. Watch out for integer division. The expression 47 / 100 yields 0, the integer quotient. This is one of the major sources of wrong output in C++ programs.
5. Check for mismatched quotes in `char` constants and strings. Each `char` constant begins and ends with an apostrophe (single quote). Each string begins and ends with a double quote.
6. Make sure your statements end in semicolons (except compound statements, which do not have a semicolon after the right brace).
7. If the cause of an error in a program is not obvious, leave the computer and study a printed listing. Change your program only after you understand the source of the error.

SUMMARY

The syntax (grammar) of the C++ language is defined by a metalanguage. In this text, we use a form of metalanguage called *syntax templates*. We describe the semantics (meaning) of C++ statements in English.

Identifiers are used in C++ to name things. Some identifiers, called *reserved words*, have predefined meanings in the language; others are created by the programmer. The identifiers you invent are restricted to those *not* reserved by the C++ language. Reserved words are listed in Appendix A.

Identifiers are associated with memory locations by declarations. A declaration may give a name to a location whose value does not change (a constant) or to one whose value does change (a variable). Every constant and variable has an associated data type. C++ provides many predefined data types, the most common of which are `int`, `float`, and `char`.

The assignment operator is used to change the value of a variable by assigning it the value of an expression. At execution time, the expression is evaluated and the result is stored into the variable. Another way to change the value of a variable is to add 1 to its value with the increment operator (++) or to subtract 1 from its value with the decrement operator (--).

Program output is accomplished by means of the output stream variable cout, along with the insertion operator (<<). Each insertion operation sends output data to the standard output device. When an endl manipulator appears instead of a data item, the computer terminates the current output line and goes on to the next line.

A C++ program is a collection of one or more function definitions (and optionally some declarations outside of any function). One of the functions *must* be named main. Execution of a program always begins with the main function. Collectively, the functions all cooperate to produce the desired results.

QUICK CHECK

1. Every C++ program consists of at least how many functions? (p. 45)
2. Use the following syntax template to decide whether your last name is a valid C++ identifier. (pp. 48–50)

Identifier

> LetterOrUnderscore LetterOrDigitOrUnderscore ...

3. Write a C++ constant declaration that gives the name DELTA to the value 0.562. (pp. 60–61)
4. Which of the following words are reserved words in C++? (*Hint:* Look in Appendix A.)

```
const  pi  float  integer  sqrt
```

(p. 50)
5. Declare an int variable named count, a float variable named sum, and a char variable named letter. (pp. 57–59)
6. Assign the value 10 to the int variable toes. (pp. 63–64)
7. You want to divide 9 by 5.
   a. How do you write the expression if you want the result to be the floating point value 1.8?
   b. How do you write it if you want only the integer quotient? (pp. 64–66)
8. What is the value of the following C++ expression?

```
5 % 2
```

(pp. 65–66)

9. Write an output statement to print out the title of this book (*Programming and Problem Solving with C++*). (pp. 68–70)
10. What does the following statement print out?

```
cout << "The answer is " << 2 + 2 << endl;
```

(pp. 68–70)
11. The following program code is incorrect. Rewrite it, using correct syntax for the comment.

```
float annualReceiptsMA;     / Total of monthly cash
                            / receipts in the
                            / Massachusetts store
```

(pp. 70–71)
12. Fill in the blanks in this program.

```
#include _____

const float PI = 3.14159;      // Ratio of circumference
                               //   to diameter

int _____()

_____

     float circumference;      // The computed circumference
                               //   of the circle
     circumference _____ PI * 7.8;

     _____ << "The circumference of a circle";

     _____ << " of diameter 7.8 is " _____ endl;

     _____ << circumference _____ endl;

     return _____;


_____
```

(pp. 71–77)
13. What should you do if a program fails to run correctly and the reason for the error is not immediately obvious? (pp. 77–81)

Answers   1. A program must have at least one function—the main function.   2. Unless your last name is hyphenated, it probably is a valid C++ identifier.

3. `const float DELTA = 0.562;`   4. `const, float`

5. `int    count;`
   `float sum;`
   `char   letter;`

6. `toes = 10;`   7. a. `9.0 / 5.0` b. `9 / 5` 8. 1

9. `cout << "Programming and Problem Solving with C++" << endl;`

10. The answer is 4

11. `float annualReceiptsMA;    // Total of monthly cash`
    `                           // receipts in the`
    `                           // Massachusetts store`

    or

    `float annualReceiptsMA;    /* Total of monthly cash */`
    `                           /* receipts in the      */`
    `                           /* Massachusetts store  */`

12. `#include `<u>`<iostream.h>`</u>

    `const float PI = 3.14159;    // Ratio of circumference`
    `                             //    to diameter`
    `int `<u>`main`</u>`()`
    `{`
    `    float circumference;     // The computed circumference`
    `                             //    of the circle`
    `    circumference `<u>`=`</u>` PI * 7.8;`
    `    `<u>`cout`</u>` << "The circumference of a circle";`
    `    `<u>`cout`</u>` << " of diameter 7.8 is " `<u>`<<`</u>` endl;`
    `    `<u>`cout`</u>` << circumference `<u>`<<`</u>` endl;`
    `    return `<u>`0`</u>`;`
    `}`

13. Get a fresh printout of the program, leave the computer, and study the program until you understand the cause of the problem. Then correct the algorithm and the program as necessary before you go back to the computer and make any changes in the program file.

EXAM PREPARATION EXERCISES

1. Mark the following identifiers either valid or invalid.

	Valid	Invalid
a. `item#1`	_____	_____
b. `data`	_____	_____
c. `y`	_____	_____

    d. 3Set   _____   _____

    e. PAY_DAY   _____   _____

    f. bin-2   _____   _____

    g. num5   _____   _____

    h. Sq Ft   _____   _____

2. Given these four syntax templates:

    mark the following "Dwits" either valid or invalid.

	Valid	Invalid
a. XYZ	_____	_____
b. 123	_____	_____
c. X1	_____	_____
d. 23Y	_____	_____
e. XY12	_____	_____
f. Y2Y	_____	_____
g. ZY2	_____	_____
h. XY23X1	_____	_____

3. Mark the following constructs either valid or invalid. Assume all variables are of type int.

	Valid	Invalid
a. x * y = c;	_____	_____
b. y = con;	_____	_____
c. const int x : 10;	_____	_____
d. int x;	_____	_____
e. a = b % c;	_____	_____

4. Match each of the following terms with the correct definition (1 through 15) given below. There is only one correct definition for each term.

    _____ a. program   _____ g. variable

    _____ b. algorithm   _____ h. constant

    _____ c. compiler   _____ i. memory

    _____ d. identifier   _____ j. syntax

    _____ e. compilation phase   _____ k. semantics

    _____ f. execution phase   _____ l. block

    (1) A symbolic name made up of letters, digits, and underscores but not beginning with a digit

    (2) A place in memory where a data value that cannot be changed is stored

    (3) A program that takes a program written in a high-level language and translates it into machine code

    (4) An input device

(5) The time spent planning a program

(6) Grammar rules

(7) A sequence of statements enclosed by braces

(8) Meaning

(9) A program that translates assembly language instructions into machine code

(10) When the machine code version of a program is being run

(11) A place in memory where a data value that can be changed is stored

(12) When a program in a high-level language is converted into machine code

(13) The part of the computer that holds both program and data

(14) A step-by-step procedure for solving a problem

(15) A sequence of instructions that enables a computer to perform a particular task

5. Compute the value of each legal expression. Indicate whether the value is an integer or a floating point value. If the expression is not legal, explain why.

   a. `10 + 3`
   b. `-9.4 - 6.2`
   c. `10.0 / 3.0`
   d. `10 / 3`
   e. `10 % 3`
   f. `10.0 % 3.0`
   g. `4 / 8`

6. If `alpha` and `beta` are int variables and `alpha = 4` and `beta = 9`, what value is stored into `alpha` in each of the following? Answer each part independently of the others.

   a. `alpha = 3 * beta;`
   b. `alpha = alpha + beta;`
   c. `alpha++;`
   d. `alpha = alpha / beta;`
   e. `alpha--;`
   f. `alpha = alpha + alpha;`
   g. `alpha = beta % 6;`

7. Which of the following are reserved words and which are programmer-defined identifiers?

	Reserved	*Programmer-Defined*
a. `char`	___	___
b. `sort`	___	___
c. `INT`	___	___
d. `long`	___	___
e. `Float`	___	___

8. Reserved words can be used as variable names. (True or False?)

9. In a C++ program consisting of just one function, that function can be named either `main` or `Main`. (True or False?)

10. If a and b are int variables and a = 5 and b = 2, what output does each of the following statements produce?

   a. `cout << "a = " << a << "b = " << b << endl;`
   b. `cout << "Sum:" << a + b << endl;`
   c. `cout << "Sum:   " << a + b << endl;`
   d. `cout << a / b << " feet" << endl;`

11. What does the following program print?

```cpp
#include <iostream.h>

const int LBS = 10;

int main()
{
    int  price;
    int  cost;
    char ch;

    price = 30;
    cost = price * LBS;
    ch = 'A';
    cout << "Cost is " << endl;
    cout << cost << endl;
    cout << "Price is " << price << "Cost is " << cost << endl;
    cout << "Grade " << ch << " costs " << endl;
    cout << cost << endl;
    return 0;
}
```

PROGRAMMING WARM-UP EXERCISES

1. Change the program in Exam Preparation Exercise 11 so that it prints the cost for 15 pounds.
2. Change the program in Exam Preparation Exercise 11 so that the price is a named constant rather than a variable.
3. Write three consecutive output statements that print the following three lines:

```
The moon
is
blue.
```

4. Enter the following program into your computer and run it. In the initial comments, replace the items within parentheses with your own information. (Omit the parentheses.)

```cpp
//********************************
// Programming Assignment One
// (your name)
// (date program was run)
// (description of the problem)
//********************************
#include <iostream.h>
```

```
const float DEBT = 300.0;      // Original value owed
const float PAYMT = 22.4;      // Payment
const float INTR = 0.02;       // Interest rate

int main()
{
    float charg;        // Interest times debt
    float reduc;        // Amount debt is reduced
    float remain;       // Remaining balance

    charg = INTR * DEBT;
    reduc = PAYMT - charg;
    remain = DEBT - reduc;
    cout << "Payment: " << PAYMT
         << " Charge: " << charg
         << " Balance owed: " << remain << endl;
    return 0;
}
```

5. Enter the following program into your computer and run it. Add comments, using the pattern shown in Exercise 4 above. (Notice how hard it is to tell what the program does without the comments.)

```
#include <iostream.h>

const int T_COST = 1376;
const int POUNDS = 10;
const int OUNCES = 12;

int main()
{
    int   totOz;
    float uCost;

    totOz = 16 * POUNDS;
    totOz = totOz + OUNCES;
    uCost = T_COST / totOz;
    cout << "Cost per unit: " << uCost << endl;
    return 0;
}
```

6. Change the program in Exercise 5 above so that it prints the total cost and total weight (labeled appropriately) before printing the cost per unit.

PROGRAMMING PROBLEMS

1. Write a C++ program that will print your initials in large block letters, each letter made up of the same character it represents. The letters should be a minimum of

seven printed lines high and should appear all in a row. For example, if your initials are DOW, your program should print out

```
DDDDDDD          00000      W        W
D      D        0     0     W        W
D       D    0           0  W        W
D       D    0           0  W   W    W
D       D    0           0  W  W W   W
D      D        0     0     W W    W W
DDDDDDD          00000      WW      WW
```

Be sure to include appropriate comments in your program, choose meaningful identifiers, and use indentation as we do in the programs in this chapter.

2. Many (but not all) C++ systems provide a header file limits.h. This header file contains declarations of constants related to the specific compiler and machine on which you are working. Two of these constants are INT_MAX and INT_MIN, the largest and smallest int values for your particular computer. Write a program to print out the values of INT_MAX and INT_MIN. The output should identify which value is INT_MAX and which value is INT_MIN. Be sure to include appropriate comments in your program, and use indentation as we do in the programs in this chapter.

3. Write a program that outputs three lines, labeled as follows:

```
7 | 4 using integer division equals   <result>
7 | 4 using floating point division equals   <result>
7 modulo 4 equals   <result>
```

where <result> stands for the result computed by your program. Use named constants for 7 and 4 everywhere in your program (including the output statements) to make the program easy to modify. Be sure to include appropriate comments in your program, choose meaningful identifiers, and use indentation as we do in the programs in this chapter.

CASE STUDY FOLLOW-UP

1. What is the advantage of using named constants instead of literal constants in the Mileage program?
2. How would you change the Mileage program to add a fifth gasoline fillup of 10.3 gallons? Assume that the starting and ending mileages remain the same.

3

Arithmetic Expressions, Function Calls, and Output

- To be able to construct and evaluate expressions that include multiple arithmetic operations.
- To understand implicit type coercion and explicit type conversion.
- To be able to call (invoke) a value-returning function.
- To be able to recognize and understand the purpose of parameters.
- To be able to use C++ library functions in expressions.
- To be able to call (invoke) a void function (one that does not return a function value).
- To be able to use C++ manipulators to format the output.
- To be able to format the statements in a program in a clear and readable fashion.

In Chapter 2, we introduced the elements of the C++ language and discussed how to construct and run very simple programs. In this chapter we revisit two topics in greater depth: writing arithmetic expressions and formatting the output to make it informative and easy to read. We also show how to make programs more powerful by using *library functions*—prewritten functions that are part of every C++ system and are available for use by any program.

 # Arithmetic Expressions

The expressions we've used so far have contained at most a single arithmetic operator. We also have been careful not to mix values of different data types in an expression. Now we look at more complicated expressions—ones that are composed of several operators and ones that contain mixed data types.

Precedence Rules

Arithmetic expressions can be made up of many constants, variables, operators, and parentheses. In what order are the operations performed? For example, in the assignment statement

```
avgTemp = FREEZE_PT + BOIL_PT / 2.0;
```

is FREEZE_PT + BOIL_PT calculated first or is BOIL_PT / 2.0 calculated first?

The five basic arithmetic operators (+ for addition, - for subtraction, * for multiplication, / for division, and % for modulus) and parentheses are ordered the same way mathematical operators are, according to *precedence rules:*

Highest precedence: ( )

                                           * / %

Lowest precedence: + -

In the example above, we divide BOIL_PT by 2.0 first and then add FREEZE_PT to the result.

You can change the order of evaluation by using parentheses. In the statement

```
avgTemp = (FREEZE_PT + BOIL_PT) / 2.0;
```

FREEZE_PT and BOIL_PT are added first, and then their sum is divided by 2.0. We evaluate subexpressions in parentheses first and then follow the precedence of the operators.

When there are multiple arithmetic operators with the same precedence, their *grouping order* (or *associativity*) is from left to right. The expression

```
int1 - int2 + int3
```

means (int1 - int2) + int3, not int1 - (int2 + int3). As another example, we would use the expression

```
(float1 + float2) / float1 * 3.0
```

to evaluate the expression in parentheses first, then divide the sum by float1, and multiply the result by 3.0. Below are some more examples.

Expression	Value
10 / 2 * 3	15
10 % 3 - 4 / 2	−1
5.0 * 2.0 / 4.0 * 2.0	5.0
5.0 * 2.0 / (4.0 * 2.0)	1.25
5.0 + 2.0 / (4.0 * 2.0)	5.25

Type Coercion and Type Casting

Integer values and floating point values are stored differently inside a computer's memory. The pattern of bits that represents the constant 2 does not look at all like the pattern of bits representing the constant 2.0. (In Chapter 10, we examine why floating point numbers need a special representation inside the computer.) What happens if we mix integer and floating point values together in an assignment statement or an arithmetic expression? Let's look first at assignment statements.

Assignment Statements If you make the declarations

```
int   someInt;
float someFloat;
```

then `someInt` can hold *only* integer values, and `someFloat` can hold *only* floating point values. The assignment statement

```
someFloat = 12;
```

may seem to store the integer value 12 into `someFloat`, but this is not true. The computer refuses to store anything other than a `float` value into `someFloat`. The compiler inserts extra machine language instructions that first convert 12 into 12.0 and then store 12.0 into `someFloat`. This implicit (automatic) conversion of a value from one data type to another is known as **type coercion.**

The statement

```
someInt = 4.8;
```

also causes type coercion. When a floating point value is assigned to an `int` variable, the fractional part is truncated (cut off). As a result, `someInt` is assigned the value 4.

With both of the assignment statements above, the program would be less confusing for someone to read if we avoided mixing data types:

```
someFloat = 12.0;
someInt = 4;
```

More often, it is not just constants but entire expressions that are involved in type coercion. Both of the assignments

```
someFloat = 3 * someInt + 2;
someInt = 5.2 / someFloat - anotherFloat;
```

lead to type coercion. Storing the result of an `int` expression into a `float` variable doesn't cause loss of information; a whole number such as 24 can be represented in floating point form as 24.0. However, storing the result of a floating point expression into an `int` variable can cause loss of information because the fractional part is truncated. It is easy to overlook the assignment of a floating point expression to an `int` variable when we try to discover why our program is producing the wrong answers.

To make our programs as clear (and error-free) as possible, we can use explicit **type casting** (or **type conversion**). A C++ *cast operation* consists of a data type name and then, within parentheses, the expression to be converted:

```
someFloat = float(3 * someInt + 2);
someInt = int(5.2 / someFloat - anotherFloat);
```

Type Coercion   The implicit (automatic) conversion of a value from one data type to another.

Type Casting   The explicit conversion of a value from one data type to another; also called type conversion.

Both of the statements

```
someInt = someFloat + 8.2;
someInt = int(someFloat + 8.2);
```

produce identical results. The only difference is in clarity. With the cast operation, it is perfectly clear to the programmer and to others reading the program that the mixing of types is intentional, not an oversight. Countless errors have resulted from unintentional mixing of types.

Note that there is a nice way to round off rather than truncate a floating point value before storing it into an int variable. Here is the way to do it:

```
someInt = int(someFloat + 0.5);
```

With pencil and paper, see for yourself what gets stored into someInt when someFloat contains 4.7. Now try it again, assuming someFloat contains 4.2. (This technique of rounding by adding 0.5 assumes that someFloat is a positive number.)

Arithmetic Expressions   So far we have been talking about mixing data types across the assignment operator (=). It's also possible to mix data types within an expression:

```
someInt * someFloat
4.8 + someInt - 3
```

Such expressions are called **mixed type (or mixed mode) expressions.**

Mixed Type Expression   An arithmetic expression that contains operands of different data types; also called mixed mode expression.

Whenever an integer value and a floating point value are joined by an operator, implicit type coercion occurs as follows.

1. The integer value is temporarily coerced to a floating point value.
2. The operation is performed.
3. The result is a floating point value.

Let's examine how the machine evaluates the expression 4.8 + someInt - 3, where someInt contains the value 2. First, the operands of the + operator have mixed types, so the value of someInt is coerced to 2.0. (This conversion is only temporary; it does not affect the value that is stored in someInt.) The addition takes place, yielding a value of 6.8. Next, the subtraction (-) operator joins a floating point value (6.8) and an integer value (3). The value 3 is coerced to 3.0, the subtraction takes place, and the result is the floating point value 3.8.

Just as with assignment statements, you can use explicit type casts within expressions to lessen the risk of errors. Writing expressions like

```
float(someInt) * someFloat
4.8 + float(someInt - 3)
```

makes it clear what your intentions are.

Not only are explicit type casts valuable for program clarity, they also can be mandatory for correct programming. Given the declarations

```
int    sum;
int    count;
float  average;
```

suppose that sum and count currently contain 60 and 80, respectively. If sum represents the sum of a group of integer values and count represents the number of values, let's find the average value:

```
average = sum / count;      // Wrong
```

Unfortunately, this statement stores the value 0.0 into average. Here's why. The expression to the right of the assignment operator is not a mixed type expression. Both operands of the / operator are of type int, so integer division is performed. 60 divided by 80 yields the integer value 0. Next, the machine implicitly coerces 0 to the value 0.0 before storing it into average. The way to find the average correctly, as well as clearly, is this:

```
average = float(sum) / float(count);
```

This statement gives us floating point division instead of integer division. As a result, the value 0.75 is stored into `average`.

As a final remark about type coercion and type conversion, you may have noticed that we have concentrated only on the `int` and `float` types. It is also possible to stir `char` values, `short` values, and `double` values into the pot. The results can be confusing and unexpected. In Chapter 10, we return to the topic with a more detailed discussion. In the meantime, you should avoid mixing values of these types within an expression.

 # Function Calls and Library Functions

Value-Returning Functions

At the beginning of Chapter 2, we showed a program consisting of three functions: `main`, `Square`, and `Cube`.

```
int main()
{
    cout << "The square of 27 is " << Square(27) << endl;
    cout << "and the cube of 27 is " << Cube(27) << endl;
    return 0;
}

int Square( int n )
{
    return n * n;
}

int Cube( int n )
{
    return n * n * n;
}
```

We said that all three functions are value-returning functions. `Square` returns a value to its caller—the square of the number sent to it. `Cube` returns a value—the cube of the number sent to it. And `main` returns a value to the operating system—the program's exit status.

Let's focus for a moment on the `Cube` function. The `main` function contains a statement

```
cout << "and the cube of 27 is " << Cube(27) << endl;
```

In this statement, the master (`main`) causes the servant (`Cube`) to compute the cube of 27 and give the result back to `main`. The sequence of symbols

MAY WE INTRODUCE

Blaise Pascal

One of the great historical figures in the world of computing was the French mathematician and religious philosopher Blaise Pascal (1623–1662), the inventor of one of the earliest known mechanical calculators.

Pascal's father, Etienne, was a noble in the French court, a tax collector, and a mathematician. Pascal's mother died when Pascal was three years old. Five years later, the family moved to Paris and Etienne took over the education of the children. Pascal quickly showed a talent for mathematics. When he was only 17, he published a mathematical essay that earned the jealous envy of René Descartes, one of the founders of modern geometry. (Pascal's work actually had been completed before he was 16.) It was based on a theorem, which he called the *hexagrammum mysticum*, or mystic hexagram, that described the inscription of hexagons in conic sections (parabolas, hyperbolas, and ellipses). In addition to the theorem (now called Pascal's theorem), his essay included over 400 corollaries.

When Pascal was about 20, he constructed a mechanical calculator that performed addition and subtraction of 8-digit numbers. That calculator required the user to dial in the numbers to be added or subtracted; then the sum or difference appeared in a set of windows. It is believed that his motivation for building this machine was to aid his father in collecting taxes. The earliest version of the machine does indeed split the numbers into six decimal digits and two fractional digits, as would be used for calculating sums of money. The machine was hailed by his contemporaries as a great advance in mathematics, and Pascal built several more in different forms. It achieved such popularity that many fake, nonfunctional copies were built by others and displayed as novelties. Several of Pascal's calculators still exist in various museums.

Pascal's box, as it is called, was long believed to be the first mechanical calculator. However, in 1950, a letter from Wilhelm Shickard to Johannes Kepler written in 1624

Cube(27)

is a **function call** or **function invocation.** The computer temporarily puts the main function on hold and starts the Cube function running. When Cube has finished doing its work, the computer goes back to main and picks up where it left off.

Function Call (Function Invocation)   The mechanism that transfers control to a function.

was discovered. This letter described an even more sophisticated calculator built by Shickard 20 years prior to Pascal's box. Unfortunately, the machine was destroyed in a fire and never rebuilt.

During his twenties, Pascal solved several difficult problems related to the cycloid curve, indirectly contributing to the development of differential calculus. Working with Pierre de Fermat, he laid the foundation of the calculus of probabilities and combinatorial analysis. One of the results of this work came to be known as Pascal's triangle, which simplifies the calculation of the coefficients of the expansion of $(X + Y)^N$, where N is a positive integer.

Pascal also published a treatise on air pressure and conducted experiments that showed that barometric pressure decreases with altitude, helping to confirm theories that had been proposed by Galileo and Torricelli. His work on fluid dynamics forms a significant part of the foundation of that field. Among the most famous of his contributions is Pascal's law, which states that pressure applied to a fluid in a closed vessel is transmitted uniformly throughout the fluid.

When Pascal was 23, his father became ill, and the family was visited by two disciples of Jansenism, a reform movement in the Catholic Church that had begun six years earlier. The family converted, and five years later one of his sisters entered a convent. Initially, Pascal was not so taken with the new movement, but by the time he was 31, his sister had persuaded him to abandon the world and devote himself to religion.

His religious works are considered no less brilliant than his mathematical and scientific writings. Some consider *Provincial Letters*, his series of 18 essays on various aspects of religion, as the beginning of modern French prose.

Pascal returned briefly to mathematics when he was 35, but a year later his health, which had always been poor, took a turn for the worse. Unable to perform his usual work, he devoted himself to helping the less fortunate. Three years later, he died while staying with his sister, having given his own house to a poor family.

In the above function call, the number 27 is known as a *parameter* (or *argument*). Parameters make it possible for the same function to work on many different values. For example, we can write statements like these:

```
cout << Cube(4);
cout << Cube(16);
```

Here's the syntax template for a function call:

FunctionCall

FunctionName (ParameterList)

The **parameter list** is a way for functions to communicate with each other. Some functions, like Square and Cube, have a single parameter in the parameter list. Other functions, like main, have no parameters in the list. And some functions have two, three, or more parameters in the parameter list, separated by commas.

Parameter List   A mechanism by which functions communicate with each other.

Value-returning functions are used in expressions in much the same way that variables and constants are. The value computed by a function simply takes its place in the expression. For example, the statement

```
someInt = Cube(2) * 10;
```

stores the value 80 into someInt. First the Cube function is executed to compute the cube of 2, which is 8. The value 8—now available for use in the rest of the expression—is multiplied by 10. Note that a function call has higher precedence than multiplication, which makes sense if you consider that the function result must be available before the multiplication takes place.

Here are several facts about value-returning functions:

- The function call is used within an expression; it does not appear as a separate statement.
- The function computes a value (*result*) that is then available for use in the expression.
- The function returns exactly one result—no more, no less.

The Cube function expects to be given (or *passed*) a parameter of type int. What happens if the caller passes a float parameter? The answer is that the compiler applies implicit type coercion. The function call Cube(6.9) computes the cube of 6, not 6.9.

Although we have been using literal constants as parameters to Cube, the parameter could just as easily be a variable or named constant. In fact, the parameter to a value-returning function can be any expression of the appropriate type. In the statement

```
alpha = Cube(int1 * int1 + int2 * int2);
```

the expression in the parameter list is evaluated first, and only its result is passed to the function. For example, if `int1` contains 3 and `int2` contains 5, the above function call passes 34 as the parameter to `Cube`.

An expression in a function's parameter list can even include calls to functions. For example, we could use the `Square` function to rewrite the above assignment statement as follows:

```
alpha = Cube(Square(int1) + Square(int2));
```

Library Functions

Certain computations, such as taking square roots or finding the absolute value of a number, are very common in programs. It would be an enormous waste of time if every programmer had to start from scratch and create functions to perform these tasks. To help make the programmer's life easier, every C++ system includes a *standard library*—a large collection of prewritten functions that any C++ programmer may use. Here is a very small sample:

Header File	Function	Parameter Type(s)	Result Type	Result
<stdlib.h>	abs(i)	int	int	Absolute value of i
<math.h>	cos(x)	float	float	Cosine of x (x is in radians)
<math.h>	fabs(x)	float	float	Absolute value of x
<stdlib.h>	labs(j)	long	long	Absolute value of j
<math.h>	pow(x, y)	float	float	x raised to the power y (if x = 0.0, y must be positive; if x $\leq$ 0.0, y must be a whole number)
<math.h>	sin(x)	float	float	Sine of x (x is in radians)
<math.h>	sqrt(x)	float	float	Square root of x (x $\geq$ 0.0)

(Technically, the entries marked `float` should all say `double`. These library functions perform their work using double precision floating point values. But because of type coercion, the functions work just as you would like them to when you pass `float` values to them.)

Using a library function is easy. First, you place an `#include` directive near the top of your program, specifying the appropriate header file. This directive ensures that the C++ preprocessor will insert declarations into your program that give the compiler some information about the function. Then, whenever you want to use the function, you just make a function call. Here's an example:

```
#include <iostream.h>
#include <math.h>        // For sqrt() and fabs()
   .
   .
   .
float alpha;
float beta;
   .
   .
   .
alpha = sqrt(7.3 + fabs(beta));
```

The C++ standard library provides dozens of functions for you to use. Appendix C lists a much larger selection than we have presented here. You should glance briefly at this appendix now, keeping in mind that much of the terminology and C++ language notation will make sense only after you have read further into the book.

Void Functions

In this chapter, the only kind of function that we have looked at is the value-returning function. C++ provides another kind of function as well. If you look at the Payroll program in Chapter 1, you see that the function definition for `CalcPay` begins with the word `void` instead of a data type like `int` or `float`:

```
void CalcPay( ... )
{
   .
   .
   .
}
```

`CalcPay` is an example of a function that doesn't return a function value to its caller. Instead, it just performs some action and then quits. We refer to a function like this as a *non-value-returning function,* a *void-returning function,* or, most briefly, a **void function.** In many programming languages, a void function is known as a **procedure.**

Void functions are invoked differently from value-returning functions. With a value-returning function, the function call appears in an expression. With a void function, the function call is a separate, stand-alone statement. In the Payroll program, `main` calls the `CalcPay` function like this:

```
CalcPay(payRate, hours, wages);
```

From the caller's perspective, a call to a void function has the flavor of a command or built-in instruction:

```
DoThis(x, y, z);
DoThat();
```

In contrast, a call to a value-returning function doesn't look like a command; it looks like a value in an expression:

```
y = 4.7 + Cube(x);
```

Value-Returning Function   A function that returns a single value to its caller and is invoked from within an expression.

Void Function (Procedure)   A function that does not return a function value to its caller and is invoked as a separate statement.

For the next few chapters, we won't be writing our own functions (except `main`). Instead, we'll be concentrating on how to use existing functions, including functions for performing stream input and output. Some of these functions are value-returning functions; others are void functions. Again, we emphasize the difference in how you invoke these two kinds of functions: A call to a value-returning function occurs in an expression, while a call to a void function occurs as a separate statement.

Formatting the Output

To format a program's output means to control how it appears visually on the screen or on a printer. If the variables i, j, and k contain the values 15, 2, and 6, respectively, the statement

```
cout << "Results: " << i << j << k;
```

outputs the stream of characters

```
Results: 1526
```

Without spacing between the numbers, this output is difficult to interpret. Let's examine how we can control both the horizontal and vertical spacing of our output to make it more appealing (and understandable). We look first at vertical spacing.

Creating Blank Lines

You already have seen how to control vertical spacing by using the `endl` manipulator in an output statement. A sequence of output statements continues to write characters across the current line until an `endl` terminates the line. Here are some examples:

Statements	Output produced

`cout << "Hi there, ";`
`cout << "Lois Lane. " << endl;`
`cout << "Have you seen ";`
`cout << "Clark Kent?" << endl;`
	`Hi there, Lois Lane.`
	`Have you seen Clark Kent?`

`cout << "Hi there, " << endl;`
`cout << "Lois Lane. " << endl;`
`cout << "Have you seen " << endl;`
`cout << "Clark Kent?" << endl;`
	`Hi there,`
	`Lois Lane.`
	`Have you seen`
	`Clark Kent?`

`cout << "Hi there, " << endl;`
`cout << "Lois Lane. ";`
`cout << "Have you seen " << endl;`
`cout << "Clark Kent?" << endl;`
	`Hi there,`
	`Lois Lane. Have you seen`
	`Clark Kent?`

What do you think the following statements print out?

```
cout << "Hi there, " << endl;
cout << endl;
cout << "Lois Lane." << endl;
```

The first output statement causes the words *Hi there,* to be printed; the `endl` causes the screen cursor to go to the next line. The next statement prints nothing but goes on to the next line. The third statement prints the words *Lois Lane.* and terminates the line. The resulting output is the three lines

```
Hi there,

Lois Lane.
```

Whenever you use an endl immediately after another endl, a blank line is produced. As you might guess, three consecutive uses of endl outputs two blank lines, four consecutive uses outputs three blank lines, and so forth.

Note that we have a great deal of flexibility in how we write an output statement in a C++ program. We could combine the three preceding statements into two statements:

```
cout << "Hi there, " << endl << endl;
cout << "Lois Lane." << endl;
```

In fact, we could do it all in one statement. One possibility is

```
cout << "Hi there, " << endl << endl << "Lois Lane." << endl;
```

Here's another:

```
cout << "Hi there, " << endl << endl
     << "Lois Lane." << endl;
```

The last example shows that you can spread a single C++ statement onto more than one line of the program. The compiler treats the semicolon, not the physical end of a line, as the end of a statement.

Inserting Blanks Within a Line

To control the horizontal spacing of the output, one technique is to send extra blank characters to the output stream. (Remember that the blank character, generated by pressing the space bar on a keyboard, is a perfectly valid character in C++.)

To prevent the output of 15, 2, and 6 from looking like this:

```
Results: 1526
```

you could print a single blank (as a char constant) between the numbers:

```
cout << "Results: " << i << ' ' << j << ' ' << k;
```

This statement produces the output

```
Results: 15 2 6
```

If you want even more spacing between items, use string constants containing blanks:

```
cout << "Results: " << i << "     " << j << "     " << k;
```

Here, the resulting output is

```
Results: 15    2    6
```

As another example, to produce this output:

```
  *   *   *   *   *   *   *   *   *
*   *   *   *   *   *   *   *   *   *
  *   *   *   *   *   *   *   *   *
```

you would use these statements:

```
cout << "  *   *   *   *   *   *   *   *   *" << endl << endl;
cout << "*   *   *   *   *   *   *   *   *" << endl << endl;
cout << "  *   *   *   *   *   *   *   *" << endl;
```

All of the blanks and asterisks are enclosed in double quotes, so they print literally as they are written in the program. The extra `endl` manipulators give you the blank lines between the rows of asterisks.

If you want blanks to be printed, you *must* enclose them in quotes. The statement

```
cout << '*' <<                              '*';
```

produces the output

```
**
```

Despite all of the blanks we included in the output statement, the asterisks print side by side because the blanks are not enclosed by quotes.

Manipulators

For some time now, we have been using the endl manipulator to terminate an output line. In C++ a manipulator is a rather curious thing that behaves like a function but travels in the disguise of a data object. Like a function, a manipulator causes some action to occur. But like a data object, a manipulator can appear in the midst of a series of insertion operations:

```
cout << someInt << endl << someFloat;
```

(Manipulators are used *only* in input and output statements.)

Here's a revised syntax template for the output statement, showing that not only expressions and strings but also manipulators are allowed:

OutputStatement

```
cout << ExprOrStringOrManipulator << ExprOrStringOrManipulator ... ;
```

The C++ standard library supplies many manipulators, but for now we look at only three of them: endl, setw, and setprecision. The endl manipulator comes "for free" when we #include the header file iostream.h to perform I/O. The other two manipulators, setw and setprecision, require that we also #include the header file iomanip.h:

```
#include <iostream.h>
#include <iomanip.h>
     ⋮
cout << setw(5) << someInt;
```

The manipulator setw—meaning "set width"—lets us control how many columns the next data item should occupy when it is output. (setw is only for formatting numbers and strings, not char data.) The parameter to setw is an integer expression called the *fieldwidth specification*; the desired number of columns is called the *field*. The next data item to be output is printed right-justified (filled with blanks on the left to fill up the field).

Let's look at an example:

```
ans  = 33    Integer
num  = 7132  Integer
```

Statement	*Output (▢ means blank)*

1. `cout << setw(4) << ans`
`      << setw(5) << num`
`      << setw(4) << "Hi";`
	▢▢33▢7132▢▢Hi
	  4 5 4

2. `cout << setw(2) << ans`
`      << setw(4) << num`
`      << setw(2) << "Hi";`
	337132Hi
	 2 4 2

3. `cout << setw(6) << ans`
`      << setw(3) << "Hi"`
`      << setw(5) << num;`
	▢▢▢▢33▢Hi▢7132
	   6 3 5

4. `cout << setw(7) << "Hi"` `      << setw(4) << num;`	▢▢▢▢▢Hi7132 7 4
5. `cout << setw(1) << ans` `      << setw(5) << num;`	33▢7132 ↑ 5 Field automatically expands to fit the two-digit value

In (1), each of the values is specified to occupy enough columns so that there is at least one space separating them. In (2), the values all run together because the fieldwidth specified for each value is just large enough to hold the value. This output obviously is not very readable. It's better to make the fieldwidth larger than the minimum size required so that some space is left between values. In (3), there are extra blanks for readability; in (4), there are not. In (5), the fieldwidth is not large enough for the value in `ans`, so it automatically expands to make room for all of the digits.

Setting the fieldwidth is a one-time action. It holds only for the very next item to be output. After this output, the fieldwidth resets to 0, meaning "extend the field to exactly as many columns as are needed." In the statement

```
cout << "Hi" << setw(5) << ans << num;
```

the fieldwidth resets to 0 after `ans` is output. As a result, we get the output

Hi   337132

You can specify a fieldwidth for floating point values just as for integer values. But you must remember to allow for the decimal point in the column count. The value 4.85 occupies four output columns, not three. If x contains the value 4.85, the statement

```
cout << setw(4) << x << endl
     << setw(6) << x << endl
     << setw(3) << x << endl;
```

produces the output

```
4.85
 4.85
4.85
```

In the third line, a fieldwidth of 3 isn't sufficient, so the field automatically expands to accommodate the number.

There are several other issues involved with output of floating point numbers. First, large floating point values are printed in scientific (E) notation. The value 123456789.5 may print on some systems as

```
1.234567E+08
```

Second, if the number is a whole number, C++ doesn't print a decimal point. The value 95.0 prints as

```
95
```

Third, you often would like to control the number of decimal places (digits to the right of the decimal point) that are displayed. For example, if you are printing monetary values as dollars and cents, you would prefer the values 12.8 and 16.38753 to print as 12.80 and 16.39.

To address the first two issues, you can include the following two statements in your program before any floating point output takes place:

```
cout.setf(ios::fixed, ios::floatfield);   // Set up floating point
cout.setf(ios::showpoint);                //   output format
```

These two statements employ some very advanced C++ notation. It's way too early in our look at C++ to explain fully the meaning of all the symbols and identifiers. But here's the general idea. setf is a void function associated with the cout stream. (Note that the dot, or period, between cout and setf is required.) The first function call ensures that floating point numbers are always printed in decimal form rather than scientific notation. The second function call specifies that the decimal point should always be printed, even for whole numbers. Our best advice is simply to use these statements just as you see them and not worry about the details.

The third issue—the number of decimal places to be displayed—is handled by the setprecision manipulator:

```
cout << setprecision(3) << x;
```

The parameter to setprecision specifies the desired number of decimal places. Unlike setw, which applies only to the very next item printed, the value sent to setprecision remains in effect for all subsequent output (until you change it with another call to setprecision). Here are some examples of using setprecision in conjunction with setw:

Value of x	Statement	Output (□ means blank)	
310.0	cout << setw(10) << setprecision(2) << x;	□□□□310.00	
310.0	cout << setw(10) << setprecision(5) << x;	□310.00000	
310.0	cout << setw(7) << setprecision(5) << x;	310.00000	(expands to 9 columns)
4.827	cout << setw(6) << setprecision(2) << x;	□□4.83	(last displayed digit is rounded off)
4.827	cout << setw(6) << setprecision(1) << x;	□□□4.8	(last displayed digit is rounded off)

Here, too, the total number of columns is expanded if the specified field-width is too narrow. However, the number of columns for fractional digits is controlled entirely by the parameter to setprecision.

The following table summarizes the three manipulators we have discussed in this section:

Header File	Manipulator	Parameter Type	Effect
`<iostream.h>`	endl	None	Terminates the current output line
`<iomanip.h>`	setw(n)	int	Sets fieldwidth to n*
`<iomanip.h>`	setprecision(n)	int	Sets floating point precision to n digits

*`setw` is only for numbers and strings, not char data. Also, `setw` applies only to the very next output item, after which the fieldwidth is reset to 0 (meaning "use only as many columns as are needed").

MATTERS OF STYLE

Program Formatting

As far as the compiler is concerned, C++ statements are *free format:* They can appear anywhere on a line, more than one can appear on a single line, and one statement can span several lines. The compiler only needs blanks (or comments or new lines) to separate important symbols, and it needs semicolons to terminate statements. However, it is extremely important that your programs be readable, both for your sake and for the sake of anyone else who has to use them.

When you write an outline for an English paper, you follow certain rules of indentation to make it readable. These same kinds of rules can make your programs easier to read.

Take a look at the following program for computing the cost per square foot of a house. Although it compiles and runs correctly, it does not conform to any formatting standards.

```
// HouseCost program
// This program computes the cost per square foot of
    // living space for a house, given the dimensions of
// the house, the number of stories, the size of the
// nonliving space, and the total cost less land
#include <iostream.h>
#include <iomanip.h>// For setw() and setprecision()
const float WIDTH = 30.0; // Width of the house
    const float LENGTH = 40.0; // Length of the house
const float STORIES = 2.5; // Number of full stories
const float NON_LIVING_SPACE = 825.0;// Garage, closets, etc.
```

```
const float PRICE = 150000.0; // Selling price less land
int main() { float grossFootage;// Total square footage
    float livingFootage;        // Living area
float costPerFoot;      // Cost/foot of living area
cout.setf(ios::fixed, ios::floatfield);  // Set up floating pt.
cout.setf(ios::showpoint);      //   output format

grossFootage = LENGTH * WIDTH * STORIES; livingFootage =
 grossFootage - NON_LIVING_SPACE; costPerFoot = PRICE /
livingFootage; cout << "Cost per square foot is "
<< setw(6) << setprecision(2) << costPerFoot << endl;
return 0; }
```

Now look at the same program with proper formatting:

```
//*****************************************************************
// HouseCost program
// This program computes the cost per square foot of
// living space for a house, given the dimensions of
// the house, the number of stories, the size of the
// nonliving space, and the total cost less land
//*****************************************************************
#include <iostream.h>
#include <iomanip.h>    // For setw() and setprecision()

const float WIDTH = 30.0;                // Width of the house
const float LENGTH = 40.0;               // Length of the house
const float STORIES = 2.5;               // Number of full stories
const float NON_LIVING_SPACE = 825.0;    // Garage, closets, etc.
const float PRICE = 150000.0;            // Selling price less land

int main()
{
    float grossFootage;        // Total square footage
    float livingFootage;       // Living area
    float costPerFoot;         // Cost/foot of living area

    cout.setf(ios::fixed, ios::floatfield);    // Set up floating pt.
    cout.setf(ios::showpoint);                 //   output format

    grossFootage = LENGTH * WIDTH * STORIES;
    livingFootage = grossFootage - NON_LIVING_SPACE;
    costPerFoot = PRICE / livingFootage;

    cout << "Cost per square foot is "
        << setw(6) << setprecision(2) << costPerFoot << endl;
    return 0;
}
```

Need we say more?

Appendix F talks about programming style. Use it as a guide when you are writing programs.

PROBLEM-SOLVING CASE STUDY

Map Measurements

Problem: You're spending a day in the city. You plan to visit the natural history museum, a record store, a gallery, and a bookshop, and then go to a concert. You have a tourist map that shows where these places are located. You want to determine how far apart they are and how far you'll walk during the entire day. Then you can decide when it would be better to take a taxi. According to the map's legend, one inch on the map equals one quarter of a mile on the ground.

Output: The distance between each of the places and the total distance, rounded to the nearest tenth of a mile. The values on which the calculations are based also should be printed for verification purposes.

Discussion: You can measure the distances between two points on the map with a ruler. The program must output miles, so you need to multiply the number of inches by 0.25. You then write down the figure, rounded to the nearest tenth of a mile. When you've done this for each pair of places, you add the distances to get the total mileage. This is essentially the algorithm we use in the program.

The only tricky part is how to round a value to the nearest tenth of a mile. In the last chapter, we showed how to round a floating point value to the nearest integer by adding 0.5 and using a type cast to truncate the result:

```
int(floatValue + 0.5)
```

To round to the nearest tenth, we first multiply the value by 10, round the result to the nearest integer, and then divide by 10 again. For example, if floatValue contains 5.162, then

```
float(int(floatValue * 10.0 + 0.5)) / 10.0
```

gives 5.2 as its result.

Let's treat all of the quantities as named constants so that it is easier to change the program later. From measuring the map, you know that the distance from the museum to the record store is 1.5 inches, from the record store to the gallery is 2.3 inches, from the gallery to the bookshop is 5.9 inches, and from the bookshop to the concert is 4.0 inches. Here is the algorithmic solution:

```
DISTANCE1 = 1.5
DISTANCE2 = 2.3
DISTANCE3 = 5.9
DISTANCE4 = 4.0
SCALE = 0.25
Set totMiles = 0.0
Set miles = float(int(DISTANCE1 * SCALE * 10.0 + 0.5)) / 10.0
Print DISTANCE1, miles
Add miles to totMiles
Set miles = float(int(DISTANCE2 * SCALE * 10.0 + 0.5)) / 10.0
Print DISTANCE2, miles
Add miles to totMiles
Set miles = float(int(DISTANCE3 * SCALE * 10.0 + 0.5)) / 10.0
Print DISTANCE3, miles
Add miles to totMiles
Set miles = float(int(DISTANCE4 * SCALE * 10.0 + 0.5)) / 10.0
Print DISTANCE4, miles
Add miles to totMiles
Print a blank line
Print totMiles
```

From the algorithm we can create tables of constants and variables that help us write the declarations in the program.

Constants

Name	Value	Description
DISTANCE1	1.5	Measurement for first distance
DISTANCE2	2.3	Measurement for second distance
DISTANCE3	5.9	Measurement for third distance
DISTANCE4	4.0	Measurement for fourth distance
SCALE	0.25	Scale factor of map

Variables

Name	Data Type	Description
totMiles	float	Total of rounded mileages
miles	float	An individual rounded mileage

Now we're ready to write the program. Let's call it Walk. We take the declarations from the tables and the executable statements from the algorithm. We have labeled the output with explanatory messages and formatted it with fieldwidth specifications. We've also added comments where needed.

Here is the program:

```
//*****************************************************************
// Walk program
// This program computes the mileage (rounded to tenths of a mile)
// for each of four distances between points in a city, given
// the measurements on a map with a scale of one inch equal to
// one quarter of a mile
//*****************************************************************
#include <iostream.h>
#include <iomanip.h>      // For setprecision()

const float DISTANCE1 = 1.5;    // Measurement for first distance
const float DISTANCE2 = 2.3;    // Measurement for second distance
const float DISTANCE3 = 5.9;    // Measurement for third distance
const float DISTANCE4 = 4.0;    // Measurement for fourth distance
const float SCALE = 0.25;       // Map scale

int main()
{
    float totMiles;        // Total of rounded mileages
    float miles;           // An individual rounded mileage

    cout.setf(ios::fixed, ios::floatfield);   // Set up floating pt.
    cout.setf(ios::showpoint);                //    output format

    totMiles = 0.0;
```

```
// Compute miles for each distance on the map

miles = float(int(DISTANCE1 * SCALE * 10.0 + 0.5)) / 10.0;
cout << "For a measurement of " << setprecision(1) << DISTANCE1
     << " the first distance is " << miles << " mile(s) long."
     << endl;
totMiles = totMiles + miles;

miles = float(int(DISTANCE2 * SCALE * 10.0 + 0.5)) / 10.0;
cout << "For a measurement of " << DISTANCE2
     << " the second distance is " << miles << " mile(s) long."
     << endl;
totMiles = totMiles + miles;

miles = float(int(DISTANCE3 * SCALE * 10.0 + 0.5)) / 10.0;
cout << "For a measurement of " << DISTANCE3
     << " the third distance is " << miles << " mile(s) long."
     << endl;
totMiles = totMiles + miles;

miles = float(int(DISTANCE4 * SCALE * 10.0 + 0.5)) / 10.0;
cout << "For a measurement of " << DISTANCE4
     << " the fourth distance is " << miles << " mile(s) long."
     << endl;
totMiles = totMiles + miles;

// Print the total miles

cout << endl;
cout << "Total mileage for the day is " << totMiles << " miles."
     << endl;
return 0;
}
```

The output from the program is

```
For a measurement of 1.5 the first distance is 0.4 mile(s) long.
For a measurement of 2.3 the second distance is 0.6 mile(s) long.
For a measurement of 5.9 the third distance is 1.5 mile(s) long.
For a measurement of 4.0 the fourth distance is 1.0 mile(s) long.

Total mileage for the day is 3.5 miles.
```

PROBLEM-SOLVING CASE STUDY

Painting Traffic Cones

Problem: The Hexagrammum Mysticum Company manufactures a line of traffic cones. The company is preparing to bid on a project that will require it to paint its cones in different colors. The paint is applied with a constant thickness. From experience, the firm finds it easier to estimate the total cost from the area to be painted. The company has hired you to write a program that will compute the surface area of a cone and the cost of painting it, given its radius, its height, and the cost per square foot of three different colors of paint.

Output: The surface area of the cone in square feet, and the costs of painting the cone in the three different colors, all displayed in floating point form.

Discussion: From interviewing the company's engineers, you learn that the cones are measured in inches. A typical cone is 30 inches high and 8 inches in diameter. The red paint costs 10 cents per square foot; the blue costs 15 cents; the green costs 18 cents. In a math text, you find that the area of a cone (not including its base, which won't be painted) equals

$$\pi r \sqrt{r^2 + h^2}$$

where r is the radius of the cone and h is its height.

The first thing the program must do is convert the cone measurements into feet and divide the diameter in half to get the radius. Then it can apply the formula to get the surface area of the cone. To determine the painting costs, it must multiply the surface area by the cost of each of the three paints. Here's the algorithm:

```
Set heightInFeet = heightInInches / 12
Set diameterInFeet = diameterInInches / 12
Set radius = diameterInFeet / 2
Set surfaceArea = pi * radius * sqrt(radius*radius + heightInFeet*heightInFeet)
Set redCost = surfaceArea * 0.10
Set blueCost = surfaceArea * 0.15
Set greenCost = surfaceArea * 0.18
Print surfaceArea
Print redCost
Print blueCost
Print greenCost
```

From the algorithm we can create tables of constants and variables to help us write the program declarations.

Constants

Name	Value	Description
INCH_HEIGHT	30.0	Height of a typical cone
INCH_DIAMETER	8.0	Diameter of the base of the cone
RED_PRICE	0.10	Price per square foot of red paint
BLUE_PRICE	0.15	Price per square foot of blue paint
GREEN_PRICE	0.18	Price per square foot of green paint
INCHES_PER_FOOT	12.0	Inches in 1 foot
PI	3.14159265	Ratio of circumference to diameter

Variables

Name	Data Type	Description
heightInFeet	float	Height of the cone in feet
diameterInFeet	float	Diameter of the cone in feet
radius	float	Radius of the cone in feet
surfaceArea	float	Surface area in square feet
redCost	float	Cost to paint a cone red
blueCost	float	Cost to paint a cone blue
greenCost	float	Cost to paint a cone green

Now we can write the program, which we'll call ConePaint. We take the declarations from the tables and the executable statements from the algorithm. We have labeled the output with explanatory messages and formatted it with fieldwidth specifications. We've also added comments where needed.

```
//*************************************************************
// ConePaint program
// This program computes the cost of painting traffic cones in
// each of three different colors, given the height and diameter
// of a cone in inches, and the cost per square foot of each of
// the paints
//*************************************************************
#include <iostream.h>
#include <iomanip.h>        // For setw() and setprecision()
#include <math.h>           // For sqrt()
```

```cpp
const float INCH_HEIGHT = 30.0;       // Height of a typical cone
const float INCH_DIAMETER = 8.0;      // Diameter of base of cone
const float RED_PRICE = 0.10;         // Price per square foot
                                      //   of red paint
const float BLUE_PRICE = 0.15;        // Price per square foot
                                      //   of blue paint
const float GREEN_PRICE = 0.18;       // Price per square foot
                                      //   of green paint
const float INCHES_PER_FOOT = 12.0;   // Inches in 1 foot
const float PI = 3.14159265;          // Ratio of circumference
                                      //   to diameter (Remove this
                                      //   declaration if your math.h
                                      //   already declares PI)
int main()
{
    float heightInFeet;      // Height of the cone in feet
    float diameterInFeet;    // Diameter of the cone in feet
    float radius;            // Radius of the cone in feet
    float surfaceArea;       // Surface area in square feet
    float redCost;           // Cost to paint a cone red
    float blueCost;          // Cost to paint a cone blue
    float greenCost;         // Cost to paint a cone green

    cout.setf(ios::fixed, ios::floatfield);   // Set up floating pt.
    cout.setf(ios::showpoint);                //    output format

    // Convert dimensions to feet

    heightInFeet = INCH_HEIGHT / INCHES_PER_FOOT;
    diameterInFeet = INCH_DIAMETER / INCHES_PER_FOOT;
    radius = diameterInFeet / 2.0;

    // Compute surface area of the cone

    surfaceArea = PI * radius *
                sqrt(radius*radius + heightInFeet*heightInFeet);

    // Compute cost for each color

    redCost = surfaceArea * RED_PRICE;
    blueCost = surfaceArea * BLUE_PRICE;
    greenCost = surfaceArea * GREEN_PRICE;

    // Print results
```

```
        cout << "The surface area is "
            << setprecision(3) << surfaceArea << " sq. ft."
            << endl;
        cout << "The painting cost for" << endl;
        cout << "   Red is   " << setw(7) << redCost << " dollars"
            << endl;
        cout << "   Blue is  " << setw(7) << blueCost << " dollars"
            << endl;
        cout << "   Green is " << setw(7) << greenCost << " dollars"
            << endl;
        return 0;
}
```

The output from the program is

```
The surface area is 2.641 sq. ft.
The painting cost for
    Red is     0.264 dollars
    Blue is    0.396 dollars
    Green is   0.475 dollars
```

TESTING AND DEBUGGING HINTS

1. Double-check every expression according to the precedence rules to be sure that the operations are performed in the desired order.
2. Avoid mixing integer and floating point values in expressions. If you must mix them, consider using explicit type casts to reduce the chance of mistakes.
3. For each assignment statement, check that the expression result has the same data type as the variable to the left of the assignment operator (=). If not, consider using an explicit type cast for clarity and safety. And remember that storing a floating point value into an int variable truncates the fractional part.
4. For every library function you use in your program, be sure to #include the appropriate header file.
5. Examine each call to a library function to see that you have the right number of parameters and that the data types of the parameters are correct.

SUMMARY

Much of the computation of a program is performed in arithmetic expressions. Expressions can contain more than one operator. The order in which the operations are performed is determined by precedence rules. In arithmetic expressions, multiplication, division, and modulus are performed first, then addition and subtraction. Multiple arithmetic operations of the same precedence are grouped from left to right. You can use parentheses to override the precedence rules.

Expressions may include function calls. C++ supports two kinds of functions: value-returning functions and void functions. A value-returning function is called by writing its name (and parameter list) as part of an expression. A void function is called by writing its name (and parameter list) as a complete C++ statement.

The C++ standard library is an integral part of every C++ system. The library contains many prewritten functions that any programmer can use. These functions are accessed by using #include directives to the C++ preprocessor, which inserts the appropriate header files into the program.

Designing a program includes careful attention to the output format. Output should be clear, understandable, and neatly arranged. Messages in the output should describe the significance of values. Blank lines (produced by successive uses of the endl manipulator) and blank spaces within lines help to organize the output and improve its appearance.

In output statements, the setw and setprecision manipulators control the appearance of values in the output. These manipulators do *not* affect the values actually stored in memory, only their appearance when displayed on the standard output device.

Not only should the output produced by a program be easy to read, but the format of the program itself should be clear and readable. C++ is a free-format language. A consistent style that uses indentation, blank lines, and spaces within lines helps you (and other programmers) understand and work with your programs.

QUICK CHECK

1. What is the result of evaluating the expression

    (1 + 2 * 2) / 2 + 1

    (pp. 94–95)

2. How would you write the following formula as a C++ expression that produces a floating point value as a result? (pp. 94–95)

$$\frac{9}{5}c + 32$$

3. Add type casts to the following statements to make the type conversions clear and explicit. Your answers should produce the same results as the original statements. (pp. 95–98)

   a. `someFloat = 5 + someInt;`
   b. `someInt = 2.5 * someInt / someFloat;`

4. You want to compute the square roots and absolute values of some floating point numbers.
   a. Which C++ library functions would you use? (pp. 103–104)
   b. Which header file(s) must you #include in order to use these functions?
5. Which part of the following function call is its parameter list? (pp. 101–102)

   `Square(someInt + 1)`

6. In the statement

   `alpha = 4 * Beta(gamma, delta) + 3;`

   would you assume that `Beta` is a value-returning function or a void function? (pp. 102–105)
7. In the statement

   `Display(gamma, delta);`

   would you assume that `Display` is a value-returning function or a void function? (pp. 102–105)
8. If you want to print the word *Hello* on one line and then print a blank line, how many consecutive `endl` manipulators should you insert after printing `"Hello"`? (pp. 106–107)
9. Assume the `float` variable pay contains the value 327.66101. Using the `setw` and `setprecision` manipulators, what output statement would you use to print pay in dollars and cents with three leading blanks? (pp. 109–113)
10. Reformat the following program to make it clear and readable. (pp. 113–115)

```
//**********************************************************
//  SumProd program
//  This program computes the sum and product of two integers
//**********************************************************
```

4. Write expressions to compute both solutions for the quadratic formula. The formula is

$$\frac{-b \pm \sqrt{b^2 - 4ac}}{2a}$$

The $\pm$ means "plus or minus" and indicates that there are two solutions to the equation: one in which the result of the square root is added to $-b$ and one in which the result is subtracted from $-b$. Assume all variables are `float` variables.

5. Complete the following C++ program. The program should find and output the perimeter and area of a rectangle, given the length and the width. Be sure to label the output. And don't forget to use comments.

```
//***********************************************
// Rectangle program
// This program finds the perimeter and the area
// of a rectangle, given the length and width
//***********************************************
#include <iostream.h>

int main()
{
    float length;          // Length of the rectangle
    float width;           // Width of the rectangle
    float perimeter;       // Perimeter of the rectangle
    float area;            // Area of the rectangle

    length = 10.7;
    width = 5.2;
```

6. Write C++ output statements that produce exactly the following output.

a. Four score
   and seven years ago
b. Four score
   and seven
   years ago
c. Four score

   and

   seven
   years ago
d. Four

      score
         and
   seven
      years
         ago

PROGRAMMING PROBLEMS

1. Write a C++ program that converts a Celsius temperature to its Fahrenheit equivalent. The formula is

$$\text{Fahrenheit} = \frac{9}{5}\,\text{Celsius} + 32$$

   Make the Celsius temperature a named constant so that its value can be changed easily. The program should print both the value of the Celsius temperature and its Fahrenheit equivalent, with appropriate identifying messages. Be sure to include appropriate comments in your program, choose meaningful identifiers, and use indentation as we do in the programs in this chapter.

2. Write a program to calculate the diameter, the circumference, and the area of a circle given a radius of 6.75. Assign the radius to a `float` variable, and then output the radius with an appropriate message. Declare a named constant `PI` with the value 3.14159. The program should output the diameter, the circumference, and the area, each on a separate line, with identifying labels. Print each value to five decimal places within a total fieldwidth of 10. Be sure to include appropriate comments in your program, choose meaningful identifiers, and use indentation as we do in the programs in this chapter.

3. You have bought a car, taking out a loan with an annual interest rate of 9%. You will make 36 monthly payments of $165.25 each. You want to keep track of the remaining balance you owe after each monthly payment. The formula for the remaining balance is

$$bal_k = pmt \left[\frac{1 - (1 + i)^{k - n}}{i} \right]$$

   where

bal_k	=	balance remaining after the kth payment
k	=	payment number $(1, 2, 3, \ldots)$
pmt	=	amount of the monthly payment
i	=	interest rate per month (annual rate ÷ 12)
n	=	total number of payments to be made

   Write a program to calculate and print the balance remaining after the first, second, and third monthly car payments. Before printing these three results, the program should output the values on which the calculations are based (monthly payment, interest rate, and total number of payments). Label all output with identifying messages, and print all money amounts to two decimal places. Be sure to include appropriate comments in your program, choose meaningful identifiers, and use indentation as we do in the programs in this chapter.

CASE STUDY FOLLOW-UP

1. Modify the Walk program to include a roundoff factor so that the rounding of `miles` can be modified easily. Currently, the program uses a literal constant (10.0) in several places to round `miles` to the nearest tenth, requiring us to make multiple changes if we want a different roundoff factor.

2. Should the roundoff factor in Question 1 be a constant or a variable? Explain.

3. In the Walk program, a particular pattern of statements is repeated four times with small variations. Identify the repeating pattern. Then circle those parts of the statements that vary with each repetition.

4

Program Input and the Software Design Process

GOALS

- To be able to construct input statements to read values into a program.
- To be able to determine the contents of variables assigned values by input statements.
- To be able to write appropriate prompting messages for interactive programs.
- To know when noninteractive input/output is appropriate and how it differs from interactive input/output.
- To be able to write programs that use data files for input and output.
- To be able to apply top-down design methodology to solve a simple problem.
- To be able to take a top-down design and code it in C++, using self-documenting code.
- To understand the basic principles of object-oriented design.

A program needs data on which to operate. We have been writing all of the data values in the program itself, in literal and named constants. If this were the only way we could enter data, we would have to rewrite a program each time we wanted to apply it to a different set of values. In this chapter, we look at ways of entering data into a program while it is running.

Once we know how to input data, process the data, and output the results, we can begin to think about designing more complicated programs. We have talked about general problem-solving strategies and writing simple programs. For a simple problem, it's easy to choose a strategy, write the algorithm, and code the program. But as problems become more complex, we have to use a more organized approach. In the second part of this chapter, we look at two general methodologies for developing software: top-down design and object-oriented design.

 Getting Data into Programs

One of the biggest advantages of computers is that a program can be used with many different sets of data. To do so, we must keep the data separate from the program until the program is executed. Then instructions in the program copy values from the data set into variables in the program. After storing these values into the variables, the program can perform calculations with them (see Figure 4-1).

The process of placing values from an outside data set into variables in a program is called *inputting*. In widely used terminology, the computer is

■ FIGURE 4-1

Separating the Data from the Program

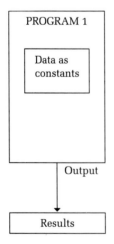

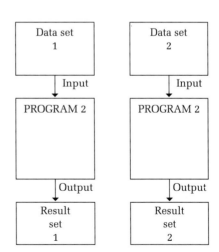

This program must be changed to work with different data values.

This program inputs its data from outside, so it can work with different data sets without being changed.

said to *read* outside data into the variables. The data for the program can come from an input device or from a file on an auxiliary storage device. We look at file input later in this chapter; here we consider the *standard input device*, the keyboard.

Input Streams and the Extraction Operator (>>)

The concept of a stream is fundamental to input and output in C++. As we stated in Chapter 3, you can think of an output stream as an endless sequence of characters going from your program to an output device. Likewise, think of an *input stream* as an endless sequence of characters coming into your program from an input device.

To use stream I/O, you must use the preprocessor directive

```
#include <iostream.h>
```

The header file `iostream.h` contains, among other things, the definitions of two data types: `istream` and `ostream`. These are data types representing input streams and output streams, respectively. The header file also contains declarations that look approximately like this:

```
istream cin;
ostream cout;
```

(We say "approximately" because the actual declarations are slightly different in a way that does not concern us right now.) The first declaration says that `cin` (pronounced "see-in") is a variable of type `istream`. The second says that `cout` (pronounced "see-out") is a variable of type `ostream`. Furthermore, `cin` is associated with the standard input device (the keyboard), and `cout` is associated with the standard output device (usually the display screen).

As you have already seen, you can output values to `cout` by using the insertion operator (<<), which is sometimes pronounced "put to":

```
cout << 3 * price;
```

In a similar fashion, you can input data from `cin` by using the *extraction operator* (>>), sometimes pronounced "get from":

```
cin >> cost;
```

When the computer executes this statement, it inputs the next number you type on the keyboard (425, for example) and stores it into the variable `cost`.

The extraction operator `>>` takes two operands. Its left-hand operand is a stream expression (in the simplest case, just the variable `cin`). Its right-hand operand is a variable of a simple type (`char`, `int`, `float`, and so forth).

You can use the `>>` operator several times in a single input statement. Each occurrence extracts (inputs) the next data item from the input stream. For example, there is no difference between the statement

```
cin >> length >> width;
```

and the pair of statements

```
cin >> length;
cin >> width;
```

Using a sequence of extractions in one statement is a convenience for the programmer.

When you are new to C++, you may get the extraction operator (`>>`) and the insertion operator (`<<`) reversed. Here is an easy way to remember which one is which: Always begin the statement with either `cin` or `cout`, and use the operator that points in the direction in which the data is going. The statement

```
cout << someInt;
```

sends data from the variable `someInt` *to* the output stream. The statement

```
cin >> someInt;
```

sends data from the input stream *to* the variable `someInt`.

Here's the syntax template for an input statement:

InputStatement

```
cin >> Variable >> Variable ... ;
```

Unlike the items specified in an output statement, which can be constants, variables, or complicated expressions, the items specified in an input statement can *only* be variable names. Why? Because an input statement indicates where input data values should be stored. Only variable names refer to memory locations where we can store values while a program is running.

When you enter input data at the keyboard, you must be sure that each data value is appropriate for the data type of the variable in the input statement.

Data Type of Variable In an >> Operation	Valid Input Data
char	A single printable character other than a blank
int	An int literal constant, optionally preceded by a sign
float	An int or float literal constant (possibly in scientific, E, notation), optionally preceded by a sign

Notice that when you input a number into a float variable, the input value doesn't have to have a decimal point. The integer value is automatically coerced to a float value. Any other mismatches, such as trying to input a float value into an int variable or a char value into a float variable, can lead to unexpected and sometimes serious results. Later in this chapter we discuss what might happen.

When looking for the next input value in the stream, the >> operator skips any leading *whitespace characters*. Whitespace characters are blanks and certain nonprintable characters like the character that marks the end of a line. (We talk about this end-of-line character in the next section.) After skipping any whitespace characters, the >> operator proceeds to extract the desired data value from the input stream. If this data value is a char value, input stops as soon as a single character is input. If the data value is int or float, input of the number stops at the first character that is inappropriate for the data type, such as a whitespace character. Here are some examples, where i, j, and k are int variables, ch is a char variable, and x is a float variable:

Statement	Data	Contents After Input
1. cin >> i;	32	i = 32
2. cin >> i >> j;	4 60	i = 4, j = 60
3. cin >> i >> ch >> x;	25 A 16.9	i = 25, ch = 'A', x = 16.9
4. cin >> i >> ch >> x;	25	
	A	
	16.9	i = 25, ch = 'A', x = 16.9
5. cin >> i >> ch >> x;	25A16.9	i = 25, ch = 'A', x = 16.9
6. cin >> i >> j >> x;	12 8	i = 12, j = 8 (Computer waits for a third number)
7. cin >> i >> x;	46 32.4 15	i = 46, x = 32.4 (15 is held for later input)

Examples (1) and (2) are straightforward examples of integer input. Example (3) shows that you do not use quotes around character data values when they are input (quotes around character constants are needed in a program, though, to distinguish them from identifiers). Example (4) demonstrates how the process of skipping whitespace characters includes going on to the next line of input if necessary. Example (5) shows that the first character encountered that is inappropriate for a numeric data type ends the number. Input for the variable i stops at the input character A, after which the A is stored into ch, and then input for x stops at the end of the input line. Example (6) shows that if you are at the keyboard and haven't entered enough values to satisfy the input statement, the computer waits (and waits and waits . . .) for more data. Example (7) shows that if more values are entered than there are variables in the input statement, the extra values remain waiting in the input stream until they can be read by the next input statement. If there are extra values left when the program ends, the computer disregards them.

The Reading Marker and the Newline Character

To help explain stream input in more detail, we introduce the concept of the *reading marker*. The reading marker works like a bookmark, but, instead of marking a place in a book, it keeps track of the point in the input stream where the computer should continue reading. The reading marker indicates the next character waiting to be read. The extraction operator >> leaves the reading marker on the character following the last piece of data that was input.

Each input line has an invisible end-of-line character (the *newline character*) that tells the computer where one line ends and the next begins. To find the next input value, the >> operator crosses line boundaries (newline characters) if it has to.

Where does the newline character come from? What is it? The answer to the first question is easy. When you are working at a keyboard, you generate a newline character yourself each time you hit the Return or Enter key. Your program also generates a newline character when it uses the endl manipulator in an output statement. The endl manipulator outputs a newline, telling the screen cursor to go to the next line. The answer to the second question varies from computer system to computer system. The newline character is a nonprintable control character that the system recognizes as meaning the end of a line, whether it's an input line or an output line.

In a C++ program, you can refer directly to the newline character by using the two symbols \n, a backslash and an n with no space between them. Although \n consists of two symbols, it refers to a single character—the newline character. Just as you can store the letter *A* into a char variable ch like this:

```
ch = 'A';
```

you can store the newline character into a variable:

```
ch = '\n';
```

You also can put the newline character into a string just as you can any printable character:

```
cout << "Hello\n";
```

This last statement has exactly the same effect as the statement

```
cout << "Hello" << endl;
```

But back to our discussion of input. Let's look at some examples using the reading marker and the newline character. In the following table, i is an `int` variable, ch is a `char` variable, and x is a `float` variable. The input statements produce the results shown. The part of the input stream printed in color is what has been extracted by input statements. The reading marker, denoted by the shaded block, indicates the next character waiting to be read. The \n denotes the newline character produced by striking the Return or Enter key.

Statements	Contents After Input	Marker Position in the Input Stream
1.		2̲5 A 16.9\n
cin >> i;	i = 25	25█A 16.9\n
cin >> ch;	ch = 'A'	25 A█16.9\n
cin >> x;	x = 16.9	25 A 16.9█\n
2.		2̲5\n A\n 16.9\n
cin >> i;	i = 25	25█\n A\n 16.9\n
cin >> ch;	ch = 'A'	25\n A█\n 16.9\n

`cin >> x;`	`x = 16.9`	25\n
		A\n
		16.9 **\n**

3.

		2 5A16.9\n
`cin >> i;`	`i = 25`	25 **A** 16.9\n
`cin >> ch;`	`ch = 'A'`	25A **16.** 9\n
`cin >> x;`	`x = 16.9`	25A16.9 **\n**

Reading Character Data with the get Function

As we have discussed, the >> operator skips any leading whitespace characters (such as blanks and newline characters) while looking for the next data value in the input stream. Suppose that ch1 and ch2 are char variables and the program executes the statement

```
cin >> ch1 >> ch2;
```

If the input stream consists of

R 1

then the extraction operator stores 'R' into ch1, skips the blank, and stores '1' into ch2. (Note that the char value '1' is not the same as the int value 1. The two are stored completely differently in a computer's memory. The extraction operator interprets the same data in different ways, depending on the data type of the variable that's being filled.)

What if we had wanted to input *three* characters from the input line: the R, the blank, and the 1? With the extraction operator, it's not possible. Whitespace characters such as blanks are skipped over.

The istream data type provides a second way in which to read character data, in addition to the >> operator. You can use the get function, which inputs the very next character in the input stream without skipping any whitespace characters. A function call looks like this:

```
cin.get(someChar);
```

You give the name of an istream variable (here, cin), then a dot (period), and then the function name and parameter list. Notice that the call to get uses the syntax for calling a void function, not a value-returning function. The function call is a complete statement; it is not part of a larger expression.

The effect of the above function call is to input the next character waiting in the stream—even if it is a whitespace character like a blank—and store it into the variable someChar. The parameter to the get function *must* be a variable, not a constant or arbitrary expression; we must tell the function where we want it to store the input character.

Using the get function, we now can input all three characters of the input line

R l

We can use three consecutive calls to the get function

```
cin.get(ch1);
cin.get(ch2);
cin.get(ch3);
```

or we can do it this way:

```
cin >> ch1;
cin.get(ch2);
cin >> ch3;
```

The first version is probably a bit clearer for someone to read and understand.

Here are some more examples of character input using both the >> operator and the get function. All of ch1, ch2, and ch3 are char variables. As before, \n denotes the newline character.

Statements	Contents After Input	Marker Position in the Input Stream
1.		A B\n
		CD\n
cin >> ch1;	ch1 = 'A'	A█B\n
		CD\n
cin >> ch2;	ch2 = 'B'	A B\n
		CD\n
cin >> ch3;	ch3 = 'C'	A B\n
		CD\n

2.   A̶ B\n
                                                           CD\n
    cin.get(ch1);   ch1 = 'A'   A B\n
                                                           CD\n
    cin.get(ch2);   ch2 = ' '   A B\n
                                                           CD\n
    cin.get(ch3);   ch3 = 'B'   A B \n
                                                           CD\n

---

3.   A̶ B\n
                                                           CD\n
    cin >> ch1;   ch1 = 'A'   A B\n
                                                           CD\n
    cin >> ch2;   ch2 = 'B'   A B \n
                                                           CD\n
    cin.get(ch3);   ch3 = '\n'   A B\n
                                                           CD\n

---

You may be puzzled about the peculiar syntax in a function call like

```
cin.get(ch1);
```

This statement uses a C++ notation called *dot notation*. There is a dot (period) between the variable name `cin` and the function name `get`. Certain predefined data types, like `istream` and `ostream`, have functions that are tightly associated with them, and dot notation is required in the function calls. If you forget to use dot notation by using

```
get(ch1);
```

you get a compile-time error message, something like "UNDECLARED IDENTIFIER." The compiler thinks you are trying to call an ordinary function named `get`, not the `get` function associated with the `istream` type.

Another example you saw in the last chapter is the function call that forces decimal points to appear in the output of all floating point numbers:

```
cout.setf(ios::showpoint);
```

(This statement uses even stranger syntax in the form of the double colon, whose purpose we won't attempt to discuss here.) Later in the chapter, we discuss the meaning behind dot notation.

THEORETICAL FOUNDATIONS

More About Functions and Parameters

When your `main` function tells the computer to go off and follow the instructions in another function, `SomeFunc`, the `main` function is *calling* `SomeFunc`. In the call to `SomeFunc`, the parameters in the parameter list are *passed* to the function. When `SomeFunc` finishes, the computer *returns* to the `main` function.

With some functions you have seen, like `sqrt` and `abs`, you can pass constants, variables, and arbitrary expressions to the function. The `get` function for reading character data, however, accepts only a variable as a parameter. The `get` function stores a value into its parameter when it returns, and only variables can have values stored into them while a program is running. Even though `get` is called as a void function—not a value-returning function—it *returns* or *passes back* a value through its parameter list. The point to remember is that you can use parameters both to send data into a function and to get results back out.

Skipping Characters with the `ignore` *Function*

Most of us have a specialized tool lying in a kitchen drawer or in a toolbox. It gathers dust and cobwebs because we almost never use it. But when we suddenly need it, we're glad we have it.

The `ignore` function associated with the `istream` type is like this specialized tool. You rarely have occasion to use `ignore`; but when you need it, you're glad it's available.

The `ignore` function is used to skip (read and discard) characters in the input stream. It is a function with two parameters, called like this:

```
cin.ignore(200, '\n');
```

The first parameter is an `int` expression; the second, a `char` value. This particular function call tells the computer to skip the next 200 input characters *or* to skip characters until a newline character is read, whichever comes first.

Here are some examples that use a char variable ch and three int variables, i, j, and k:

Statements	Contents After Input	Marker Position in the Input Stream
1.		**9**57 34 1235\n 128 96\n
`cin >> i >> j;`	i = 957, j = 34	957 34█ 1235\n 128 96\n
`cin.ignore(100, '\n');`		957 34 1235\n █128 96\n
`cin >> k;`	k = 128	957 34 1235\n 128█96\n
2.		**A** 22 B 16 C 19\n
`cin >> ch;`	ch = 'A'	A█22 B 16 C 19\n
`cin.ignore(100, 'B');`		A 22 B█16 C 19\n
`cin >> i;`	i = 16	A 22 B 16█C 19\n
3.		**A**BCDEF\n
`cin.ignore(2, '\n');`		AB**C**DEF\n
`cin >> ch;`	ch = 'C'	ABC**D**EF\n

Example (1) shows the most common use of the ignore function, which is to skip the rest of the data on the current input line. Example (2) demonstrates the use of a character other than '\n' as the second parameter. We skip over all input characters until a 'B' has been found, then read the next input number into i. In both (1) and (2), we are focusing on the second parameter to the ignore function, and we arbitrarily choose any large number like 100 for the first parameter. In (3), we change our focus and concentrate on the first parameter. Our intention is to skip the next two input characters on the current line.

Interactive Input/Output

Remember in Chapter 1 that we defined an interactive program as one in which the user communicates directly with the computer. Many of the programs that you write will be interactive. There is a certain "etiquette" involved in writing interactive programs that has to do with instructions for the user (the person executing your program).

To get data into an interactive program, we begin with *input prompts*, printed messages that explain what the user should enter. Without these messages, the user has no idea what to type into a program. A program also should print out all of the data values typed in so that the user can verify that they were entered correctly. Printing out the input values is called *echo printing*. Here's a program segment showing the proper use of prompts:

```
cout << "Enter the part number:" << endl;              // Prompt
cin >> partNumber;
cout << "Enter the quantity of this part ordered:"      // Prompt
     << endl;
cin >> quantity;
cout << "Enter the unit price for this part:"           // Prompt
     << endl;
cin >> unitPrice;
totalPrice = quantity * unitPrice;
cout << "Part " << partNumber                           // Echo print
     << ", quantity " << quantity
     << ", at $ " << setprecision(2) << unitPrice
     << " each" << endl;
cout << "totals $ " << totalPrice << endl;
```

And here's the output, with the user's input shown in color:

```
Enter the part number:
4671
Enter the quantity of this part ordered:
10
Enter the unit price for this part:
27.25
Part 4671, quantity 10, at $ 27.25 each
totals $ 272.50
```

The amount of information you put into your prompts depends on who is going to be using a program. If you are writing a program for people who are not familiar with computers, your messages should be more detailed. For example, "Type a four-digit part number, then press the key marked RE-TURN." If the program is going to be used frequently by the same people, you could shorten the prompts: "Enter PN." and "Enter Qty." If the program is for very experienced users, you can prompt for several values at once and have them type all of the values on one input line:

```
Enter PN, Qty, Unit Price:
4176 10 27.25
```

In programs that use large amounts of data, this method saves the user keystrokes and time. However, it also makes it easier for the user to enter values in the wrong order.

Prompts are not the only way in which programs interact with users. It can be helpful to have a program print out some general instructions at the beginning ("Press RETURN after typing each data value. Enter a negative number when done."). When data is not entered in the correct form, a message that indicates the problem should be printed. For users who haven't worked much with computers, it's important that these messages be informative and "friendly." The message

```
ILLEGAL DATA VALUES!!!!!!!
```

is likely to upset an inexperienced user. Moreover, it doesn't offer any constructive information. A much better message would be

```
That is not a valid part number.
Part numbers must be no more than four digits long.
Please reenter the number in its proper form:
```

In Chapter 5, we introduce the statements that allow us to test for erroneous data.

Noninteractive Input/Output

Although we tend to use examples of interactive I/O in this text, many programs are written using noninteractive I/O. A common example of noninteractive I/O on large computer systems is batch processing. Remember that in batch processing (Chapter 1), the user and the computer do not interact while the program is running. This method is most effective when a program is going to input or output large amounts of data. An example of batch processing is a program that inputs a file containing semester grades for thousands of students and prints grade reports to be mailed out.

When a program must read in many data values, the usual practice is to prepare them ahead of time, storing them into a file. This allows the user to go back and make changes or corrections to the data as necessary before running the program. When a program is designed to print lots of data, the output can be sent directly to a high-speed printer or another disk file. After the program has been run, the user can examine the data at leisure. In the next section, we discuss input and output with disk files.

Programs designed for noninteractive I/O do not print prompting messages for input. It is a good idea, however, to echo-print each data value that is read. Echo printing allows the person reading the output to verify that the input values were prepared correctly. Because noninteractive programs tend to print large amounts of data, their output often is in the form of a table—columns with descriptive headings.

Most C++ programs are written for interactive use. But the flexibility of the language allows you to write noninteractive programs as well. The biggest difference is in the input/output requirements. Noninteractive programs are generally more rigid about the organization and format of the input and output data.

File Input and Output

In everything we've done so far, we've assumed that the input to our programs comes from the keyboard and that the output from our programs goes to the screen. We look now at input/output to and from files.

Files

Earlier we defined a file as a named area in secondary memory that holds a collection of information (for example, the program code we have typed into the editor). The information in a file usually is stored on an auxiliary storage device, such as a disk (see Figure 4-2).

Our programs can read data from a file in the same way they read data from the keyboard. And they can write output to a disk file in the same way they write output to the screen.

Why would we want a program to read data from a file instead of the keyboard? If a program is going to read a large quantity of data, it is easier to enter the data into a file with an editor than to enter it while the program is running. With the editor, we can go back and correct mistakes. Also, we do not have to enter the data all at once; we can take a break and come back later. And if we want to rerun the program, having the data stored in a file allows us to do so without reentering the data.

Why would we want the output from a program to be written to a disk file? The contents of a file can be displayed on a screen or printed. This gives us the option of looking at the output over and over again without having to rerun the program. Also, the output stored in a file can be read into another program as input. For example, the Payroll program writes its output to a file named `payFile`. We can take `payFile` and read it into another program, perhaps one that prints out paychecks.

■ FIGURE 4-2

3.5-inch and 5.25-inch Floppy Disks

Through the header file `fstream.h`, the C++ standard library defines two

Using Files

If we want a program to use file I/O, we have to do four things:

1. Request the preprocessor to include the header file `fstream.h`.
2. Use declaration statements to declare the files we are going to use.
3. Prepare each file for reading or writing by using a function named `open`.
4. Specify the name of the file in each input or output statement.

Including the Header File `fstream.h`   Suppose we want the Mileage program (page 83) to read data from a file and to write its output to a file. The first thing we must do is use the preprocessor directive

```
#include <fstream.h>
```

Through the header file `fstream.h`, the C++ standard library defines two data types, `ifstream` and `ofstream` (standing for *input file stream* and *output file stream*). Consistent with the general idea of streams in C++, the `ifstream` data type represents a stream of characters coming from an input file, and `ofstream` represents a stream of characters going to an output file.

All of the `istream` operations you have learned about—the extraction operator (`>>`), the `get` function, and the `ignore` function—are also valid for the `ifstream` type. And all of the `ostream` operations, like the insertion operator (`<<`) and the `endl`, `setw`, and `setprecision` manipulators, apply also to the `ofstream` type. To these basic operations, the `ifstream` and `ofstream` types add some more operations designed specifically for file I/O.

Declaring File Streams   In a program, you declare stream variables the same way that you declare any variable—you specify the data type and then the variable name:

```
int       someInt;
float     someFloat;
ifstream inFile;
ofstream outFile;
```

(You don't have to declare the stream variables cin and cout. The header file iostream.h already does this for you.)

For our Mileage program, let's name the input and output file streams inMPG and outMPG. We declare them like this:

```
ifstream inMPG;        // Holds gallon amounts and mileages
ofstream outMPG;       // Holds miles per gallon output
```

Note that the ifstream type is for input files only, and the ofstream type is for output files only. With these data types, you cannot read from and write to the same file. If you wanted to do so, you would use a third data type named fstream, the details of which we don't explore in this book.

Opening Files   The third thing we have to do is prepare each file for reading or writing, an act called *opening a file*. Opening a file causes the computer's operating system to perform certain actions that allow us to proceed with file I/O.

In our example, we want to read from the file stream inMPG and write to the file stream outMPG. We open the relevant files by using these statements:

```
inMPG.open("inmpg.dat");
outMPG.open("outmpg.dat");
```

These statements are both function calls (notice the telltale parameters—the mark of a function). In each function call, the parameter is a string enclosed by quotes. The first statement is a call to a function named open, which is associated with the ifstream data type. The second is a call to another function (also named open) associated with the ofstream data type. As we discussed earlier, we use dot notation (as in inMPG.open) to call certain library functions that are tightly associated with data types.

Exactly what does an open function do? First, it associates a stream variable used in your program with a physical file on disk. Our first function call creates a connection between the stream variable inMPG and the actual disk file, inmpg.dat. (Names of file streams must be identifiers; they are variables in your program. But some computer systems do not use this format for file names on disk. For example, many systems include a dot in file names.) Similarly, the second function call associates the stream variable outMPG with the disk file outmpg.dat. Associating a program's name for a file (outMPG) with the actual name for the file (outmpg.dat) is much the same as associating a program's name for the standard output device (cout) with the actual device (the screen).

The next thing the open function does depends on whether the file is an input file or an output file. With an input file, the open function sets the file reading marker to the first piece of data in the file. (Each input file has its own reading marker.)

With an output file, the open function checks to see whether the file already exists. If the file doesn't exist, open creates a new, empty file for you. If the file does exist, open erases the old contents of the file. Then the writing marker is set at the beginning of the empty file (see Figure 4-3). As output proceeds, each successive output operation advances the writing marker to add data to the end of the file.

Because the reason for opening files is to *prepare* the files for reading or writing, you must open the files before using any input or output statements that refer to the files. In a program, it's a good idea to open files right away to be sure that the files are prepared before the program attempts any file I/O.

```
    ⋮

int main()
{
        ⋮  } Declarations

    // Open the files

    inMPG.open("inmpg.dat");
    outMPG.open("outmpg.dat");

        ⋮

}
```

Specifying Files in Input/Output Statements   There is just one more thing we have to do in order to use files. As we said earlier, all istream operations are also valid for the ifstream type, and all ostream operations are valid for the ofstream type. So, to read from or write to a file, all we need to do in our input and output statements is substitute the appropriate file stream variable for cin or cout. In our Mileage program, we would use a statement like

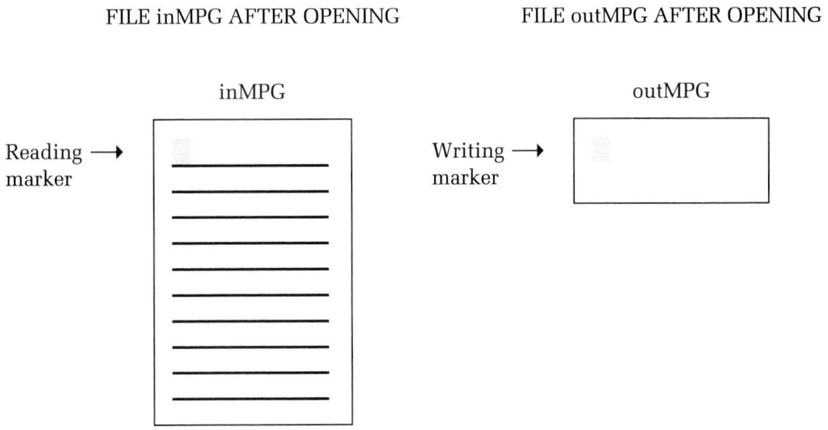

■ FIGURE 4-3

The Effect of
Opening a File

FILE inMPG AFTER OPENING   FILE outMPG AFTER OPENING

inMPG   outMPG

Reading →   Writing →
marker   marker

```
inMPG >> amt1 >> amt2 >> amt3 >> amt4 >> startMiles >> endMiles;
```

to instruct the computer to read data from the file inMPG instead of from cin.
And all of the output statements that write to the file outMPG would specify
outMPG, not cout, as the destination:

```
outMPG << "the mileage per gallon is " << mpg << endl;
```

What is nice about C++ stream I/O is that we have a uniform syntax for performing I/O operations, regardless of whether we're working with the keyboard and screen, with files, or with other I/O devices.

An Example Program Using Files

Here's the Mileage program reworked. Now it reads its input from the file
inMPG and writes its output to the file outMPG. Compare this program with
the original version on page 83 and notice that the constants have disappeared because the data is now input at execution time.

```
//*************************************************************
// Mileage program
// This program computes miles per gallon given four amounts
// for gallons used, and starting and ending mileage
//*************************************************************
#include <iostream.h>
#include <fstream.h>      // For file I/O
```

```
int main()
{
    float     amt1;          // Number of gallons for fillup 1
    float     amt2;          // Number of gallons for fillup 2
    float     amt3;          // Number of gallons for fillup 3
    float     amt4;          // Number of gallons for fillup 4
    float     startMiles;    // Starting mileage
    float     endMiles;      // Ending mileage
    float     mpg;           // Computed miles per gallon
    ifstream  inMPG;         // Holds gallon amounts and mileages
    ofstream  outMPG;        // Holds miles per gallon output

    // Open the files

    inMPG.open("inmpg.dat");
    outMPG.open("outmpg.dat");

    // Get data

    inMPG >> amt1 >> amt2 >> amt3 >> amt4
          >> startMiles >> endMiles;

    // Compute miles per gallon

    mpg = (endMiles - startMiles) / (amt1 + amt2 + amt3 + amt4);

    // Output results

    outMPG << "For the gallon amounts" << endl;
    outMPG << amt1 << ' ' << amt2 << ' '
           << amt3 << ' ' << amt4 << endl;
    outMPG << "and a starting mileage of " << startMiles << endl;
    outMPG << "and an ending mileage of " << endMiles << endl;
    outMPG << "the mileage per gallon is " << mpg << endl;
    return 0;
}
```

In this program, what happens if you mistakenly specify cout instead of outMPG in one of the output statements? Nothing disastrous; the output of that one statement merely goes to the screen instead of the output file. And what if, by mistake, you specify cin instead of inMPG in the input statement? The consequences are not as pleasant. When you run the program, the computer will appear to go dead (to *hang*). Here's the reason.

Execution reaches the input statement and the computer waits for you to enter the data from the keyboard. But you don't know that the computer is waiting. There's no message on the screen prompting you for input, and you are assuming (wrongly) that the program is getting its input from a data file. So the computer waits, and you wait, and the computer waits, and you wait. Every programmer at one time or another has had the experience of thinking the computer has hung, when, in fact, it is working just fine, silently waiting for keyboard input.

Input Failure

When a program inputs data from the keyboard or an input file, things can go wrong. Let's suppose that we're executing a program. It prompts us to enter an integer value, but we absentmindedly type some letters of the alphabet. The input operation fails because of the invalid data. In C++ terminology, the cin stream has entered the *fail state*. Once a stream has entered the fail state, any further I/O operations using that stream are considered to be null operations—that is, they have no effect at all. Unfortunately for us, *the computer does not halt the program or give any error message*. The computer just continues executing the program, silently ignoring each additional attempt to use that stream.

Invalid data is the most common reason for input failure. When your program inputs an int value, it is expecting to find only digits in the input stream, possibly preceded by a plus or minus sign. If there is a decimal point somewhere within the digits, does the input operation fail? Not necessarily; it depends on where the reading marker is. Let's look at an example.

Assume that a program has int variables i, j, and k, whose contents are currently 10, 20, and 30, respectively. The program now executes the following two statements:

```
cin >> i >> j >> k;
cout << "i: " << i << "  j: " << j << "  k: " << k;
```

If we type these characters for the input data:

```
1234.56 7 89
```

then the program produces this output:

```
i: 1234  j: 20  k: 30
```

Let's see why.

Remember that when reading int or float data, the extraction operator >> stops reading at the first character that is inappropriate for the data type (whitespace or otherwise). In our example, the input operation for i succeeds. The computer extracts the first four characters from the input stream and stores the integer value 1234 into i. The reading marker is now on the decimal point:

```
1234.56 7 89
```

The next input operation (for j) fails; an int value cannot begin with a decimal point. The cin stream is now in the fail state, and the current value of j (20) remains unchanged. The third input operation (for k) is ignored, as are all the rest of the statements in our program that read from cin.

Another way to make a stream enter the fail state is to try to open an input file that doesn't exist. Suppose that you have a data file on your disk named myfile.dat. In your program you have the following statements:

```
ifstream inFile;

inFile.open("myfil.dat");
inFile >> i >> j >> k;
```

In the call to the open function, you misspelled the name of your disk file. At run time, the attempt to open the file fails, so the stream inFile enters the fail state. The next three input operations (for i, j, and k) are null operations. Without issuing any error message, the program proceeds to use the (unknown) contents of i, j, and k in calculations. The results of these calculations are certain to be puzzling.

The point of this discussion is not to make you nervous about I/O but to make you aware. The Testing and Debugging section at the end of this chapter offers suggestions for avoiding input failure. And in Chapters 5 and 6, you will learn about program statements that let you test the state of a stream.

 ## Software Design

Over the last two chapters and the first part of this one, we have introduced elements of the C++ language that let us input data, perform calculations, and output results. The programs we wrote were short and straightforward because the problems to be solved were simple. We are ready to write programs for more complicated problems, but first we need to step back and look at the overall process of programming.

As you learned in Chapter 1, the programming process consists of a problem-solving phase and an implementation phase. The problem-solving phase includes *analysis* (analyzing and understanding the problem to be solved) and *design* (designing a solution to the problem). Given a complex problem—one that results in a 10,000-line program, for example—it's simply not reasonable to skip the design process and go directly to writing C++ code. What we need is a systematic way of designing a solution to a problem, no matter how complicated the problem is.

In the remainder of this chapter, we describe two important methodologies for designing solutions to more complex problems: *top-down design* and *object-oriented design*. These methodologies help you create solutions that can be easily implemented as C++ programs. The resulting programs are readable, understandable, and easy to debug and modify.

 Top-Down Design

The design technique we'll be using for the next several chapters is **top-down design** (it's also called *structured design*, *stepwise refinement*, and *modular programming*). It allows us to use the divide-and-conquer approach, which we talked about in Chapter 1.

Top-Down Design   A technique for developing a program in which the problem is divided into more easily handled subproblems, the solutions of which create a solution to the overall problem.

In top-down design, we work from the abstract (a list of the major steps in our solution) to the particular (algorithmic steps that can be translated directly into C++ code). You can also think of this as working from a high-level solution, leaving the details of implementation unspecified, down to a fully detailed solution.

The easiest way to solve a problem is to give it to someone else and say, "Solve this problem." This is the most abstract level of a problem solution: a single-statement solution that encompasses the entire problem without specifying any of the details of implementation. It's at this point that we programmers are called in. Our job is to turn the abstract solution into a concrete solution, a program.

We start by breaking the solution into a series of major steps. In the process, we move to a lower level of abstraction—that is, some of the implementation details (but not too many) are now specified. Each of the major steps becomes an independent subproblem that we can work on separately. In a very large project, one person (the *chief architect* or *team leader*) formulates the subproblems and then gives them to other members of the programming team, saying, "Solve this problem." In the case of a small project, we give the subproblems to ourselves. Then we choose one subproblem at a time and break it into another series of steps that, in turn, become smaller subproblems. The process continues until each subproblem cannot be divided further or has an obvious solution.

Why do we work this way? Why not simply write out all of the details? Because it is much easier to focus on one problem at a time. For example, suppose you are working on a program to print out certain values and discover that you need a complex formula to calculate an appropriate fieldwidth for printing one of the values. Calculating fieldwidths is not the purpose of the program. If you shift your focus to the calculation, you are more likely to forget some detail of the overall printing process. What you do is write down an abstract step—"Calculate the fieldwidth required"—and go on with the problem at hand. Once you've completed the general solution, you can go back to solving the step that does the calculation.

By subdividing the problem, you create a hierarchical structure called a *tree structure*. Each level of the tree is a complete solution to the problem that is less abstract (more detailed) than the level above it. Figure 4-4 shows a generic solution tree for a problem. Steps that are shaded have enough implementation details to be translated directly into C++ statements. These are **concrete steps.** Those that are not shaded are **abstract steps;** they reappear as subproblems in the next level down. Each box in the figure represents a **module.** Modules are the basic building blocks in a top-down design. The diagram in Figure 4-4 is also called a *module structure chart*.

Concrete Step   A step for which the implementation details are fully specified.

Abstract Step   A step for which some implementation details remain unspecified.

Module   A self-contained collection of steps that solves a problem or subproblem; can contain both concrete and abstract steps.

Modules

A module begins life as an abstract step in the next higher level of the solution tree. It is completed when it solves a given subproblem—that is, when it specifies a series of steps that does the same thing as the higher-level abstract step. At this stage, a module is **functionally equivalent** to the abstract step. (Don't confuse our use of *function* with C++ functions. Here we use the term to refer to the specific role that the module or step plays in an algorithmic solution.)

Functional Equivalence   A property of a module that performs exactly the same operation as the abstract step it defines. A pair of modules are also functionally equivalent to each other when they perform exactly the same operation.

■ FIGURE 4-4   Hierarchical Solution Tree

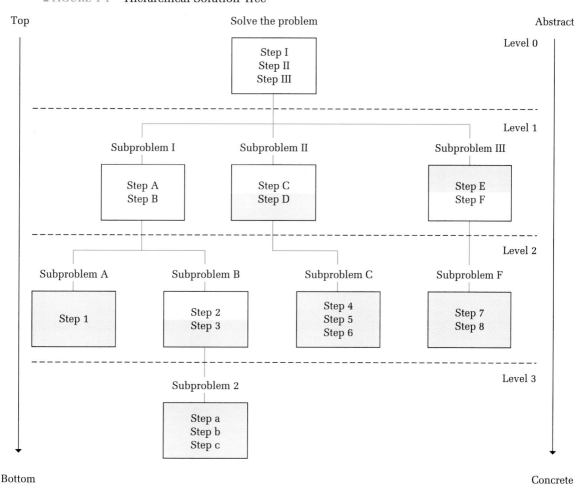

In a properly written module, the only steps that directly address the given subproblem are concrete steps; abstract steps are used for significant new subproblems. This is called **functional cohesion.**

Functional Cohesion   A property of a module in which all concrete steps are directed toward solving just one problem, and any significant subproblems are written as abstract steps.

The idea behind functional cohesion is that each module should do just one thing and do it well. Functional cohesion is not a well-defined property; there is no quantitative measure of cohesion. It is a product of the human need to organize things into neat chunks that are easy to understand and remember. Knowing which details to make concrete and which to leave abstract is a matter of experience, circumstance, and personal style. For example, you might decide to include a fieldwidth calculation in a printing module if there isn't so much detail in the rest of the module that it becomes confusing. On the other hand, if the calculation is performed several times, it makes sense to write it as a separate module and just refer to it each time you need it.

Writing Cohesive Modules   Here's one approach to writing modules that are cohesive:

1. Think about how you would solve the subproblem by hand.
2. Begin writing down the major steps.
3. If a step is simple enough so that you can see how to implement it directly in C++, it is at the concrete level; it doesn't need any further refinement.
4. If you have to think about implementing a step as a series of smaller steps or as several C++ statements, it is still at an abstract level.
5. If you are trying to write a series of steps and start to feel overwhelmed by details, you probably are bypassing one or more levels of abstraction. Stand back and look for pieces that you can write as more abstract steps.

We could call this the "procrastinator's technique." If a step is cumbersome or difficult, put it off to a lower level; don't think about it today, think about it tomorrow. Of course, tomorrow does come, but the whole process can be applied again to the subproblem. A trouble spot often seems much simpler when you can focus on it. And eventually the whole problem is broken up into manageable units.

As you work your way down the solution tree, you make a series of design decisions. If a decision proves awkward or wrong (and many times it will), you can backtrack (go back up the tree to a higher-level module) and try something else. You don't have to scrap your whole design—only the small part you are working on. There may be many intermediate steps and trial solutions before you reach a final design.

Pseudocode   You'll find it easier to implement a design if you write the steps in pseudocode. *Pseudocode* is a mixture of English statements and C++-like control structures that can be translated easily into C++. (We've been using pseudocode in the algorithms in the Problem-Solving Case Studies.) When a concrete step is written in pseudocode, it should be possible to rewrite it directly as a C++ statement in a program.

Remember that the problem-solving phase of the programming process takes time. If you spend the bulk of your time analyzing and designing a solution, coding and implementing the program will take very little time.

Implementing the Design

The product of top-down design is a hierarchical solution to a problem with multiple levels of abstraction. Figure 4-5 shows a top-down design for the ConePaint program in Chapter 3. This kind of solution forms the basis for the implementation phase of programming.

How do we translate a top-down design into a C++ program? If you look closely at Figure 4-5, you can see that the concrete steps (those that are shaded) can be assembled into a complete algorithm for solving the problem. The order in which they are assembled is determined by their position in the tree. We start at the top of the tree, at level 0, with the first step, "Convert dimensions to feet." Because it is abstract, we must go to the next level, level 1. There we find a series of concrete steps that correspond to this step; this series of steps becomes the first part of our algorithm. Because the conversion process is now concrete, we can go back to level 0 and go on to the next step, finding the radius of the cone. This step is concrete; we can copy it directly into the algorithm. The last three steps at level 0 are abstract, so we work with each of them in order at level 1, making them concrete. Here's the resulting algorithm:

```
Set heightInFeet = heightInInches / 12
Set diameterInFeet = diameterInInches / 12
Set radius = diameterInFeet / 2
Set surfaceArea = pi * radius * sqrt(radius*radius + heightInFeet*heightInFeet)
Set redCost = surfaceArea * 0.10
Set blueCost = surfaceArea * 0.15
Set greenCost = surfaceArea * 0.18
Print surfaceArea
Print redCost
Print blueCost
Print greenCost
```

From this algorithm we can construct a table of the constants and variables required, and then write the declarations and executable statements of the program.

In practice, you write your design not as a tree diagram but as a series of modules grouped by levels of abstraction, as we've done below.

Main Module   *Level 0*

```
Convert dimensions to feet
Set radius = diameterInFeet / 2
Compute surface area
Compute costs
Print results
```

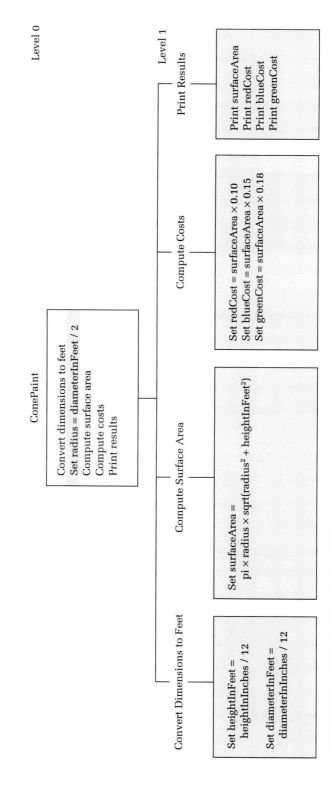

■ FIGURE 4-5   Solution Tree for ConePaint Program

Convert Dimensions to Feet *Level 1*

Set heightInFeet = heightInInches / 12
Set diameterInFeet = diameterInInches / 12

Compute Surface Area

Set surfaceArea = pi * radius * sqrt(radius*radius +
  heightInFeet*heightInFeet)

Compute Costs

Set redCost = surfaceArea * 0.10
Set blueCost = surfaceArea * 0.15
Set greenCost = surfaceArea * 0.18

Print Results

Print surfaceArea
Print redCost
Print blueCost
Print greenCost

If you look at the C++ program for ConePaint, you can see that it closely resembles this solution. The main difference is that the one concrete step at level 0 has been inserted at the proper point among the other concrete steps. You can also see that the names of the modules have been paraphrased as comments in the code.

The type of implementation that we've introduced here is called *flat* or *inline implementation*. We are flattening the two-dimensional, hierarchical structure of the solution by writing all of the steps as one long sequence. This kind of implementation is adequate when a solution is short and has only a few levels of abstraction. And the programs it produces are clear and easy to understand, assuming appropriate comments and good style.

Longer programs, with more levels of abstraction, are difficult to work with as flat implementations. In Chapter 7, you'll see that it is preferable to implement a hierarchical solution by using a *hierarchical implementation*. There we implement many of the modules by writing them as separate C++ functions, and the abstract steps in the design are replaced with calls to those functions.

One of the advantages of implementing modules as functions is that they can be called from different places in a program. For example, if a problem requires that the volume of a cylinder be computed in several places, we could write a single function to perform the calculation and simply call it in each place. This gives us a *semihierarchical implementation*. The implementation does not preserve a pure hierarchy because abstract steps at various levels of the solution tree share one implementation of a module (see Figure 4-6). A shared module actually falls outside the hierarchy because it doesn't really belong at any one level.

Another advantage of implementing modules as functions is that you can pick them up and use them in other programs. Over time, you will build a library of your own functions to complement those that are supplied by the C++ standard library.

We postpone a detailed discussion of hierarchical implementations until Chapter 7. For now, our programs remain short enough for flat implementations to suffice. Chapters 5 and 6 examine topics such as flow of control, preconditions and postconditions, interface design, side effects, and others you'll need to develop hierarchical implementations.

From now on, we use the following outline for the top-down designs in our case studies:

Problem statement
Input description
Output description
Discussion
Assumptions (if any)
Main module
Remaining modules by levels
Module structure chart

"This was your first effort at TOP-DOWN design, wasn't it?"

Cartoon by M. LAD. TOPOLSKY

■ FIGURE 4-6   A Semihierarchical Module Structure Chart with a Shared Module

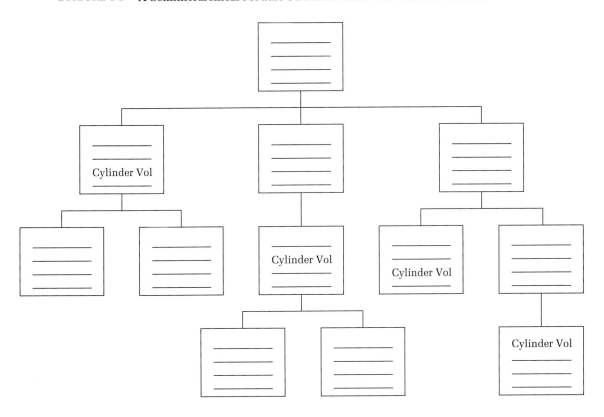

Cylinder Vol

| Set volume = $\pi r^2 h$ |

Object-Oriented Design (A Preview)

A second software design methodology, one that is gaining acceptance rapidly, is known as **object-oriented design** (**OOD**). In this section, we present only a preview of OOD. We postpone a thorough treatment until later in the book when we have introduced additional C++ language features. Even though we won't be using OOD for some time yet, it's important to recognize that top-down design is not the only technique used by programmers to design problem solutions.

Let's begin our look at OOD by making an observation about top-down design. Top-down design can be thought of as the design of a problem solution by focusing on actions and algorithms. In top-down design, data plays a secondary role in support of actions to be performed.

In contrast, OOD focuses on entities ("objects") and operations on those objects. For example, a banking problem may require a checkingAccount object with associated operations OpenAccount, WriteCheck, MakeDeposit, and IsOverdrawn. The checkingAccount object consists of both data (the account number and the current balance, for example) and operations, all bundled together.

The first step in OOD is to identify the major objects in the problem, together with their associated operations. The final problem solution is ultimately expressed in terms of these objects and operations. In OOD, data plays a leading role. Algorithms are used to implement operations on the objects and to guide the interaction of objects with each other.

Object-Oriented Design   A technique for developing a program in which the solution is expressed in terms of objects—self-contained entities composed of data and operations on that data.

Like top-down design, OOD uses the divide-and-conquer approach to problem solving. Both techniques break up large problems into smaller units that are easier to handle. The difference is that in top-down design the units are modules representing algorithms, whereas the units in OOD are objects.

Several programming languages, called *object-oriented programming languages*, have been created specifically to support OOD. Examples are C++, Smalltalk, CLOS, Eiffel, and Object-Pascal. In these languages, a *class* is a programmer-defined data type from which objects are created. Although we did not say it at the time, we have been using classes and objects to perform input and output in C++. cin is an object of a data type (class) named istream, and cout is an object of a class ostream. As we explained earlier, the header file iostream.h defines the classes istream and ostream and also declares cin and cout to be objects of those classes:

```
istream cin;
ostream cout;
```

Similarly, the header file fstream.h defines classes ifstream and ofstream, from which you can declare your own input file stream and output file stream objects.

In Figure 4-7, we picture the `cin` and `cout` objects as entities that have a private part and a public part. The private part includes data that the user cannot access and doesn't need to know about in order to use the object. The public part, shown as ovals in the side of the object, consists of operations that are available to programmers wishing to use the object. In C++, these public operations are written as functions and are called *member functions*. Except for the << and >> operations, a member function is invoked by giving the name of the class object, then a dot, and then the function name and parameter list:

```
cin.ignore(100, '\n');
cin.get(someChar);
cin >> someInt;
```

OOD leads to programs that are collections of objects. Each object is responsible for one part of the entire solution, and the objects communicate with each other by calling one another's member functions. OOD is especially suitable for large software projects for three reasons. First, objects within a program often model real-life objects in the problem to be solved. In a banking problem, it may be easier to design a solution by thinking about what objects are required—a savings account object, a checking account object, a teller object, a cash drawer object—than by thinking about what actions are required (do this step, then that step, then the next step, and so

■ FIGURE 4-7

Objects and Their
Operations

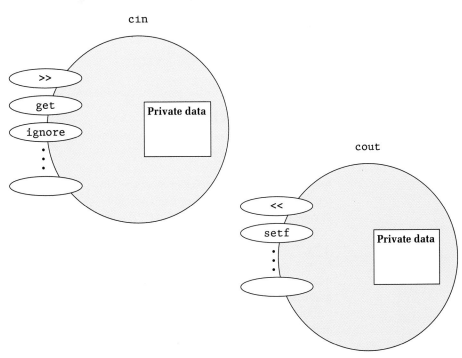

on). Second, with the expanding use of OOD, more and more individuals and software companies are supplying libraries of prewritten classes and objects. In many cases, it is possible to browse through a class library, choose classes and objects you need for your problem, and assemble them to form a substantial portion of your program. Putting existing pieces together in this fashion is an excellent example of the building-block approach we discussed in Chapter 1. Third, OOD employs a concept called *inheritance*, which allows you to adapt an existing class to meet your particular needs without having to inspect and modify the source code for that class. Together, OOD, class libraries, and inheritance can dramatically reduce the time and effort required to design, implement, and maintain large software systems.

In this section, we have presented only an introduction to OOD. A more complete discussion requires knowledge of topics that we explore in Chapters 4 through 14: flow of control, programmer-written functions, and structured data types. In Chapter 15, we learn how to write our own classes and create our own objects, and we return to OOD in Chapter 16. Until then, our programs are relatively small and we use top-down design to arrive at our problem solutions.

An important perspective to keep in mind is that top-down design and object-oriented design are not separate, disjoint techniques. OOD decomposes a problem into objects. Objects not only contain data; they also have associated operations. The operations on objects require algorithms. Sometimes the algorithms are complicated and must be decomposed into subalgorithms by using top-down design. Experienced programmers are familiar with both methodologies and know when to use one or the other, or a combination of the two.

SOFTWARE ENGINEERING TIP

Documentation

As you create your top-down or object-oriented design, you are developing documentation for your program. *Documentation* includes the written problem specifications, design, development history, and actual code of a program.

Good documentation helps other programmers read and understand a program and is invaluable when software is being debugged and modified (maintained). If you haven't looked at your program for six months and need to change it, you'll be happy that you documented it well. Of course, if someone else has to use and modify your program, documentation is indispensable.

Documentation is both external and internal to the program. External documentation includes the specifications, the development history, and the design documents. Internal documentation includes the program format and **self-documenting code**—

meaningful identifiers and comments. You can use the pseudocode from your top-down designs as comments in your programs.

This kind of documentation may be sufficient for someone reading or maintaining your programs. However, if a program is going to be used by people who are not programmers, you must provide a user's manual as well.

Be sure to keep documentation up-to-date. Indicate any changes you make in a program in all of the pertinent documentation. Use self-documenting code to make your programs more readable.

Self-Documenting Code Program code containing meaningful identifiers as well as judiciously used clarifying comments.

Now let's look at two case studies that demonstrate top-down design.

P ROBLEM-SOLVING CASE STUDY

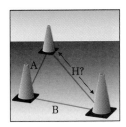

Pythagorean Theorem Applied to Right Triangles

Problem: Determine the length of the hypotenuse of a right triangle given the lengths of the other two sides.

Input: Two floating point numbers, one for each known side of the triangle.

Output: Print the input data with a message that identifies each number (echo printing). Print the length of the hypotenuse with an identifying message. All numbers are to be printed to four decimal places.

Discussion: The Pythagorean Theorem states that the square of the hypotenuse of a right triangle is equal to the sum of the squares of the other two sides. To compute the length of the hypotenuse, then, you square the lengths of the other two sides, add the squares, and then find the square root of the sum. We use the same method in our programming solution.

Assumptions: The two lengths are positive floating point numbers (checking for erroneous data is not done).

Main Module   *Level 0*

Get data
Print data
Find length of hypotenuse
Print length of hypotenuse

Get Data   *Level 1*

Print "Enter the lengths of the two sides."
Read lengthOfA, lengthOfB

Print Data

Print blank line
Print "The length of side A is ", lengthOfA
Print "The length of side B is ", lengthOfB

Find Length of Hypotenuse

Compute sum of squares
Set hypotenuse = sqrt(sumOfSquares)

Print Length of Hypotenuse

Print "The length of the hypotenuse is ", hypotenuse

Compute Sum of Squares   *Level 2*

Set sumOfSquares = lengthOfA * lengthOfA + lengthOfB * lengthOfB

PROBLEM-SOLVING CASE STUDY cont'd.

Module Structure Chart:

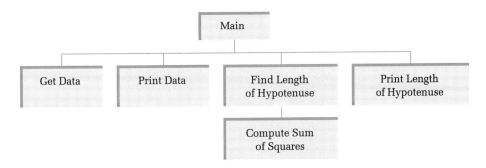

Variables

Name	Data Type	Description
lengthOfA	float	Length of one of the known sides
lengthOfB	float	Length of the other known side
sumOfSquares	float	Sum of the squares of the two known sides
hypotenuse	float	Length of the hypotenuse

Here is the complete program. Notice how we've used the module names as comments to help distinguish the modules from one another in our flat implementation.

```
//************************************************************
// Triangle program
// This program finds the length of the hypotenuse of a right
// triangle, given the lengths of the other two sides
//************************************************************
#include <iostream.h>
#include <iomanip.h>      // For setw() and setprecision()
#include <math.h>         // For sqrt()

int main()
{
    float lengthOfA;      // Length of one of the known sides
    float lengthOfB;      // Length of the other known side
    float sumOfSquares;   // Sum of the squares of the known sides
    float hypotenuse;     // Length of the hypotenuse
```

```
        cout.setf(ios::fixed, ios::floatfield);    // Set up floating pt.
        cout.setf(ios::showpoint);                 //    output format

        // Get data

        cout << "Enter the lengths of the two sides." << endl;
        cin >> lengthOfA >> lengthOfB;

        // Print data

        cout << endl;
        cout << "The length of side A is "
             << setw(8) << setprecision(4) << lengthOfA << endl;
        cout << "The length of side B is "
             << setw(8) << lengthOfB << endl;

        // Compute sum of squares

        sumOfSquares = lengthOfA * lengthOfA + lengthOfB * lengthOfB;

        // Find length of hypotenuse

        hypotenuse = sqrt(sumOfSquares);

        // Print length of hypotenuse

        cout << "The length of the hypotenuse is "
             << hypotenuse << endl;
        return 0;
}
```

This is an interactive program. The data is input while the program is executing. If the user enters this data:

```
95.019 123.45
```

the dialogue with the user looks like this:

```
Enter the lengths of the two sides.
95.019 123.45

The length of side A is  95.0190
The length of side B is 123.4500
The length of the hypotenuse is 155.7835
```

PROBLEM-SOLVING CASE STUDY

Weighted Average of Test Scores

Problem: Find the weighted average of three test scores. The data for each test is a score (an integer number) followed by its associated weight (a floating point number); each pair of numbers is on a separate line. The data is stored in a file called `scoreFile`.

Input: Three lines of data, each listing a test score (integer) and weight (floating point).

Output: Print the input data with headings (echo printing). Print the weighted average with an explanation. All floating point values are to be displayed to two decimal places.

Discussion: It is common to give different weights to tests in order to arrive at a student's grade in a course. For example, if two tests are worth 30 percent each and a final exam is worth 40 percent, we multiply the first test grade by 0.30, the second test grade by 0.30, and the final grade by 0.40. We then add these three values to get a weighted average. We use this by-hand algorithm to solve the problem.

Because the data is going to be read from a file, we have to #include the header file `fstream.h`, declare an input file stream, prepare the file for reading (open it), and remember to use the file stream instead of `cin` in the input statements.

Assumptions: The three weights add up to 1.00, and the input data is correct (checking for erroneous input data is not done).

Main Module   *Level 0*

> Prepare file for reading
> Get data
> Print data
> Find weighted average
> Print weighted average

Prepare File for Reading   *Level 1*

> Open scoreFile

Get Data

```
Read test1, weight1 from scoreFile
Read test2, weight2 from scoreFile
Read test3, weight3 from scoreFile
```

Print Data

```
Print heading
Print test1, weight1
Print test2, weight2
Print test3, weight3
```

Find Weighted Average

```
Set ave = test1 * weight1
    + test2 * weight2 + test3 * weight3
```

Print Weighted Average

```
Print blank line
Print "Weighted average = ", ave
```

Print Heading

Level 2

```
Print "Test Score     Weight"
Print blank line
```

Module Structure Chart:

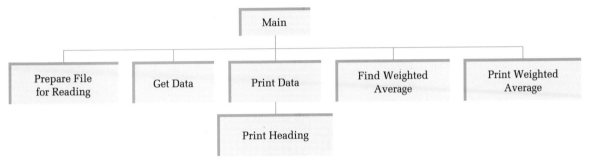

Variables

Name	Data Type	Description
test1	int	Score for first test
test2	int	Score for second test
test3	int	Score for third test
weight1	float	Weight for first test
weight2	float	Weight for second test
weight3	float	Weight for third test
ave	float	Weighted average of the tests
scoreFile	ifstream	Input data file

Here is the complete program. There are no prompting messages because the input is taken from a file.

```
//***********************************************************
// TestAverage program
// This program finds the weighted average of three test scores
//***********************************************************
#include <iostream.h>
#include <fstream.h>      // For file I/O
#include <iomanip.h>      // For setw() and setprecision()

int main()
{
    int     test1;            // Score for first test
    int     test2;            // Score for second test
    int     test3;            // Score for third test
    float   weight1;          // Weight for first test
    float   weight2;          // Weight for second test
    float   weight3;          // Weight for third test
    float   ave;              // Weighted average of the tests
    ifstream scoreFile;       // Input data file
```

```
cout.setf(ios::fixed, ios::floatfield);    // Set up floating pt.
cout.setf(ios::showpoint);                 //   output format

// Prepare file for reading

scoreFile.open("scores.dat");

// Get data

scoreFile >> test1 >> weight1;
scoreFile >> test2 >> weight2;
scoreFile >> test3 >> weight3;

// Print heading

cout << "Test Score   Weight" << endl << endl;

// Print data

cout << setw(7) << test1
     << setw(11) << setprecision(2) << weight1 << endl;
cout << setw(7) << test2 << setw(11) << weight2 << endl;
cout << setw(7) << test3 << setw(11) << weight3 << endl;

// Find weighted average

ave = test1 * weight1 + test2 * weight2 + test3 * weight3;

// Print weighted average

cout << endl;
cout << "Weighted average = " << ave << endl;
return 0;

}
```

If the file `scoreFile` (that is, the physical disk file `scores.dat`) contains this data:

```
90   0.30
85   0.25
78   0.45
```

the output from the program looks like this:

```
Test Score   Weight

        90    0.30
        85    0.25
        78    0.45

Weighted average = 83.35
```

TESTING AND DEBUGGING

An important part of implementing a program is testing it (checking the results). By now you should realize that there is nothing magical about the computer. It is infallible only if the person writing the instructions and entering the data is infallible. Don't trust it to give you the correct answers until you've verified enough of them by hand to convince yourself that the program is working.

From here on, these Testing and Debugging sections offer tips on how to test your programs and what to do if a program doesn't work the way you expect it to work. But don't wait until you've found a bug to read the Testing and Debugging sections. It's much easier to prevent bugs than it is to fix them.

When testing programs that input data values from a file, it's possible for input operations to fail. And when input fails in C++, the computer doesn't issue a warning message or terminate the program. The program simply continues executing, ignoring any further input operations on that file. The two most common reasons for input failure are invalid data and the *end-of-file error*.

An end-of-file error occurs when the program has read all of the input data available in the file and needs more data to fill the variables in its input statements. It might be that the data file simply was not prepared properly. Perhaps it contains fewer data items than the program requires. Or perhaps the format of the input data is wrong. Leaving out whitespace between numeric values is guaranteed to cause trouble. For example, we may want a data file to contain three integer values—25, 16, and 42. Look what happens with this data:

```
2516  42
```

and this code:

```
inFile >> i >> j >> k;
```

BACKGROUND INFORMATION

Programming at Many Scales

To help you relate to the topics in this book, we describe in broad terms the way programming in its many forms is done in the "real world." Obviously, we can't cover every situation, but we try to describe the state of the art.

Programming projects range in size from small-scale, in which a student or computer hobbyist writes a short program to try out something new, to large-scale multicompany programming projects involving hundreds of people. Between these two extremes are efforts of many other sizes. There are people who use programming in their professions, even though it isn't their primary job. For example, a scientist might write a special-purpose program to analyze data from a particular experiment.

Even among professional programmers, there are many specialized programming areas. An individual might have a specialty in business data processing, in writing compilers or developing word processors (a specialty known as "tool making"), in research and development support, in graphical display development, in writing entertainment software, or in one of many other areas. However, one individual can produce only fairly small programs (a few tens of thousands of lines of code at best). Work of this kind is called *programming in the small*.

A larger application, such as the development of a new operating system, might require hundreds of thousands or even millions of lines of code. Such large-scale projects require teams of programmers, many of them specialists, who must be organized in some manner or they waste valuable time just trying to communicate with one another.

Usually, a hierarchical organization is set up along the lines of the module structure chart. One person, the *chief architect* or *project director*, determines the basic structure of the program and then delegates the responsibility of implementing the major components. These components may be modules produced by a top-down design, or they may be classes and objects resulting from an object-oriented design. In smaller projects, the components may be delegated directly to programmers. In larger projects, the components may be given to team leaders, who divide them into subcomponents, which are then delegated to individual programmers or groups of programmers. At

The first two input operations use up the data in the file, leaving the third with no data to read. The stream `inFile` enters the fail state, so k isn't assigned a new value and the computer quietly continues executing at the next statement in the program.

If the data file is prepared correctly and there is still an end-of-file error, the problem is in the program logic. For some reason, the program is attempting too many input operations. It could be a simple oversight such as specifying too many variables in a particular input statement. It could be a misuse of the `ignore` function, causing values to be skipped inadvertently. Or it could be a serious flaw in the algorithm. You should check all of these possibilities.

each stage, the person in charge must have the knowledge and experience necessary to define the next-lower level of the hierarchy and to estimate the resources necessary to implement it. This sort of organization is called *programming in the large*.

Programming languages and software tools can help a great deal in supporting programming in the large. For example, if a programming language lets programmers develop, compile, and test parts of a program independently before they are put together, then it enables several people to work on the program simultaneously. Of course, it is hard to appreciate the complexity of programming in the large when you are writing a small program for a class assignment. However, the experience you gain in this course will be valuable as you begin to develop larger programs.

The following is a classic example of what happens when a large program is developed without careful organization and proper language support. In the 1960s, IBM developed a major new operating system called OS/360, which was one of the first true examples of programming in the large. After the operating system was written, more than 1000 significant errors were found. Despite years of trying to fix these errors, IBM never did get the number of errors below 1000, and sometimes the "fixes" produced far more errors than they eliminated.

What led to this situation? Hindsight analysis showed that the code was badly organized and that different pieces were so interrelated that nobody could keep it all straight. A seemingly simple change in one part of the code caused several other parts of the system to fail. Eventually, at great expense, an entirely new system was created using better organization and tools.

In those early days of computing, everyone expected occasional errors to occur, and it was still possible to get useful work done with a faulty operating system. Today, however, computers are used more and more in critical applications such as medical equipment and aircraft control systems where errors can prove fatal. Many of these applications depend on large-scale programming. If you were stepping onto a modern jetliner right now, you might well pause and wonder, "Just what sort of language and tools did they use when they wrote the programs for this thing?" Fortunately, most large software development efforts today use a combination of good methodology, appropriate language, and extensive organizational tools—an approach known as *software engineering*.

The other major source of input failure, invalid data, happens when numeric and character data are mixed inappropriately in the input. The stream fails if it is supposed to read a numeric value, but the reading m is positioned at a character that isn't allowed in the number.

There are several possible causes of invalid data. The most common error in the preparation or entry of the data. Another cause is using wrong variable name (which happens to be of the wrong data type input statement. Declaring a variable to be of the wrong data type is tion on the problem. Last, leaving out a variable (or including an ex in an input statement can cause the reading marker to end up positi the wrong type of data.

Another oversight, one that doesn't cause input failure but causes programmer frustration, is to use `cin` or `cout` in an I/O statement when you meant to specify a file stream. If you mistakenly use `cin` instead of an input file stream, the program stops and waits for input from the keyboard. If you mistakenly use `cout` instead of an output file stream, you get unexpected output on the screen.

By giving you a framework that can help you organize and keep track of the details involved in designing and implementing a program, top-down design (and, later, object-oriented design) should help you avoid these errors in the first place.

In later chapters, you'll see that you can test modules separately. If you make sure that each module works by itself, your program should work when you put all the modules together. Testing modules separately is less work than trying to test an entire program. In a smaller section of code, it's less likely that multiple errors will combine to produce behavior that's difficult to analyze.

Testing and Debugging Hints

1. Input and output statements always begin with the name of a stream variable, and the `>>` and `<<` operators point in the direction in which the data is going. The statement

```
cout << n;
```

sends data *to* the output stream `cout`, and the statement

```
cin >> n;
```

sends data *to* the variable `n`.

2. When a program inputs from or outputs to a file, be sure each I/O statement from or to the file uses the name of the file stream, not `cin` or `cout`.

3. When you open a data file for input, make sure that the parameter to the `open` function supplies the correct name of the file as it exists on disk.

4. Be sure that each input statement specifies the correct number of variables and that each of those variables is of the correct data type.

5. If your input data is mixed (character and numeric values), be sure to deal with intervening blanks.

6. Echo-print the input data to verify that each value is where it belongs and is in the proper format. (This is crucial because an input failure in C++ doesn't produce an error message or terminate the program.)

SUMMARY

Programs operate on data. If data and programs are kept separate, the data is available to use with other programs, and the same program can be run with other sets of input data.

The extraction operator (>>) inputs data from the keyboard or a file, storing the data into the variable specified as its right-hand operand. The extraction operator skips any leading whitespace characters to find the next data value in the input stream. The get function does not skip leading whitespace characters; it inputs the very next character and stores it into the char variable specified in its parameter list. Both the >> operator and the get function leave the reading marker positioned at the next character to be read. The next input operation begins reading at the point indicated by the marker.

The newline character (denoted by \n in a C++ program) marks the end of a data line. You create a newline character each time you press the Return or Enter key. Your program generates a newline each time you use the endl manipulator or explicitly output the \n character. Newline is a control character; it does not print. It controls the movement of the screen cursor or the position of a line on a printer.

Interactive programs prompt the user for each data entry and directly inform the user of results and errors. Designing interactive dialogue is an exercise in the art of communication.

Noninteractive input/output allows data to be prepared before a program is run and allows the program to run again with the same data in the event that a problem crops up during processing.

Data files often are used for noninteractive processing and to permit the output from one program to be used as input to another program. There are four things you have to do to use these files: (1) include the header file fstream.h; (2) declare the file streams along with your other variable declarations; (3) prepare the files for reading or writing by calling the open function; and (4) specify the name of the file stream in each input or output statement that uses it.

Top-down design and object-oriented design are methods for tackling large programming problems. Top-down design begins with an abstract solution that then is divided into major steps. Each step becomes a subproblem that is analyzed and subdivided further. A concrete step is one that can be translated directly into C++; those that need more refining are abstract steps. A module is a collection of concrete and abstract steps that solves a subproblem. Programs can be built out of modules using a flat implementation, a hierarchical implementation, or a semihierarchical implementation.

Object-oriented design produces a problem solution by focusing on objects and their associated operations. The first step is to identify the major objects in the problem and choose appropriate operations on those objects.

An object is an instance of a data type called a class. During object-oriented design, classes can be designed from scratch, obtained from class libraries and used as-is, or customized from existing classes by using the technique of inheritance. The result of the design process is a program consisting of self-contained objects that manage their own data and communicate by invoking each other's operations.

Careful attention to program design, program formatting, and documentation produces highly structured and readable programs.

QUICK CHECK

1. Write a C++ statement that inputs values from the standard input stream into two `float` variables, x and y. (pp. 133–136)
2. Your program is reading from the standard input stream. The next three characters waiting in the stream are a blank, a blank, and the letter *A*. Indicate what character is stored into the `char` variable ch by each of the following statements. (Assume the same initial stream contents for each.)

   a. `cin >> ch;`
   b. `cin.get(ch);`

   (pp. 136–140)
3. Input prompts should acknowledge the user's experience.
   a. What sort of message would you have a program print to prompt a novice user to input a social security number?
   b. How would you change the wording of the prompting message for an experienced user? (pp. 142–144)
4. If a program is going to input 1000 numbers, is interactive input appropriate? (pp. 144–145)
5. What are the four things that you have to remember to do in order to use data files in a C++ program? (pp. 146–149)
6. How many levels of abstraction are there in a top-down design before you reach the point at which you can begin coding a program? (pp. 153–160)
7. When is a flat implementation of a top-down design appropriate? (pp. 157–160)
8. Modules are the building blocks of top-down design. What are the building blocks of object-oriented design? (pp. 161–164)

Answers 1. `cin >> x >> y;` 2. a. 'A' b. ' ' (a blank) 3. a. `Please type a nine-digit so-`
`cial security number, then press the key marked RETURN.` b. `Enter SSN.` 4. No. Batch
input is more appropriate for programs that input large amounts of data. 5. (1) Include the
header file `fstream.h`. (2) Declare the file streams along with your other variable declarations.
(3) Call the open function to prepare each file for reading or writing. (4) Specify the name of the
file stream in each I/O statement that uses it. 6. There is no fixed number of levels of abstraction. You keep refining the solution through as many levels as necessary until the steps are all
concrete. 7. A flat implementation is appropriate when a design is short and has just one or
two levels of abstraction. 8. The building blocks are objects, each of which has associated
operations.

1. What is the main advantage of having a program input its data rather than writing all the data values as constants in the program?
2. Given these two lines of data:

   ```
   17 13
   7 3 24 6
   ```

   and this input statement:

   ```
   cin >> int1 >> int2 >> int3;
   ```

   a. What is the value of each variable after the statement is executed?
   b. What happens to any leftover data values in the input stream?
3. The newline character signals the end of a line.
   a. How do you generate a newline character from the keyboard?
   b. How do you generate a newline character in a program's output?
4. When reading char data from an input stream, what is the difference between using the >> operator and using the get function?
5. Integer data values can be read into float variables. (True or False?)
6. You may use either spaces or newlines to separate numeric data values being entered into a C++ program. (True or False?)
7. Consider this input data:

   ```
   14 21 64
   19 67 91
   73 89 27
   23 96 47
   ```

   What are the values of the int variables a, b, c, and d after the following program segment is executed?

   ```
   cin >> a;
   cin.ignore(200, '\n');
   cin >> b >> c;
   cin.ignore(200, '\n');
   cin >> d;
   ```

8. Given the input data

   ```
   123W 56
   ```

   what is printed by the output statement when the following code segment is executed?

   ```
   int1 = 98;
   int2 = 147;
   cin >> int1 >> int2;
   cout << int1 << ' ' << int2;
   ```

9. Given the input data

   11 12.35 ABC

   what is the value of each variable after the following statements are executed? Assume that i is of type int, x is of type float, and ch1 is of type char.

   a. cin >> i >> x >> ch1 >> ch1;
   b. cin >> ch1 >> i >> x;

10. Define the following terms as they apply to interactive input/output.
    a. Input prompt
    b. Echo printing

11. Correct the following program so that it reads a value from the file inData and writes it to the file outData.

    ```
    #include <iostream.h>

    int main()
    {
        int     n;
        ifstream inData;

        outData.open("results.dat");
        cin >> n;
        outData << n << endl;
        return 0;
    }
    ```

12. Use your corrected version of the program in Exercise 11 to answer the following questions.
    a. If the file inData initially contains the value 144, what does it contain after the program is executed?
    b. If the file outData is initially empty, what are its contents after the program is executed?

13. List three characteristics of programs that are designed using a highly organized methodology such as top-down design or object-oriented design.

PROGRAMMING WARM-UP EXERCISES

1. Your program has three char variables: ch1, ch2, and ch3. Given the input data

   A B C\n

   write the input statement(s) required to store the A into ch1, the B into ch2, and the C into ch3. Note that each pair of input characters is separated by two blanks.

2. Change your answer to Exercise 1 so that the *A* is stored into ch1 and the next two blanks are stored into ch2 and ch3.
3. Write a single input statement that reads the input lines

```
10.25     7.625\n
8.5\n
1.0\n
```

and stores the four values into the float variables length1, height1, length2, and height2.

4. Write a series of statements that input the first letter of each of the following names into the char variables chr1, chr2, and chr3.

```
Peter\n
Kitty\n
Kathy\n
```

5. Write a set of variable declarations and a series of input statements to read the following lines of data into variables of the appropriate type. You can make up the variable names. Notice that the values are separated from one another by a single blank and that there are no blanks to the left of the first character on each line.

```
A 100 2.78 g 14\n
207.98 w q 23.4 92\n
R 42 L 27 R 63\n
```

6. Write a program segment that reads nine integer values from a file and writes them to the screen, three numbers per output line. The file is organized one value to a line.
7. Write a code segment for an interactive program to input values for a person's age, height, and weight, and the initials of their first and last names. The numeric values are all integers. Assume that the person using the program is a novice user. How would you rewrite the code for an experienced user?
8. Fill in the blanks in the following program, which should read four values from the file dataIn and output them to the file resultsOut.

```
#include _____
#include _____

int main()
{
    int          val1;
    int          val2;
    int          val3;
    int          val4;
    _____  dataIn;
    ofstream     _____;
```

```
_____ ("myinput.dat");
_____ ("myoutput.dat");
_____ >> val1 >> val2 >> val3 >> val4;
_____ << val1 << val2 << val3 << val4 << endl;
    return 0;
}
```

9. Use top-down design to write an algorithm for starting the engine of an automobile with a manual transmission.

10. Use top-down design to write an algorithm for logging on to your computer system, and entering and running a program. The algorithm should be simple enough for a novice user to follow.

11. The quadratic formula is

$$x = \frac{-b \pm \sqrt{b^2 - 4ac}}{2a}$$

Use top-down design to write an algorithm to read the three coefficients of a quadratic polynomial from a file (inQuad) and write the two floating point solutions to another file (outQuad). Assume that the discriminant (the portion of the formula inside the square root) is nonnegative. You may use the standard library function sqrt. (Express your solution as pseudocode, not as a C++ program.)

PROGRAMMING PROBLEMS

1. Write a top-down design and a C++ program to read an invoice number, the quantity ordered, and the unit price (all integers), and compute the total price. The program should write out the invoice number, quantity, unit price, and total price with identifying phrases. Format your program with consistent indentation, and use appropriate comments and meaningful identifiers. If you are using an interactive system, write the program to be run interactively, with informative prompts for each data value.

2. How tall is a rainbow? Because of the way in which light is refracted by water droplets, the angle between the level of your eye and the top of a rainbow is always the same. If you know the distance to the rainbow, you can multiply it by the tangent of that angle to find the height of the rainbow. The magic angle is 42.3333333 degrees. The C++ standard library works in radians, however, so you have to convert the angle to radians with this formula:

$$\text{radians} = \text{degrees} \times \frac{\pi}{180}$$

where π equals 3.14159265.

Through the header file math.h, the C++ standard library provides a tangent function named tan. This is a value-returning function that takes a floating point parameter and returns a floating point result:

```
x = tan(someAngle);
```

If you multiply the tangent by the distance to the rainbow, you get the height of the rainbow.

Write a top-down design and a C++ program to read a single floating point value—the distance to the rainbow—and compute the height of the rainbow. The program should print the distance to the rainbow and its height with phrases that identify which number is which. Display the floating point values to four decimal places. Format your program with consistent indentation, and use appropriate comments and meaningful identifiers. If you are using an interactive system, write the program so that it prompts the user for the input value.

3. Sometimes you can see a second, fainter rainbow outside a bright rainbow. This second rainbow has a magic angle of 52.25 degrees. Modify the program in Problem 2 so that it prints the height of the main rainbow, the height of the secondary rainbow, and the distance to the main rainbow, with a phrase identifying each of the numbers.

CASE STUDY FOLLOW-UP

1. In the TestAverage problem, look at the module structure chart and identify each module as abstract or concrete.
2. Redraw the module structure chart for the TestAverage problem using Prepare File for Reading, Get and Echo Data, Find Weighted Average, and Print Weighted Average as level 1 modules. Add any appropriate modules at levels below these modules.

5

Conditions, Logical Expressions, and Selection Control Structures

- To be able to construct a simple logical (Boolean) expression to evaluate a given condition.
- To be able to construct a complex logical expression to evaluate a given condition.
- To be able to construct an If-Then-Else statement to perform a specific task.
- To be able to construct an If-Then statement to perform a specific task.
- To be able to construct a set of nested If statements to perform a specific task.
- To be able to determine the precondition and postcondition for a module, and use them to perform an algorithm walk-through.
- To be able to trace the execution of a C++ program.
- To be able to test and debug a C++ program.

So far, the statements in our programs have been executed in their physical order. The first statement is executed, then the second, and so on until all of the statements have been executed. But what if we want the computer to execute the statements in some other order? Suppose we want to check the validity of input data and then perform a calculation *or* print an error message, not both. To do so, we must be able to ask a question and then, based on the answer, choose one or another course of action.

The If statement allows us to execute statements in an order that is different from their physical order. We can ask a question with it and do one thing if the answer is yes (true) or another if the answer is no (false). In the first part of this chapter, we deal with asking questions; in the second part, we deal with the If statement itself.

 Flow of Control

The order in which statements are executed in a program is called the **flow of control.** In a sense, the computer is under the control of one statement at a time. When a statement has been executed, control is turned over to the next statement (like a baton being passed in a relay race).

Flow of Control   The order in which the computer executes statements in a program.

Flow of control is normally sequential (see Figure 5-1). That is, when one statement is finished executing, control passes to the next statement in the program. Where we want the flow of control to be nonsequential, we use **control structures,** special statements that transfer control to a statement other than the one that physically comes next. Control structures are so important that we focus on them in the remainder of this chapter and in the next four chapters.

Control Structure   A statement used to alter the normally sequential flow of control.

■ FIGURE 5-1

Sequential Control

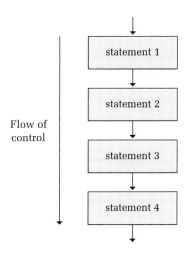

Flow of
control

Selection

We use a selection (or branching) control structure when we want the computer to choose between alternative actions. We make an assertion, a claim that is either true or false. If the assertion is true, the computer executes one statement. If it is false, it executes another (see Figure 5-2). The computer's ability to solve practical problems is a product of its ability to make decisions and execute different sequences of instructions.

The Payroll program in Chapter 1 shows the selection process at work. The computer must decide whether or not a worker has earned overtime pay. It does this by testing the assertion that the person has worked more than 40 hours. If the assertion is true, the computer follows the instructions

■ FIGURE 5-2

Selection
(Branching) Control
Structure

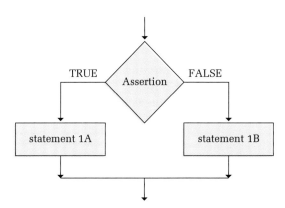

for computing overtime pay. If the assertion is false, the computer simply computes the regular pay. Before we examine selection control structures in C++, let's look closely at how we get the computer to make decisions.

 ## Conditions and Logical Expressions

To ask a question in C++, we don't phrase it as a question; we state it as an assertion. If the assertion we make is true, the answer to the question is yes. If the statement is not true, the answer to the question is no. For example, if we want to ask, "Are we having spinach for dinner tonight?" we would say, "We are having spinach for dinner tonight." If the assertion is true, the answer to the question is yes. If not, the answer is no.

So, asking questions in C++ means making an assertion that is either true or false. The computer *evaluates* the assertion, checking it against some internal condition (the values stored in certain variables, for instance) to see whether it is true or false.

Logical Expressions

In C++, assertions take the form of *logical expressions* (also called *Boolean expressions**). Just as an arithmetic expression is made up of numeric values and operations, a logical expression is made up of logical values and operations.

Here are some examples of logical expressions:

- A Boolean variable or constant
- An expression followed by a relational operator followed by an expression
- A logical expression followed by a logical operator followed by a logical expression

Let's look at each of these in detail.

Boolean Data   Some programming languages include a data type named Boolean, which has only two literal constants: *true* and *false*. In these languages, if you declare a variable dataOK to be of type Boolean, you can store either the value *true* or the value *false* into the variable:

```
dataOK = true;
```

---

*The word Boolean ('bōōl-ē-un) is a tribute to George Boole, a nineteenth-century English mathematician who described a system of logic using variables with just two values, True and False. (See the May We Introduce box on page 198.)

The C++ language doesn't have a Boolean data type. In C++, the value 0 represents *false,* and any nonzero value represents *true.* Programmers usually use the int type to represent Boolean data:

```
int dataOK;
    .
    .
    .
dataOK = 1;    // Store "true" into dataOK
    .
    .
    .
dataOK = 0;    // Store "false" into dataOK
```

Many C++ programmers prefer to define their own Boolean data type by using a *Typedef statement.* This statement allows you to introduce a new name for an existing data type. Here is the syntax template:

TypedefStatement

> **typedef** ExistingTypeName NewTypeName ;

Here's an example:

```
typedef int Boolean;
```

All this statement does is cause the compiler to substitute the word int for every occurrence of the word Boolean in the rest of the program. If a program uses these statements:

```
typedef int Boolean;
    .
    .
    .
float   price;
int     quantity;
Boolean dataOK;
```

then the compiler substitutes int for Boolean in the declarations:

```
float   price;
int     quantity;
int     dataOK;
```

Notice that we have capitalized the identifier `Boolean` according to the style we described in Chapter 2. We begin our variable names with lower-case letters, and we begin the names of programmer-written functions and programmer-defined data types with uppercase letters.

To complete the construction of our own Boolean type in C++, we define two named constants, `TRUE` and `FALSE`:

```
typedef int Boolean;
const Boolean TRUE = 1;
const Boolean FALSE = 0;
   .
   .
   .
Boolean dataOK;
   .
   .
   .
dataOK = TRUE;
   .
   .
   .
dataOK = FALSE;
```

As you can see, we haven't *really* created a new data type. `Boolean` is just a synonym for `int`, and `TRUE` and `FALSE` are synonyms for 1 and 0. Why do we go to the trouble of doing this? First, it helps us to mentally separate `int` data (numeric values) from Boolean data (truth values) as we design and implement programs. Second, we end up with self-documenting code. Someone looking at our programs can see right away that the identifiers `Boolean`, `TRUE`, and `FALSE` refer to logical (Boolean) data and not integer values.

Throughout the rest of this text, whenever we need Boolean data in a C++ program, we incorporate the following statements into the program:

```
typedef int Boolean;
const Boolean TRUE = 1;
const Boolean FALSE = 0;
```

Relational Operators   One way of assigning values to Boolean variables is to use an assignment statement, like this:

```
itemFound = TRUE;
```

We also can assign values to Boolean variables by setting them equal to the result of comparing two expressions with a *relational operator*. Relational operators test a relationship between two values.

Let's look at an example. In this program fragment, `lessThan` is a Boolean variable and `i` and `j` are `int` variables:

Value of **x**	Value of **y**	Value of **x** $\vert\vert$ **y**
TRUE	TRUE	TRUE
TRUE	FALSE	TRUE
FALSE	TRUE	TRUE
FALSE	FALSE	FALSE

The following table summarizes the results of applying the ! operator to a logical expression (represented by Boolean variable x).

Value of **x**	Value of !**x**
TRUE	FALSE
FALSE	TRUE

Technically, the C++ operators !, &&, and || are not required to have logical expressions as operands. Their operands can be of any simple data type, even floating point types. You sometimes encounter C++ code that looks like this:

```
float    height;
Boolean badData;
    .
    .
    .
cin >> height;
badData = !height;
```

The ! operator yields 1 (TRUE) if its operand—whatever the data type—has the value zero (FALSE). The ! operator yields 0 (FALSE) if its operand has any nonzero value (TRUE). So, what the assignment statement above really is saying is, "Set badData to TRUE if height equals 0.0." Although the assignment statement works correctly according to the C++ language, many programmers find the following statement to be more readable:

```
badData = (height == 0.0);
```

Throughout this text, we apply the logical operators *only* to logical expressions, not to arithmetic expressions.

Caution: It's easy to confuse the logical operators && and || with two other C++ operators, & and |. We don't discuss the & and | operators here, but we'll tell you that they are used for manipulating individual bits within a memory cell—a role quite different from that of the logical operators. If you accidentally use & instead of &&, or | instead of ||, you won't get an error message from the compiler. But your program probably will compute wrong answers. Some programmers pronounce && as "and-and" and || as "or-or" to avoid making mistakes.

Short-Circuit Evaluation   Consider the logical expression

```
i == 1 && j > 2
```

Some programming languages use *full evaluation* of logical expressions. With full evaluation, the computer first evaluates both subexpressions (both i == 1 and j > 2) before applying the && operator to produce the final result.

In contrast, C++ uses **short-circuit** (or **conditional**) **evaluation** of logical expressions. Evaluation proceeds from left to right, and the computer stops evaluating subexpressions as soon as possible—that is, as soon as it knows the truth value of the entire expression. How can the computer know if a lengthy logical expression is TRUE or FALSE if it doesn't examine all the subexpressions? Let's look first at the AND operation.

An AND operation yields the value TRUE only if both of its operands are TRUE. In the expression above, suppose that the value of i happens to be 95. The first subexpression is FALSE, so it isn't necessary even to look at the second subexpression. The computer stops evaluation and produces the final result of FALSE.

Short-Circuit (Conditional) Evaluation Evaluation of a logical expression in left-to-right order with evaluation stopping as soon as the final truth value can be determined.

With the OR operation, the left-to-right evaluation stops as soon as a TRUE subexpression is found. Remember that an OR produces a result of TRUE if either one or both of its operands are TRUE. Given this expression:

```
c <= d || e == f
```

if the first subexpression is TRUE, evaluation stops and the entire result is TRUE. The computer doesn't waste time with an unnecessary evaluation of the second subexpression.

Precedence of Operators

In Chapter 3, we discussed the rules of precedence, the rules that govern the evaluation of complex arithmetic expressions. C++'s rules of precedence also govern relational and logical operators. Here's a list showing the order of precedence for the arithmetic, relational, and logical operators (with the assignment operator thrown in as well):

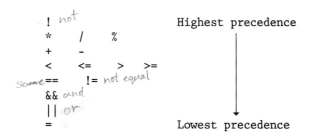

Operators on the same line in the list have the same precedence. If there is more than one operator with the same precedence in an expression, most of the operators group (associate) from left to right. For example, the expression

    a / b * c

means (a / b) * c, not a / (b * c). However, the ! operator groups from right to left. Although you'd never have occasion to use this expression:

    !!badData

the meaning of it is !(!badData) rather than the meaningless (!!)badData. Appendix B, Precedence of Operators, lists the order of precedence for all operators in C++. In skimming the appendix, you can see that a few of the operators associate from right to left (for the same reason we just described for the ! operator).

Parentheses are used to override the order of evaluation in an expression. If you're not sure whether parentheses are necessary, use them anyway. The compiler disregards unnecessary parentheses. So if they clarify an expression, use them. Some programmers like to include extra parentheses when assigning a relational expression to a Boolean variable:

    dataInvalid = (inputVal == 0);

MAY WE INTRODUCE

George Boole

Boolean algebra is named for its inventor, English mathematician George Boole, born in 1815. His father, a tradesman, began teaching him mathematics at an early age. But Boole initially was more interested in classical literature, languages, and religion—interests he maintained throughout his life. By the time he was 20, he had taught himself French, German, and Italian. He was well versed in the writings of Aristotle, Spinoza, Cicero, and Dante, and wrote several philosophical papers himself.

At 16, to help support his family, he took a position as a teaching assistant in a private school. His work there and a second teaching job left him little time to study. A few years later, he opened a school and began to learn higher mathematics on his own. In spite of his lack of formal training, his first scholarly paper was published in the *Cambridge Mathematical Journal* when he was just 24. Boole went on to publish over 50 papers and several major works before he died in 1864, at the peak of his career.

Boole's *The Mathematical Analysis of Logic* was published in 1847. It would eventually form the basis for the development of digital computers. In the book, Boole set forth the formal axioms of logic (much like the axioms of geometry) on which the field of symbolic logic is built.

Boole drew on the symbols and operations of algebra in creating his system of logic. He associated the value 1 with the universal set (the set representing everything in the universe) and the value 0 with the empty set, and restricted his system to these two quantities. He then defined operations that are analogous to subtraction, addition, and multiplication. Variables in the system have symbolic values. For example, if a Boolean variable P represents the set of all plants, then the expression $1 - P$ refers to the set of

The parentheses are not needed; the assignment operator has the lowest precedence of all the operators we've just listed. So we could write the statement as

```
dataInvalid = inputVal == 0;
```

but some people find the parenthesized version more readable.

One final comment about parentheses: C++, like other programming languages, requires that parentheses always be used in pairs. Whenever you write a complicated expression, take a minute to go through and pair up all of the opening parentheses with their closing counterparts.

all things that are not plants. We can simplify the expression by using $-P$ to mean "not plants." ($0 - P$ is simply 0 because we can't remove elements from the empty set.) The subtraction operator in Boole's system corresponds to the ! (NOT) operator in C++. In a C++ program, we might set the value of the Boolean variable `plant` to TRUE when the name of a plant is entered, and !`plant` is TRUE when the name of anything else is input.

The expression $0 + P$ is the same as P. However, $0 + P + F$, where F is the set of all foods, is the set of all things that are either plants or foods. So the addition operator in Boole's algebra is the same as the C++ || (OR) operator.

The analogy can be carried to multiplication: $0 \times P$ is 0, and $1 \times P$ is P. But what is $P \times F$? It is the set of things that are both plants and foods. In Boole's system, the multiplication operator is the same as the && (AND) operator.

In 1854, Boole published *An Investigation of the Laws of Thought, on Which Are Founded the Mathematical Theories of Logic and Probabilities*. In the book, he described theorems built on his axioms of logic and extended the algebra to show how probabilities could be computed in a logical system. Five years later, Boole published *Treatise on Differential Equations*, then *Treatise on the Calculus of Finite Differences*. The latter is one of the cornerstones of numerical analysis, which deals with the accuracy of computations. (In Chapter 10, you'll see the important role numerical analysis plays in computer programming.)

Boole received little recognition and few honors for his work. Given the importance of Boolean algebra in modern technology, it is hard to believe that his system of logic was not taken seriously until the early twentieth century. George Boole was truly one of the founders of computer science.

PEANUTS reprinted by permission of United Feature Syndicate, Inc.

SOFTWARE ENGINEERING TIP

Changing English Statements into Logical Expressions

In most cases, you can write a logical expression directly from an English statement or mathematical term in an algorithm. But you have to watch out for some tricky situations. Remember our sample logical expression:

```
midtermGrade == 'A' || finalGrade == 'A'
```

In English, you would be tempted to write this expression: "Midterm grade or final grade equals A." In C++, you can't write the expression as you would in English. That is,

```
midtermGrade || finalGrade == 'A'
```

won't work because the || operator is connecting a char value (midtermGrade) and a logical expression (finalGrade == 'A'). The two operands of || should be logical expressions. (Note that this expression is wrong in terms of logic, but it isn't "wrong" to the C++ compiler. Recall that the || operator may legally connect two expressions of any data type, so this example won't generate a syntax error message. The program will run, but it won't work the way you intended.)

A variation of this mistake is to express the English assertion "*i* equals either 3 or 4" as

```
i == 3 || 4
```

Again, the syntax is correct but the semantics are not. This expression always evaluates to TRUE. The first subexpression, i == 3, may be TRUE or FALSE. But the second subexpression, 4, is nonzero (TRUE). Therefore, the || operation causes the entire expression to be TRUE. We repeat: Use the || operator (and the && operator) only to connect two logical expressions. Here's what we want:

```
i == 3 || i == 4
```

In math books, you might see a notation like this:

$$12 < y < 24$$

which means "y is between 12 and 24." This expression is legal in C++ but gives an unexpected result. First, the relation $12 < y$ is evaluated, giving the int result 1 (TRUE) or 0

(FALSE). The computer then compares this 1 or 0 with the number 24. Because both 1 and 0 are less than 24, the result is always TRUE. To write this expression correctly in C++, use the && operator:

```
12 < y && y < 24
```

Relational Operators with Floating Point Types

The relational operators can be applied to any of the three basic data types: int, float, and char. We've talked about comparing int and char values. Here we look at float values.

Do not compare floating point numbers for equality. Because small errors in the rightmost decimal places are likely to arise when calculations are performed on floating point numbers, two float values rarely are exactly equal. For example, consider the following code that uses two float variables named oneThird and x:

```
oneThird = 1.0 / 3.0;
x = oneThird + oneThird + oneThird;
```

We would expect x to contain the value 1.0, but it probably doesn't. The first assignment statement stores an *approximation* of ⅓ into oneThird, perhaps 0.333333. The second statement stores a value like 0.999999 into x. If we now ask the computer to compare x with 1.0, the comparison yields FALSE.

Instead of testing floating point numbers for equality, we test for *near* equality. To do so, we compute the difference between the two numbers and test to see if the result is less than some maximum allowable difference. For example, we often use comparisons like this:

```
fabs(r - s) < 0.00001
```

where fabs is the floating point absolute value function from the C++ standard library. The expression fabs(r - s) computes the absolute value of the difference between two float variables r and s. If the difference is less than 0.00001, the two numbers are close enough to call them equal. We discuss this problem with floating point accuracy in more detail in Chapter 10.

 # The If Statement

Now that we've seen how to write logical expressions, let's use them to alter the normal flow of control in a program. The *If statement* is the fundamental control structure that allows branches in the flow of control. With it, we can ask a question and choose a course of action: *If* a certain condition exists, *then* perform one action, *else* perform a different action.

The computer actually performs just one of the two actions under any given set of circumstances. Yet we have to write *both* actions into the program. Why? Because, depending on the circumstances, the computer can choose to execute *either* of them. The If statement gives us a way of including both actions in a program and gives the computer a way of deciding which action to take.

The If-Then-Else Form

In C++, the If statement comes in two forms: the *If-Then-Else* form and the *If-Then* form. Let's look first at the If-Then-Else. Here is its syntax template:

IfStatement (the If-Then-Else form)

```
if ( Expression )
        Statement1A
else
        Statement1B
```

The expression in parentheses can be of any simple data type. Almost without exception, this will be a logical (Boolean) expression. If the value of the expression is nonzero (TRUE), the computer executes Statement1A. If the value of the expression is zero (FALSE), Statement1B is executed. Statement1A often is called the *then-clause*; Statement1B, the *else-clause*. Figure 5-3 illustrates the flow of control of the If-Then-Else. In the figure, Statement2 is the next statement in the program after the entire If statement.

Notice that a C++ If statement uses the reserved words `if` and `else` but does not include the word *then*. Still, we use the term *If-Then-Else* because it corresponds to how we say things in English: "*If* something is true, *then* do this, *else* do that."

The code fragment below shows how to write an If statement in a program. Observe the indentation of the then-clause and the else-clause, which makes the statement easier to read. And notice the placement of the statement following the If statement.

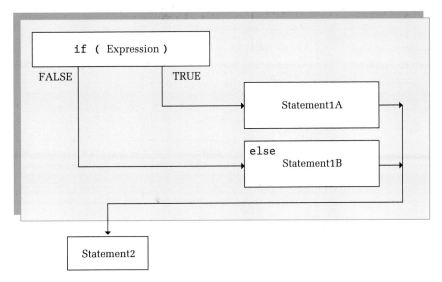

```
if (hours <= 40.0)
    pay = rate * hours;
else
    pay = rate * (40.0 + (hours - 40.0) * 1.5);
cout << pay;
```

In terms of instructions to the computer, the above code fragment says, "If hours is less than or equal to 40.0, compute the regular pay and then go on to execute the output statement. But if hours is greater than 40, compute the regular pay and the overtime pay, and then go on to execute the output statement." Figure 5-4 shows the flow of control of this If statement.

If-Then-Else often is used to check the validity of input. For example, before we ask the computer to divide with a data value, we should be sure that the value is not zero. (Even computers can't divide something by zero. If you try, the computer halts the execution of your program.) If the divisor is zero, our program should print out an error message. Here's the code:

```
if (divisor != 0)
    result = dividend / divisor;
else
    cout << "Division by zero is not allowed." << endl;
```

Before we look any further at If statements, take another look at the syntax template for the If-Then-Else. According to the template, there is no semicolon at the end of an If statement. In both of the program fragments

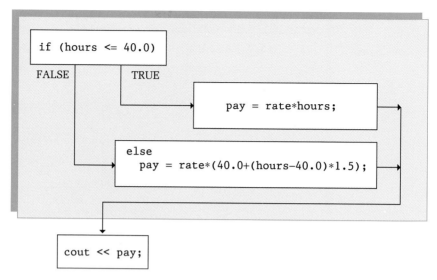

above—the worker's pay and the division-by-zero examples—there seems to be a semicolon at the end of each If statement. However, the semicolons belong to the statements in the else-clauses in those examples; assignment statements end in semicolons, as do output statements. The If statement doesn't have its own semicolon at the end.

Blocks (Compound Statements)

In our division-by-zero example, suppose that when the divisor is equal to zero we want to do *two* things: print the error message *and* set a variable named `result` equal to a special value like 9999. We would need two statements in the same branch, but the syntax template seems to limit us to one.

What we really want to do is turn the else-clause into a *sequence* of statements. This is easy. Remember from Chapter 2 that the compiler treats the block (compound statement)

```
{
    ⋮
}
```

like a single statement. If you put a { } pair around the sequence of statements you want in a branch of the If statement, the sequence of statements becomes a single block. For example:

```
if (divisor != 0)
    result = dividend / divisor;
else
{
    cout << "Division by zero is not allowed." << endl;
    result = 9999;
}
```

If the value of divisor is zero, the computer both prints the error message and sets the value of result to 9999 before continuing with whatever statement follows the If statement.

Blocks can be used in both branches of an If-Then-Else. For example:

```
if (divisor != 0)
{
    result = dividend / divisor;
    cout << "Division performed." << endl;
}
else
{
    cout << "Division by zero is not allowed." << endl;
    result = 9999;
}
```

When you use blocks in an If statement, there's a rule of C++ syntax to remember: *Never use a semicolon after the right brace of a block.* Semicolons are used only to terminate simple statements such as assignment statements, input statements, and output statements. If you look at the examples above, you won't see a semicolon after the right brace that signals the end of each block.

MATTERS OF STYLE

Braces and Blocks

C++ programmers use different styles when it comes to locating the left brace of a block. The style we use puts the left and right braces directly below the words if and else, each brace on its own line:

```
if (n >= 2)
{
    alpha = 5;
    beta = 8;
}
else
{
    alpha = 23;
    beta = 12;
}
```

Another popular style is to place the left braces at the end of the `if` line and the `else` line; the right braces still line up directly below the words `if` and `else`. This way of formatting the If statement originated with programmers using the C language, the predecessor of C++.

```
if (n >= 2) {
    alpha = 5;
    beta = 8;
}
else {
    alpha = 23;
    beta = 12;
}
```

It makes no difference to the C++ compiler which style you use (and there are other styles as well). It's a matter of personal preference. Whichever style you use, though, you should always use the same style throughout a program. Inconsistency can confuse the person reading your program and give the impression of carelessness.

The If-Then Form

Sometimes you run into a situation where you want to say, "*If* a certain condition exists, *then* perform some action; otherwise, don't do anything." In other words, you want the computer to skip a sequence of instructions if a certain condition isn't met. You could do this by leaving the `else` branch empty, using only the null statement:

```
if (a <= b)
    c = 20;
else
    ;
```

Better yet, you could simply leave off the else part. The resulting statement is the If-Then form of the If statement. This is its syntax template:

IfStatement (the If-Then form)

> **if** (Expression)
> Statement

Here's an example of an If-Then. Notice the indentation and the placement of the statement that follows the If-Then.

```
if (age < 18)
    cout << "Not an eligible ";
cout << "voter." << endl;
```

This statement means that if age is less than 18, first print "Not an eligible " and then print "voter." If age is not less than 18, skip the first output statement and go directly to print "voter." Figure 5-5 shows the flow of control for an If-Then.

Like the two branches in an If-Then-Else, the one branch in an If-Then can be a block. For example, let's say you are writing a program to compute income taxes. One of the lines on the tax form says, "Subtract line 23 from line 17 and enter result on line 24; if result is less than zero, enter zero and check box 24A." You can use an If-Then to do this in C++:

■ FIGURE 5-5

If-Then Flow of Control

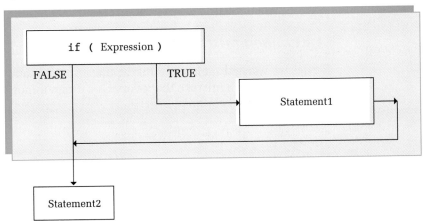

```
result = line17 - line23;
if (result < 0.0)
{
    cout << "Check box 24A" << endl;
    result = 0.0;
}
line24 = result;
```

This code does exactly what the tax form says it should. It computes the result of subtracting line 23 from line 17. Then it looks to see if `result` is less than zero. If it is, the fragment prints a message telling the user to check box 24A and then sets `result` to zero. Finally, the calculated result (or zero, if the result is less than zero) is stored into a variable named `line24`.

What happens if we leave out the left and right braces in the code fragment above? Let's look at it:

```
result = line17 - line23;               // Incorrect version
if (result < 0.0)
    cout << "Check box 24A" << endl;
    result = 0.0;
line24 = result;
```

Despite the way we have indented the code, the compiler takes the then-clause to be a single statement—the output statement. If `result` is less than zero, the computer executes the output statement, then sets `result` to zero, and then stores result into `line24`. So far, so good. But if `result` is initially greater than or equal to zero, the computer skips the then-clause and proceeds to the statement following the If statement—the assignment statement that sets `result` to zero. The unhappy outcome is that `result` ends up as zero no matter what its initial value was! The moral here is not to rely on indentation alone; you can't fool the compiler. If you want a compound statement for a then- or else-clause, you must include the left and right braces.

A Common Mistake

Earlier we warned against confusing the = operator and the == operator. Here is an example of a mistake that every C++ programmer is guaranteed to make at least once in his or her career:

```
cin >> n;
if (n = 3)                              // Wrong
    cout << "n equals 3";
else
    cout << "n doesn't equal 3";
```

This code segment *always* prints out

```
n equals 3
```

no matter what was input for n. Here is the reason.

We've used the wrong operator in the If test. The expression n = 3 is not a logical expression; it's called an *assignment expression*. (If an assignment is written as a separate statement ending with a semicolon, it's an assignment *statement*.) An assignment expression has a *value* (above, it's 3) and a *side effect* (storing 3 into n). In the If statement of our example, the computer finds the value of the tested expression to be 3. Because 3 is a nonzero (TRUE) value, the then-clause is executed, no matter what the value of n is. Worse yet, the side effect of the assignment expression is to store 3 into n, destroying what was there.

Our intention is not to focus on assignment expressions; we discuss their use later in the book. What's important now is that you see the effect of using = when you meant to use ==. The program compiles correctly but runs incorrectly. When debugging a faulty program, always look at your If statements to see whether you've made this particular mistake.

Nested If Statements

There are no restrictions on what the statements in an If can be. Therefore, an If within an If is okay. In fact, an If within an If within an If is legal. The only limitation here is that people cannot follow a structure that is too involved. And readability is one of the marks of a good program.

When we place an If within an If, we are creating a *nested control structure*. Control structures nest much like mixing bowls do, smaller ones tucked inside larger ones. Here's an example, written in pseudocode:

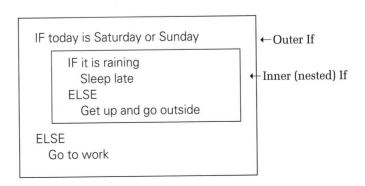

In general, any problem that involves a *multi-way branch* (more than two alternative courses of action) can be coded using nested If statements. For example, to print out the name of a month given its number, we could use a sequence of If statements (unnested):

```
if (month == 1)
    cout << "January";
if (month == 2)
    cout << "February";
if (month == 3)
    cout << "March";
        .
        .
        .
if (month == 12)
    cout << "December";
```

But the equivalent nested If structure,

```
if (month == 1)
    cout << "January";
else
    if (month == 2)               // Nested If
        cout << "February";
    else
        if (month == 3)           // Nested If
            cout << "March";
        else
            if (month == 4)       // Nested If
                    .
                    .
                    .
```

is more efficient because it makes fewer comparisons. The first version—the sequence of independent If statements—always tests every condition (all 12 of them), even if the first one is satisfied. In contrast, the nested If solution skips all remaining comparisons after one alternative has been selected.

In the last example, notice how the indentation of the then- and else-clauses causes the statements to move continually to the right. We use a special indentation style with deeply nested If-Then-Else statements to indicate that the complex structure is just choosing one of a set of alternatives. This general multi-way branch is known as an *If-Then-Else-If* control structure:

```
if (month == 1)
    cout << "January";
```

```
else if (month == 2)          // Nested If
    cout << "February";
else if (month == 3)          // Nested If
    cout << "March";
else if (month == 4)          // Nested If
    .
    .
    .
else
    cout << "December";
```

This style prevents the indentation from marching continuously to the right. But, more importantly, it visually conveys the idea that we are using a 12–way branch based on the variable month.

It's important to note one difference between the sequence of If statements and the nested If: More than one alternative can be taken by the sequence of Ifs, but the nested If can select only one. To see why this is important, consider the analogy of filling out a questionnaire. Some questions are like a sequence of If statements, asking you to circle all the items in a list that apply to you (such as all your hobbies). Other questions ask you to circle only one item in a list (your age group, for example) and are thus like a nested If structure. Both kinds of questions occur in programming problems. Being able to recognize which type of question is being asked permits you to immediately select the appropriate control structure.

Another particularly helpful use of the nested If is when you want to compare a series of consecutive ranges of values. For example, the first Problem-Solving Case Study in this chapter involves printing different messages for different ranges of temperatures. We present two solutions for one of the modules, one using a sequence of If statements, the other using a nested If structure. As you'll see, the nested If version uses fewer comparisons, so it's more efficient.

As fast as modern computers are, many applications require so much computation that inefficient algorithms can waste hours of computer time. Always be on the lookout for ways to make your programs more efficient, as long as doing so doesn't make them difficult for other programmers to understand. It's usually better to sacrifice a little efficiency for the sake of readability.

The Dangling Else

When If statements are nested, you may find yourself confused about the if-else pairings: To which if does an else belong? For example, suppose that if a student's average is below 60, we want to print "Failing"; if it is at least 60 but less than 70, we want to print "Passing but marginal"; and if it is 70 or greater, we don't want to print anything.

We code this information with an If-Then-Else nested within an If-Then:

```
if (average < 70.0)
    if (average < 60.0)
        cout << "Failing";
    else
        cout << "Passing but marginal";
```

How do we know to which `if` the `else` belongs? Here is the rule that the C++ compiler follows: In the absence of braces, an `else` is always paired with the closest preceding `if` that doesn't already have an `else` paired with it. We indented the code to reflect this pairing.

Suppose we write the fragment like this:

```
if (average >= 60.0)       // Incorrect version
    if (average < 70.0)
        cout << "Passing but marginal";
else
    cout << "Failing";
```

Here we want the `else` branch attached to the outer If statement, not the inner, so we indent the code as you see it. But indentation does not affect the execution of the code. Even though the `else` aligns with the first `if`, the compiler pairs it with the second `if`. An `else` that follows a nested If-Then is called a *dangling else*. It doesn't logically belong with the nested If but is attached to it by the compiler.

To attach the `else` to the first `if`, not the second, you can turn the outer then-clause into a block:

```
if (average >= 60.0)       // Correct version
{
    if (average < 70.0)
        cout << "Passing but marginal";
}
else
    cout << "Failing";
```

The { } pair indicates that the inner If statement is complete, so the `else` must belong to the outer `if`.

Testing the State of an I/O Stream

In Chapter 4, we talked about the concept of input and output streams in C++. We introduced the data types istream, ostream, ifstream, and ofstream. We said that any of the following can cause an input stream to enter the fail state:

- Invalid input data
- An attempt to read beyond the end of a file
- An attempt to open a nonexistent file for input

C++ provides a way in which to determine if a stream is in the fail state. In a logical expression, you simply use the name of the stream variable as if it were a Boolean variable:

```
if (cin)
     .
     .
if ( !inFile )
     .
     .
```

When you do this, you are said to be **testing the state of the stream.** The result of the test is either a nonzero value (meaning the last I/O operation on that stream succeeded) or zero (meaning the last I/O operation failed).

Conceptually, you want to think of a stream variable in a logical expression as being a Boolean variable with a value TRUE (the stream state is okay) or FALSE (the state isn't okay).

Testing the State of a Stream   The act of using a C++ stream variable in a logical expression as if it were a Boolean variable; the result is nonzero (TRUE) if the last I/O operation on that stream succeeded, and zero (FALSE) otherwise.

In an If statement, the way you phrase the logical expression depends on what you want the then-clause to do. The statement

```
if (inFile)
    :
    :
```

executes the then-clause if the last I/O operation on `inFile` succeeded. The statement

```
if ( !inFile )
    :
    :
```

executes the then-clause if `inFile` is in the fail state. (And remember that once a stream is in the fail state, it remains so. Any further I/O operations on that stream are null operations.)

Here's an example that shows how to check whether an input file was opened successfully:

```
#include <iostream.h>
#include <fstream.h>        // For file I/O

int main()
{
    int       height;
    int       width;
    ifstream inFile;

    inFile.open("mydata.dat");           // Attempt to open input file
    if ( !inFile )                       // Was it opened?
    {
        cout << "Can't open the input file.";   // No--print message
        return 1;                                // Terminate program
    }
    inFile >> height >> width;
        :
        :

    return 0;
}
```

In this program, we begin by attempting to open the disk file `mydata.dat` for input. Immediately, we check to see whether the attempt succeeded. If it was successful, the value of the expression `!inFile` in the If statement is zero (FALSE) and the then-clause is skipped. The program proceeds to read data from the file and then, presumably, to perform some computations. It concludes by executing the statement

```
return 0;
```

With this statement, the `main` function returns control to the computer's operating system. Recall that the function value returned by `main` is known as the exit status. The value 0 signifies normal completion of the program. Any other value (typically 1, 2, 3, ...) means that something went wrong.

Let's trace through the program again, assuming we weren't able to open the input file. Upon return from the `open` function, the stream `inFile` is in the fail state. In the If statement, the value of the expression `!inFile` is nonzero (TRUE). Thus, the then-clause is executed. The program prints an error message to the user and then terminates, returning an exit status of 1 to inform the operating system of an abnormal termination of the program. (Our choice of the value 1 for the exit status is purely arbitrary. System programmers sometimes use several different values in a program to signal different reasons for program termination. But most people just use the value 1.)

Whenever you open a data file for input, be sure to test the stream state before proceeding. If you forget to, and the computer cannot open the file, your program quietly continues executing and ignores any input operations on the file.

*P*ROBLEM-SOLVING CASE STUDY

An Electronic Activity Director

Problem: You've taken a job at a year-round resort where the owner has just installed a computerized sign. She wants you to program the sign to show the current temperature and a recommended activity. Your program should read the temperature and print out the activity appropriate for that temperature using the following guidelines:

Activity	Temperature
Swimming	Temperature > 85
Tennis	70 < temperature ≤ 85
Golf	32 < temperature ≤ 70
Skiing	0 < temperature ≤ 32
Dancing	Temperature ≤ 0

Input: Temperature, an `int` value.

Output:
A prompt for input
Temperature (echo print)
Appropriate activity

Discussion: We must compare the temperature with the limits of each activity. Once the correct range is found, the corresponding activity is printed. We can make this comparison using If statements.

Main Module   *Level 0*

> Get temperature
> Print activity

Get Temperature   *Level 1*

> Prompt for temperature value input
> Read temperature
> Echo-print temperature

Print Activity

> Print "The recommended activity is"
> IF temperature > 85
>   Print "swimming."
> IF temperature <= 85 AND temperature > 70
>   Print "tennis."
> IF temperature <= 70 AND temperature > 32
>   Print "golf."
> IF temperature <= 32 AND temperature > 0
>   Print "skiing."
> IF temperature <= 0
>   Print "dancing."

Module Print Activity has five consecutive If statements and a total of eight comparisons. The algorithm performs all five If statements, even if the first condition happens to be satisfied. It would make more sense to code this module as a set of nested If-Then-Elses. With If-Then-Else, we stop testing as soon as a condition is satisfied. The middle Ifs seem to require compound logical conditions with two parts. However, the If-Then-Else structure makes the two-part conditions unnecessary; we don't execute the `else` branch unless one of the parts is already satisfied. Here's the rewritten module:

Print Activity (a better version)

```
Print "The recommended activity is"
IF temperature > 85
    Print "swimming."
ELSE IF temperature > 70
    Print "tennis."
ELSE IF temperature > 32
    Print "golf."
ELSE IF temperature > 0
    Print "skiing."
ELSE
    Print "dancing."
```

Module Structure Chart:

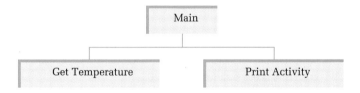

Because this algorithm has just one variable, `temperature`, we won't bother with the list of variables.

```
//************************************************************
// Activity program
// This program outputs an appropriate activity
// for a given temperature
//************************************************************
#include <iostream.h>
```

```
int main()
{
    int temperature;    // The outside temperature

    // Get temperature

    cout << "Enter the outside temperature:" << endl;
    cin >> temperature;
    cout << "The current temperature is " << temperature << '.'
        << endl;

    // Print activity

    cout << "The recommended activity is ";
    if (temperature > 85)
        cout << "swimming." << endl;
    else if (temperature > 70)
        cout << "tennis." << endl;
    else if (temperature > 32)
        cout << "golf." << endl;
    else if (temperature > 0)
        cout << "skiing." << endl;
    else
        cout << "dancing." << endl;

    return 0;
}
```

Here are two sample runs of the Activity program. The user's input is in color.

```
Enter the outside temperature:
-20
The current temperature is -20.
The recommended activity is dancing.

Enter the outside temperature:
52
The current temperature is 52.
The recommended activity is golf.
```

Figure 5-6 shows how the flow of control works in module Print Activity.

■ FIGURE 5-6

Flow of Control for Module Print Activity

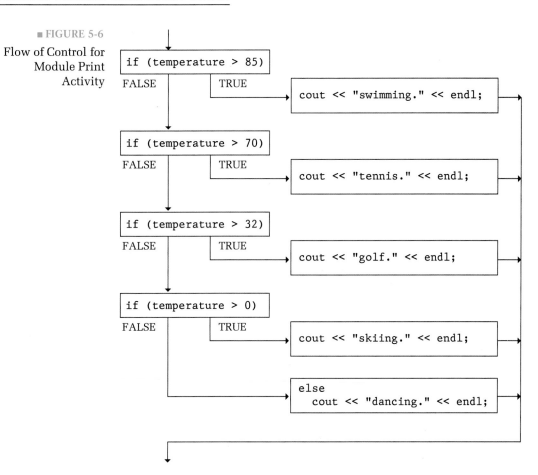

In this problem, the nested If version of the solution has four relational operators; the other solution had eight. Because it uses fewer operations to accomplish the same task, the nested Ifs are more efficient.

Notice the indentation we use for the nested If statements. When a deeply nested selection structure represents a series of alternate choices, in which each choice depends on the previous one being FALSE, we format the code as a series of branches. Each of the nested If statements begins with `else if`. The `else` indicates that the `if` is executed only if the preceding conditions are FALSE. Besides making the code look more like a series of If statements, this style avoids deep indentations that leave no room for writing a statement.

PROBLEM-SOLVING CASE STUDY

Warning Notices

Problem: Many universities send warning notices to freshmen who are in danger of failing a class. Your program should calculate the average of three test grades and print out a student's ID number, average, and whether or not the student is passing. Passing is a 60-point average or better. If the student is passing with less than a 70 average, the program should indicate that he or she is marginal.

Input: Student ID number (of type `long`) followed by three test grades (of type `int`). On many personal computers, the maximum `int` value is 32767. The student ID number is of type `long` (meaning long integer) to accommodate larger values such as nine-digit Social Security numbers.

Output:
A prompt for input
The input values (echo print)
Student ID number, average grade, passing/failing message, marginal indication, and error message if any of the test scores are negative

Discussion: To calculate the average, we have to read in the three test scores, add them, and divide by 3.

To print the appropriate message, we have to determine whether or not the average is below 60. If it is at least 60, we have to determine if it is less than 70.

If you were doing this by hand, you probably would notice if a test grade was negative and question it. If the semantics of your data imply that the values should be nonnegative, then your program should test to be sure they are. We test to make sure each grade is nonnegative, using a Boolean variable to report the result of the test. Here is the main module for our algorithm.

Main Module   *Level 0*

> Get data
> Test data
> IF data OK
>   Calculate average
>   Print message indicating status
> ELSE
>   Print "Invalid Data: Score(s) less than zero."

Which of these steps require(s) expansion? *Get data*, *Test data*, and *Print message indicating status* all require multiple statements in order to solve their particular subproblem. On the other hand, we can translate *Print "Invalid Data: . . . "* directly into a C++ output statement. What about the step *Calculate average*? We can write it as a single C++ statement, but there's another level of detail that we must fill in—the actual formula to be used. Because the formula is at a lower level of detail than the rest of the main module, we chose to expand *Calculate average* as a Level 1 module.

Get Data   *Level 1*

> Prompt for input
> Read studentID, test1, test2, test3
> Print studentID, test1, test2, test3

Test Data

> IF test1 < 0 OR test2 < 0 OR test3 < 0
>   Set dataOK = FALSE
> ELSE
>   Set dataOK = TRUE

Calculate Average

> Set average = (test1 + test2 + test3) / 3.0

Print Message Indicating Status

```
Print average
IF average >= 60.0
    Print "Passing"
    IF average < 70.0
        Print " but marginal"
    Print '.'
ELSE
    Print "Failing."
```

Module Structure Chart:

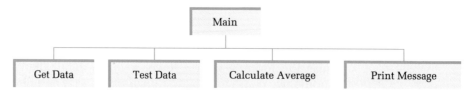

Get Data	Test Data	Calculate Average	Print Message

Variables

Name	Data Type	Description
average	float	Average of three test scores
studentID	int	Student's identification number
test1	int	Score for first test
test2	int	Score for second test
test3	int	Score for third test
dataOK	Boolean	TRUE if data is correct

```
//*****************************************************************
// Notices program
// This program determines (1) a student's average based on three
// test scores and (2) the student's passing/failing status
//*****************************************************************
#include <iostream.h>
#include <iomanip.h>     // For setprecision()
```

```
typedef int Boolean;
const Boolean TRUE = 1;
const Boolean FALSE = 0;

int main()
{
    float    average;      // Average of three test scores
    long     studentID;    // Student's identification number
    int      test1;        // Score for first test
    int      test2;        // Score for second test
    int      test3;        // Score for third test
    Boolean  dataOK;       // TRUE if data is correct

    cout.setf(ios::fixed, ios::floatfield);  // Set up floating pt.
    cout.setf(ios::showpoint);               //    output format

    // Get data

    cout << "Enter a Student ID number and three test scores:"
         << endl;
    cin >> studentID >> test1 >> test2 >> test3;
    cout << "Student number: " << studentID << "  Test Scores: "
         << test1 << ", " << test2 << ", " << test3 << endl;

    // Test data

    if (test1 < 0 || test2 < 0 || test3 < 0)
        dataOK = FALSE;
    else
        dataOK = TRUE;

    if (dataOK)
    {
        // Calculate average

        average = float(test1 + test2 + test3) / 3.0;

        // Print message

        cout << "Average score is "
             << setprecision(2) << average << "--";
        if (average >= 60.0)
```

```
        {
            cout << "Passing";              // Student is passing
            if (average < 70.0)
                cout << " but marginal";    // But marginal
            cout << '.' << endl;
        }
        else                                // Student is failing
            cout << "Failing." << endl;
    }
    else                                    // Invalid data
        cout << "Invalid Data:  Score(s) less than zero." << endl;

    return 0;
}
```

Here's a sample run of the program. Again, the input is in color.

```
Enter a Student ID number and three test scores:
9483681  73  62  68
Student Number: 9483681  Test Scores: 73, 62, 68
Average score is 67.67--Passing but marginal.
```

And here's a sample run with invalid data:

```
Enter a Student ID number and three test scores:
9483681  73  -10  62
Student Number: 9483681  Test Scores: 73, -10, 62
Invalid Data:  Score(s) less than zero.
```

In this program, we use a nested If structure that's easy to understand although somewhat inefficient. We assign a value to dataOK in one statement before testing it in the next. We could reduce the code by saying

```
dataOK = ! (test1 < 0 || test2 < 0 || test3 < 0);
```

Using DeMorgan's Law, we also could write this statement as

```
dataOK = (test1 >= 0 && test2 >= 0 && test3 >= 0);
```

In fact, we could reduce the code even more by eliminating the variable dataOK and using

```
if (test1 >= 0 && test2 >= 0 && test3 >= 0)
        :
        :


in place of


if (dataOK)
        :
        :
```

To convince yourself that these three variations work, try them by hand with some test data.

If these statements do the same thing, how do you choose which one to use? If your goal is efficiency, the compound condition in the If statement is best. If you are trying to express as clearly as possible what your code is doing, the longer form shown in the program may be best. The other variations lie somewhere in between. (However, some people would find the compound condition in the If statement to be not only the most efficient but also the clearest to understand.) There are no absolute rules to follow here, but the general guideline is to strive for clarity, even if you must sacrifice a little efficiency.

*P*ROBLEM-SOLVING *CASE STUDY*

The Lumberyard

Problem: You've been hired by a local lumberyard to help computerize its operations. Your first assignment is to write a program that computes the total amount of an item ordered in standard units, given its type, dimensions, and the number of pieces ordered. The yard sells two kinds of items: dimensioned lumber and plywood panels. First, the program should read a letter—either 'L' for lumber or 'P' for plywood—to determine the type. Next, it should read four integer numbers. For lumber, the first two numbers are the width and depth in inches; the third number is the length in feet; and the fourth number is the number of pieces ordered. So

L 2 4 8 14

means 14 pieces of 2-inch by 4-inch lumber, each 8 feet long. To compute the quantity ordered, you have to calculate the total volume ordered. The unit for lumber volume is the board foot, which is equivalent to 1 square foot of lumber, 1 inch thick, or 144 cubic inches. The quantity ordered in the sample input is 74.67 board feet. To determine the board feet, we use this formula:

(2 in. × 4 in. × (8 ft x 12 in./ft) × 14 pieces)/144 cubic in. per board foot

For plywood, the first two numbers are the thickness of the sheet, expressed as a fraction; the third number is the length of the sheet in feet; and the last number is the number of sheets ordered. The lumberyard only stocks plywood sheets in 4-foot widths, so there's no need to enter the width. The entry

P 3 4 8 6

means 6 sheets of ¾-inch-thick plywood, 8 feet long (and 4 feet wide). Again, to compute the quantity ordered, you have to calculate the total volume ordered. At this lumberyard, the unit for plywood volume is a full sheet. A full sheet is 4 feet (48 inches) wide, 8 feet (96 inches) long, and 1 inch thick, or 4608 cubic inches. For the sample input, the quantity ordered is 4.5 full sheets. We use this formula:

(6 sheets × ¾ in. × (8 ft × 12 in./ft) × 48 in.)/4608 cubic in. per sheet

Input: A letter (code) and four integer numbers (size1, size2, size3, numOrdered).

Output:
A prompt for input
The input values (echo print)
Result of calculating the quantity ordered

Discussion: To do this problem by hand, you would read the letter and four numbers and examine the letter to decide what to do. If the letter is 'L', you first would change all the units to inches and then multiply the four numbers together to get the total volume. Then you would divide the result by 1 board foot (144 cubic inches). If the letter is a 'P', you would change all the units to inches again, divide the first number by the second to get the thickness, then multiply the dimensions (don't forget the width) by the number of pieces to get the volume in cubic inches. You would divide this quantity by the volume of one full sheet (4608 cubic inches) to get the number of sheets.

The process can be translated directly into a program. "Read the letter and four numbers" becomes an input statement. We use an If-Then-Else statement to "examine the letter" and decide which formula to use. Each branch of the If-Then-Else has two steps. In the first, we calculate the appropriate result. In the second, we print the result and say whether it is in board feet or full sheets.

Main Module *Level 0*

```
Get data
IF code equals 'L'
    Calculate lumber amount
ELSE
    Calculate plywood amount
```

Get Data *Level 1*

```
Prompt for input
Read code, size1, size2, size3, numOrdered
Echo-print input data
```

Calculate Lumber Amount

```
Set boardFeet = size1 * size2 * size3 * 12 *
                numOrdered / BOARD_FT_INCHES
Print boardFeet
```

Calculate Plywood Amount

```
Set fullSheets = size1 / size2 * size3 * 12 * WIDTH_INCHES *
                 numOrdered / PLYWOOD_INCHES
Print fullSheets
```

Module Structure Chart:

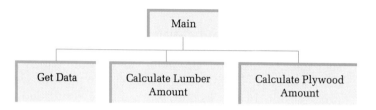

Constants

Name	Value	Description
BOARD_FT_INCHES	144.0	Cubic inches in 1 board foot
PLYWOOD_INCHES	4608.0	Cubic inches in 1 full sheet of plywood
WIDTH_INCHES	48	Width in inches of every sheet of plywood

In the following list of variables, notice that the data type listed for `size1`, `size2`, `size3`, and `numOrdered` is `long` (long integer) rather than `int`. In the calculation of the amount of wood ordered, the values of these variables are multiplied together. If the variables were of type `int`, their product could easily exceed the maximum `int` value, which is 32767 on many personal computers.

Variables

Name	Data Type	Description
code	char	Indicates lumber or plywood item
size1	long	First dimension
size2	long	Second dimension
size3	long	Third dimension
numOrdered	long	Number ordered
boardFeet	float	Result for lumber item
fullSheets	float	Result for plywood item

To save space, from here on we omit the list of constants and variables from the Problem-Solving Case Studies. But we recommend that you continue writing those lists as you design your own algorithms. The lists save you a lot of work when you are writing the declarations for your programs. Here is the program that implements our design.

```
//*****************************************************************
// LumberYard program
// This program reads a letter and four integer numbers.  If
// the letter is 'L', the four numbers are interpreted as the
// dimensions and quantity ordered of a lumber item, and the
// board-foot equivalent is output.  If the letter is 'P', the
// four numbers are the dimensions and quantity ordered of a
// plywood item, and the full-sheet equivalent is output.
//*****************************************************************
#include <iostream.h>
#include <iomanip.h>      // For setprecision()

const float BOARD_FT_INCHES = 144.0;    // Cubic inches in
                                        //   one board foot
const float PLYWOOD_INCHES = 4608.0;    // Cubic inches in
                                        //   one plywood sheet
const int   WIDTH_INCHES = 48;          // Width in inches of
                                        //   plywood sheet

int main()
{
    char   code;         // Indicates lumber or plywood item
    long   size1;        // First dimension
    long   size2;        // Second dimension
    long   size3;        // Third dimension
    long   numOrdered;   // Number ordered
    float  boardFeet;    // Result for lumber item
    float  fullSheets;   // Result for plywood item

    cout.setf(ios::fixed, ios::floatfield);  // Set up floating pt.
    cout.setf(ios::showpoint);               //    output format

    // Get data

    cout << "Enter letter code, three integer dimensions, "
         << "and quantity ordered:" << endl;             // Prompt
    cin >> code >> size1 >> size2 >> size3 >> numOrdered;

    cout << "For the order data:" << endl;
    cout << code << ' ' << size1 << ' ' << size2 << ' '
         << size3 << ' ' << numOrdered << endl;      // Echo print

    if (code == 'L')
    {
        // Calculate lumber amount

        boardFeet =  float(size1 * size2 * size3 * 12 * numOrdered)
                     / BOARD_FT_INCHES;
        cout << "the board-foot equivalent is "
             << setprecision(2) << boardFeet << endl;
    }
```

```
        else
        {
            // Calculate plywood amount

            fullSheets = float(size1) / float(size2) *
                        float(size3 * 12 * WIDTH_INCHES * numOrdered) /
                        PLYWOOD_INCHES;
            cout << "the full-sheet equivalent is "
                << setprecision(2) << fullSheets << endl;
        }
        return 0;
}
```

This is a sample run of the program:

```
Enter letter code, three integer dimensions, and quantity ordered:
L 2 6 10 45
For the order data:
L 2 6 10 45
the board-foot equivalent is 450.00
```

This sample shows what happens when code is 'P':

```
Enter letter code, three integer dimensions, and quantity ordered:
P 1 2 9 7
For the order data:
P 1 2 9 7
the full-sheet equivalent is 3.94
```

We examine this program in more detail in the next section.

TESTING AND DEBUGGING

In Chapter 1, we discussed the problem-solving and implementation phases of computer programming. Testing is an integral part of both phases. Here we test both phases of the process used to develop the LumberYard program. Testing in the problem-solving phase is done after the solution is developed but before it is implemented. In the implementation phase, we test after the algorithm is translated into a program, and again after the program has compiled successfully. The compilation itself constitutes another stage of testing that is performed automatically.

The Problem-Solving Phase: The Algorithm Walk-Through

To test at the problem-solving phase, we do a *walk-through* of the algorithm. For each module in the top-down design, we establish an assertion called a precondition and another called a postcondition. A **precondition** is an assertion that must be true before a module is executed in order for the module to execute correctly. A **postcondition** is an assertion that should be true after the module has executed, if it has done its job correctly. To test a module, we "walk through" the algorithmic steps to confirm that they produce the required postcondition given the stated precondition.

Precondition   An assertion that must be true before a module begins executing.

Postcondition   An assertion that should be true after a module has executed.

Our lumberyard algorithm has four modules: the main module, Get Data, Calculate Lumber Amount, and Calculate Plywood Amount. Usually there is no precondition for a main module. Our main module's postcondition is that it outputs the correct result given the correct input. More specifically, the postcondition for the main module is

- the computer has read five input values (a letter and four integers).
- either the number of board feet ordered or the number of full sheets of plywood ordered has been calculated and displayed.

Because Get Data is the first module executed in the algorithm and because it does not assume anything about the contents of the variables it is about to manipulate, it has no precondition. Its postcondition is that it has input a letter into `code`, and integer values into `size1`, `size2`, `size3`, and `numOrdered`.

The precondition for module Calculate Lumber Amount is that `code` equals 'L', and that `size1`, `size2`, `size3`, and `numOrdered` contain integer values. Its postcondition is that the number of board feet ordered has been computed from those values and printed out.

The precondition for module Calculate Plywood Amount is that `code` equals 'P', and that `size1`, `size2`, `size3`, and `numOrdered` contain integer values. Its postcondition is that the number of full sheets ordered has been computed and printed out.

Below we summarize the module preconditions and postconditions in tabular form. In the table, we use *AND* with its usual meaning in an assertion—the logical AND operation. Also, a phrase like "`someVariable` is assigned" is an abbreviated way of asserting that `someVariable` has already been assigned a meaningful value.

Module	Precondition	Postcondition
Main	—	A letter and four integer values have been input AND Either the number of board feet or the number of plywood sheets has been calculated and displayed
Get Data	—	`code`, `size1`, `size2`, `size3`, and `numOrdered` have been input
Calculate Lumber Amount	`code` equals 'L' AND `size1`, `size2`, `size3`, and `numOrdered` are assigned	The number of board feet has been computed and printed
Calculate Plywood Amount	`code` equals 'P' AND `size1`, `size2`, `size3`, and `numOrdered` are assigned	The number of plywood sheets has been computed and printed

Now that we've established the preconditions and postconditions, we walk through the main module. At this point, we are concerned only with the steps in the main module, so for now we assume that each lower-level module executes correctly. At each step, we must determine the current conditions. If the step is a reference to another module, we have to verify that the precondition of that module is met by the current conditions.

First we assume that Get Data correctly inputs a letter and four integer values. Then the If statement checks to see if the letter is an 'L'. If it is, the computer takes the Calculate Lumber Amount branch. Assuming Calculate Lumber Amount correctly calculates and prints the quantity ordered (remember, we're assuming that the lower-level modules are correct for now), that branch of the If statement is correct.

If the letter in `code` is not an 'L', the computer takes the Calculate Plywood Amount branch. Here we have a problem. The precondition of Calculate Plywood Amount asserts that the value of `code` is 'P', but the only condition that has been established is that `code` does not contain an 'L'. As we have written it, the algorithm calculates the quantity of full sheets ordered if anything other than an 'L' is entered for `code`. So the algorithm works as long as the data is entered correctly, but it does not catch incorrect data. This is poor design, and we return to the problem later. But first let's finish up the walk-through.

The next step is to examine each module at level 1 and answer this question: If the level-2 modules (if any) are assumed to be correct, will this level-1 module do what it is supposed to do? We simply repeat the walk-through process for each module, starting with its particular precondition. In this example, there are no level-2 modules, so the level-1 modules must be complete.

Get Data correctly reads in five values—code, size1, size2, size3, and numOrdered—thereby satisfying its postcondition. (The next refinement is to code this instruction in C++. Whether it is coded correctly or not is *not* an issue in this phase; we deal with the code when we perform testing in the implementation phase.)

Calculate Lumber Amount assigns to variable boardFeet the result of multiplying the contents of size1, size2, size3 (itself multiplied by the literal 12), and numOrdered, and dividing by BOARD_FT_INCHES. That's the correct formula for computing board feet, so the step is correct and the calculated value is printed. Calculate Lumber Amount meets its required postcondition.

Calculate Plywood Amount assigns to the variable fullSheets the result of dividing size1 by size2, multiplying by size3 (itself multiplied by the literal 12), WIDTH_INCHES, and numOrdered, and dividing by PLYWOOD_INCHES. This is the correct formula for computing full sheets of plywood, so this step is correct and the calculated value is printed. Calculate Plywood Amount also meets its required postcondition.

Once we've completed the algorithm walk-through, we have to correct any discrepancies and repeat the process. When we know that the modules do what they are supposed to do, we start translating the top-down design into our programming language.

We need to fix the problem we discovered in the algorithm—namely, that the main module does not guarantee the required precondition for Calculate Plywood Amount. We have to change the main module so that the assertion "code equals 'P'" is true before Calculate Plywood Amount is entered. Here's the revised main module:

Main Module   *Level 0*

```
Get data
IF code equals 'L'
    Calculate lumber amount
IF code equals 'P'
    Calculate plywood amount
```

The main module now sees to it that data has been input to the five variables and that code contains the letter 'P' before Calculate Plywood Amount is executed. This change corrects the problem we found in the walk-through, but we also should output an error message when a letter other than 'L' or 'P' is entered.

A standard postcondition for any program is that the user has been notified of invalid data. You should *validate* every input value for which any restrictions apply. A data validation If statement tests an input value and outputs an error message if the value is not acceptable. (We are validating the data when we test for negative scores in the Notices program.) The best place to validate data is immediately after it is input. In the lumberyard algorithm, we would add a data validation test to the Get Data module.

Get Data   *Level 1*

```
Prompt for input
Read code, size1, size2, size3, numOrdered
Echo-print input data
IF code is not 'L' or 'P'
    Print an error message
```

To satisfy the data validation postcondition, the lumberyard algorithm also should test the other input values. For example, a negative size or order quantity would be invalid. More elaborate checks might test for invalid combinations of dimensions. We leave you the task of other data validations in Programming Warm-Up Exercise 12.

The Implementation Phase

Now that we've talked about testing in the problem-solving phase, we can turn to testing in the implementation phase. In this phase, you need to test at several points.

Code Walk-Through   After the code is written, you should go over it line by line to be sure that you've faithfully reproduced the top-down design—a process known as a *code walk-through*. In a team programming situation, you ask other team members to walk through the algorithm and code with you, to double-check the design and code.

Execution Trace   You also should take some actual values and hand-calculate what the output should be by doing an *execution trace* (or *hand trace*). When the program is executed, you can use these same values as input and check the results.

The computer is a very literal device—it does exactly what we tell it to do, which may or may not be what we want it to do. We try to make sure that a program does what we want by tracing the execution of the statements.

We use a nonsense program below to demonstrate the technique. We keep track of the values of the program variables on the right-hand side. Variables with undefined values are indicated with a dash. When a variable is assigned a value, that value is listed in the appropriate column.

	Value of		
Statement	a	b	c
`const int x = 5;`			
`int main()`			
`{`			
`    int a, b, c;`	—	—	—
`    b = 1;`	—	1	—
`    c = x + b;`	—	1	6
`    a = x + 4;`	9	1	6
`    a = c;`	6	1	6
`    b = c;`	6	6	6
`    a = a + b + c;`	18	6	6
`    c = c % x;`	18	6	1
`    c = c * a;`	18	6	18
`    a = a % b;`	0	6	18
`    cout << a << b`			
`         << c;`	0	6	18
`    return 0;`	0	6	18
`}`			

Now that you've seen how the technique works, let's apply it to the LumberYard program. We list just the executable statement portion here, modified to reflect the results of our algorithm walk-through.

	Value of						
Statement	code	size1	size2	size3	numOrdered	boardFeet	fullSheets
`cout << "Enter letter code, three integer "` `    << "dimensions, and quantity ordered:" << endl;`	—	—	—	—	—	—	—
`cin >> code >> size1 >> size2 >> size3` `    >> numOrdered;`	P	1	2	8	20	—	—
`cout << "For the order data:" << endl;`	P	1	2	8	20	—	—
`cout << code << ' ' << size1 << ' ' << size2 << ' '` `    << size3 << ' ' << numOrdered << endl;`	P	1	2	8	20	—	—
`if ( ! (code == 'L' || code == 'P') )` `    cout << "The item code is invalid." << endl;`	P —	1 —	2 —	8 —	20 —	— —	— —
`if (code == 'L')` `{`	P	1	2	8	20	—	—
`    // Calculate lumber amount`							
`    boardFeet = float(size1 * size2 * size3 * 12 *` `            numOrdered) / BOARD_FT_INCHES;`	—	—	—	—	—	—	—

`    cout << "the board-foot equivalent is "`
 `        << setprecision(2) << boardFeet << endl;`
 `}`
	—	—	—	—	—	—	—

`if (code == 'P')` `{`	P	1	2	8	20	—	—
`    // Calculate plywood amount`							

`    fullSheets = float(size1) / float(size2) *`
 `            float(size3 * 12 * WIDTH_INCHES *`
 `            numOrdered) / PLYWOOD_INCHES;`
	P	1	2	8	20	—	10.0

`    cout << "the full-sheet equivalent is "`
 `        << setprecision(2) << fullSheets << endl;`
 `}`
	P	1	2	8	20	—	10.0

`return 0;`	P	1	2	8	20	—	10.0

Neither of the then-clauses of the first two If statements are executed for this input data, so we do not fill in any of the variable columns to their right. We always create columns for all of the variables, even though we know that some will stay empty. Why? Because it's possible that we'll encounter an error that refers to an empty variable; having a column for the variable reminds us to check for just such an error.

When a program contains branches, it's a good idea to retrace its execution with different input data so that each branch is traced at least once. In the next section, we describe how to develop data sets that test each of a program's branches.

Testing Selection Control Structures   To test a program with branches, we have to execute each branch at least once and verify the results. For example, in the student warning notices program (Notices), there are four If-Then-Else statements (see Figure 5-7). We need a series of data sets to test the different branches. For example, we could use the following sets of data for the input values of test1, test2, and test3:

	test1	test2	test3
Set 1	100	100	100
Set 2	60	60	63
Set 3	50	50	50
Set 4	−50	50	50

■ FIGURE 5-7

Branching Structure
for Notices Program

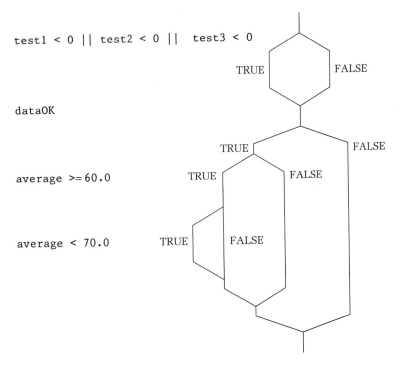

Figure 5-8 shows the flow of control through the branching structure of the Notices program for each of these data sets. Set 1 is valid and gives an average of 100, which is passing and not marginal. Set 2 is valid and gives an average of 61, which is passing but marginal. Set 3 is valid and gives an average of 50, which is failing. Set 4 has an invalid test grade, which generates an error message.

Every branch in the program is executed at least once through this series of test runs; eliminating any of the test data sets would leave at least one branch untested. This series of data sets provides *minimum complete coverage* of the program's branching structure. Whenever you test a program with branches in it, you should design a series of tests that covers all of the branches. It may help to draw diagrams like those in Figure 5-8 so that you can see which branches are being executed.

Because an action in one branch of a program often affects processing in a later branch, it is critical to test as many *combinations of branches*, or paths, through a program as possible; this way we can be sure that there are no interdependencies that could cause problems. Of course, some combinations of branches may be impossible to follow. For example, if the `else` is taken in the first branch of program Notices, the `else` in the second branch cannot be taken. Shouldn't we try all possible paths? Yes, in theory we should. However, the number of paths in even a small program is quite large. For example, there are 16 possible paths in the LumberYard program.

■ FIGURE 5-8   Flow of Control Through Notices Program for Each of Four Data Sets

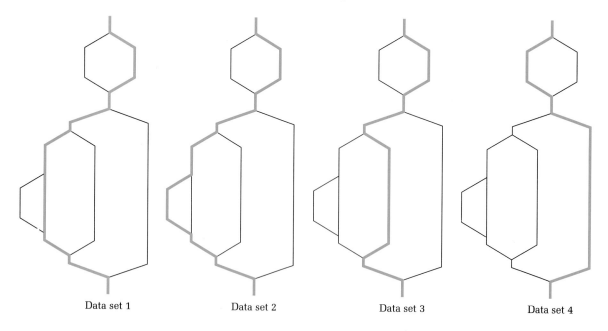

Data set 1   Data set 2   Data set 3   Data set 4

The approach to testing that we've used here is called *code coverage* because the test data is designed by looking at the code of the program. Another approach to testing, *data coverage*, attempts to test as many allowable data values as possible without regard to the program code. Complete data coverage is as impractical as complete code coverage for many programs. For example, program Notices reads four integer values and thus has approximately $(2 * \text{INT\_MAX})^4$ possible inputs. (INT_MAX and INT_MIN are constants declared in the header file limits.h. They represent the largest and smallest possible int values, respectively, on your particular computer and C++ compiler.)

Often, testing is a combination of these two strategies. Instead of trying every possible data value (data coverage), we examine the code (code coverage) and look for ranges of values for which processing is identical. Then we test the values at the boundaries and, sometimes, a value in the middle of each range. For example, a simple condition, such as

```
alpha < 0
```

divides the integers into two ranges:

INT_MIN through −1
0 through INT_MAX

Thus, we should test the four values INT_MIN, −1, 0, and INT_MAX. A compound condition, such as

```
alpha >= 0 && alpha <= 100
```

divides the integers into three ranges:

INT_MIN through −1
0 through 100
101 through INT_MAX

Thus, we have six values to test. In addition, to verify that the relational operators are correct, we should test for values of 1 (> 0) and 99 (< 100).

Conditional branches are only one factor in developing a testing strategy. We consider more of these factors in later chapters.

Tests Performed Automatically During Compilation and Execution

Once a program is coded and test data has been prepared, it is ready for compiling. The compiler has two responsibilities: to report any errors and (if there are no errors) to translate the program into object code.

Errors can be syntactic or semantic. The compiler finds syntactic errors. For example, the compiler warns you when reserved words are misspelled, identifiers are undeclared, semicolons are missing, and operand types are mismatched. But it won't find all of your typing errors. If you type > instead of < , you won't get an error message. It's up to you to design test data and carefully check the code to detect semantic errors.

Semantic errors (also called *logic errors*) are mistakes that give you the wrong answer. They are more difficult to locate than syntactic errors and usually surface when a program is executing. C++ detects only the most obvious semantic errors—those that result in an invalid operation (dividing by zero, for example). Although semantic errors sometimes are caused by typing errors, they are more often a product of faulty design. The mistake we found in the algorithm walk-through for the lumberyard problem is a typical semantic error.

By walking through the algorithm and the code, tracing the execution of the program, and developing a thorough test strategy, you should be able to avoid, or at least quickly locate, semantic errors in your programs.

Figure 5-9 illustrates the testing process we've been discussing. The figure shows where syntax and semantic errors occur and in which phase they can be corrected.

■ FIGURE 5-9   Testing Process

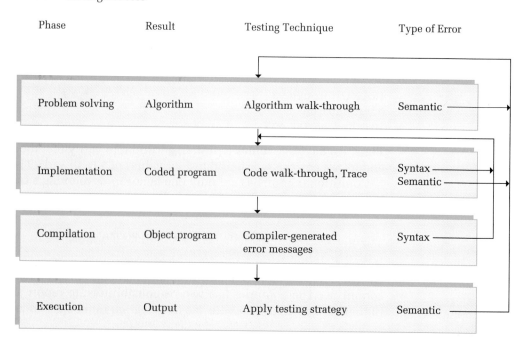

Phase	Result	Testing Technique	Type of Error
Problem solving	Algorithm	Algorithm walk-through	Semantic
Implementation	Coded program	Code walk-through, Trace	Syntax / Semantic
Compilation	Object program	Compiler-generated error messages	Syntax
Execution	Output	Apply testing strategy	Semantic

Testing and Debugging Hints

1. C++ has three pairs of operators that are similar in appearance but very different in effect: == and =, && and &, and || and |. Double-check all of your logical expressions to be sure you're using the "equals-equals," "and-and," and "or-or" operators.

2. If you use extra parentheses for clarity, be sure that the opening and closing parentheses match up. To verify that parentheses are properly paired, start with the innermost pair and draw a line connecting them. Do the same for the others, working your way out to the outermost pair. For example,

   ```
   if (((total/scores) > 50) && ((total/(scores - 1)) < 100))
   ```

   And here is a quick way to tell whether you have an equal number of opening and closing parentheses. The scheme uses a single number (the "magic number"), whose value initially is 0. Scan the expression from left to right. At each opening parenthesis, add 1 to the magic number; at each closing parenthesis, subtract 1. At the final closing parenthesis, the magic number should be 0. For example,

   ```
   if (((total/scores) > 50) && ((total/(scores - 1)) < 100))
      0  123            2   1   23        4          32    10
   ```

3. Don't use =< to mean "less than or equal to"; only the symbol <= works. Likewise, => is invalid for "greater than or equal to"; you must use >= for this operation.

4. In an If statement, remember to use a { } pair if the then-clause or else-clause is a sequence of statements. And be sure not to put a semicolon after the right brace.

5. Echo-print all input data. This way you know that your input data are what they are supposed to be.

6. Test for bad data. If a data value must be positive, use an If statement to test the value. If the value is negative or 0, an error message should be printed; otherwise processing should continue. For example, the Activity program could have the following statement inserted after the second output statement (the echo print):

   ```
   if (temperature > 120 || temperature < -35)
       cout << "Temperature data is in error." << endl;
   else
   {
       .
       .
       .
   ```

   This If statement tests the limits of reasonable temperatures and executes the rest of the program only if the data value is reasonable.

7. Take some sample values and try them by hand as we did for the Notices program. (There's more on this in Chapter 6.)

8. If your program reads data from an input file, it should verify that the file was opened successfully. Immediately after the call to the **open** function, an If statement should test the state of the file stream.

9. If your program produces an answer that does not agree with a value you've calculated by hand, try these suggestions:
   a. Redo your arithmetic.
   b. Recheck your input data.
   c. Carefully go over the section of code that does the calculation. If you're in doubt about the order in which the operations are performed, insert clarifying parentheses.
   d. Check for integer overflow. The value of an int variable may have exceeded INT_MAX in the middle of a calculation. Some systems give an error message when this happens, but most do not.
   e. Check the conditions in branching statements to be sure that the correct branch is taken under all circumstances.

SUMMARY

Using logical expressions is a way of asking questions while a program is running. The program evaluates each logical expression, producing a nonzero value if the expression is true or the value zero if the expression is not true.

The If statement allows you to take different paths through a program based on the value of a logical expression. The If-Then-Else is used to choose between two courses of action; the If-Then is used to choose whether or not to take a particular course of action. The branches of an If-Then or If-Then-Else can be any statement, simple or compound. They can even be another If statement.

The algorithm walk-through requires us to define a precondition and a postcondition for each module in an algorithm. Then we have to verify that those assertions are true at the beginning and end of each module. By testing our design in the problem-solving phase, we can eliminate errors that can be more difficult to detect in the implementation phase.

An execution trace is a way of finding program errors once we've entered the implementation phase. It's a good idea to trace a program before you run it, so that you have some sample results against which to check the program's output.

QUICK CHECK

1. Write a C++ expression that compares the variable letter to the constant 'Z' and yields TRUE if letter is less than 'Z'. (pp. 188–192)
2. Write a C++ expression that yields TRUE if letter is between 'A' and 'Z' inclusive. (pp. 188–196)
3. What form of the If statement would you use to make a C++ program print out "Is a letter" if the value in letter is between 'A' and 'Z' inclusive, and print out "Is not a letter" if the value in letter is outside that range? (pp. 202–204)
4. What form of the If statement would you use to make a C++ program print out "Is a letter" only if the value in letter is between 'A' and 'Z' inclusive? (pp. 206–209)

5. On a telephone, each of the digits 2 through 9 has a segment of the alphabet associated with it. What kind of control structure would you use to decide which segment a given letter falls into and to print out the corresponding digit? (pp. 209–212)
6. What is one postcondition that every program should have? (pp. 230–234)
7. In what phase of the program development process should you carry out an execution trace? (pp. 234–237)
8. You've written a program that prints out the corresponding digit on a phone given a letter of the alphabet. Everything seems to work right except that you can't get the digit '5' to print out; you keep getting the digit '6'. What steps would you take to find and fix this bug? (pp. 237–239)

Answers 1. `letter < 'Z'` 2. `letter >= 'A' && letter <= 'Z'` 3. The If-Then-Else form 4. The If-Then form 5. A nested If statement 6. The user has been notified of invalid data values. 7. The implementation phase 8. Carefully review the section of code that should print out '5'. Check the branching condition and the output statement there. Try some sample values by hand.

EXAM PREPARATION EXERCISES

1. Given these values for Boolean variables x, y, and z:

   x = TRUE, y = FALSE, z = TRUE

   evaluate the following logical expressions. In the blank next to each expression, write a T if the result is TRUE or an F if the result is FALSE.

   _____ a. `x && y || x && z`
   _____ b. `(x || !y) && (!x || z)`
   _____ c. `x || y && z`
   _____ d. `!(x || y) && z`

2. Given these values for variables i, j, p, and q:

   i = 10, j = 19, p = TRUE, q = FALSE

   add parentheses (if necessary) to the expressions below so that they evaluate to TRUE.

   a. `i == j || p`
   b. `i >= j || i <= j && p`
   c. `!p || p`
   d. `!q && q`

3. Given these values for the int variables i, j, m, and n:

   i = 6, j = 7, m = 11, n = 11

   what is the output of the following code?

   ```
   cout << "Madam";
   if (i < j)
       if (m != n)
           cout << "How";
       else
           cout << "Now";
   ```

   (*continued on next page*)

```
cout << "I'm";
if (i >= m)
    cout << "Cow";
else
    cout << "Adam";
```

4. Given the int variables x, y, and z, where x is 3, y is 7, and z is 6, what is the output from each of the following code fragments?

a.
```
if (x <= 3)
    cout << x + y << endl;
cout << x + y << endl;
```

b.
```
if (x != -1)
    cout << "The value of x is " << x << endl;
else
    cout << "The value of y is " << y << endl;
```

c.
```
if (x != -1)
{
    cout << x << endl;
    cout << y << endl;
    cout << z << endl;
}
else
    cout << "y" << endl;
    cout << "z" << endl;
```

5. Given this code fragment:

```
if (height >= minHeight)
    if (weight >= minWeight)
        cout << "Eligible to serve." << endl;
    else
        cout << "Too light to serve." << endl;
else
    if (weight >= minWeight)
        cout << "Too short to serve." << endl;
    else
        cout << "Too short and too light to serve." << endl;
```

a. What is the output when height exceeds minHeight and weight exceeds minWeight?

b. What is the output when height is less than minHeight and weight is less than minWeight?

6. Match each logical expression in the left column with the logical expression in the right column that tests for the same condition.

_____ a. x < y && y < z		(1) !(x != y) && y == z
_____ b. x > y && y >= z		(2) !(x <= y || y < z)
_____ c. x != y || y == z		(3) (y < z || y == z) || x == y
_____ d. x == y || y <= z		(4) !(x >= y) && !(y >= z)
_____ e. x == y && y == z		(5) !(x == y && y != z)

7. The following expressions make sense but are invalid according to C++'s rules of syntax. Rewrite them so that they are valid logical expressions. (All the variables are of type int.)

 a. `x < y <= z`
 b. `x`, `y`, and `z` are greater than 0
 c. `x` is equal to neither `y` nor `z`
 d. `x` is equal to `y` and `z`

8. Given these values for Boolean variables `x`, `y`, and `z`:

 x = TRUE, y = TRUE, z = FALSE

 indicate whether each expression is TRUE (T) or FALSE (F).

 _____ a. `!(y || z) || x`
 _____ b. `z && x && y`
 _____ c. `! y || (z || !x)`
 _____ d. `z || (x && (y || z))`
 _____ e. `x || x && z`

9. For each of the following problems, decide which is more appropriate, an If-Then-Else or an If-Then. Explain your answers.

 a. Students who are candidates for admission to a college submit their SAT scores. If a student's score is equal to or above a certain value, print a letter of acceptance for the student. Otherwise, print a rejection notice.

 b. For employees who work more than 40 hours a week, calculate overtime pay and add it to their regular pay.

 c. In solving a quadratic equation, whenever the value of the discriminant (the quantity under the square root sign) is negative, print out a message noting that the roots are complex (imaginary) numbers.

 d. In a computer-controlled sawmill, if a cross section of a log is greater than certain dimensions, adjust the saw to cut 4-inch by 8-inch beams; otherwise, adjust the saw to cut 2-inch by 4-inch studs.

10. What causes the error message "UNEXPECTED ELSE" when this code fragment is compiled?

```
if (mileage < 24.0)
{
    cout << "Gas ";
    cout << "guzzler.";
};
else
    cout << "Fuel efficient.";
```

11. The following code fragment is supposed to print "Type AB" when Boolean variables `typeA` and `typeB` are both TRUE, and print "Type O" when both variables are FALSE. Instead, it prints "Type O" whenever just one of the variables is FALSE. Insert a { } pair to make the code segment work the way it should.

```
if (typeA || typeB)
    if (typeA && typeB)
        cout << "Type AB";
else
    cout << "Type O";
```

12. The nested If structure below has five possible branches depending on the values read into char variables ch1, ch2, and ch3. To test the structure, you need five sets of data, each set using a different branch. Create the five test data sets.

```
cin >> ch1 >> ch2 >> ch3;
if (ch1 == ch2)
    if (ch2 == ch3)
        cout << "All initials are the same." << endl;
    else
        cout << "First two are the same." << endl;
else if (ch2 == ch3)
    cout << "Last two are the same." << endl;
else if (ch1 == ch3)
    cout << "First and last are the same." << endl;
else
    cout << "All initials are different." << endl;
```

a. Test data set 1: ch1 = _____ ch2 = _____ ch3 = _____
b. Test data set 2: ch1 = _____ ch2 = _____ ch3 = _____
c. Test data set 3: ch1 = _____ ch2 = _____ ch3 = _____
d. Test data set 4: ch1 = _____ ch2 = _____ ch3 = _____
e. Test data set 5: ch1 = _____ ch2 = _____ ch3 = _____

13. If x and y are Boolean variables, do the following two expressions test the same condition?

```
x != y
(x || y) && !(x && y)
```

14. The following If condition is made up of three relational expressions:

```
if (i >= 10 && i <= 20 && i != 16)
    j = 4;
```

If i contains the value 25 when this If statement is executed, which relational expression(s) will the computer evaluate? (Remember that C++ uses short-circuit evaluation.)

PROGRAMMING WARM-UP EXERCISES

1. Declare eligible to be a Boolean variable, and assign it the value TRUE.
2. Write a statement that sets the Boolean variable available to TRUE if numberOrdered is less than or equal to numberOnHand minus numberReserved.
3. Write a statement containing a logical expression that assigns TRUE to the Boolean variable isCandidate if satScore is greater than or equal to 1100, gpa is not less than 2.5, and age is greater than 15. Otherwise, isCandidate should be FALSE.
4. Given the declarations

```
Boolean leftPage;
int     pageNumber;
```

write a statement that sets leftPage to TRUE if pageNumber is even. (*Hint:* Consider what the remainders are when you divide different integers by two.)

5. Write an If statement (or a series of If statements) that assigns to the variable biggest the greatest value contained in variables i, j, and k. Assume the three values are distinct.

6. Rewrite the following sequence of If-Thens as a single If-Then-Else.

```
if (year % 4 == 0)
    cout << year << " is a leap year." << endl;
if (year % 4 != 0)
{
    year = year + 4 - year % 4;
    cout << year << " is the next leap year." << endl;
}
```

7. Simplify the following program segment, taking out unnecessary comparisons. Assume that age is an int variable.

```
if (age > 64)
    cout << "Senior voter";
if (age < 18)
    cout << "Under age";
if (age >= 18 && age < 65)
    cout << "Regular voter";
```

8. The following program fragment is supposed to print out the values 25, 60, and 8, in that order. Instead, it prints out 50, 60, and 4. Why?

```
length = 25;
width = 60;
if (length = 50)
    height = 4;
else
    height = 8;
cout << length << ' ' << width << ' ' << height << endl;
```

9. The following C++ program segment is almost unreadable because of the inconsistent indentation and the random placement of left and right braces. Fix the indentation and align the braces properly.

```
// This is a nonsense program
if (a > 0)
if (a < 20)
        {
    cout << "A is in range." << endl;
b = 5;
    }
        else
    else
```

```
                                   {
            cout << "A is too large." << endl;
                b = 3;
            }
                else
            cout << "A is too small." << endl;
                    cout << "All done." << endl;
```

10. Given the `float` variables `x1`, `x2`, `y1`, `y2`, and `m`, write a program segment to find the slope of a line through the points (`x1`, `y1`) and (`x2`, `y2`). Use the formula

$$m = \frac{(y1 - y2)}{(x1 - x2)}$$

to determine the slope of the line. If `x1` equals `x2`, the line is vertical and the slope is undefined. The segment should write the slope with an appropriate label. If the slope is undefined, it should write the message "Slope undefined".

11. Given the `float` variables `a`, `b`, `c`, `root1`, `root2`, and `discriminant`, write a program segment to determine whether the roots of a quadratic polynomial are real or complex (imaginary). If the roots are real, find them and assign them to `root1` and `root2`. If they are complex, write the message "No real roots."

    The formula for the solution to the quadratic equation is

$$\frac{-b \pm \sqrt{b^2 - 4ac}}{2a}$$

The ± means "plus or minus" and indicates that there are two solutions to the equation: one in which the result of the square root is added to $-b$ and one in which the result is subtracted from $-b$. The roots are real if the discriminant (the quantity under the square root sign) is not negative.

12. Continue to validate the data in the lumberyard case study. Test for negative numeric values. Also check for invalid plywood thicknesses. Valid thicknesses are ¼, ⅜, ½, ⅝, ¾, ⅞, ¼, ⅞, and ¾.

13. The following program reads data from an input file without checking to see if the file was opened successfully. Insert statements that will print an error message and terminate the program if the file cannot be opened.

```cpp
#include <iostream.h>
#include <fstream.h>        // For file I/O

int main()
{
    int      m;
    int      n;
    ifstream info;
```

```
        info.open("indata.dat");
        info >> m >> n;
        cout << "The sum of " << m << " and " << n
            << " is " << m + n << endl;
        return 0;
    }
```

PROGRAMMING PROBLEMS

1. Using a top-down design, write a C++ program that inputs a single letter and prints out the corresponding digit on the telephone. The letters and digits on a telephone are grouped this way:

2 = ABC	4 = GHI	6 = MNO	8 = TUV
3 = DEF	5 = JKL	7 = PRS	9 = WXY

    No digit corresponds to either Q or Z. For these two letters, your program should print a message indicating that they are not used on a telephone.
        The program might operate like this:

    ```
    Enter a single letter, and I will tell you what the corresponding
    digit is on the telephone.
    R
    The digit 7 corresponds to the letter R on the telephone.
    ```

    Here's another example:

    ```
    Enter a single letter, and I will tell you what the corresponding
    digit is on the telephone.
    Q
    There is no digit on the telephone that corresponds to Q.
    ```

    Your program should print a message indicating that there is no matching digit for any nonalphabetic character the user enters. Also, the program should recognize only uppercase letters. Include the lowercase letters with the invalid characters.
        Prompt the user with an informative message for the input value, as shown above. The program should echo-print the input letter as part of the output.
        Use proper indentation, appropriate comments, and meaningful identifiers throughout the program.

2. People who deal with historical dates use a number called the Julian day to calculate the number of days between two events. The Julian day is the number of days that have elapsed since January 1, 4713 B.C. For example, the Julian day for October 16, 1956, is 2435763. There are formulas for computing the Julian Day from a given date and vice versa.

One very simple formula computes the day of the week from a given Julian day:

Day of the week = (Julian day + 1) % 7

where % is the C++ modulus operator. This formula gives a result of 0 for Sunday, 1 for Monday, and so on up to 6 for Saturday. For Julian day 2435763, the result is 2 (a Tuesday). Your job is to write a C++ program that inputs a Julian day, computes the day of the week using the formula, and then prints out the name of the day that corresponds to that number. If the maximum int value on your machine is small (32767, for instance), use the long data type instead of int. Be sure to echo-print the input data and to use proper indentation and comments.

Your output might look like this:

```
Enter a Julian day number:
2451545
Julian day number 2451545 is a Saturday.
```

3. You can compute the date for any Easter Sunday from 1982 to 2048 as follows (all variables are of type int):

```
a is year % 19
b is year % 4
c is year % 7
d is (19 * a + 24) % 30
e is (2 * b + 4 * c + 6 * d + 5) % 7
Easter Sunday is March (22 + d + e)*
```

Write a program that inputs the year and outputs the date (month and day) of Easter Sunday for that year. Echo-print the input as part of the output. For example:

```
Enter the year (for example, 1997):
1985
Easter is Sunday, April 7, in 1985.
```

4. The algorithm for computing the date of Easter can be extended easily to work with any year from 1900 to 2099. There are four years, 1954, 1981, 2049, and 2076, for which the algorithm gives a date that is seven days later than it should be. Modify the program for Problem 3 to check for these years and subtract 7 from the day of the month. This correction does not cause the month to change. Be sure to change the documentation for the program to reflect its broadened capabilities.

5. Write a C++ program that calculates and prints the diameter, the circumference, or the area of a circle, given the radius. The program inputs two data items. The first is a character—'D' (for diameter), 'C' (for circumference), or 'A' (for area)—to indicate the calculation needed. The next data value is a floating point number

---

*Notice that this formula can give a date in April.

with two digits after the decimal point indicating the radius of the particular circle.

The program should echo-print the input data. The output should be appropriately labeled and formatted to two decimal places. For example, if the input is

```
A 6.75
```

your program should print something like this:

```
The area of a circle with radius 6.75 is 143.14.
```

Here are the formulas you'll need:

Diameter $= 2r$
Circumference $= 2\pi r$
Area of a circle $= \pi r^2$

where r is the radius. Use 3.14159265 for π.

6. The factorial of a number n is $n * (n-1) * (n-2) * \ldots * 2 * 1$. Stirling's formula approximates the factorial for large values of n:

$$\frac{n^n \sqrt{2\pi n}}{e^n}$$

where $\pi = 3.14159265$ and $e = 2.718282$.

Write a C++ program that inputs an integer value (but stores it into a `float` variable n), calculates the factorial of n using Stirling's formula, assigns the (rounded) result to a `long` integer variable, and then prints the result appropriately labeled.

Depending on the value of n, you should obtain one of these results:

- A numerical result.
- If n equals 0, the factorial is defined to be 1.
- If n is less than 0, the factorial is undefined.
- If n is too large, the result exceeds LONG_MAX.

(LONG_MAX is a constant declared in the header file `limits.h`. It gives the maximum `long` value for your particular machine and C++ compiler.)

Because Stirling's formula is used to calculate the factorial of very large numbers, the factorial will approach LONG_MAX quickly. If the factorial exceeds LONG_MAX, it will cause an arithmetic overflow in the computer, in which case the program will either stop running or continue with a strange-looking integer result, perhaps negative. Before you write the program, then, you first must write a small program that lets you determine, by trial and error, the largest value of n for which your computer system can compute a factorial using Stirling's formula. After you've determined this value, you can write the program using nested Ifs that print different messages depending on the value of n. If n is within the acceptable range for your computer system, write the number and the result with an appropriate message. If n is 0, write the message, "The number is 0. The factorial is 1.". If the number is less than 0, write "The number is less than 0. The factorial is undefined.". If the number is greater than the largest value of n for which your computer system can compute a factorial, write "The number is too large.".

Suggestion: Don't compute Stirling's formula directly. The values of n^n and e^n can be huge, even in floating point form. Take the natural logarithm of the formula and manipulate it algebraically to work with more reasonable floating point values. If r is the result of these intermediate calculations, the final result is e^r. Make use of the standard library functions `log` and `exp`, available through the header file `math.h`. These functions, described in Appendix C, compute the natural logarithm and natural exponentiation, respectively.

CASE STUDY FOLLOW-UP

1. In the Activity program, the `endl` manipulator appears five times, once in each output statement. Show how to eliminate this duplication of code by using `endl` just once after the appropriate message is printed.
2. For the Activity program, insert validation tests to exclude temperatures beyond 125 degrees and below −40 degrees. Provide constructive error messages to the user.
3. How would you modify the prompt in the Activity program so that the user avoids violating the constraints in Question 2?
4. Write the preconditions and postconditions for the modules in the Notices program.
5. Change the revised LumberYard program (page 236) so that if a code other than 'L' or 'P' is entered, the other two tests are avoided. Also, if the code is an 'L', do not test for the 'P'.

6

Looping

- To be able to construct syntactically correct While loops.
- To be able to construct count-controlled loops with a While statement.
- To be able to construct event-controlled loops with a While statement.
- To be able to use the end-of-file condition to control the input of data.
- To be able to use flags to control the execution of a While statement.
- To be able to construct counting loops with a While statement.
- To be able to construct summing loops with a While statement.
- To be able to choose the correct type of loop for a given problem.
- To be able to construct nested While loops.
- To be able to write the invariant conditions for a loop and use them to verify the loop.
- To be able to choose data sets that test a looping program comprehensively.

In Chapter 5, we said that the flow of control in a program can differ from the physical order of the statements. The *physical order* is the order in which the statements appear in a program; the order in which we want the statements to be executed is called the *logical order*.

The If statement is one way of making the logical order different from the physical order. Looping control structures are another. A **loop** executes the same statement (simple or compound) over and over, as long as a condition or set of conditions is met.

Loop   A control structure that causes a sequence of statements to be executed repeatedly.

In this chapter, we discuss different types of loops and how they are constructed using the While statement. We also discuss *nested loops* (loops that contain other loops) and introduce a notation for comparing the amount of work done by different algorithms.

 ## The While Statement

The While statement, like the If statement, tests a condition. Here is the syntax template for the While statement:

WhileStatement

```
while ( Expression )
    Statement
```

and this is an example of one:

```
while (inputVal != 25)
    cin >> inputVal;
```

The While statement is a looping control structure. The statement to be executed each time through the loop is called the *body* of the loop. In the example above, the body of the loop is the input statement that reads in a value for `inputVal`.

Just like the condition in an If statement, the condition in a While statement can be an expression of any simple data type. Nearly always, it is a logical (Boolean) expression. The While statement says, "If the value of the expression is nonzero (TRUE), execute the body and then go back and test the expression again. If the expression's value is zero (FALSE), skip the body." So the loop body is executed over and over as long as the expression is TRUE when it is tested. When the expression is FALSE, the program skips the body and execution continues at the statement immediately following the loop. Of course, if the expression is FALSE to begin with, the body is not even executed. Figure 6-1 shows the flow of control of the While statement, where Statement1 is the body of the loop and Statement2 is the statement following the loop.

The body of a loop can be a compound statement (block), which allows us to execute any group of statements repeatedly. Most often you'll use While loops in the following form:

```
while (Expression)
{
    .
    .
    .
}
```

In this structure, if the expression is TRUE, the entire sequence of statements in the block is executed, and then the expression is checked again. If it is still TRUE, the statements are executed again. The cycle continues until the expression becomes FALSE.

■ FIGURE 6-1

While Statement
Flow of Control

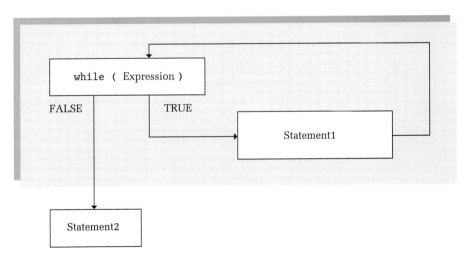

■ FIGURE 6-2   A Comparison of If and While

IF-THEN STATEMENT

| if (Expression) |
FALSE   TRUE

| Statement1 |

| Statement2 |

WHILE STATEMENT

| while (Expression) |
FALSE   TRUE

| Statement1 |

| Statement2 |

Although in some ways the If and While statements are alike, there are fundamental differences between them (see Figure 6-2). In the If structure, Statement1 is either skipped or executed exactly once. In the While structure, Statement1 can be skipped, executed once, or executed over and over. The If is used to *choose* a course of action; the While is used to *repeat* a course of action.

Phases of Loop Execution

The body of a loop is executed in several phases:

- The moment that the flow of control reaches the first statement inside the loop body is the **loop entry**.
- Each time the body of a loop is executed, a pass is made through the loop. This pass is called an **iteration**.
- Before each iteration, control is transferred to the **loop test** at the beginning of the loop.
- When the last iteration is complete and the flow of control has passed to the first statement following the loop, the program has **exited the loop**. The condition that causes a loop to be exited is the **termination condition**. In the case of a While loop, the termination condition is that the While expression becomes zero (FALSE).

Loop Entry   The point at which the flow of control reaches the first statement inside a loop.

Iteration   An individual pass through, or repetition of, the body of a loop.

Loop Test   The point at which the While expression is evaluated and the decision is made either to begin a new iteration or skip to the statement immediately following the loop.

Loop Exit   The point at which the repetition of the loop body ends and control passes to the first statement following the loop.

Termination Condition   The condition that causes a loop to be exited.

Notice that the loop exit occurs only at one point: when the loop test is performed. Even though the termination condition may become satisfied midway through the execution of the loop, the current iteration is completed before the computer checks the While expression again.

The concept of looping is fundamental to programming. In this chapter, we spend some time looking at typical types of loops and ways of implementing them with the While statement. These looping situations come up again and again when you are analyzing problems and doing top-down designs.

 Loops Using the While Statement

In solving problems, you will come across two major types of loops: **count-controlled loops,** which repeat a specified number of times, and **event-controlled loops,** which repeat until something happens within the loop.

Count-Controlled Loop   A loop that executes a specified number of times.

Event-Controlled Loop   A loop that terminates when something happens inside the loop body to signal that the loop should be exited.

If you are making an angel food cake and the recipe reads, "Beat the mixture 300 strokes," you are executing a count-controlled loop. If you are making a pie crust and the recipe reads, "Cut with a pastry blender until the mixture resembles coarse meal," you are executing an event-controlled loop; you don't know ahead of time the exact number of loop iterations.

Count-Controlled Loops

A count-controlled loop uses a variable we call the *loop control variable* in the loop test. Before we enter a count-controlled loop, we have to *initialize* (set the initial value of) the loop control variable and then test it. Then, as part of each iteration of the loop, we must *increment* (increase by 1) the loop control variable. Here's an example:

```
loopCount = 1;                        // Initialization
while (loopCount <= 10)               // Test
{
     .
     .                                // Repeated actions
     .
    loopCount = loopCount + 1;        // Incrementation
}
```

Here `loopCount` is the loop control variable. It is set to 1 before loop entry. The While statement tests the expression

```
loopCount <= 10
```

and executes the loop body as long as the expression is TRUE. The dots inside the compound statement represent a sequence of statements to be repeated. The last statement in the loop body increments `loopCount` by adding 1 to it.

Look at the statement in which we increment the loop control variable. Notice its form:

```
variable = variable + 1;
```

This statement adds 1 to the value of the variable, and the result replaces the old value. Variables that are used this way are called *counters*. In our example, `loopCount` is incremented with each iteration of the loop—we use it to count the iterations. The loop control variable of a count-controlled loop is always a counter.

We've encountered another way of incrementing a variable in C++. The incrementation operator (++) increments the variable that is its operand. The statement

```
loopCount++;
```

has precisely the same effect as the assignment statement

```
loopCount = loopCount + 1;
```

When designing loops, it is the programmer's responsibility to see that the condition to be tested is set correctly (initialized) before the While statement begins. The programmer also must make sure the condition changes within the loop so that it becomes FALSE at some point; otherwise, the loop is never exited.

```
loopCount = 1;              ← Variable loopCount must be initialized
while (loopCount <= 10)
{
    .
    .
    .
    loopCount++;            ← loopCount must be incremented
}
```

A loop that does not exit is called an *infinite loop* because, in theory, the loop executes forever. In the code above, omitting the incrementation of loopCount at the bottom of the loop leads to an infinite loop; the While expression is always TRUE because the value of loopCount is forever 1. If your program goes on running for much longer than you expect it to, chances are that you've created an infinite loop. You may have to issue an operating system command to stop the program.

How many times does the loop in our example execute—9 or 10? To determine this, we have to look at the initial value of the loop control variable and then at the test to see what its final value is. Here we've initialized loopCount to 1, and the test indicates that the loop body is executed for each value of loopCount up through 10. If loopCount starts out at 1 and runs up to 10, the loop body is executed 10 times. If we want the loop to execute 11 times, we have to either initialize loopCount to 0 or change the test to

```
loopCount <= 11
```

Event-Controlled Loops

There are several kinds of event-controlled loops: sentinel-controlled, end-of-file-controlled, and flag-controlled. In all of these loops, the termination condition depends on some event occurring while the loop body is executing.

Sentinel-Controlled Loops Loops often are used to read in and process long lists of data. Each time the loop body is executed, a new piece of data is read and processed. Often a special data value, called a *sentinel* or *trailer*

value, is used to signal the program that there is no more data to be processed. Looping continues as long as the data value read is *not* the sentinel; the loop stops when the program recognizes the sentinel. In other words, reading the sentinel value is the event that controls the looping process.

A sentinel value must be something that never shows up in the normal input to a program. For example, if a program reads calendar dates, we could use February 31 as a sentinel value:

```
// This code is incorrect:

while ( !(month == 2 && day == 31) )
{
    cin >> month >> day;                    // Get a date
        .
        .                                   // Process it
        .
}
```

There is a problem in the loop in the example above. The values of month and day are not defined before the first pass through the loop. Somehow we have to initialize these variables. We could assign them arbitrary values, but then we would run the risk of those values being processed as data. Also, it's inefficient to initialize variables with values that are never used.

We can solve the problem by reading the first set of data values *before* entering the loop. This is called a *priming read.* (The idea is similar to priming a pump by pouring a bucket of water into the mechanism before starting it.) Let's add the priming read to the loop:

```
// This is still incorrect:

cin >> month >> day;                       // Get a date--priming read
while ( !(month == 2 && day == 31) )
{
    cin >> month >> day;                   // Get a date
        .
        .                                  // Process it
        .
}
```

There is still a problem here. Notice that the first thing the program does inside the loop is to get a date, destroying the values obtained by the priming read. Thus, the first date in the data list is never processed. Given the priming read, the *first* thing that the loop body should do is process the data that have already been read. But then at what point do we read the next data set? We do this *last.* In this way, the While condition is applied to the next data set before it gets processed. Here's how it looks:

```
// This version is correct:

cin >> month >> day;                    // Get a date--priming read
while ( !(month == 2 && day == 31) )
{
      .
      .                                 // Process it
      .
    cin >> month >> day;                // Get the next date
}
```

This segment works fine. The first data set is read in; if it is not the sentinel, it gets processed. At the end of the loop, the next data set is read in, and we go back to the beginning of the loop. If the new data set is not the sentinel, it gets processed just like the first. When the sentinel value is read, the While expression becomes FALSE, and the loop exits (*without* processing the sentinel).

Many times the problem dictates the value of the sentinel. For example, if the problem does not allow data values of 0, then the sentinel value should be 0. Sometimes a combination of values is invalid. The combination of February and 31 as a date is such a case. Sometimes a range of values (negative numbers, for example) is the sentinel. And when you process char data, one line of input at a time, the newline character ('\n') often serves as the sentinel. Here's a code segment that reads and prints all of the characters on an input line (inChar is of type char):

```
cin.get(inChar);               // Get first character
while (inChar != '\n')
{
    cout << inChar;            // Echo it
    cin.get(inChar);          // Get next character
}
```

(Notice that for this particular task we use the get function, not the >> operator, to input a character. Remember that the >> operator skips whitespace characters—including blanks and newlines—to find the next data value in the input stream. In this example, we want to input *every* character, even a blank and especially the newline character.)

When you are choosing a value to use as a sentinel, what happens if there aren't any invalid data values? Then you may have to input an extra value in each iteration, a value whose only purpose is to signal the end of the data. For example, look at this code segment:

```
cin >> dataValue >> sentinel;         // Get first data value
while (sentinel == 1)
```

```
{
    .
    .                                    // Process it
    .
    cin >> dataValue >> sentinel;   // Get next data value
}
```

The second value on each line of the following data set is used to indicate whether or not there are more data. In this data set, when the sentinel value is 0, there are no more data; when it is 1, there are more data.

Data values	*Sentinel values*
↘	✓
10	1
0	1
-5	1
8	1
-1	1
47	0

What happens if you forget to enter the sentinel value? In an interactive program, the loop executes again, prompting for input. At that point, you can enter the sentinel value, but your program logic may be wrong if you already entered what you thought was the sentinel value. If the input to the program is from a file, once all the data have been read from the file, the loop body is executed again. However, there aren't any data left—because the computer has reached the end of the file—so the file stream enters the fail state. In the next section, we describe a way to use the end-of-file situation as an alternative to using a sentinel.

Before we go on, we mention an issue that is related not to the design of loops but to C++ language usage. In Chapter 5, we talked about the common mistake of using the assignment operator (=) instead of the relational operator (==) in an If condition. This same mistake can happen when you write While statements. See what happens when we use the wrong operator in the previous example:

```
cin >> dataValue >> sentinel;
while (sentinel = 1)                      // Whoops
{
    .
    .
    .
    cin >> dataValue >> sentinel;
}
```

This mistake creates an infinite loop. The While expression is now an assignment expression, not a relational expression. The expression's value is 1 (interpreted by the computer as TRUE), and its side effect is to store the value 1 into sentinel, replacing the value that was just input into the variable. Because the While expression is always TRUE, the loop never stops.

End-of-File-Controlled Loops You already have learned that an input stream (such as cin or an input file stream) goes into the fail state (a) if it encounters unacceptable input data, (b) if the program tries to open a nonexistent input file, or (c) if the program tries to read past the end of an input file. Let's look at the third of these three possibilities.

After a program has read the last piece of data from an input file, the computer is at the end of the file (EOF, for short). At this moment, the stream state is all right. But if we try to input even one more data value, the stream goes into the fail state. We can use this fact to our advantage. To write a loop that inputs an unknown number of data items, we can use the failure of the input stream as a "sentinel."

In Chapter 5, we described how to test the state of an I/O stream. In a logical expression, we use the name of the stream as though it were a Boolean variable:

```
if (inFile)
    .
    .
    .
```

In a test like this, the result is nonzero (TRUE) if the most recent I/O operation succeeded, or zero (FALSE) if it failed. In a While statement, testing the state of a stream works the same way. Suppose we have a data file containing integer values. If inData is the name of the file stream in our program, here's a loop that reads and echoes all of the data values in the file:

```
inData >> intVal;          // Get first value
while (inData)             // While the input succeeded ...
{
    cout << intVal << endl;  // Echo it
    inData >> intVal;      // Get next value
}
```

Let's trace this code, assuming there are three values in the file: 10, 20, and 30. The priming read inputs the value 10. The While condition is TRUE because the input succeeded. Therefore, the computer executes the loop body. First the body prints out the value 10, and then it inputs the second data value, 20. Looping back to the loop test, the expression inData is TRUE because the input succeeded. The body executes again, printing the value 20 and reading the value 30 from the file. Looping back to the test, the expression is TRUE. Even though we are at the end of the file, the stream state is still okay—the previous input operation succeeded. The body executes a third time, printing the value 30 and executing the input statement. This time, the input statement fails; we're trying to read beyond the end of the file. The stream inData enters the fail state. Looping back to the loop test, the value of the expression is zero (FALSE) and we exit the loop.

When we write EOF-controlled loops like the one above, we are expecting that end-of-file is the reason for stream failure. But keep in mind that *any* input error causes stream failure. The above loop terminates, for example, if input fails because of invalid characters in the input data. This fact emphasizes again the importance of echo printing. It helps us verify that all the data were read correctly before EOF was encountered.

EOF-controlled loops are similar to sentinel-controlled loops in that the program doesn't know in advance how many data items are to be input. In the case of sentinel-controlled loops, the program reads until it encounters the sentinel value. With EOF-controlled loops, it reads until it reaches the end of the file.

Is it possible to use an EOF-controlled loop when we read from the standard input device (via the cin stream) instead of a data file? On many systems, yes. With the UNIX operating system, you can type Ctrl/D (that is, you hold down the Ctrl key and tap the D key) to signify end-of-file during interactive input. With the MS-DOS operating system, the end-of-file keystrokes are Ctrl/Z. Other systems use similar keystrokes. Here's a program segment that tests for EOF on the cin stream in UNIX:

```
cout << "Enter an integer (or Ctrl/D to quit): ";
cin >> someInt;
while (cin)
{
    cout << someInt << " doubled is " << 2 * someInt << endl;
    cout << "Next number (or Ctrl/D to quit): ";
    cin >> someInt;
}
```

Flag-Controlled Loops   A *flag* is a Boolean variable that is used to control the logical flow of a program. We can set a Boolean variable to TRUE before a While loop; then, when we want to stop executing the loop, we reset it to FALSE. That is, we can use the Boolean variable to record whether or not the event that controls the process has occurred. For example, the following program segment reads and sums values until the input value is negative. (nonNegative is the Boolean flag; all of the other variables are of type int.)

```
sum = 0;
nonNegative = TRUE;              // Initialize flag
while (nonNegative)
{
    cin >> number;
```

[handwritten margin notes:]
typedef int Boolean;
const Boolean True = 1;
const Boolean False = 0;
Boolean NonNegative;

```
    if (number < 0)              // Test input value
        nonNegative = FALSE;     // Set flag if event occurred
    else
        sum = sum + number;
}
```

Notice that we can code sentinel-controlled loops with flags. In fact, this code uses a negative value as a sentinel.

You do not have to initialize flags to TRUE; you can initialize them to FALSE. If you do, you must use the NOT operator (!) in the While expression and reset the flag to TRUE when the event occurs. Compare the code segment above with the one below; both perform the same task. (Assume that `negative` is a Boolean variable.)

```
sum = 0;
negative = FALSE;               // Initialize flag
while ( !negative )
{
    cin >> number;
    if (number < 0)             // Test input value
        negative = TRUE;        // Set flag if event occurred
    else
        sum = sum + number;
}
```

As one more example, look at the While statement in the Payroll program of Chapter 1 (page 35). This is a sentinel-controlled loop because an employee number (empNum) with a value of 0 is used to stop the loop. We could have used a flag instead, as follows. (`moreData` is a Boolean variable.)

```
cin >> empNum;
moreData = (empNum != 0);       // moreData is TRUE if empNum != 0
while (moreData)
{
        .
        .
        .
    cin >> empNum;              // Get the next employee number
    moreData = (empNum != 0);   // Update the flag accordingly
}
```

Looping Subtasks

We have been looking at ways to use loops to affect the flow of control in programs. Looping by itself does nothing. The loop body must perform a task in order for the loop to accomplish something. In this section, we look at three tasks—counting, summing, and keeping track of a previous value—that often are used in loops.

Counting   A common task in a loop is to keep track of the number of times the loop has been executed. For example, the program fragment below reads and counts input characters until it comes to a period. (inChar is of type char; count is of type int.) The loop in this example has a counter variable; but the loop is not a count-controlled loop because the variable is not being used as a loop control variable.

```
count = 0;                    // Initialize counter
cin.get(inChar);              // Read the first character
while (inChar != '.')
{
    count++;                  // Increment counter
    cin.get(inChar);          // Get the next character
}
```

The loop continues until a period is read. After the loop is finished, count contains one less than the number of characters read. That is, it counts the number of characters up to, but not including, the sentinel value (the period). Notice that if a period is the first character, the loop body is not entered and count contains a zero, as it should. We use a priming read here because the loop is sentinel-controlled.

The counter variable in this example is called an **iteration counter** because its value equals the number of iterations through the loop.

Iteration Counter   A counter variable that is incremented with each iteration of a loop.

According to our definition, the loop control variable of a count-controlled loop is an iteration counter. However, as you've just seen, not all iteration counters are loop control variables.

Summing   Another common looping task is to sum a set of data values. Notice in the example below that the summing operation is written the same way, regardless of how the loop is controlled.

```
sum = 0;                      // Initialize the sum
count = 1;
while (count <= 10)
{
    cin >> number;            // Input a value
    sum = sum + number;       // Add the value to sum
    count++;
}
```

We initialize sum to 0 before the loop starts so that the first time the loop body executes, the statement

```
sum = sum + number;
```

adds the current value of sum (0) to number to form the new value of sum. After the entire code fragment has executed, sum contains the total of the 10 values read, count contains 11, and number contains the last value read.

Here count is being incremented in each iteration. For each new value of count, there is a new value for number. Does this mean we could decrement count by 1 and inspect the previous value of number? No. Once a new value has been read into number, the previous value is gone forever unless we've saved it in another variable. You'll see how to do that in the next section.

Let's look at another example. We want to count and sum the first 10 odd numbers in a data set. We need to test each number to see if it is even or odd. (We can use the modulus operator to find out. If number % 2 equals 1, number is odd; otherwise, it's even.) If the input value is even, we do nothing. If it is odd, we increment the counter and add the value to our sum. We use a flag to control the loop because this is not a normal count-controlled loop. In the following code segment, all of the variables are of type int except the Boolean flag, lessThanTen.

```
count = 0;                          // Initialize event counter
sum = 0;                            // Initialize sum
lessThanTen = TRUE;                 // Initialize loop control flag
while (lessThanTen)
{
    cin >> number;                  // Get the next value
    if (number % 2 == 1)            // Is the value odd?
    {
        count++;                    // Yes--Increment counter
        sum = sum + number;         // Add value to sum
        lessThanTen = (count < 10); // Update loop control flag
    }
}
```

In this example, there is no relationship between the value of the counter variable and the number of times the loop is executed. We could have written the While expression this way:

```
while (count < 10)
```

but this might mislead a reader into thinking that the loop is count-controlled in the normal way. So, instead, we choose to control the loop with the flag lessThanTen, to emphasize that count is incremented only when an odd number is read. The counter in this example is an **event counter;** it is initialized to 0 and incremented only when a certain event occurs. The counter in the previous example was an *iteration counter;* it was initialized to 1 and incremented during each iteration of the loop.

Event Counter A variable that is incremented each time a particular event occurs.

Keeping Track of a Previous Value Sometimes we want to remember the previous value of a variable. Suppose we want to write a program that counts the number of not-equal operators (!=) in a file that contains a C++ program. We can do so by simply counting the number of times an exclamation mark (!) followed by an equal sign (=) appears in the input. One way in which to do this is to read the input file one character at a time, keeping track of the two most recent characters, the current value and the previous value. In each iteration of the loop, a new current value is read and the old current value becomes the previous value. When EOF is reached, the loop is finished. Here's a program that counts not-equal operators this way:

```cpp
//***********************************************************
// NotEqualCount program
// This program counts the occurrences of "!=" in a data file
//***********************************************************
#include <iostream.h>
#include <fstream.h>        // For file I/O

int main()
{
    int      count;        // Number of != operators
    char     prevChar;     // Last character read
    char     currChar;     // Character read in this loop iteration
    ifstream inFile;       // Data file

    inFile.open("myfile.dat");          // Attempt to open input file
    if ( !inFile )                      // Was it opened?
    {
        cout << "** Can't open input file **" // No--print message
            << endl;
        return 1;                       // Terminate program
    }
    count = 0;                  // Initialize counter
    inFile.get(prevChar);       // Initialize previous value
    inFile.get(currChar);       // Initialize current value
    while (inFile)              // While previous input succeeded...
    {
```

```
            if (currChar == '=' &&    // Test for event
                prevChar == '!')
                count++;              // Increment counter
            prevChar = currChar;     // Replace previous value
                                     //    with current value
            inFile.get(currChar);    // Get next value
    }
    cout << count << " != operators were found." << endl;
    return 0;
}
```

Study this loop carefully. It's going to come in handy. There are many times when you must keep track of the last value read in addition to the current value.

THEORETICAL FOUNDATIONS

Finite State Machines

Our program for counting not-equal operators is only one way of accomplishing the task. Another is to design the program using a finite state machine. A *finite state machine* is an idealized model of a very simple computer. It consists of a set of *states* and a set of *transition rules* for changing from one state to another.

For example, a thermostat is a finite state machine with two states: on and off. And it has just two transition rules:

- If the measured temperature is less than the set temperature, switch from off to on.
- If the measured temperature is more than a degree warmer than the set temperature, switch from on to off.

Only one transition rule can be valid at a time.

THERMOSTAT STATE DIAGRAM

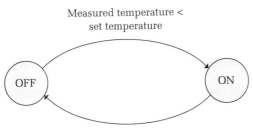

Measured temperature <
set temperature

OFF   ON

Measured temperature >
set temperature + 1

All around us are devices that can be modeled as finite state machines—traffic lights, automatic transmissions, washing machines, and elevators, for example. Each has specific states of operation and a set of rules for switching among them. In the following traffic light state diagram, notice that the lights are set to blinking red from 1:00 A.M. to 6:00 A.M.

TRAFFIC LIGHT STATE DIAGRAM

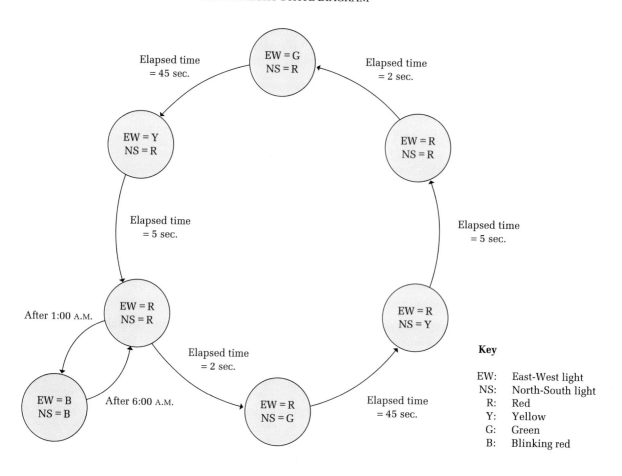

Finite state machines are not general-purpose computers. There are many problems that they cannot solve. But when a problem can be modeled as a set of states and transition rules, we can use a standard approach to writing an algorithm that solves it. Many of these problems are most easily solved with means-ends analysis, which we described in Chapter 1.

Let's rework the NotEqualCount program as a finite state machine. Here's the state diagram of the problem:

STATE DIAGRAM FOR "!=" COUNTER

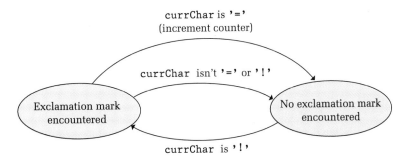

currChar is '='
(increment counter)

currChar isn't '=' or '!'

Exclamation mark
encountered

No exclamation mark
encountered

currChar is '!'

The first part of defining a finite state machine is to provide a way in which to keep track of the current state. Because there are only two states in this problem, we can use a single Boolean *state variable*, called exclamEncountered. When the variable is TRUE, the machine is in one state; when the variable is FALSE, it is in the other. (In our traffic light example, we would define two char variables eastWest and northSouth to be the state variables.)

Next, we have to determine which state the machine is in. For this, we use an If-Then-Else structure with one branch for each possible state.

```
if (exclamEncountered)
    .
    .          // Test for each transition rule from the state where
    .          //    exclamEncountered == TRUE
else
    .
    .          // Test for each transition rule from the state where
    .          //    exclamEncountered == FALSE
```

Within each state branch, we test for each transition rule that starts from that particular state. There are two rules that start from the exclamation-mark-encountered state and one that starts from the no-exclamation-mark-encountered state. Associated with each transition rule is some action that may be as simple as switching to another state, or much more complex.

```
if (exclamEncountered)               // State == '!' encountered
{
    if (currChar == '=')             // Rule: If currChar is '=',
    {
        count++;                 //          increment count
        exclamEncountered = FALSE; //        and switch states
    }
```

```
            else if (currChar != '!')        // Rule: If currChar isn't
                                             //          '=' or '!',
                exclamEncountered = FALSE;   //       switch states
        }
        else                                 // State == no '!' encountered
            if (currChar == '!')             // Rule: If currChar is '!',
                exclamEncountered = TRUE;    //       switch states
```

Next, we wrap these state tests and transition rules in a loop that applies them to each input character. In addition, we must specify a starting state for the finite state machine by initializing all of the state variables. In this case, we just have to set exclamEncountered to FALSE. Here's the new program:

```
//**********************************************************************
// FiniteState program
// This program counts the occurrences of "!=" in a data file
// by simulating a finite state machine
//**********************************************************************
#include <iostream.h>
#include <fstream.h>        // For file I/O

typedef int Boolean;
const Boolean TRUE = 1;
const Boolean FALSE = 0;

int main()
{
    int        count;          // Number of != operators
    char       currChar;       // Current character
    Boolean    exclamEncountered;  // State variable
    ifstream inFile;           // Data file

    inFile.open("myfile.dat");
    if ( !inFile )
    {
        cout << "** Can't open input file **" << endl;
        return 1;
    }
    count = 0;
    exclamEncountered = FALSE;              // Initialize starting state
    inFile.get(currChar);
    while (inFile)
    {
        if (exclamEncountered)             // State == '!' encountered
        {
            if (currChar == '=')           // Rule: If currChar is '=',
            {
                count++;                   //          increment count
                exclamEncountered = FALSE; //          and switch states
            }
```

```
            else if (currChar != '!')      // Rule: If currChar isn't
                                           //          '=' or '!',
                exclamEncountered = FALSE; //       switch states
        }
        else                               // State == no '!' encountered
            if (currChar == '!')           // Rule: If currChar is '!',
                exclamEncountered = TRUE;  //       switch states
        inFile.get(currChar);
    }
    cout << count << " != operators were found." << endl;
    return 0;
}
```

The thing to notice about this program is that it keeps track of the previous input value without actually storing it into a variable. Instead, it simply remembers the one aspect of the value that pertains to the problem—namely, whether it was an exclamation mark or something else.

Program FiniteState is longer than program NotEqualCount. For such a simple problem, it's clearly less efficient to use a finite state machine approach than to store the previous value. However, for problems that are more complex—ones that involve many different states—finite state machines give us a way in which to organize the states so that we don't leave out any combinations.

Finite state machine models are used extensively in the development of compilers and operating systems. They also are an important tool in researching theoretical issues of computing.

 # How to Design Loops

It's one thing to understand how a loop works when you look at it and something else again to design a loop that solves a given problem. In this section, we look at how to design loops. We can divide the design process into two tasks: designing the control flow and designing the processing that takes place in the loop. And we can break each task into three phases: the task itself, initialization, and update. It's also important to specify the state of the program when it exits the loop, since a loop that leaves variables and files in a mess is not well designed.

There are seven different points to consider in designing a loop:

1. What is the condition that ends the loop?
2. How should the condition be initialized?
3. How should the condition be updated?
4. What is the process being repeated?
5. How should the process be initialized?
6. How should the process be updated?
7. What is the state of the program on exiting the loop?

We use these questions as a checklist. The first three help us design the parts of the loop that control its execution. The next three help us design the processing within the loop. The last question reminds us to make sure that the loop exits in an appropriate manner.

Designing the Flow of Control

The most important step in loop design is deciding what should make the loop stop. If the termination condition isn't well thought out, there's the potential for infinite loops and other mistakes. So here is our first question:

- What is the condition that ends the loop?

This question usually can be answered through a close examination of the problem statement. For example:

Key Phrase in Problem Statement	*Termination Condition*
"Sum 365 temperatures"	The loop ends when a counter reaches 365 (count-controlled loop).
"Process all the data in the file"	The loop ends when EOF occurs (EOF-controlled loop).
"Process until 10 odd integers have been read"	The loop ends when 10 odd numbers have been input (event counter).
"The end of the data is indicated by a negative test score"	The loop ends when a negative input value is encountered (sentinel-controlled loop).

Now we need statements that make sure the loop gets started correctly and statements that allow the loop to reach the termination condition. So we have to ask the next two questions:

- How should the condition be initialized?
- How should the condition be updated?

The answers to these questions depend on the type of termination condition.

Count-Controlled Loops If the loop is count-controlled, we initialize the condition by giving the loop control variable an initial value. For count-controlled loops that use an iteration counter, the initial value is usually 1. If the process requires the counter to run through a specific range of values, the initial value should be the lowest value in that range.

The condition is updated by increasing the value of the counter by 1 for each iteration. (Occasionally, you may come across a problem that requires a counter to count from some value *down* to a lower value. In this case, the initial value is the greater value, and the counter is decremented by 1 for each iteration.) So, for count-controlled loops that use an iteration counter, these are the answers to the questions:

- Initialize the iteration counter to 1.
- Increment the iteration counter at the end of each iteration.

If the loop is controlled by a variable that is counting an event within the loop, the control variable usually is initialized to 0 and is incremented each time the event occurs. For count-controlled loops that use an event counter, these are the answers to the questions:

- Initialize the event counter to 0.
- Increment the event counter each time the event occurs.

Sentinel-Controlled Loops In sentinel-controlled loops, a priming read may be the only initialization necessary. If the source of input is a file rather than the keyboard, it also may be necessary to open the file in preparation for reading. To update the condition, a new value is read at the end of each iteration. So, for sentinel-controlled loops, we answer our questions this way:

- Open the file, if necessary, and input a value before entering the loop (priming read).
- Input a new value for processing at the end of each iteration.

EOF-Controlled Loops EOF-controlled loops require the same initialization as sentinel-controlled loops. You must open the file, if necessary, and perform a priming read. Updating the loop condition happens implicitly; the stream state is updated to reflect success or failure every time a value is input. However, if the loop doesn't read any data, it will never reach EOF, so updating the loop condition means the loop must keep reading data.

Flag-Controlled Loops In flag-controlled loops, the Boolean flag variable must be initialized to TRUE or FALSE and then updated when the condition changes.

- Initialize the flag variable to TRUE or FALSE, as appropriate.
- Update the flag variable as soon as the condition changes.

In a flag-controlled loop, the flag variable essentially remains unchanged until it is time for the loop to end. Then the code detects some condition within the process being repeated that changes the value of the flag (through an assignment statement). Because the update depends on what the process does, at times we have to design the process before we can decide how to update the condition.

Designing the Process Within the Loop

Once we've determined the looping structure itself, we can fill in the details of the process. In designing the process, we first must decide what we want a single iteration to do. Assume for a moment that the process is going to execute only once. What tasks must the process perform?

- What is the process being repeated?

To answer this question, we have to take another look at the problem statement. The definition of the problem may require the process to sum up data values or to keep a count of data values that satisfy some test. For example:

Count the number of integers in the file howMany.

This statement tells us that the process to be repeated is a counting operation.

Here's another example:

Read a stock price for each business day in a week and compute the average price.

In this case, part of the process involves reading a data value. We have to conclude from our knowledge of how an average is computed that the process also involves summing the data values.

In addition to counting and summing, another common loop process is reading data, performing a calculation, and writing out the result. Many other operations can appear in looping processes. We've mentioned only the simplest here; we'll look at some other processes later on.

After we've determined the operations to be performed if the process is executed only once, we design the parts of the process that are necessary for it to be repeated correctly. We often have to add some steps to take into account the fact that the loop executes more than once. This part of the design typically involves initializing certain variables before the loop and then reinitializing or updating them before each subsequent iteration.

- How should the process be initialized?
- How should the process be updated?

For example, if the process within a loop requires that several different counts and sums be performed, each must have its own statements to initialize variables, increment counting variables, or add values to sums. Just deal with each counting or summing operation by itself—that is, first write the initialization statement, and then write the incrementing or summing statement. After you've done this for one operation, you go on to the next.

The Loop Exit

When the termination condition occurs and the flow of control passes to the statement following the loop, the variables used in the loop still contain values. And if the `cin` stream has been used, the reading marker has been left at some point in the stream. Or maybe an output file has new contents. If these variables or files are used elsewhere in the program, the loop must leave them ready to be used. So, the final step in designing a loop is answering this question:

- What is the state of the program on exiting the loop?

Now we have to consider the consequences of our design and double-check its validity. For example, suppose we've used an event counter and later processing depends on the number of events. It's important to be sure (with an algorithm walk-through) that the value left in the counter is the exact number of events—that it is not off by 1.

Look at this code segment:

```
commaCount = 1;            // This code is incorrect
cin.get(inChar);
while (inChar != '\n')
{
    if (inChar == ',')
        commaCount++;
    cin.get(inChar);
}
cout << commaCount << endl;
```

This loop reads characters from an input line and counts the number of commas on the line. However, when the loop terminates, `commaCount` equals the actual number of commas plus 1 because the loop initializes the event counter to 1 before any events take place. By determining the state of `commaCount` at loop exit, we've detected a flaw in the initialization. `commaCount` should be initialized to zero.

Designing correct loops depends as much on experience as it does on the application of design methodology. At this point, you may want to read through the first two problem-solving case studies at the end of the chapter to see how the loop design process is applied to some real problems.

Nested Logic

In Chapter 5, we described nested If statements. It's also possible to nest While statements. Both While and If statements contain statements and are themselves statements. So the body of a While statement or the branch of an

If statement can contain other While and If statements. By nesting, we can create complex control structures.

Suppose we want to extend our code for counting commas on one line, repeating it for all the lines in a file. We put an EOF-controlled loop around it:

```
cin.get(inChar);                // Initialize outer loop
while (cin)                     // Outer loop test
{
    commaCount = 0;             // Initialize inner loop
                               //    (Priming read is taken care of
                               //     by outer loop's priming read)
    while (inChar != '\n')      // Inner loop test
    {
        if (inChar == ',')
            commaCount++;
        cin.get(inChar);        // Update inner termination condition
    }
    cout << commaCount << endl;
    cin.get(inChar);            // Update outer termination condition
}
```

In this code, notice that we have omitted the priming read for the inner loop. The priming read for the outer loop has already "primed the pump." It would be a mistake to include another priming read just before the inner loop; the character read by the outer priming read would be destroyed before we could test it.

Let's examine the general pattern of a simple nested loop:

```
Initialize outer loop
while (Outer loop condition)
{
    .
    .
    .
    Initialize inner loop
    while (Inner loop condition)
    {
        Inner loop processing and update
    }
    .
    .
    .
    Outer loop update
}
```

Notice that each loop has its own initialization, test, and update. The dots represent places where processing may take place in the outer loop. It's possible for an outer loop to do no processing other than to execute the inner loop repeatedly. On the other hand, the inner loop might be just a small part of the processing done by the outer loop; there could be many statements preceding or following the inner loop.

Let's look at another example. For nested count-controlled loops, the pattern looks like this (where outCount is the counter for the outer loop, inCount is the counter for the inner loop, and limit1 and limit2 are the number of times each loop should be executed):

```
outCount = 1;                    // Initialize outer loop counter
while (outCount <= limit1)
{
    .
    .
    inCount = 1;                 // Initialize inner loop counter
    while (inCount <= limit2)
    {
        .
        .
        inCount++;               // Increment inner loop counter
    }
    .
    .
    outCount++;                  // Increment outer loop counter
}
```

Here, both the inner and outer loops are count-controlled loops, but the pattern can be used with any combination of loops. The following program fragment shows a count-controlled loop nested within an EOF-controlled loop. The outer loop inputs an integer value telling how many asterisks to print out across a row of the screen. (We use the numbers to the right of the code to trace the execution of the program below.)

```
cin >> starCount;                            1
while (cin)                                   2
{
    loopCount = 1;                            3
    while (loopCount <= starCount)            4
    {
        cout << '*';                          5
        loopCount++;                          6
    }
    cout << endl;                             7
    cin >> starCount;                         8
}
cout << "Goodbye" << endl;                    9
```

To see how this code works, let's trace its execution with these data values (<EOF> denotes the end-of-file keystrokes pressed by the user):

```
3
1
<EOF>
```

We'll keep track of the variables `starCount` and `loopCount`, as well as the logical expressions. To do this, we've numbered each line (except those containing only a left or right brace). As we trace the program, we indicate the first execution of line 3 by 3.1, the second by 3.2, and so on. Each loop iteration is enclosed by a large brace (see Table 6-1).

Table 6-1   *Code Trace*

Statement	Variables		Logical Expressions		
	starCount	*loopCount*	*cin*	*loopCount <= starCount*	*Output*
1.1	3	—	—	—	—
2.1	3	—	T	—	—
3.1	3	1	—	—	—
4.1	3	1	—	T	—
5.1	3	1	—	—	*
6.1	3	2	—	—	—
4.2	3	2	—	T	—
5.2	3	2	—	—	*
6.2	3	3	—	—	—
4.3	3	3	—	T	—
5.3	3	3	—	—	*
6.3	3	4	—	—	—
4.4	3	4	—	F	—
7.1	3	4	—	—	\n (newline)
8.1	1	4	—	—	—
2.2	1	4	T	—	—
3.2	1	1	—	—	—
4.5	1	1	—	T	—
5.4	1	1	—	—	*
6.4	1	2	—	—	—
4.6	1	2	—	F	—
7.2	1	2	—	—	\n (newline)
8.2	1	2	—	—	—
(null operation)					
2.3	1	2	F	—	—
9.1	1	2	—	—	Goodbye

Here's a sample run of the program. The user's input is in color. Again, the symbols <EOF> denote the end-of-file keystrokes pressed by the user (the symbols would not appear on the screen).

```
3
***
1
*
<EOF>
Goodbye
```

Because `starCount` and `loopCount` are variables, their values remain the same until they are explicitly changed, as indicated by the repeating values in Table 6-1. Only when the test is made are the values of the logical expressions `cin` and `loopCount <= starCount` shown. We've used dashes in those columns at all other times.

Designing Nested Loops

To design a nested loop, we begin with the outer loop. The process being repeated includes the nested loop as one of its steps. Because that step is more complex than a single statement, our top-down design methodology tells us to make it a separate module. We can come back to it later and design the nested loop just as we would any other loop.

For example, here's the design process for the code segment above:

1. *What is the condition that ends the loop?* EOF is reached in the input.
2. *How should the condition be initialized?* A priming read should be performed before the loop starts.
3. *How should the condition be updated?* An input statement should occur at the end of each iteration.
4. *What is the process being repeated?* Using the value of the current input integer, the code should print that many asterisks across one output line.
5. *How should the process be initialized?* No initialization is necessary.
6. *How should the process be updated?* A sequence of asterisks is output and then a newline character is output. There are no counter variables or sums to update.
7. *What is the state of the program on exiting the loop?* The `cin` stream is in the fail state (because the program tried to read past EOF), `starCount` contains the last integer read from the input stream, and the rows of asterisks have been printed along with a concluding message.

From the answers to these questions, we can write this much of the algorithm:

```
Read starCount
WHILE NOT EOF
   Print starCount asterisks
   Output newline
   Read starCount
Print "Goodbye"
```

After designing the outer loop, it's obvious that the process in its body (printing a sequence of asterisks) is a complex step that requires us to design an inner loop. So we repeat the methodology for the corresponding lower-level module:

1. *What is the condition that ends the loop?* An iteration counter exceeds the value of `starCount`.
2. *How should the condition be initialized?* The iteration counter should be initialized to 1.
3. *How should the condition be updated?* The iteration counter is incremented at the end of each iteration.
4. *What is the process being repeated?* The code should print a single asterisk on the standard output device.
5. *How should the process be initialized?* No initialization is needed.
6. *How should the process be updated?* No update is needed.
7. *What is the state of the program on exiting the loop?* A single row of asterisks has been printed, the writing marker is at the end of the current output line, and `loopCount` contains a value one greater than the current value of `starCount`.

Now we can write the algorithm:

```
Read starCount
WHILE NOT EOF
   Set loopCount = 1
   WHILE loopCount <= starCount
      Print '*'
      Increment loopCount
   Output newline
   Read starCount
Print "Goodbye"
```

Of course, nested loops themselves can contain nested loops (called *doubly nested loops*), which can contain nested loops (*triply nested loops*), and so on. You can use this design process for any number of levels of nesting.

The trick is to defer details using the top-down methodology—that is, focus on the outermost loop first, and treat each new level of nested loop as a module within the loop that contains it.

It's also possible for the process within a loop to include more than one loop. For example, here's an algorithm that reads and prints people's names from a file, omitting the middle name in the output:

```
Read and print first name (ends with a comma)
WHILE NOT EOF
    Read and discard characters from middle name (ends with a comma)
    Read and print last name (ends at newline)
    Output newline
    Read and print first name (ends with a comma)
```

The steps for reading the first name, middle name, and last name require us to design three separate loops. All of these loops are sentinel-controlled.

This kind of complex control structure would be difficult to read if written out in full. There are simply too many variables, conditions, and steps to remember at one time. In the next two chapters, we examine the control structure that allows us to break programs down into more manageable chunks—the subprogram.

THEORETICAL FOUNDATIONS

The Magnitude of Work

There is usually more than one way to solve a problem. This may leave the programmer trying to choose the most efficient algorithm by deciding how much **work** is necessary to execute it.

Work   A measure of the effort expended by the computer in performing a computation.

How do we measure the amount of work required to execute an algorithm? We use the total number of *steps* executed as a measure of work. One statement, such as an assignment, may require only one step; another, such as a loop, may require many steps. We define a step as any operation roughly equivalent in complexity to a comparison, an I/O operation, or an assignment.

Given an algorithm with just a sequence of statements (no branches or loops), the number of steps performed is directly related to the number of statements. When we introduce branches, however, we make it possible to skip some statements in the algorithm. Branches allow us to subtract steps without physically removing them from the algorithm because only one branch is executed at a time. But because we always want to express work in terms of the worst-case scenario, we use the number of steps in the longest branch.

Now consider the effect of a loop. If a loop repeats a sequence of 15 simple statements 10 times, it performs 150 steps. Loops allow us to multiply the work done in an algorithm without physically adding statements.

Now that we have a measure for the work done in an algorithm, we can compare algorithms. For example, if Algorithm A always executes 3124 steps and Algorithm B always does the same task in 1321 steps, then we can say that Algorithm B is more efficient—that is, it takes fewer steps to accomplish the same task.

If an algorithm always takes the same number of steps regardless of how many data values it processes, we say that it executes in *constant time*. Be careful: Constant time doesn't mean small; it means that the amount of work done does not depend on the number of data values.

If a loop executes a fixed number of times, the work done is greater than the physical number of statements but is still constant. But what happens if the number of loop iterations can change from one run to the next? Suppose a data file contains N data values to be processed in a loop. If the loop reads and processes one value during each iteration, then the loop executes N iterations. The amount of work done thus depends on a variable, the number of data values. Algorithms that perform work directly proportional to the number of data values are said to execute in *linear time*. If we have a loop that executes N times, the number of steps to be executed is linearly dependent on N.

Specifically, the work done by an algorithm with a data-dependent loop is

Steps performed
by the loop

$$\overbrace{S_1 * N} + \underbrace{S_0}$$

Steps performed
outside the loop

where S_1 is the number of steps in the loop body (a constant for a given loop), N is the number of iterations (a variable), and S_0 is the number of steps outside the loop. (We can use this same formula for constant-time loops, but N would be a constant.) Notice that if N grows very large, the term $S_1 * N$ dominates the execution time. That is, S_0 becomes an insignificant part of the total execution time.

What about a data-dependent loop that contains a nested loop? The number of steps in the inner loop, S_2, and the number of iterations performed by the inner loop, L, must be multiplied by the number of iterations in the outer loop:

Steps performed by the nested loop		Steps performed by the outer loop		Steps performed outside the outer loop
$\overbrace{(S_2 * L * N)}$	$+$	$\overbrace{(S_1 * N)}$	$+$	$\overbrace{S_0}$

By itself, the inner loop performs $S_2 * L$ steps, but because it is repeated N times by the outer loop, it accounts for a total of $S_2 * L * N$ steps. If L is a constant, then the algorithm still executes in linear time.

Now, suppose that for each of the N outer loop iterations, the inner loop performs N steps ($L = N$). Here the formula for the total steps is

$$(S_2 * N * N) + (S_1 * N) + S_0$$

or

$$(S_2 * N^2) + (S_1 * N) + S_0$$

Because N^2 grows much faster than N (for large values of N), the inner loop term $(S_2 * N^2)$ accounts for the majority of steps executed and the work done. So the corresponding execution time is essentially proportional to N^2. If we have a doubly nested loop, where each loop depends on N, then the expression is

$$(S_3 * N^3) + (S_2 * N^2) + (S_1 * N) + S_0$$

and the work and time are proportional to N^3 whenever N is reasonably large.

The table below shows the number of steps required for each increase in the exponent of N.

N	N^0 (Constant)	N^1 (Linear)	N^2 (Quadratic)	N^3 (Cubic)
1	1	1	1	1
10	1	10	100	1,000
100	1	100	10,000	1,000,000
1,000	1	1,000	1,000,000	1,000,000,000
10,000	1	10,000	100,000,000	1,000,000,000,000

As you can see, each time the exponent increases by 1, the number of steps is multiplied by an additional order of magnitude (factor of 10). That is, if N is made 10 times greater, the work involved in an N^2 algorithm increases by a factor of 100, and the work involved in an N^3 algorithm increases by a factor of 1000. To put this in more concrete terms, an algorithm with a doubly nested loop, in which each loop depends on the number of data values, takes 1000 steps for 10 input values and 1 trillion steps for 10,000 values. On a computer that executes 1 million instructions per second, the latter case would take more than 11 days to run.

The table also shows that the steps outside of the innermost loop account for an insignificant portion of the total number of steps as N gets bigger. Because the innermost loop dominates the total time, we classify an algorithm according to the highest order of N that appears in its work expression, called the *order of magnitude,* or simply the *order* of that expression. So we talk about algorithms being "order N squared" (or cubed or so on) or we describe them with what is called "Big-O notation." We express this order by putting the highest-order term in parentheses with a capital O in front. For example, $O(1)$ is constant time; $O(N)$ is linear time; $O(N^2)$ is quadratic time; and $O(N^3)$ is cubic time.

Determining the orders of different algorithms allows us to compare the work they require without having to program and execute them. For example, if you had an $O(N^2)$ algorithm and a linear algorithm that performed the same task, you probably would choose the linear algorithm. We say *probably* because an $O(N^2)$ algorithm actually may execute fewer steps than an $O(N)$ algorithm for small values of N. Remember that if N is small, the constants and lower-order terms in the work expression may be significant.

Although we generally ignore the lower-order terms, they do exist, giving us a polynomial expression when all the terms are written out. Thus, such algorithms are said to execute in *polynomial time* and form a broad class of algorithms that encompasses everything we've discussed so far.

In addition to polynomial-time algorithms, we encounter a logarithmic-time algorithm in Chapter 12. There are also factorial ($O(N!)$), exponential ($O(N^N)$), and hyperexponential ($O(N^{N^N})$) class algorithms, which can require vast amounts of time to execute and are beyond the scope of this course. For now, the important point to remember is that the looping control structure allows an algorithm to perform more work than the physical number of statements it contains.

PROBLEM-SOLVING CASE STUDY

Average Income by Gender

Problem: You've been hired by a law firm that is working on a sex discrimination case. Your firm has obtained a file of incomes, incFile, which contains the salaries for every employee in the company. Each salary amount is preceded by 'F' for female or 'M' for male. As a first pass in the analysis of these data, you've been asked to compute the average income for females and the average income for males.

Input: A file, incFile, of floating point salary amounts, with one amount per line. Each amount is preceded by a character ('F' for female, 'M' for male). This code is the first character on each input line and is followed by a blank, which separates the code from the amount.

PROBLEM-SOLVING CASE STUDY cont'd.

Output:

All the input data (echo print)
The number of females and their average income
The number of males and their average income

Discussion: The problem breaks down into three main steps. First, we have to process the data, counting and summing the salary amounts for each sex. Next, we compute the averages. Finally, we have to print the calculated results.

The first step is the most difficult. It involves a loop with several subtasks. We'll use our checklist of questions to develop these subtasks in detail.

1. *What is the condition that ends the loop?* The termination condition is EOF on the file incFile. It leads to the pseudocode While statement

   WHILE NOT EOF on incFile

2. *How should the condition be initialized?* We must open the file for input, and a priming read must take place.
3. *How should the condition be updated?* We must input a new data line with a gender code and amount at the end of each iteration. Here's the resulting algorithm:

   Open incFile for input (and verify the attempt)
   Read sex and amount from incFile
   WHILE NOT EOF on incFile

      .
      : (Process being repeated)
      Read sex and amount from incFile

4. *What is the process being repeated?* From our knowledge of how to compute an average, we know that we have to count the number of amounts and divide this number into the sum of the amounts. Because we have to do this separately for females and males, the process consists of four parts: counting the females and summing their incomes, and then counting the males and summing their incomes. We develop each of these in turn.
5. *How should the process be initialized?* femaleCount and femaleSum should be set to zero. maleCount and maleSum also should be set to zero.
6. *How should the process be updated?* When a female income is input, femaleCount is incremented, and the income is added to femaleSum. Oth-

erwise, an income is assumed to be for a male, so `maleCount` is incremented, and the amount is added to `maleSum`.

7. *What is the state of the program on exiting the loop?* The file stream
`incFile` is in the fail state; `femaleCount` contains the number of input values preceded by 'F'; `femaleSum` contains the sum of the values preceded
by 'F'; `maleCount` contains the number of values not preceded by 'F'; and
`maleSum` holds the sum of those values.

From the description of how the process is updated, we can see that the
loop must contain an If-Then-Else structure, with one branch for female incomes and the other for male incomes. Each branch must increment the correct event counter and add the income amount to the correct total. After the
loop has exited, we have enough information to compute and print the averages, dividing each total by the corresponding count.

Assumptions: There is at least one male and one female among all the
data sets. The only gender codes in the file are 'M' and 'F'—any other codes
are counted as 'M'. (This last assumption invalidates the results if there are
any illegal codes in the data. Programming Warm-Up Exercise 11 asks you to
change the program as necessary to address this problem.)
Now we're ready to write the complete algorithm:

Main Module   *Level 0*

> Separately count females and males, and sum incomes
> Compute average incomes
> Output results

Separately Count Females and Males, and Sum Incomes   *Level 1*

> Initialize ending condition
> Initialize process
> WHILE NOT EOF on incFile
>   Update process
>   Update ending condition

Compute Average Incomes

> Set femaleAverage = femaleSum / femaleCount
> Set maleAverage = maleSum / maleCount

PROBLEM-SOLVING CASE STUDY cont'd.

Output Results

> Print femaleCount and femaleAverage
> Print maleCount and maleAverage

Initialize Ending Condition

Level 2

> Open incFile for input (and verify the attempt)
> Read sex and amount from incFile

Initialize Process

> Set femaleCount = 0
> Set femaleSum = 0.0
> Set maleCount = 0
> Set maleSum = 0.0

Update Process

> Echo-print sex and amount
> IF sex is 'F'
>   Increment femaleCount
>   Add amount to femaleSum
> ELSE
>   Increment maleCount
>   Add amount to maleSum

Update Ending Condition

> Read sex and amount from incFile

Module Structure Chart:

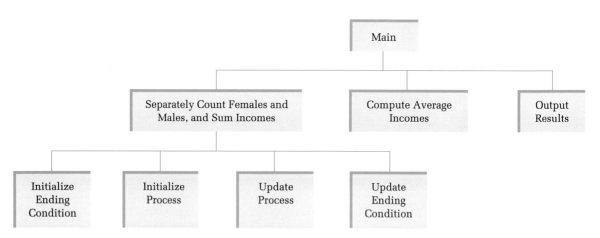

Now we can write the program:

```
//*****************************************************************
// Incomes program
// This program reads a file of income amounts classified by
// gender and computes the average income for each gender
//*****************************************************************
#include <iostream.h>
#include <iomanip.h>     // For setprecision()
#include <fstream.h>     // For file I/0

int main()
{
    char      sex;             // Coded 'F' = female, 'M' = male
    int       femaleCount;     // Number of female income amounts
    int       maleCount;       // Number of male income amounts
    float     amount;          // Amount of income for a person
    float     femaleSum;       // Total of female income amounts
    float     maleSum;         // Total of male income amounts
    float     femaleAverage;   // Average female income
    float     maleAverage;     // Average male income
    ifstream  incFile;         // File of income amounts

    cout.setf(ios::fixed, ios::floatfield);   // Set up floating pt.
    cout.setf(ios::showpoint);                //    output format
    cout << setprecision(2);

    // Separately count females and males, and sum incomes

    // Initialize ending condition
```

```cpp
        incFile.open("incfile.dat");          // Open input file
        if ( !incFile )                        //    and verify attempt
        {
            cout << "** Can't open input file **" << endl;
            return 1;
        }
        incFile >> sex >> amount;              // Perform priming read

        // Initialize process

        femaleCount = 0;
        femaleSum = 0.0;
        maleCount = 0;
        maleSum = 0.0;

        while (incFile)
        {
            // Update process

            cout << "Sex: " << sex << " Amount: " << amount << endl;
            if (sex == 'F')
            {
                femaleCount++;
                femaleSum = femaleSum + amount;
            }
            else
            {
                maleCount++;
                maleSum = maleSum + amount;
            }

            // Update ending condition

            incFile >> sex >> amount;
        }

        // Compute average incomes

        femaleAverage = femaleSum / float(femaleCount);
        maleAverage = maleSum / float(maleCount);

        // Output results

        cout << "For " << femaleCount << " females, the average "
             << "income is " << femaleAverage << endl;
        cout << "For " << maleCount << " males, the average "
             << "income is " << maleAverage << endl;
        return 0;
    }
```

Testing: With an EOF-controlled loop, the obvious test cases are a file with data and an empty file. We should test input values of both 'F' and 'M' for the gender, and try some typical data (so we can compare the results with our hand-calculated values) and some atypical data (to see how the process behaves). An atypical data set for testing a counting operation is an empty file, which should result in a count of zero. Any other result for the count indicates an error. For a summing operation, atypical data might include negative or zero values.

The Incomes program is not designed to handle empty files or negative income values. An empty file causes both `femaleCount` and `maleCount` to equal zero at the end of the loop. Although this is correct, the statements that compute average income cause the program to crash because they divide by zero. And a negative income would be treated like any other value, even though it is probably a mistake.

To correct these problems, we should insert If statements to test for the error conditions at the appropriate points in the program. When an error is detected, the program should print an error message instead of carrying out the usual computation. This prevents a crash and allows the program to keep running. We call a program that can recover from erroneous input and keep running a *robust program*.

*P*ROBLEM-SOLVING CASE STUDY

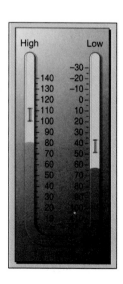

High and Low Temperatures

Here's another problem in loop design. In this case we design a count-controlled loop that finds the minimum and maximum values in a data set.

Problem: A heating oil company uses the temperature range for each day to determine its customers' typical oil use and to schedule deliveries. The firm has hired you to take hourly outdoor temperature readings for each 24-hour period and find the day's high and low temperatures from this data. Because you won't be getting much sleep on this job, you decide that it would be a good idea to have the computer keep track of the maximum and minimum values.

Input: Twenty-four integer numbers representing hourly temperatures.

Output:
The temperatures (echo print)
The day's high temperature
The day's low temperature

Discussion: This problem is easy to do by hand. We simply scan the list, looking for the highest and lowest values. How do we simulate this process in an algorithm? Well, let's look carefully at what we actually are doing.

To find the largest number in a list of numbers, we compare the first with the second and remember which one is larger. Then we compare that number with the third one, remembering the larger number. We repeat the process until we run out of numbers. The one we remember is the largest. We use the same process to find the smallest number, only we remember the smaller number instead of the larger one.

Now that we understand the process, we can design an algorithm for it:

1. *What is the condition that ends the loop?* Because there will be exactly 24 values in the list, we can use a counter to control the loop. When it exceeds 24, the loop exits.
2. *How should the condition be initialized?* The counter should be set to 1.
3. *How should the condition be updated?* The counter should be incremented at the end of each iteration.
4. *What is the process being repeated?* The process reads a value, echoprints it, and checks to see if it should replace the current high or low value.
5. *How should the process be initialized?* In other words, what values should the first number be compared to? We have to give the variables high and low starting values that are to change immediately. So we set high to the smallest number possible (INT_MIN), and we set low to the greatest number possible (INT_MAX). In this way, the first temperature read is less than low and greater than high and replaces the values in each. (If your C++ system doesn't supply the header file limits.h, in which INT_MIN and INT_MAX are defined, you could use numbers like 30000 and −30000 instead.)
6. *How should the process be updated?* In each iteration, a new temperature is input and compared with high and low. If it exceeds high, it replaces the old value of high. If it is less than low, it replaces the old value of low. Otherwise, high and low are unchanged. This tells us that the loop contains two If-Then structures, one each for comparing the input value against high and low.
7. *What is the state of the program on exiting the loop?* Twenty-four temperature values have been input and echo-printed. The loop control variable equals 25, high contains the largest of the input values, and low contains the smallest.

PROBLEM-SOLVING CASE STUDY cont'd.

Assumptions: At least 24 integer numbers will be input before EOF is reached. None of the data values is equal to INT_MAX or INT_MIN.

Main Module   *Level 0*

```
Initialize process
Initialize loop ending condition
WHILE hour <= number of hours in time period
    Update process
    Update loop ending condition
Print high and low temperatures
```

Initialize Process   *Level 1*

```
Set high = machine's minimum integer
Set low = machine's maximum integer
```

Initialize Loop Ending Condition

```
Set hour = 1
```

Update Process

```
Read temperature
Echo-print temperature
Lowest temperature so far?
Highest temperature so far?
```

Update Loop Ending Condition

```
Increment hour
```

PROBLEM-SOLVING CASE STUDY cont'd.

Print High and Low Temperatures

> Print "High temperature is ", high
> Print "Low temperature is ", low

Lowest Temperature So Far?   *Level 2*

> IF temperature < low
>   Set low = temperature

Highest Temperature So Far?

> IF temperature > high
>   Set high = temperature

Module Structure Chart:

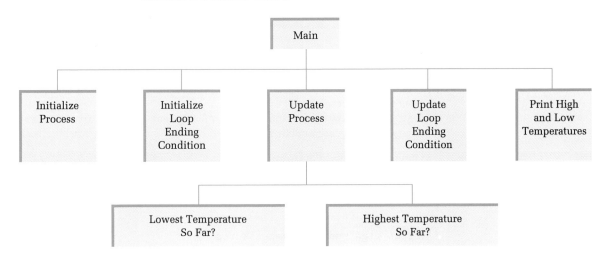

```cpp
//****************************************************************
// TempStat program
// This program calculates the high and low temperatures
// from 24 hourly temperature readings
//****************************************************************
#include <iostream.h>
#include <limits.h>          // For INT_MAX and INT_MIN

const int NUM_HRS = 24;   // Number of hours in time period

int main()
{
    int temperature;       // An hourly temperature reading
    int high;              // Highest temperature so far
    int low;               // Lowest temperature so far
    int hour;              // Loop control variable for hours in a day

    // Initialize process

    high = INT_MIN;                 // Set high to impossibly low value
    low = INT_MAX;                  // Set low to impossibly high value

    // Initialize loop ending condition

    hour = 1;

    while (hour <= NUM_HRS)
    {
        // Update process

        cin >> temperature;
        cout << temperature << endl;
        if (temperature < low)          // Lowest temperature so far?
            low = temperature;
        if (temperature > high)         // Highest temperature so far?
            high = temperature;

        // Update loop ending condition

        hour++;
    }

    // Print high and low temperatures

    cout << endl
         << "High temperature is " << high << endl
         << "Low temperature is " << low << endl;
    return 0;
}
```

Testing: Program TempStat reads 24 integer values. We can test the While statement by entering data values until the program outputs the high and low temperatures. If the program doesn't input exactly 24 numbers, there must be an error in the control of the loop.

We should try data sets that present the high and low temperatures in different orders. For example, we should try one set with the highest temperature as the first value and another set with it as the last. We should do the same for the lowest temperature. We also should try a data set in which the temperature goes up and down several times, and another in which the temperatures are all the same. Finally, we should test the program on some typical sets of data and check the output with results we've determined by hand. For example, given these data:

```
45 47 47 47 50 50 55 60 70 70 72 75
75 75 75 74 74 73 70 70 69 67 65 50
```

the final output of the high and low temperatures would look like this:

```
High temperature is 75
Low temperature is 45
```

What happens if we combine the two If-Then statements into one If-Then-Else, as shown below?

```
if (temperature < low)
    low = temperature;
else if (temperature > high)
    high = temperature;
```

At first glance, the single statement looks more efficient. Why should you ask if temperature is larger than high if you know it is lower than low? But this code segment gives the wrong answer if the highest temperature is the first value read in because of the way high and low are initialized.

In Programming Warm-Up Exercise 8, you are asked to redo the TempStat program using an initialization scheme that removes this data dependency. (*Hint:* Use a priming read and set high and low to that first value.)

PROBLEM-SOLVING CASE STUDY

Shipping Invoices

Problem: The Mill Hollow Boring and Bearing Company occasionally has to ship products outside its delivery area. The company has asked you to write a program that prints shipping invoices. Only one invoice is printed at a time, but each invoice may have several items on it.

The input—in a file `inFile`—is a series of data sets, one set per item, each on a separate line. Each data set contains the quantity of an item shipped, a description of the item, and the unit price of the item. The end of the data is indicated by an item quantity of zero or less. After the last data set is processed, the total number of items and the total amount should be output.

Input: A file `inFile`, where each line of input contains the quantity shipped of an item (`int`), followed by a blank, followed by a 30–character description of the item, followed by another blank and then the unit price of the item (`float`). The end of the data is indicated by an item quantity of zero or less. Here is a sample of the input data:

```
15 Titanium bearing assembly      14.35
42 Bore insert (Part no. 36JX425) 9.29
18 Assembly bolt packet           12.45
0
```

Output: An invoice with four columns of information: the quantity of each item shipped, a description of each item, the unit price of each item, and the billing amount for the given number of items. Each column should have an appropriate heading, as should the overall invoice. After the last item has been printed, the total number of units shipped and the total amount of the invoice should be printed.

Discussion: This program simply reads each line of data and prints out the quantity, description, price, and amount for the given number of units. Running sums of the quantity and amount values must be kept. There are two loops in this program: a sentinel-controlled loop to control the reading of the data sets and a nested count-controlled loop to read and print the string of 30 characters in the item description.

Outer Loop Design: The loop exits when a sentinel value of 0 or less is input for an item quantity. The termination condition is initialized by opening the file `inFile` and performing a priming read of the quantity. The condition is updated by reading a new quantity at the end of each iteration. The process is to read and print the data for an item, and to add the quantity and dollar amount for the item to running totals. The process is initialized by setting the totals to 0. It is updated by reading the data for an item, printing a line of the invoice, and adding the appropriate values to the totals.

When the loop ends, the following is true: The reading marker is positioned just beyond the sentinel value in the input file; an invoice line has been printed for each item; `quantity` contains the last quantity input; `price` contains the last price input; `inputChar` contains the last character in the final description; `blank` contains the character separating the last quantity and description; `amount` contains the price times the quantity of the last item ordered; `counter` equals 31; and the quantity of items ordered and their costs have been summed in `totalUnits` and `totalAmount`, respectively.

Inner Loop Design: The loop exits when the loop control variable exceeds 30. The loop control variable is initialized to 1 and incremented at the end of each iteration. The process is to read and print one character. No initialization or update is necessary because the reading and writing markers advance automatically. At loop exit, the reading marker should be on the character following the item description; the item description should be printed on the current line; and the loop control variable should be equal to 31.

In addition to printing an invoice line for each item, we must print *headings* at the top of the page and above each column. Programs that use loops often produce large amounts of output, and it is common to organize that output in columns with headings.

The first step in designing columnar output is to determine what is going to be printed. The next step is to make a sketch on graph paper of how the output should look. Line up the headings and put in some actual values. Once you have an acceptable design, count the number of character positions associated with each heading or data value.

Figure 6-3 shows a sample design for the output here. From it we can determine the appropriate fieldwidths for aligning headings with columns of values.

We now have enough information to write the algorithm:

Problem-Solving Case Study cont'd.

■ FIGURE 6-3   Formatting Output

```
                    Mill Hollow Boring and Bearing Company
                         128 East Southwest Street
                    North Old Newgate, New Hampshire   01010

                              Shipping Invoice

Quantity                    Description                    Price        Amount

    9999     XXXXXXXXXXXXXXXXXXXXXXXXXXXXXX    99999.99     9999999.99
    9999     XXXXXXXXXXXXXXXXXXXXXXXXXXXXXX    99999.99     9999999.99
Total Units Ordered:  99999999                           Total:  9999999.99
```

Main Module   *Level 0*

> Print headings
> Print body of invoice
> Print totals

Print Headings   *Level 1*

> Print centered "Mill Hollow Boring and Bearing Company"
> Print centered "128 East Southwest Street"
> Print centered "North Old Newgate, New Hampshire 01010"
> Print blank line
> Print centered "Shipping Invoice"
> Print blank line
> Print "Quantity", "Description", "Price", "Amount" to align with columns
> Print blank line

PROBLEM-SOLVING CASE STUDY cont'd.

Print Body of Invoice

Initialize process
Initialize ending condition
WHILE quantity > 0
    Update process
    Update ending condition

Print Totals

Print blank line
Print "Total Units Ordered:", totalUnits ,"Total:", totalAmount

Initialize Process

Level 2

Set totalUnits = 0
Set totalAmount = 0.0

Initialize Ending Condition

Open inFile for input (and verify the attempt)
Read quantity from inFile

Update Process

Print quantity (aligned with heading)
Read and print description (aligned with heading)
Read price from inFile
Print price (aligned with heading)
Set amount = quantity * price
Print amount (aligned with heading)
Add quantity to totalUnits
Add amount to totalAmount

Update Ending Condition

> Read quantity from inFile

Read and Print Description   *Level 3*

> Read (and ignore) a blank from inFile
> Print four spaces
> Set counter = 1
> WHILE counter <= DESCR_LENGTH
>   Read a character from inFile
>   Print the character
>   Increment counter

Module Structure Chart:

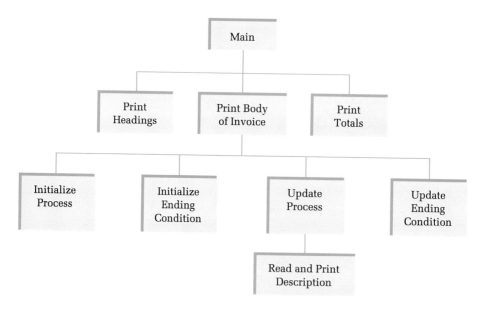

Here is the program:

```
//**************************************************************
// Invoice program
// This program prints a shipping invoice given quantities,
// item descriptions, and unit prices as read from a data file
//**************************************************************
#include <iostream.h>
#include <iomanip.h>      // For setw() and setprecision()
#include <fstream.h>      // For file I/O

const int DESCR_LENGTH = 30;     // Characters in an item description

int main()
{
    int      quantity;         // Number of items ordered
    int      totalUnits;       // Total items in invoice
    int      counter;          // Loop control variable for printing
                               //    description
    float    price;            // Unit price for an item
    float    amount;           // Amount for quantity of items
    float    totalAmount;      // Total amount of invoice
    char     blank;            // Dummy variable to hold blanks
    char     inputChar;        // Holds one character of description
    ifstream inFile;           // File containing item quantities,
                               //    descriptions, and prices

    cout.setf(ios::fixed, ios::floatfield);  // Set up floating pt.
    cout.setf(ios::showpoint);               //    output format
    cout << setprecision(2);

    // Print headings

    cout << setw(50) << "Mill Hollow Boring and Bearing Company"
         << endl;
    cout << setw(43) << "128 East Southwest Street" << endl;
    cout << setw(50) << "North Old Newgate, New Hampshire  01010"
         << endl;
    cout << endl;
    cout << setw(38) << "Shipping Invoice" << endl;
    cout << endl;
    cout << "Quantity" << setw(22) << "Description"
         << setw(19) << "Price" << setw(11) << "Amount" << endl;
    cout << endl;

    // Print body of invoice
```

```
// Initialize process

totalUnits = 0;
totalAmount = 0.0;

// Initialize ending condition

inFile.open("invoice.dat");
if ( !inFile )
{
    cout << "** Can't open input file **" << endl;
    return 1;
}
inFile >> quantity;

while (quantity > 0)
{
    // Update process

    cout << setw(6) << quantity;

    // Read and print description

    inFile.get(blank);              // Discard extra blank
    cout << "      ";
    counter = 1;                    // Initialize loop control
                                    //    variable
    while (counter <= DESCR_LENGTH)
    {
        inFile.get(inputChar);      // Process
        cout << inputChar;
        counter++;                  // Update loop control
    }                               //    variable

    inFile >> price;
    cout << setw(10) << price;
    amount = quantity * price;
    cout << setw(12) << amount << endl;
    totalUnits = totalUnits + quantity;
    totalAmount = totalAmount + amount;

    // Update ending condition

    inFile >> quantity;
}
```

```
// Print totals

cout << endl;
cout << "Total Units Ordered:" << setw(9) << totalUnits
     << setw(21) << "Total:" << setw(12) << totalAmount << endl;
return 0;
}
```

Testing: Because program Invoice is so complex, we discuss testing for it both here and in the next section. Here we look at the important points to watch for in testing data sets with typical values.

The output from this program, given valid test data, is an invoice consisting of three sections. The first section is the company name and address and the column headings. Carefully examine this section of the output for spelling mistakes, proper centering of the name and address, and correct spacing of the column headings.

The second section is the list of items being shipped. There should be one line in this section for each line of input. Check that the first and last lines of data have been processed correctly—it's in these lines that errors in loop control most often appear. Make sure that the columns of numbers are aligned under the appropriate headings. Compare the output in the Amount column with your hand-calculated results.

The third section of the output consists of the totals. Look for spelling and spacing errors, and compare the printed values against your hand-calculated results.

TESTING AND DEBUGGING

The Loop Invariant

In Chapter 5, we saw that an algorithm walk-through can be used to test a design before it is implemented. With this technique, we verify that each module's precondition is true before it executes and that its postcondition is true after it executes. Loops present some special problems in performing a walk-through because each iteration can behave differently. In order to test a data-dependent loop design, we would have to try every possible combination of input. In many cases, this is not practical because the possibilities are too numerous, if not infinite.

What we would like to do is treat a loop as a separate module, so we can use our standard walk-through technique. But in order to establish a fixed

precondition and postcondition for a loop, we must determine those characteristics that do not vary from one iteration to the next. The collection of all
these characteristics is called the **loop invariant,** an assertion that must always be true for the loop to execute correctly.

Loop Invariant   An assertion about the characteristics of a loop that must always be true for a loop to execute properly. The invariant is true on loop
entry, at the start of each loop iteration, and on exit from the loop. It is not
necessarily true at each point in the body of the loop.

At first, you might think that the invariant is just the While condition that
controls the loop. But an invariant must be TRUE when the loop exits; the
While condition is FALSE when the loop exits. Here are some examples:

While-Loop Condition	*Related Invariant Condition*
`loopControlVariable` < 366 (`loopControlVariable` is initialized to 1 before the loop.)	1 <= `loopControlVariable` <= 366
`oddCount` < 10 (`oddCount` is initialized to 0 before the loop.)	`oddCount` equals the number of odd numbers input AND 0 <= `oddCount` <= 10
`inputVal` >= 0 (`inputVal` is initialized before the loop.)	Only nonnegative data values are processed AND `inputVal` < 0 when the loop exits

You can see that an invariant condition is related to each While condition
but that they are not identical. The loop invariant and the While condition
must be true for the loop to execute; the loop invariant and the termination
condition (the negation of the While condition) must be true after the loop
exits. Let's state this relationship more precisely using logic symbols. Suppose we have a loop with While condition C:

```
while (C)
    Statement
```

Suppose further that the loop invariant is I and that P is the loop postcondition (the assertion that is true immediately after loop exit). Then the following should be true:

$(I$ AND (NOT $C)) \rightarrow P$

- One invoice line has been printed for each loop iteration AND
  The number of lines output is 1 less than the number of data sets input.

The invariant for the outer loop of the Invoice program is then the logical AND of all these assertions.

Loop Testing Strategy

Even if a loop has been properly designed and verified, it is still important to test it rigorously, because there is always the chance of an error creeping in during the implementation phase. Because loops allow us to input many data sets in one run, and because there is the potential for each iteration to be affected by preceding ones, the test data for a looping program is usually more extensive than for a program with just sequential or branching statements. To test a loop thoroughly, we have to check for the proper execution of both a single iteration and multiple iterations.

Remember that a loop has seven parts (corresponding to the seven questions in our checklist). A test strategy must test each part. Although all seven parts aren't implemented separately in every loop, the checklist reminds us that some loop operations may serve multiple purposes, each of which should be tested. For example, the incrementing statement in a count-controlled loop may be updating both the process and the ending condition. So it's important to verify that it performs both actions properly with respect to the rest of the loop.

The loop invariant is a good place to start in designing test data. The invariant tells us what the acceptable ranges of variables are and what sorts of I/O operations we should see. To test a loop, we try to devise data sets that could cause the variables to go out of range or leave the files in improper states that violate either the loop postcondition or the postcondition of the module containing the loop.

In addition to tests based on the invariant, it's good practice to test a loop for four special cases: (1) when the loop is skipped entirely, (2) when the loop body is executed just once, (3) when the loop executes some normal number of times, and (4) when the loop fails to exit.

Statements following a loop often depend on its processing. If a loop can be skipped, those statements may not execute correctly. If it's possible to execute a single iteration of a loop, the results can show whether the body performs correctly in the absence of the effects of previous iterations, which can be very helpful when you're trying to isolate the source of an error. Obviously, it's important to test a loop under normal conditions, with a wide variety of inputs. If possible, you should test the loop with real data in addition to mock data sets. Count-controlled loops should be tested to be sure they execute exactly the right number of times. And finally, if there is any chance that a loop might never exit, your test data should try to make that happen.

where the symbol " → " is the *logical implication* (
nounced *implies*. In other words, we want to ensure tl
true *and* the While condition is false, *then* the loop pos

The loop invariant usually consists of other condit
related to the While condition. For example, it typical
of all the variables used in the loop and the status of a

To create the invariant, we begin with the loop p
swer to the last question on the loop design checklis
the program on exiting the loop?)—because it force
final condition of the variables and files. Then we w
ing the other questions on the checklist.

Let's write the invariant for the outer loop in th
begin with the part of the invariant associated with
that on loop exit, totalAmount contains the sum of
amounts. Then we look at how the process is initiali:
the related invariant condition:

- totalAmount >= 0 AND
  At the start of each iteration, totalAmount equals t
  of amount that have been computed.

In the same way, we look at the termination con(
update of totalUnits to determine the portion of th
it:

- totalUnits >= 0 AND
  At the start of each iteration, totalUnits equals
  of quantity that have been input so far.

Here are the invariant conditions for the othe
file:

- price either is undefined or contains a floating
  price contains the item price input in the
  iteration.
- amount either is undefined or contains a floatin
  amount contains the product quantity * pric
  cently completed iteration.
- quantity contains the most recently input qua
- counter either is undefined or contains the va
- inputChar either is undefined or contains th
  description input in the previous iteration.
- blank either is undefined or contains the cha
  and the item description input in the previou
- The reading marker in inFile is positione
  quantity input.

In addition to the status of variables and
some general invariant conditions. For exampl

Testing a program can be as challenging as writing it. To test a program, you have to step back, take a fresh look at what you've written, and then attack it in every way possible to make it fail. This isn't always easy to do, but it's necessary if your programs are going to be reliable. (A *reliable program* is one that works consistently and without errors regardless of whether the input data is valid or invalid.)

To verify an algorithm, we use the loop invariant as a bridge between the statements that precede and follow the loop. We have to show that the invariant is true before entering the loop. If the loop is designed correctly, the invariant should still be true when the termination condition is reached.

To show that the invariant is true before loop entry, we compare the current set of conditions (the postconditions from the preceding statements) with the invariant. If the invariant is a subset of the current conditions, then the loop is ready to start. If the invariant contains an assertion that has not been established, then something is missing in our preparations for executing the loop. Most often, the missing item is an initialization such as assigning a beginning value to a loop control variable or performing a priming read.

Once we know that the invariant is true at loop entry, we must show that the invariant is true at the start of each iteration. We do this by walking through the body of the loop and determining the postcondition of each statement. Then we compare the postcondition of the last statement in the loop to the invariant. If any part of the invariant is not satisfied by these conditions, there is something wrong with the loop. Otherwise, we know that the invariant is true at the beginning of the next iteration.

When the loop exits, its termination condition is true (that is, the While condition is false). The postcondition of the loop is, in part, the conjunction (logical AND) of the termination condition and the invariant. The postcondition also includes any conditions that existed before the loop that have not changed.

Let's tie all this together with an example: summing the integers 1 through 10.

```
// SumUp program

int main()
{
    int sum;
    int number;

    sum = 0;
    number = 1;
```

```
while (number <= 10)
{
    sum = sum + number;
    number++;
}
}
```

To verify this program, we begin by determining the loop postcondition. When the loop finishes executing, here's what should be true:

sum contains the sum of the integers from 0 through 10 AND
number equals 11 AND
The number of loop iterations executed equals 10.

Now we have to do the following:

1. Define the loop invariant.
2. Show that the invariant is true before loop entry.
3. Show that the invariant is true at the start of each iteration.
4. Show that at loop exit the invariant is still true, the termination condition is true, and the AND of these two conditions implies that the postcondition is true.

This is the loop invariant:

sum contains the sum of the integers from 0 through number − 1 AND
1 <= number <= 11 AND
The number of loop iterations executed equals number − 1.

At loop entry, the following conditions have been established: sum is equal to 0, and number is equal to 1. Comparing these conditions to the invariant, we see that sum is equal to number − 1; number is in the range 1 through 11; and the number of iterations executed is 0, which equals number − 1.

Next, we walk through the loop body. The first statement adds the value of number to sum, so sum now contains the sum of the integers from 0 through number. The next statement increments number, which means that sum now contains the sum of the integers from 0 through number − 1. At the end of this iteration, number − 1 also equals the number of iterations. Because number cannot be greater than 10 at the start of an iteration, we also know that number cannot be greater than 11 at this point. So the invariant is true for the start of the next iteration.

We can tell that the loop terminates correctly from the fact that number is initially less than 10 and is incremented in each loop iteration. So number eventually becomes greater than 10, and the loop will terminate.

Finally, let's form the logical AND of the loop invariant and the termination condition:

sum contains the sum of the integers from 0
  through number − 1 AND
1 <= number <= 11 AND   } Invariant
The number of loop iterations executed equals
  number − 1 AND
number > 10   } Termination condition

This assertion is the conjunction of four individual assertions. The conjunction of the second and fourth assertions

1 <= number <= 11 AND number > 10

implies that number must equal 11. Thus, our four assertions are reduced to three:

sum contains the sum of the integers from 0 through number − 1 AND
number = 11 AND
The number of loop iterations executed equals number − 1.

If all three of these are true, we can substitute the value 11 for number in the first and third assertions, giving us the desired postcondition:

sum contains the sum of the integers from 0 through 10 AND
number = 11 AND
The number of loop iterations executed equals 10.

This may seem like an awful lot of work to show something that's obvious anyway: The code *is* correct. But what is obvious in simple code may not be obvious in more complicated code. That's where verification methods can really help.

Testing and Debugging Hints

1. Plan your test data carefully to test all sections of a program.
2. Beware of infinite loops, where the expression in the While statement never becomes FALSE. The symptom: The program doesn't stop. If you are on a system that monitors the execution time of a program, you may see a message like "TIME LIMIT EXCEEDED."

   If you have created an infinite loop, check your logic and the syntax of your loops. Be sure there's no semicolon immediately after the right parenthesis of the While condition:

   ```
   while (Expression);
     Statement
   ```

   This causes an infinite loop in most cases; the compiler thinks the loop body is the null statement (the do-nothing statement terminated by a semicolon). In a count-controlled loop, make sure the loop control variable is incremented within the loop. In a flag-controlled loop, make sure the flag eventually changes.

And, as always, watch for the = versus == problem in While conditions as well as in If conditions. The statement

```
while (someVar = 5)        // Wrong
{
    .
    .
    .
}
```

produces an infinite loop. The value of the assignment (not relational) expression is always 5, which is interpreted by the machine as TRUE.

3. Check the loop termination condition carefully, and be sure that something in the loop causes it to be met. Watch closely for values that cause one iteration too many or too few (the "off-by-1" syndrome).

4. Write out the loop invariant—the consistent, predictable part of its behavior in each iteration. Look for patterns that the invariant establishes. Are they just what you want? Perform an algorithm walk-through to verify that all of the appropriate preconditions and postconditions occur in the right places.

5. Trace the execution of the loop by hand with a code walk-through. Simulate the first few passes and the last few passes very carefully to see how the loop really behaves.

6. Use a *debugger* if your system provides one. A debugger is a program that runs your program in "slow motion," allowing you to execute one instruction at a time and to examine the contents of variables as they change. If you haven't already, check to see if a debugger is available on your system.

7. If all else fails, use *debug output statements*—output statements inserted into a program to help debug it. They output a message that indicates the flow of execution in the program or reports the values of variables at certain points in the program.

For example, if you want to know the value of variable beta at a certain point in a program, you could insert this statement:

```
cout << "beta = " << beta << endl;
```

If this output statement is in a loop, you will get as many values of beta as there are iterations of the body of the loop.

After you have debugged your program, you can remove the debug output statements or just precede them with // so that they'll be treated as comments. (This practice is referred to as *commenting out* a piece of code.) You can remove the double slashes if you need to use the statements again.

8. An ounce of prevention is worth a pound of debugging. Use the checklist questions, write the loop invariant, and design your loop correctly at the outset. It may seem like extra work, but it pays off in the long run.

SUMMARY

The While statement is a looping construct that allows the program to repeat a statement as long as an expression is TRUE. When the expression becomes FALSE, the statement is skipped, and execution continues with the first statement following the loop.

With the While statement you can construct several types of loops that you will use again and again. These types of loops fall into two categories: count-controlled loops and event-controlled loops.

In a count-controlled loop, the loop body is repeated a specified number of times. You initialize a counter variable right before the While statement. This variable is the loop control variable. The control variable is tested against the limit in the expression of the While. The last statement in the loop body increments the control variable.

Event-controlled loops continue executing until something inside the body signals that the looping process should stop. Event-controlled loops include those that test for a sentinel value in the data, end-of-file, or a change in a flag variable.

Sentinel-controlled loops are input loops that use a special data value as a signal to stop reading. EOF-controlled loops are loops that continue to input (and process) data values until there is no more data. To implement them with a While statement, you must test the state of the input stream by using the name of the stream variable as if it were a Boolean variable. The test yields zero (FALSE) when there are no more data values. A flag is a variable that is set in one part of the program and tested in another. In a flag-controlled loop, you must set the flag before the While, test it in the expression, and change it somewhere in the body of the loop.

Counting is a looping operation that keeps track of how many times a loop is repeated or how many times some event occurs. This count can be used in computations or to control the loop. A counter is a variable that is used for counting. It may be the loop control variable in a count-controlled loop, an iteration counter in a counting loop, or an event counter that counts the number of times a particular condition occurs in a loop.

Summing is a looping operation that keeps a running total of certain values. It is like counting in that the variable that holds the sum is initialized outside the loop. The summing operation, however, adds up unknown values; the counting operation adds a constant (1) to the counter each time.

When you design a loop, there are seven points to consider: How the termination condition is initialized, tested, and updated; how the process in the loop is initialized, performed, and updated; and the state of the program upon loop exit. By answering the checklist questions, you can bring each of these points into focus.

To design a nested loop structure, begin with the outermost loop. When you get to where the inner loop must appear, make it a separate module and come back to its design later.

Looping programs often produce a large amount of output that can be easier to read in table form, with a heading for each column. Tables are easy to print using fieldwidth specifications.

A loop invariant is a set of conditions that specify what must be true on loop entry, at the beginning of each iteration, and at loop exit in order for the loop to work properly. Writing out the loop invariant is a part of the verification process for programs that contain loops.

The process of testing a loop is based on the loop invariant, the answers to the checklist questions, and the patterns it might encounter (for example, executing a single iteration, multiple iterations, an infinite number of iterations, or no iterations at all).

QUICK CHECK

1. Write the first line of a While statement that loops until the value of Boolean variable done becomes TRUE. (pp. 254–257)
2. What are the four parts of a count-controlled loop? (pp. 257–259)
3. Should you use a priming read with an EOF-controlled loop? (pp. 263–264)
4. How is a flag variable used to control a loop? (pp. 264–265)
5. What is the difference between a counting operation in a loop and a summing operation in a loop? (pp. 265–269)
6. What is the difference between a loop control variable and an event counter? (pp. 265–269)
7. What kind of loop would you use in a program that reads the closing price of a stock for each day of the week? (pp. 273–277)
8. How would you extend the loop in Question 7 to make it read prices for 52 weeks? (pp. 277–283)
9. With what kind of loop is the following invariant most likely associated? (pp. 305–311)

   $1 <= day <= 366$ AND
   day indicates the number of the iteration that is about to be executed.

10. How would you test a program that is supposed to count the number of females and the number of males in a data set? (Assume that females are coded with 'F' in the data; males, with 'M'.) (pp. 305–311)

Answers 1. while (!done) 2. The process being repeated, plus initializing, testing, and incrementing the loop control variable. 3. Yes. 4. The flag is set outside the loop; the While checks the flag; and an If inside the loop resets the flag when the termination condition occurs. 5. A counting operation increments by a fixed value with each iteration of the loop; a summing operation adds unknown values to the total.   6. A loop control variable controls the loop; an event counter simply counts certain events during execution of the loop.   7. Because there are five days in a business week, you would use a count-controlled loop that runs from 1 to 5. 8. Nest the original loop inside a count-controlled loop that runs from 1 to 52.   9. A count-controlled loop.   10. Run the program with data sets that have a different number of females and males, only females, only males, illegal values (other characters), and an empty input file.

EXAM PREPARATION EXERCISES

1. In one or two sentences, explain the difference between loops and branches.
2. What does the following loop print out? (number is of type int.)

```
number = 1;
while (number < 11)
{
    number++;
    cout << number << endl;
}
```

output
1
2
3
:
11

3. By rearranging the order of the statements (don't change the way they are written), make the loop in Exercise 2 print the numbers from 1 through 10.
4. When the following code is executed, how many iterations of the loop are performed?

```
number = 2;
done = FALSE;
while ( !done )
{
    number = number * 2;
    if (number > 64)
        done = TRUE;
}
```

5. What is the output of this nested loop structure?

```
i = 4;
while (i >= 1)
{
    j = 2;
    while (j >= 1)
    {
        cout << j << ' ';
        j--;
    }
    cout << i << endl;
    i--;
}
```

output
2   1   4
2   1   3
2   1   2
2   1   1.

6. The following code segment is supposed to write out the even numbers between 1 and 15. (n is an int variable.) It has two flaws in it.

```
n = 2;
while (n != 15)
{
    n = n + 2;
    cout << n << ' ';
}
```

a. What is the output of the code as written?

b. Correct the code so that it works as intended.

7. The following code segment is supposed to copy one line from the standard input device to the standard output device.

```
cin.get(inChar);
while (inChar != '\n')
{
    cin.get(inChar);
    cout << inChar;
}
```

a. What is the output if the input line consists of the characters ABCDE?

b. Rewrite the code so that it works properly.

8. Does the following program segment need any priming reads? If not, explain why. If so, add the input statement(s) in the proper place. (letter is of type char.)

```
while (cin)
{
    while (letter != '\n')
    {
        cout << letter;
        cin.get(letter);
    }
    cout << endl;
    cout << "Another line read..." << endl;
    cin.get(letter);
}
```

9. Write the loop invariant for the following loop. (sum and count are of type int.)

```
sum = 0;
count = 0;
while (count < 22)
{
    sum = sum + count;
    count++;
}
```

10. What sentinel value would you choose for a program that reads telephone numbers as integers?

11. Consider this program:

```
#include <iostream.h>

typedef int Boolean;
const Boolean TRUE = 1;
const Boolean FALSE = 0;

const int LIMIT = 8;

int main()
{
    int     sum;
    int     i;
    int     number;
    Boolean finished;

    sum = 0;
    i = 1;
    finished = FALSE;
    while (i <= LIMIT && !finished)
    {
        cin >> number;
        if (number > 0)
            sum = sum + number;
        else if (number == 0)
            finished = TRUE;
        i++;
    }
    cout << "End of test. " << sum << ' ' << number << endl;
    return 0;
}
```

and these data values:

```
5 6 -3 7 -4 0 5 8 9
```

a. What are the contents of sum and number after exit from the loop?

b. Does the data fully test the program? Explain your answer.

12. Write the invariant for an EOF-controlled loop that reads integer values, counts them, sums them, and sums the squares of the values.

13. Here is a simple count-controlled loop:

```
count = 1;
while (count < 20)
    count++;
```

a. List three ways of changing the loop so that it executes 20 times instead of 19.

b. Which of those changes makes the value of count range from 1 through 21?

14. What is the output of the following program segment? (All variables are of type int.)

```
i = 1;
while (i <= 5)
{
    sum = 0;
    j = 1;
    while (j <= i)
    {
        sum = sum + j;
        j++;
    }
    cout << sum << ' ';
    i++;
}
```

PROGRAMMING WARM-UP EXERCISES

1. Write a program segment that sets a Boolean variable `dangerous` to TRUE and stops reading in data if `pressure` (a `float` variable being read in) exceeds 510.0. Use `dangerous` as a flag to control the loop.
2. Write a program segment that counts the number of times the integer 28 occurs in a file of 100 integers.
3. Write a nested loop code segment that produces this output:

```
1
1 2
1 2 3
1 2 3 4
```

4. Write a program segment that reads a file of student scores for a class (any size) and finds the class average.
5. a. Write a statement that prints the following headings in the format shown.

```
        Sales

Week1    Week2    Week3
```

   b. Write a statement that lines values up under each week's heading. The values are stored in the `int` variables `week1`, `week2`, and `week3`. The last digit of each number should fall under the 1, 2, or 3 of its column heading.
6. Write a program segment that reads in integers and then counts and prints out the number of positive integers and the number of negative integers. If a value is zero, it should not be counted. The process should continue until end-of-file occurs.
7. Write a program segment that adds up the even integers from 16 through 26, inclusive.
8. Rewrite program TempStat (page 296) using a different initialization scheme. One temperature should be read before the loop, and all values (except `hour`) should be initialized to the first temperature. Trace your program to make sure it works.

9. Write a program segment that prints out the sequence of all the hour and minute combinations in a day, starting with 1:00 A.M. and ending with 12:59 A.M.

10. Rewrite the code segment for Exercise 9 so that it prints the times in 10-minute intervals, arranged as a table with six columns and 24 rows.

11. Change program Incomes (page 290) so that it
    a. prints an error message when a negative income value is input and then goes on processing any remaining data. The erroneous data should not be included in any of the calculations. Thoroughly test the modified program with your own data sets.
    b. does not crash when there are no males in the input file or no females (or the file is empty). However, it should print an appropriate error message. Test the revised program with your own data sets.
    c. rejects data sets that are coded with a letter other than 'F' or 'M' and prints an error message before continuing to process the remaining data.

12. Develop a thorough set of test data for program Incomes as modified in Exercise 11.

PROGRAMMING PROBLEMS

1. Write a top-down design and a C++ program that inputs an integer and a character. The output should be a diamond composed of the character and extending the width specified by the integer. For example, if the integer is 11 and the character is an asterisk (*), the diamond would look like this:

```
     *
    ***
   *****
  *******
 *********
***********
 *********
  *******
   *****
    ***
     *
```

If the input integer is an even number, it should be increased to the next odd number. Use meaningful variable names, proper indentation, appropriate comments, and good prompting messages.

2. Write a top-down design and a C++ program that inputs an integer larger than 1 and calculates the sum of the squares from 1 to that integer. For example, if the integer equals 4, the sum of the squares is 30 $(1 + 4 + 9 + 16)$. The output should be the value of the integer and the sum, properly labeled. A negative input value signals the end of the data.

3. You are putting together some music tapes for a party. You've arranged a list of songs in the order in which you want to play them. However, you would like to minimize the empty tape left at the end of each side of a cassette (the cassette plays for 45 minutes on a side). So you want to figure out the total time for a group of songs and see how well they fit. Write a top-down design and a C++ program to help you do this. The program should input a reference number and a

time for each song, until it encounters a reference number of 0. The times should each be entered in the form of minutes and seconds (two integer values). For example, if song number 4 takes 7 minutes and 42 seconds to play, the data entered for that song would be

4 7 42

The program should echo-print the data for each song and the current running time total. The last data entry (reference number 0) should not be added to the total time. After all of the data have been read, the program should print a message indicating the time remaining on the tape.

If you are writing this program to read data from a file, the output should be in the form of a table with columns and headings. For example:

Song Number	Song Time Minutes	Seconds	Total Time Minutes	Seconds
------	-------	-------	-------	-------
1	5	10	5	10
2	7	42	12	52
5	4	19	17	11
3	4	33	21	44
4	10	27	32	11
6	8	55	41	6
0	0	1	41	6

There are 3 minutes and 54 seconds of tape left.

If you are using interactive input, your output should have prompting messages interspersed with the results. For example:

```
Enter the song number:
  1
Enter the number of minutes:
  5
Enter the number of seconds:
  10
Song number 1, 5 minutes and 10 seconds
Total time is 5 minutes and 10 seconds.
For the next song,
Enter the song number:
  .
  .
  .
```

Use meaningful variable names, proper indentation, and appropriate comments. If you're writing an interactive program, use good prompting messages. The program should discard any invalid data sets (negative numbers, for example) and print an error message indicating that the data set has been discarded and what was wrong with it.

4. Using top-down design, write a program that prints out the approximate number of words in a file of text. For our purposes, this is the same as the number of gaps

following words. A *gap* is defined as one or more spaces in a row, so a sequence of spaces counts as just one gap. The newline character also counts as a gap. Anything other than a space or newline is considered to be part of a word. For example, there are 19 words in the following hint, according to our definition. (*Hint:* Only count a space as a gap if the previous character read is something other than a space.) The program should echo-print the data.

Use meaningful variable names, proper indentation, and appropriate comments. Thoroughly test the program with your own data sets.

CASE STUDY FOLLOW-UP

1. Modify the TempStat program to work with any number of temperature readings, using a temperature of −999 to signal the end of the data. What type of event-controlled loop does your solution employ?
2. If we want the program to input any number of temperature readings and still use a count-controlled loop, how would we revise the program and input data?
3. In the Shipping Invoices case study, identify the two types of loop used.

7

Functions

- To be able to write a program that uses functions to reflect the structure of your top-down design.
- To be able to write a module of your own design as a void function.
- To be able to define a void function to do a specified task.
- To be able to distinguish between value and reference parameters.
- To be able to use actual and formal parameters correctly.
- To be able to do the following tasks, given a top-down design of a problem:

    Determine what the formal parameter list should be for each module.

    Determine which formal parameters should be reference parameters and which should be value parameters.

    Code the program correctly.

- To be able to define and use local variables correctly.
- To be able to write a program that uses multiple calls to a single function.

You have been using C++ functions since we introduced standard library routines such as `sqrt` and `abs` in Chapter 3. By now, you should be quite comfortable with the idea of calling these subprograms to perform a task. So far, we have not considered how the programmer can create his or her own functions other than `main`. That is the topic of this chapter and the next.

You might wonder why we waited until now to look at user-defined subprograms. The reason, and the major purpose for using subprograms, is that we write our own value-returning functions and void functions to help organize and simplify large and complex programs. Until now, our programs have been relatively small and simple, so we didn't need to write subprograms. Now that we've covered the basic control structures, we are ready to introduce subprograms so we can begin writing larger and more complex programs.

 # Top-Down Structured Design with Void Functions

As a brief refresher, let's review the two kinds of subprograms that the C++ language works with: value-returning functions and void functions. A value-returning function receives some data through its parameter list, computes a single function value, and returns this function value to the calling code. The caller invokes (calls) a value-returning function by using its name and parameter list in an expression:

```
y = 3.8 * sqrt(x);
```

In contrast, a void function (*procedure*, in some languages) does not return a function value. Nor is it called from within an expression. Instead, the function call appears as a complete, stand-alone statement. An example is the `get` function associated with the `istream` and `ifstream` data types:

```
cin.get(inputChar);
```

In this chapter, we concentrate exclusively on creating our own void functions. In Chapter 8, we examine how to write value-returning functions.

From the early chapters on, you have been designing your programs as collections of modules. Many of these modules are naturally implemented as *user-defined void functions*. We now look at how to turn the modules in your algorithms into user-defined void functions.

When to Use Functions

In general, you can code any module as a function, although some are so simple that this really is unnecessary. Thus, in designing a program, we frequently need to decide which modules should be implemented as functions. The decision should be based on whether the overall program is easier to understand as a result. There are other factors that can affect this decision, but for now this is the simplest heuristic (strategy) to use.

If a module is a single line only, it is usually best to write it directly in the program. Turning it into a function only complicates the overall program, which defeats the purpose of using subprograms. On the other hand, if a module is many lines long, it is easier to understand the program if the module is turned into a function.

Keep in mind that whether you choose to code a module as a function or not affects only the readability of the program and may make it more or less convenient to change the program later. Your choice does not affect the correct functioning of the program.

Writing Modules as Void Functions

It is quite simple to turn a module into a void function in C++. Basically, a void function looks like the `main` function except that the function heading uses `void` rather than `int` as the data type. Additionally, a void function does not use a statement like

```
return 0;
```

as does `main`. A void function does not return a function value to its caller.

Let's look at a program using void functions. A friend of yours is returning from a long trip, and you want to write a program that prints the following message:

```
***************
***************
 Welcome Home!
***************
***************
***************
***************
```

Here is a design for the program.

Main   *Level 0*

```
Print two lines of asterisks
Print "Welcome Home!"
Print four lines of asterisks
```

Print 2 Lines   *Level 1*

```
Print "**************"
Print "**************"
```

Print 4 Lines

```
Print "**************"
Print "**************"
Print "**************"
Print "**************"
```

If we write the two Level 1 modules as void functions, the `main` function is simply

```cpp
int main()
{
    Print2Lines();
    cout << " Welcome Home!" << endl;
    Print4Lines();
    return 0;
}
```

Notice how similar this code is to the main module of our top-down design. It contains two function calls—one to a function named `Print2Lines` and another to a function named `Print4Lines`. Both of these functions are *parameterless*—that is, they have no parameters within the parentheses.

The following code should look familiar to you, but look carefully at the function heading.

```
void Print2Lines()                          // Function heading
{
    cout << "***************" << endl;
    cout << "***************" << endl;
}
```

This segment is a *function definition*. A function definition is the code that extends from the function heading to the end of the block that is the body of the function. The function heading begins with the word void, signalling the compiler that this is not a value-returning function. The body of the function executes some ordinary statements and does *not* finish with a return statement to return a function value.

Now look again at the function heading. Just like any other identifier in C++, the name of a function is not allowed to include blanks, even though our paper-and-pencil module names do. Following the function name is an empty parameter list—that is, there is nothing between the parentheses. Later we'll see what goes inside the parentheses if a function uses parameters. Now let's put main and the other two functions together to form a complete program.

```
//***********************************************************
// Welcome program
// This program prints a "Welcome Home" message
//***********************************************************
#include <iostream.h>

void Print2Lines();                         // Function prototypes
void Print4Lines();

int main()
{
    Print2Lines();                          // Function call
    cout << " Welcome Home!" << endl;
    Print4Lines();                          // Function call
    return 0;
}

//***********************************************************

void Print2Lines()                          // Function heading

// This function prints two lines of asterisks
```

```
{
    cout << "****************" << endl;
    cout << "****************" << endl;
}


//*****************************************************************

void Print4Lines()                          // Function heading

// This function prints four lines of asterisks

{
    cout << "****************" << endl;
    cout << "****************" << endl;
    cout << "****************" << endl;
    cout << "****************" << endl;
}
```

C++ function definitions can appear in any order. We could have chosen to place the main function last instead of first, but C++ programmers typically put main first and any supporting functions after it.

In the Welcome program, the two statements just before the main function are called *function prototypes*. These declarations are necessary because of the C++ rule requiring you to declare an identifier before you can use it. Our main function uses the identifiers Print2Lines and Print4Lines, but the definitions of those functions don't appear until later. We must supply the function prototypes to inform the compiler in advance that Print2Lines and Print4Lines are the names of functions, that they do not return function values, and that they have no parameters. We say more about function prototypes later in the chapter.

Because the Welcome program is so simple to begin with, it may seem more complicated with its modules written as functions. However, it is clear that it much more closely resembles our top-down design. This is especially true of the main function. If you handed this code to someone, the person could look at the main function (which, as we said, usually appears first) and tell you immediately what the program does—it prints two lines of something, prints "Welcome Home!", and prints four lines of something. If you asked the person to be more specific, he or she could then look up the details in the other function definitions. The person is able to begin with a top-level view of the program and then study the lower-level modules as necessary, without having to read the entire program or look at a module structure chart. As our programs grow to include many modules nested several levels deep, the ability to read a program in the same manner as a top-down design greatly aids in the development and debugging process.

An Overview of User-Defined Functions

Now that we've seen an example of how a program is written with functions, let's look briefly and informally at some of the more important points of function construction and use.

Flow of Control in Function Calls

We said that C++ function definitions can be arranged in any order, although `main` usually appears first. During compilation, the functions are translated in the order in which they physically appear. When the program is executed, however, control begins at the first statement in the `main` function, and the program proceeds in logical sequence. When a function call is encountered, logical control is passed to the first statement in that function's body. The statements in the function are executed in logical order. After the last one is executed, control returns to the point immediately following the function call. Because function calls alter the logical order of execution, functions are considered control structures. Figure 7-1 illustrates this physical versus logical ordering of functions. In the figure, functions A, B, and C are written in the physical order A, B, C but are executed in the order C, B, A.

■ FIGURE 7-1

Physical Versus
Logical Order of
Functions

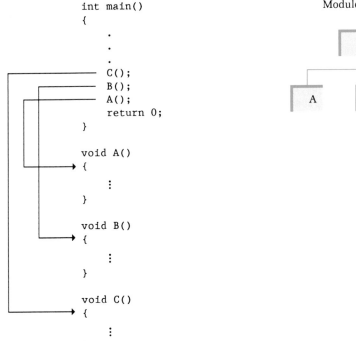

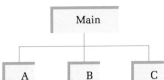
Module Structure Chart

MAY WE INTRODUCE

Charles Babbage

The British mathematician Charles Babbage (1791–1871) is generally credited with designing the world's first computer. Unlike today's electronic computers, however, Babbage's machine was mechanical. It was made of gears and levers, the predominant technology of the 1820s and 1830s.

Babbage actually designed two different machines. The first, called the Difference Engine, was to be used in computing mathematical tables. For example, the Difference Engine could produce a table of squares:

x	x^2
1	1
2	4
3	9
4	16
$\vdots$	$\vdots$

It was essentially a complex calculator that could not be programmed. Babbage's Difference Engine was designed to improve the accuracy of the computation of tables, not the speed. At that time, all tables were produced by hand, a tedious and error-prone job. Because much of science and engineering depended on accurate table information, an error could have serious consequences. Even though the Difference Engine could perform the calculations only a little faster than a human could, it did so without error. In fact, one of its most important features was that it would stamp its output directly onto copper plates, which could then be placed into a printing press, thereby avoiding even typographical errors.

By 1833, the project to build the Difference Engine had run into financial trouble. The engineer whom Babbage had hired to do the construction was dishonest and had drawn the project out as long as possible so as to extract more money from Babbage's

In the Welcome program, execution begins with the first executable statement in the main function (the call to Print2Lines). When Print2Lines is called, control passes to its first statement and subsequent statements in its body. After the last statement in Print2Lines has executed, control returns to the main function at the point following the call (the output statement that prints "Welcome Home!").

sponsors in the British government. Eventually the sponsors became tired of waiting for the machine and withdrew their support. At about the same time, Babbage lost interest in the project because he had developed the idea for a much more powerful machine, which he called the Analytical Engine—a truly programmable computer.

The idea for the Analytical Engine came to Babbage as he toured Europe to survey the best technology of the time in preparation for constructing the Difference Engine. One of the technologies that he saw was the Jacquard automatic loom, in which a series of paper cards with punched holes was fed through the machine to produce a woven cloth pattern. The pattern of holes constituted a program for the loom and made it possible to weave patterns of arbitrary complexity automatically. In fact, its inventor even had a detailed portrait of himself woven by one of his machines.

Babbage realized that this sort of device could be used to control the operation of a computing machine. Instead of calculating just one type of formula, such a machine could be programmed to perform arbitrarily complex computations, including the manipulation of algebraic symbols. As his associate, Ada Lovelace (the world's first computer programmer), elegantly put it, "We may say most aptly that the Analytical Engine weaves algebraical patterns." It is clear that Babbage and Lovelace fully understood the power of a programmable computer and even contemplated the notion that someday such machines could achieve artificial thought.

Unfortunately, Babbage never completed construction of either of his machines. Some historians believe that he never finished them because the technology of the period could not support such complex machinery. But most feel that Babbage's failure was his own doing. He was both brilliant and somewhat eccentric (it is known that he was afraid of Italian organ grinders, for example). As a consequence, he had a tendency to abandon projects in midstream so that he could concentrate on newer and better ideas. He always believed that his new approaches would enable him to complete a machine in less time than his old ideas would.

When he died, Babbage had many pieces of computing machines and partial drawings of designs, but none of the plans were complete enough to produce a single working computer. After his death, his ideas were dismissed and his inventions ignored. Only after modern computers were developed did historians recognize the true importance of his contributions. Babbage recognized the potential of the computer an entire century before one was fully developed. Today, we can only imagine how different the world would be if he had succeeded in constructing his Analytical Engine.

Function Parameters

Looking at the Welcome program, you can see that `Print2Lines` and `Print4Lines` are very similar functions. They differ only in the number of lines that they print. Do we really need two different functions in this program? Maybe we should write only one function that prints *any* number of lines, where the "any number of lines" is passed as a parameter by the caller (main). Here is a second version of the program, which uses only one function to do the printing. We call it NewWelcome.

```
//****************************************************************
// NewWelcome program
// This program prints a "Welcome Home" message
//****************************************************************
#include <iostream.h>

void PrintLines( int );                        // Function prototype

int main()
{
    PrintLines(2);
    cout << " Welcome Home!" << endl;
    PrintLines(4);
    return 0;
}


//****************************************************************

void PrintLines( int numLines )

// This function prints lines of asterisks, where
// numLines specifies how many lines to print

{
    int count;        // Loop control variable

    count = 1;
    while (count <= numLines)
    {
        cout << "***************" << endl;
        count++;
    }
}
```

In the function heading of PrintLines, you see some code between the parentheses that looks like a variable declaration. This is a *parameter declaration*. As you learned in earlier chapters, parameters represent a way for two functions to communicate with each other. Parameters enable the calling function to input (pass) values to another function to use in its processing and—in some cases—to allow the called function to output (return) results to the caller. The parameters in the call to a function are the **actual parameters.** The parameters listed in the function heading are the **formal**

parameters. (Some programmers use the terms *actual argument* and *formal argument* instead of *actual parameter* and *formal parameter*. Others use the term *argument* in place of *actual parameter*, and *parameter* in place of *formal parameter*.)

Formal Parameter   A variable declared in a function heading.

Actual Parameter   A variable or expression listed in a call to a function.

In the NewWelcome program, the actual parameters in the two function calls are the constants 2 and 4, and the formal parameter in the PrintLines function is named numLines. The main function first calls PrintLines with an actual parameter of 2. When control is turned over to PrintLines, the formal parameter numLines is initialized to 2. Within PrintLines, the count-controlled loop executes twice and the function returns. The second time PrintLines is called, the formal parameter numLines is initialized to the value of the actual parameter, 4. The loop executes four times, after which the function returns.

Although there is no benefit in doing so, we could write the main function this way:

```
int main()
{
    int lineCount;

    lineCount = 2;
    PrintLines(lineCount);
    cout << " Welcome Home!" << endl;
    lineCount = 4;
    PrintLines(lineCount);
    return 0;
}
```

In this version, the actual parameter in each call to PrintLines is a variable rather than a constant. Each time main calls PrintLines, a copy of the actual parameter's value is passed to the function to initialize the formal parameter numLines. This version shows that when you pass a variable as an actual parameter, the actual and formal parameters can have different names.

The NewWelcome program brings up a second major reason for using functions—namely, a function can be called from many places in the main function (or from other functions). Use of multiple calls can save a great deal of effort in coding many problem solutions. If there is a task that must be done in more than one place in a program, we can avoid repetitive coding by writing it as a function and then calling it wherever we need it. Another example that illustrates this use of functions appears in the Problem-Solving Case Study at the end of this chapter.

If more than one parameter is passed to a function, the formal and actual parameters are matched by their relative positions in the two parameter lists. For example, if you want `PrintLines` to print lines consisting of any selected character, not only asterisks, you might rewrite the function so that its heading is

```
void PrintLines( int   numLines,
                 char whichChar )
```

and a call to the function might look like this:

```
PrintLines(3, '#');
```

The first actual parameter, 3, is matched with `numLines` because `numLines` is the first formal parameter. Likewise, the second actual parameter, `'#'`, is matched with the second formal parameter, `whichChar`.

 # Syntax and Semantics of Void Functions

Function Call (Invocation)

To call (or invoke) a void function, we use its name as a statement, with the actual parameters in parentheses following the name. A **function call** in a program results in the execution of the body of the called function. This is the syntax template of a function call to a void function:

FunctionCall (to a void function)

> FunctionName (ActualParameterList);

Function Call (To a Void Function)   A statement that transfers control to a void function. In C++, this statement is the name of the function, followed by a list of actual parameters.

According to the syntax template for a function call, the parameter list is optional. A function is not required to have parameters. However, as the syntax template also shows, the parentheses are required even if the parameter list is empty.

If there are two or more parameters in the parameter list, you must separate them with commas. Here is the syntax template for ActualParameterList:

ActualParameterList

> Expression , Expression ...

When a function call is executed, the actual parameters are passed to the formal parameters according to their positions, left to right, and then control transfers to the first executable statement in the function body. When the last statement in the function has executed, control returns to the point from which the function was called.

Function Declarations and Definitions

In C++, you must declare every identifier before it can be used. In the case of functions, a function's declaration must physically precede any function call.

A function declaration announces to the compiler the name of the function, the data type of the function's return value (either void or a data type like int or float), and the data types of the parameters it uses. The NewWelcome program shows a total of three function declarations. The first declaration (the statement labeled "Function prototype") does not include the body of the function. The remaining two declarations—for main and PrintLines—include bodies for the functions.

In C++ terminology, a function declaration that omits the body is called a **function prototype**, and a declaration that does include the body is a **function definition**. We can use a Venn diagram to picture the fact that all definitions are declarations, but not all declarations are definitions:

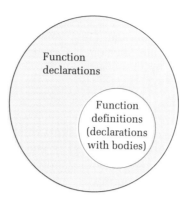

Function Prototype   A function declaration without the body of the function.
Function Definition   A function declaration that includes the body of the function.

Whether we are talking about functions or variables, the general idea in C++ is that a declaration becomes a definition if it also allocates memory space for the item. For example, a function prototype is merely a declaration—that is, it specifies the properties of a function: its name, its data type, and the data types of its parameters. But a function definition does more; it causes the compiler to allocate memory for the instructions in the body of the function. (Technically, all of the variable declarations we've used so far have been variable *definitions* as well as declarations—they allocate memory for the variable. In Chapter 8, we see examples of variable declarations that aren't variable definitions.)

The rule throughout C++ is that you can declare an item as many times as you wish, but you can define it only once. In the NewWelcome program, we could include many function prototypes for PrintLines (though we'd have no reason to), but only one function definition is allowed.

Function Prototypes   We have said that the definition of the main function usually appears first in a program, followed by the definitions of all other functions. To satisfy the requirement that identifiers be declared before they are used, C++ programmers typically place all function prototypes near the top of the program, before the definition of main.

A function prototype (known as a *forward declaration* in some languages) specifies in advance the data type of the function value to be returned (or the word void) and the data types of the parameters. A prototype for a void function has the following form:

FunctionPrototype (for a void function)

> **void** FunctionName **(** FormalParameterList **);**

As you can see in the syntax template, no body is included for the function, and a semicolon terminates the declaration. The formal parameter list is optional and has the form

FormalParameterList (in a function prototype)

> DataType **&** VariableName , DataType**&** VariableName . . .

The ampersand (&) attached to the name of a data type is optional and has a special significance that we cover later in the chapter.

In a function prototype, the formal parameter list must specify the data types of the parameters, but their names are optional. You could write either

```
void DoSomething( int, float );
```

or

```
void DoSomething( int velocity, float angle );
```

Sometimes it's useful for documentation purposes to supply names for the parameters, but the compiler ignores them.

Function Definitions   You learned in Chapter 2 that a function definition consists of two parts: the function heading and the function body, which is syntactically a block (compound statement). Here's the syntax template for a function definition, specifically for a void function:

FunctionDefinition (for a void function)

> **void** FunctionName **(** FormalParameterList **)**
> {
>   Statement
>   .
>   .
>   .
> }

Notice that the function heading does *not* end in a semicolon the way a function prototype does. It is a common syntax error to put a semicolon at the end of the line.

The syntax of the parameter list differs slightly from that of a function prototype in that you *must* specify the names of all the formal parameters. Also, it's our style preference (but not a language requirement) to declare each formal parameter on a separate line:

FormalParameterList (in a function definition)

DataType **&** VariableName **,**
DataType **&** VariableName
$\vdots$

Local Variables

Because a function body is a block, any function—not only the `main` function—can include variable declarations within its body. These variables are **local variables** because they are accessible only within the block in which they are declared. As far as the calling code is concerned, they don't exist. If you tried to print the contents of a local variable from another function, a compile-time error such as "UNDECLARED IDENTIFIER" would occur. You saw an example of a local variable in the NewWelcome program—the `count` variable declared within the `PrintLines` function.

Local Variable   A variable declared within a block and not accessible outside of that block.

In contrast to local variables, variables declared outside of all the functions in a program are called *global variables*. We return to the topic of global variables in Chapter 8.

Local variables occupy memory space only while the function is executing. At the moment the function is called, memory space is created for its local variables. When the function returns, its local variables are destroyed.[*] Therefore, every time the function is called, its local variables start out with their values undefined. Because every call to a function is independent of every other call to that same function, you must initialize the local variables

---

[*]We'll see an exception to this rule in the next chapter.

within the function itself. And because local variables are destroyed when the function returns, you cannot use them to store values between calls to the function.

The following code segment illustrates each of the parts of the function declaration and calling mechanism that we have discussed.

```
#include <iostream.h>

void TryThis( int, int, float );        // Function prototype

int main()                              // Function definition
{
    int   int1;                         // Variables local to main
    int   int2;
    float someFloat;
        .
        .
        .

    TryThis(int1, int2, someFloat);     // Function call with three
                                        //    actual parameters

        .
        .
        .
}

void TryThis( int   param1,             // Function definition with
              int   param2,             //    three formal parameters
              float param3 )
{
    int   i;                            // Variables local to TryThis
    float x;
        .
        .
        .
}
```

The Return Statement

The main function uses the statement

```
return 0;
```

to return the value 0 (or 1 or some other value) to its caller, the operating system. Every value-returning function must return its function value this way.

A void function does not return a function value. Control returns from the function when it "falls off" the end of the body—that is, after the final statement has executed. As you saw in the NewWelcome program, the PrintLines function simply prints some lines of asterisks and then returns.

Alternatively, there is a second form of the `return` statement. It looks like this:

```
return;
```

This statement is valid *only* for void functions. It can appear anywhere in the body of the function; it causes control to exit the function immediately and return to the caller. Here's an example:

```
void SomeFunc( int n )
{
    if (n > 50)
    {
        cout << "The value is out of range.";
        return;
    }
    n = 412 * n;
    cout << n;
}
```

In this (nonsense) example, there are two ways for control to exit the function. At function entry, the value of n is tested. If it is greater than 50, the function prints a message and returns immediately without executing any more statements. If n is less than or equal to 50, the If statement's then-clause is skipped and control proceeds to the assignment statement. After the last statement, control returns to the caller.

Another way of writing the above function is to use an If-Then-Else structure:

```
void SomeFunc( int n )
{
    if (n > 50)
        cout << "The value is out of range.";
    else
    {
        n = 412 * n;
        cout << n;
    }
}
```

If you asked different programmers about these two versions of the function, you would get differing opinions. Some prefer the first version, saying that it is most straightforward to use `return` statements whenever it logically makes sense to do so. Others insist on the *single-entry/single-exit* approach in the second version. With this philosophy, control enters a function at one point only (the first executable statement) and exits at one point only (the end of the body). They argue that multiple exits from a function make the program logic hard to follow and difficult to debug. Other programmers take a position somewhere between these two philosophies, allowing occasional use of the `return` statement when the logic is clear. Our advice is to use `return` sparingly; overuse can lead to confusing code.

MATTERS OF STYLE

Naming Void Functions

When you choose a name for a void function, keep in mind how calls to it will look. A call is written as a statement; therefore, it should sound like a command or an instruction to the computer. For this reason, it is a good idea to choose a name that is an imperative verb or has an imperative verb as part of it. (In English, an imperative verb is one representing a command: *Listen! Look! Do something!*) For example, the statement

```
Lines(3);
```

has no verb to suggest that it's a command. Adding the verb *Print* makes the name sound like an action:

```
PrintLines(3);
```

When you are picking a name for a void function, write down sample calls with different names until you come up with one that sounds like a command to the computer.

Header Files

From the very beginning we have been using #include directives, requesting the C++ preprocessor to insert the contents of header (.h) files into our programs:

```
#include <iostream.h>
#include <math.h>        // For sqrt() and fabs()
#include <fstream.h>     // For file I/O
#include <limits.h>      // For INT_MAX and INT_MIN
```

Exactly what are in these header files?

It turns out that there is nothing magical about header files. Their contents are nothing more than a series of C++ declarations. There are declarations of named constants such as INT_MAX and INT_MIN, and there are declarations of stream variables like cin and cout. But most of the items in a header file are function prototypes.

Suppose that your program needs to use the library function sqrt in a statement like this:

```
y = sqrt(x);
```

Every identifier must be declared before it can be used. If you forget to #include the header file math.h, the compiler gives you an "UNDECLARED IDENTIFIER" error message. The file math.h contains function prototypes for sqrt and all of the other math-oriented library functions. With this header file included in your program, the compiler not only knows that the identifier sqrt is the name of a function but it also can verify that your function call is correct with respect to the number of parameters and their data types.

Header files save you the trouble of specifying all of the library function prototypes yourself at the beginning of your program. With just one line—the #include directive—you cause the preprocessor to go out and find the header file and insert the prototypes into your program. In later chapters, we see how to create our own header files that contain declarations specific to our programs.

Parameters

When a function is executed, it uses the actual parameters given to it in the function call. How is this done? The answer to this question depends on the nature of the formal parameters. C++ supports two kinds of formal parameters: **value parameters** and **reference parameters.** With a value parameter, which is declared without an ampersand (&) at the end of the data type name, the function receives a copy of the actual parameter's value. With a reference parameter, which is declared by adding an ampersand to the data type name, the function receives the location (memory address) of the actual parameter. Before we examine in detail the difference between these two kinds of parameters, let's look at an example of a function heading with a mixture of reference and value parameter declarations.

```
void Example( int&  param1,      // A reference parameter
              int   param2,      // A value parameter
              float param3 )     // Another value parameter
```

With simple data types—int, char, float, and so on—a value parameter is the default (assumed) kind of parameter. In other words, if you don't do anything special (add an ampersand), a parameter is assumed to be a value parameter. To specify a reference parameter, you have to go out of your way to do something extra (attach an ampersand).

Value Parameter   A formal parameter that receives a copy of the contents of the corresponding actual parameter.

Reference Parameter   A formal parameter that receives the location (memory address) of the caller's actual parameter.

Let's look at both kinds of parameters, starting with value parameters.

Value Parameters

In the NewWelcome program, the PrintLines function heading is

```
void PrintLines( int numLines )
```

The formal parameter numLines is a value parameter because its data type name doesn't end in "&". If the function is called using an actual parameter lineCount

```
PrintLines(lineCount);
```

then the formal parameter numLines receives a copy of the value of lineCount. At this moment, there are two copies of the data—one in the actual parameter lineCount and one in the formal parameter numLines. If a statement inside the PrintLines function were to change the value of num-Lines, this change would not affect the actual parameter lineCount (remember, there are two copies of the data). Using value parameters thus helps us avoid unintentional changes to actual parameters.

Because value parameters are passed copies of their actual parameters, anything that has a value may be passed to a value parameter. This includes constants, variables, and even arbitrarily complicated expressions. (The expression is simply evaluated and a copy of the result is sent to the corresponding value parameter.) For the PrintLines function, the following function calls are all valid:

```
PrintLines(3);
PrintLines(lineCount);
PrintLines(2 * abs(10 - someInt));
```

There must be the same number of actual parameters in a function call as there are formal parameters in the function heading.* Also, each actual parameter should have the same data type as the formal parameter in the same position. Notice how each formal parameter in the following example is matched to the actual parameter in the same position (the data type of each actual parameter is what you would assume from its name):

Function heading: `void ShowMatch(float num1, int num2, char letter)`

Function call: `ShowMatch(floatVariable, intVariable, charVariable);`

If the matched parameters are not of the same data type, implicit type coercion takes place. For example, if a formal parameter is of type `int`, an actual parameter that is a `float` expression is coerced to an `int` value before it is passed to the function. As usual in C++, you can avoid unintended type coercion by using an explicit type cast or, better yet, by not mixing data types at all.

As we have stressed, a value parameter receives a copy of the actual parameter and therefore the actual parameter cannot be directly accessed or changed. When a function returns, the contents of any value parameters are destroyed, along with the contents of the local variables. The difference between value parameters and local variables is that the values of local variables are undefined when a function starts to execute, whereas value parameters are automatically initialized to the values of the corresponding actual parameters.

Because the contents of value parameters are destroyed when the function returns, they cannot be used to return information to the calling code. What if we *do* want to return information by modifying the actual parameters? We must use the second kind of parameter available in C++: reference parameters. Let's look at these now.

Reference Parameters

A reference parameter is one that you declare by attaching an ampersand to the name of its data type. It is called a reference parameter because the called function can refer to the corresponding actual parameter directly. Specifically, the function is allowed to inspect *and modify* the caller's actual parameter.

---

*This statement is not the whole truth. C++ has a special language feature—*default parameters*—that lets you call a function with fewer actual parameters than formal parameters. We do not cover default parameters in this book.

When a function is invoked using a reference parameter, it is the *location* (memory address) of the actual parameter, not its value, that is passed to the function. There is only one copy of the information, and it is used by both the caller and the called function. When a function is called, the actual parameter and formal parameter become synonyms for the same location in memory. Whatever value is left by the called function in this location is the value that the caller will find there. Therefore, you must be careful using a formal reference parameter because any change made to it affects the actual parameter in the calling code. Let's look at an example.

The Activity program in Chapter 5 reads in a temperature and prints out an appropriate activity. Here is its design.

Main   *Level 0*

> Get temperature
> Print activity

Get Temperature   *Level 1*

> Prompt for temperature value input
> Read temperature
> Echo-print temperature

Print Activity

> Print "The recommended activity is"
> IF temperature > 85
>   Print "swimming."
> ELSE IF temperature > 70
>   Print "tennis."
> ELSE IF temperature > 32
>   Print "golf."
> ELSE IF temperature > 0
>   Print "skiing."
> ELSE
>   Print "dancing."

Let's write the two Level 1 modules as void functions, GetTemp and PrintActivity, so that the main function looks like the main module of our top-down design. Here is the resulting program.

```
//**********************************************************************
// Activity program
// This program outputs an appropriate activity
// for a given temperature
//**********************************************************************
#include <iostream.h>

void GetTemp( int& );                        // Function prototypes
void PrintActivity( int );

int main()
{
    int temperature;      // The outside temperature

    GetTemp(temperature);                    // Function call
    PrintActivity(temperature);              // Function call
    return 0;
}

//**********************************************************************

void GetTemp( int& temp )                    // Reference parameter

// This function prompts for a temperature to be entered,
// reads the input value into temp, and echo-prints it

{
    cout << "Enter the outside temperature:" << endl;
    cin >> temp;
    cout << "The current temperature is " << temp << endl;
}

//**********************************************************************

void PrintActivity( int temp )               // Value parameter

// Given the value of temp, this function prints a message
// indicating an appropriate activity

{
    cout << "The recommended activity is ";
    if (temp > 85)
        cout << "swimming." << endl;
    else if (temp > 70)
```

```
        cout << "tennis." << endl;
    else if (temp > 32)
        cout << "golf." << endl;
    else if (temp > 0)
        cout << "skiing." << endl;
    else
        cout << "dancing." << endl;
}
```

In the Activity program, the actual parameters in the two function calls are both named `temperature`. The formal parameter in `GetTemp` is a reference parameter named `temp`. The formal parameter in `PrintActivity` is a value parameter, also named `temp`.

The `main` function tells `GetTemp` where to leave the temperature by giving it the location of the variable `temperature` when it makes the function call. We *must* use a reference parameter here so that `GetTemp` knows where to deposit the result. In a sense, the formal parameter `temp` is just a convenient placeholder in the function definition. When `GetTemp` is called with `temperature` as its actual parameter, all the references to `temp` inside the function actually are made to `temperature`. If the function were to be called again with a different variable as an actual parameter, all the references to `temp` would actually refer to that other variable until the function returned control to `main`.

In contrast, `PrintActivity`'s formal parameter is a value parameter. When `PrintActivity` is called, `main` sends a copy of the value of `temperature` for the function to work with. It's appropriate to use a value parameter in this case because `PrintActivity` is not supposed to modify the actual parameter `temperature`.

Because actual and formal parameters can have different names, we can call a function with different actual parameters. Suppose we wanted to change the Activity program to print an activity for both the indoor and outdoor temperatures. We could declare integer variables in the `main` function named `indoorTemp` and `outdoorTemp`, then write the body of `main` as:

```
GetTemp(indoorTemp);
PrintActivity(indoorTemp);
GetTemp(outdoorTemp);
PrintActivity(outdoorTemp);
return 0;
```

In `GetTemp` and `PrintActivity`, the formal parameters would receive values from, or pass values to, either `indoorTemp` or `outdoorTemp`.

The following table summarizes the different kinds of parameters that we've seen.

Kind of Parameter	Usage
Actual parameter	Appears in a function *call*. The corresponding formal parameter may be either a reference or a value parameter.
Formal value parameter	Appears in a function *heading*. Receives a *copy* of the value stored in the corresponding actual parameter.
Formal reference parameter	Appears in a function *heading*. Receives the *address* of the corresponding actual parameter.

An Analogy

Before we talk more about parameter passing, let's look at an analogy from daily life. You're at the local discount catalog showroom to buy a Father's Day present. To place your order, you fill out an order form. The form has places to write in the quantity of each item desired and its catalog number, and places where the order clerk will fill in the prices. You write down what you want and hand the form to the clerk. You wait for the clerk to check whether the items are available and calculate the cost. He returns the form, and you see that the items are in stock and the price is $48.50. You pay the clerk and go on about your business.

This illustrates how function calls work. The clerk is like a void function. You, acting as the main function, ask him to do some work for you. You give him some information: the item numbers and quantities. These are his input parameters. You wait until he returns some information to you: the availability of the items and their prices. These are the clerk's output parameters. The clerk does this task all day long with different input values. Each order activates the same process. The shopper waits until the clerk returns information based on the specific input.

The order form is analogous to the actual parameters of a function call. The spaces on the form represent variables in the main function. When you hand the form to the clerk, some of the places contain information and some are empty. The clerk holds the form while doing his job so he can write information in the blank spaces. These blank spaces correspond to reference parameters; you expect the clerk to return results to you in the spaces.

When the main function calls another function, reference parameters allow the called function to access and change the variables in the actual parameter list. When the called function finishes, main continues, making use of whatever new information the called function left in the variables.

The formal parameter list is like the set of shorthand or slang terms the clerk uses to describe the spaces on the order form. For example, he may think in terms of "units," "codes," and "receipts." These are his terms (formal parameters) for what the order form calls "quantity," "catalog number," and "price" (the actual parameters). But he doesn't waste time reading the names on the form every time; he knows that the first item is the units (quantity), the second is the code (catalog number), and so on. In other words, he looks only at the position of each space on the form. This is how actual parameters are matched to formal parameters—by their relative positions in the two parameter lists.

Matching Actual Parameters with Formal Parameters

Earlier we said that with reference parameters, the actual parameter and formal parameter become synonyms for the same memory location. When a function returns control to its caller, the link between the actual and the formal parameters is broken. They are synonymous only during a particular call to the function. The only evidence that a matchup between the two parameters ever occurred is that the contents of the actual parameter may have changed (see Figure 7-2).

Only a variable can be passed as an actual parameter to a reference parameter because a function can assign a new value to the actual parameter. (In contrast, remember that an arbitrarily complicated expression can be passed to a value parameter.) Suppose that we have a function with the following heading:

```
void DoThis( float val,    // Value parameter
             int&  count )  // Reference parameter
```

Then the following function calls are all valid.

■ FIGURE 7-2   Using a Formal Reference Parameter to Access an Actual Parameter

When flow of control is in the `main` function,
`temperature` can be accessed as shown by the arrow.

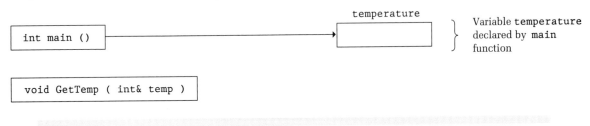

When flow of control is in function `GetTemp`, every
reference to `temp` accesses the variable `temperature`.

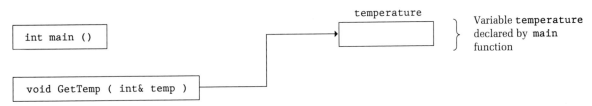

```
DoThis(someFloat, someInt);
DoThis(9.83, intCounter);
DoThis(4.9 * sqrt(y), myInt);
```

In the DoThis function, the first parameter is a value parameter, so any expression is allowed as the actual parameter. The second parameter is a reference parameter, so the actual parameter *must* be a variable name. The statement

```
DoThis(y, 3);
```

generates a compile-time error because the second parameter isn't a variable name. Earlier we said the syntax template for an actual parameter list is

ActualParameterList

Expression	, Expression	. . .

But you must keep in mind that Expression is restricted to a variable name if the formal parameter is a reference parameter.

There is another important difference between value and reference parameters when it comes to matching actual parameters with formal parameters. With value parameters, we said that implicit type coercion occurs if the matched parameters have different data types (the value of the actual parameter is coerced to the data type of the formal parameter). With reference parameters, if the matched parameters have different data types, a curious thing happens. C++ copies the value of the actual parameter into a temporary variable of the correct type and passes the address of the *temporary variable* to the formal parameter. When the function returns, the temporary variable is discarded. Any changes that you expected the function to make to your actual parameter were not made at all. To avoid this unpleasant result, always verify that the actual parameter has exactly the same data type as the formal parameter.

The following table summarizes the appropriate forms of actual parameters.

Formal Parameter	*Actual Parameter*
Value	A variable, constant, or arbitrary expression (type coercion may take place)
Reference	A variable only, of exactly the same data type as the formal parameter

Finally, it is up to the programmer to make sure that the formal and actual parameter lists match up semantically as well as syntactically. For example, suppose we had written the indoor/outdoor modification to the Activity program as follows.

```
int main()
{
    .
    .
    .
    GetTemp(indoorTemp);
    PrintActivity(indoorTemp);
    GetTemp(outdoorTemp);
    PrintActivity(indoorTemp);    // Wrong actual parameter
    return 0;
}
```

The parameter list in the last function call matches the formal parameter list in its number and type of parameters, so no syntax error would be signaled. However, the output would be erroneous because the actual parameter is the wrong temperature value. Similarly, if a function has two formal parameters of the same data type, you must be careful that the actual parameters are in the right order. If they are in the wrong order, no syntax error will result, but the answers will be wrong.

THEORETICAL FOUNDATIONS

Parameter-Passing Mechanisms

There are three major ways of passing parameters to and from subprograms. C++ supports only two of these mechanisms; however, it's useful to know about all three in case you have occasion to use them in another language.

C++ reference parameters employ a mechanism called *pass-by-address* or *pass-by-location*. A memory address is passed to the function. Another name for this is *pass-by-reference* because the function can refer directly to the actual parameter.

C++ value parameters are an example of *pass-by-value*. The function receives a copy of the value of the actual parameter. Pass-by-value can be less efficient than pass-by-address because the value of a parameter may occupy many memory locations (as we see in Chapter 11), whereas an address usually occupies only a single location. For the simple data types int, char, and float, the efficiency of either mechanism is about the same.

A third method of passing parameters is called *pass-by-name*. The actual parameter is passed to the function as a character string that must be interpreted by special run-time support software (called a *thunk*) supplied by the compiler. For example, if the name of a variable is passed to a function, the run-time interpreter looks up the name of the parameter in a table of declarations to find the address of the variable. Pass-by-name can have unexpected results. If an actual parameter has the same spelling as a local variable in the function, the function will refer to the local version of the variable instead of the variable in the calling code.

Some versions of pass-by-name allow an expression or even a code segment to be passed to a function. Each time the function refers to the parameter, an *interpreter* performs the action specified by the parameter. An interpreter is similar to a compiler and nearly as complex. Thus, pass-by-name is the least efficient of the three parameter passing mechanisms. Pass-by-name is supported by the ALGOL and LISP programming languages, but not by C++.

There are two different ways of matching actual parameters with formal parameters, although C++ supports only one of them. Most programming languages, C++ among them, match actual and formal parameters by their relative positions in the two parameter lists. This is called *positional* matching, *relative* matching, or *implicit* matching. A few languages, such as Ada, also support *explicit* or *named* matching. In explicit matching, the actual parameter list specifies the name of the formal parameter to be associated with each actual parameter.

Explicit matching allows actual parameters to be written in any order in the function call. The real advantage is that each call documents precisely which values are being passed to which formal parameters.

 ## Designing Functions

We've looked at some examples of functions and defined the syntax of function prototypes and function definitions. But how do we design functions? First, we need to be more specific about what functions do. We've said that they allow us to organize our programs more like our top-down designs, but what really is the advantage of doing that?

The body of a function is like any other segment of code, except that it is contained in a separate block within the program. Isolating a segment of code in a separate block means that its implementation details can be "hidden" from view. As long as you know how to call a function and what its purpose is, you can use it without knowing how it actually works. For example, you don't know how the code for a library function like sqrt is written (its implementation is hidden from view), yet you still can use it effectively.

The specification of what a function does and how it is invoked defines its **interface** (see Figure 7-3). By hiding a module implementation, or **encapsulating** the module, we can make changes to it without changing the main function, as long as the interface remains the same. For example, you might rewrite the body of a function using a more efficient algorithm.

Heading: `void PrintActivity ( int temp )`
Precondition: `temp` is a temperature value in a valid range
Postcondition: A message has been printed indicating an
               appropriate activity given temperature `temp`

Implementation

Interface   A connecting link at a shared boundary that permits independent systems to meet and act on or communicate with each other. Also, the formal description of the purpose of a subprogram and the mechanism for communicating with it.

Encapsulation   Hiding a module implementation in a separate block with a formally specified interface.

Encapsulation is what we do in the top-down design process when we postpone the solution of a difficult subproblem. We write down its purpose and what information it takes and returns, and then we write the rest of our design as if the subproblem already had been solved. We could hand this interface specification to someone else, and that person could develop a function for us that solves the subproblem. We needn't be concerned about how it works, as long as it conforms to the interface specification. Interfaces and encapsulation are the basis for *team programming*, in which a group of programmers work together to solve a large problem.

Thus, designing a function can (and should) be divided into two tasks: designing the interface and designing the implementation. We already know how to design an implementation—it is a segment of code that corresponds to an algorithm. To design the interface, we focus on the *what*, not the *how*. We must define the behavior of the function (what it does) and the mechanism for communicating with it.

You already know how to specify formally the behavior of a function. Because a function corresponds to a module, its behavior is defined by the precondition and postcondition of the module. All that remains is to define the mechanism for communicating with the function. To do so, make a list of the following items:

1. *Incoming values* that the function receives from the caller.
2. *Outgoing values* that the function produces and returns to the caller.

3. *Incoming/outgoing values*—values the caller has that the function changes (receives and returns).

Decide which identifiers inside the module match the values in this list. These identifiers become the variables in the formal parameter list for the function. Then the formal parameters are declared in the function heading. All other variables that the function needs are local and must be declared within the body of the function. This process may be repeated for all the modules at each level.

Let's look more closely at designing the interface. First we examine function preconditions and postconditions. After that, we consider in more detail the notion of incoming, outgoing, and incoming/outgoing parameters.

Writing Assertions as Program Comments

We have been writing module preconditions and postconditions as informal, English-language assertions. From now on, we include preconditions and postconditions as comments to document the interfaces of C++ functions. Here's an example:

```
void PrintAverage( float sum,
                   int   count )

// Precondition:
//     sum is assigned  &&  count > 0
// Postcondition:
//     The average sum/count has been output on one line

{
    cout << "Average is " << sum / float(count) << endl;
}
```

The precondition is an assertion describing everything that the function requires to be true at the moment the caller invokes the function. The postcondition describes the state of the program at the moment the function finishes executing.

You can think of the precondition and postcondition as a contract. The contract states that if the precondition is true at function entry, then the postcondition must be true at function exit. The *caller* is responsible for ensuring the precondition, and the *function code* must ensure the postcondition. If the caller fails to satisfy its part of the contract (the precondition), the contract is off; the function cannot guarantee that the postcondition will be true.

Above, the precondition warns the caller to make sure that sum has been assigned a meaningful value and to be sure that count is positive. If this precondition is true, the function guarantees it will satisfy the postcondition. If count isn't positive when PrintAverage is invoked, the effect of the function is undefined. (For example, if count equals zero, the postcondition surely isn't satisfied—the program crashes!)

Sometimes the caller doesn't need to satisfy any precondition before calling a function. In this case, the precondition can be written as the value TRUE or simply omitted. In the following example, no precondition is necessary:

```
void Get2Ints( int& int1,
               int& int2 )

// Postcondition:
//      User has been prompted to enter two integers
//   && int1 == first input value
//   && int2 == second input value

{
    cout << "Please enter two integers: ";
    cin >> int1 >> int2;
}
```

In assertions written as C++ comments, we use either && or AND to denote the logical AND operator; either || or OR to denote a logical OR; either ! or NOT to denote a logical NOT; and == to denote "equals." (Notice that we do *not* use = to denote "equals." Even when we write program comments, we want to keep C++'s == operator distinct from the assignment operator.)

There is one final notation we use when we express assertions as program comments. Preconditions implicitly refer to values of variables at the moment the function is invoked. Postconditions implicitly refer to values at the moment the function returns. But sometimes you need to write a postcondition that refers to parameter values that existed at the moment the function was invoked. To signify "at the time of entry to the function," we attach the symbols @entry to the end of the variable name. Below is an example of the use of this notation. The Swap function exchanges, or swaps, the values of its two parameters.

```
void Swap( int& firstInt,
           int& secondInt )

// Precondition:
//      firstInt and secondInt are assigned
// Postcondition:
//      firstInt == secondInt@entry
//   && secondInt == firstInt@entry

{
    int temporaryInt;
```

```
        temporaryInt = firstInt;
        firstInt = secondInt;
        secondInt = temporaryInt;
}
```

*M*ATTERS OF STYLE

Function Preconditions and Postconditions

Preconditions and postconditions, when well written, are a concise but accurate description of the behavior of a function. A person reading your program should be able to see at
a glance how to use the function by looking only at its interface (the function heading and
the precondition and postcondition). The reader should never have to look into the code
of the function body to understand the purpose of the function or how to use it.

A function interface describes *what* the function does, not the details of *how* it does
it. For this reason, the postcondition should mention (by name) each outgoing parameter and its value but should not mention any local variables. Local variables are implementation details; they are irrelevant to the function's interface.

Documenting the Direction of Data Flow

Another helpful piece of documentation in a function interface is the direction of **data flow** for each parameter in the parameter list. Data flow is the
flow of information between the function and its caller. We said earlier that
each parameter can be classified as an *incoming* parameter, an *outgoing* parameter, or an *incoming/outgoing* parameter. (Some people refer to these as
input parameters, *output* parameters, and *input/output* parameters.)

> **Data Flow**   The flow of information from the calling code to a function and
> from the function back to the calling code.

For an incoming parameter, the direction of data flow is one-way—into the
function. The function inspects and uses the current value of the parameter
but does not modify it. In the function heading, we attach the comment

```
/* in */
```

to the declaration of the formal parameter. (Remember that C++ comments come in two forms. The first, which we use most often, starts with two slashes and extends to the end of the line. The second form encloses a comment between /* and */ and allows us to embed a comment within a line of code.) Here is the PrintAverage function with comments added to the formal parameter declarations:

```
void PrintAverage( /* in */ float sum,
                   /* in */ int   count )
// Precondition:
//      sum is assigned  &&  count > 0
// Postcondition:
//      The average sum/count has been output on one line

{
    cout << "Average is " << sum / float(count) << endl;
}
```

Pass-by-value is appropriate for each parameter that is incoming only. As you can see in the function body, PrintAverage does not modify the values of the parameters sum and count. It merely uses their current values. The direction of data flow is one-way—into the function.

The data flow for an outgoing parameter is one-way—out of the function. The function produces a new value for the parameter without using the old value in any way. The comment /* out */ identifies an outgoing parameter. Here we've added comments to the Get2Ints function heading:

```
void Get2Ints( /* out */ int& int1,
               /* out */ int& int2 )
```

Pass-by-reference must be used for an outgoing parameter. If you look back at the body of Get2Ints, you'll see that the function stores new values into the two variables (by means of the input statement), replacing whatever values they originally contained.

Finally, the data flow for an incoming/outgoing parameter is two-way—into and out of the function. The function uses the old value and also produces a new value for the parameter. We use /* inout */ to document this two-way direction of data flow. Here is an example of a function that uses two parameters, one of them incoming only and the other one incoming/outgoing:

```
void Calc( /* in */     int  alpha,
           /* inout */ int& beta  )

// Precondition:
//    alpha and beta are assigned
// Postcondition
//    beta == beta@entry * 7 - alpha

{
    beta = beta * 7 - alpha;
}
```

This function first inspects the incoming value of beta so that it can evaluate the expression to the right of the equal sign. Then it stores a new value into beta by using the assignment operation. The data flow for beta is therefore considered a two-way flow of information. Pass-by-value is appropriate for alpha (it's incoming only), but pass-by-reference is required for beta (it's an incoming/outgoing parameter).

MATTERS OF STYLE

Formatting Function Headings

From here on, we follow a specific style when coding our function headings. Comments appear next to the formal parameters to explain how each parameter is used. Also, embedded comments indicate which of the three data flow categories each parameter belongs to (in, out, or inout).

```
void Print( /* in */     float val,     // Value to be printed
            /* inout */ int&  count )   // Number of lines printed
                                        //   so far
```

Notice that the first parameter is a value parameter. The second is a reference parameter, presumably because the function changes the value of the counter.

We use comments in the form of rows of asterisks (or dashes or some other character) before and after a function to make the function stand out from the surrounding code. Each function also has its own block of introductory comments, just like those at the start of a program, as well as its precondition and postcondition.

It's important to put as much care into documenting each function as you would into the documentation at the beginning of a program.

The following table summarizes the correspondence between a parameter's data flow and the appropriate parameter-passing mechanism.

Data Flow for a Parameter	Parameter-Passing Mechanism
Incoming	Pass-by-value
Outgoing	Pass-by-reference
Incoming/outgoing	Pass-by-reference

There are exceptions to the guidelines in this table. C++ requires that I/O stream variables be passed by reference because of the way streams and files are implemented. We encounter one more exception in Chapter 11.

SOFTWARE ENGINEERING TIP

Conceptual Versus Physical Hiding of a Function Implementation

In many programming languages, the encapsulation of an implementation is purely conceptual. If you want to know how a function is implemented, you simply look at the function body. C++, however, permits function implementations to be written and stored separately from the main function.

Larger C++ programs are often split up and stored into separate files on a disk. One file might contain just the source code for the main function; another file, the source code for one or two functions invoked by main; and so on. This organization is called a *multifile program*. To translate the source code into object code, the compiler is invoked for each file independently of the others. A program called the *linker* then collects all the resulting object code into a single executable program.

When you write a program that invokes a function located in another file, it isn't necessary for that function's source code to be available. All that's required is for you to include a function prototype so that the compiler can check the syntax of the call to the function. After the compiler is done, the linker finds the object code for that function and links it with your main function's object code. We do this kind of thing all the time when we invoke library functions. C++ systems supply only the object code, not the source code, for library functions like sqrt. The source ccde for their implementations are physically hidden from view.

One advantage of physical hiding is that it helps the programmer avoid the temptation to take advantage of any unusual features of a function's implementation. For example, suppose we were changing the Activity program to read temperatures and output activities repeatedly. Knowing that function GetTemp doesn't perform range checking on the input value, we might be tempted to use −1000 as a sentinel for the loop:

```
int main()
{
    int temperature;

    GetTemp(temperature);
    while (temperature != -1000)
    {
        PrintActivity(temperature);
        GetTemp(temperature);
    }
    return 0;
}
```

This code works fine for now, but later we might want to improve GetTemp so that it checks for a valid temperature range (as it should).

```
void GetTemp( /* out */ int& temp )

// This function prompts for a temperature to be entered, reads
// the input value, checks to be sure it is in a valid temperature
// range, and echo-prints it

// Postcondition:
//      User has been prompted for a temperature value (temp)
//   && Error messages and additional prompts have been printed
//      in response to invalid data
//   && IF no valid data was encountered before EOF
//          Value of temp is undefined
//      ELSE
//          -50 <= temp <= 130  &&  temp has been printed

{
    cout << "Enter the outside temperature (-50 through 130): ";
    cin >> temp;
```

```
    while (cin &&                               // While not EOF and
           (temp < -50 || temp > 130))          //    temp is invalid...
    {
        cout << "Temperature must be"
             << " -50 through 130." << endl;
        cout << "Enter the outside temperature: ";
        cin >> temp;
    }
    if (cin)                                     // If not EOF...
        cout << "The current temperature is "
             << temp << endl;
}
```

Unfortunately, if we make this improvement, the main function will be stuck in an infinite loop because GetTemp won't let us enter the sentinel value −1000. If the original implementation of GetTemp had been physically hidden, we would not have relied on its unusual feature of not performing error checking. Instead, we would have written the main function in a way that is unaffected by the improvement to GetTemp:

```
int main()
{
    int temperature;

    GetTemp(temperature);
    while (cin)                         // While not EOF...
    {
        PrintActivity(temperature);
        GetTemp(temperature);
    }
    return 0;
}
```

Later in the book, you learn how to write multifile programs and hide implementations physically. In the meantime, conscientiously avoid writing code that depends on the internal workings of a function.

PROBLEM-SOLVING CASE STUDY

Comparison of Furniture-Store Sales

   Problem: A new regional sales manager for the Chippendale Furniture Stores has just come into town. She wants to see a monthly, department-by-department comparison, in the form of bar graphs, of the two Chippendale stores in town. The daily sales for each department are kept in each store's accounting files. Data on each store are stored in the following form:

Department ID number
Number of business days for the department
Daily sales for day 1
Daily sales for day 2
.
.
.

Daily sales for last day in period
Department ID number
Number of business days for the department
Daily sales for day 1
.
.
.

The bar graph to be printed is of the following form:

```
Bar Graph Comparing Departments of Store#1 and Store#2

Store  Sales in 1,000s of dollars
   #   0         5        10        15        20        25
       |.........|.........|.........|.........|.........|

       Dept 1030
   1   ***********************
       Dept 1030
   2   *****************************************
       

       Dept 1210
   1   *************************************************
       Dept 1210
   2   ****************************************
       

       Dept 2040
   1   **********************************************
       Dept 2040
   2   *****************************
```

PROBLEM-SOLVING CASE STUDY cont'd.

As you can see from the bar graph, each star represents $500 in sales. No stars are printed if a department's sales are less than or equal to $250.

Input: Two data files (`store1` and `store2`), each containing

Department ID number (`int`)
Number of business days (`int`)
Daily sales (several `float` values)

repeated for each department.

Output: A bar graph showing total sales for each department.

Discussion: Reading the input data from both files is straightforward. We need to open the files (let's call them `store1` and `store2`) and read a department ID number, the number of business days, and the daily sales for that department. After processing each department, we can read the data for the next department, continuing until we run out of departments (EOF is encountered). Because the process is the same for reading `store1` and `store2`, we can use one function for reading both files. All we have to do is pass the file name as a parameter to the function. We want total sales for each department, so this function has to sum the daily sales for a department as they are read. A function can be used to print the output heading. Another function can be used to print out each department's sales for the month in graphic form.

There are three loops in this program: one in the `main` function (to read and process the file data), one in the function that gets the data for one department (to read all the daily sales amounts), and one in the function that prints the bar graph (to print the stars in the graph). The loop for the `main` function tests for EOF on *both* `store1` and `store2`. One graph for each store must be printed for each iteration of this loop.

The loop for the `GetData` function requires an iteration counter that ranges from 1 through the number of days for the department. Also, a summing operation is needed to total the sales for the period.

At first glance, it might seem that the loop for the `PrintData` function is like any other counting loop, but let's look at how we would do this process by hand. Suppose we wanted to print a bar for the value 1850. We first would make sure the number was greater than 250, then print a star and subtract 500 from the original value. We would check again to see if the new value was greater than 250, then print a star and subtract 500. This process would repeat until the resulting value was less than or equal to 250. Thus, the loop requires a counter that is decremented by 500 for each iteration, with a termination value of 250 or less. A star is printed for each iteration of the loop.

Function `PrintHeading` does not receive any values from `main`, nor does it return any. Thus, its parameter list is empty.

Function `GetData` receives the data file from `main` and returns it, modified, after having read some values. The function returns the values of the department ID and its sales for the month to `main`. Thus, `GetData` has three formal parameters: the data file (with data flow Inout), department ID (data flow Out), and department sales (data flow Out).

Function `PrintData` must receive the department ID, store number, and department sales from the `main` function to print the bar graph for an input record. Therefore, the function has those three items as its formal parameters, all with data flow In.

Assumptions: Each file is in order by department ID. The same departments are in each store.

Main   *Level 0*

```
Open data files (and verify success)
Print heading
Get data for a Store 1 department
Get data for a Store 2 department
WHILE NOT EOF on file store1 AND NOT EOF on file store2
    Print data for the Store 1 department
    Print data for the Store 2 department
    Get data for a Store 1 department
    Get data for a Store 2 department
```

Print Heading (No parameters)   *Level 1*

```
Print chart title
Print heading
Print bar graph scale
```

into a C++ logical expression.

The second limitation is that the `assert` function is appropriate only for testing a program that is under development. A production program (one that has been completed and released to the public) must be robust and must furnish helpful error messages to the user of the program. You can imagine how baffled a user would be if the program suddenly quit and displayed an error message like

```
Assertion failed: sysRes <= resCount, file newproj.cpp, line 298
```

Despite these limitations, you'll want to use the `assert` function as a regular tool for testing and debugging your programs.

Testing and Debugging Hints

1. Follow documentation guidelines carefully when writing functions (see Appendix F). As your programs become more complex and prone to errors, it becomes increasingly important to adhere to documentation and formatting standards. Even if the function name seems to describe the process being done, describe that process in comments. Include comments stating the function precondition (if any) and postcondition to make the function interface complete. Use comments to explain the purposes of all the formal parameters and local variables in a function.
2. Provide a function prototype near the top of your program for each function you've written. Make sure that the prototype and its corresponding function heading are an *exact* match (except for the absence of parameter names in the prototype).
3. Be sure to put a semicolon at the end of a function prototype. But do *not* put a semicolon at the end of the function heading in a function definition. Because function prototypes look so much like function headings, it's common to get one of them wrong.
4. Be sure the formal parameter list gives the data type of each parameter.
5. Use value parameters unless a result is to be returned through a parameter. Reference parameters can change the contents of an actual parameter; value parameters cannot.
6. In a formal parameter list, be sure the data type of each reference parameter ends with an ampersand (&). Without the ampersand, the parameter is a value parameter.
7. Make sure that the actual parameter list of every function call matches the formal parameter list in number and order of items, and be very careful with their data types. The compiler will trap any mismatch in the number of parameters. But if there is a mismatch in data types, there is no compile-time error. With pass-by-reference, the compiler creates a

temporary variable whose address is passed to the function, and the results may not be what you expect. With pass-by-value, implicit type coercion takes place.

8. Remember that a reference parameter requires a variable as an actual parameter, whereas a value parameter can have any expression that supplies a value of the same data type (except as noted in hint 7) as an actual parameter.

9. Become familiar with *all* the tools available to you when you're trying to locate the sources of bugs—the algorithm walk-through, hand tracing, the system's debugger program, the `assert` function, and debug output statements.

Summary

C++ allows us to write programs in modules expressed as functions. The structure of a program, therefore, can parallel its top-down design even when the program is complicated. To make your `main` function look exactly like Level 0 of your top-down design, simply write each lower-level module as a function. The `main` function then executes these other functions in logical sequence.

An important means of communication between two functions is the use of two parameter lists: the formal parameter list (which includes the data type of each identifier) in the function heading, and the actual parameter list in the calling code. The items in these lists must agree in number and position, and they should agree in data type.

Part of the top-down design process involves determining what data must be received by a lower-level module and what information must be returned from it. The names of these data values, together with the precondition and postcondition of a module, define its interface. The names of the data values become the formal parameter list, and the module name becomes the name of the function. With void functions, a call to the function is accomplished by writing the function's name as a statement, enclosing the appropriate actual parameters in parentheses.

C++ has two kinds of formal parameters: reference and value. Reference parameters have data types ending in "&" in the formal parameter list, whereas value parameters do not. Parameters that return values from a function should be reference parameters; all others should be value parameters. This minimizes the risk of errors, because only a copy of the value of an actual parameter is passed to a value parameter, and thus the original value cannot be changed.

In addition to the variables declared in its formal parameter list, a function may have local variables declared within it. These variables are accessible only within the block in which they are declared. Local variables must be initialized each time the function containing them is called because their values are destroyed when the function returns.

You may call functions from more than one place in a program. The positional matching mechanism allows the use of different variables as actual parameters to the same function. Multiple calls to a function, from different places and with different actual parameters, can be used to simplify greatly the coding of many complex programs.

QUICK CHECK

1. If a design has one Level 0 module and three Level 1 modules, how many C++ functions is the program likely to have? (pp. 324–328)
2. Does a C++ function have to be declared before it can be used in a function call? (p. 328)
3. What is the difference between a function declaration and a function definition in C++? (pp. 335–338)
4. Given the function heading

   ```
   void QuickCheck( int    size,
                    float& length,
                    char   initial )
   ```

   indicate which parameters are value parameters and which are reference parameters. (pp. 342–343)
5. a. What would a call to the QuickCheck function look like if the actual parameters were the variables radius (a float), number (an int), and letter (a char)? (p. 334)
   b. How is the matchup between these actual parameters and the formal parameters made? What information is actually passed from the calling code to the QuickCheck function, given these actual parameters? (pp. 342–350)
   c. Which of these actual parameters is (are) protected from being changed by the QuickCheck function? (pp. 342–350)
6. Where in a function are local variables declared, and what are their initial values equal to? (pp. 338–339)
7. Assume that you are designing a program and you need a void function that reads any number of floating point values and returns their average. The number of values to be read is in an integer variable named dataPoints, declared in the calling code.
   a. How many parameters will there be in the formal parameter list, and what will their data type(s) be? (pp. 352–354)
   b. Which of the formal parameters should be passed by reference and which should be passed by value? (pp. 352–354)
8. Describe one way in which you can use a function to simplify the coding of an algorithm. (pp. 333–334)

Answers   1. Four (including main)   2. Yes   3. A definition is a declaration that includes the function body.   4. length is a reference parameter; size and initial are value parameters.
5. a. QuickCheck(number, radius, letter); b. The matchup is done on the basis of the pa-

rameters' positions in each list. Copies of the values of size and initial are passed to the function; the location (memory address) of length is passed to the function. c. size and initial are protected from change because it is only copies of their values that are sent to the function. 6. In the block that forms the body of the function. Their initial values are undefined. 7. a. There will be two parameters: an int containing the number of values to be read and a float containing the computed average. b. The int should be a value parameter; the float should be a reference parameter. 8. The coding may be simplified if the function is called from more than one place in the program.

EXAM PREPARATION EXERCISES

1. Define the following terms:

function call	formal parameter
parameter list	actual parameter
parameterless function	local variable

2. Identify the following items in the program fragment shown below.

function prototype	function definition
function heading	formal parameters
actual parameters	function call
local variables	function body

```
void Test( int, int, int );

int main()
{
    int a;
    int b;
    int c;
       .
       .
       .
    Test(a, c, b);
    Test(b, a, c);
       .
       .
       .
}

void Test( int d,
           int e,
           int f )
{
    int g;
    int h;
       .
       .
       .
}
```

3. For the program in Exercise 2, fill in the blanks with variable names to show the matching that takes place between the actual and the formal parameter lists in each of the two calls to the Test function.

	First Call to Test		*Second Call to* Test	
	Formal	*Actual*	*Formal*	*Actual*
1.	____	____	1. ____	____
2.	____	____	2. ____	____
3.	____	____	3. ____	____

4. What is the output of the following program?

```
#include <iostream.h>

void Print( int, int );

int main()
{
    int n;

    n = 3;
    Print(5, n);
    Print(n, n);
    Print(n * n, 12);
    return 0;
}

void Print( int a,
            int b )
{
    int c;

    c = 2 * a + b;
    cout << a << ' ' << b << ' ' << c << endl;
}
```

5. Using a reference parameter (passing by reference), a function can obtain the initial value of an actual parameter as well as change the value of the actual parameter. (True or False?)
6. Using a value parameter, the value of a variable can be passed to a function and used for computation there, without any modification of the actual parameter. (True or False?)
7. Given the declarations

```
const int ANGLE = 90;

char letter;
int  number;
```

indicate whether each of the following actual parameters would be valid using pass-by-value, pass-by-reference, or both.

a. `letter`
b. `ANGLE`
c. `number`
d. `number + 3`
e. `23`
f. `ANGLE * number`
g. `abs(number)`

8. A variable named `widgets` is stored in memory location 13571. When the statements

```
widgets = 23;
Drop(widgets);
```

are executed, what information is passed to the formal parameter in function Drop? (Assume the formal parameter is a reference parameter.)

9. Assume that, in Exercise 8, the formal parameter for function `Drop` is named `clunkers`. After the function body performs the assignment

```
clunkers = 77;
```

what is the value in `widgets`? in `clunkers`?

10. Using the data values

```
3 2 4
```

show what is printed by the following program.

```cpp
#include <iostream.h>

void Test( int&, int&, int& );

int main()
{
    int a;
    int b;
    int c;

    Test(a, b, c);
    b = b + 10;
    cout << "The answers are " << b << ' ' << c << ' ' << a;
    return 0;
}

void Test( int& z,
           int& x,
           int& a )
{
```

```
        cin >> z >> x >> a;                  12    10    3
        a = z * x + a;
    }
```

11. The program below has a function named Change. Fill in the values of all variables before and after the function is called. Then fill in the values of all variables after the return to the main function. (If any value is undefined, write *u* instead of a number.)

```
#include <iostream.h>

void Change( int, int& );

int main()
{
    int a;
    int b;

    a = 10;
    b = 7;
    Change(a, b);
    cout << a << ' ' << b << endl;
    return 0;
}

void Change( int  x,
             int& y )
{
    int b;

    b = x;
    y = y + b;
    x = y;
}
```

Variables in main just before Change is called:

a ___10___
b ___7___

Variables in Change at the moment control enters the function:

x ___10___
y ___7___
b ___undefined___

Variables in main after return from Change:

a ___10___
b ___17___

12. Show the output of the following program.

```cpp
#include <iostream.h>

void Test( int&, int );

int main()
{
    int d;
    int e;

    d = 12;
    e = 14;
    Test(d, e);
    cout << "In the main function after the first call, "
         << "the variables equal " << d << ' ' << e << endl;
    d = 15;
    e = 18;
    Test(e, d);
    cout << "In the main function after the second call, "
         << "the variables equal " << d << ' ' << e << endl;
    return 0;
}

void Test( int& s,
           int  t )
{
    s = 3;
    s = s + 2;
    t = 4 * s;
    cout << "In function Test, the variables equal "
         << s << ' ' << t << endl;
}
```

variables   5   14 (handwritten)

variables   5   20. (handwritten)

13. Number the marked statements in the following program to show the order in which they are executed (the logical order of execution).

```cpp
#include <iostream.h>

void DoThis( int&, int& );

int main()
{
    int number1;
    int number2;

    cout << "Exercise ";
    DoThis(number1, number2);
    cout << number1 << ' ' << number2 << endl;
    return 0;
}
```

(handwritten numbers to left of marked statements: 1, 2, 5)

(continued on next page)

```
            void DoThis( int& value1,
                          int& value2 )
        {
            int value3;

  3         cin >> value3 >> value1;
  4         value2 = value1 + 10;
        }
```

14. If the program in Exercise 13 were run with the data values 10 and 15, what would be the values of the following variables just before execution of the **return** statement in the **main** function?

    number1 _____ number2 _____ value3 _____

PROGRAMMING WARM-UP EXERCISES

1. Write the function heading for a void function named **PrintMax** that accepts a pair of integers and prints out the greater of the two. Document the data flow of each parameter with /* in */, /* out */, or /* inout */.
2. Write the heading for a void function that corresponds to the following list.

    Module Rocket Simulation

Incoming	thrust (floating point)
Incoming/Outgoing	weight (floating point)
Incoming	timeStep (integer)
Incoming	totalTime (integer)
Outgoing	velocity (floating point)
Outgoing	outOfFuel (Boolean)

3. Write a void function that reads in a specified number of **float** values and returns their average. A call to this function might look like

    GetMeanOf(5, mean);

    where the first parameter specifies the number of values to be read, and the second parameter contains the result. Document the data flow of each parameter with /* in */, /* out */, or /* inout */.
4. Given the function heading

    ```
    void Halve( /* inout */ int& firstNumber,
                /* inout */ int& secondNumber )
    ```

    write the body of the function so that when it returns, the original values in **firstNumber** and **secondNumber** are halved.
5. Add comments to the preceding **Halve** function that state the function precondition and postcondition.
6. a. Write a single void function to replace the repeated pattern of statements you identified in Case Study Follow-Up Exercise 3 of Chapter 3. Document the data flow of the formal parameters with /* in */, /* out */, or /* inout */. Include comments giving the function precondition and postcondition.
   b. Show the function calls with actual parameters.

7. a. Write a void function that reads in data values of type int (heartRate) until a normal heart rate (between 60 and 80) is read or EOF occurs. The function has one parameter, named normal, that contains TRUE if a normal heart rate was read or FALSE if EOF occurred. (Assume that a data type Boolean has already been defined.)

   b. Write a statement that invokes your function. You may use the same variable name for the actual and formal parameters.

8. Consider the following function definition.

```
void Rotate( /* inout */ int& firstValue,
             /* inout */ int& secondValue,
             /* inout */ int& thirdValue  )
{
    int temp;

    temp = firstValue;
    firstValue = secondValue;
    secondValue = thirdValue;
    thirdValue = temp;
}
```

   a. Add comments to the function that tell a reader what the function does and what is the purpose of each parameter and local variable.

   b. Write a program that reads three values into variables, echo-prints them, calls the Rotate function with the three variables as parameters, and then prints the parameters after the function returns.

9. Modify the function in Exercise 8 to perform the same sort of operation on four values. Modify the program you wrote for part b of Exercise 8 to work with the new version of this function.

10. Write a void function named CountUpper that counts the number of uppercase letters on one line of input. The function should return this number to the calling code in a parameter named upCount.

11. Write a void function named AddTime that has three parameters: hours, minutes, and elapsedTime. elapsedTime is an integer number of minutes to be added to the starting time passed in through hours and minutes. The resulting new time is returned through hours and minutes. For example:

Before Call *to* AddTime	*After Call* *to* AddTime
hours = 12	hours = 16
minutes = 44	minutes = 2
elapsedTime = 198	elapsedTime = 198

12. Write a void function named GetNonBlank that returns the first nonblank character it encounters in the standard input stream. In your function, use the cin.get function to read each character. (This GetNonBlank function is just for practice. It's unnecessary because you could use the >> operator, which skips leading blanks, to accomplish the same result.)

13. Write a void function named SkipToBlank that skips all characters in the standard input stream until a blank is encountered. In your function, use the

`cin.get` function to read each character. (This function is just for practice. There's already a library function, `cin.ignore`, that allows you to do the same thing.)

14. Modify the function in Exercise 13 so that it returns a count of the number of characters that were skipped.

PROGRAMMING PROBLEMS

1. Using functions, rewrite the program developed for Programming Problem 4 in Chapter 6.

   Develop a top-down design and write a C++ program to determine the number of words encountered in the input stream. For the sake of simplicity, we define a word to be any sequence of characters except whitespace characters (blanks and newlines). Words may be separated by any number of whitespace characters. A word may be any length, from a single character to an entire line of characters. If you are writing the program to read data from a file, then it should echo-print the input. For an interactive implementation, you do not need to echo-print for this program.

   For example, for the following data, the program would indicate that 26 words were entered.

   ```
   This isn't exactly an example of g00d english, but it
   does demonstrate that a w0rd is just a se@uence of
   characters          with0u+ any blank$.   #####   .......
   ```

   (*Hint:* One way to solve this problem involves turning the `SkipToBlank` function of Programming Warm-Up Exercise 13 into a `SkipToWhitespace` function.)

   Now that your programs are becoming more complex, it is even more important for you to use proper indentation and style, meaningful identifiers, and plenty of comments.

2. Write a C++ program that reads characters representing binary (base 2) numbers from a data file and translates them to decimal (base 10) numbers. The decimal numbers should be output in a column with an appropriate heading. Each binary number has been placed "backwards" in the file. That is, the rightmost digit is the first encountered, the second digit from the right is encountered next, and so on. The program reads the digits one at a time. As each digit is read, the program should translate that digit into the corresponding decimal value by multiplying it by the appropriate power of 2 (depending on where the digit was in the number). There is only one number per input line, but there is an arbitrary number of blanks before each number. The program should check for bad data; if it encounters anything except a zero or a one, it should output the message "Bad integer on input."

   As always, use plenty of comments, proper documentation and coding style, and meaningful identifiers throughout this program. You must decide which of your design modules should be coded as functions to make the program easier to understand.

3. Develop a top-down design and write a C++ program to print a calendar for one year, given the year and the day of the week that January 1 falls on. It may help to think of this task as printing 12 calendars, one for each month, given the day of

the week on which a month starts and the number of days in the month. Each successive month starts on the day of the week that follows the last day of the preceding month. Days of the week should be numbered 0 through 6 for Sunday through Saturday. Years that are divisible by 4 are leap years. (Determining leap years actually is more complicated than this, but for this program it will suffice.) Here is a sample run for an interactive program:

```
What year do you want a calendar for?
2002
What day of the week does January 1 fall on?
(Enter 0 for Sunday, 1 for Monday, etc.)
2
            2002

            January
    S   M   T   W   T   F   S
   _____
            1   2   3   4   5
    6   7   8   9  10  11  12
   13  14  15  16  17  18  19
   20  21  22  23  24  25  26
   27  28  29  30  31

            February
    S   M   T   W   T   F   S
   _____
                            1   2
    3   4   5   6   7   8   9
   10  11  12  13  14  15  16
   17  18  19  20  21  22  23
   24  25  26  27  28
                    .
                    .
                    .

            December
    S   M   T   W   T   F   S
   _____
    1   2   3   4   5   6   7
    8   9  10  11  12  13  14
   15  16  17  18  19  20  21
   22  23  24  25  26  27  28
   29  30  31
```

When writing your program, be sure to use proper indentation and style, meaningful identifiers, and plenty of comments.

4. Write a top-down design and a C++ program with functions to help you balance your checking account. The program should let you enter the initial balance for the month, followed by a series of transactions. For each transaction entered, the program should echo-print the transaction data, the current balance for the account, and the total service charges. Service charges are $0.10 for a deposit and $0.15 for a check. If the balance drops below $500.00 at any point during the month, a service charge of $5.00 is assessed for the month. If the balance drops below $50.00, the program should print a warning message. If the balance becomes negative, an additional service charge of $10.00 should be assessed for each check until the balance becomes positive again.

A transaction takes the form of a letter, followed by a blank and a `float` number. If the letter is a C, then the number is the amount of a check. If the letter is a D, then the number is the amount of a deposit. The last transaction consists of the letter E, with no number following it. A sample run might look like this:

```
Enter the beginning balance:
879.46
Enter a transaction:
C 400.00
Transaction: Check in amount of $400.00
Current balance: $479.46
Service charge: Check - $0.15
Service charge: Below $500 - $5.00
Total service charges: $5.15
Enter a transaction:
D 100.0
Transaction: Deposit in amount of $100.00
Current balance: $579.46
Service charge: Deposit - $0.10
Total service charges: $5.25
Enter a transaction:
E
Transaction: End
Current balance: $579.46
Total service charges: $5.25
Final balance: $574.21
```

As usual, your program should use proper style and indentation, meaningful identifiers, and appropriate comments. Also, be sure to check for data errors such as invalid transaction codes or negative amounts.

5. In this problem you are to design and implement a Roman numeral calculator. The subtractive Roman numeral notation commonly in use today (such as IV, meaning "4") was used only rarely during the time of the Roman Republic and Empire. For ease of calculation, the Romans most frequently used a purely additive notation in which a number was simply the sum of its digits (4 equals IIII, in this notation). Each number starts with the digit of highest value and ends with the digit of smallest value. This is the notation we use in this problem.

Your program inputs two Roman numbers and an arithmetic operator and prints out the result of the operation, also as a Roman number. The values of the Roman digits are as follows:

I	1
V	5
X	10
L	50
C	100
D	500
M	1000

Thus, the number MDCCCCLXXXXVI represents 1996. The arithmetic operators that your program should recognize in the input are +, -, *, and /. These should perform the C++ operations of integer addition, subtraction, multiplication, and division.

One way of approaching this problem is to convert the Roman numbers into integers, perform the required operation, and then convert the result back into a Roman number for printing. The following might be a sample run of the program:

```
Enter the first number:
MCCXXVI
The first number is 1226
Enter the second number:
LXVIIII
The second number is 69
Enter the desired arithmetic operation:
+
The sum of MCCXXVI and LXVIIII is MCCLXXXXV (1295)
```

Your program should use proper style and indentation, appropriate comments, and meaningful identifiers. It also should check for errors in the input, such as illegal digits or arithmetic operators, and take appropriate actions when these are found. The program also may check to ensure that the numbers are in purely additive form—that is, digits are followed only by digits of the same or lower value.

6. Develop a top-down design and write a program to produce a bar chart of gourmet-popcorn production for a cooperative farm group on a farm-by-farm basis. The input to the program is a series of data sets, one per line, with each set representing the production for one farm. The output is a bar chart that identifies each farm and displays its production in pints of corn per acre.

Each data set consists of the name of a farm, followed by a comma and one or more spaces, a `float` number representing acres planted, one or more spaces, and an `int` number representing pint jars of popcorn produced.

The output is a single line for each farm, with the name of the farm starting in the first column on a line and the bar chart starting in column 30. Each mark in the bar chart represents 250 pint jars of popcorn per acre. The production goal for the year is 5000 jars per acre. A vertical bar should appear in the chart for farms with lower production, and a special mark is used for farms with production greater than or equal to 5000 jars per acre. For example, given the input file

```
Orville's Acres,  114.8  43801
Hoffman's Hills,  77.2  36229
Jiffy Quick Farm,  89.4  24812
Jolly Good Plantation,  183.2  104570
Organically Grown Inc.,  45.5  14683
```

the output would be

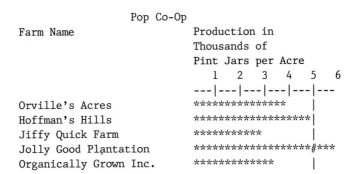

```
                          Pop Co-Op
Farm Name                 Production in
                          Thousands of
                          Pint Jars per Acre
                           1   2   3   4   5   6
                          ---|---|---|---|---|---
Orville's Acres           **************    |
Hoffman's Hills           ******************|
Jiffy Quick Farm          ***********       |
Jolly Good Plantation     *******************#***
Organically Grown Inc.    *************      |
```

This problem should decompose neatly into several functions. You should write your program in proper programming style, with plenty of comments and no global variables. It should handle data errors (such as a farm name longer than 29 characters) without crashing.

CASE STUDY FOLLOW-UP

1. Write a separate function for the Graph program that prints a bar of asterisks, given the department sales value.
2. Rewrite the existing `PrintData` function so that it calls the function you wrote for Question 1.

8

Scope, Lifetime, and More on Functions

GOALS

- To be able to do the following tasks, given a C++ program composed of several functions:

    Determine whether a variable is being referenced globally.

    Determine which variables are local variables.

    Determine which variables are accessible within a given block.

- To be able to determine the lifetime of each variable in a program.
- To understand and be able to avoid unwanted side effects.
- To know when to use a value-returning function.
- To be able to design and code a value-returning function for a specific task.
- To be able to invoke a value-returning function properly.

As programs get larger and more complicated, the number of identifiers in a program increases. We invent function names, variable names, constant identifiers, and so on. Some of these identifiers we declare inside blocks. Other identifiers—function names, for example—we declare outside of any block. This chapter examines the C++ rules by which a function may access identifiers that are declared outside its own block. Using these rules, we return to the discussion of interface design that we began in Chapter 7.

Finally, we look at the second kind of subprogram provided by C++: the *value-returning function*. Unlike void functions, which return results (if any) through the parameter list, a value-returning function returns a single result—the function value—to the expression from which it was called. In this chapter, you learn how to write user-defined value-returning functions.

 ## Scope and Lifetime

Scope of Identifiers

As we saw in Chapter 7, local variables are those declared inside a block, such as the body of a function. Recall that local variables cannot be accessed outside the block that contains them. The same access rule applies to declarations of named constants: local constants may be accessed only in the block in which they are declared.

Any block, not only a function body, can contain variable and constant declarations. For example, this If statement contains a block that declares a local variable n:

```
if (alpha > 3)
{
    int n;

    cin >> n;
    beta = beta + n;
}
```

As with any local variable, n cannot be accessed by any statement outside the block containing its declaration.

If we list all the places from which an identifier could be accessed legally, we would describe that identifier's **scope of visibility** or **scope of access**, often just called its **scope**.

Scope The region of program code where it is legal to reference (use) an identifier.

C++ defines three categories of scope for any identifier.*

1. **Class scope**
   This term refers to the data type called a *class*, which we introduced briefly in Chapter 4. We postpone a detailed discussion of class scope until Chapter 15.
2. **Local scope**
   The scope of an identifier declared inside a block extends from the point of declaration to the end of that block.
3. **Global** (or **file**) **scope**
   The scope of an identifier declared outside all functions and classes extends from the point of declaration to the end of the entire file containing the program code.

C++ function names have global scope. (There is an exception to this rule, which we discuss in Chapter 15 when we examine C++ classes.) Once a function name has been declared, the function can be invoked by any other function in the rest of the program. In C++ there is no such thing as a local function—that is, you cannot nest a function definition inside another function definition.

Global variables and constants are those declared outside all functions. In the following code fragment, gamma is a global variable and can be accessed directly by statements in main and SomeFunc.

```
int gamma;     // Global variable

int main()
{
    .
    .
    .
}

void SomeFunc()
{
    .
    .
    .
}
```

When a function declares a local identifier with the same name as a global identifier, the local identifier takes precedence within the function. This principle is called **name precedence** or **name hiding.**

---

*Technically, C++ defines four scope categories. The fourth relates to a statement called a goto statement, which we do not discuss in this book.

Name Precedence   The precedence that a local identifier in a function has over a global identifier with the same name in any references that the function makes to that identifier; also called *name hiding*.

Here's an example that uses both local and global declarations:

```
#include <iostream.h>

void SomeFunc( float );

const int a = 17;      // A global constant
int b;                 // A global variable
int c;                 // Another global variable

int main()
{
    b = 4;                      // Assignment to global b
    c = 6;                      // Assignment to global c
    SomeFunc(42.8);
    return 0;
}

void SomeFunc( float c )    // Prevents access to global c
{
    float b;                // Prevents access to global b

    b = 2.3;                // Assignment to local b
    cout << "a = " << a;    // Output global a (17)
    cout << " b = " << b;   // Output local b (2.3)
    cout << " c = " << c;   // Output local c (42.8)
}
```

In this example, function SomeFunc accesses global constant a but declares its own local variables b and c. Thus, the output would be

```
a = 17 b = 2.3 c = 42.8
```

Local variable b takes precedence over global variable b, effectively hiding global b from the statements in function SomeFunc. Formal parameter c also blocks access to global variable c from within the function. Formal parameters act just like local variables in this respect.

Scope Rules

When you write C++ programs, you rarely declare global variables. There are negative aspects to using global variables, which we discuss later. But when a situation crops up where you have a compelling need for global variables, it pays to know how C++ handles these declarations. The rules for accessing identifiers that aren't declared locally are called **scope rules.**

> **Scope Rules**   The rules that determine where in the program an identifier may be accessed, given the point where that identifier is declared.

In addition to local and global access, the C++ scope rules define what happens when blocks are nested within other blocks. Anything declared in a block that contains a nested block is **nonlocal** to the inner block. (Global identifiers are nonlocal with respect to all blocks in the program.) If a block accesses any identifier declared outside its own block, it is a *nonlocal access.*

> **Nonlocal Identifier**   Any identifier declared outside a given block is said to be nonlocal with respect to that block.

Here are the detailed scope rules, excluding class scope and certain language features we have not yet discussed:

1. A function name has global scope. Function definitions cannot be nested within function definitions.
2. The scope of a formal parameter is identical to the scope of a local variable declared in the outermost block of the function body.
3. The scope of a global variable or constant extends from its declaration to the end of the file, except as noted in rule 5.
4. The scope of a local variable or constant extends from its declaration to the end of the block in which it is declared. This scope includes any nested blocks, except as noted in rule 5.
5. The scope of an identifier does not include any nested block that contains a locally declared identifier with the same name (local identifiers have name precedence).

Here is a sample program that demonstrates C++ scope rules. To simplify the example, only the declarations and headings are spelled out. Note how the While-loop body labeled Block3, declared within function Block2, contains its own local variable declarations.

```
// ScopeRules program

#include <iostream.h>

void Block1( int, char& );
void Block2();

int  a1;          // One global variable
char a2;          // Another global variable

int main()
{
     .
     .
     .
}

//**********************************************************************

void Block1( int   a1,          // Prevents access to global a1
             char& b2 )         // Has same scope as c1 and d2
{
    int c1;         // A variable local to Block1
    int d2;         // Another variable local to Block1
     .
     .
     .
}

//**********************************************************************

void Block2()
{
    int a1;         // Prevents access to global a1
    int b2;         // Local to Block2; no conflict with b2 in Block1

    while (...)
    {               // Block3
        int c1;     // Local to Block3; no conflict with c1 in Block1
        int b2;     // Prevents nonlocal access to b2 in Block2; no
                    //   conflict with b2 in Block1
         .
         .
         .
    }
}
```

Let's look at the ScopeRules program in terms of the blocks it defines and see just what these rules mean. Figure 8-1 shows the headings and declarations in the ScopeRules program with the scopes of visibility indicated by boxes.

Anything inside a box can refer to anything in a larger surrounding box, but outside-in references aren't allowed. Thus, a statement in Block3 could access any identifier declared in Block2 or any global variable. A statement in Block3 could not access identifiers declared in Block1 because it would have to enter the Block1 box from outside.

Notice that the formal parameters for a function are inside the function's box, but the function name itself is outside. If the name of the function were inside the box, no function could call another function. This demonstrates merely that function names are globally accessible.

Imagine the boxes in Figure 8-1 as rooms whose walls are made of two-way mirrors, with the reflective side facing out and the see-through side facing in. If you stood in the room for Block3, you would be able to see out

■ FIGURE 8-1

Scope Diagram for
ScopeRules
Program

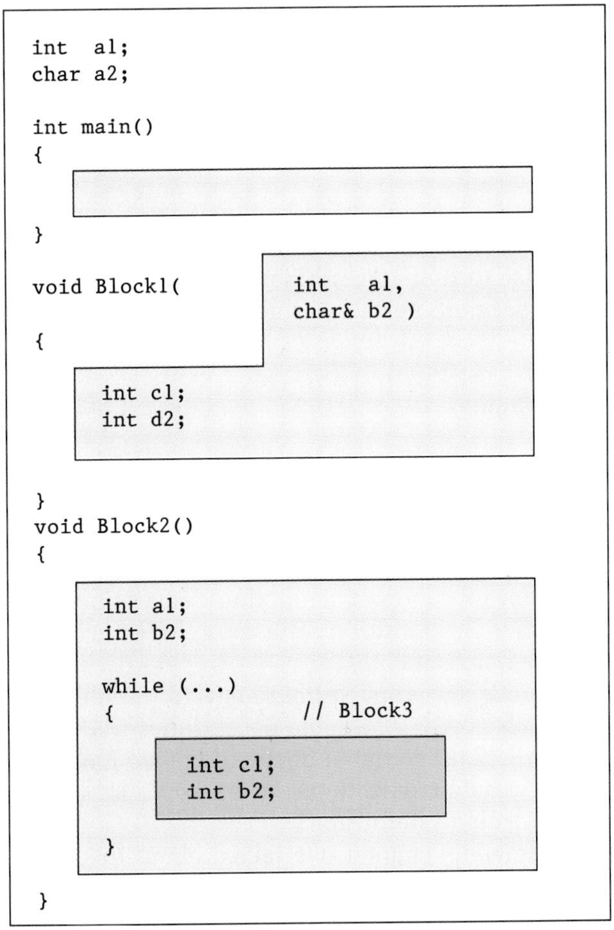

```
int   a1;
char a2;

int main()
{



}

void Block1(        int      a1,
                    char& b2 )

{
        int c1;
        int d2;



}
void Block2()
{
        int a1;
        int b2;

        while (...)
        {               // Block3

                int c1;
                int b2;

        }

}
```

through all the surrounding rooms to the declarations of the global variables (and anything between). You would not be able to see into any other rooms (such as Block1), however, because their mirrored outer surfaces would block your view. Because of this analogy, the term *visible* is often used in describing a scope of access. For example, variable a2 is visible throughout the program, meaning that it can be accessed from anywhere in the program.

Figure 8-1 does not tell the whole story; it represents only scope rules 1 through 4. We also must keep rule 5 in mind. Variable a1 is declared in two different places in the ScopeRules program. Because of name precedence, Block2 and Block3 access the a1 declared in Block2 rather than the global a1. Similarly, the scope of the variable b2 declared in Block2 does *not* include the "hole" created by Block3, because Block3 declares its own variable b2.

Name precedence is implemented by the compiler as follows. When a statement refers to an identifier, the compiler first checks the local declarations. If the identifier isn't local, the compiler works its way outward through each level of nesting until it finds an identifier with the same name. There it stops. If there is an identifier with the same name declared at a level even further out, it is never reached. If the compiler reaches the global declarations (including identifiers inserted by #include directives) and still can't find the identifier, an error message such as "UNDECLARED IDENTIFIER" will result.

Such a message most likely indicates a misspelling or an incorrect capitalization, or it could mean that the identifier was not declared before the reference to it or was not declared at all. It may also indicate, however, that the blocks are nested so that the identifier's scope doesn't include the reference.

Variable Declarations and Definitions

In Chapter 7, you learned that C++ terminology distinguishes between a function declaration and a function definition. A function prototype is a declaration only—that is, it doesn't cause memory space to be reserved for the function. In contrast, a function declaration that includes the body is called a function definition. The compiler reserves memory for the instructions in the function body.

C++ applies the same terminology to variable declarations. A variable declaration becomes a variable definition if it also reserves memory for the variable. All of the variable declarations we have used from the beginning have been variable definitions. What would a variable declaration look like if it were *not* also a definition?

In the previous chapter, we talked about the concept of a multifile program, a program that physically occupies several files containing individual pieces of the program. C++ has a reserved word extern that lets you reference a global variable located in another file. A "normal" declaration such as

Initializations in Declarations One of the most common things we do in programs is first declare a variable and then, in a separate statement, assign an initial value to the variable. Here's a typical example:

```
int sum;

sum = 0;
```

C++ allows you to combine these two statements into one. The result is known as an *initialization in a declaration*. Here we initialize sum in its declaration:

```
int sum = 0;
```

In a declaration, the expression that specifies the initial value is called an *initializer*. Above, the initializer is the constant 0.

An automatic variable is initialized to the specified value each time control enters the block:

```
void SomeFunc( int someParam )
{
    int i = 0;                    // Initialized each time
    int n = 2 * someParam + 3;    // Initialized each time
        .
        .
        .
}
```

In contrast, initialization of a static variable (either a global variable or a local variable explicitly declared static) occurs once only, the first time control reaches its declaration. Furthermore, the initializer must be a constant expression (one with only constant values as operands). Here's an example:

```
void AnotherFunc( int param )
{
    static char ch = 'A';       // Initialized once only
    static int  m  = param + 1; // Illegal. Constant expression
                                //    required
        .
        .
        .
}
```

Although an initialization gives a variable an initial value, it is perfectly acceptable to reassign it another value during program execution.

The following table summarizes initialization of static and automatic variables.

	Automatic variables	*Static variables*
Initialized when?	Each time control reaches the declaration	Once only, the first time control reaches the declaration
Initializer	Any expression*	Constant expression only*

*Implicit type coercion takes place if the data type of the initializer is different from the data type of the variable.

There are differing opinions about initializing a variable in its declaration. Some programmers never do it, preferring to keep an initialization close to the executable statements that depend on that variable. For example,

```
int loopCount;
    .
    .
    .
loopCount = 1;
while (loopCount <= 20)
{
        .
        .
        .
}
```

Other programmers maintain that one of the most frequent causes of program bugs is forgetting to initialize variables before using their contents; initializing each variable in its declaration eliminates these bugs. As with any controversial topic, most programmers seem to take a position somewhere between these two extremes.

Interface Design

We return now to the issue of interface design, which we first discussed in Chapter 7. Recall that the data flow through a function interface can take three forms: incoming only, outgoing only, and incoming/outgoing. Any item that can be classified as purely incoming should be coded as a value parameter. Items in the remaining two categories (outgoing and incoming/outgoing) must be reference parameters; the only way the function can deposit results into the caller's actual parameters is to have the addresses of those parameters. For emphasis, we repeat the following table from Chapter 7.

Data Flow for a Parameter	Parameter-Passing Mechanism
Incoming	Pass-by-value
Outgoing	Pass-by-reference
Incoming/outgoing	Pass-by-reference

As we said in the last chapter, there are exceptions to the guidelines in this table. C++ requires that I/O stream variables be passed by reference because of the way streams and files are implemented. We encounter another exception in Chapter 11.

Sometimes it is tempting to skip the interface design step when writing a function, letting it communicate with other functions by referencing global variables. Don't! Without the interface design step, you would actually be creating a poorly structured and undocumented interface. Except in well-justified circumstances, the use of global variables is a poor programming practice that can lead to program bugs. These bugs are extremely hard to locate and usually take the form of unwanted side effects.

Side Effects

Suppose you made a call to the sqrt library function in your program:

```
y = sqrt(x);
```

You expect that the call to sqrt will compute the square root of the variable x. You'd be surprised if sqrt also changed the value of your variable x because sqrt, by definition, does not make such changes. This would be an example of an unexpected and unwanted **side effect.**

Side Effect   Any effect of one function on another that is not a part of the explicitly defined interface between them.

Side effects are sometimes caused by a combination of reference parameters and careless coding in a function. Perhaps an assignment statement in

■ FIGURE 8-2

Side Effects

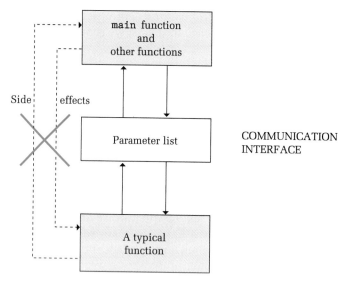

the function stores a temporary result into one of the reference parameters, accidentally changing the value of an actual parameter back in the calling code. As we mentioned before, using value parameters avoids this type of side effect by preventing the change from reaching the actual parameter.

Side effects can also occur when a function accesses a global variable. An error in the function might cause the value of a global variable to be changed in an unexpected way, causing an error in other functions that access that variable.

The symptoms of a side effect error are misleading because the trouble appears in one part of the program when it really is caused by something in another part. To avoid such errors, the only external effect that a function should have is to transfer information through the well-structured interface of the parameter list (see Figure 8-2). If functions access nonlocal variables *only* through their parameter lists, and if all incoming-only parameters are value parameters, then each function is essentially isolated from other parts of the program and there are no side effects.

When a function is free of side effects, we can treat it as an independent module and reuse it in other programs. We cannot reuse functions with side effects.

Here is a short example of a program that runs but produces incorrect results because of global variables and side effects.

```
//**********************************************************************
// Trouble program
// This is an example of poor program design, which
// causes an error when the program is executed
```

```
//*****************************************************************
#include <iostream.h>

void CountChars();

int  count;            // Supposed to count input lines, but does it?
char ch;               // Holds one input character

int main()
{
    count = 0;
    while (cin)
    {
        count++;
        CountChars();
    }
    cout << count << " lines of input processed." << endl;
    return 0;
}

//*****************************************************************

void CountChars()

// Counts the number of characters on one input line
// and prints the count

{
    count = 0;                                      // Side effect
    cin.get(ch);
    while (ch != '\n')
    {
        count++;                                    // Side effect
        cin.get(ch);
    }
    cout << count << " characters on this line." << endl;
}
```

The Trouble program is supposed to count and print the number of characters on each line of input. After the last line has been processed, it should
print the number of lines. Strangely enough, each time the program is run, it
reports that the number of lines of input is the same as the number of characters in the last line of input. This is because function CountChars accesses
the global variable count and uses it to store the number of characters on
each line of input.

There is no reason for count to be a global variable. If a local variable
count is declared in main and another local variable count is declared in
CountChars, the program works correctly. There is no conflict between the

two variables because each is visible only inside its own block. Also, ch should be declared locally in CountChars, of course, because that is the only place where it is used.

The Trouble program also demonstrates one common exception to the rule of not accessing global variables. Technically, cin and cout are global variables declared in the header file iostream.h. Function CountChars reads and writes directly to these streams. To be absolutely correct, cin and cout should be passed as reference parameters to the function. However, cin and cout are fundamental I/O facilities supplied by the standard library, and it is conventional for C++ functions to access them directly.

Global Constants

Contrary to what you might think, it is also acceptable to reference named constants globally. Because the values of global constants cannot be changed while the program is running, no side effects can occur. You have seen numerous examples of programs using global constants, such as the Lumber-Yard program of Chapter 5 and the TempStat and Invoice programs of Chapter 6, to name a few.

There are two advantages to referencing constants globally: 1) ease of change and 2) consistency. If we have to change the value of a constant, it's easier to change only one global declaration than to change a local declaration in every function. By declaring a constant in only one place, we also ensure that all parts of the program use exactly the same value.

This is not to say that you should declare *all* constants globally. If a constant is needed in only one function, then it makes sense to declare it locally within that function.

At this point, you may want to turn to the first two problem-solving case studies at the end of this chapter. These case studies further illustrate the interface design process and the use of value and reference parameters.

 ## Value-Returning Functions

In Chapter 7 and the first part of this chapter, we have been writing our own void functions. We now look at the second kind of subprogram in C++, the value-returning function. You already know several value-returning functions supplied by the C++ standard library: sqrt, abs, fabs, and others. From the caller's perspective, the main difference between void functions and value-returning functions is the way in which they are called. A call to a void function is a complete statement; a call to a value-returning function is part of an expression.

From a design perspective, value-returning functions are used when there is only one result returned by a function and that result is to be used directly in an expression. For example, suppose we are writing a program that calculates a prorated refund of tuition for students who withdraw in the middle of a semester. The amount to be refunded is the total tuition times the remaining fraction of the semester (the number of days remaining divided by the total number of days in the semester). The people who use the program want to be able to enter the dates on which the semester begins and ends and the date of withdrawal, and they want the program to calculate the fraction of the semester that remains.

Because each semester begins and ends within one calendar year, we can calculate the number of days in a period by determining the day number of each date and subtracting the starting day number from the ending day number. The day number is the number associated with each day of the year if you count sequentially from January 1. December 31 has the day number 365, except in leap years, when it is 366. For example, if a semester begins on 1/3/97 and ends on 5/17/97, the calculation is as follows.

The day number of 1/3/97 is 3
The day number of 5/17/97 is 137
The length of the semester is $137 - 3 + 1 = 135$

We add 1 to the difference of the days because we count the first day as part of the period.

The algorithm for calculating the day number for a date is complicated by leap years and by months of different lengths. We could code this algorithm as a void function named ComputeDay. The refund could then be computed by the following code segment.

```
ComputeDay(startMonth, startDay, startYear, start);
ComputeDay(lastMonth, lastDay, lastYear, last);
ComputeDay(withdrawMonth, withdrawDay, withdrawYear, withdraw);
fraction = float(last - withdraw + 1) / float(last - start + 1);
refund = tuition * fraction;
```

The first three parameters to ComputeDay are received by the function, and the last one is returned to the caller. Because ComputeDay returns only one value, we can write it as a value-returning function instead of a void function. Let's look at how the code segment would be written if we had a value-returning function named Day that returned the day number of a date in a given year.

```
start = Day(startMonth, startDay, startYear);
last = Day(lastMonth, lastDay, lastYear);
withdraw = Day(withdrawMonth, withdrawDay, withdrawYear);
fraction = float(last - withdraw + 1) / float(last - start + 1);
refund = tuition * fraction;
```

The second version of the code segment is much more intuitive. Because Day is a value-returning function, you know immediately that all its parame-

MAY WE INTRODUCE

Ada Lovelace

On December 10, 1815, a daughter—Augusta Ada Byron—was born to Anna Isabella (Annabella) Byron and George Gordon, Lord Byron. In England at that time, Byron's fame derived not only from his poetry but also from his wild, scandalous behavior. The marriage was strained from the beginning, and Annabella left Byron shortly after Ada's birth. By April of 1816, the two had signed separation papers. Byron left England, never to return. Throughout the rest of his life, he regretted being unable to see his daughter. At one point, he wrote of her:

> I see thee not. I hear thee not.
> But none can be so wrapt in thee.

Before he died in Greece at age 36, he exclaimed,

> Oh my poor dear child! My dear Ada! My God, could I but have seen her!

Meanwhile, Annabella, who would eventually become a baroness in her own right, and who was educated as both a mathematician and a poet, carried on with Ada's upbringing and education. Annabella gave Ada her first instruction in mathematics, but it soon became clear that Ada was gifted in the subject and should receive more extensive tutoring. Ada received further training from Augustus DeMorgan, famous today for one of the basic theorems of Boolean algebra, the logical foundation for modern computers. By age 8, Ada had also demonstrated an interest in mechanical devices and was building detailed model boats.

When she was 18, Ada visited the Mechanics Institute to hear Dr. Dionysius Lardner's lectures on the "Difference Engine," a mechanical calculating machine being built by Charles Babbage. She became so interested in the device that she arranged to be introduced to Babbage. It was said that, upon seeing Babbage's machine, Ada was the only person in the room to understand immediately how it worked and to recognize its significance. Ada and Charles Babbage became lifelong friends. She worked with him helping to document his designs, translating writings about his work, and developing programs for his machines. In fact, today Ada is recognized as the first computer

ters receive values and that it returns just one value (the day number for a date).

Let's look at the function definition for Day. Don't worry about how Day works; for now, we are concerned mainly with its syntax and structure.

```
int Day( /* in */ int month,        // Month number, 1 - 12
         /* in */ int dayOfMonth,   // Day of month, 1 - 31
         /* in */ int year       )  // Year. For example, 1997
```

programmer in history, and the modern Ada programming language is named in her honor.

When Babbage designed his Analytical Engine, Ada foresaw that it could go beyond arithmetic computations and become a general manipulator of symbols, and that it would thus have far-reaching capabilities. She even suggested that such a device could eventually be programmed with rules of harmony and composition so that it could produce "scientific" music. In effect, Ada foresaw the field of artificial intelligence more than 150 years ago.

In 1842, Babbage gave a series of lectures in Turin, Italy, on his Analytical Engine. One of the attendees was Luigi Menabrea, who was so impressed that he wrote an account of Babbage's lectures. At age 27, Ada decided to translate the account into English with the intent of adding a few of her own notes about the machine. In the end, her notes were twice as long as the original material, and the document, "The Sketch of the Analytical Engine," became the definitive work on the subject.

It is obvious from Ada's letters that her "notes" were entirely her own and that Babbage was sometimes making unsolicited editorial changes. At one point, Ada wrote to him,

> I am much annoyed at your having altered my Note. You know I am always willing to make any required alterations myself, but that I cannot endure another person to meddle with my sentences.

Ada gained the title Countess of Lovelace when she married Lord William Lovelace. The couple had three children, whose upbringing was left to Ada's mother, while Ada pursued her work in mathematics. Her husband was supportive of her work, but for a woman of that day, such behavior was considered almost as scandalous as some of her father's exploits.

Ada Lovelace died of cancer in 1852, just one year before a working Difference Engine was built in Sweden from one of Babbage's designs. Like her father, Ada lived only to age 36, and even though they led very different lives, she had undoubtedly admired him and taken inspiration from his unconventional, rebellious nature. In the end, Ada asked to be buried beside him at the family's estate.

```
// This function computes the day number within a year, given
// the date. It accounts correctly for leap years. The
// calculation is based on the fact that months average 30 days
// in length. Thus, (month - 1) * 30 is roughly the number of
// days in the year at the start of any month. A correction
// factor is used to account for cases where the average is
// incorrect and for leap years. The day of the month is then
// added to get the specific day number
```

```
// Precondition:
//      1 <= month <= 12
//   && dayOfMonth is in valid range for the month
//   && year is assigned
// Postcondition:
//      Function value == day number in the range 1 - 365
//                              (or 1 - 366 for a leap year)

{
    int correction;    // Correction factor to account for leap year
                       //    and months of different lengths

    // Test for leap year

    if (year % 4 == 0 && (year % 100 != 0 || year % 400 == 0))
    {
        if (month >= 3)            // If date is after February 29
            correction = 1;        //    then add one for leap year
    }
    else
        correction = 0;

    // Correct for different length months

    if (month == 3)
        correction = correction - 1;
    else if (month == 2 || month == 6 || month == 7)
        correction = correction + 1;
    else if (month == 8)
        correction = correction + 2;
    else if (month == 9 || month == 10)
        correction = correction + 3;
    else if (month == 11 || month == 12)
        correction = correction + 4;
    return (month - 1) * 30 + correction + dayOfMonth;
}
```

The first thing to note about the function definition is that it looks like a void function, except for the fact that the heading begins with the data type int instead of the word void. The second thing to observe is the return statement at the end, which includes an integer expression between the word return and the semicolon.

A value-returning function returns one value, not through a parameter but by means of a return statement. The data type at the beginning of the heading declares the type of value that the function will return. This data type is called the *function type*, although a more proper term is **function value type** (or *function return type* or *function result type*).

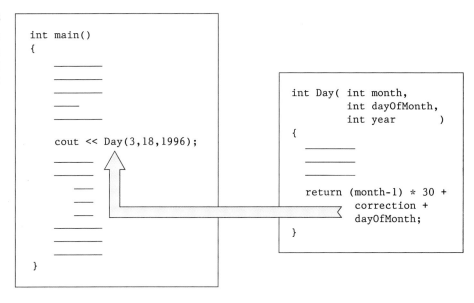

Function Value Type   The data type of the result value returned by a function.

The last statement in the Day function evaluates the expression

```
(month - 1) * 30 + correction + dayOfMonth
```

and returns the result as the function value (see Figure 8-3).

You now have seen two forms of the return statement. The form

```
return;
```

is valid *only* in void functions. It causes control to exit the function immediately and return to the caller. The second form is

```
return Expression;
```

This form is valid *only* in a value-returning function. It returns control to the caller, sending back the value of Expression as the function value. (If the data type of Expression is different from the declared function type, its value is coerced to the correct type.)

In Chapter 7, we presented a syntax template for the function definition of a void function. We now update the syntax template to cover both void functions and value-returning functions:

FunctionDefinition

DataType FunctionName (FormalParameterList)
{
    Statement
       .
       .
       .
}

If DataType is `void`, the function is a void function; otherwise, it is a value-returning function. Notice from the shading in the syntax template that DataType is optional. If you omit the data type of a function, `int` is assumed. We mention this point only because you sometimes encounter programs where DataType is missing from the function heading. Many programmers do not consider this practice to be good programming style.

The formal parameter list for a value-returning function has exactly the same form as for a void function: a list of parameter declarations, separated by commas. Also, a function prototype for a value-returning function looks just like the prototype for a void function except that it begins with a data type instead of `void`.

Let's look at two more examples of value-returning functions. The C++ standard library provides a power function, `pow`, that raises a floating point number to a floating point power. The library does not supply a power function for `int` values, so we'll build one of our own. The function receives two integers, x and n (where $n \geq 0$), and computes x^n. We use a simple approach, multiplying repeatedly by x. Because the number of iterations is known in advance, a count-controlled loop is appropriate. The loop counts down to 0 from the initial value of n. For each iteration of the loop, x is multiplied by the previous product.

```
int Power( /* in */ int x,      // Base number
           /* in */ int n )     // Power to raise base to

// This function computes x to the n power

// Precondition:
//     x is assigned  &&  n >= 0  &&  (x to the n) <= INT_MAX
```

```
// Postcondition:
//      Function value == x to the n power

{
    int result;        // Holds intermediate powers of x

    result = 1;
    while (n > 0)
    {
        result = result * x;
        n--;
    }
    return result;
}
```

Notice the notation that we use in the postcondition of a value-returning function. Because a value-returning function returns a single value, it is most concise if you simply state what that value equals. Except in complicated examples, the postcondition looks like this:

```
// Postcondition
//      Function value == ...
```

Another function that is frequently used in calculating probabilities is the factorial. For example, 5 factorial (written 5! in mathematical notation) is $5 \times 4 \times 3 \times 2 \times 1$. Zero factorial is, by definition, equal to 1. This function has one integer parameter. As with the Power function, we use repeated multiplication, but we decrement the multiplier on each iteration.

```
int Factorial( /* in */ int x )    // Number whose factorial is
                                   //    to be computed
// This function computes x!

// Precondition:
//      x >= 0  &&  x! <= INT_MAX
// Postcondition:
//      Function value == x!

{
    int result;        // Holds partial products

    result = 1;
    while (x > 0)
    {
        result = result * x;
        x--;
    }
```

```
        return result;
}
```

A call to the `Factorial` function might look like this:

```
combinations = Factorial(n) / (Factorial(m) * Factorial(n - m));
```

Boolean Functions

Value-returning functions are not restricted to returning numerical results. We can also use them to evaluate a condition and return a Boolean result. Boolean functions can be useful when a branch or loop depends on some complex condition. Rather than code the condition directly into the If or While statement, we can call a Boolean function to form the controlling expression.

Suppose we are writing a program that works with triangles. The program reads three angles as floating point numbers. Before performing any calculations on those angles, however, we want to check that they really form a triangle by adding the angles to confirm that their sum equals 180 degrees. We can write a value-returning function that takes the three angles as parameters and returns a Boolean result. Such a function would look like this (recall from Chapter 5 that you should test floating point numbers only for near equality):

```
#include <math.h>    // For fabs()
 .
 .
 .
typedef int Boolean;
const Boolean TRUE = 1;
const Boolean FALSE = 0;
 .
 .
 .
Boolean IsTriangle( /* in */ float angle1,     // First angle
                    /* in */ float angle2,     // Second angle
                    /* in */ float angle3 )    // Third angle

// This function checks to see if its three incoming values
// add up to 180 degrees, forming a valid triangle

// Precondition:
//     angle1, angle2, and angle3 are assigned
// Postcondition:
//     Function value == TRUE, if (angle1 + angle2 + angle3) is
//                                 within 0.00000001 of 180.0 degrees
//                          == FALSE, otherwise

{
```

```
        return (fabs(angle1 + angle2 + angle3 - 180.0) < 0.00000001);
    }
```

The following program fragment shows how function `IsTriangle` might be called:

```
cin >> angleA >> angleB >> angleC;
if (IsTriangle(angleA, angleB, angleC))            // Function call
    cout << "The three angles form a valid triangle.";
else
    cout << "Those angles do not form a triangle.";
```

The If statement is much easier to understand with the function than it would be if the entire condition were coded directly. When a conditional test is at all complicated, a Boolean function is in order.

The C++ standard library provides a number of helpful Boolean functions that let you test the contents of char variables. To use them, you #include the header file `ctype.h`. Here are some of the available functions; Appendix C contains a more complete list.

Header File	Function	Function Type	Function Value
`<ctype.h>`	`isalpha(ch)`	`int`	Nonzero, if ch is a letter ('A'–'Z', 'a'–'z'); 0, otherwise
`<ctype.h>`	`isalnum(ch)`	`int`	Nonzero, if ch is a letter or a digit ('A'–'Z', 'a'–'z', '0'–'9'); 0, otherwise
`<ctype.h>`	`isdigit(ch)`	`int`	Nonzero, if ch is a digit ('0'–'9'); 0, otherwise
`<ctype.h>`	`islower(ch)`	`int`	Nonzero, if ch is a lowercase letter ('a'–'z'); 0, otherwise
`<ctype.h>`	`isspace(ch)`	`int`	Nonzero, if ch is a whitespace character (blank, newline, tab, carriage return, form feed); 0, otherwise
`<ctype.h>`	`isupper(ch)`	`int`	Nonzero, if ch is an uppercase letter ('A'–'Z'); 0, otherwise

Although Boolean is not a built-in data type in C++, the "is..." functions behave like Boolean functions. They return an int value that is nonzero (true) or zero (false). These functions are convenient to use and make programs more readable. For example, the test

```
if (isalnum(inputChar))
```

is easier to read and less prone to error than if you coded the test the long way:

```
if (inputChar >= 'A' && inputChar <= 'Z' ||
    inputChar >= 'a' && inputChar <= 'z' ||
    inputChar >= '0' && inputChar <= '9'   )
```

In fact, this complicated logical expression doesn't work correctly on some machines. We'll see why when we examine character data in Chapter 10.

MATTERS OF STYLE

Naming Value-Returning Functions

In Chapter 7, we said that it's good style to use imperative verbs when naming void functions. The reason is that a call to a void function is a statement and should look like a command to the computer:

```
PrintResults(a, b, c);
DoThis(x);
DoThat();
```

This naming scheme, however, doesn't work well with value-returning functions. A statement like

```
z = 6.7 * ComputeMaximum(d, e, f);
```

sounds awkward when you read it aloud: "Set z equal to 6.7 times the *compute maximum* of d, e, and f."

With a value-returning function, the function call represents a value within an expression. Things that represent values, such as variables and value-returning functions, are best given names that are nouns or, occasionally, adjectives. See how much better this statement sounds when you pronounce it out loud:

```
z = 6.7 * Maximum(d, e, f);
```

You would read this as, "Set z equal to 6.7 times the *maximum* of d, e, and f." Other names that suggest values rather than actions are SquareRoot, Cube, Factorial, StudentCount, SumOfSquares, and SocialSecurityNum. As you see, they are all nouns or noun phrases.

Boolean value-returning functions (and variables) are often named using adjectives or phrases beginning with *Is*. Here are a few examples:

```
while (Valid(m, n))
if (Odd(n))
if (IsTriangle(s1, s2, s3))
```

When you are choosing a name for a value-returning function, try to stick with nouns or adjectives so that the name suggests a value, not a command to the computer.

Interface Design and Side Effects

The interface to a value-returning function is designed in much the same way as for a void function. We simply write down a list of what the function needs and what it must return. Because value-returning functions return only one value, there is only one item labeled "outgoing" in the list (the function return value). Everything else in the list is labeled "incoming," and there aren't any "incoming/outgoing" parameters.

Returning more than one value from a value-returning function (by modifying the actual parameters) is an unwanted side effect and should be avoided. If your interface design calls for multiple values to be returned or for the values of actual parameters to be changed, then you should use a void function instead of a value-returning function.

A rule of thumb is never to use reference parameters in the formal parameter list of a value-returning function, but to use value parameters exclusively. Let's look at an example that demonstrates the importance of this rule. Suppose we define the following function:

```
int SideEffect( int& n )
{
    int result = n * n;

    n++;                    // Side effect
    return result;
}
```

This function returns the square of its incoming value, but it also increments the actual parameter before returning. Now suppose we call this function with the following statement:

```
y = x + SideEffect(x);
```

BACKGROUND INFORMATION

Ignoring a Function Value

A peculiarity of the C++ language is that it lets you ignore the value returned by a value-returning function. For example, you could write the following statement in your program without any complaint from the compiler:

```
sqrt(x);
```

When this statement is executed, the value returned by `sqrt` is promptly discarded. This function call has absolutely no effect except to waste the computer's time by calculating a value that is never used.

Clearly, the above call to `sqrt` is a mistake. No programmer would write that statement intentionally. But C++ programmers occasionally write value-returning functions in a way that allows the caller to ignore the function value. Here is a specific example from the C++ standard library.

The library provides a function named `remove`, the purpose of which is to delete a disk file from the system. It takes a single parameter—a string specifying the name of the file—and it returns a function value. This function value is an integer notifying you of the status: zero if the operation succeeded, and nonzero if it failed. (Notice that this use of zero and nonzero is backwards from the result of testing the state of an I/O stream.) Here is how you might call the `remove` function:

If x is originally 2, what value is stored into y? The answer depends on the order in which your compiler evaluates the expression. If it first calls the function, then the answer is 7. If it accesses x first in preparation for adding it to the function result, the answer is 6. This is precisely why reference parameters shouldn't be used with value-returning functions. Obviously, a function that creates such an unpredictable situation has no place in a well-written program.

An exception is the case where an I/O stream variable is passed to a value-returning function; remember, C++ allows a stream variable to be passed only to a reference parameter. Within a value-returning function, the only operation that should be performed is testing the state of the stream (for EOF or I/O errors). A value-returning function should not perform input or output operations. Such operations are considered to be side effects of the

```
status = remove("junkfile.dat");
if (status != 0)
    PrintErrorMsg();
```

On the other hand, if you assume that the system always succeeds at deleting a file, you can ignore the returned status by calling `remove` as though it were a void function:

```
remove("junkfile.dat");
```

The `remove` function is sort of a hybrid between a void function and a value-returning function. Conceptually, it is a void function; its principal purpose is to delete a file, not to compute a value to be returned. Literally, however, it's a value-returning function. It does return a function value—the status of the operation (which you can choose to ignore).

In this book, we don't write hybrid functions. We prefer to keep the concept of void function distinct from value-returning function. But there are two reasons why every C++ programmer should know about the topic of ignoring a function value. First, if you accidentally call a value-returning function as if it were a void function, the compiler won't prevent you from making the mistake. Second, you sometimes encounter this style of coding in other people's programs and in the C++ standard library. Several of the library functions are technically value-returning functions, but the function value is used merely to return something of secondary importance like a status value.

function. (We should point out that not everyone agrees with this point of view. Some programmers feel that performing I/O within a value-returning function is perfectly acceptable. You will find strong opinions on both sides of this issue.)

There is another advantage to using only value parameters in a value-returning function definition: you can use constants and expressions as actual parameters. For example, we can call the `IsTriangle` function in the following manner using literals and an expression:

```
if (IsTriangle(30.0, 60.0, 30.0 + 60.0))
    cout << "A 30–60–90 angle combination forms a triangle.";
else
    cout << "Something is wrong.";
```

When to Use Value-Returning Functions

There aren't any formal rules for determining when to use a void function and when to use a value-returning function, but here are some guidelines:

1. If the module must return more than one value or modify any actual parameters, do not use a value-returning function.
2. If the module must perform I/O, do not use a value-returning function. (This guideline is not universally agreed upon.)
3. If there is only one value returned from the module and it is a Boolean value, a value-returning function is appropriate.
4. If there is only one value returned and that value is to be used immediately in an expression, a value-returning function is appropriate.
5. When in doubt, use a void function. You can recode any value-returning function as a void function by adding an extra outgoing parameter to carry back the computed result.
6. If both a void function and a value-returning function are acceptable, use the one you feel more comfortable implementing.

Value-returning functions were included in C++ to provide a way of simulating the mathematical concept of a function. The C++ standard library supplies a set of commonly used mathematical functions through the header file math.h. A list of these appears in Appendix C.

PROBLEM-SOLVING *CASE STUDY*

Reformat Names

Problem: Write a program that reads names in the form

```
Mary     Brown
 Sam   Green
```

and prints them out in the form

```
Brown, M.
Green, S.
```

The input may contain any number of blanks preceding the first name and between the first and last names. Each person's name is on a separate line of input.

Problem-Solving Case Study cont'd.

Input: A series of names, with one person's name (first and last) on each line of input in the form

```
First Last
```

where there may be any number of blanks preceding the first name and one or more blanks between the two names.

The number of input lines is unknown. The program should continue to process input lines until EOF occurs.

Output: A corresponding series of lines of the form

```
Last, F.
```

Discussion: This task is an easy one to do by hand. We would read the two names; write down the last, followed by a comma; and write down the first letter of the first name, followed by a period. Basically, this is how we program the problem. The hard part is trying to simulate "reading the two names." The program has to read one character at a time, examine it, and decide what to do with it.

Let's analyze this process by hand, going character-by-character through the input. The first character is either a blank or a letter. If it is a letter, we need to save it because it is the first initial.

Once we have the first initial, we are not interested in the rest of the first name. So we must continue to read and ignore characters until we reach the last name. How do we recognize the beginning of the last name? It is the first letter after the blanks following the first name. Once we find the last name, we continue reading and printing each character until we reach the end of the input line. Then we print a comma followed by a blank and the first initial, which we saved, followed by a period.

Now that we have analyzed the problem, we can do our top-down design.

Assumptions: Middle names are not present in the input. The end of an input line comes immediately after the person's last name.

Main   *Level 0*

```
Get initial
WHILE NOT EOF
    Print last name
    Print initial
    Get initial
```

Get Initial (Out: initial)   *Level 1*

> Read initial, skipping leading blanks

Print Last (No parameters)

> Find last name
> Print name

Print Initial (In: initial)

> Print ", ", initial, '.'

Find Last (Out: First character of last name)   *Level 2*

> Skip rest of first name
> Read first character of last name, skipping
>   leading blanks

Print Name (In: First character of last name)

> WHILE ch != '\n'
>   Print ch
>   Read ch

Skip First Name (No parameters)   *Level 3*

> Skip characters up to first blank

This design goes to four levels. We can see from the design that Get Initial, Print Initial, and Skip First Name are only one line of C++ code each. (Skip First Name can be implemented as a call to the `cin.ignore` function.)

Let's not code these modules as functions but, instead, put each line of code into the level above. The resulting module structure chart consists of three levels rather than four.

Module Structure Chart:

Here is the module structure chart for the Transpose program. The chart emphasizes the importance of interface design. The arrows indicate which identifiers are received or returned by each module.

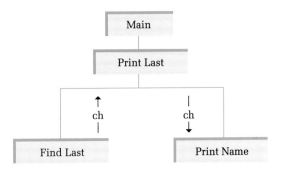

According to the structure chart, we have four modules to implement as C++ functions. In addition to `main`, let's name the functions `PrintLast`, `FindLast`, and `PrintName`. Before coding the problem, we should clearly spell out the function interfaces. Each interface mentions references to global variables (normally, only `cin` and `cout`).

`main`: Calls `PrintLast`. No parameters are passed between `main` and `PrintLast`. Reads from `cin` and writes to `cout`.

`PrintLast`: Is called by `main`. Calls `FindLast` and `PrintName`. Returns nothing to `main` (no formal parameters). Must obtain the first character of the last name from `FindLast` (actual parameter). Must pass the first character of the last name to `PrintName` (actual parameter).

`FindLast`: Is called by `PrintLast`. Returns the first character of the last name to `PrintLast` (formal reference parameter). Reads from `cin`.

`PrintName`: Is called by `PrintLast`. Receives the first character of the last name from `PrintLast` (formal value parameter). Reads from `cin` and writes to `cout`. Returns nothing.

This design is only one of many ways in which to structure the solution. In fact, it has some flaws. After presenting the C++ program, we discuss ways of improving the design.

Here is the program. You'll see that we have omitted the precondition and postcondition from the comments at the beginning of each function. Case Study Follow-Up Question 1 asks you to fill them in.

```cpp
//****************************************************************
// Transpose program
// This program reformats names to be in the form of last name,
// comma, blank, first initial, period.  The input is in the form
// of first name, blanks, last name with one person's name per
// input line
//****************************************************************
#include <iostream.h>

void FindLast( char& );
void PrintLast();
void PrintName( char );

int main()
{
    char initial;        // Holds first initial

    cin >> initial;
    while (cin)
    {
        PrintLast();
        cout << ", " << initial << '.' << endl;
        cin >> initial;
    }
    return 0;
}


//****************************************************************

void PrintLast()

// Skips the rest of the characters in the first name,
// then prints the person's last name

// Precondition:  Exercise
// Postcondition: Exercise

{
    char ch;     // Holds first letter of last name

    FindLast(ch);
```

```
        PrintName(ch);
}

//**************************************************************

void FindLast( /* out */ char& ch )   // First character of last name

// Scans the input stream for the first letter of a person's last
// name by skipping the nonblank characters in the first name,
// then skipping the blanks between the first and last name

// Precondition:  Exercise
// Postcondition: Exercise

{
    cin.ignore(100, ' ');        // Ignore all characters up to
                                 //   (and including) a blank
    cin >> ch;                   // Input first letter of last name,
}                                //   ignoring blanks along the way

//**************************************************************

void PrintName( /* in */ char ch )    // First character of last name

// Prints a person's last name by printing the incoming
// parameter and then reading and echoing each character
// until a newline is found

// Precondition:  Exercise
// Postcondition: Exercise

{
    while (ch != '\n')
    {
        cout << ch;
        cin.get(ch);
    }
}
```

Testing: The test data for the Transpose program should include names of different lengths, ranging from a single character to many characters. Some of the names should be preceded by one or more blanks, and the number of blanks separating the two names should be varied. It also would be instructive to try the program with some invalid data, such as a line with no names, one name, more than two names, and so on.

Further Discussion: This problem is actually too simple to require such an involved structure. For example, some of the functions have only two lines of code in the body. We could just as easily have written these statements directly in place of the call to those functions. However, the problem does illustrate such concepts as interface design, pass-by-value, and pass-by-reference.

We don't mean to imply that you should never write a function with as few as two statements. In some cases, decomposition of a problem makes a two-line function quite appropriate. When deciding whether to code a module directly in the next higher level or as a function, ask yourself the following question: Which way will make the overall program easier to read, understand, and modify later? With experience, you will develop your own set of guidelines for making this decision. For example, if a two-line module is to be called from several places in the program, you should code it as a function. Look also at the Software Engineering Tip box for further guidelines.

SOFTWARE ENGINEERING TIP

Control Abstraction, Functional Cohesion, and Communication Complexity

The Transpose program contains two different While loops. The control structure for this program has the potential to be fairly complex. Yet if you look at the individual modules, the most complicated control structure is a While loop without any If or While statements nested within it.

The complexity of a program is hidden by reducing each of the major control structures to an abstract action performed by a function call. In the Transpose program, for example, reading and printing a person's last name is an abstract action that appears as a call to PrintName. The logical properties of the action are separated from its implementation (a While loop). This aspect of a design is called **control abstraction.**

Control Abstraction   The separation of the logical properties of an action from its implementation.

Control abstraction can serve as a guideline for deciding which modules to code as functions and which to code directly. If a module contains a control structure, it is a good candidate for being implemented as a function. For example, function `FindLast` lacks control abstraction. Its body is a sequence of two statements, which could just as well be located in the `PrintLast` function. But even if a module does not contain a control structure, you still want to consider other factors. Is it lengthy, or is it called from more than one place? If so, you should use a function.

Somewhat related to control abstraction is the concept of **functional cohesion,** which states that a module should perform exactly one abstract action.

Functional Cohesion   The principle that a module should perform exactly one abstract action.

If you can state the action that a module performs in one sentence with no conjunctions (*and*s), then it is highly cohesive. A module that has more than one primary purpose is lacking in cohesion. For example, function `PrintLast` skips the remainder of the first name *and* prints the last name; a more cohesive design would do away with `PrintLast` and simply call `FindLast` and `PrintName`. Note that `PrintLast` is also lacking in control abstraction.

A module that only partially fulfills a purpose also lacks cohesion. Such a module should be combined with whatever other modules are directly related to it. For example, it would make no sense to have a separate function that prints the first letter of the last name because printing the last name is one abstract action.

A third and related aspect of a module's design is its **communication complexity,** the amount of information that passes through a module's interface. A module's communication complexity is often an indicator of its cohesiveness. Usually, if a module requires a large number of parameters, it is either trying to accomplish too much or it is only partially fulfilling a purpose. You should step back and see if there is an alternative way of dividing up the problem so that a minimal amount of information is communicated between modules.

Communication Complexity   A measure of the quantity of information passing through a module's interface.

PROBLEM-SOLVING CASE STUDY

Comparison of Furniture-Store Sales, Part 2

Problem: In Chapter 7, we wrote the Graph program making some assumptions: each file is in order by department IDs, and the same departments are in each store. What if there are errors in the data files? We have not paid too much attention to data error checking (also called *data validation*) in our programs, yet errors do occur. Let's redo the design for the Graph program to add some data validation. There are no changes to the Input and Output specifications of the program, so we won't repeat them here.

Discussion: We'll begin by reviewing our old design for the Graph program.

Main   *Level 0*

Open data files (and verify success)
Print heading
Get data for a Store 1 department
Get data for a Store 2 department
WHILE NOT EOF on file store1 AND NOT EOF on file store2
   Print data for the Store 1 department
   Print data for the Store 2 department
   Get data for a Store 1 department
   Get data for a Store 2 department

Print Heading (No parameters)   *Level 1*

Print chart title
Print heading
Print bar graph scale

Get Data (Inout: dataFile; Out: deptID, deptSales)

```
Read deptID from dataFile
IF EOF on dataFile
    Return
Read numDays from dataFile
Set deptSales = 0.0
Set day (loop control variable) = 1
WHILE day <= numDays
    Read sale from dataFile
    Add sale to deptSales
    Increment day
```

Print Data (In: deptID, storeNum, deptSales)

```
Print deptID
Print storeNum
WHILE deptSales > 250.0
    Print a '*'
    Subtract 500.0 from deptSales
Terminate current output line
```

We can check for mismatched department IDs in the main function by comparing the IDs before we call PrintData. We can check for too few data values by inserting tests for EOF in the GetData function. We can also add a test to the main function that tells us if the two files do not have the same number of data sets.

Assumptions: Sales do not exceed $25,000 for one department.

Here is our new design.

Main   *Level 0*

> Open data files (and verify success)
> Print heading
> Get data for a Store 1 department
> Get data for a Store 2 department
> WHILE NOT EOF on file store1 AND NOT EOF on file store2
>   IF deptID1 != deptID2
>   Print error message indicating mismatched IDs
>   ELSE
>   Print data for the Store 1 department
>   Print data for the Store 2 department
>   Get data for a Store 1 department
>   Get data for a Store 2 department
> IF EOF on store1 AND NOT EOF on store2
>   Print "Ran out of data for Store 1 before Store 2."
> ELSE IF EOF on store2 AND NOT EOF on store1
>   Print "Ran out of data for Store 2 before Store 1."

Print Heading (No parameters)   *Level 1*

> Print chart title
> Print heading
> Print bar graph scale

Get Data (Inout: dataFile; Out: deptID, deptSales)

```
Read deptID from dataFile
IF EOF on dataFile
   Return
Read numDays from dataFile
IF EOF on dataFile
   Print "Data error: No data following dept. ID."
   Return
Set deptSales = 0.0
Set day (loop control variable) = 1
WHILE day <= numDays
   Read sale from dataFile
   IF EOF on dataFile
      Print "Data error: Ran out of data in mid-set."
      Return
   Add sale to deptSales
   Increment day
```

Print Data (In: deptID, storeNum, deptSales)

```
Print deptID
Print storeNum
WHILE deptSales > 250.0
   Print a '*'
   Subtract 500.0 from deptSales
Terminate current output line
```

The module structure chart for the design has not changed. The following C++ program parallels our new design.

```cpp
//**************************************************************
// Graph program
// This program generates bar graphs of monthly sales
// by department for two Chippendale furniture stores, permitting
// department-by-department comparison of sales
//**************************************************************
#include <iostream.h>
#include <iomanip.h>      // For setw()
```

```
#include <fstream.h>      // For file I/O

void GetData( ifstream&, int&, float& );
void PrintData( int, int, float );
void PrintHeading();

int main()
{
    int       deptID1;       // Department ID number for Store 1
    int       deptID2;       // Department ID number for Store 2
    float     sales1;        // Department sales for Store 1
    float     sales2;        // Department sales for Store 2
    ifstream store1;         // Accounting file for Store 1
    ifstream store2;         // Accounting file for Store 2

    store1.open("store1.dat");
    store2.open("store2.dat");
    if ( !store1 || !store2 )              // Make sure files
    {                                      //    were opened
        cout << "** Can't open input file(s) **" << endl;
        return 1;
    }


    PrintHeading();

    GetData(store1, deptID1, sales1);         // Priming reads
    GetData(store2, deptID2, sales2);
    while (store1 && store2)                   // While not EOF...
    {
        cout << endl;
        if (deptID1 != deptID2)               // Data validation test
            cout << "Data error: Department IDs don't match."
                 << endl;
        else
        {
            PrintData(deptID1, 1, sales1);
            PrintData(deptID2, 2, sales2);
        }
        GetData(store1, deptID1, sales1);
        GetData(store2, deptID2, sales2);
    }
    if ( !store1 && store2 )                   // Data validation test
        cout << "Ran out of data for Store 1 before Store 2."
             << endl;
    else if ( !store2 && store1 )
        cout << "Ran out of data for Store 2 before Store 1."
             << endl;
```

```
        return 0;
}

//********************************************************************

void PrintHeading()

// Prints the title for the bar chart, a heading, and the numeric
// scale for the chart.  The scale uses one mark per $500

// Postcondition:
//      The heading for the bar chart has been printed

{
    cout
        << "Bar Graph Comparing Departments of Store #1 and Store #2"
        << endl << endl
        << "Store  Sales in 1,000s of dollars" << endl
        << "  #    0         5        10        15        20        25"
        << endl
        << "         |.........|.........|.........|.........|.........|"
        << endl;
}

//********************************************************************

void GetData( /* inout */ ifstream& dataFile,    // Input file
              /* out */     int&       deptID,     // Department number
              /* out */     float&    deptSales ) // Department's
                                                   //   monthly sales

// Takes an input accounting file as a parameter, reads the
// department ID number and number of days of sales from that file,
// then reads one sales figure for each of those days, computing a
// total sales figure for the month.  This figure is returned in
// deptSales.  (If input of any of the department's data fails
// due to end-of-file, deptID and deptSales are undefined.)

// Precondition:
//      dataFile has been successfully opened
// Postcondition:
//      IF input of any of the department data failed
//          deptID and deptSales are undefined
//      ELSE
//          The data file reading marker has advanced past one
//          department's data
//        && deptID == department ID number as read from the file
```

```
//          && deptSales == sum of the sales values for the department

{
    int   numDays;   // Number of business days in the month
    int   day;       // Loop control variable for reading daily sales
    float sale;      // One day's sales for the department

    dataFile >> deptID;
    if ( !dataFile )              // Check for "normal" EOF
        return;

    dataFile >> numDays;
    if ( !dataFile )              // Data validation test
    {
        cout << "Data error: No data following dept. ID." << endl;
        return;
    }
    deptSales = 0.0;
    day = 1;                      // Initialize loop control variable
    while (day <= numDays)
    {
        dataFile >> sale;
        if ( !dataFile )          // Data validation test
        {
            cout << "Data error: Ran out of data in mid-set."
                 << endl;
            return;
        }
        deptSales = deptSales + sale;
        day++;                    // Update loop control variable
    }
}

//****************************************************************

void PrintData( /* in */ int   deptID,      // Department ID number
                /* in */ int   storeNum,    // Store number
                /* in */ float deptSales )  // Total sales for the
                                            //    department

// Prints the department ID number, the store number, and a
// bar graph of the sales for the department.  The bar graph
// is printed at a scale of one mark per $500

// Precondition:
//     deptID contains a valid department number
//  && storeNum contains a valid store number
//  && 0.0 <= deptSales <= 25000.0
```

Problem-Solving Case Study cont'd.

```
// Postcondition:
//    A line of the bar chart has been printed with one * for
//     each $500 in sales, with fractions over $250 rounded up
//    && No stars have been printed for sales <= $250

{
    cout << setw(12) << "Dept " << deptID << endl;
    cout << setw(3) << storeNum << "    ";
    while (deptSales > 250.0)
    {
        cout << '*' ;                    // Print '*' for each $500
        deptSales = deptSales - 500.0;   // Update loop control
    }                                    //   variable
    cout << endl;
}
```

Testing: In addition to the testing that was recommended for the original Graph program in Chapter 7, the new program should be run with data sets that verify the new data validation code. For example, a data set with mismatched department ID numbers should be tried, as well as some incomplete data sets.

We have not changed the overall design of the Graph program—it still consists of the same collection of modules. However, we have changed the roles of some of the modules to make them more robust in dealing with invalid data. For example, if either file ends prematurely or the department IDs are not the same for both stores, then an error message is printed. (More data validation could be added to this program, such as testing for negative sales.)

Each of the error messages in the Graph program describes the exact error that caused the message to be printed. This is effective programming practice because it aids the user of the program in determining what is wrong with the data. (Imagine how hard this would be if all the error messages just said "Data error.")

PROBLEM-SOLVING CASE STUDY

Starship Weight and Balance

Problem: The company you work for has just upgraded its fleet of corporate aircraft by adding the Beechcraft Starship-1. As with any airplane, it is essential that the pilot know the total weight of the loaded plane at takeoff and its center of gravity. If the plane weighs too much, it won't be able to lift off. If its center of gravity is outside the limits established for the plane, it might be impossible to control. Either situation can lead to a crash. You have been asked to write a program that determines the weight and center of gravity of this new plane, based on the number of crew members and passengers as well as the weight of the baggage, closet contents, and fuel.

The Beechcraft
Starship-1

Input: Number of crew members, number of passengers, weight of closet contents, baggage weight, fuel in gallons.

Output: Total weight, center of gravity.

Discussion: As with most real-world problems, the basic solution is simple but is complicated by special cases. We use value-returning functions to hide the complexity so that the main function remains simple.

The total weight is basically the sum of the empty weight of the airplane plus the weight of each of the following: crew members, passengers, baggage, contents of the storage closet, and fuel. We use the standard average weight of a person, 170 pounds, to compute the total weight of the people. The weight of the baggage and the contents of the closet are given. Fuel weighs 6.7 pounds per gallon. Thus, the total weight is

$$\text{totalWeight} = \text{emptyWeight} + (\text{crew} + \text{passengers}) * 170 + \text{baggage} + \text{closet} + \text{fuel} * 6.7$$

To compute the center of gravity, each weight is multiplied by its distance from the front of the airplane, and the products—called *moment arms* or simply *moments*—are then summed and divided by the total weight (see Figure 8-4).

The formula is thus

centerOfGravity = (emptyMoment + crewMoment + passengerMoment + cargoMoment + fuelMoment) / totalWeight

The Starship-1 manual gives the distance from the front of the plane to the crew's seats, closet, baggage compartment, and fuel tanks. There are four rows of passenger seats, so this calculation depends on where the individual passengers sit. We have to make some assumptions about how passengers arrange themselves. Each row has two seats. The most popular seats are in row 2 because they are near the entrance and face forward. Once row 2 is filled, passengers usually take seats in row 1, facing their traveling companions. Row 3 is usually the next to fill up, even though it faces backward, because row 4 is a fold-down bench seat that is less comfortable than the armchairs in the forward rows. The following table gives the distance from the nose of the plane to each of the "loading stations."

Loading Station	Distance from Nose (inches)
Crew seats	143
Row 1 seats	219
Row 2 seats	265
Row 3 seats	295
Row 4 seats	341
Closet	182
Baggage	386

■ FIGURE 8-4   A Passenger Moment Arm

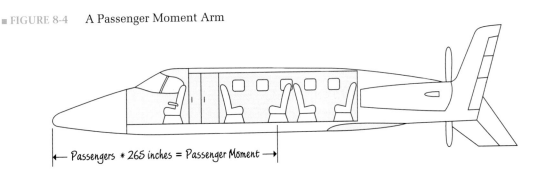

← Passengers * 265 inches = Passenger Moment →

The distance for the fuel varies because there are several tanks, and the tanks are in different places. As fuel is added to the plane, it automatically flows into the different tanks so that the center of gravity changes as the tanks are filled. There are four formulas for computing the distance from the nose to the "center" of the fuel tanks, depending on how much fuel is being loaded into the plane. The following table lists these distance formulas.

Gallons of Fuel (G)	Distance (D) Formula
0–59	$D = 314.6 * G$
60–360	$D = 305.8 + (-0.01233 * (G - 60))$
361–520	$D = 303.0 + (0.12500 * (G - 361))$
521–565	$D = 323.0 + (-0.04444 * (G - 521))$

We define one value-returning function for each of the different moments, and we name these functions CrewMoment, PassengerMoment, CargoMoment, and FuelMoment. The center of gravity is then computed with the formula we gave earlier and the following parameters:

centerOfGravity = (CrewMoment(crew) + PassengerMoment(passengers) + CargoMoment(closet, baggage) + FuelMoment(fuel) + emptyMoment) / totalWeight

The empty weight of the Starship is 9887 pounds, and its empty center of gravity is 319 inches from the front of the airplane. Thus, the empty moment is 3,153,953 inch-pounds.

We now have enough information to write the algorithm to solve this problem. In addition to printing the results, we'll also print a warning message that states the assumptions of the program and tells the pilot to double-check the results by hand if the weight or center of gravity is near the allowable limits.

Main   *Level 0*

Get data
Set totalWt =
    EMPTY_WEIGHT + (passengers + crew) * 170 +
    baggage + closet + fuel * 6.7
Set centerOfGravity =
    (CrewMoment(crew) + PassengerMoment(passengers) +
    CargoMoment(closet, baggage) + FuelMoment(fuel) +
    EMPTY_MOMENT) / totalWt
Print totalWt and centerOfGravity
Print warning

Get Data (Out: crew, passengers, closet, baggage, fuel)   *Level 1*

Prompt for number of crew, number of passengers,
    weight in closet and baggage compartments,
    and gallons of fuel
Read crew, passengers, closet, baggage, fuel
Echo-print the input

Crew Moment (In: crew)
    Out: Function value

Return crew * 170 * 143

Passenger Moment (In: passengers)
   Out: Function value

```
Set moment = 0.0
IF passengers > 6
   Add (passengers − 6) * 170 * 341 to moment
   Set passengers = 6
IF passengers > 4
   Add (passengers − 4) * 170 * 295 to moment
   Set passengers = 4
IF passengers > 2
   Add (passengers − 2) * 170 * 219 to moment
   Set passengers = 2
IF passengers > 0
   Add passengers * 170 * 265 to moment
Return moment
```

Cargo Moment (In: closet, baggage)
   Out: Function value

```
Return closet * 182 + baggage * 386
```

Fuel Moment (In: fuel)
   Out: Function value

```
Set fuelWt = fuel * 6.7
IF fuel < 60
   Set fuelDistance = fuel * 314.6
ELSE IF fuel < 361
   Set fuelDistance = 305.8 + (−0.01233 * (fuel − 60))
ELSE IF fuel < 521
   Set fuelDistance = 303.0 + ( 0.12500 * (fuel − 361))
ELSE
   Set fuelDistance = 323.0 + (−0.04444 * (fuel − 521))
Return fuelDistance * fuelWt
```

Print Warning (No parameters)

> Print a warning message about the assumptions of the program
> and when to double-check the results

Module Structure Chart:

In the following chart, you'll see a new notation. The box corresponding to each value-returning function has an upward arrow originating at its right side. This arrow signifies the function value that is returned.

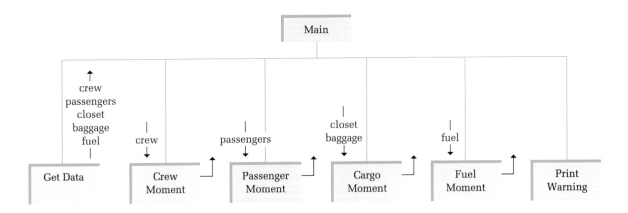

Here is the program that implements our algorithm.

```
//******************************************************************
// Starship program
// This program computes the total weight and center of gravity
// of a Beechcraft Starship-1, given the number of crew members
// and passengers, weight of closet and baggage compartment cargo,
// and gallons of fuel loaded.  It assumes that each person
// weighs 170 pounds, and that the fuel weighs 6.7 pounds per
// gallon.  Thus, the output is approximate and should be hand-
// checked if the Starship is loaded near its limits
//******************************************************************
#include <iostream.h>
#include <iomanip.h>      // For setw() and setprecision()
```

```
const float PERSON_WT = 170.0;        // Average person weighs
                                      //   170 lbs.
const float LBS_PER_GAL = 6.7;        // Jet-A weighs 6.7 lbs.
                                      //   per gal.
const float EMPTY_WEIGHT = 9887.0;    // Standard empty weight
const float EMPTY_MOMENT = 3153953.0; // Standard empty moment

float CargoMoment( int, int );
float CrewMoment( int );
float FuelMoment( int );
void  GetData( int&, int&, int&, int&, int& );
float PassengerMoment( int );
void  PrintWarning();

int main()
{
    int    crew;            // Number of crew on board (1 or 2)
    int    passengers;      // Number of passengers (0 through 8)
    int    closet;          // Weight in closet (160 lbs. maximum)
    int    baggage;         // Weight of baggage (525 lbs. max.)
    int    fuel;            // Gallons of fuel (10 through 565 gals.)
    float  totalWt;         // Total weight of the loaded Starship
    float  centerOfGravity; // Center of gravity of loaded Starship

    cout.setf(ios::fixed, ios::floatfield);   // Set up floating pt.
    cout.setf(ios::showpoint);                //   output format

    GetData(crew, passengers, closet, baggage, fuel);

    totalWt =
        EMPTY_WEIGHT + float(passengers + crew) * PERSON_WT +
        float(baggage + closet) + float(fuel) * LBS_PER_GAL;
    centerOfGravity =
        (CrewMoment(crew) + PassengerMoment(passengers) +
        CargoMoment(closet, baggage) + FuelMoment(fuel) +
        EMPTY_MOMENT) / totalWt;

    cout << "Total weight is " << setprecision(2) << totalWt
         << " pounds." << endl;
    cout << "Center of gravity is " << centerOfGravity
         << " inches from the front of the plane." << endl;
    PrintWarning();
    return 0;
}

//*****************************************************************
```

```cpp
void GetData( /* out */ int& crew,          // Number of crew members
              /* out */ int& passengers,    // Number of passengers
              /* out */ int& closet,        // Weight of closet cargo
              /* out */ int& baggage,       // Weight of baggage
              /* out */ int& fuel        )  // Gallons of fuel

// Prompts for the input of crew, passengers, closet, baggage, and
// fuel values and returns the five values after echo printing them

// Postcondition:
//     All parameters (crew, passengers, closet, baggage, and fuel)
//     have been prompted for, input, and echo printed

{
    cout << "Enter the number of crew members." << endl;
    cin >> crew;
    cout << "Enter the number of passengers." << endl;
    cin >> passengers;
    cout << "Enter the weight, in pounds, of cargo in the" << endl
         << " closet, rounded up to the nearest whole number."
         << endl;
    cin >> closet;
    cout << "Enter the weight, in pounds, of cargo in the" << endl
         << " aft baggage compartment, rounded up to the" << endl
         << " nearest whole number." << endl;
    cin >> baggage;
    cout << "Enter the number of U.S. gallons of fuel" << endl
         << " loaded, rounded up to the nearest whole number."
         << endl;
    cin >> fuel;
    cout << endl;
    cout << "Starship loading data as entered:" << endl
         << "    Crew:          " << setw(6) << crew << endl
         << "    Passengers:    " << setw(6) << passengers << endl
         << "    Closet weight: " << setw(6) << closet << " pounds"
         << endl
         << "    Baggage weight:" << setw(6) << baggage << " pounds"
         << endl
         << "    Fuel:          " << setw(6) << fuel << " gallons"
         << endl << endl;
}

//****************************************************************

float CrewMoment( /* in */ int crew )    // Number of crew members

// Computes the crew moment arm in inch-pounds from the number of
```

```
// crew members.  Global constant PERSON_WT is used as the weight
// of each crew member

// Precondition:
//     crew == 1  OR  crew == 2
// Postcondition:
//     Function value == Crew moment arm, based on the crew parameter

{
    const float CREW_DISTANCE = 143.0;  // Distance to crew seats
                                        //    from front

    return float(crew) * PERSON_WT * CREW_DISTANCE;
}

//*****************************************************************

float PassengerMoment( /* in */ int passengers )   // Number of
                                                   //    passengers

// Computes the passenger moment arm in inch-pounds from the number
// of passengers.  Global constant PERSON_WT is used as the weight
// of each passenger.  It is assumed that the first two passengers
// sit in row 2, the second two in row 1, the next two in row 3,
// and remaining passengers sit in row 4

// Precondition:
//     0 <= passengers <= 8
// Postcondition:
//     Function value == Passenger moment arm, based on the
//                       passengers parameter

{
    const float ROW1_DIST = 219.0;  // Distance to row 1 seats
                                    //    from front
    const float ROW2_DIST = 265.0;  // Distance to row 2 seats
    const float ROW3_DIST = 295.0;  // Distance to row 3 seats
    const float ROW4_DIST = 341.0;  // Distance to row 4 seats

    float moment = 0.0;             // Running total of moment as
                                    //    rows are added

    if (passengers > 6)                      // For passengers 7 and 8
    {
        moment = moment +
                float(passengers - 6) * PERSON_WT * ROW4_DIST;
        passengers = 6;                      // 6 remain
```

```
        }
        if (passengers > 4)                    // For passengers 5 and 6
        {
            moment = moment +
                    float(passengers - 4) * PERSON_WT * ROW3_DIST;
            passengers = 4;                     // 4 remain
        }
        if (passengers > 2)                    // For passengers 3 and 4
        {
            moment = moment +
                    float(passengers - 2) * PERSON_WT * ROW1_DIST;
            passengers = 2;                     // 2 remain
        }
        if (passengers > 0)                    // For passengers 1 and 2
            moment = moment +
                    float(passengers) * PERSON_WT * ROW2_DIST;
        return moment;
    }

//*****************************************************************

float CargoMoment( /* in */ int closet,      // Weight in closet
                   /* in */ int baggage )    // Weight of baggage

// Computes the total moment arm for cargo loaded into the
// front closet and aft baggage compartment

// Precondition:
//     0 <= closet <= 160  &&  0 <= baggage <= 525
// Postcondition:
//     Function value == Cargo moment arm, based on the closet and
//                       baggage parameters

{
    const float CLOSET_DIST = 182.0;    // Distance from front
                                        //   to closet
    const float BAGGAGE_DIST = 386.0;   // Distance from front
                                        //   to bagg. comp.

    return float(closet) * CLOSET_DIST +
           float(baggage) * BAGGAGE_DIST;
}

//*****************************************************************
```

```
float FuelMoment( /* in */ int fuel )    // Fuel in gallons

// Computes the moment arm for fuel on board.  There are four
// different formulas for this calculation, depending on
// the amount of fuel, due to fuel tank layout.
// This function uses the global constant LBS_PER_GAL
// to compute the weight of the fuel

// Precondition:
//      10 <= fuel <= 565
// Postcondition:
//      Function value == Fuel moment arm, based on the
//                        fuel parameter

{
    float fuelWt;          // Weight of fuel in pounds
    float fuelDistance;    // Distance from front of plane

    fuelWt = float(fuel) * LBS_PER_GAL;
    if (fuel < 60)
        fuelDistance = float(fuel) * 314.6;
    else if (fuel < 361)
        fuelDistance = 305.8 + (-0.01233 * float(fuel - 60));
    else if (fuel < 521)
        fuelDistance = 303.0 + ( 0.12500 * float(fuel - 361));
    else
        fuelDistance = 323.0 + (-0.04444 * float(fuel - 521));
    return fuelDistance * fuelWt;
}

//*****************************************************************

void PrintWarning()

// Warns the user of assumptions made by the program
// and when to double check the program's results

// Postcondition:
//      An informational warning message has been printed

{
    cout << endl
         << "Notice:  This program assumes that passengers" << endl
         << "  fill the seat rows in order 2, 1, 3, 4, and" << endl
         << "  that each passenger and crew member weighs "
         << PERSON_WT << " pounds." << endl
         << "  It also assumes that Jet-A fuel weighs "
         << LBS_PER_GAL << " pounds" << endl
         << "  per U.S. gallon.  The center of gravity" << endl
```

```
                    << "  calculations for fuel are approximate.  If" << endl
                    << "  the aircraft is loaded near its limits, the" << endl
                    << "  pilot's operating handbook should be used" << endl
                    << "  to compute weight and center of gravity" << endl
                    << "  with more accuracy." << endl;
    }
```

Testing: Because someone could use the output of this program to make decisions that could result in property damage, injury, or death, it is essential to test the program thoroughly. In particular, it should be checked for maximum and minimum input values in different combinations. In addition, a wide range of test cases should be tried and verified against results calculated by hand. If possible, the program's output should be checked against sample calculations done by experienced pilots for actual flights.

Notice that the `main` function neglects to guarantee any of the function preconditions before calling the functions. If this program were actually to be used by pilots, it should have data validation checks added in function `GetData`.

TESTING AND DEBUGGING

One of the advantages of a modular design is that you can test it long before the code has been written for all of the modules. If we test each module individually, then we can assemble the modules into a complete program with much greater confidence that the program is correct. In this section, we introduce a technique for testing a module separately.

Stubs and Drivers

Suppose you were given the code for a module and your job was to test it. How would you test a single module by itself? First of all, it must be called by something (unless it is the `main` function). Second, it may have calls to other modules that aren't available to you. To test the module, you must fill in these missing links.

When a module contains calls to other modules, we can write dummy functions called **stubs** to satisfy those calls. A stub usually consists of an output statement that prints a message like, "Function such-and-such just got called." Even though the stub is a dummy, it allows us to determine whether the function is called at the right time by the `main` function or another function.

> **Stub** A dummy function that assists in testing part of a program. A stub has the same name and interface as a function that actually would be called by the part of the program being tested, but it is usually much simpler.

A stub can also be used to print the set of values that are passed to it; this tells us whether or not the module under test is supplying the proper information. Sometimes the stub will assign new values to its reference parameters to simulate data being read or results being computed to give the module something to keep working on. Because we can choose the values that are returned by the stub, we have better control over the conditions of the test run.

Here is a stub that simulates function `PrintName` in the Transpose program.

```
void PrintName( /* in */ char ch )    // First character of last name

// Stub for function PrintName in the Transpose program

{
    cout << "PrintName was called with ch = " << ch << endl;
}
```

Here is a stub that simulates a call to `FindLast` by returning an arbitrarily chosen character.

```
void FindLast( /* out */ char& ch )   // First character of last name

// Stub for function FindLast in the Transpose program

{
    cout << "FindLast was called here. Returning 'X'." << endl;
    ch = 'X';
}
```

Each of these stubs is simpler than the function it simulates, which is typical because the object of using stubs is to provide a simple, predictable environment for testing a module.

In addition to supplying a stub for each call within the module, you must provide a dummy program—a **driver**—to call the module itself. A driver program contains the bare minimum of code required to call the module being tested.

> **Driver**   A simple `main` function that is used to call a function being tested. The use of a driver permits direct control of the testing process.

By surrounding a module with a driver and stubs, you gain complete control of the conditions under which it executes. This allows you to test different situations and combinations that may reveal errors. For example, the following program is a driver for the `FuelMoment` function in the Starship program. Because `FuelMoment` doesn't call any other functions, no stubs are necessary.

```cpp
//*************************************************************
// FuelMomentDriver program
// This program provides an environment for testing the
// FuelMoment function in isolation from the Starship program
//*************************************************************
#include <iostream.h>

const float LBS_PER_GAL = 6.7;

float FuelMoment( int );

int main()
{
    int testVal;     // Test value for fuel in gallons

    cout << "Fuel moment for gallons from 10 through 565"
        << " in steps of 15:" << endl;
    testVal = 10;
    while (testVal <= 565)
    {
        cout << FuelMoment(testVal) << endl;
        testVal = testVal + 15;
    }
    return 0;
}

//*************************************************************

float FuelMoment( /* in */ int fuel )      // Fuel in gallons
{
    float fuelWt;           // Weight of fuel in pounds
    float fuelDistance;     // Distance from front of plane
```

```
    fuelWt = float(fuel) * LBS_PER_GAL;
    if (fuel < 60)
        fuelDistance = float(fuel) * 314.6;
    else if (fuel < 361)
        fuelDistance = 305.8 + (-0.01233 * float(fuel - 60));
    else if (fuel < 521)
        fuelDistance = 303.0 + ( 0.12500 * float(fuel - 361));
    else
        fuelDistance = 323.0 + (-0.04444 * float(fuel - 521));
    return fuelDistance * fuelWt;
}
```

Stubs and drivers are important tools in team programming. The programmers develop the overall design and the interfaces between the modules. Each programmer then designs and codes one or more of the modules and uses drivers and stubs to test the code. When all of the modules have been coded and tested, they are assembled into what should be a working program.

For team programming to succeed, it is essential that all of the module interfaces be defined explicitly and that the coded modules adhere strictly to the specifications for those interfaces. Obviously, global variable references must be carefully avoided in a team-programming situation because it is impossible for each person to know how the rest of the team is using every variable.

Testing and Debugging Hints

1. Make sure that variables used as actual parameters to a function are declared in the block where the function call is made.
2. Carefully define the precondition, postcondition, and parameter list to eliminate side effects. Variables used only in a function should be declared as local variables. *Do not* use global variables in your programs. (*Exception:* It is acceptable to reference the global variables cin and cout.)
3. If the compiler displays a message such as "UNDECLARED IDENTIFIER," check that identifiers aren't misspelled (and that they are, in fact, declared), that identifiers are declared before they are referenced, and that the scope of the identifier includes the reference to it.
4. If you intend to use a local name that is the same as a nonlocal name, a misspelling in the local declaration will wreak havoc. The C++ compiler won't complain, but will cause every reference to the local name to go to the nonlocal name instead.
5. Remember that the same identifier cannot be used in both the formal parameter list and the outermost local declarations of a function.

6. With a value-returning function, be sure the function heading and prototype begin with the correct data type for the function return value.

7. With a value-returning function, don't forget to use a statement

```
return Expression;
```

to return the function value. Make sure the expression is of the correct type, or implicit type coercion will occur.

8. Remember that a call to a value-returning function is part of an expression, whereas a call to a void function is a separate statement. (C++ softens this distinction, however, by letting you call a value-returning function as if it were a void function, ignoring the return value. Be careful here.)

9. In general, don't use reference parameters in the formal parameter list of a value-returning function. A reference parameter must be used, however, when an I/O stream variable is passed as a parameter.

10. If necessary, use debug output statements to indicate when a function is called and if it is executing correctly. The values in the actual parameters can be printed immediately before (to show the incoming values) and immediately after (to show the outgoing values) the call to the function. You may want to use debug output statements in the function itself to indicate what happens each time it is called.

SUMMARY

The scope of an identifier refers to the parts of the program in which it is visible. C++ functions have global scope, as do variables and constants that are declared outside all functions. Variables and constants declared within a block have local scope; they are not visible outside the block. The formal parameters of a function have the same scope as local variables declared in the outermost block of a function.

With rare exceptions, it is not considered good practice to declare global variables and reference them directly from a function. All communication between the modules of a program should be through the formal and actual parameter lists (and via the function value sent back by a value-returning function). The use of global constants, on the other hand, is considered to be an acceptable programming practice because it adds consistency and makes a program easier to change while avoiding the pitfalls of side effects. Well-designed and well-documented functions that are free of side effects can often be reused in other programs. Many programmers keep a library of functions that they use repeatedly.

The lifetime of a variable is the period of time during program execution when memory is allocated to it. Global variables have static lifetime (memory remains allocated for the duration of the program's execution). By default, local variables have automatic lifetime (memory is allocated and deallocated at block entry and block exit). A local variable may be given static lifetime by using the word `static` in its declaration. This variable has the lifetime of a global variable but the scope of a local variable.

C++ allows a variable to be initialized in its declaration. For a static variable, the initialization occurs once only—when control first reaches its declaration. An automatic variable is initialized each time control reaches the declaration.

C++ provides two kinds of subprograms, void functions and value-returning functions, for us to use. A value-returning function is called from within an expression and returns a single result that is used in the evaluation of the expression. For the function value to be returned, the last statement executed by the function must be a `return` statement containing an expression of the appropriate data type.

All the scope rules, as well as the rules about reference and value parameters, apply to both void functions and value-returning functions. It is considered poor programming practice, however, to use reference parameters in a value-returning function declaration. Doing so increases the potential for side effects. (An exception is when I/O stream variables are passed as parameters. Other exceptions are noted in later chapters.)

We can use stubs and drivers to test functions in isolation from the rest of a program. They are particularly useful in the context of team-programming projects.

Quick Check

1. a. How can you tell if a variable that is referenced inside a function is local or global? (pp. 390–395)
   b. Where are local variables declared? (pp. 390–395)
   c. When does the scope of an identifier declared in block A exclude a block nested within block A? (pp. 390–395)
2. A program consists of two functions, main and DoCalc. A variable x is declared outside both functions. DoCalc declares two variables, a and b, within its body; b is declared as `static`. In what function(s) are each of a, b, and x visible, and what is the lifetime of each variable? (pp. 390–395, 397–398)
3. Why should you use value parameters whenever possible? Why should you avoid the use of global variables? (pp. 400–404, 415–416)
4. For each of the following, decide whether a value-returning function or a void function is the most appropriate implementation. (pp. 404–417)
   a. Selecting the larger of two values for further processing in an expression.
   b. Printing a paycheck.
   c. Computing the area of a hexagon.
   d. Testing whether an incoming value is valid and returning TRUE if it is.
   e. Computing the two roots of a quadratic equation.

5. What would the heading for a value-returning function named `Min` look like if it had two `float` parameters, `num1` and `num2`, and returned a `float` result? (pp. 404–417)
6. What would a call to `Min` look like if the actual parameters were a variable named `deductions` and the literal `2000.0`? (pp. 404–417)

Answers 1. a. If the variable is not declared in either the body of the function or its formal parameter list, then the reference is global. b. Local variables are declared within a block (compound statement). c. When the nested block declares an identifier with the same name. 2. x is visible to both functions, but a and b are visible only within DoCalc. x and b are static variables; once memory is allocated to them, they are "alive" until the program terminates. a is an automatic variable; it is "alive" only while DoCalc is executing. 3. Both using value parameters and avoiding global variables will minimize side effects. Also, pass-by-value allows the actual parameters to be arbitrary expressions. 4. a. Value-returning function b. Void function c. Value-returning function d. Value-returning function e. Void function
5. float Min(float num1,
              float num2)
6. smaller = Min(deductions, 2000.0);

EXAM PREPARATION EXERCISES

1. If a function contains a locally declared variable with the same name as a global variable, no confusion results because references to variables in functions are first interpreted as references to local variables. (True or False?)
2. Variables declared at the beginning of a block are accessible to all statements in that block, including those in nested blocks (assuming the nested blocks don't declare local variables with the same names). (True or False?)
3. Define the following terms.

local variable	scope
global variable	side effects
lifetime	name precedence (name hiding)

4. What is the output of the following C++ program? (This program is an example of poor interface design practices.)

```
#include <iostream.h>

void DoGlobal();
void DoLocal();
void DoReference( int& );
void DoValue( int );

int x;

int main()
{
```

Handwritten annotations:
x = 3 after call to Do Reference
x = 16 "   "   "   Do Value
x = 14 "   "   "   " Do Local
x = 7   "   "   "   " Do Global

```
        x = 15;
        DoReference(x);
        cout << "x = " << x << " after the call to DoReference."
             << endl;
        x = 16;
        DoValue(x);
        cout << "x = " << x << " after the call to DoValue."
             << endl;
        x = 17;
        DoLocal();
        cout << "x = " << x << " after the call to DoLocal."
             << endl;
        x = 18;
        DoGlobal();
        cout << "x = " << x << " after the call to DoGlobal."
             << endl;
        return 0;
}

void DoReference( int& a )
{
        a = 3;
}

void DoValue( int b )
{
        b = 4;
}

void DoLocal()
{
        int x;

        x = 5;
}

void DoGlobal()
{
        x = 7;
}
```

5. What is the output of the following program?

```
#include <iostream.h>

void Test();

int main()
{
```

```
        Test();
        Test();
        Test();
        return 0;
    }

    void Test()
    {
        int i = 0;
        static int j = 0;

        i++;
        j++;
        cout << i << ' ' << j << endl;
    }
```

11
12
13

6. The following function calculates the sum of the numbers from 1 through n. However, it has an unintended side effect. What is it?

```
    void SumInts( int& n,
                  int& sum )
    {
        sum = 0;
        while (n >= 1)
        {
          sum = sum + n;
          n = n - 1;
        }
    }
```

7. Given the function heading

```
    Boolean HighTaxBracket( int inc,
                            int ded )
```

is the following statement a legal call to the function if `income` and `deductions` are of type `int`?

```
    if (HighTaxBracket(income, deductions))
        cout << "Upper Class";
```

8. The statement

```
    Power(k, 1, m);
```

is a call to the void function whose definition is on the next page. Rewrite the function as a value-returning function, then write a function call that assigns the function value to the variable `m`.

```
void Power( float   base,
            int     exponent,
            float&  answer    )
{
    int i;

    answer = 1.0;
    i = 1;
    while (i <= exponent)
    {
        answer = answer * base;
        i++;
    }
}
```

9. You are given the following Test function and a C++ program in which the variables a, b, c, and result are declared to be of type float. In the calling code, a = –5.0, b = 0.1, and c = 16.2. What is the value of result when each of the following calls returns?

```
float Test( float x,
            float y,
            float z )
{
    if (x > y || y > z)
        return 0.5;
    else
        return -0.5;
}
```

```
a. result = Test(5.2, 5.3, 5.6);
b. result = Test(fabs(a), b, c);
```

10. What is wrong with each of the following C++ function definitions?

```
a. void Test1( int m,
              int n )
   {
       return 3 * m + n;
   }
b. float Test2( int   i,
                float x )
   {
       i = i + 7;
       x = 4.8 + float(i);
   }
```

11. Explain why it is risky to use a reference parameter as a formal parameter of a value-returning function.

PROGRAMMING WARM-UP EXERCISES

1. The following program is written with very poor style. For one thing, global variables are used in place of parameters. Rewrite it without global variables, using good programming style.

```
#include <iostream.h>
void MashGlobals();
int a, b, c;
int main()
{
cin >> a >> b >> c;
MashGlobals();
cout << "a=" << a << ' ' << "b=" << b << ' '
<< "c=" << c << endl;
return 0;
}
void MashGlobals()
{
int temp;
temp = a + b;
a = b + c;
b = temp;
}
```

2. Write the heading for a value-returning function Epsilon that receives two float parameters named high and low and returns a float result.

3. Write the heading for a value-returning function named NearlyEqual that receives three float parameters—num1, num2, and difference—and returns a Boolean result.

4. Given the heading you wrote in Exercise 3, write the body of the function. The function returns TRUE if the absolute value of the difference between num1 and num2 is less than the value in difference and returns FALSE otherwise.

5. Write a value-returning function named CompassHeading that returns the sum of its four float parameters: trueCourse, windCorrAngle, variance, and deviation.

6. Write a value-returning function named FracPart that receives a floating point number and returns the fractional part of that number. Use a single parameter named x. For example, if the incoming value of x is 16.753, the function return value is 0.753.

7. Write a value-returning function named Circumf that finds the circumference of a circle given the radius. The formula for calculating the circumference of a circle is π multiplied by twice the radius. Use 3.14159 for π.

8. Given the function heading

```
float Hypotenuse( float side1,
                  float side2 )
```

write the body of the function to return the length of the hypotenuse of a right triangle. The formal parameters represent the lengths of the other two sides. The formula for the hypotenuse is

$$\sqrt{side1^2 + side2^2}$$

9. Write a value-returning function named `FifthPow` that returns the fifth power of its `float` parameter.

10. Write a value-returning function named `Min` that returns the smallest of its three integer parameters.

11. The following If conditions work correctly on most, but not all, machines. Rewrite them using the "`is...`" functions from the C++ standard library (header file `ctype.h`).

   a. `if (inChar >= '0' && inChar <= '9')`
        `DoSomething();`

   b. `if (inChar >= 'A' && inChar <= 'Z' ||`
        `inChar >= 'a' && inChar <= 'z'   )`
        `DoSomething();`

   c. `if (inChar >= 'A' && inChar <= 'Z' ||`
        `inChar >= '0' && inChar <= '9'   )`
        `DoSomething();`

   d. `if (inChar < 'a' || inChar > 'z')`
        `DoSomething();`

12. Write a Boolean value-returning function `IsPrime` that receives an integer parameter n, tests it to see if it is a prime number, and returns TRUE if it is. (A prime number is an integer greater than or equal to 2 whose only divisors are 1 and the number itself.) A call to this function might look like this:

```
if (IsPrime(n))
    cout << n << " is a prime number.";
```

   (*Hint:* If n is not a prime number, it is exactly divisible by an integer in the range 2 through $\sqrt{n}$.)

13. Write a value-returning function named `Postage` that returns the cost of mailing a package, given the weight of the package in pounds and ounces and the cost per ounce.

PROGRAMMING PROBLEMS

1. If a principal amount (*P*), for which the interest is compounded *Q* times per year, is placed in a savings account, then the amount of interest earned after *N* years is given by the following formula, where *I* is the annual interest rate as a floating point number:

$$amount = P * (1 + I/Q)^{N*Q}$$

   Write a C++ program that inputs the values for *P*, *I*, *Q*, and *N* and outputs the interest earned for each year up through year *N*. You should use a value-returning function to compute the amount of interest. Your program should prompt the user appropriately, label output values, and have good style.

2. Euclid's algorithm is a method for finding the greatest common divisor (GCD) of two positive integers. It states that, for any two positive integers M and N such that $M \le N$, the GCD is calculated as follows:

a. Divide N by M.
b. If the remainder $R = 0$, then the GCD $= M$.
c. If $R > 0$, then M becomes N, and R becomes M, and repeat step (a) until $R = 0$.

Write a program that uses a value-returning function to find the GCD of two numbers. The `main` function reads pairs of numbers from a file stream named `dataFile`. For each pair read in, the two numbers and the GCD should be labeled properly and written to a file stream named `gcdList`.

3. The distance to the landing point of a projectile, launched at an angle `angle` (in radians) with an initial velocity of `velocity` (in feet per second), ignoring air resistance, is given by the formula

$$distance = \frac{velocity^2 * \sin(2*angle)}{32.2}$$

Write a C++ program that implements a game in which the user first enters the distance to a target. The user then enters the angle and velocity for launching a projectile. If the projectile comes within a tenth of one percent of the distance to the target, the user wins the game. If the projectile doesn't come close enough, the user is told how far off the projectile is and is allowed to try again. If after five tries there isn't a winning input, then the user loses the game.

To simplify input for the user, your program should allow the angle to be input in degrees. The formula for converting degrees to radians is

$$radians = \frac{degrees * 3.14159265}{180.0}$$

Each of the formulas in this problem should be implemented as a C++ value-returning function in your program. Your program should prompt the user for input appropriately, label the output values, and have proper programming style.

4. Write a program that computes the number of days between two dates. One way of doing this is to have the program compute the Julian day number for each of the dates and subtract one from the other. The Julian day number is the number of days that have elapsed since noon on January 1, 4713 B.C. The following algorithm may be used to calculate the Julian day number.

Given `year` (an integer, such as 1997), `month` (an integer from 1 through 12), and `day` (an integer from 1 through 31), if `month` is 1 or 2, then subtract 1 from `year` and add 12 to `month`.

If the date comes from the Gregorian calendar (later than October 15, 1582), then compute an intermediate result with the following formula (otherwise, let `intRes1` equal 0):

intRes1 = 2 – year / 100 + year / 400   (integer division)

Compute a second intermediate result with the formula

intRes2 = int(365.25 * year)

Compute a third intermediate result with the formula

intRes3 = int(30.6001 * (month + 1))

Finally, the Julian day number is computed with the formula

julianDay = intRes1 + intRes2 + intRes3 + day + 1720994.5

Your program should make appropriate use of value-returning functions in solving this problem. These formulas require nine significant digits; you may have to use the floating point type double or long double. Your program should prompt appropriately for input (the two dates). You should use proper style with plenty of comments.

CASE STUDY FOLLOW-UP

1. Supply the missing precondition and postcondition in the comments at the beginning of each function in the Transpose program.
2. Rewrite the revised Graph program (pp. 429–433), adding data validation tests for negative sales amounts, a negative number of business days, and sales greater than $25,000.
3. In the Starship program, the main function neglects to guarantee any of the function preconditions before calling the functions. Modify the GetData function to validate the input data. When control returns from GetData, the main function should be able to assume that all the data values are within the proper ranges.

9

Additional Control Structures

GOALS

- To be able to write a Switch statement for a multi-way branching problem.
- To be able to write a Do-While statement and contrast it with a While statement.
- To be able to write a For statement as an alternative to a While statement.
- To understand the purpose of the break and continue statements.
- To be able to choose the most appropriate looping statement for a given problem.
- To be able to express a loop invariant as a comment within a program.

In the preceding chapters, we introduced C++ statements for sequence, selection, loop, and subprogram. In some cases, we introduced more than one way of implementing these structures. For example, selection may be implemented by an If-Then statement or an If-Then-Else statement. The If-Then is sufficient to implement any selection structure, but C++ provides the If-Then-Else for convenience because the two-way branch is frequently used in programming.

This chapter introduces five new statements that are also nonessential to, but nonetheless convenient for, programming. One, the Switch statement, makes it easier to write selection structures that have many branches. Two new looping statements, For and Do-While, make it easier to program certain types of loops. The other two statements, `break` and `continue`, are control statements that are used as part of larger looping and selection structures.

 # The Switch Statement

The Switch statement is a selection control structure that allows us to list any number of branches. In other words, it is a control structure for multi-way branches. A Switch is similar to nested If statements. The value of the **switch expression**—an expression whose value is matched with a label attached to a branch—determines which one of the branches is executed. For example, look at the following statement:

```
switch (letter)
{
    case 'X' : Statement1;
               break;
    case 'L' :
    case 'M' : Statement2;
               break;
    case 'S' : Statement3;
               break;
    default  : Statement4;
}
Statement5;
```

In this example, `letter` is the switch expression. The statement means "If `letter` is 'X', execute Statement1 and break out of the Switch statement, continuing with Statement5. If `letter` is 'L' or 'M', execute Statement2 and continue with Statement5. If `letter` is 'S', execute Statement3 and continue with Statement5. If `letter` is none of the characters mentioned, execute

Statement4 and continue with Statement5." The `break` statement causes an immediate exit from the Switch statement. We'll see shortly what happens if we omit the `break` statements.

Switch Expression The expression whose value determines which switch label is selected. It cannot be a floating point expression.

The syntax template for the Switch statement is

SwitchStatement

```
switch (IntegralExpression)
{
        SwitchLabel... Statement
                 .
                 .
                 .
}
```

IntegralExpression is an expression of integral type—`char`, `short`, `int`, `long`, or `enum` (we discuss `enum` in the next chapter). The optional SwitchLabel in front of a statement is either a *case label* or a *default label*:

SwitchLabel

```
  case ConstantExpression :

  default :
```

In a case label, ConstantExpression is an integral expression whose operands must be literal or named constants. The following are examples of constant integral expressions (`CLASS_SIZE` is a named constant of type `int`):

```
3
CLASS_SIZE
'A'
2 * CLASS_SIZE + 1
```

The data type of ConstantExpression is coerced, if necessary, to match the type of the switch expression.

In our opening example that tests the value of `letter`, the following are case labels:

```
case 'X' :
case 'L' :
case 'M' :
case 'S' :
```

As the example shows, a single statement may be preceded by more than one case label. Each case constant may appear only once in a given Switch statement. If a value appears more than once, a syntax error results. Also, there can be only one default label in a Switch statement.

The flow of control through a Switch statement goes like this. First, the switch expression is evaluated. If the value matches one of the constants in a case label, control branches to the statement following that case label. From there, control proceeds sequentially until either a break statement or the end of the Switch statement is encountered. If the value of the switch expression doesn't match any case constant, then one of two things happens. If there is a default label, control branches to the statement following that label. If there is no default label, all statements within the Switch are skipped and control simply proceeds to the statement following the entire Switch statement.

The following Switch statement prints an appropriate comment based on a student's grade (grade is of type char):

```
switch (grade)
{
    case 'A' :
    case 'B' : cout << "Good Work";
               break;
    case 'C' : cout << "Average Work";
               break;
    case 'D' :
    case 'F' : cout << "Poor Work";
               numberInTrouble++;
               break;                    // Unnecessary, but a good habit
}
```

Notice that the final break statement is unnecessary. But programmers often include it anyway. One reason is that it's easier to insert another case label at the end if there is already a break statement present.

If grade does not contain one of the specified characters, none of the statements within the Switch is executed. Unless a precondition of the

Switch statement is that `grade` is definitely one of 'A', 'B', 'C', 'D', or 'F', it would be wise to include a default label to account for an invalid grade:

```cpp
switch (grade)
{
    case 'A' :
    case 'B' : cout << "Good Work";
               break;
    case 'C' : cout << "Average Work";
               break;
    case 'D' :
    case 'F' : cout << "Poor Work";
               numberInTrouble++;
               break;
    default  : cout << grade << " is not a legal letter grade.";
               break;
}
```

A Switch statement with a break statement after each case alternative behaves exactly like an If-Then-Else-If control structure. For example, our Switch statement is equivalent to the following code:

```cpp
if (grade == 'A' || grade == 'B')
    cout << "Good Work";
else if (grade == 'C')
    cout << "Average Work";
else if (grade == 'D' || grade == 'F')
{
    cout << "Poor Work";
    numberInTrouble++;
}
else
    cout << grade << " is not a legal letter grade.";
```

Is either of these two versions better than the other? There is no absolute answer to this question. For this particular example, our opinion is that the Switch statement is easier to understand because of its two-dimensional, table-like form. But some may find the If-Then-Else-If version easier to read. When implementing a multi-way branching structure, our advice is to write down both a Switch and an If-Then-Else-If and then compare them for readability. Keep in mind that C++ provides the Switch statement as a matter of convenience. Don't feel obligated to use a Switch statement for every multi-way branch.

Finally, we said we would look at what happens if you omit the **break** statements inside a Switch statement. Let's rewrite our letter grade example without the break statements:

```
switch (grade)      // Wrong version
{
    case 'A' :
    case 'B' : cout << "Good Work";
    case 'C' : cout << "Average Work";
    case 'D' :
    case 'F' : cout << "Poor Work";
               numberInTrouble++;
    default  : cout << grade << " is not a legal letter grade.";
}
```

If grade happens to be 'H', control branches to the statement at the default label and the output is

```
H is not a legal letter grade.
```

Unfortunately, this case alternative is the only one that works correctly. If grade is 'A', the resulting output is this:

```
Good WorkAverage WorkPoor WorkA is not a legal letter grade.
```

Remember that after a branch is taken to a specific case label, control proceeds sequentially until either a break statement or the end of the Switch statement is encountered. Forgetting a break statement in a case alternative is a very common source of errors in C++ programs.

The Do-While Statement

The Do-While statement is a looping control structure in which the loop condition is tested at the end (bottom) of the loop. This format guarantees that the loop body is executed at least once. The syntax template for the Do-While is this:

DoWhileStatement

```
do
    Statement
while ( Expression ) ;
```

As usual in C++, Statement is either a single statement or a block. Also, note that the Do-While ends with a semicolon.

The Do-While statement

```
do
{
   Statement1;
   Statement2;
     .
     .
     .
   StatementN;
} while (Expression);
```

means "Execute the statements between do and while as long as Expression is still nonzero (TRUE) at the end of the loop."

Let's compare a While loop and a Do-While loop that do the same task: they find the first period in a file of data. Assume that there is at least one period in the file.

While Solution

```
dataFile >> inputChar;
while (inputChar != '.')
     dataFile >> inputChar;
```

Do-While Solution

```
do
     dataFile >> inputChar;
while (inputChar != '.');
```

The While solution requires a priming read so that inputChar has a value before the loop is entered. This isn't required for the Do-While solution because the input statement within the loop is executed before the loop condition is evaluated.

Let's look at another example. Suppose a program needs to read a person's age interactively. The program requires that the age be positive. The following loops ensure that the input value is positive before the program proceeds any further.

While Solution

```
cout << "Enter your age: ";
cin >> age;
while (age <= 0)
{
     cout << "Your age must be positive." << endl;
     cout << "Enter your age: ";
     cin >> age;
}
```

MAY WE INTRODUCE

Admiral Grace Murray Hopper

From 1943 until her death on New Year's Day in 1992, Admiral Grace Murray Hopper was intimately involved with computing. In 1991, she was awarded the National Medal of Technology "for her pioneering accomplishments in the development of computer programming languages that simplified computer technology and opened the door to a significantly larger universe of users."

Admiral Hopper was born Grace Brewster Murray in New York City on December 9, 1906. She attended Vassar and received a Ph.D. in mathematics from Yale. For the next 10 years, she taught mathematics at Vassar.

In 1943, Admiral Hopper joined the U.S. Navy and was assigned to the Bureau of Ordnance Computation Project at Harvard University as a programmer on the Mark I. After the war, she remained at Harvard as a faculty member and continued work on the navy's Mark II and Mark III computers. In 1949, she joined Eckert-Mauchly Computer Corporation and worked on the UNIVAC I. It was there that she made a legendary contribution to computing: She discovered the first computer "bug"—a moth caught in the hardware.

Admiral Hopper had a working compiler in 1952, at a time when the conventional wisdom was that computers could do only arithmetic. Although not on the committee that designed the computer language COBOL, she was active in its design, implementation, and use. COBOL (which stands for COmmon Business-Oriented Language) was

Do-While Solution

```
do
{
    cout << "Enter your age: ";
    cin >> age;
    if (age <= 0)
        cout << "Your age must be positive." << endl;
} while (age <= 0);
```

Notice that the Do-While solution does not require the prompt and input steps to appear twice—once before the loop and once within it—but it does test the input value twice.

We can also use the Do-While to implement a count-controlled loop *if* we know in advance that the loop body is always executed at least once. Below are two versions of a loop to sum the integers from 1 through n.

developed in the early 1960s and is still widely used in business data processing.

Admiral Hopper retired from the navy in 1966, only to be recalled within a year to full-time active duty. Her mission in the navy was to oversee the navy's efforts at maintaining uniformity in programming languages. It has been said that just as Admiral Hyman Rickover was the father of the nuclear navy, Rear Admiral Hopper was the mother of computerized data automation in the navy. She served with the Naval Data Automation Command until she retired again in 1986 with the rank of rear admiral. At the time of her death, she was a senior consultant at Digital Equipment Corporation.

During her lifetime, Admiral Hopper received honorary degrees from more than 40 colleges and universities. She was honored by her peers on several occasions, including the first Computer Sciences "Man of the Year" award given by the Data Processing Management Association and the "Contributions to Computer Science Education Award" given by the Special Interest Group for Computer Science Education of the ACM (Association for Computing Machinery).

Admiral Hopper loved young people and enjoyed giving talks on college and university campuses. She often handed out colored wires, which she called nanoseconds because they were cut to the length of about one foot—the distance that light travels in a nanosecond (billionth of a second). Her advice to young people was, "You manage things, you lead people. We went overboard on management and forgot about leadership."

When asked which of her many accomplishments she was most proud of, she answered, "All the young people I have trained over the years."

While Solution

```
sum = 0;
counter = 1;
while (counter <= n)
{
    sum = sum + counter;
    counter++;
}
```

Do-While Solution

```
sum = 0;
counter = 1;
do
{
    sum = sum + counter;
    counter++;
} while (counter <= n);
```

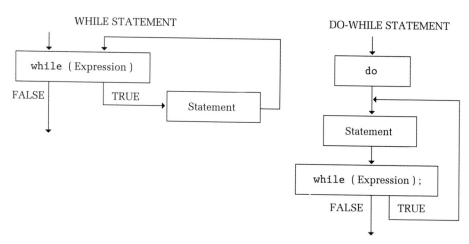

If n is a positive number, both of these versions are equivalent. But if n is 0 or negative, the two loops give different results. In the While version, the final value of sum is 0 because the loop body is never entered. In the Do-While version, the final value of sum is 1 because the body executes once and *then* the loop test is made.

Because the While statement tests the condition before executing the body of the loop, it is called a *pretest loop*. The Do-While statement does the opposite and thus is known as a *posttest loop*. Figure 9-1 compares the flow of control in the While and Do-While loops.

After we look at two other new looping constructs, we offer some guidelines for determining when to use each type of loop.

 # The For Statement

The For statement is designed to simplify the writing of count-controlled loops. The following statement prints out the integers from 1 through n:

```
for (count = 1; count <= n; count++)
    cout << count << endl;
```

This For statement means "Initialize the loop control variable count to 1. While count is less than or equal to n, execute the output statement and increment count by 1. Stop the loop after count has been incremented to n + 1."

In C++, a For statement is merely a compact notation for a While loop. In fact, the compiler essentially translates a For statement into an equivalent While loop as follows:

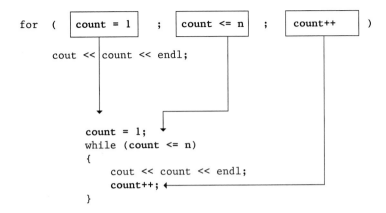

The syntax template for a For statement is

ForStatement

for (InitStatement Expression1 ; Expression2)
      Statement

Expression1 is the While condition. InitStatement can be one of the following: the null statement (just a semicolon), a declaration statement (which always ends in a semicolon), or an expression statement (an expression ending in a semicolon). Therefore, there is always a semicolon before Expression1. (You don't see a semicolon in the syntax template. If we included one, you would have to use *two* semicolons—one to terminate InitStatement and another before Expression1.)

Most often, a For statement is written such that InitStatement initializes a loop control variable and Expression2 increments or decrements the loop control variable. Here are two loops that execute the same number of times (50):

```
for (loopCount = 1; loopCount <= 50; loopCount++)
   .
   .
   .

for (loopCount = 50; loopCount >= 1; loopCount--)
   .
   .
   .
```

Just like While loops, Do-While and For loops may be nested. For example, the nested For structure

```
for (lastNum = 1; lastNum <= 7; lastNum++)
{
    for (numToPrint = 1; numToPrint <= lastNum; numToPrint++)
        cout << numToPrint;
    cout << endl;
}
```

prints the following triangle of numbers.

```
1
12
123
1234
12345
123456
1234567
```

Although For statements are used most frequently for count-controlled loops, C++ allows you to write *any* While loop by using a For statement. To use For loops intelligently, you should know the following facts.

1. In the syntax template, InitStatement can be the null statement, and Expression2 is optional. If Expression2 is omitted, there is no statement for the compiler to insert at the bottom of the loop. As a result, you could write the While loop

```
while (inputVal != 999)
    cin >> inputVal;
```

as the equivalent For loop

```
for ( ; inputVal != 999; )
    cin >> inputVal;
```

2. According to the syntax template, Expression1—the While condition—is optional. If you omit it, the expression 1 (meaning TRUE) is assumed. The loop

```
for ( ; ; )
    cout "Hi" << endl;
```

is equivalent to the While loop

```
while (1)
    cout << "Hi" << endl;
```

Both of these are infinite loops that print "Hi" endlessly.

3. The initializing statement, InitStatement, can be a declaration with initialization:

```
for (int i = 1; i <= 20; i++)
    cout << "Hi" << endl;
```

But you have to be careful here. The variable i is *not* local to the body of the loop. Its scope extends to the end of the block surrounding the For statement. In other words, it's as if i had been declared outside the loop. The following sequence of statements, therefore, produces a compile-time error:

```
for (int i = 1; i <= 20; i++)
    cout << "Hi" << endl;
for (int i = 1; i <= 100; i++)   // Error--i already defined
    cout << "Ed" << endl;
```

As you have seen by now, the For statement in C++ is a very flexible structure. Its use can range from a simple count-controlled loop to a general-purpose, "anything goes" While loop. Some programmers find it an intellectual challenge to see how much they can squeeze into the heading (the first line) of a For statement. For example, the program fragment

```
cin >> ch;
while (ch != '.')
    cin >> ch;
```

can be compressed into the following For loop:

```
for (cin >> ch; ch != '.'; cin >> ch)
    ;
```

Because all the work is done in the For heading, there is nothing for the loop body to do. The body is simply the null statement.

With For statements, our advice is to keep things simple. The trickier the code is, the harder it will be for another person (or you!) to understand your code and track down errors. In this book, we use For loops for count-controlled loops only.

The Break and Continue Statements

The break statement, which we introduced with the Switch statement, is also used with loops. A break statement causes an immediate exit from the innermost Switch, While, Do-While, or For statement in which it appears. Notice the word *innermost*. If break is in a loop that is nested inside another loop, control exits the inner loop but not the outer.

One of the more common ways of using break with loops is to set up an infinite loop and use If tests to exit the loop. Suppose we want to input 10 pairs of integers, performing data validation and computing the square root of the sum of each pair. For data validation, assume that the first number must be less than 100 and the second must be greater than 50. Also, after each input, we want to test the state of the stream for EOF. Here's a loop using break statements to accomplish the task (assume TRUE has been defined as the integer 1):

```
loopCount = 1;
while (TRUE)
{
    cin >> num1;
    if ( !cin || num1 >= 100)
        break;
    cin >> num2;
    if ( !cin || num2 <= 50)
        break;
    cout << sqrt(float(num1 + num2)) << endl;
    loopCount++;
    if (loopCount > 10)
        break;
}
```

Note that we could have used a For loop to count from 1 to 10, breaking out of it as necessary. However, this loop is both count-controlled and event-controlled, so we prefer to use a While loop.

The above loop contains three distinct exit points. Some people vigorously oppose this style of programming, as it violates the single-entry, single-exit philosophy we discussed with multiple returns from a function. Is there any advantage to using an infinite loop in conjunction with break? To answer this question, let's rewrite the loop without using break statements. The loop must terminate when num1 is invalid or num2 is invalid or loop-Count exceeds 10. We'll use Boolean flags to signal invalid data in the While condition:

```
num1Valid = TRUE;
num2Valid = TRUE;
loopCount = 1;
while (num1Valid && num2Valid && loopCount <= 10)
{
    cin >> num1;
    if ( !cin || num1 >= 100)
        num1Valid = FALSE;
    else
    {
        cin >> num2;
        if ( !cin || num2 <= 50)
            num2Valid = FALSE;
        else
        {
            cout << sqrt(float(num1 + num2)) << endl;
            loopCount++;
        }
    }
}
```

One could argue that the first version is easier to follow and understand than this second version. The primary task of the loop body—computing the square root of the sum of the numbers—is more prominent in the first version. In the second version, the computation is obscured by being buried within nested Ifs. The second version also has a more complicated control flow.

The disadvantage of using break with loops is that it can become a crutch for those who are too impatient to think carefully about loop design. It's easy to overuse (and abuse) the technique. Here's an example, printing the integers 1 through 5:

```
i = 1;
while (TRUE)
{
    cout << i;
    if (i == 5)
        break;
    i++;
}
```

There is no real justification for setting up the loop this way. Conceptually, it is a pure count-controlled loop, and a simple For loop does the job:

```
for (i = 1; i <= 5; i++)
    cout << i;
```

The For loop is easier to understand and is less prone to error.

A good rule of thumb is: Use `break` within loops only as a last resort. Specifically, use it only to avoid baffling combinations of multiple Boolean flags and nested Ifs.

Another statement that alters the flow of control in a C++ program is the `continue` statement. This statement, valid only in loops, terminates the current loop iteration (but not the entire loop). It causes an immediate branch to the bottom of the loop—skipping the rest of the statements in the loop body—in preparation for the next iteration. Here is an example of a reading loop in which we want to process only the positive numbers in an input file:

```
for (dataCount = 1; dataCount <= 500; dataCount++)
{
    dataFile >> inputVal;
    if (inputVal <= 0)
        continue;
    cout << inputVal;
    .
    .
    .

}
```

If `inputVal` is less than or equal to 0, control branches to the bottom of the loop. Then, as with any For loop, the computer increments `dataCount` and performs the loop test before going on to the next iteration.

The `continue` statement is not used often, but we present it for completeness (and because you may run across it in other people's programs). Its primary purpose is to avoid obscuring the main process of the loop by indenting it within an If statement. For example, the above code would be written without a `continue` statement as follows:

```
for (dataCount = 1; dataCount <= 500; dataCount++)
{
    dataFile >> inputVal;
    if (inputVal > 0)
    {
        cout << inputVal;
        .
        .
        .
    }
}
```

Be sure to note the difference between `continue` and `break`. The `continue` statement means "Abandon the current iteration of the loop, and go on to the next iteration." The `break` statement means "Exit the entire loop immediately."

Guidelines for Choosing a Looping Statement

Here are some guidelines to help you decide when to use each of the three looping statements (While, Do-While, and For).

1. If the loop is a simple count-controlled loop, the For statement is a "natural." Concentrating the three loop control actions—initialize, test, and increment/decrement—into one location (the heading of the For statement) reduces the chances of forgetting to include one of them.
2. If the loop is an event-controlled loop whose body is always executed at least once, a Do-While statement is appropriate.
3. If the loop is an event-controlled loop and nothing is known about the first execution, use a While or a For statement.
4. When in doubt, use a While statement.
5. An infinite loop with `break` statements sometimes clarifies the code but more often reflects an undisciplined loop design. Use it only after careful consideration of While, Do-While, and For.

Loop Invariants as Program Comments

We've been writing preconditions and postconditions as comments at the beginning of our functions. These assertions help to document the interface between the function and the calling code. From here on, we also include loop invariants as comments in our loops. These assertions help to document important facts about the state of the program while the loop is executing.

Recall from Chapter 6 that a loop invariant is an assertion that must be true each time the loop iterates and when the loop exits. For a loop to be correct, the logical AND of the loop invariant and the loop termination condition must imply that the loop postcondition is true.

We said that the invariant "must be true each time the loop iterates." Let's be more specific. When we place a comment with an assertion somewhere in a program, the assertion should be true when control reaches that precise location. We place a loop invariant at some point in the loop, claiming that it is true with respect to that point in the loop. The most useful location for a loop invariant is immediately before the loop test because at this point an iteration has just completed. Here is an example that uses a Do-While loop to sum the integers 1 through 10. To help explain the loop invariant, we also include a loop postcondition.

```
sum = 0;
count = 1;
do
{
```

```
    sum = sum + count;
    count++;

        // Invariant:
        //     sum == 1 + 2 + ... + count-1
        //   && 2 <= count <= 11

} while (count <= 10);

// Assert:
//      sum == 1 + 2 + ... + 10
//   && count == 11
```

The first time control reaches the position of the loop invariant, sum equals 1 and count equals 2. Therefore, the invariant is true. (Notice that sum equals the sum of the integers from 1 up through 1—there's just one number in this sum.) At the end of the second iteration, sum equals 3 (that is, 1 + 2) and count equals 3, so the invariant is again true. At the end of the tenth iteration, sum contains the sum of 1 through 10 and count equals 11. The invariant is still true. At this time, control exits the loop. Now let's verify that

Invariant AND Termination condition → Postcondition

(Remember that the right arrow, pronounced *implies*, is the logical implication operator.) We manipulate the assertions as follows. The loop invariant is

(sum = 1 + 2 + . . . + count−1) AND (2 ≤ count ≤ 11)

and the loop termination condition is

count > 10

The following sequence of implications leads us to the loop postcondition:

(sum = 1 + 2 + . . . + count−1) AND (2 ≤ count ≤ 11) AND (count > 10) →
(sum = 1 + 2 + . . . + count−1) AND (count = 11) →
(sum = 1 + 2 + . . . + 10) AND (count = 11)

Placing a loop invariant into a While loop (or a For loop) is complicated by the fact that its loop test is at the top, not the bottom. To locate the loop invariant just before the loop test, we need two copies of the invariant, one before the loop starts and one at the end of an iteration:

```
// Invariant: ...
while ( ... )
{
      .
      .
      .

    // Invariant: ...
}
```

To avoid duplicating the invariant this way, we include only one copy at the top of the loop body, along with the remark "prior to test." This remark is a reminder that the invariant is logically, if not physically, located just before the loop test. Here is a While loop to sum the integers 1 through 10:

```
sum = 0;
count = 1;
while (count <= 10)
{
        // Invariant (prior to test):
        //      sum == 1 + 2 + ... + count-1
        //   && 1 <= count <= 11

    sum = sum + count;
    count++;
}
```

In comparing this example to the Do-While version, there are two things to notice. First, the two versions use different invariants for count. In the Do-While loop, the lower limit is 2 because count has already been incremented by the time the invariant is reached. In the While loop version, the invariant is first encountered *before* the loop begins. At that moment, count equals 1.

The second thing to notice is that the invariant for sum seems to be wrong the first time the invariant is encountered. Before the loop begins, the assertion is

$$sum = 1 + 2 + \ldots + 0$$

Is this a true assertion? The answer is yes, and here's why. The assertion, if written out in full, is actually this: "For all integers in the range 1 through 0 in increasing order, sum is the sum of these integers." Because there aren't any integers that satisfy the "For all" part, the assertion is trivially true. Here's another example of a loop invariant that is trivially true before the first execution of the loop body:

```
for (i = 1; i <= 50; i++)

        // Invariant (prior to test):
        //      The values 1, 2, ... , i-1 have been output
        //   && 1 <= i <= 51

    cout << i << endl;
```

After i has been initialized to 1 but before the loop test occurs, the assertion

The values 1, 2, ... , 0 have been output

is trivially true because there are no integers in this range. The second part of the invariant is also true—namely, that i is in the range 1 through 51, inclusive. The first loop iteration prints the value 1 and increments i to 2. Prior to the loop test, the invariant is true; the value 1 has been output, and i is in the stated range. On the final iteration, the value 50 is printed and i becomes 51. Prior to the loop test, you can see that the invariant is true. After the loop test, control exits the loop and the invariant is still true.

When loops don't use counters, loop invariants are harder to write. For example, what is the invariant for the following loop?

```
do
{
    cout << "Enter your age: ";
    cin >> age;
} while (age <= 0);
```

This loop continues to iterate as long as age ≤ 0. We might be tempted to write the invariant this way:

```
do
{
    cout << "Enter your age: ";
    cin >> age;

        // Invariant (WRONG):
        //      age has been input
        // && age <= 0

} while (age <= 0);
```

This invariant is true for every iteration *except* the final iteration, which occurs when the user finally types a positive number. Suppose that the user types 5 as the input value. Immediately after the input statement and before the loop test, the invariant is false. This is not the correct invariant.

With loops that input data and immediately test the data in the loop condition, there are two keys to expressing a loop invariant correctly. The first is to think about the *history* of the loop—what has happened so far since the loop began. The second is to exclude the current input value from any claim about its value. In the above loop, we can't claim that age is negative or 0 or positive immediately after reading it in—that's for the loop test to determine. Here is a reasonable way to write the invariant for the above loop:

```
do
{
    cout << "Enter your age: ";
```

```
    cin >> age;

    // Invariant:
    //     age has been input
    //  && For all values of age prior to
    //     current value, age <= 0

} while (age <= 0);
```

After the loop terminates, the conjunction of the termination condition and the invariant yields the postcondition

(age > 0) AND (For all values of age prior to the current value, age ≤ 0)

Writing loop invariants as program comments is not always easy to do. Sometimes an invariant consists of 15 or 20 separate assertions. Although these assertions may all be important when you design and verify the loop, it's not practical to include them all as comments. For documentation purposes, what is important is to summarize concisely the task accomplished by the loop, mentioning values of key variables such as counters, summing variables, and input or output variables. Using mathematical notation wherever possible helps keep the comments brief and precise. And remember to express an invariant as an assertion, not as a general informational comment. Assertions don't look like "This loop will do such-and-such" or "This loop does so-and-so." An assertion is a truth-valued statement—one that is either true or false (true, one hopes).

One final remark about loop invariants: If you write an infinite loop with `break` statements to allow multiple exits from the loop, you need a different loop invariant for each of the exit points. The loop invariants are all bound to be different because the state of the program changes between any two exit points. The prospect of creating four or five different invariants for a given loop may keep you from becoming too casual about using `break` statements!

P ROBLEM-SOLVING CASE STUDY

The Rich Uncle

Problem: Your rich uncle has just died, and in his desk you find two wills. One of them, dated several months ago, leaves you and your relatives a substantial part of his fortune; the other, dated last week, gives it all to his next-door neighbor. Being suspicious that the second will is a forgery, you decide to write a program to analyze writing style in order to compare the wills. The program reads and prints alphanumeric characters from a file named `inFile`. When the entire file has been read, it prints a summary table showing the percentage of characters that were uppercase letters, lowercase letters, decimal digits, blanks, and end-of-sentence punctuation marks ('?', '!', '.').

Input: Text in the file `inFile`.

Output: A copy of the text in file `inFile`, and a table giving the name of each category and what percentage of the total the category represents.

Discussion: Doing this task by hand would be tedious but quite straightforward. You would set up five places to make hash marks, one for each of the categories of symbols to be counted. You would then read the text character by character, determine which category to put each character into, and make a hash mark in the appropriate place.

As a human, you can look at a character and tell immediately which category to mark. We can simulate this process by using the library functions `isupper`, `islower`, and `isdigit` (described in Chapter 8) along with a Switch statement with branches for the other categories.

Assumptions: None.

Main   *Level 0*

```
Initialize counters to zero
Open inFile (and verify success)
Read a character from inFile
WHILE NOT EOF on inFile
    Print the character
    Increment proper counter
    Read a character from inFile
Calculate and print percentages
```

At this point, we realize that the instructions do not indicate whether the percentages to be taken are percentages of the total number of characters read, including those that do not fit any of the categories or percentages of the total number of characters that fall into the five categories. We assume that all characters should be counted. We thus add a counter (named `left-OverCount`) for all characters that do not fall into the five categories.

Increment Proper Counter (Inout: upperCount, lowerCount, digitCount, blankCount, puncCount, leftOverCount; In: ch) *Level 1*

```
IF ch is uppercase
    Increment upperCount
ELSE IF ch is lowercase
    Increment lowerCount
ELSE IF ch is a digit
    Increment digitCount
ELSE
    SWITCH ch
        Blank: Increment blankCount
        Punctuation mark: Increment puncCount
        Anything else: Increment leftOverCount
```

Calculate and Print Percentages (In: upperCount, lowerCount, digitCount, blankCount, puncCount, leftOverCount)

```
Set total = sum of all 6 counters
Print "Percent that are uppercase letters:",
    upperCount / total * 100
Print "Percent that are lowercase letters:",
    lowerCount / total * 100
Print "Percent that are decimal digits:",
    digitCount / total * 100
Print "Percent that are blanks:",
    blankCount / total * 100
Print "Percent that are end-of-sentence punctuation:",
    puncCount / total * 100
```

Module Structure Chart:

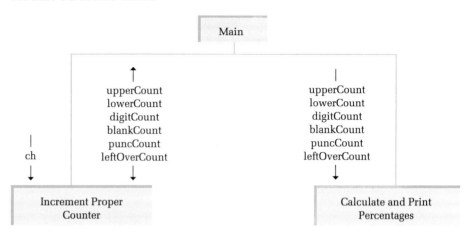

```
//*********************************************************************
// CategoryCount program
// An input file is opened and echo-printed.  A table is printed to
// show the percentage of characters in the file that belong to
// five categories: uppercase letters, lowercase letters, decimal
// digits, blanks, and end-of-sentence punctuation marks.
// ASSUMPTION:  Percentages are based on total number of
// characters in the file
//*********************************************************************
#include <iostream.h>
#include <iomanip.h>      // For setprecision()
#include <fstream.h>      // For file I/O
#include <ctype.h>        // For isupper(), islower(), isdigit()

void CalculateAndPrint( int, int, int, int, int, int );
void IncrementProperCounter( int&, int&, int&, int&,
                             int&, int&, char );

int main()
{
    int      upperCount = 0;        // Number of uppercase letters
    int      lowerCount = 0;        // Number of lowercase letters
    int      digitCount = 0;        // Number of digits
    int      blankCount = 0;        // Number of blanks
    int      puncCount = 0;         // Number of punctuation marks
    int      leftOverCount = 0;     // Number of other characters
    char     inputChar;             // Current input character
    ifstream inFile;                // Input text file
```

```
        cout.setf(ios::fixed, ios::floatfield);    // Set up floating pt.
        cout.setf(ios::showpoint);                  //   output format
        cout << setprecision(2);

        inFile.open("myfile.txt");
        if ( !inFile )
        {
            cout << "** Can't open input file **" << endl;
            return 1;
        }

        inFile.get(inputChar);
        while (inFile)
        {
                // Invariant (prior to test):
                //     All previous values of inputChar
                //     have been read, echoed, and categorized

            cout << inputChar;
            IncrementProperCounter(upperCount, lowerCount, digitCount,
                                   blankCount, puncCount,
                                   leftOverCount, inputChar);
            inFile.get(inputChar);
        }
        CalculateAndPrint(upperCount, lowerCount, digitCount,
                          blankCount, puncCount, leftOverCount);
        return 0;
}

//****************************************************************

void IncrementProperCounter
    ( /* inout */ int& upperCount,        // Counter
      /* inout */ int& lowerCount,        // Counter
      /* inout */ int& digitCount,        // Counter
      /* inout */ int& blankCount,        // Counter
      /* inout */ int& puncCount,         // Counter
      /* inout */ int& leftOverCount,     // Counter
      /* in */    char ch            )    // Current character

// Increments the proper counter for a given character, ch
```

```
// Precondition:
//     All parameters are assigned
// Postcondition:
//     upperCount == upperCount@entry + 1, if ch == 'A' ... 'Z'
//  && lowerCount == lowerCount@entry + 1, if ch == 'a' ... 'z'
//  && digitCount == digitCount@entry + 1, if ch == '0' ... '9'
//  && blankCount == blankCount@entry + 1, if ch == ' '
//  && puncCount  == puncCount@entry + 1,  if ch == '.'  or  '?'
//                                                       or  '!'
//  && leftOverCount == leftOverCount@entry + 1, otherwise

{
    if (isupper(ch))
        upperCount++;
    else if (islower(ch))
        lowerCount++;
    else if (isdigit(ch))
        digitCount++;
    else
        switch (ch)
        {
            case ' ': blankCount++;
                      break;
            case '.':
            case '?':
            case '!': puncCount++;
                      break;
            default:  leftOverCount++;
                      break;            // Unnecessary here, but OK
        }
}

//***************************************************************

void CalculateAndPrint( /* in */ int upperCount,      // Counter
                        /* in */ int lowerCount,      // Counter
                        /* in */ int digitCount,      // Counter
                        /* in */ int blankCount,      // Counter
                        /* in */ int puncCount,       // Counter
                        /* in */ int leftOverCount )  // Counter

// Calculates the total number of characters and prints the
// percentage for each category of characters (except leftOverCount)
```

```
// Precondition:
//     All parameters are assigned
// Postcondition:
//     upperCount, lowerCount, digitCount, blankCount, puncCount,
//     and leftOverCount have been summed, and the percentage of
//     the sum for each counter (except leftOverCount) has been
//     output

{
    int total;          // Total number of characters in the file

    total = upperCount + lowerCount + digitCount +
            blankCount + puncCount + leftOverCount;
    cout << "Percent that are uppercase letters: "
        << float(upperCount) / float(total) * 100.0 << endl;
    cout << "Percent that are lowercase letters: "
        << float(lowerCount) / float(total) * 100.0 << endl;
    cout << "Percent that are decimal digits: "
        << float(digitCount) / float(total) * 100.0 << endl;
    cout << "Percent that are blanks: "
        << float(blankCount) / float(total) * 100.0 << endl;
    cout << "Percent that are end-of-sentence punctuation: "
        << float(puncCount) / float(total) * 100.0 << endl;
}
```

Testing: To be tested thoroughly, the CategoryCount program must be run with all possible combinations of the categories of characters being counted. Listed below is the minimum set of cases that must be tested.

1. All the categories of characters are present.
2. Four of the categories are present; one is not. (This alone requires five test runs.)
3. Only characters that fall into one of the five categories are present.
4. Other characters are present.

The percentages listed below came from a sample run of the program on a large text file. To save space, we show only the percentages, not the echo print of the input.

```
Percent that are uppercase letters: 2.05
Percent that are lowercase letters: 82.32
Percent that are decimal digits: 0.05
Percent that are blanks: 7.03
Percent that are end-of-sentence punctuation: 1.27
```

PROBLEM-SOLVING *CASE STUDY*

Monthly Rainfall Averages

Problem: Meteorologists have recorded monthly rainfall amounts at several sites throughout a region of the country. You have been asked to write an interactive program that lets the user enter one year's rainfall amounts at a particular site and prints out the average of the 12 values. After the data for a site is processed, the program asks whether the user would like to repeat the process for another recording site. A user response of 'y' means yes and 'n' means no. The program must trap erroneous input data (negative values for rainfall amounts and invalid responses to the "Do you wish to continue?" prompt).

Input: For each recording site, 12 floating point rainfall amounts. For each "Do you wish to continue?" prompt, either a 'y' or an 'n'.

Output: For each recording site, the floating point average of the 12 rainfall amounts, displayed to two decimal places.

Discussion: A solution to this problem requires several looping structures. At the topmost level of the design, we need a loop to process the data from all the sites. Each iteration must process one site's data, then ask the user whether to continue with another recording site. The program does not know in advance how many recording sites there are, so the loop cannot be a count-controlled loop. Although we can make any of For, While, or Do-While work correctly, we'll use a Do-While under the assumption that the user definitely wants to process at least one site's data. Therefore, we can set up the loop so that it processes the data from a recording site and then, at the *bottom* of the loop, decides whether to iterate again.

Another loop is required to input 12 monthly rainfall amounts and form their sum. Using the summing technique we are familiar with by now, we initialize the sum to zero before starting the loop, and each loop iteration reads another number and adds it to the accumulating sum. A For loop is appropriate for this task, because we know that exactly 12 iterations must occur.

We'll need two more loops to perform data validation—one loop to ensure that a rainfall amount is negative and another to verify that the user types only 'y' or 'n' when prompted to continue. As we saw earlier in the chapter, Do-While loops are well suited to this kind of data validation. We want the loop body to execute at least once, reading an input value and testing for valid data. As long as the user keeps entering invalid data, the loop continues. Control exits the loop only when the user finally gets it right.

Assumptions: The user processes data for at least one site.

Main   *Level 0*

```
DO
    Get 12 rainfall amounts and sum them
    Print sum / 12
    Prompt user to continue
    Get yes or no response ('y' or 'n')
WHILE response is 'y'
```

Get 12 Amounts (Out: sum)   *Level 1*

```
Set sum = 0
FOR count going from 1 through 12
    Prompt user for a rainfall amount
    Get and verify one rainfall amount
    Add amount to sum
```

Get Yes Or No (Out: response)

```
DO
    Read response
    IF response isn't 'y' or 'n'
        Print error message
WHILE response isn't 'y' or ''n'
```

Get One Amount (Out: amount)   *Level 2*

```
DO
    Read amount
    IF amount < 0.0
        Print error message
WHILE amount < 0.0
```

Module Structure Chart:

Main

sum   response

Get 12 Amounts   Get Yes Or No

amount

Get One Amount

```
//*****************************************************************
// Rainfall program
// This program inputs 12 monthly rainfall amounts from a
// recording site and computes the average monthly rainfall.
// This process is repeated for as many recording sites as
// the user wishes.
//*****************************************************************
#include <iostream.h>
#include <iomanip.h>      // For setprecision()

void Get12Amounts( float& );
void GetOneAmount( float& );
void GetYesOrNo( char& );

int main()
{
    float sum;           // Sum of 12 rainfall amounts
    char  response;      // User response ('y' or 'n')

    cout.setf(ios::fixed, ios::floatfield);    // Set up floating pt.
    cout.setf(ios::showpoint);                 //   output format
    cout << setprecision(2);
```

```
        do
        {
            Get12Amounts(sum);
            cout << "Average rainfall is " << sum / 12.0
                << " inches" << endl << endl;
            cout << "Do you have another recording site? (y or n) ";
            GetYesOrNo(response);

                // Invariant:
                //     Rainfall amounts have been processed for
                //     current site and all previous sites
                //  && All previous values of response were 'y'

        } while (response == 'y');
        return 0;
}


//******************************************************************

void Get12Amounts( /* out */ float& sum )     // Sum of 12 rainfall
                                              // amounts

// Inputs 12 monthly rainfall amounts, verifying that
// each is nonnegative, and returns their sum

// Postcondition:
//     12 rainfall amounts have been read and verified to be
//     nonnegative
//  && sum == sum of the 12 input values

{
    int   count;      // Loop control variable
    float amount;     // Rainfall amount for one month

    sum = 0;
    for (count = 1; count <= 12; count++)
    {
            // Invariant (prior to test):
            //     sum == sum of the first count-1 input values
            //  && 1 <= count <= 13

        cout << "Enter rainfall amount " << count << ':' << endl;
        GetOneAmount(amount);
        sum = sum + amount;
    }
}
```

```
//*******************************************************************

void GetYesOrNo( /* out */ char& response )    // User response char

// Inputs a character from the user and, if necessary,
// repeatedly prints an error message and inputs another
// character if the character isn't 'y' or 'n'

// Postcondition:
//      response has been input (repeatedly, if necessary, along
//      with an error message)
//   && response == 'y' or 'n'

{
    do
    {
        cin >> response;
        if (response != 'y' && response != 'n')
            cout << "Please type y or n: ";

                // Invariant:
                //      No previous value of response was 'y' or 'n'

    } while (response != 'y' && response != 'n');
}


//*******************************************************************

void GetOneAmount( /* out */ float& amount )    // Rainfall amount
                                                // for one month

// Inputs one month's rainfall amount and, if necessary,
// repeatedly prints an error message and inputs another
// value if the value is negative

// Postcondition:
//      amount has been input (repeatedly, if necessary, along
//      with an error message)
//   && amount >= 0.0

{
    do
    {
        cin >> amount;
        if (amount < 0.0)
            cout << "Amount cannot be negative. Enter again:"
                << endl;
```

```
                          // Invariant:
                          //      All previous values of amount were < 0.0

         } while (amount < 0.0);
}
```

Testing: We should test two separate aspects of the Rainfall program. First, we should verify that the program works correctly given valid input data. Supplying arbitrary rainfall amounts of zero or greater, we must confirm that the program correctly adds up the values and divides by 12 to produce the average. Also, we should make sure that the program behaves correctly whether we type 'y' or 'n' when prompted to continue.

The second aspect to test is the data validation code that we included in the program. When entering a particular rainfall amount, we should type negative numbers repeatedly to verify that an error message is printed and that we are unable to escape the Do-While loop until we eventually type a nonnegative number. Similarly, when prompted to type 'y' or 'n' to process another recording site, we must press several incorrect keys to exercise the loop in the GetYesOrNo function. Here's a sample run showing the testing of the data validation code:

```
Enter rainfall amount 1:
0
Enter rainfall amount 2:
0
Enter rainfall amount 3:
0
Enter rainfall amount 4:
3.4
Enter rainfall amount 5:
9.6
Enter rainfall amount 6:
1.2
Enter rainfall amount 7:
-3.4
Amount cannot be negative. Enter again:
-9
Amount cannot be negative. Enter again:
-4.2
Amount cannot be negative. Enter again:
1.3
Enter rainfall amount 8:
0
Enter rainfall amount 9:
0
Enter rainfall amount 10:
0
```

```
Enter rainfall amount 11:
0
Enter rainfall amount 12:
0
Average rainfall is 1.29 inches

Do you have another recording site? (y or n) d
Please type y or n: q
Please type y or n: Y
Please type y or n: n
```

TESTING AND DEBUGGING

The same testing techniques we used with While loops apply to Do-While and For loops. There are, however, a few additional considerations with these loops.

The body of a Do-While loop always executes at least once. Thus, you should try data sets that show the result of executing a Do-While loop the minimal number of times.

With a data-dependent For loop, it is important to test for proper results when the loop executes zero times. This occurs when the starting value is greater than the ending value (or less than the ending value if the loop control variable is being decremented).

When a program contains a Switch statement, you should test it with enough different data sets to ensure that each branch is selected and executed correctly. You should also test the program with a switch expression whose value is not in any of the case labels.

Testing and Debugging Hints

1. In a Switch statement, make sure there is a `break` statement at the end of each case alternative. Otherwise, control "falls through" to the code in the next case alternative.
2. Case labels in a Switch statement are made up of values, not variables. They may, however, include named constants and expressions involving only constants.
3. A switch expression cannot be a floating point expression, and case constants cannot be floating point constants.
4. If there is a possibility that the value of the switch expression might not match one of the case constants, it's best to provide a `default` alternative.
5. Double-check long Switch statements to make sure that you haven't omitted any branches.

6. The Do-While loop is a posttest loop. If there is a possibility that the loop body should be skipped entirely, use a While statement or a For statement.
7. The For statement heading (the first line) always has three pieces within the parentheses. Most often, the first piece initializes a loop control variable, the second piece tests the variable, and the third piece increments or decrements the variable. The three pieces must be separated by semicolons. Any of the pieces can be omitted, but the semicolons still must be present.
8. With nested control structures, the break statement can exit only one level of nesting—the innermost Switch or loop in which the break is located.

Summary

The Switch statement is a multi-way selection statement. It allows the program to choose among a set of branches. A Switch containing break statements can always be simulated by an If-Then-Else-If structure. If a Switch can be used, however, it often makes the code easier to read and understand. A Switch statement cannot be used with floating point values as labels.

The Do-While is a general-purpose looping statement. It is like the While loop except that its test occurs at the end of the loop, guaranteeing at least one execution of the loop body. As with a While loop, a Do-While continues as long as the loop condition is nonzero (true).

The For statement is also a general-purpose looping statement, but its most common use is to implement count-controlled loops. The initialization, testing, and incrementation (or decrementation) of the loop control variable are centralized in one location, the first line of the For statement.

The For, Do-While, and Switch statements are the ice cream and cake of C++. We can live without them if we absolutely must, but they are very nice to have.

Quick Check

1. Given a switch expression that is the int variable nameVal, write a Switch statement that prints your first name if nameVal = 1, your middle name if nameVal = 2, and your last name if nameVal = 3. (pp. 460–464)
2. How would you change the answer to Question 1 so that it prints an error message if the value is not 1, 2, or 3? (pp. 460–464)
3. What is the primary difference between a While loop and a Do-While loop? (pp. 464–468)
4. A certain problem requires a count-controlled loop that starts at 10 and counts down to 1. Write the heading (the first line) of a For statement that controls this loop. (pp. 468–471)
5. Within a loop, how does a continue statement differ from a break statement? (pp. 472–474)

6. What C++ looping statement would you choose for a loop that is both count-controlled and event-controlled and whose body might not execute even once? (p. 475)

7. When a loop invariant is written as a program comment, where in the loop does it logically, if not physically, belong? (pp. 475–479)

Answers

1. ```
switch (nameVal)
{
    case 1 : cout << "Mary";
             break;
    case 2 : cout << "Lynn";
             break;
    case 3 : cout << "Smith";
             break;   // Not required
}
```

2. ```
switch (nameVal)
{
    case 1  : cout << "Mary";
              break;
    case 2  : cout << "Lynn";
              break;
    case 3  : cout << "Smith";
              break;
    default : cout << "Invalid name value.";
              break;    // Not required
}
```

3. The body of a Do-While always executes at least once; the body of a While may not execute at all.

4. `for (count = 10; count >= 1; count--)`   5. A `continue` statement terminates the current iteration and goes on to the next iteration (if possible). A `break` statement causes an immediate loop exit.   6. Either a While or a For statement   7. Immediately before the loop test.

EXAM PREPARATION EXERCISES

1. Define the following terms:

   switch expression
   pretest loop
   posttest loop

2. A switch expression may be an expression that results in a value of type `int`, `float`, or `char`. (True or False?)

3. The values in case labels may appear in any order, but duplicate case labels are not allowed within a given Switch statement. (True or False?)

4. All possible values for the switch expression must be included among the case labels for a given Switch statement. (True or False?)

5. Rewrite the following code fragment using a Switch statement.

```
if (n == 3)
    alpha++;
else if (n == 7)
    beta++;
else if (n == 10)
    gamma++;
```

6. What is printed by the following code fragment if n equals 3?

```
switch (n + 1)
{
    case 2  : cout << "Bill";
    case 4  : cout << "Mary";
    case 7  : cout << "Joe";
    case 9  : cout << "Anne";
    default : cout << "Whoops!";
}
```

7. If a While loop whose condition is delta <= alpha is converted into a Do-While loop, the loop condition of the Do-While loop is delta > alpha. (True or False?)
8. A Do-While statement always ends in a semicolon. (True or False?)
9. What is printed by the following program fragment, assuming the input value is 0? (All variables are of type int.)

```
cin >> n;
i = 1;
do
{
    cout << i;
    i++;
} while (i <= n);
```

10. What is printed by the following program fragment, assuming the input value is 0? (All variables are of type int.)

```
cin >> n;
for (i = 1; i <= n; i++)
    cout << i;
```

11. What is printed by the following program fragment? (All variables are of type int.)

```
for (i = 4; i >= 1; i--)
{
    for (j = i; j >= 1; j--)
        cout << j << ' ';
    cout << i << endl;
}
```

12. What is printed by the following program fragment? (All variables are of type int.)

```
for (row = 1; row <= 10; row++)
{
    for (col = 1; col <= 10 - row; col++)
        cout << '*';
    for (col = 1; col <= 2*row - 1; col++)
        cout << ' ';
    for (col = 1; col <= 10 - row; col++)
        cout << '*';
    cout << endl;
}
```

13. A break statement located inside a Switch statement that is within a While loop causes control to exit the loop immediately. (True or False?)

14. Given the For statement

```
for (count = 3; count <= 20; count++)
    cout << "Hello" << endl;
```

which one of the following invariants for count is correct just prior to the loop test?

    a. $1 \le \text{count} \le 20$
    b. $3 \le \text{count} \le 20$
    c. $2 < \text{count} < 20$
    d. $3 < \text{count} < 21$
    e. $3 \le \text{count} \le 21$

PROGRAMMING WARM-UP EXERCISES

1. Write a Switch statement that does the following:

    If the value of grade is
    'A', add 4 to sum
    'B', add 3 to sum
    'C', add 2 to sum
    'D', add 1 to sum
    'F', print "Student is on probation"

2. Modify the code for Exercise 1 so that an error message is printed if grade does not equal one of the five possible grades.

3. Rewrite the Day function of Chapter 8 (pages 406–408), replacing the If-Then-Else-If structure with a Switch statement.

4. Write a program segment that reads and sums until it has summed 10 data values or until a negative value is read, whichever comes first. Use a Do-While loop for your solution.

5. Rewrite the following code segment using a Do-While loop instead of a While loop.

```
cout << "Enter 1, 2, or 3: ";
cin >> response;
```

```
while (response != 1 && response != 2 && response != 3)
{
    cout << "Enter 1, 2, or 3: ";
    cin >> response;
}
```

6. Rewrite the following code segment using a While loop.

```
cin >> ch;
if (cin)
    do
    {
        cout << ch;
        cin >> ch;
    } while (cin);
```

7. Rewrite the following code segment using a For loop.

```
sum = 0;
count = 1;
while (count <= 1000)
{
    sum = sum + count;
    count++;
}
```

8. Rewrite the following For loop as a While loop.

```
for (m = 93; m >= 5; m--)
    cout << m << ' ' << m * m << endl;
```

9. Rewrite the following For loop using a Do-While loop.

```
for (k = 9; k <= 21; k++)
    cout << k << ' ' << 3 * k << endl;
```

10. Write a value-returning function that accepts two int parameters, base and exponent, and returns the value of base raised to the exponent power. Use a For loop in your solution.

11. Make the logic of the following loop easier to understand by using an infinite loop with break statements.

```
sum = 0;
count = 1;
do
{
    cin >> int1;
    if ( !cin || int1 <= 0)
        cout << "Invalid first integer.";
```

```
        else
        {
            cin >> int2;
            if ( !cin || int2 > int1)
                cout << "Invalid second integer.";
            else
            {
                cin >> int3;
                if ( !cin || int3 == 0)
                    cout << "Invalid third integer.";
                else
                {
                    sum = sum + (int1 + int2) / int3;
                    count++;
                }
            }
        }
    }
} while (cin && int1 > 0 && int2 <= int1 && int3 != 0 &&
        count <= 100);
```

12. Write a While loop (and any pre-loop initializations) corresponding to the following loop invariant and loop postcondition.

```
// Invariant (prior to test):
//      prod == 1 * 2 * ... * (count-1)
//   && 1 <= count <= 12
```

```
// Postcondition:
//      prod == 1 * 2 * ... * 11
//   && count == 12
```

13. The following loop is supposed to add the integers 1 through 100, but the loop is wrong (it's off by one). Prove that it is wrong by determining the loop postcondition. (Write the loop invariant for the code as it stands, then use the AND of the loop invariant and the termination condition to find the postcondition.)

```
sum = 0;
i = 0;
while (i <= 100)
{
    i++;
    sum = sum + i;
}
```

PROGRAMMING PROBLEMS

1. Develop a top-down design and write a C++ program that inputs a two-letter abbreviation for one of the 50 states and prints out the full name of the state. If the abbreviation isn't valid, the program should print an error message and ask for an abbreviation again. The names of the 50 states and their abbreviations are:

header file defines the constants CHAR_MAX and CHAR_MIN, SHRT_MAX and SHRT_MIN, INT_MAX and INT_MIN, and LONG_MAX and LONG_MIN. The unsigned types have a minimum value of zero and maximum values defined by UCHAR_MAX, USHRT_MAX, UINT_MAX, and ULONG_MAX. To find out the values specific to your computer you could print them out like this:

```
#include <limits.h>
  .
  .
  .
cout << "Max. long = " << LONG_MAX << endl;
cout << "Min. long = " << LONG_MIN << endl;
  .
  .
  .
```

Constants In C++, integer constants can be specified in three different number bases: decimal (base-10), octal (base-8), and hexadecimal (base-16). Just as the decimal number system has 10 digits—0 through 9—the octal system has 8 digits—0 through 7. The hexadecimal system has digits 0, 1, 2, 3, 4, 5, 6, 7, 8, 9, A, B, C, D, E, and F, which correspond to the decimal values 0 through 15. Octal and hexadecimal values are used in system software (compilers, linkers, and operating systems, for example) to refer directly to individual bits in a memory cell and to control hardware devices. These manipulations of low-level objects in a computer are the subject of more advanced study and are outside the scope of this book.

The following table shows examples of integer constants in C++. Notice that an L or a U (either uppercase or lowercase) can be added to the end of a constant to signify long or unsigned, respectively.

Constant	Type	Remarks
1658	int	Decimal (base-10) integer.
03172	int	Octal (base-8) integer. Begins with 0 (zero). Decimal equivalent is 1658.
0x67A	int	Hexadecimal (base-16) integer. Begins with 0 (zero), then either x or X. Decimal equivalent is 1658.
65535U	unsigned int	Unsigned constants end in U or u.
421L	long	Explicit long constant. Ends in L or l.
53100	long	Implicit long constant, assuming the machine's maximum int is, say, 32767.
389123487UL	unsigned long	Unsigned long constants end in UL or LU in any combination of uppercase and lowercase letters.

You'll notice that this table presents only numeric constants for the integral types. We discuss char constants later in a separate section.

Here is the syntax template for an integer constant:

IntegerConstant

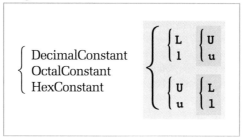

DecimalConstant is a nonzero digit followed, optionally, by a sequence of decimal digits:

DecimalConstant

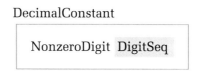

NonzeroDigit, DigitSeq, and Digit are defined as follows:

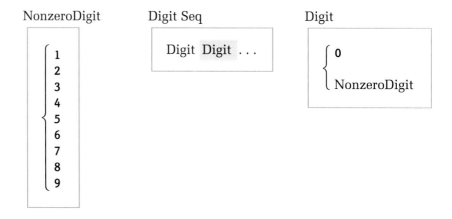

The second form of integer constant, OctalConstant, has the following syntax:

OctalConstant   OctalDigit

0 OctalDigit . . .	0 1 2 3 4 5 6 7

Finally, HexConstant is defined as

HexConstant   HexDigit

0 { **X** / **x** } HexDigit . . .	0 1 2 3 4 5 6 7 8 9 A a B b C c D d E e F f

Floating Point Types

Ranges of Values   Below is a table that gives sample ranges of values for the three floating point types, `float`, `double`, and `long double`. In this table we show, for each type, the maximum positive value and the minimum positive value (a tiny fraction that is very close to zero). Negative numbers have the same range but the opposite sign. Ranges of values are expressed in exponential (scientific) notation, where 3.4E+38 means 3.4×10^{38}.

Type	Size in Bytes*	Minimum Positive Value*	Maximum Positive Value*
float	4	3.4E–38	3.4E+38
double	8	1.7E–308	1.7E+308
long double	10	3.4E–4932	1.1E+4932

* These values are for one particular machine. Your machine's values may be different.

The standard header file `float.h` defines the constants `FLT_MAX` and `FLT_MIN`, `DBL_MAX` and `DBL_MIN`, and `LDBL_MAX` and `LDBL_MIN`. To determine the ranges of values for your machine, you could write a short program that prints out these constants.

Constants   When you use a floating point constant like 5.8 in a C++ program, its type is assumed to be `double` (double precision). If you store the value into a `float` variable, the computer coerces its type from `double` to `float` (single precision). If you insist on a constant being of type `float` rather than `double`, you can append an F or an f at the end of the constant. Similarly, a suffix of L or l signifies a `long double` constant. Here are some examples of floating point constants in C++:

Constant	Type	Remarks
6.83	double	By default, floating point constants are of type double.
6.83F	float	Explicit `float` constants end in F or f.
6.83L	long double	Explicit `long double` constants end in L or l.
4.35E-9	double	Exponential notation, meaning 4.35×10^{-9}.

Here's the syntax template for a floating point constant in C++:

FloatingPtConstant

$$
\left\{
\begin{array}{l}
\text{DigitSeq Exponent} \\
\text{DigitSeq . DigitSeq Exponent} \\
\text{. DigitSeq Exponent}
\end{array}
\right.
\quad
\left\{
\begin{array}{l}
\text{F} \\
\text{f} \\
\text{L} \\
\text{l}
\end{array}
\right.
$$

DigitSeq is the same as defined in the section on integer constants—a sequence of decimal (base-10) digits. The form of Exponent is the following:

Exponent

$$
\left\{
\begin{array}{l}
\text{E} \\
\text{e}
\end{array}
\right.
\left\{
\begin{array}{l}
+ \\
-
\end{array}
\right.
\text{DigitSeq}
$$

Additional C++ Operators

C++ has a rich, sometimes bewildering, variety of operators that allow you to manipulate values of the simple data types. Operators you have learned about so far include the assignment operator (=), the arithmetic operators (+, -, *, /, %), the increment and decrement operators (++, --), the relational operators (==, !=, <, <=, >, >=), and the logical operators (!, &&, ||). Another operator—at least the compiler formally treats it as an operator—is the pair of symbols ( ). This is either the function call operator, as in

```
ComputeSum(x, y);
```

or the type cast operator, as in

```
y = float(someInt);
```

C++ also has operators that are more specialized and seldom found in other programming languages. Here is a table of these additional operators. As you inspect the table, don't panic—a quick scan will do.

Operator		Remarks
Combined assignment operators		
+=	Add and assign	
-=	Subtract and assign	
*=	Multiply and assign	
/=	Divide and assign	
Increment and decrement operators		
++	Pre-increment	Example: `++someVar`
++	Post-increment	Example: `someVar++`
--	Pre-decrement	Example: `--someVar`
--	Post-decrement	Example: `someVar--`
Bitwise operators		Integer operands only
<<	Left shift	
>>	Right shift	
&	Bitwise AND	
|	Bitwise OR	
^	Bitwise EXCLUSIVE OR	
~	Complement (invert all bits)	
More combined assignment operators		Integer operands only
%=	Modulus and assign	
<<=	Shift left and assign	
>>=	Shift right and assign	
&=	Bitwise AND and assign	
|=	Bitwise OR and assign	
^=	Bitwise EXCLUSIVE OR and assign	
Other operators		
()	Cast	
sizeof	Size of operand in bytes	Form: `sizeof` Expr or `sizeof`(Type)
?:	Conditional operator	Form: Expr1 `?` Expr2 `:` Expr3

The operators in this table, along with those you are already familiar with, comprise most—but not all—of the C++ operators. We introduce a few more operators in later chapters as the need arises.

Assignment Operators and Assignment Expressions

C++ has several assignment operators. The equal sign (**=**) is the basic assignment operator. When combined with its two operands, it forms an **assignment expression** (*not* an assignment statement). Every assignment expression has:

- a *value*, and
- a *side effect:* the value is stored into the object denoted by the left-hand side.

For example, the expression

```
delta = 2 * 12
```

has the value 24 and the side effect of storing this value into `delta`.

In C++, any expression becomes an **expression statement** when it is terminated by a semicolon. All three of the following are valid C++ statements, although the first two have no effect whatsoever:

```
23;
2 * (alpha + beta);
delta = 2 * 12;
```

The third expression statement *is* useful because of its side effect of storing 24 into `delta`.

Assignment Expression   A C++ expression with (1) a value and (2) the side effect of storing the expression value into a memory location.
Expression Statement   A statement formed by appending a semicolon to an expression.

Because an assignment is an expression, not a statement, you can use it anywhere an expression is allowed. Here is a statement that stores the value 20 into `firstInt`, the value 30 into `secondInt`, and the value 35 into `thirdInt`:

```
thirdInt = (secondInt = (firstInt = 20) + 10) + 5;
```

Some C++ programmers use this style of coding, but others find it hard to read and error-prone.

In Chapter 5, we cautioned against the mistake of using the = operator in place of the == operator:

```
if (alpha = 12)    // Wrong
       .
       .
       .
```

```
else
    ⋮
```

The condition in the If statement is an assignment expression, not a relational expression. The value of the expression is 12 (interpreted by the computer as TRUE), so the else-clause is never executed. Worse yet, the side effect of the assignment expression is to store 12 into `alpha`, destroying its previous contents.

In addition to the = operator, C++ has several combined assignment operators (+=, *=, and the others listed in our table of operators). These operators have the following semantics:

Statement	*Equivalent Statement*
`i += 5;`	`i = i + 5;`
`pivotPoint *= n + 3;`	`pivotPoint = pivotPoint * (n + 3);`

The combined assignment operators are another example of "icing on the cake." They are sometimes convenient for writing a line of code more compactly, but you can do just fine without them.

Increment and Decrement Operators

The increment and decrement operators (++ and --) operate only on variables, not on constants or arbitrary expressions. Suppose a variable `someInt` contains the value 3. The expression `++someInt` denotes pre-incrementation. The side effect of incrementing `someInt` occurs first, so the resulting value of the expression is 4. In contrast, the expression `someInt++` denotes post-incrementation. The value of the expression is 3, and *then* the side effect of incrementing `someInt` takes place. The following code illustrates the difference between pre- and post-incrementation:

```
int1 = 14;
int2 = ++int1;
// Assert: int1 == 15  &&  int2 == 15

int1 = 14;
int2 = int1++;
// Assert: int1 == 15  &&  int2 == 14
```

Using side effects in the middle of larger expressions is always a bit dangerous. It's easy to make semantic errors, and the code may be confusing to read. Look at this example:

```
a = (b = c++) * --d / (e += f++);
```

Some people make a game of seeing how much they can do in as few keystrokes as possible. But they should remember that serious software development requires writing code that other programmers can read and understand. Overuse of side effects hinders this goal. By far, the most common use of the ++ and -- operators is to do the incrementation or decrementation as a separate expression statement:

```
count++;
```

Here, the value of the expression is unused, but we get the desired side effect of incrementing count. In this example, it doesn't matter whether we use pre-incrementation or post-incrementation. The choice is up to you.

Bitwise Operators

The bitwise operators listed in the operator table (<<, >>, &, |, and so forth) are used for manipulating individual bits within a memory cell. This book does not explore the use of these operators; the topic of bit-level operations is beyond an introduction to computer science and computer programming. However, we point out two things about the bitwise operators.

First, the built-in operators << and >> are the left shift and right shift operators, respectively. Their purpose is to take the bits within a memory cell and shift them to the left or right. Of course, we have been using these operators all along, but in an entirely different context—program input and output. The header file iostream.h uses an advanced C++ technique called *operator overloading* to give additional meanings to these two operators. An overloaded operator is one that has multiple meanings, depending on the data types of its operands. Looking at the << operator, the compiler determines by context whether a left shift operation or an output operation is desired. Specifically, if the first (left-hand) operand denotes an output stream, then it is an output operation. If the first operand is an integer variable, it is a left shift operation.

Second, we repeat our caution from Chapter 5: Do not confuse the && and || operators with the & and | operators. The statement

```
if (i == 3 & j == 4)     // Wrong
    k = 20;
```

is syntactically correct because & is a valid operator (the bitwise AND operator). The program containing this statement compiles correctly but executes incorrectly. Although we do not examine what the bitwise AND and OR operators do, just be careful to use the relational operators && and || in your logical expressions.

The Cast Operator

You have seen that C++ is very liberal about letting the programmer mix data types in expressions, in assignment operations, in parameter passage, and in returning a function value. However, implicit type coercion takes place when values of different data types are mixed together. Instead of relying on implicit type coercion in a statement like

```
intVar = floatVar;
```

we have recommended using an explicit type cast to show that the type conversion is intentional:

```
intVar = int(floatVar);
```

In C++, the cast operation comes in two forms:

```
intVar = int(floatVar);      // Functional notation
intVar = (int) floatVar;     // Prefix notation—parentheses required
```

The first form is called functional notation because it looks like a function call. It isn't really a function call (there is no user-defined or predefined subprogram named int), but it has the syntax and visual appearance of a function call. The second form, prefix notation, doesn't look like any familiar language feature in C++. In this notation, the parentheses surround the name of the data type instead of the expression being converted. Prefix notation is the only form available in the C language; C++ added the functional notation.

Although most C++ programmers use the functional notation for the cast operation, there is one restriction on its use. The data type name must be a single identifier. If the type name consists of more than one identifier, you *must* use prefix notation. For example,

```
myVar = unsigned int(someFloat);      // No
myVar = (unsigned int) someFloat;     // Yes
```

The sizeof Operator

The sizeof operator is a unary operator that yields the size, in bytes, of its operand. The operand can be a variable name, as in

```
sizeof someInt
```

or the operand can be the name of a data type, enclosed in parentheses:

```
sizeof(float)
```

You could find out the sizes of various data types on your machine by using code like this:

```
cout << "Size of a short is " << sizeof(short) << " bytes." << endl;
cout << "Size of an int is " << sizeof(int) << " bytes." << endl;
cout << "Size of a long is " << sizeof(long) << " bytes." << endl;
    .
    .
    .
```

The ?: Operator

The last operator in our operator table is the ?: operator, sometimes called the conditional operator. It is a ternary (three-operand) operator with the following syntax:

ConditionalExpression

> Expression1 ? Expression2 : Expression3

Here's how it works. First, the computer evaluates Expression1. If it is nonzero (true), then the value of the entire expression is Expression2; otherwise, the value of the entire expression is Expression3. (Only one of Expression2 and Expression3 is evaluated.) A classic example of its use is to set a variable max equal to the larger of two variables a and b. Using an If statement, we would do it this way:

```
if (a > b)
    max = a;
else
    max = b;
```

With the ?: operator, we can use the following assignment statement:

```
max = (a > b) ? a : b;
```

1)
ch = (ch == 'm') ? 'M' : ' ';

means

if (ch == 'm')
   ch = 'M';
else
   ch = ' ';

Here is another example. The absolute value of a number x is defined as

$$|x| = \begin{cases} x, & \text{if } x \geq 0 \\ -x, & \text{if } x < 0 \end{cases}$$

To compute the absolute value of a variable x and store it into y, you could use the **?:** operator as follows:

```
y = (x >= 0) ? x : -x;
```

In both the **max** and the absolute value examples, we used parentheses around the expression being tested. These parentheses are unnecessary because, as we'll see shortly, the conditional operator has very low precedence. But it is customary to include the parentheses for clarity.

2) if (value % 2 == 0)
   flag = 0;
else
   flag = 1;

means

flag = (value % 2 == 0) ? 0 : 1;

Operator Precedence

Below is a summary of operator precedence for the C++ operators that we have encountered so far, excluding the bitwise operators. (Appendix B contains the complete list.)

Precedence (highest to lowest)

	Operator	Associativity
	()	Left to right
unary:	++ -- ! + - (cast) sizeof	Right to left
	* / %	Left to right
	+ -	Left to right
	< <= > >=	Left to right
	== !=	Left to right
	&&	Left to right
	||	Left to right
	?:	Right to left
	= += -= etc.	Right to left

3)

The column labeled *Associativity* describes grouping order. Within a precedence level, most operators group from left to right. For example,

```
a - b + c
```

means

```
(a - b) + c
```

and not

```
a - (b + c)
```

Certain operators, though, group from right to left. Look at the assignment operators, for example. The expression

```
sum = count = 0
```

means

```
sum = (count = 0)
```

This associativity makes sense because the assignment operation is naturally a right-to-left operation.

A word of caution: Although operator precedence and associativity dictate the *grouping* of operators with their operands, C++ does not define the *order* in which subexpressions are evaluated. Therefore, using side effects in expressions requires extra care. For example, if i currently contains 5, the statement

```
j = ++i + i;
```

stores either 11 or 12 into j, depending on the particular compiler being used. Let's see why. There are three operators in the expression statement above: =, ++, and +. The ++ operator has the highest precedence, so it operates just on i, not the expression i + i. The addition operator has higher precedence than the assignment operator, giving implicit parentheses as follows:

```
j = (++i + i);
```

So far, so good. But now we ask this question: In the addition operation, is the left operand or the right operand evaluated first? The C++ language doesn't define the order. If a compiler generates code to evaluate the left operand first, the result is 6 + 6, or 12. Another compiler might generate code to evaluate the right operand first, yielding 5 + 6, or 11. To be assured of left-to-right evaluation in this example, you should force the ordering with two separate statements:

```
++i;
j = i + i;
```

The moral here is that if you use multiple side effects in expressions, you increase the risk of unexpected or inconsistent results. For the newcomer to C++, it's better to avoid unnecessary side effects altogether.

 # Working with Character Data

Because char is an integral type and sizeof(char) equals 1, a char variable can store a small (one-byte) integer constant. For example,

```
char counter;
    .
    .
    .
counter = 3;
```

On computers with a very limited amount of memory space, programmers sometimes use the char type to save memory when they are working with small integers. But it is far more common to use char variables to store character data, such as the character 'A' or 'e' or '+':

```
char someChar;
    .
    .
    .
someChar = 'A';
```

A natural question to ask is, How does the computer know the difference between integer data and character data when the data is sitting in a memory cell? The answer is, The computer *can't* tell the difference! To explain this surprising fact, we have to look more closely at how character data is stored in a computer.

Character Sets

Each computer uses a particular character set, the set of all possible characters with which it is capable of working. There are two character sets widely in use today: the ASCII character set and the EBCDIC character set. ASCII is used by virtually all personal computers and minicomputers, and EBCDIC is found primarily on IBM mainframe computers. ASCII consists of 128 different characters, and EBCDIC has 256 characters. Appendix E shows the characters that are available in these two character sets.

Each character has an **external representation**—the way it looks on an I/O device like a printer—and an **internal representation**—the way it is stored inside the computer's memory unit. If you use the char constant 'A' in a C++ program, its external representation is the letter *A*. That is, if you print it out you see an *A*, as you would expect. Its internal representation, though, is an integer value. The 128 ASCII characters have internal representations 0 through 127; the EBCDIC characters, 0 through 255. For example, the ASCII table in Appendix E shows that the character 'A' has internal representation 65, and the character 'b' has internal representation 98.

External Representation The printable (character) form of a data value.
Internal Representation The form in which a data value is stored inside the memory unit.

Let's look again at the statement

```
someChar = 'A';
```

Assuming our machine uses the ASCII character set, the compiler translates the constant 'A' into the integer 65. We could also have written the statement as

```
someChar = 65;
```

Both statements have exactly the same effect—that of storing 65 into some-Char. However, the second version is *not* recommended. It is not as understandable as the first version, and it is nonportable (the program won't work correctly on a machine that uses EBCDIC, which uses a different internal representation—193—for 'A').

Earlier we mentioned that the computer cannot tell the difference between character and integer data in memory. Both are stored internally as integers. However, when we perform I/O operations, the computer does the right thing—it uses the external representation that corresponds to the data type of the expression being printed. Look at this code segment, for example:

```
// This example assumes use of the ASCII character set
int someInt = 97;
char someChar = 97;

cout << someInt << endl;
cout << someChar << endl;
```

When these statements are executed, the output is

```
97
a
```

When the << operator outputs someInt, it prints the sequence of characters 9 and 7. To output someChar, it prints the single character a. Even though both variables contain the value 97 internally, the data type of each variable determines how it is printed.

What do you think will be output by the following sequence of statements?

```
char ch = 'D';

ch++;
cout << ch;
```

If you answered E, you are right. The first statement declares ch and initializes it to the integer value 68 (assuming ASCII). The next statement increments ch to 69, and then its external representation (the letter *E*) is printed. Extending this idea of incrementing a char variable, we could print the letters *A* through *G* as follows:

```
char ch;

for (ch = 'A'; ch <= 'G'; ch++)
    cout << ch;
```

This code initializes ch to 'A' (65 in ASCII). Each time through the loop, the external representation of ch is printed. On the final loop iteration, the *G* is printed and ch is incremented to 'H' (72 in ASCII). The loop test is then false, so the loop terminates.

C++ char *Constants*

In C++, char constants come in two different forms. The first form, which we have been using regularly, is a single printable character enclosed by apostrophes (single quotes):

```
'A'   '8'   ')'   '+'
```

Notice that we said *printable* character. Character sets include both printable characters and *control characters* (or *nonprintable characters*). Control characters are not meant to be printed but are used to control the screen, printer, and other hardware devices. If you look at the ASCII character table, you see that the printable characters are those with integer values 32–126. The remaining characters (with values 0–31 and 127) are nonprintable control characters. In the EBCDIC character set, the control characters are those with values 0–63 and 250–255 (and some that are intermingled with the printable characters). One control character you already know about is the newline character, which causes the screen cursor to advance to the next line.

To accommodate control characters, C++ provides a second form of char constant: the *escape sequence*. An escape sequence is one or more characters preceded by a backslash (\). You are familiar with the escape sequence \n, which represents the newline character. Here is the complete description of the two forms of char constant in C++:

1. A single printable character—except an apostrophe (') or backslash (\)—enclosed by apostrophes.

2. One of the following escape sequences, enclosed by apostrophes:

\n	Newline (Line feed in ASCII)
\t	Horizontal tab
\v	Vertical tab
\b	Backspace
\r	Carriage return
\f	Form feed
\a	Alert (a bell or beep)
\\	Backslash
\'	Single quote (apostrophe)
\"	Double quote (quotation mark)
\0	Null character (all zero bits)
\ddd	Octal equivalent (1, 2, or 3 octal digits specifying the integer value of the desired character)
\xddd	Hexadecimal equivalent (1 or more hexadecimal digits specifying the integer value of the desired character)

Even though an escape sequence consists of two or more characters, each escape sequence represents a single character in the character set. The alert character (\a) is the same as what is called the BEL character in ASCII and EBCDIC. To ring the bell (well, these days, beep the beeper) on your computer or terminal, you can output the alert character like this:

```
cout << '\a';
```

In the list of escape sequences above, the entries labeled *Octal equivalent* and *Hexadecimal equivalent* let you refer to any character in your machine's character set by specifying its integer value in either octal or hexadecimal form.

Note that you can use an escape sequence within a string just as you can use any printable character within a string. The statement

```
cout << "\aWhoops!\n";
```

beeps the beeper, displays Whoops!, and terminates the output line. The statement

```
cout << "She said \"Hi\"";
```

outputs She said "Hi" and does not terminate the output line.

Programming Techniques

What kinds of things can we do with character data in a program? The possibilities are endless and depend, of course, on the particular problem we are solving. But several techniques are so widely used that it's worth taking a look at them.

Comparing Characters   In previous chapters, you have seen examples of comparing characters for equality. We have used tests such as

```
if (ch == 'a')
```

and

```
while (inputChar != '\n')
```

Characters can also be compared by using <, <=, >, and >=. For example, if the variable firstLetter contains the first letter of a person's last name, we can test to see if the last name starts with *A* through *H* by using this test:

```
if (firstLetter >= 'A' && firstLetter <= 'H')
```

On one level of thought, a test like this is reasonable if you think of < as meaning "comes before" in the character set and > as meaning "comes after." On another level, the test makes even more sense when you consider that the underlying representation of a character is an integer number. The machine literally compares the two integer values using the mathematical meaning of less than or greater than.

When you write a logical expression to check whether a character lies within a certain range of values, you sometimes have to keep in mind the character set your machine uses. In Chapter 8, we hinted that a test like

```
if (ch >= 'a' && ch <= 'z')
```

works correctly on some machines but not on others. In ASCII, this If test behaves correctly because the lowercase letters occupy 26 consecutive positions in the character set. In EBCDIC, however, there is a gap between the lowercase letters *i* and *j* that includes nonprintable characters, and there is another gap between *r* and *s*. (There are similar gaps between the uppercase letters *I* and *J* and between *R* and *S*.) If your machine uses EBCDIC, you must rephrase the If test to be sure you include *only* the desired characters. A better approach, though, is to take advantage of the "is..." functions supplied by the standard library through the header file ctype.h. If you replace the above If test with this one:

```
if (islower(ch))
```

then your program is more portable; the test works correctly on any machine, regardless of its character set. It's a good idea to become well acquainted with these character-testing library functions (Appendix C). They can save you time and help you to write more portable programs.

Converting Digit Characters to Integers Suppose you want to convert a digit that is read in character form to its numeric equivalent. Because the digit characters '0' through '9' are consecutive in both the ASCII and EBCDIC character sets, subtracting '0' from any digit in character form gives the digit in numeric form:

'0' - '0' = 0
'1' - '0' = 1
'2' - '0' = 2
.
.
.

For example, in ASCII, '0' has internal representation 48 and '2' has internal representation 50. Therefore, the expression

'2' - '0' = 50 - 48 = 2

Why would you want to do this? Recall that when the extraction operator (>>) reads data into an int variable, the input stream fails if an invalid character is encountered. (And once the stream has failed, no further input will succeed). Suppose you're writing a program that prompts an inexperienced user to enter a number from 1 through 5. If the input variable is of type int and the user accidentally types a letter of the alphabet, the program is in trouble. To defend against this possibility, you might read the user's response as a character and convert it to a number, performing error checking along the way. Here's a code segment that demonstrates the technique:

```
#include <ctype.h>    // For isdigit()

typedef int Boolean;
const Boolean TRUE = 1;
const Boolean FALSE = 0;
  .
  .
  .

void GetResponse( /* out */ int& response )

// Postcondition:
//      User has been prompted to enter a digit from 1
//      through 5 (repeatedly, and with error messages,
//      if data is invalid)
// && 1 <= response <= 5
```

```
{
    char    inChar;
    Boolean badData = FALSE;

    do
    {
        cout << "Enter a number from 1 through 5: ";
        cin >> inChar;
        if ( !isdigit(inChar) )
            badData = TRUE;                      // It's not a digit
        else
        {
            response = int(inChar - '0');
            if (response < 1 || response > 5)
                badData = TRUE;                  // It's a digit, but
        }                                        // it's out of range
        if (badData)
            cout << "Please try again." << endl;

        // Invariant:
        //     All previous values of inChar were either
        //     nondigit chars or were out of range
        //  && IF current inChar is a digit char
        //         response == numeric equivalent of inChar

    } while (badData);
}
```

Converting to Lowercase and Uppercase When working with character data, you sometimes find that you need to convert a lowercase letter to uppercase, or vice versa. Fortunately, the programming technique required to do these conversions is easy—a simple call to a library function is all it takes. Through the header file ctype.h, the standard library provides not only the "is..." functions we have discussed, but also two value-returning functions named toupper and tolower. Here are their descriptions:

Header File	Function	Function Type	Function Value
<ctype.h>	toupper(ch)	char*	Uppercase equivalent of ch, if ch is a lowercase letter; ch, otherwise
<ctype.h>	tolower(ch)	char	Lowercase equivalent of ch, if ch is an uppercase letter; ch, otherwise

* Technically, both the parameter and the return value are of type int. But conceptually, the functions operate on character data.

Notice that the value returned by each function is just the original character if the condition is not met. For example, `tolower('M')` returns the character 'm', whereas `tolower('+')` returns '+'.

A common use of these two functions is to let the user respond to certain input prompts by using either uppercase or lowercase letters. For example, if you want to allow either *Y* or *y* for a "Yes" response from the user, and either *N* or *n* for "No," you might do this:

```
cout << "Enter Y or N: ";
cin >> inputChar;
if (toupper(inputChar) == 'Y')
{
    .
    .
    .

}
else if (toupper(inputChar) == 'N')
{
    .
    .
    .

}
else
    PrintErrorMsg();
```

Below is a function named `Lower`, which is our implementation of the `tolower` function. (You wouldn't actually want to waste time by writing this function because `tolower` is already available to you.) This function returns the lowercase equivalent of an uppercase letter. In ASCII, each lowercase letter is exactly 32 positions beyond the corresponding uppercase letter. And in EBCDIC, the lowercase letters are 64 positions *before* their corresponding uppercase letters. To make our `Lower` function work on both ASCII-based and EBCDIC-based machines, we define a constant DISTANCE to have the value

```
'a' - 'A'
```

In ASCII, the value of this expression is 32. In EBCDIC, the value is −64.

```
#include <ctype.h>      // For isupper()
    .
    .
    .
char Lower( /* in */ char ch )

// Postcondition:
```

```
//        Function value == lowercase equivalent of ch, if ch is
//                          an uppercase letter
//                       == ch, otherwise

{
    const int DISTANCE = 'a' - 'A';  // Fixed distance between
                                     // uppercase and lowercase
                                     // letters
    if (isupper(ch))
        return ch + DISTANCE;
    else
        return ch;
}
```

More on Floating Point Numbers

We have used floating point numbers off and on since they were introduced in Chapter 2, but we have not examined them in depth. Floating point numbers have some special properties when used on the computer. Thus far, we've almost ignored these properties, but now it's time to consider them in detail.

Representation of Floating Point Numbers

Let's assume we have a computer where each memory location is the same size and is divided into a sign plus five decimal digits. When a variable or constant is defined, the location assigned to it consists of five digits and a sign. When an int variable or constant is defined, the interpretation of the number stored in that place is quite straightforward. When a float variable or constant is defined, the number stored there has both a whole number part and a fractional part, so it must be coded to represent both parts.

Let's see what such coded numbers might look like. The range of whole numbers we can represent with five digits is −99,999 through +99,999:

−99999 through +99999

| + | 9 | 9 | 9 | 9 | 9 | Largest positive number |

| + | 0 | 0 | 0 | 0 | 0 | Zero |

| − | 9 | 9 | 9 | 9 | 9 | Largest negative number |

Our **precision** (the number of digits we can represent) is five digits, and each number within that range can be represented exactly.

What happens if we allow one of those digits (the leftmost one, for example) to represent an exponent?

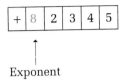

Exponent

Then +82345 represents the number $+2345 * 10^8$. The range of numbers we now represent is much larger:

$-9999 * 10^9$ through $9999 * 10^9$

or

$-9,999,000,000,000$ through $+9,999,000,000,000$

However, our precision is now only four digits; that is, any four-digit number can be represented exactly in our system. But what happens to numbers with more digits? The four leftmost digits are represented correctly, and the rightmost digits, or least **significant digits,** are lost (assumed to be 0). Figure 10-2 shows what happens. Note that 1,000,000 can be represented exactly but −4,932,416 cannot, because this coding scheme limits us to four significant (nonzero) digits.

To extend our coding scheme to represent floating point numbers, we must be able to represent negative exponents. As examples,

$7394 * 10^{-2} = 73.94$

and

$22 * 10^{-4} = .0022$

	NUMBER	POWER OF TEN NOTATION	CODED REPRESENTATION						VALUE
			Sign	Exp					
	+99,999	$+9999 * 10^1$	+	1	9	9	9	9	+99,990
			Sign	Exp					
	−999,999	$−9999 * 10^2$	−	2	9	9	9	9	−999,900
			Sign	Exp					
	+1,000,000	$+1000 * 10^3$	+	3	1	0	0	0	+1,000,000
			Sign	Exp					
	−4,932,416	$−4932 * 10^3$	−	3	4	9	3	2	−4,932,000

■ FIGURE 10-2
Coding Using Positive Exponents

Because our scheme does not allow for a sign for the exponent, we shall change it slightly. The sign that we have will be the sign of the exponent, and a sign can be added to the far left to represent the sign of the number itself (see Figure 10-3).

All the numbers between $9999 * 10^{-9}$ and $9999 * 10^9$ can now be represented accurately to four digits. Adding negative exponents to our scheme has allowed representation of fractional numbers.

Figure 10-4 shows how we would encode some floating point numbers. Note that our precision is still only four digits. The numbers 0.1032, −5.406, and 1,000,000 can be represented exactly. The number 476.0321, however, with seven significant digits, is represented as 476.0; the "321" cannot be represented. (We should point out that some computers perform *rounding* rather than simple truncation when excess digits are discarded. Using our assumption of four significant digits, such a machine would store 476.0321 as 476.0 but would store 476.0823 as 476.1. We continue our discussion assuming simple truncation rather than rounding.)

Arithmetic with Floating Point Numbers

When we use integer arithmetic, our results are exact. Floating point arithmetic, however, is seldom exact. We can illustrate this by adding three floating point numbers x, y, and z, using our coding scheme.

First, we add x to y and then we add z to the result. Next, we perform the operations in a different order, adding y to z, and then adding x to that result. The associative law of arithmetic says that the two answers should be the same—but are they? Let's use the following values for x, y, and z:

$$x = -1324 * 10^3 \qquad y = 1325 * 10^3 \qquad z = 5424 * 10^0$$

On the next page is the result of adding z to the sum of x and y.

■ **FIGURE 10-3**

Coding Using Positive and Negative Exponents

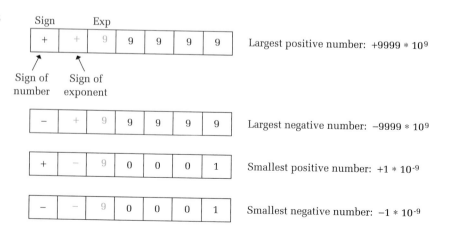

■ FIGURE 10-4

Coding of Some Floating Point Numbers

NUMBER	POWER OF TEN NOTATION	CODED REPRESENTATION							VALUE
		Sign		Exp					
0.1032	$+1032 * 10^{-4}$	+	−	4	1	0	3	2	0.1032
−5.4060	$-5406 * 10^{-3}$	−	−	3	5	4	0	6	−5.406
−0.003	$-3000 * 10^{-6}$	−	−	6	3	0	0	0	−0.0030
476.0321	$+4760 * 10^{-1}$	+	−	1	4	7	6	0	476.0
1,000,000	$+1000 * 10^{3}$	+	+	3	1	0	0	0	1,000,000

$$
\begin{array}{ll}
(x) & -1324 * 10^3 \\
(y) & \underline{1325 * 10^3} \\
& 1 * 10^3 \quad = 1000 * 10^0
\end{array}
$$

$$
\begin{array}{ll}
(x+y) & 1000 * 10^0 \\
(z) & \underline{5424 * 10^0} \\
& 6424 * 10^0 \quad \leftarrow (x+y)+z
\end{array}
$$

Now here is the result of adding x to the sum of y and z:

$$
\begin{array}{ll}
(y) & 1325000 * 10^0 \\
(z) & \underline{5424 * 10^0} \\
& 1330424 * 10^0 \quad = 1330 * 10^3 \text{ (truncated to four digits)}
\end{array}
$$

$$
\begin{array}{ll}
(y+z) & 1330 * 10^3 \\
(x) & \underline{-1324 * 10^3} \\
& 6 * 10^3 \quad = 6000 * 10^0 \leftarrow x+(y+z)
\end{array}
$$

These two answers are the same in the thousands place, but different thereafter. The error behind this discrepancy is called **representational error.**

Because of representational errors, it is unwise to use a floating point number as a loop control variable. Because precision may be lost in calculations involving floating point numbers, it is difficult to predict when (or even *if*) a loop control variable of type float (or double or long double) will become equal to the termination value. A count-controlled loop with a floating point control variable may behave in an unpredictable fashion.

Also because of representational errors, we should never compare floating point numbers for exact equality. Rarely are two floating point numbers exactly equal, and thus they should be compared only for near equality. If the difference between the two numbers is less than some acceptable small value, we can consider them equal for the purposes of the given problem.

Implementation of Floating Point Numbers in the Computer

Let's formally define some of the terms we used informally in the previous section.

Significant Digits   Those digits from the first nonzero digit on the left to the last nonzero digit on the right (plus any zero digits that are exact).

Precision   The maximum number of significant digits.

Representational Error   Arithmetic error that occurs when the precision of the true result of an arithmetic operation is greater than the precision of the machine.

All computers limit the precision of a floating point number, although most machines use binary rather than decimal arithmetic. In our representation, we used only 5 digits to simplify the examples, and some computers really are limited to only 4 or 5 digits of precision. A more typical system might provide 6 significant digits for `float` values, 15 digits for `double` values, and 19 for the `long double` type. We have shown only a single-digit exponent, but most systems allow 2 digits for the `float` type and up to 4-digit exponents for type `long double`.

When you declare a floating point variable, part of the memory location is assumed to contain the exponent, and the number itself (called the *mantissa*) is assumed to be in the balance of the location. The system is called floating point representation because the number of significant digits is fixed, and the decimal point conceptually floats (is moved to different positions as necessary). In our coding scheme, every number is stored as four digits, with the leftmost being nonzero, and the exponent adjusted accordingly. The number 1,000,000 was stored as

+	+	3	1	0	0	0

and 0.1032 was stored as

+	−	4	1	0	3	2

This allowed for the maximum precision possible.

Underflow and Overflow In addition to representational errors, there are two other problems to watch out for in floating point arithmetic: *underflow* and *overflow*.

Underflow is the condition that arises when the value of a calculation is too small to be represented. Going back to our decimal representation, let's look at a calculation involving small numbers:

$$\begin{array}{r} 4210 * 10^{-8} \\ * \quad 2000 * 10^{-8} \\ \hline 8420000 * 10^{-16} \end{array} \quad = 8420 * 10^{-13}$$

This value cannot be represented in our scheme because an exponent of -13 is too small. Our minimum is -9. One way to resolve the problem is to set the result of the calculation to 0.0. Obviously, any answer depending on this calculation will not be exact.

Overflow is a more serious problem because there is no logical recourse when it occurs. For example, the result of the calculation

$$\begin{array}{r} 9999 * 10^{9} \\ * \quad 1000 * 10^{9} \\ \hline 9999000 * 10^{18} \end{array} \quad = 9999 * 10^{21}$$

cannot be stored, so what should we do? To be consistent with our response to underflow, we could set the result to $9999 * 10^9$ (the maximum representable value in this case). Yet this seems intuitively wrong. The alternative is to stop with an error message.

C++ does not define what should happen in the case of overflow or underflow. Different implementations of C++ solve the problem in different ways. You might try to cause an overflow with your system and see what happens. Some systems print a run-time error message such as "FLOATING POINT OVERFLOW". On other systems, you may get the largest number that can be represented.

We have been discussing problems with floating point numbers, but integer numbers also can overflow both negatively and positively. Most implementations of C++ ignore integer overflow. To see how your system handles the situation, you should try adding 1 to INT_MAX and -1 to INT_MIN. On most systems, adding 1 to INT_MAX sets the result to INT_MIN, a negative number.

Sometimes you can avoid overflow by carefully arranging computations. Suppose you would like to know how many different poker hands are possible. There are 52 cards in a poker deck and 5 cards in one hand. What we are looking for is the number of combinations of 52 cards taken 5 at a time. The standard mathematical formula for the number of combinations of n things taken r at a time is

$$\frac{n!}{r!\,(n-r)!}$$

Thus, we could use the `Factorial` function we wrote in Chapter 8 and write this formula in an assignment statement:

```
hands = Factorial(52) / (Factorial(5) * Factorial(47));
```

The only problem is that 52! is a very large number (approximately $8.0658 * 10^{67}$). And 47! is also rather big (approximately $2.5862 * 10^{59}$). Both of these numbers are well beyond the capacity of most systems to represent exactly as integers (52! requires 68 digits of precision). Even though they can be represented on many machines as floating point numbers, some of the precision is still lost. By rearranging the calculations, however, we can achieve an exact result on any system with 9 or more digits of precision. How? Consider that most of the multiplications in computing 52! are cancelled when it is divided by 47!

$$\frac{52!}{5! * 47!} = \frac{52 * 51 * 50 * 49 * 48 * 47 * 46 * 45 * 44 * \ldots}{(5 * 4 * 3 * 2 * 1) * (47 * 46 * 45 * 44 * \ldots)}$$

So, we really only have to compute

```
hands = 52 * 51 * 50 * 49 * 48 / Factorial(5);
```

which means the numerator is 311,875,200 and the denominator is 120. On a system with 9 digits of precision, we thus have an exact answer of 2,598,960 poker hands.

Cancellation Error　Another type of error that can happen with floating point numbers is called *cancellation error*, a form of representational error that occurs when numbers of widely differing magnitudes are added or subtracted. Let's look at an example:

$(1 + 0.00001234 − 1) = 0.00001234$

The laws of arithmetic say this equation should be true. But is it true if the computer does the arithmetic?

$$
\begin{array}{r}
100000000 * 10^{-8} \\
+ \quad 1234 * 10^{-8} \\
\hline
100001234 * 10^{-8}
\end{array}
$$

To four digits, the sum is $1000 * 10^{-3}$. Now the computer subtracts 1:

$$
\begin{array}{r}
1000 * 10^{-3} \\
- 1000 * 10^{-3} \\
\hline
0
\end{array}
$$

The result is 0, not .00001234.

Sometimes you can avoid adding two floating point numbers that are drastically different in size by carefully arranging the calculations in a program. Suppose a problem requires many small floating point numbers to be added to a large floating point number. The result is more accurate if the program first sums the smaller numbers to obtain a larger number and then adds the sum to the large number.

At this point, you may want to turn to the first Problem-Solving Case Study at the end of the chapter. This case study involves floating point computations, and it addresses some of the issues you have learned about in this section.

SOFTWARE ENGINEERING TIP

Choosing a Numeric Data Type

A first encounter with all the numeric data types of C++ may leave you feeling overwhelmed. To help in choosing an alternative, you may even feel tempted to toss a coin. You should resist this temptation, because each data type exists for a reason. Here are some guidelines:

1. In general, int is preferable.

    As a rule, you should use floating point types *only* when absolutely necessary—that is, when you definitely need fractional values. Not only is floating point arithmetic subject to representational errors, it also is significantly slower than integer arithmetic on most computers.

    For ordinary integer data, use int instead of char or short. It's easy to make overflow errors with these smaller data types. (For character data, though, the char type is appropriate.)

2. Use long only if the range of int values on your machine is too restrictive.

    Compared to int, the long type requires more memory space and execution time.

3. Use double and long double only if you need enormously large or small numbers, or if your machine's float values do not carry enough digits of precision.

    The cost of using double and long double is increased memory space and execution time.

4. Avoid the unsigned forms of integral types.

    These types are primarily for manipulating bits within a memory cell, a topic this book does not cover. You might think that declaring a variable as unsigned prevents you from accidentally storing a negative number into the variable. However, the C++ compiler does *not* prevent you from doing so. Later in this chapter, we explain why.

By following these guidelines, you'll find that the simple types you use most often are int and float, along with char for character data. Only rarely do you need the longer and shorter variations of these fundamental types.

*B*ACKGROUND INFORMATION

Practical Implications of Limited Precision

A discussion of representational, overflow, underflow, and cancellation errors may seem purely academic. In fact, these errors have serious practical implications in many problems. We close this section with three examples illustrating how limited precision can have disastrous effects.

During the Mercury space program, several of the spacecraft splashed down a considerable distance from their computed landing points. This delayed the recovery of the spacecraft and the astronaut, putting both in some danger. Eventually, the problem was traced to an imprecise representation of the Earth's rotation period in the program that calculated the landing point.

As part of the construction of a hydroelectric dam, a long set of high-tension cables had to be constructed to link the dam to the nearest power distribution point. The cables were to be several miles long, and each one was to be a continuous unit. (Because of the high power output from the dam, shorter cables couldn't be spliced together.) The cables were constructed at great expense and strung between the two points. It turned out that they were too short, however, so another set had to be manufactured. The problem was traced to errors of precision in calculating the length of the catenary curve (the curve that a cable forms when hanging between two points).

An audit of a bank turned up a mysterious account with a large amount of money in it. The account was traced to an unscrupulous programmer who had used limited precision to his advantage. The bank computed interest on its accounts to a precision of a tenth of a cent. The tenths of cents were not added to the customers' accounts, so the programmer had the extra tenths for all the accounts summed and deposited into an account in his name. Because the bank had thousands of accounts, these tiny amounts added up to a large amount of money. Because the rest of the bank's programs did not use as much precision in their calculations, the scheme went undetected for many months.

The moral of this discussion is twofold: 1) The results of floating point calculations are often imprecise, and these errors can have serious consequences; and 2) If you are working with extremely large numbers or extremely small numbers, you need more information than this book provides and should consult a numerical methods text.

User-Defined Simple Types

The concept of a data type is fundamental to all of the widely used programming languages. One of the strengths of the C++ language is that it allows programmers to create new data types, tailored to meet the needs of a particular program. Much of the remainder of this book is about user-defined data types. In this section, we examine how to create our own simple types.

The Typedef Statement

In Chapter 5, we introduced the Typedef statement, whose syntax is given by

TypedefStatement

> **typedef** ExistingTypeName NewTypeName **;**

To simulate a Boolean data type, we used Typedef to introduce `Boolean` as a synonym for `int`:

```
typedef int Boolean;
const Boolean TRUE = 1;
const Boolean FALSE = 0;
      .
      .
      .
Boolean dataOK;
      .
      .
      .
dataOK = TRUE;
```

The Typedef statement provides a very limited way in which to define our own data types. In fact, Typedef does not create a new data type at all; it merely creates an additional name for an existing data type. As far as the compiler is concerned, the domain and operations of our `Boolean` type are identical to the domain and operations of the `int` type.

Despite the fact that Typedef cannot truly create a new data type, it is a valuable tool for writing self-documenting programs. Program code that uses the identifiers `Boolean`, `TRUE`, and `FALSE` is more descriptive than code that uses `int`, 1, and 0.

Names of user-defined types obey the same scope rules that apply to identifiers in general. Most types like `Boolean` are defined globally, although it is reasonable to define a new type within a subprogram if that is the only place it is used. The guidelines that determine where a named constant should be defined also apply to data types.

Enumeration Types

C++ allows the user to define a new simple type by listing (enumerating) the literal values that make up the domain of the type. These literal values must be *identifiers*, not numbers. The identifiers are separated by commas, and the list is enclosed in braces. Data types defined in this way are called **enumeration types.** Here's an example:

Type

↓

```
enum Days {SUN, MON, TUE, WED, THU, FRI, SAT};
```

This declaration creates a new data type named Days. Whereas Typedef merely creates a synonym for an existing type, an enumeration type like Days is a new type and is distinct from any existing type.

The values in the Days type—SUN, MON, TUE, and so forth—are called **enumerators**. The enumerators are *ordered*, in the sense that SUN < MON < TUE . . . < FRI < SAT. Applying relational operators to enumerators is like applying them to characters: the relation that is tested is "comes before" or "comes after" in the ordering of the data type.

Enumeration Type   A user-defined data type whose domain is an ordered set of literal values expressed as identifiers.

Enumerator   One of the values in the domain of an enumeration type.

Earlier we saw that the internal representation of a char constant is a non-negative integer. The 128 ASCII characters are represented in memory as the integers 0 through 127. Values in an enumeration type are also represented internally as integers. By default, the first enumerator has the integer value 0, the second has the value 1, and so forth. Our declaration of the Days enumeration type is similar to the following set of declarations:

```
typedef int Days;
const int SUN = 0;
const int MON = 1;
const int TUE = 2;
      .
      .
      .
const int SAT = 6;
```

If there is some reason that you want different internal representations for the enumerators, you can specify them explicitly like this:

```
enum Days {SUN = 4, MON = 18, TUE = 9, ...};
```

There is rarely any reason to assign specific values to enumerators. With the Days type, we are interested in the days of the week, not in the way the machine stores them internally. We do not discuss this feature any further, although you may occasionally see it in C++ programs.

Notice the style we use to capitalize enumerators. Because enumerators are, in essence, named constants, we capitalize the entire identifier. This is purely a style choice. Many C++ programmers use both uppercase and lowercase letters when they invent names for the enumerators.

Here is the syntax template for the declaration of an enumeration type. It is a simplified version; later in the chapter we expand it.

EnumDeclaration

enum Name { Enumerator , Enumerator ... } ;

An enumerator has the following form:

Enumerator

Identifier = ConstIntExpression

where the optional ConstIntExpression is an integer expression composed only of literal or named constants.

The identifiers used as enumerators must follow the rules for any C++ identifier. For example,

```
enum Vowel {'A', 'E', 'I', 'O', 'U'};    // No
```

is not legal because the items are not identifiers. In the declaration

```
enum Places {1st, 2nd, 3rd};    // No
```

type Places is not legal because identifiers cannot begin with digits. In the declarations

```
enum Starch {CORN, RICE, POTATO, BEAN};
enum Grain {WHEAT, CORN, RYE, BARLEY, SORGHUM};    // No
```

type `Starch` and type `Grain` are legal by themselves, but together they are not. Identifiers in the same scope must be unique. `CORN` cannot be defined twice.

Suppose you are writing a program for a veterinary office. The program must keep track of different kinds of animals. The following enumeration type might be used for this purpose.

Type identifier   Literal values in the domain

```
enum Animals {RODENT, CAT, DOG, BIRD, REPTILE, HORSE, BOVINE, SHEEP};

Animals inPatient;  ⎫  Creation of two variables of type Animals
Animals outPatient; ⎭
```

`RODENT` is a literal, one of the values in the data type `Animals`. Be sure you understand that `RODENT` is not a variable name. Instead, `RODENT` is one of the values that can be stored into the variables `inPatient` and `outPatient`. Let's look at the kinds of operations we might want to perform on variables of enumeration types.

Assignment   The assignment statement

```
inPatient = DOG;
```

does not assign to `inPatient` the character string "DOG", nor the contents of a variable named `DOG`. It assigns the *value* `DOG`, which is one of the values in the domain of the data type `Animals`.

Assignment is a valid operation, as long as the value being stored is of type `Animals`. Both of the statements

```
inPatient = DOG;
outPatient = inPatient;
```

are acceptable. Each expression on the right-hand side is of type `Animals`— `DOG` is a literal of type `Animals`, and `inPatient` is a variable of type `Animals`. Although we know that the underlying representation of `DOG` is the integer 2, the compiler prevents us from using this assignment:

```
inPatient = 2;
```

Here is the precise rule:

Implicit type coercion is defined from an enumeration type to int *but not from* int *to an enumeration type.*

Applying this rule to the statements

```
someInt = DOG;     // Valid
inPatient = 2;     // Error
```

we see that the first statement stores 2 into someInt (because of implicit type coercion), but the second produces a compile-time error. The restriction against storing an int value into a variable of type Animals is to keep you from accidentally storing an out-of-range value:

```
inPatient = 65;     // No
```

We said earlier that an enum declaration is similar to a Typedef statement and several const declarations, all of type int. For example, the declaration

```
enum Boolean {FALSE, TRUE};
```

is like the sequence of statements

```
typedef int Boolean;
const int FALSE = 0;
const int TRUE = 1;
```

However, there is an important difference. Because of the type coercion rule, the compiler issues an error message at the assignment statement in the following code:

```
enum Boolean {FALSE, TRUE};

Boolean isGreater;
float    a;
float    b;
   .
   .
   .
isGreater = (a > b);    // Error
```

The data type of the right-hand side is int. (Remember that a relational expression yields the int value 1 or 0, meaning TRUE or FALSE.) Type coercion from int to an enumeration type is not defined, so we cannot store an int value into a Boolean variable. Therefore, it is better not to define Boolean as an enumeration type but to use a Typedef along with const declarations for TRUE and FALSE.

Incrementation   Suppose you want to "increment" the value in inPatient so that it becomes the next value in the domain:

```
inPatient = inPatient + 1;    // No
```

This statement is illegal for the following reason. The right-hand side is okay because implicit type coercion lets you add inPatient to 1; the result is an int value. But the assignment operation is not valid because you can't store an int value into inPatient. The statement

```
inPatient++;    // No
```

is also invalid because the compiler considers it to have the same semantics as the assignment statement above. However, you can escape the type coercion rule by using an *explicit* type conversion—a type cast—as follows:

```
inPatient = Animals(inPatient + 1);    // Yes
```

When you use the type cast, the compiler assumes that you know what you are doing and allows it.

Incrementing a variable of enumeration type is very useful in loops. Sometimes we need a loop that processes all the values in the domain of the type. We might try the following For loop:

```
Animals patient;

for (patient=RODENT; patient <= SHEEP; patient++)  // No
    ⋮
    ⋮
```

However, as we explained above, the compiler will complain about the expression patient++. To increment patient, we must use an assignment expression and a type cast:

```
for (patient=RODENT; patient <= SHEEP; patient=Animals(patient + 1))
    ⋮
    ⋮
```

The only caution here is that when control exits the loop, the value of pa-tient is one *greater than* the largest value in the domain (SHEEP). If you want to use patient outside the loop, you must reassign it a value that is within the appropriate range for the Animals type.

Comparison The most common operation performed on values of enumer-ation types is comparison. When you compare two values, their ordering is determined by the order in which you listed the enumerators in the type declaration. For instance, the expression

```
inPatient <= BIRD
```

is TRUE if inPatient contains the value RODENT, CAT, DOG, or BIRD.

You can also use values of an enumeration type in a Switch statement. Because RODENT, CAT, and so on are literals, they can appear in case labels:

```
switch (inPatient)
{
    case RODENT  :
    case CAT     :
    case DOG     :
    case BIRD    : cout << "Cage ward";
                   break;
    case REPTILE : cout << "Terrarium ward";
                   break;
    case HORSE   :
    case BOVINE  :
    case SHEEP   : cout << "Barn";
}
```

Input and Output Stream I/O is defined only for the basic built-in types (int, float, and so on), not for enumeration types. Values of enumeration types must be input or output indirectly.

To input values, the usual strategy is to read a number or a letter code and translate it to one of the identifiers in the enumeration type. For example, the veterinary office program could read the kind of animal as a series of characters, then assign one of the values of type Animals to that patient. The following program fragment reads in an animal represented by its first two letters and converts it to one of the values in type Animals.

```
cin >> ch1 >> ch2;
switch (ch1)
{
    case 'R' : if (ch2 == 'o')
                   inPatient = RODENT;
```

```
            else
                  inPatient = REPTILE;
            break;
    case 'C' : inPatient = CAT;
            break;
    case 'D' : inPatient = DOG;
            break;
    case 'B' : if (ch2 == 'i')
                  inPatient = BIRD;
            else
                  inPatient = BOVINE;
            break;
    case 'H' : inPatient = HORSE;
            break;
    default : inPatient = SHEEP;
}
```

Enumeration type values cannot be printed directly either. Printing is done by using a Switch statement that prints a character string corresponding to the value.

```
switch (inPatient)
{
    case RODENT  : cout << "Rodent";
                break;
    case CAT     : cout << "Cat";
                break;
    case DOG     : cout << "Dog";
                break;
    case BIRD    : cout << "Bird";
                break;
    case REPTILE : cout << "Reptile";
                break;
    case HORSE   : cout << "Horse";
                break;
    case BOVINE  : cout << "Bovine";
                break;
    case SHEEP   : cout << "Sheep";
}
```

You might ask, Why not use just a pair of letters or an integer number as a code to represent each animal in a program? We use enumeration types to make our programs more readable; they are another way to make code self-documenting.

Returning a Function Value   We have been using value-returning functions to compute and return values of built-in types such as `int`, `float`, and `char`:

```
int Factorial( int );
float CargoMoment( int );
```

C++ allows a function return value to be of *any* data type—built-in or user-defined—except an array (a data type we introduce in the next chapter).

In the last section, we wrote a Switch statement to convert a pair of `char` values into a value of type `Animals`. Let's write a value-returning function that performs this task. Notice how the function heading declares the data type of the return value to be `Animals`.

```
Animals CharToAnimal( /* in */ char ch1,
                      /* in */ char ch2 )
{
    switch (ch1)
    {
        case 'R' : if (ch2 == 'o')
                       return RODENT;
                   else
                       return REPTILE;
        case 'C' : return CAT;
        case 'D' : return DOG;
        case 'B' : if (ch2 == 'i')
                       return BIRD;
                   else
                       return BOVINE;
        case 'H' : return HORSE;
        default  : return SHEEP;
    }
}
```

In this function, why didn't we include a break statement after each case alternative? Because when each alternative executes a `return` statement, control immediately exits the function. It's not possible for control to "fall through" to the next alternative.

Here is a sample of code that calls the `CharToAnimal` function:

```
enum Animals {RODENT, CAT, DOG, BIRD, REPTILE, HORSE, BOVINE, SHEEP};

Animals CharToAnimal( char, char );
    .
    .
    .
int main()
{
    Animals inPatient;
    Animals outPatient;
    char    char1;
```

```
char      char2;
         .
         .
         .
cin >> char1 >> char2;
inPatient = CharToAnimal(char1, char2);
         .
         .
         .
cin >> char1 >> char2;
outPatient = CharToAnimal(char1, char2);
         .
         .
         .
}
```

Named and Anonymous Data Types

The enumeration types we have looked at, Animals and Days, are called **named types** because their declarations included names for the types. Variables of these new data types are declared separately using the type identifiers Animals and Days.

Named Type   A user-defined type whose declaration includes a type identifier that gives a name to the type.

C++ also lets us introduce a new type directly in a variable declaration. Instead of the declarations

```
enum CoinType {NICKEL, DIME, QUARTER, HALF_DOLLAR};
enum StatusType {OK, OUT_OF_STOCK, BACK_ORDERED};

CoinType    change;
StatusType status;
```

we could write

```
enum {NICKEL, DIME, QUARTER, HALF_DOLLAR} change;
enum {OK, OUT_OF_STOCK, BACK_ORDERED} status;
```

A new type declared in a variable declaration is called an **anonymous type** because it does not have a name—that is, it does not have a type identifier associated with it.

Anonymous Type   A type that does not have an associated type identifier.

If we can create a data type in a variable declaration, why bother with a separate type declaration that creates a named type? Named types, like named constants, make a program more readable, more understandable, and easier to modify. Also, declaring a type and declaring a variable of that type are two distinct concepts; it is better to keep them separate. In addition, assignment of one enumeration type variable to another is valid only if they are both of the same *named* type. In the following code segment, the assignment statement is not allowed:

```
enum {NICKEL, DIME, QUARTER, HALF_DOLLAR} amount;
enum {NICKEL, DIME, QUARTER, HALF_DOLLAR} thisCoin;
      .
      .
      .
amount = thisCoin;    // No
```

Even though the two anonymous data types have the same domain, the compiler considers them to be two distinct data types and won't let you assign thisCoin to amount.

We now give a more complete syntax template for an enumeration type declaration. This template shows that the type name is optional (yielding an anonymous type) and that a list of variables may optionally be included in the declaration.

EnumDeclaration

enum Name { Enumerator , Enumerator ... } VariableName , VariableName ... ;

User-Written Header Files

As you create your own user-defined data types, you sometimes find that a data type can be useful in more than one program. An example is the Boolean type we have been using in several programs. Instead of typing the statements

```
typedef int Boolean;
const Boolean TRUE = 1;
const Boolean FALSE = 0;
```

at the beginning of every program that uses the `Boolean` type, we can put these three statements into a separate file named, say, `bool.h`. Then we use `bool.h` just as we use system-supplied header files such as `iostream.h` and `math.h`. By using an `#include` directive, we ask the C++ preprocessor to insert physically the contents of the file into our program. (Although many C++ systems use `.h` to denote header files, other systems use `.hpp` or `.hxx`.)

When you enclose the name of a header file in angle brackets, as in

```
#include <iostream.h>
```

the preprocessor looks for the file in the standard *include directory*, a directory that contains all the header files supplied by the C++ system. On the other hand, you can enclose the name of a header file in double quotes, like this:

```
#include "bool.h"
```

In this case, the preprocessor looks for the file in the programmer's current directory. This mechanism allows us to write our own header files that contain type declarations and constant declarations. We can use a simple `#include` directive instead of retyping the declarations in every program that makes use of them (see Figure 10-5).

From now on, the program examples in this book use the directive

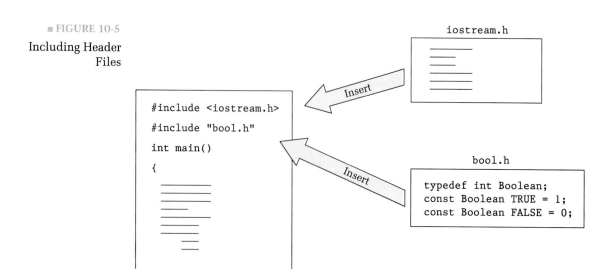

```
#include "bool.h"
```

instead of explicitly defining the Boolean type each time it is needed.

# More on Type Coercion

As you have learned over the course of several chapters, C++ performs implicit type coercion whenever values of different data types are used in

1. arithmetic and relational expressions
2. assignment operations
3. parameter passage
4. return of the function value from a value-returning function

For item 1—mixed-type expressions—the C++ compiler follows one set of rules for type coercion. For items 2, 3, and 4, the compiler follows a second set of rules. Let's examine each of these two rules.

Type Coercion in Arithmetic and Relational Expressions

Suppose that an arithmetic expression consists of one operator and two operands—for example, 3.4*sum or var1/var2. If the two operands are of different data types, then one of them is temporarily **promoted** (or **widened**) to match the data type of the other. To understand exactly what promotion means, let's look at the rule for type coercion in an arithmetic expression.

Step 1: Each char, short, or enumeration value is promoted (widened) to int. If both operands are now int, the result is an int expression.
Step 2: If Step 1 still leaves a mixed-type expression, the following precedence of types is used:

lowest ——→ highest

int, unsigned int, long, unsigned long, float, double, long double

The value of the operand of "lower" type is promoted to that of the "higher" type, and the result is an expression of that type.

A simple example is the expression someFloat+2. This expression has no char, short, or enumeration values in it, so step 1 still leaves a mixed-type expression. In step 2, int is a "lower" type than float, so the value 2 is coerced temporarily to the float value, say, 2.0. Then the addition takes place, and the type of the entire expression is float.

This description of type coercion also holds for relational expressions such as

```
someInt <= someFloat
```

The value of `someInt` is temporarily coerced to floating point representation before the comparison takes place. The only difference between arithmetic expressions and relational expressions is that the resulting type of a relational expression is always `int`—the value 1 (true) or 0 (false).

Promotion (Widening)   The conversion of a value from a "lower" type to a "higher" type according to a programming language's precedence of data types.

Here is a table that describes the result of promoting a value from one simple type to another in C++:

From	To	Result of Promotion
`double`	`long double`	Same value, occupying more memory space
`float`	`double`	Same value, occupying more memory space
Integral type	Floating point type	Floating point equivalent of the integer value; fractional part is zero
Integral type	Its `unsigned` counterpart	Same value, if original number is nonnegative; a radically different positive number, if original number is negative
Signed integral type	Longer signed integral type	Same value, occupying more memory space
`unsigned` integral type	Longer integral type (either signed or unsigned)	Same nonnegative value, occupying more memory space

NOTE: The result of promoting a `char` to an `int` is compiler-dependent. Some compilers treat `char` as `unsigned char`, so promotion always yields a nonnegative integer. With other compilers, `char` means `signed char`, so promotion of a negative value yields a negative integer.

The note at the bottom of the table suggests a potential problem if you are trying to write a portable C++ program. If you use the `char` type only to store character data, there is no problem. C++ guarantees that each character in a machine's character set (such as ASCII) is a nonnegative value. Using character data, promotion from char to int gives the same result on any machine with any compiler.

But if you try to save memory by using the char type for manipulating small signed integers, then promotion of these values to the int type can produce different results on different machines! That is, one machine may promote negative char values to negative int values, whereas the same program on another machine might promote negative char values to *positive* int values. The moral is this: Unless you are squeezed to the limit for memory space, do not use char to manipulate small signed numbers. Use char only to store character data.

Type Coercion in Assignments, Parameter Passage, and Return of a Function Value

In general, promotion of a value from one type to another does not cause loss of information. Think of promotion as moving your baseball cards from a small shoe box to a larger shoe box. All of the cards still fit into the new box and there is room to spare. On the other hand, **demotion** (or **narrowing**) of data values can potentially cause loss of information. Demotion is like moving a shoe box full of baseball cards into a smaller box—something has to be thrown out.

Demotion (Narrowing)   The conversion of a value from a "higher" type to a "lower" type according to a programming language's precedence of data types. Demotion may cause loss of information.

Consider an assignment operation

$v = e$

where v is a variable and e is an expression. Regarding the data types of v and e, there are three possibilities:

1. If the types of v and e are the same, no type coercion is necessary.
2. If the type of v is "higher" than that of e (using the type precedence we explained with promotion), then the value of e is promoted to v's type before being stored into v.
3. If the type of v is "lower" than that of e, the value of e is demoted to v's type before being stored into v.

Demotion, which you can think of as shrinking a value, may cause loss of information:

- Demotion from a longer integral type to a shorter integral type (such as `long` to `int`) results in discarding the leftmost (most significant) bits in the binary number representation. The result may be a drastically different number.
- Demotion from a floating point type to an integral type causes truncation of the fractional part (and an undefined result if the whole-number part will not fit into the destination variable). The result of truncating a negative number is machine-dependent.
- Demotion from a longer floating point type to a shorter floating point type (such as `double` to `float`) may result in a loss of digits of precision.

Our description of type coercion in an assignment operation also holds for parameter passage (the mapping of actual parameters onto formal parameters) and for returning a function value with a `return` statement. For example, assume that `INT_MAX` on your machine is 32767 and that you have the following function:

```
void DoSomething( int n )
{
    .
    .
    .
}
```

If the function is called with the statement

```
DoSomething(50000);
```

then the value 50000 (which is implicitly of type `long` because it is larger than `INT_MAX`) is demoted to a completely different, smaller value that fits into an `int` location. In a similar fashion, execution of the function

```
int SomeFunc( float x )
{
    .
    .
    .
    return 70000;
}
```

causes demotion of the value 70000 to a smaller `int` value because `int` is the declared type of the function return value.

One interesting consequence of implicit type coercion is the futility of declaring a variable to be `unsigned`, hoping that the compiler will prevent you from making a mistake like this:

```
unsignedVar = -5;
```

The compiler does not complain at all. It generates code to coerce the int value to an unsigned int value. If you now print out the value of unsigned-Var, you'll see a strange-looking positive integer. As we have pointed out before, unsigned types are most appropriate for advanced techniques that manipulate individual bits within memory cells. It's best to avoid using unsigned for ordinary numeric computations.

PROBLEM-SOLVING CASE STUDY

Finding the Area Under a Curve

Problem: Find the area under the curve of the function X^3 over an interval specified by the user. In other words, given a pair of floating point numbers, find the area under the graph of X^3 between those two numbers (see Figure 10-6).

Input: Two floating point numbers specifying the interval over which to find the area, and an integer number of intervals to use in approximating the area.

■ FIGURE 10-6

Area Under Graph of X^3 Between 0 and 3

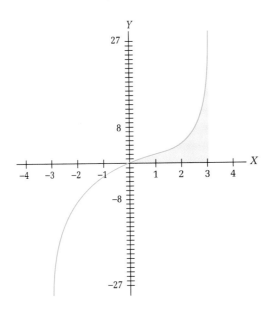

Output: The input data (echo-print) and the value calculated for the area over the given interval.

Discussion: Our approach is to compute an approximation to this area. If the area under the curve is divided into equal, narrow, rectangular strips, the sum of the areas of these rectangles is close to the actual area under the curve (see Figure 10-7). The narrower the rectangles, the more accurate the approximation should be.

We can use a value-returning function to compute the area of each rectangle. The user enters the low and high values for X, as well as the number of rectangles into which the area should be subdivided (`divisions`). The width of a rectangle is then

```
(high - low) / divisions
```

The height of a rectangle equals the value of X^3 when X is at the horizontal midpoint of the rectangle. The area of a rectangle equals its height times its width. Because the leftmost rectangle has its midpoint at

```
(low + width/2.0)
```

■ FIGURE 10-7

Approximation of
Area Under a Curve

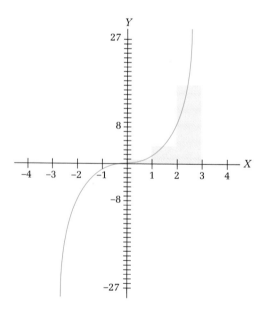

its area equals the following (see Figure 10-8):

(low + width/2.0)³ * width

The second rectangle has its left edge at the point where X equals

low + width

and its area equals the following (see Figure 10-9):

(low + width + width/2.0)³ * width

The left edge of each rectangle is at a point that is width greater than the left edge of the rectangle to its left. Thus, we can step through the rectangles by using a count-controlled loop with the number of iterations equal to the value of divisions. This loop contains a second counter (not the loop control variable) starting at low and counting by steps of width up to (high − width). Two counters are necessary because the second counter must be of type float, and it is poor programming technique to have a loop control

■ FIGURE 10-8

Area of the Leftmost
Rectangle

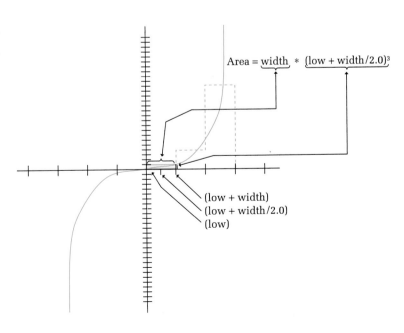

variable be a `float` variable. For each iteration of this loop, we compute the area of the corresponding rectangle and add this value to the total area under the curve.

We want a value-returning function to compute the area of a rectangle, given the position of its left edge and its width. Let's also make X^3 a separate function named `Funct`, so we can substitute other mathematical functions in its place without changing the rest of the design. Our program can then be converted quickly to find the area under the curve of any single-variable function.

Here is our design:

Main   *Level 0*

```
Get data
Set width = (high − low) / divisions
Set area = 0.0
Set leftEdge = low
FOR count going from 1 through divisions
    Set area = area + RectArea(leftEdge, width)
    Set leftEdge = leftEdge + width
Print area
```

■ FIGURE 10-9

Area of the Second
Rectangle

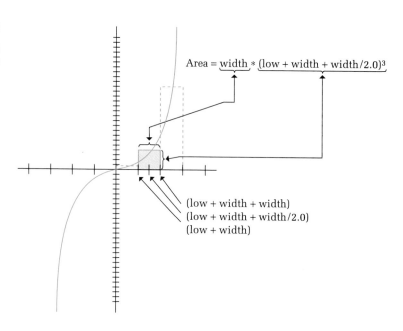

$$\text{Area} = \underline{\text{width}} * \underline{(\text{low} + \text{width} + \text{width}/2.0)^3}$$

(low + width + width)
(low + width + width/2.0)
(low + width)

Problem-Solving Case Study cont'd.

RectArea (In: leftEdge, width)   *Level 1*
    Out: Function value

> Return Funct(leftEdge + width/2.0) * width

Get Data (Out: low, high, divisions)

> Prompt for low and high
> Read low, high
> Prompt for divisions
> Read divisions
> Echo-print input data

Funct (In: x)   *Level 2*
    Out: Function value

> Return x * x * x

Module Structure Chart:

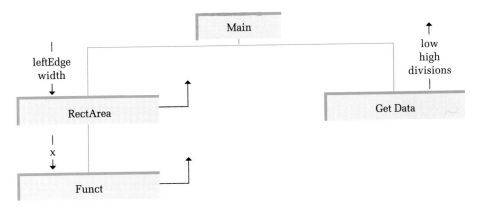

The Area program implements our design.

```
//******************************************************************
// Area program
// This program finds the area under the curve of a mathematical
// function in a specified interval. Input consists of two float
// values and one int. The first two are the low, high values for
// the interval. The third is the number of slices to be used in
// approximating the area. As written, this program finds the
// area under the curve of the function x cubed; however, any
// single-variable function may be substituted for the function
// named Funct
//******************************************************************
#include <iostream.h>
#include <iomanip.h>      // For setprecision()

float Funct( float );
void GetData( float&, float&, int& );
float RectArea( float, float );

int main()
{
    float low;         // Lowest value in the desired interval
    float high;        // Highest value in the desired interval
    float width;       // Computed width of a rectangular slice
    float leftEdge;    // Left edge point in a rectangular slice
    float area;        // Total area under the curve
    int   divisions;   // Number of slices to divide the interval by
    int   count;       // Loop control variable

    cout.setf(ios::fixed, ios::floatfield);   // Set up floating pt.
    cout.setf(ios::showpoint);                //    output format

    GetData(low, high, divisions);
    width = (high - low) / float(divisions);
    area = 0.0;
    leftEdge = low;

    // Calculate and sum areas of slices

    for (count = 1; count <= divisions; count++)
    {
            // Invariant (prior to test):
            //     area == sum of areas of first count-1 rectangles
            //  && leftEdge == low + (count-1)*width
            //  && 1 <= count <= divisions+1

        area = area + RectArea(leftEdge, width);
        leftEdge = leftEdge + width;
    }
```

```
                    // Print result

                    cout << "The result is equal to "
                        << setprecision(7) << area << endl;
                    return 0;
              }

     //***********************************************************

     void GetData( /* out */ float& low,          // Bottom of interval
                   /* out */ float& high,         // Top of interval
                   /* out */ int&   divisions )   // Division factor

     // Prompts for the input of low, high, and divisions values
     // and returns the three values after echo printing them

     // Postcondition:
     //     All parameters (low, high, and divisions)
     //     have been prompted for, input, and echo printed

     {
         cout << "Enter low and high values of desired interval"
             << " (floating point)." << endl;
         cin >> low >> high;
         cout << "Enter the number of divisions to be used (integer)."
             << endl;
         cin >> divisions;
         cout << "The area is computed over the interval "
             << setprecision(7) << low << endl
             << "to " << high << " with " << divisions
             << " subdivisions of the interval." << endl;
     }

     //***********************************************************

     float RectArea( /* in */ float leftEdge,     // Left edge point of
                                                  //   rectangle
                     /* in */ float width   )     // Width of rectangle

     // Computes the area of a rectangle that starts at leftEdge and is
     // "width" units wide. The rectangle's height is given by the value
     // computed by Funct at the horizontal midpoint of the rectangle

     // Precondition:
     //     leftEdge and width are assigned
     // Postcondition:
     //     Function value == area of specified rectangle
```

```
{
    return Funct(leftEdge + width / 2.0) * width;
}


//***************************************************************

float Funct( /* in */ float x )    // Value to be cubed

// Computes x cubed. You may replace this function with any
// single-variable function

// Precondition:
//      The absolute value of x cubed does not exceed the
//      machine's maximum float value
// Postcondition:
//      Function value == x cubed

{
    return x * x * x;
}
```

Testing: We should test this program with sets of data that include positive, negative, and zero values. It is especially important to try to input values of 0 and 1 for the number of divisions. The results from the program
should be compared against values calculated by hand using the same algorithm and against the true value of the area under the curve of X^3, which is
given by the formula

$$\frac{1}{4} * (\text{high}^4 - \text{low}^4)$$

(This formula comes from the mathematical topic of calculus. What we have
been referring to as the area under the curve in the interval a to b is called
the *integral* of the function from a to b.)

Let's consider for a moment the effects of representational error on this
program. The user specifies the low and high values of the interval, as well
as the number of subdivisions to be used in computing the result. The more
subdivisions used, the more accurate the result should be because the rectangles are narrower and thus approximate more closely the shape of the
area under the curve. It seems that we can obtain precise results by using a
large number of subdivisions. In fact, however, there is a point beyond
which an increase in the number of subdivisions *decreases* the precision of
the results. If we specify too many subdivisions, the area of an individual
rectangle becomes so small that the computer can no longer represent its
value accurately. Adding all those inaccurate values produces a total area
that has an even greater error.

PROBLEM-SOLVING *CASE STUDY*

Rock, Paper, Scissors

Problem: Play the children's game "rock, paper, scissors." In this game, two people simultaneously choose one of the following: rock, paper, or scissors. Whether a player wins or loses depends not only on that player's choice but also on the opponent's choice. The rules are:

Rock breaks scissors; rock wins.
Paper covers rock; paper wins.
Scissors cut paper; scissors win.
All matching combinations are ties.
The overall winner is the player who wins the most individual games.

Input: A series of letters representing player A's plays (fileA, one letter per line) and a series of letters representing player B's plays (fileB, one letter per line), with each play indicated by 'R' (Rock), 'P' (Paper), or 'S' (Scissors).

Output: For each game, the game number and the player who won that game; at the end, the total number of games won by each player, and the overall winner.

THE FAR SIDE   By GARY LARSON

Before paper and scissors

Discussion: We assume that everyone has played this game and understands it. Therefore, our discussion centers on how to simulate the game in a program.

For input, we have to use alphanumeric characters to stand for rock, paper, and scissors. We can input 'R', 'P', and 'S' and convert the letters to a user-defined enumeration type made up of the literals ROCK, PAPER, and SCISSORS.

Each player creates a file composed of a series of the letters 'R', 'P', and 'S', representing a series of individual games. The letters are read, one from each file, and converted into the appropriate enumeration type literals. Let's call each literal a play. The plays are compared, and a winner is determined. The number of games won is incremented for the winning player. The game is over when there are no more plays (the files are empty).

Assumptions: The game is over when one of the files runs out of plays.

Main   *Level 0*

```
Open data files (and verify success)
Get plays
WHILE NOT EOF on fileA AND NOT EOF on fileB
   IF plays are legal
      Process plays
   ELSE
      Print an error message
   Get plays
Print big winner
```

Get Plays (Out: playForA, playForB, legal)   *Level 1*

```
Read charForA (player A's play) from fileA
Read charForB (player B's play) from fileB
IF EOF on fileA OR EOF on fileB
   Return
Set legal = (charForA is 'R', 'P', or 'S') AND
            (charForB is 'R', 'P', or 'S')
IF legal
   Set playForA = ConversionValue(charForA)
   Set playForB = ConversionValue(charForB)
```

Problem-Solving Case Study cont'd.

Process Plays (In: gameNumber, playForA, playForB; Inout: winsForA, winsForB)

```
IF playForA == playForB
    Print gameNumber, " is a tie"
ELSE IF playForA == PAPER AND playForB == ROCK OR
            playForA == SCISSORS AND playForB == PAPER OR
            playForA == ROCK AND playForB == SCISSORS
    Record a win for Player A, incrementing winsForA (the number
            of games won by Player A)
ELSE
    Record a win for Player B, incrementing winsForB
```

Print Big Winner (In: winsForA, winsForB)

```
Print winsForA
Print winsForB
IF winsForA > winsForB
    Print "Player A has won the most games."
ELSE IF winsForB > winsForA
    Print "Player B has won the most games."
ELSE
    Print "Players A and B have tied."
```

ConversionValue (In: someChar)   *Level 2*
   Out: Function value

```
SWITCH someChar
    'R': Return ROCK
    'P': Return PAPER
    'S': Return SCISSORS
```

Record A Win (In: player, gameNumber; Inout: numOfWins)

```
Print message saying which player has won game number gameNumber
Increment numOfWins by 1
```

Now we are ready to code the simulation of the game. We must remember to initialize our counters. We assumed that we knew the game number for each game, yet nowhere have we kept track of the game number. We need to add a counter to our loop in the main module. Here's the revised main module:

Main

```
Open data files (and verify success)
Set winsForA and winsForB = 0
Set gameNumber = 0
Get plays
WHILE NOT EOF on fileA AND NOT EOF on fileB
   Increment gameNumber by 1
   IF plays are legal
      Process plays
   ELSE
      Print an error message
   Get plays
Print big winner
```

Module Structure Chart:

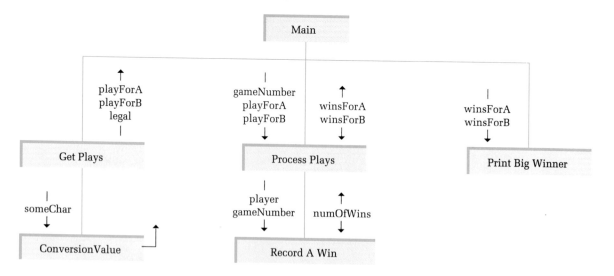

Here's the program that implements our design. It assumes we have created our own header file `bool.h`, whose contents are the statements

```
typedef int Boolean;
const Boolean TRUE = 1;
const Boolean FALSE = 0;
```

The preprocessor directive #include "bool.h" causes these declarations to be inserted into our program.

```
//*************************************************************
// Game program
// This program simulates the children's game 'rock, paper, and
// scissors.' Each game consists of inputs from two players,
// coming from fileA and fileB. A winner is determined for each
// individual game, and for the games overall
//*************************************************************
#include <iostream.h>
#include <fstream.h>      // For file I/O
#include "bool.h"         // For Boolean type

enum PlayType {ROCK, PAPER, SCISSORS};

PlayType ConversionVal( char );
void GetPlays( PlayType&, PlayType&, Boolean& );
void PrintBigWinner( int, int );
void ProcessPlays( int, PlayType, PlayType, int&, int& );
void RecordAWin( char, int, int& );

ifstream fileA;        // Player A's plays
ifstream fileB;        // Player B's plays

int main()
{
    PlayType playForA;              // Player A's play
    PlayType playForB;              // Player B's play
    int      winsForA = 0;          // Number of games A wins
    int      winsForB = 0;          // Number of games B wins
    int      gameNumber = 0;        // Number of games played
    Boolean  legal;                 // True if play is legal

    // Open the input files

    fileA.open("filea.dat");
    fileB.open("fileb.dat");
    if ( !fileA || !fileB )
    {
        cout << "** Can't open input file(s) **" << endl;
        return 1;
    }
```

```
        // Play a series of games and keep track of who wins

        GetPlays(playForA, playForB, legal);
        while (fileA && fileB)
        {
                // Invariant (prior to test):
                //      gameNumber pairs of input data have been
                //      input and processed

            gameNumber++;
            if (legal)
                ProcessPlays(gameNumber, playForA, playForB, winsForA,
                            winsForB);
            else
                cout << "Game number " << gameNumber
                        << " contained an illegal play." << endl;
            GetPlays(playForA, playForB, legal);
        }

        // Print overall winner

        PrintBigWinner(winsForA, winsForB);

        return 0;
    }

    //********************************************************************

    void GetPlays( /* out */ PlayType& playForA,      // A's play
                   /* out */ PlayType& playForB,      // B's play
                   /* out */ Boolean&  legal    )     // True if plays
                                                      //    are legal

// Reads the players' plays from the data files, converts the plays
// from char form to PlayType form, and reports whether the plays
// are legal. If end-of-file is encountered on either file, the
// outgoing parameters are undefined. Files fileA and fileB are
// accessed globally

// Precondition:
//      fileA and fileB have been successfully opened
// Postcondition:
//      IF input from either file failed due to end-of-file
//          playForA, playForB, and legal are undefined
//      ELSE
```

```
//              Player A's play has been read from fileA and Player B's
//              play has been read from fileB
//        && IF both plays are legal
//              legal == TRUE
//            && playForA == PlayType equivalent of Player A's play
//                          char
//            && playForB == PlayType equivalent of Player B's play
//                          char
//        ELSE
//              legal == FALSE
//            && playForA and playForB are undefined

{
    char charForA;        // Player A's input
    char charForB;        // Player B's input

    fileA >> charForA;            // Skip whitespace, including newline
    fileB >> charForB;
    if ( !fileA || !fileB)
        return;

    legal = (charForA=='R' || charForA=='P' || charForA=='S') &&
            (charForB=='R' || charForB=='P' || charForB=='S');
    if (legal)
    {
        playForA = ConversionVal(charForA);
        playForB = ConversionVal(charForB);
    }
}

//*****************************************************************

PlayType ConversionVal( /* in */ char someChar )    // Play character

// Converts a character into an associated value of PlayType

// Precondition:
//      someChar == 'R' or 'P' or 'S'
// Postcondition:
//      Function value == ROCK, if someChar == 'R'
//                     == PAPER, if someChar == 'P'
//                     == SCISSORS, if someChar == 'S'

{
    switch (someChar)
    {
```

```
        case 'R': return ROCK;        // No break needed after
        case 'P': return PAPER;       //   return statement
        case 'S': return SCISSORS;
    }
}

//*****************************************************************

void ProcessPlays( /* in */     int      gameNumber,    // Game number
                   /* in */     PlayType playForA,      // A's play
                   /* in */     PlayType playForB,      // B's play
                   /* inout */ int&     winsForA,       // A's wins
                   /* inout */ int&     winsForB   )    // B's wins

// Determines whether there is a winning play or a tie. If there
// is a winner, the number of wins of the winning player is
// incremented. In all cases, a message is written

// Precondition:
//     All parameters are assigned
// Postcondition:
//     IF Player A won
//         winsForA == winsForA@entry + 1
//     ELSE IF Player B won
//         winsForB == winsForB@entry + 1
//  && A message, including gameNumber, has been written specifying
//     either a tie or a winner

{
    if (playForA == playForB)
        cout << "Game number " << gameNumber << " is a tie."
            << endl;
    else if (playForA == PAPER && playForB == ROCK ||
             playForA == SCISSORS && playForB == PAPER ||
             playForA == ROCK && playForB == SCISSORS)
        RecordAWin('A', gameNumber, winsForA);       // Player A wins
    else
        RecordAWin('B', gameNumber, winsForB);       // Player B wins
}

//*****************************************************************

void RecordAWin( /* in */    char player,        // Winning player
                 /* in */    int gameNumber,     // Game number
                 /* inout */ int& numOfWins )    // Win count

// Outputs a message telling which player has won the current game
// and updates that player's total
```

```
// Precondition:
//     player == 'A' or 'B'
//   && gameNumber and numOfWins are assigned
// Postcondition:
//     A winning message, including player and gameNumber, has
//     been written
//   && numOfWins == numOfWins@entry + 1

{
    cout << "Player " << player << " has won game number "
        << gameNumber << '.' << endl;
    numOfWins++;
}


//****************************************************************

void PrintBigWinner( /* in */ int winsForA,      // A's win count
                     /* in */ int winsForB )     // B's win count

// Prints number of wins for each player and the
// overall winner (or tie)

// Precondition:
//     winsForA and winsForB are assigned
// Postcondition:
//     The values of winsForA and winsForB have been output
//   && A message indicating the overall winner (or a tie) has been
//     output

{
    cout << endl;
    cout << "Player A has won " << winsForA << " games." << endl;
    cout << "Player B has won " << winsForB << " games." << endl;
    if (winsForA > winsForB)
        cout << "Player A has won the most games." << endl;
    else if (winsForB > winsForA)
        cout << "Player B has won the most games." << endl;
    else
        cout << "Players A and B have tied." << endl;
}
```

Testing: We tested the Game program with the following files. They are listed side by side so that you can see the pairs that made up each game. Note that each combination of 'R', 'S', and 'P' is used at least once. In addition, there is an erroneous play character in each file.

fileA	fileB
R	R
S	S
S	S
R	S
R	P
P	P
P	P
R	S
S	T
A	P
P	S
P	R
S	P
R	S
R	S
P	P
S	R

Given the data in these files, the program produced the following output.

```
Game number 1 is a tie.
Game number 2 is a tie.
Game number 3 is a tie.
Player A has won game number 4.
Player B has won game number 5.
Game number 6 is a tie.
Game number 7 is a tie.
Player A has won game number 8.
Game number 9 contained an illegal play.
Game number 10 contained an illegal play.
Player B has won game number 11.
Player A has won game number 12.
Player A has won game number 13.
Player A has won game number 14.
Player A has won game number 15.
Game number 16 is a tie.
Player B has won game number 17.

Player A has won 6 games.
Player B has won 3 games.
Player A has won the most games.
```

An examination of the output shows it to be correct: player A did win six games, player B did win three games, and player A won the most games. This one set of test data is not enough to test the program completely. It should be run with test data where player B wins, where player A and player B tie, where `fileA` is longer than `fileB`, and where `fileB` is longer than `fileA`.

PROBLEM-SOLVING *CASE STUDY*

Birthday Reminder

Problem: Everyone has at least one friend who always remembers everyone's birthday. Each year when we receive appropriate greetings on our birthday from this friend, we promise to do better about remembering others' birthdays. Let's write a program that prints the names of those friends who have a birthday in a given month.

Input: A month entered from the keyboard, with first letter capitalized.

Output: The names (and birthdays) of all friends with a birthday in that month.

Discussion: If we were solving this problem by hand, we would turn our calendar to the month in question and list the names written there. That is exactly what our program does: it recognizes which month is being requested and calls a function that writes out the information for that month. The information for each month is represented as a series of output statements.

We represent the months as an enumeration type whose domain is the values JANUARY, FEBRUARY, MARCH, . . . DECEMBER. Thus, we must convert the month as input in character form into this type. We can perform the conversion by checking just the first one, two, or three characters of the input string. February, September, October, November, and December have unique first characters. April, August, and January can be distinguished by their first two characters. June, July, March, and May require three characters to distinguish them.

Assumptions: None.

Main   *Level 0*

```
Get month
SWITCH month
    JANUARY        : Print January info
    FEBRUARY       : Print February info
    MARCH          : Print March info
    APRIL          : Print April info
    MAY            : Print May info
    JUNE           : Print June info
    JULY           : Print July info
    AUGUST         : Print August info
    SEPTEMBER      : Print September info
    OCTOBER        : Print October info
    NOVEMBER       : Print November info
    DECEMBER       : Print December info
```

Get Month (Out: month)   *Level 1*

```
Read firstChar, secondChar, thirdChar
SWITCH firstChar
    'F'   : Set month = FEBRUARY
    'S'   : Set month = SEPTEMBER
    'O'   : Set month = OCTOBER
    'N'   : Set month = NOVEMBER
    'D'   : Set month = DECEMBER
    'J'   : Set month = appropriate J month
    'A'   : Set month = appropriate A month
    'M'   : Set month = appropriate M month
```

Print January (No parameters)

```
Print all the information for January
```

.
.
.

Problem-Solving Case Study cont'd.

Print December (No parameters)

> Print all the information for December

J Month (In: secondChar, thirdChar)
Out: Function value

Level 2

> IF secondChar is an 'a'
>   Return JANUARY
> ELSE IF thirdChar is an 'l'
>   Return JULY
> ELSE
>   Return JUNE

A Month (In: secondChar)
Out: Function value

> IF secondChar is a 'p'
>   Return APRIL
> ELSE
>   Return AUGUST

M Month (In: thirdChar)
Out: Function value

> IF thirdChar is an 'r'
>   Return MARCH
> ELSE
>   Return MAY

The print modules are composed of output statements that print all the information for the month. To test the program, we code all the print modules as stubs, which print one line stating that the month has been printed.

Module Structure Chart:

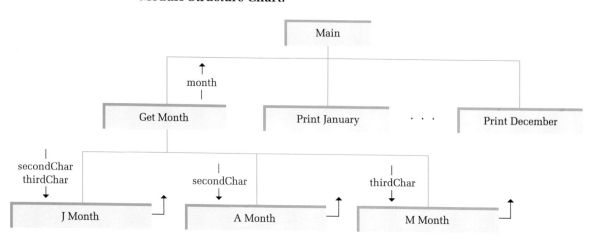

```
//****************************************************************
// BirthdayReminder program
// This program takes a month as input and prints the
// list of birthdays associated with that month
//****************************************************************
#include <iostream.h>

enum Months
{
    JANUARY, FEBRUARY, MARCH, APRIL, MAY, JUNE,
    JULY, AUGUST, SEPTEMBER, OCTOBER, NOVEMBER, DECEMBER
};

Months A_Month( char );
Months J_Month( char, char );
Months M_Month( char );
void GetMonth( Months& );
void PrintJanuary();
void PrintFebruary();
void PrintMarch();
void PrintApril();
void PrintMay();
void PrintJune();
void PrintJuly();
void PrintAugust();
void PrintSeptember();
void PrintOctober();
void PrintNovember();
void PrintDecember();
```

```cpp
int main()
{
    Months month;

    GetMonth(month);
    switch (month)
    {
        case JANUARY   : PrintJanuary();
                         break;
        case FEBRUARY  : PrintFebruary();
                         break;
        case MARCH     : PrintMarch();
                         break;
        case APRIL     : PrintApril();
                         break;
        case MAY       : PrintMay();
                         break;
        case JUNE      : PrintJune();
                         break;
        case JULY      : PrintJuly();
                         break;
        case AUGUST    : PrintAugust();
                         break;
        case SEPTEMBER : PrintSeptember();
                         break;
        case OCTOBER   : PrintOctober();
                         break;
        case NOVEMBER  : PrintNovember();
                         break;
        case DECEMBER  : PrintDecember();
    }
    return 0;
}

//*****************************************************************

void GetMonth( /* out */ Months& month )    // User's desired month

// Inputs a month after prompting the user

// Postcondition:
//     User has been prompted to enter a month
//  && Only the characters needed to determine the month are read
//     (the remaining characters on the input line are read and
//     discarded)
//  && month == value of type Months corresponding to user's input
```

```
{
    char firstChar;
    char secondChar;
    char thirdChar;

    cout << "Please enter month, capitalizing first letter."
         << endl;
    cin.get(firstChar);
    cin.get(secondChar);
    cin.get(thirdChar);
    cin.ignore(500, '\n');        // Skip remaining characters
                                  //    through newline
    switch (firstChar)
    {
        case 'F': month = FEBRUARY;
                break;
        case 'S': month = SEPTEMBER;
                break;
        case 'O': month = OCTOBER;
                break;
        case 'N': month = NOVEMBER;
                break;
        case 'D': month = DECEMBER;
                break;
        case 'J': month = J_Month(secondChar, thirdChar);
                break;
        case 'A': month = A_Month(secondChar);
                break;
        case 'M': month = M_Month(thirdChar);
                break;
    }
}

//*************************************************************************

Months J_Month( /* in */ char secondChar,      // 2nd input char
                /* in */ char thirdChar  )      // 3rd input char

// Determines month beginning with J

// Precondition:
//      secondChar and thirdChar are assigned
// Postcondition:
//      Function value == JANUARY, if secondChar == 'a'
//                     == JULY, if thirdChar == 'l'
//                     == JUNE, otherwise
```

```
{
    if (secondChar == 'a')
        return JANUARY;
    else if (thirdChar == 'l')
        return JULY;
    else
        return JUNE;
}

//**********************************************************************

Months A_Month( /* in */ char secondChar )    // 2nd input char

// Determines month beginning with A

// Precondition:
//      secondChar is assigned
// Postcondition:
//      Function value == APRIL, if secondChar == 'p'
//                     == AUGUST, otherwise

{
    if (secondChar == 'p')
        return APRIL;
    else
        return AUGUST;
}

//**********************************************************************

Months M_Month( /* in */ char thirdChar )    // 3rd input char

// Determines month beginning with M

// Precondition:
//      thirdChar is assigned
// Postcondition:
//      Function value == MARCH, if thirdChar == 'r'
//                     == MAY, otherwise

{
    if (thirdChar == 'r')
        return MARCH;
    else
        return MAY;
}
```

```
//*******************************************************************

void PrintJanuary()
{
    cout << "January printed" << endl;
}

//*******************************************************************

void PrintFebruary()
{
    cout << "February printed" << endl;
}

//*******************************************************************

void PrintMarch()
{
    cout << "March printed" << endl;
}


                    .
                    .
                    .


//*******************************************************************

void PrintDecember()
{
    cout << "December printed" << endl;
}
```

Testing: To test this program, we must run it 12 times. For each run, a different month is used as input, the appropriate print function is called, and the corresponding message is printed. If you want to use this program, you have to create the output statements to print the data for your friends. The stubs we use to test the rest of the program merely show that each print function is called correctly. We have more to say about testing this program in the Testing and Debugging section that follows.

TESTING AND DEBUGGING

Floating Point Data

When a problem requires the use of floating point numbers that are extremely large, small, or precise, it is important to keep in mind the limitations of the particular system you are using. When testing a program that performs floating point calculations, determine the acceptable margin of error beforehand, and then design your test data to try to push the program beyond those limits. Carefully check the accuracy of the computed results. (Remember that when you "hand calculate" the correct results, a pocket calculator may have *less* precision than your computer system.) If the program produces acceptable results when given worst-case data, it probably performs correctly on typical data.

Coping with Input Errors

Several times in this book we had our programs test for invalid data and write an error message. Writing an error message is certainly necessary, but it is only the first step. We must also decide what the program should do next. The problem itself and the severity of the error should determine what action is taken in any error condition. The approach taken also depends on whether or not the program is being run interactively.

In a program that reads its data only from an input file, there is no interaction with the person who entered the data. The program, therefore, should try to adjust for the bad data items, if at all possible.

If the invalid data item is not essential, the program can skip it and continue; for example, if a program averaging test grades encounters a negative test score, it could simply skip the negative score. If an educated guess can be made about the probable value of the bad data, it can be set to that value before being processed. In either event a message should be written stating that an invalid data item was encountered and outlining the steps that were taken. Such messages form an *exception report*.

If the data item is essential and no guess is possible, processing should be terminated. A message should be written to the user with as much information as possible about the invalid data item.

In an interactive environment, the program can prompt the user to supply another value. The program should indicate to the user what is wrong with the original data. Another possibility is to write out a list of actions and ask the user to choose among them.

These suggestions on how to handle bad data assume that the program recognizes when bad data have been entered. There are two approaches to error detection: passive and active. Passive error detection leaves it to the system to detect errors. This may seem easier, but the programmer relinquishes control of processing when an error occurs. An example of passive error detection is the system's division-by-zero error.

Active error detection means having the program check for possible errors and determine an appropriate action if an error is encountered. An example of active error detection would be to read a value and use an If statement to see if the value is zero before dividing it into another number.

The BirthdayReminder program uses *no* error detection. If the input is typed incorrectly, the program either produces no output at all (if the first character of the month is invalid) or erroneous output (if the second or third characters are invalid). Let's rewrite the GetMonth, J_Month, A_Month, and M_Month functions to incorporate active error detection. The first character must be checked to see whether it is one of the valid first letters. If not, the error must be reported. If the first character is an 'A', a 'J', or an 'M', the second or third character (or both) must be checked.

The first character should be checked where it is read, in the body of Get-Month. To handle invalid characters, we add a default label to the Switch statement. The second and/or third character should be checked in the function that uses it. Functions J_Month, A_Month, and M_Month need an extra parameter to let GetMonth know whether an error occurred. If an error has occurred, GetMonth must notify the user and request another input. This implies that the Switch statement must be in a loop that continues until a month has been recognized.

This scheme does not check the entire spelling of each month. It checks to see only that there are enough letters to recognize a month.

We said that J_Month, A_Month, and M_Month need an extra parameter to report to GetMonth whether an error occurred. A Boolean flag is appropriate for reporting an error, but now we have a problem. These three functions are value-returning functions and return only one value. We need to return *two* values—the appropriate month and a Boolean flag. Let's change these value-returning functions into void functions, returning two results through the parameter list. Because void functions should be named using imperative verbs, we rename the three functions as CheckJ, CheckA, and CheckM.

The following code assumes that we have defined our own Boolean type.

```
void CheckA( char, Months&, Boolean& );
void CheckJ( char, char, Months&, Boolean& );
void CheckM( char, Months&, Boolean& );
void GetMonth( Months& );
      .
      .
      .
//******************************************************************

void GetMonth( /* out */ Months& month )    // User's desired month

// Inputs a month after prompting the user

// Postcondition:
//      User has been prompted to enter a month
//   && Only the characters needed to determine the month are read
//      (the remaining characters on the input line are read and
//      discarded)
//   && On invalid input, the user has been repeatedly prompted to
//      type a correct month
//   && month == value of type Months corresponding to user's input
```

```
        return someShort;
```

within an `int` function.

14. Active error detection leaves error hunting to C++ and the operating system, whereas passive error detection requires the programmer to do the error hunting. (True or False?)

PROGRAMMING WARM-UP EXERCISES

1. Find out the maximum and minimum values for each of the C++ simple types on your machine. On most systems, these values are declared as named constants in the files `limits.h` and `float.h` in the standard include directory.

2. Using a combination of printable characters and escape sequences within *one* string, write a single output statement that does the following in the order shown:

   - Prints `Hello`
   - Prints a (horizontal) tab character
   - Prints `There`
   - Prints two blank lines
   - Prints `"Ace"` (including the double quotes)

3. Write a While loop that copies all the characters (including whitespace characters) from an input file `inFile` to an output file `outFile`, except that every lowercase letter is converted to uppercase. Assume that both files have been opened successfully before the loop begins. The loop should terminate when end-of-file is detected.

4. Given the following declarations

   ```
   int n;
   char ch1;
   char ch2;
   ```

   and given that n contains a two-digit number, translate n into two single characters where `ch1` holds the higher-order digit, and `ch2` holds the lower-order digit. For example, if n = 59, `ch1` would equal '5', and `ch2` would equal '9'. Then output the two digits as characters in the same order as the original numbers. (*Hint:* Consider how you might use the / and % operators in your solution.)

5. In a program you are writing, a `float` variable `beta` may potentially contain a very large number. Before multiplying `beta` by 100.0, you want the program to test whether it is safe to do so. Write an If statement that tests for a possible overflow *before* multiplying by 100.0. Specifically, if the multiplication would lead to overflow, print a message and don't perform the multiplication; otherwise, go ahead with the multiplication.

6. Declare an enumeration type for the course numbers of computer courses at your school.

7. Declare an enumeration type for the South American countries.

8. Declare an enumeration type for the work days of the week (Monday through Friday).

9. Write a value-returning function that converts the first two letters of a work day into the type declared in Exercise 8.

10. Write a void function that prints a value of the type declared in Exercise 8.

11. Using a loop control variable `today` of the type declared in Exercise 8, write a For loop that prints out all five values in the domain of the type. To print each value, invoke the function of Exercise 10.

12. Below is a function that is supposed to return the average of two integers, rounded to the nearest integer.

```
int Avg( /* in */ int1,
         /* in */ int2 )
{
    return float(int1) / float(int2);
}
```

Sometimes this function returns an incorrect result. Describe what the problem is in terms of type promotion or demotion, and fix the problem.

PROGRAMMING PROBLEMS

1. Read in the lengths of the sides of a triangle and determine whether the triangle is an isosceles triangle (two sides are equal), an equilateral triangle (three sides are equal), or a scalene triangle (no sides are equal). Use an enumeration type whose enumerators are ISOSCELES, EQUILATERAL, and SCALENE.

   The lengths of the sides of the triangle are to be entered as integer values. For each set of sides, print out the kind of triangle or an error message saying that the three sides do not make a triangle. (For a triangle to exist, any two sides together must be longer than the remaining side.) Continue analyzing triangles until end-of-file occurs.

2. Write a C++ program that reads a single character from 'A' through 'Z' and produces output in the shape of a pyramid composed of the letters up to and including the letter that is input. The top letter in the pyramid should be 'A', and on each level, the next letter in the alphabet should fall between the letter that was introduced in the level above it. For example, if the input is 'E', the output looks like the following:

```
    A
   ABA
  ABCBA
 ABCDCBA
ABCDEDCBA
```

3. Read in a floating point number character by character, ignoring any characters other than digits and a decimal point. Convert the valid characters into a single floating point number, and print the result. Your algorithm should convert the whole number part to an integer and the fractional part to an integer, and combine the two integers as follows:

   Set result = wholePart + fractionalPart / ($10^{\text{number of digits in fraction}}$)

   For example, `3A4.21P6` would be converted into 34 and 216, and the result would be the sum

   $$34 + \frac{216}{1000}$$

■ FIGURE 11-1

Atomic (Simple)
and Structured
Data Types

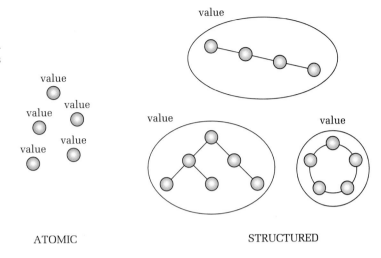

ATOMIC   STRUCTURED

values and imposes a specific arrangement on them (see Figure 11-1). The
method used to access the individual components of a structured type depends on how the components are arranged. As we discuss various ways of
structuring data, we'll look at the corresponding access mechanisms.

Figure 11-2 shows the structured types available in C++. This figure is a
portion of the complete diagram presented in Figure 2-1.

In this chapter and the next two chapters, we examine array data types.
The struct and union types are the topic of Chapter 14, and Chapter 15 ex-
plores a very powerful structured type—the class.

■ FIGURE 11-2

C++ Structured
Types

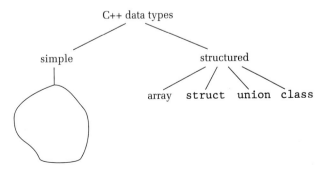

One-Dimensional Arrays

If we wanted to read a list of 1000 values and print them in reverse order, we could write a program of this form:

```cpp
//***************************
// ReverseList program
//***************************
#include <iostream.h>

int main()
{
    int value0;
    int value1;
    int value2;
        .
        .
    int value999;

    cin >> value0;
    cin >> value1;
    cin >> value2;
        .
        .
    cin >> value999;

    cout << value999 << endl;
    cout << value998 << endl;
    cout << value997 << endl;
        .
        .
    cout << value0 << endl;
    return 0;
}
```

This program is over 3000 lines long, and we have to use 1000 separate variables. Note that all the variables have the same name except for an appended number that distinguishes them. Wouldn't it be convenient if we could put the number into a counter variable and use For loops to go from 0 through 999, and then from 999 back down to 0? For example, if the counter variable were number, we could replace the 2000 original input/output statements with the following four lines of code (we enclose number in brackets to set it apart from value):

```
for (number = 0; number < 1000; number++)
    cin >> value[number];
for (number = 999; number >= 0; number--)
    cout << value[number] << endl;
```

This code fragment is correct in C++ *if* we declare value to be a *one-dimensional array*—that is, a collection of variables, all of the same type, where the first part of each variable name is the same, and the last part is an *index value* enclosed in square brackets. In our example, the value stored in number is called the *index*.

The declaration of a one-dimensional array is similar to the declaration of a simple variable (a variable of a simple data type), with one exception: you must also declare the size of the array. To do so, you indicate within brackets the number of components in the array:

```
int value[1000];
```

This declaration creates an array with 1000 components, all of type int. The first component has index value 0, the second component has index value 1, and the last component has index value 999.

Here is the complete ReverseList program, using array notation. This is certainly much shorter than our first version of the program.

```
//**************************
// ReverseList program
//**************************
#include <iostream.h>

int main()
{
    int value[1000];
    int number;

    for (number = 0; number < 1000; number++)
        cin >> value[number];
    for (number = 999; number >= 0; number--)
        cout << value[number] << endl;
    return 0;
}
```

Now that we have demonstrated how useful one-dimensional arrays can be, we define them formally and explain how individual components are accessed.

Declaring Arrays

A **one-dimensional array** is a structured collection of components (often called *elements*) that can be accessed individually by specifying the position of a component with a single index value. (In Chapter 13, we introduce multi-dimensional arrays, arrays that have more than one index value.)

One-Dimensional Array A structured collection of components, all of the same type, that is given a single name. Each component (array element) is accessed by an index that indicates the component's position within the collection.

Here is a syntax template describing the simplest form of a one-dimensional array declaration:

ArrayDeclaration

DataType ArrayName **[** ConstIntExpression **]** ;

In the syntax template, DataType describes what is stored in each component of the array. Array components may be of almost any type, but for now we limit our discussion to atomic components. ConstIntExpression is an integer expression composed only of literal or named constants. This expression, which specifies the number of components in the array, must have a value greater than zero. If the value is n, the range of index values is 0 through $n - 1$, not 1 through n. For example, the declarations

```
float angle[4];
int   testScore[10];
```

create the arrays shown in Figure 11-3. The `angle` array has four components, each capable of holding one `float` value. The `testScore` array has a total of 10 components, all of type `int`.

Accessing Individual Components

To access an individual array component, we write the array name, followed by an expression enclosed in square brackets. The expression specifies

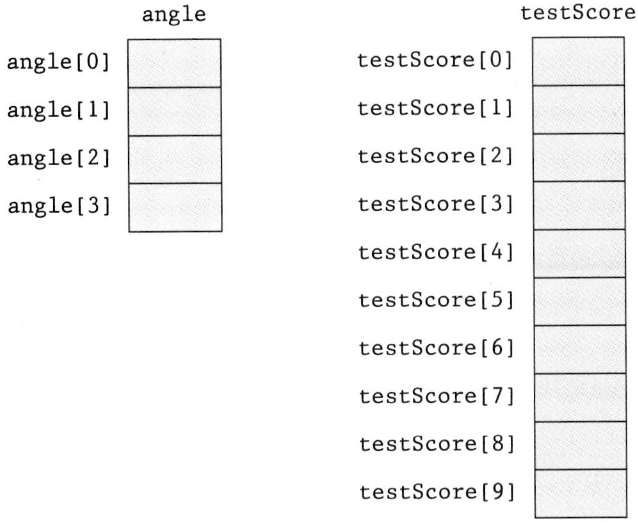

■ FIGURE 11-3
angle and
testScore Arrays

which component to access. The syntax template for accessing an array component is

ArrayComponentAccess

ArrayName [IndexExpression]

The index expression may be as simple as a constant or a variable name or as complex as a combination of variables, operators, and function calls. Whatever the form of the expression, it must result in an integer value. Index expressions can be of type char, short, int, long, or enumeration types because these are all integral types.

The simplest form of index expression is a constant. Using our angle array, the sequence of assignment statements

```
angle[0] = 4.93;
angle[1] = -15.2;
angle[2] = 0.5;
angle[3] = 1.67;
```

fills the array components one at a time (see Figure 11-4).

Each array component—angle[2], for instance—can be treated exactly the same as a simple variable. We can assign it a value

```
angle[2] = 9.6;
```

■ FIGURE 11-4
angle Array with Values

	angle
angle[0]	4.93
angle[1]	−15.2
angle[2]	0.5
angle[3]	1.67

or read a value into it

```
cin >> angle[2];
```

or write its contents

```
cout << angle[2];
```

or pass it as a parameter

```
y = sqrt(angle[2]);
```

or use it in an arithmetic expression.

```
x = 6.8 * angle[2] + 7.5;
```

Let's look at index expressions that are more complicated than constants. Suppose we declare a 1000-element array of `int` values with the statement

```
int value[1000];
```

and execute the following two statements.

```
value[counter] = 5;
if (value[number+1] % 10 != 0)
     ⋮
```

In the first statement, 5 is stored into an array component. If `counter` is 0, 5 is stored into the first component of the array. If `counter` is 1, 5 is stored into the second place in the array, and so forth.

In the second statement, an array component is selected by the expression `number+1`. The specific array component accessed is divided by 10 and checked to see if the remainder is nonzero. If `number+1` is 0, the value in the first component is being tested; if `number+1` is 1, the second place is tested; and so on. Figure 11-5 shows the indexing expression as a constant, a variable, and a more complex expression.

Out-of-Bounds Array Indices

Given the declaration

```
float alpha[100];
```

the valid range of index values is 0 through 99. What happens if we execute the statement

```
alpha[i] = 62.4;
```

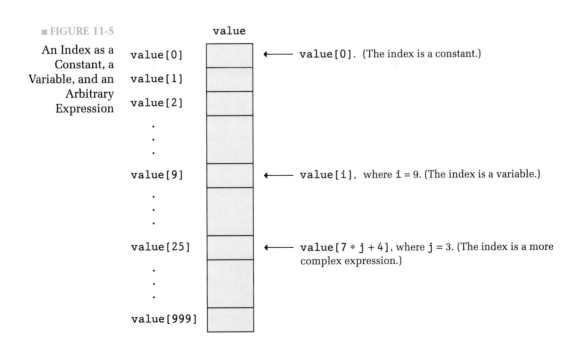

■ FIGURE 11-5

An Index as a Constant, a Variable, and an Arbitrary Expression

when i < 0 or when i > 99? The result is that a memory location outside the array is accessed. C++ does not check for invalid (*out-of-bounds*) array indices either at compile time or at run time. If i happens to be 100 in the statement above, the computer stores 62.4 into the next memory location past the end of the array, destroying whatever value was contained there. It is entirely the programmer's responsibility to make sure that an array index does not step off either end of the array.

Out-of-Bounds Array Index   An index value that, in C++, is either less than zero or greater than the array size minus one.

Array-processing algorithms often use For loops to step through the array elements one at a time. Here is a loop to zero out our 100-element alpha array (i is an int variable):

```
for (i = 0; i < 100; i++)
    alpha[i] = 0.0;
```

We could also write the first line as

```
for (i = 0; i <= 99; i++)
```

However, C++ programmers commonly use the first version so that the number in the loop test (100) is the same as the array size. With this pattern, it is important to remember to test for *less-than*, not less-than-or-equal.

Assertions can help convince you (and others) that an array-processing loop executes the correct number of times. In assertions written as comments, we often need to refer to a range of array elements:

```
// alpha[i] through alpha[j] have been printed
```

To specify such ranges, it is more convenient to use an abbreviated notation consisting of two dots:

```
// alpha[i]..alpha[j] have been printed
```

or, more briefly:

```
// alpha[i..j] have been printed
```

(Note that this dot-dot notation is not valid syntax in C++ language statements. We are talking only about comments in a program.) Here is the loop to zero out the `alpha` array, documented with a loop invariant and a loop postcondition:

```
for (i = 0; i < 100; i++)

        // Invariant (prior to test):
        //     alpha[0..i-1] == 0.0
        // && 0 <= i <= 100

    alpha[i] = 0.0;

// Assert:
//     alpha[0..99] == 0.0  &&  i == 100
```

Notice that the loop invariant states that $i \leq 100$, whereas the While condition is $i < 100$. Remember that a loop invariant is logically positioned just before the loop test:

```
        Invariant
            |
            ↓
for (i = 0; i < 100; i++)
```

After the final loop iteration, which sets `alpha[99]` to zero, i is incremented to 100. Prior to the final loop test, then, the invariant $i \leq 100$ is true because i equals 100; however, the loop condition is now FALSE and control exits the loop.

C++ does not prevent us from running off the end of an array. Writing loop invariants can give us an extra measure of safety by forcing us to think carefully about the number of iterations in an array-processing loop.

Initializing Arrays in Declarations

You learned in Chapter 8 that C++ allows you to initialize a variable in its declaration:

```
int delta = 25;
```

The value 25 is called an initializer. You also can initialize an array in its declaration, and the initializer has a special syntax. You specify a list of initial values for the array elements, separate them with commas, and enclose the list within braces:

```
int age[5] = {23, 10, 16, 37, 12};
```

In this declaration, `age[0]` is initialized to 23, `age[1]` is initialized to 10, and so on. There must be at least one initial value between the braces. If you specify too many initial values, you get a syntax error. If you specify too few, the remaining array elements are initialized to zero. It's always a good idea to specify exactly the right number of initial values.

Arrays follow the same rule as simple variables about the time(s) at which initialization occurs. A static array (one that is either global or declared as `static` within a block) is initialized once only, when control reaches its declaration. An automatic array (one that is local and not declared as `static`) is reinitialized each time control reaches its declaration.

An interesting feature of C++ is that you are allowed to omit the size of an array when you initialize it in a declaration:

```
float temperature[] = {0.0, 112.37, 98.6};
```

The compiler figures out the size of the array (here, 3) according to how many initial values are listed. In general, this feature is not particularly useful. In Chapter 12, though, we'll see that it can be convenient for initializing certain kinds of `char` arrays called strings.

(Lack of) Aggregate Array Operations

Some programming languages allow **aggregate operations** on arrays. An aggregate operation is one that manipulates the array as an entire unit.

Aggregate Operation   An operation on a data structure as a whole, as opposed to an operation on an individual component of the data structure.

C++ does not provide aggregate operations on arrays. If **x** and **y** are declared as

```
int x[50];
int y[50];
```

there is no aggregate assignment of y to x:

```
x = y;      // No
```

To copy array y into array x, you must do it yourself, element by element:

```
for (index = 0; index < 50; index++)
    x[index] = y[index];
```

Similarly, there is no aggregate comparison of arrays:

```
if (x == y)     // No
```

nor can you perform aggregate I/O of arrays:

```
cout << x;      // No
```

or aggregate arithmetic on arrays:

```
x = x + y;      // No
```

(C++ allows one exception for I/O, as we discuss in Chapter 12. Aggregate I/O is permitted for strings, which are special kinds of char arrays.) Finally, it's not possible to return an entire array as the value of a value-returning function:

```
return x;      // No
```

The only thing you can do to an array as a whole is to pass it as a parameter to a function:

```
DoSomething(x);
```

Passing an array as a parameter gives the function access to the entire array. Later in the chapter, we look at parameter passage in detail.

Examples of Declaring and Accessing Arrays

We now look in detail at some specific examples of declaring and accessing arrays. Here are some declarations that a program might use to analyze occupancy rates in an apartment building:

```
const int BUILDING_SIZE = 350;    // Number of apartments

int occupants[BUILDING_SIZE];     // occupants[i] is the number of
                                  //    occupants in apartment i
int totalOccupants;               // Total number of occupants
int counter;                      // Loop control and index variable
```

occupants is a 350-element array of type int (see Figure 11-6). occupants[0] = 3 if the first apartment has three occupants; occupants[1] = 5 if the second apartment has five occupants; and so on. If values have been stored into the array, then the following code totals the number of occupants in the building.

```
totalOccupants = 0;
for (counter = 0; counter < BUILDING_SIZE; counter++)

        // Invariant (prior to test):
        //     totalOccupants == sum of occupants[0..counter-1]
        //  && 0 <= counter <= BUILDING_SIZE

    totalOccupants = totalOccupants + occupants[counter];
```

The first time through the loop, counter is 0. We add the contents of totalOccupants (which is 0) to the contents of occupants[0], storing the

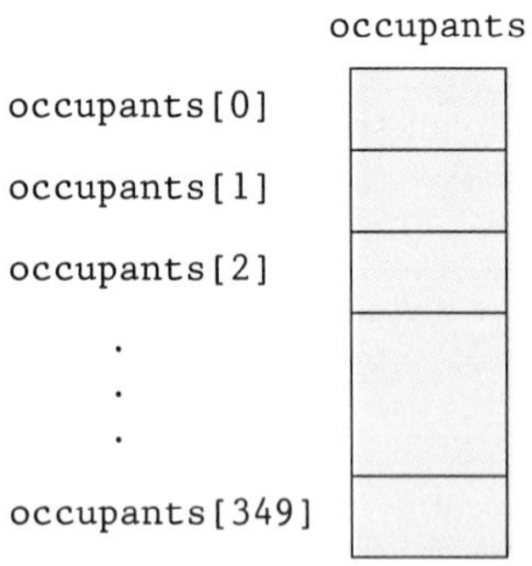

■ FIGURE 11-6

occupants Array

result into `totalOccupants`. Next, `counter` becomes 1 and the loop test occurs. The second loop iteration adds the contents of `totalOccupants` to the contents of `occupants[1]`, storing the result into `totalOccupants`. Now `counter` becomes 2 and the loop test is made. You can confirm that the loop invariant is true just before the test occurs: `totalOccupants` equals the sum of `occupants[0]` through `occupants[1]`, and $0 \leq counter \leq 350$ because `counter` is 2. Eventually, the loop adds the contents of `occupants[349]` to the sum and increments `counter` to 350. Just before the loop test occurs, the loop invariant is true because `totalOccupants` is the sum of `occupants[0]` through `occupants[349]` and `counter` equals 350. At this point, the loop condition is false, and control exits the loop.

Note how we used the named constant `BUILDING_SIZE` in both the array declaration and the For loop. When constants are used in this manner, changes can be made easily. If the number of apartments changes from 350 to 400, only the `const` declaration of `BUILDING_SIZE` needs to be changed. If the literal value 350 were used in place of `BUILDING_SIZE`, several of the statements in the code above, and probably many more throughout the rest of the program, would have to be changed.

Because an array index is an integer value, we can access the components by their position in the array—that is, the first, the second, the third, and so on, until the last. Using an `int` index is the most common way of thinking about an array. C++, however, provides more flexibility by allowing an index to be of any integral type. (The index expression still must evaluate to an integer in the range from 0 through one less than the array size.) The next example shows an array where the indices are values of an enumeration type.

```
enum Drink {ORANGE, COLA, ROOT_BEER, GINGER_ALE, CHERRY, LEMON};

float salesAmt[6]; // Array of 6 floats, to be indexed by Drink type
Drink flavor;      // Variable of the index type
```

`Drink` is an enumeration type in which the enumerators `ORANGE`, `COLA`, ..., `LEMON` have internal representations 0 through 5, respectively. `salesAmt` is a group of six `float` components representing dollar sales figures for each kind of drink (see Figure 11-7). The following code prints the values in the array (see Chapter 10 to review how to increment values of enumeration types in For loops).

```
for (flavor = ORANGE; flavor <= LEMON; flavor = Drink(flavor + 1))

        // Invariant (prior to test):
        //     salesAmt[0..int(flavor)-1] have been output
        //     && ORANGE <= flavor <= int(LEMON) + 1

    cout << salesAmt[flavor] << endl;
```

■ FIGURE 11-7

salesAmt Array

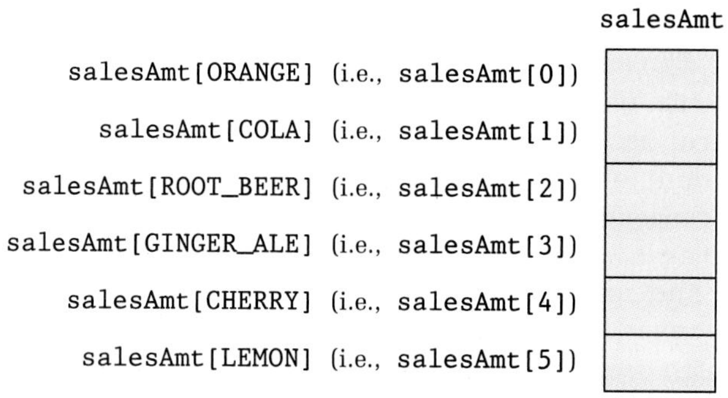

salesAmt

salesAmt[ORANGE] (i.e., salesAmt[0])

salesAmt[COLA] (i.e., salesAmt[1])

salesAmt[ROOT_BEER] (i.e., salesAmt[2])

salesAmt[GINGER_ALE] (i.e., salesAmt[3])

salesAmt[CHERRY] (i.e., salesAmt[4])

salesAmt[LEMON] (i.e., salesAmt[5])

Here is one last example.

```
const int NUM_STUDENTS = 10;

char grade[NUM_STUDENTS];    // Array of 10 student letter grades
int  idNumber;               // Student ID number (0 through 9)
```

The grade array is pictured in Figure 11-8. Values are shown in the components, which implies that some processing of the array has already occurred. Following are some simple examples showing how the array may be used.

■ FIGURE 11-8

grade Array with Values

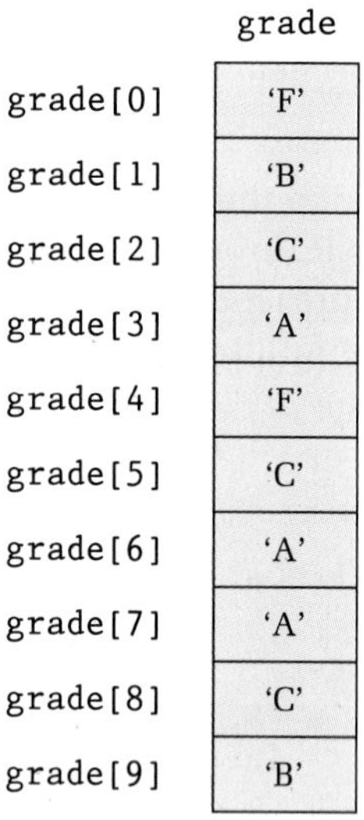

grade

grade[0]   'F'

grade[1]   'B'

grade[2]   'C'

grade[3]   'A'

grade[4]   'F'

grade[5]   'C'

grade[6]   'A'

grade[7]   'A'

grade[8]   'C'

grade[9]   'B'

```
cin >> grade[2];
```

reads the next nonwhitespace character from the input stream and stores it into the component in grade indexed by 2;

```
grade[3] = 'A';
```

assigns the character 'A' to the component in grade indexed by 3;

```
idNumber = 5;
```

assigns 5 to the index variable idNumber;

```
grade[idNumber] = 'C';
```

assigns the character 'C' to the component of grade indexed by idNumber (that is, by 5); and

```
for (idNumber = 0; idNumber < NUM_STUDENTS; idNumber++)
    cout << grade[idNumber];
```

loops through the grade array, printing each component. For this loop, the output would be FBCAFCAACB. And, finally,

```
for (idNumber = 0; idNumber < NUM_STUDENTS; idNumber++)
    cout << "Student " << idNumber
         << " Grade " << grade[idNumber] << endl;
```

loops through grade, printing each component in a more readable form. idNumber is used as the index, but it also has semantic content—it is the student's identification number. The output would be

```
Student 0 Grade F
Student 1 Grade B
      .
      .
      .
Student 9 Grade B
```

Passing Arrays as Parameters

In Chapter 8, we said that if a variable is passed to a function and it is not to be changed by the function, then the variable should be passed by value instead of by reference. We specifically excluded stream variables (such as those representing data files) from this rule and said that there would be one more exception. Arrays are this exception.

By default, C++ simple variables are always passed by value. To pass a simple variable by reference, you must append an ampersand (&) to the data type name in the formal parameter list:

```
int SomeFunc( float param1,      // Passed by value
              char& param2 )     // Passed by reference
{
   .
   .
   .
}
```

It is impossible to pass a C++ array by value; arrays are *always* passed by reference. Therefore, you never use "&" when declaring an array as a formal parameter. When an array is passed as a parameter, its **base address**—the memory address of the first element of the array—is sent to the function. The function then knows where the caller's actual array is located and can access any element of the array.

Base Address   The memory address of the first element of an array.

Here is a C++ function that will zero out a one-dimensional float array of any size:

```
void ZeroOut( /* out */ float arr[],
              /* in */  int   numElements )
{
    int i;

    for (i = 0; i < numElements; i++)

            // Invariant (prior to test):
            //     arr[0..i-1] == 0.0
            // && 0 <= i <= numElements

        arr[i] = 0.0;
}
```

In the formal parameter list, the declaration of `arr` does not include a size within the brackets. If you include a size, the compiler ignores it. The compiler only wants to know that it is a `float` array, not a `float` array of any particular size. Therefore, you must include a second parameter—the number of array elements—in order for this function to work correctly.

The calling code can invoke the `ZeroOut` function for a `float` array of any size. The following code fragment makes function calls to zero out two arrays of different sizes. Notice how an array parameter is declared in a function prototype.

```
void ZeroOut( float[], int );      // Function prototype
    .
    .
    .

int main()
{
    float velocity[30];
    float refractionAngle[9000];
        .
        .
        .
    ZeroOut(velocity, 30);
    ZeroOut(refractionAngle, 9000);
        .
        .
        .
}
```

With simple variables, pass-by-value prevents a function from modifying the caller's actual parameter. You cannot pass arrays by value in C++, but you can still prevent the function from modifying the caller's array. To do so, you use the reserved word `const` in the declaration of the formal parameter. Below is a function that copies one `int` array into another. The first parameter—the destination array—is expected to be modified, but the second array is not.

```
void Copy( /* out */          int destination[],
           /* in */    const int source[],
           /* in */          int size           )
{
    int i;

    for (i = 0; i < size; i++)

            // Invariant (prior to test):
            //      For all k, where 0 <= k <= i-1,
            //           destination[k] == source[k]
            // && 0 <= i <= size
```

```
                destination[i] = source[i];
}
```

The word `const` guarantees that any attempt to modify the `source` array within the `Copy` function results in a compile-time error.

Here's a table that summarizes parameter passage for simple variables and one-dimensional arrays:

Parameter	Formal Parameter Declaration for Pass-by-Value	Formal Parameter Declaration for Pass-by-Reference
Simple variable	int cost	int& price
Array	Impossible*	int arr[]

*However, prefixing the array declaration with the word const prevents the function from modifying the parameter.

One final remark about parameter passage: It is a common mistake to pass an array *element* to a function when passing the entire array was intended. For example, our `ZeroOut` function expects the base address of a `float` array to be sent as the first parameter. In the following code fragment, the function call is an error.

```
float velocity[30];
   .
   .
ZeroOut(velocity[30], 30);     // No
```

First of all, `velocity[30]` denotes a single array element—one floating point number—and not an entire array. Worse yet, there is no array element with an index of 30. The indices for the `velocity` array run from 0 through 29.

Processing Arrays

Three types of array processing occur especially often: using part of the declared array (a subarray), using two or more arrays in parallel (parallel arrays), and using index values that have specific meaning within the problem (indices with semantic content). We describe each of these methods briefly here, and leave further examples to the case studies at the end of the chapter.

BACKGROUND INFORMATION

C, C++, and Parameter Passage of Arrays

Some programming languages allow arrays to be passed either by value or by reference. Remember that with passage by value, a copy of the actual parameter is sent to the function. When an array is passed by value, the entire array is copied. Not only is extra space required in the function to hold the copy, but the copying itself takes time. Passage by reference requires only that the address of the actual parameter be passed to the function, so when an array is passed by reference, just the address of the first array component is passed. Thus, passing large arrays by reference saves both memory and time.

The C programming language—the direct predecessor of C++—was originally designed to be a system programming language. System programs, such as compilers, assemblers, linkers, and operating systems, must be both fast and economical with memory space. In the design of the C language, passing arrays by value was judged to be an unnecessary language feature. Serious system programmers never used pass-by-value when working with arrays. Therefore, both C and C++ pass arrays only by reference.

Of course, using a reference parameter can lead to inadvertent errors if the values are changed within the function. In early versions of the C language, there was no way to protect the caller's array from being modified by the function.

C++ (and recent versions of C) added the ability to declare a formal array parameter as const. By declaring the array as const, a compile-time error occurs if the function attempts to modify the array. As a result, C++ supports the efficiency of passing arrays by reference yet also provides the protection (through const) of passage by value.

Whenever your design of a function's interface identifies an array parameter as incoming-only (to be inspected but not modified by the function), declare the array as const to obtain the same protection as passage by value.

Subarray Processing

The *size* of an array—the declared number of array components—is established at compile time. We have to declare it to be as big as it would ever need to be. Because the exact number of values to be put into the array is often dependent on the data itself, however, we may not fill all of the array components with values. The problem is that, to avoid processing empty ones, we must keep track of how many components are actually filled.

As values are put into the array, we keep a count of how many components are filled. We then use this count to process only components that have values stored in them. Any remaining places are not processed. For example, if there are 250 students in a class, a program to analyze test grades would set aside 250 locations for the grades. However, some students will surely be absent on the day of the test. So the number of test grades is counted, and that number, rather than 250, is used to control the processing of the array.

We often call the actual number of values in an array the *length* of the array. If the length of an array is less than its declared size, functions that use array parameters should also have the length passed as a parameter. For example,

```
void Print( /* in */ const char grade[],      // Array for up to
                                              //    250 students
            /* in */          int  length  )  // Number of grades
                                              //    actually in array
```

The first two case studies at the end of this chapter—Comparison of Two Lists and Frequency of Certain Characters—demonstrate the technique of subarray processing.

Parallel Arrays

In many problems, there are several pieces of information that go together. For example, we might have ID numbers and grades for a particular group of students. We can set up an int (or long) array for the ID numbers and a char array for the grades. We can then access the components in the arrays in parallel. A particular ID number goes with a particular grade because they have the same position in their respective arrays; that is, they have the same index value. In Figure 11-9, the grade in grade[0] is the grade for the student whose ID number is in idNum[0]; the grade in grade[1] is the grade for the student whose ID number is in idNum[1]; and so on.

Another example of parallel arrays is the second case study in this chapter (Frequency of Certain Characters).

Parallel Arrays should be the same size.

■ FIGURE 11-9

Parallel Arrays

	idNum			grade	
idNum[0]	18345		grade[0]	'F'	
idNum[1]	30241		grade[1]	'B'	
idNum[2]	28274		grade[2]	'A'	
.			.		
.			.		
.			.		
idNum[9]	73002		grade[9]	'D'	

Indices with Semantic Content

In some problems, the index has meaning beyond simple position; that is, the index has *semantic content*. An example is the `salesAmt` array we showed earlier. This array is indexed by a value of enumeration type `Drink`. The index of a specific sales amount is the kind of soft drink sold; for example, `salesAmt[ROOT_BEER]` is the dollar sales figure for root beer.

The third of the three case studies that now follow (Frequency of All Characters) illustrates the use of indices with semantic content.

P*ROBLEM-SOLVING CASE STUDY*

Comparison of Two Lists

Problem: You are writing a program for an application that does not tolerate erroneous input data. Therefore, the data are prepared by entering them twice into one file. The file contains two lists of positive integer numbers, separated by a negative number. These two lists of numbers should be identical; if they are not, then a data entry error has occurred. For example, if the input file contains the sequence of numbers 17, 14, 8, –5, 17, 14, 8, then the two lists of three numbers are identical. However, the sequence 17, 14, 8, –5, 17, 12, 8 shows a data entry error.

You decide to write a separate program to compare the lists and print out any pairs of numbers that are not the same. The exact number of integers in each list is unknown, but each list has no more than 500.

Input: A file (`dataFile`) containing two lists of positive integers. The lists are separated by a negative integer and are of equal length.

Output: The statement that the lists are identical, or a list of the pairs of values that do not match.

Discussion: Because the lists are in the same file, the first list has to be read and stored until the negative number is read. Then the second list can be read and compared with the first list.

If we were checking the lists by hand, we would write the numbers from the first list on a pad of paper, one per line. The line number would correspond to the number's position in the list; that is, the first number would be on the first line, the second number on the second line, and so on. The first number in the second list would then be compared to the number on the first line, the second number to the number on the second line, and so forth.

We use an array named `firstList` to represent the pad of paper. Its declaration looks like this:

```
const int MAX_NUMBER = 500;        // Maximum in each list

int firstList[MAX_NUMBER];         // Holds first list
```

Because the first array component has index 0, we must think of our pad of paper as having its lines numbered from 0, not 1.

Now we can complete the top-down design and program for our problem.

Assumption: The two lists to be compared are of equal length.

Data Structures: A one-dimensional int array (firstList) to hold the first list of numbers. See Figure 11-10.

Main   *Level 0*

> Open dataFile (and verify success)
> Read first list
> Set allOK = TRUE
> Compare lists, changing allOK if necessary
> IF allOK
>   Print "The two lists are identical"

In the module Read First List, the first input value is stored into firstList[0], the second into firstList[1], the third into firstList[2]. This implies that we need a counter to keep track of which number is being read. When the negative number is encountered, the counter tells us how many of the 500 places set aside were actually needed. We can use this value (call it length) to control the reading and comparing loop in the Compare Lists module. This is an example of subarray processing.

Read First List (Inout: dataFile; Out: length, firstList)   *Level 1*

> Set counter = 0
> Read number from dataFile
> WHILE number >= 0
>   Set firstList[counter] = number
>   Increment counter
>   Read number from dataFile
> Set length = counter

PROBLEM-SOLVING CASE STUDY cont'd.

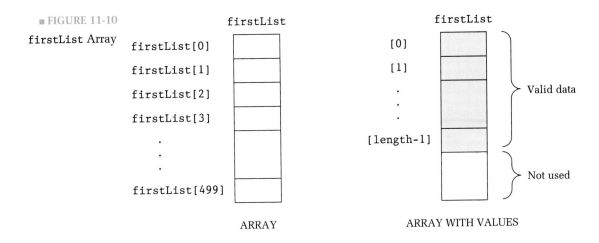

■ FIGURE 11-10

firstList Array

ARRAY

ARRAY WITH VALUES

Compare Lists (In: firstList, length; Inout: dataFile, allOK)

> FOR counter going from 0 through length−1
>   Read number from second list
>   IF numbers not the same
>   Set allOK = FALSE
>   Print both numbers

Numbers Not the Same   *Level 2*

> number != firstList[counter]

Print Both Numbers

> Print firstList[counter], number

Because the last two modules are only one line each, they are coded directly in the Compare Lists module.

PROBLEM-SOLVING CASE STUDY *cont'd.*

Module Structure Chart:

```
//*********************************************************************
// CheckLists program
// There are two lists of integers in a data file, separated by a
// negative integer.  This program compares the two lists.  If they
// are identical, a message is printed.  If not, nonmatching pairs
// are printed.  Assumption:  The lists are of equal length
//*********************************************************************
#include <iostream.h>
#include <iomanip.h>      // For setw()
#include <fstream.h>      // For file I/O
#include "bool.h"         // For Boolean type
```
user defined → directive.

```
const int MAX_NUMBER = 500;      // Maximum in each list

void CompareLists( Boolean&, const int[], int, ifstream& );
void ReadFirstList( int[], int&, ifstream& );
```
← to locate pointer

```
int main()
{
    int      firstList[MAX_NUMBER];   // Holds first list
    Boolean  allOK;                   // True if lists are identical
    int      length;                  // Length of first list
    ifstream dataFile;                // Input file

    dataFile.open("lists.dat");
    if ( !dataFile )
    {
        cout << "** Can't open input file **" << endl;
        return 1;
    }

    ReadFirstList(firstList, length, dataFile);
    allOK = TRUE;
    CompareLists(allOK, firstList, length, dataFile);
    if (allOK)
        cout << "The two lists are identical" << endl;
```

```
            return 0;
        }

//*****************************************************************

void ReadFirstList(
            /* out */    int       firstList[],   // Filled first list
            /* out */    int&      length,        // Number of values
            /* inout */  ifstream& dataFile    )  // Input file

// Reads the first list from the data file
// and counts the number of values in the list

// Precondition:
//     dataFile has been successfully opened for input
//     && The no. of input values in the first list <= MAX_NUMBER
// Postcondition:
//     length == number of input values in the first list
//     && firstList[0..length-1] contain the input values

{
    int counter;     // Index variable
    int number;      // Variable used for reading

    counter = 0;
    dataFile >> number;
    while (number >= 0)
    {
            // Invariant (prior to test):
            //     firstList[0..counter-1] contain the
            //     first "counter" input values
            //   && All previous values of number were >= 0

        firstList[counter] = number;
        counter++;
        dataFile >> number;
    }
    length = counter;
}

//*****************************************************************

void CompareLists(
            /* inout */  Boolean&  allOK,        // True if lists match
            /* in */     const int firstList[],  // 1st list of numbers
            /* in */     int       length,       // Length of 1st list
            /* inout */  ifstream& dataFile    )  // Input file
```

```
// Reads the second list of numbers
// and compares it to the first list

// Precondition:
//     allOK is assigned
//  && length <= MAX_NUMBER
//  && firstList[0..length-1] are assigned
//  && The two lists are of equal length
// Postcondition:
//     Values from the second list have been read from the
//     input file
//  && IF all values in the two lists match
//         allOK == allOK@entry
//     ELSE
//         allOK == FALSE
//      && The positions and contents of mismatches have been
//         printed

{
    int counter;     // Loop control and index variable
    int number;      // Variable used for reading

    for (counter = 0; counter < length; counter++)
    {
        // Invariant (prior to test):
        //     firstList[0..counter-1] have been compared with
        //     the corresponding input values
        //  && 0 <= counter <= length
        //  && allOK == FALSE, if any mismatches occurred
        //             == allOK@entry, otherwise

        dataFile >> number;
        if (number != firstList[counter])
        {
            allOK = FALSE;
            cout << "Position " << counter << ": "
                 << setw(4) << firstList[counter] << " != "
                 << setw(4) << number << endl;
        }
    }
}
```

Testing: The program is run with two sets of data, one in which the two lists are identical and one in which there are errors. The data and the results from each are shown below.

PROBLEM-SOLVING CASE STUDY cont'd.

Data Set One	Data Set Two
21	21
32	32
76	76
22	22
21	21
-4	-4
21	21
32	32
76	176
22	12
21	21

Output:
The two lists are identical.

Output:
Position 3:   76 != 176
Position 4:   22 != 12

P *ROBLEM-SOLVING* CASE STUDY

Frequency of Certain Characters

Problem: You've found a secret message, written in some sort of code. After doing some research, you decide to see if it is a simple substitution cypher—a code in which each letter is replaced by a different letter. Your research tells you that the way to break this type of code is to count the occurrences of each letter in the text and compare them to the average occurrence of letters in any English text. For example, the most common letter is probably a substitute for *e*. You decide to write a program to count the occurrences of certain characters in a text file. Rather than count every character in the message, you decide to look just at certain characters that appear to be the most common. The characters you are interested in are input from the keyboard.

Input: A list of the characters to be counted, as read from the keyboard (the character '#' ends the list); and text to be processed character by character (in file dataFile).

Output: The characters to be counted and their frequency.

Discussion: If you were doing this by hand, you would make a list of the characters you wanted to count. Then you would process the text by taking each character and checking to see whether it was on your list. If it was, you would make a hash mark beside it.

This algorithm can be used directly in a program. The list of characters can be read into an array of type char. To see whether or not a character is in the list, you scan the list, comparing the character with the ones in the list. To simulate making a hash mark, you use a second, parallel array that is the same size as the character list, but whose components are of type int. If you find the character in the list, you add 1 to the component with the same index in the second array. For example, if the first character in our list is an 'A', then each time you find an 'A', the first slot in the integer array is incremented.

Data Structures: A one-dimensional array of type char to hold the characters being counted (charList) and a one-dimensional array of type int to hold the corresponding frequencies (freqList).

Main *Level 0*

```
Open dataFile (and verify success)
Get charList
Zero out freqList
Read inputChar from dataFile
WHILE NOT EOF on dataFile
    Scan list for inputChar
    IF found
        Increment appropriate element of freqList
    Read inputChar from dataFile
Print charList and freqList
```

Get CharList (parameters discussed later) *Level 1*

```
Set counter = 0
Read a character ch
WHILE ch isn't '#'
    Set charList[counter] = ch
    Increment counter
    Read ch
Set length = counter
```

PROBLEM-SOLVING CASE STUDY cont'd.

Because you don't know how many characters are in the list, charList has to be large enough to hold all the characters in the character set except one. ('#' is a sentinel value and is not counted.) When charList has been read, counter holds the length of the array; that is, when the list is searched for a character, only those components from charList[0] through charList[length−1] need be examined. This is another example of subarray processing. Note that counter is being used both as a counter and as an index.

Zero FreqList (parameters discussed later)

FOR index going from 0 through length−1
    Set freqList[index] = 0

Scan List (parameters discussed later)

Set index = 0
WHILE index < length AND inputChar != charList[index]
    Increment index
Set found = (index < length)

The algorithm for the Scan List module is called a *sequential search*. We start with the first array element and step through the array one element at a time. We continue searching until we either find the item we're looking for or reach the end of the array. If found is TRUE, the value of index is the position in array charList where inputChar was found. If inputChar is not in the array, then index becomes equal to length, and found is FALSE.

The While condition assumes the use of short-circuit evaluation of logical expressions (Chapter 5). If index equals length, the condition is immediately determined to be FALSE. The second half of the condition is not evaluated (which would reference a nonexistent array element, charList[length]).

Increment FreqList

Increment freqList[index] by 1

Print CharList and FreqList (parameters discussed later)

> FOR index going from 0 through length–1
>   Print charList[index], " occurred ", freqList[index], " time(s)"

Because the Increment FreqList module is only one simple statement, it is coded directly in the main module. Let's look at the interfaces of the other functions.

Function	In	Out	Comments
GetCharList		charList length	length will be last value of counter.
ZeroFreqList	length	freqList	
ScanList	charList length inputChar	found index	If found is TRUE, index gives place found.
Print	freqList charList length		

Remember that any variables in the *Out* column must be reference parameters. Those listed only in the *In* column, except for arrays, should be value parameters. Because C++ always passes arrays by reference, an array listed only in the *In* column should be declared as const in the formal parameter list.

Module Structure Chart:

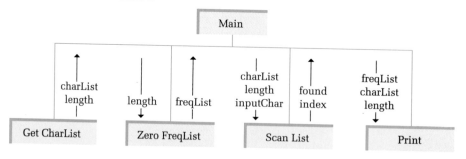

PROBLEM-SOLVING CASE STUDY cont'd.

```
//*****************************************************************
// CharCount program
// This program counts the frequency of occurrence of certain
// characters in a text file.  The specific characters to be
// counted are read from the standard input device
//*****************************************************************
#include <iostream.h>
#include <iomanip.h>       // For setw()
#include <fstream.h>       // For file I/O
#include "bool.h"          // For Boolean type

const int  MAX_LENGTH = 256;       // Max. number of different
                                   //    characters
const char SENTINEL_CHAR = '#';    // Marks the end of the character
                                   //    list

void GetCharList( char[], int& );
void Print( const int[], const char[], int );
void ScanList( const char[], int, char, int&, Boolean& );
void ZeroFreqList( int[], int );

int main()
{
    char      charList[MAX_LENGTH];   // Chars to be counted
    int       freqList[MAX_LENGTH];   // Frequency counts
    int       length;                 // Number of chars to count
    int       index;                  // Position of a located char
    char      inputChar;              // Temporary char
    Boolean   found;                  // True if char found in list
    ifstream  dataFile;               // Input file to be analyzed

    dataFile.open("text.dat");
    if ( !dataFile )
    {
        cout << "** Can't open input file **" << endl;
        return 1;
    }

    GetCharList(charList, length);
    ZeroFreqList(freqList, length);

    // Count occurrences of desired characters in text on dataFile

    dataFile.get(inputChar);              // Don't skip whitespace
    while (dataFile)                      // While not EOF...
    {
```

```
                    // Invariant (prior to test):
                    //     For all previous values of inputChar,
                    //     freqList contains the counts of characters
                    //     that were found in charList

            ScanList(charList, length, inputChar, index, found);
            if (found)
                freqList[index]++;
            dataFile.get(inputChar);              // Don't skip whitespace
        }

        Print(freqList, charList, length);
        return 0;
    }


//******************************************************************

void GetCharList( /* out */ char charList[],     // List of chars
                  /* out */ int& length     )    // Length of list

// Reads the list of characters from standard input
// until SENTINEL_CHAR is encountered

// Postcondition:
//     User has been prompted to enter the list of characters
//     && length == number of characters in the list
//     && charList[0..length-1] contain the input characters
// Note:
//     If the user enters more than MAX_LENGTH characters
//     or types duplicate characters, the effect of this
//     function is undefined
{
    int counter;     // Index variable
    char ch;         // Used for reading

    cout << "Please enter your list of characters." << endl
         << "Enter at most " << MAX_LENGTH << " characters," << endl
         << "and terminate the list with a pound sign (#)." << endl;
    counter = 0;
    cin.get(ch);
    while (ch != SENTINEL_CHAR)
    {
                    // Invariant (prior to test):
                    //     charList[0..counter-1] contain the
                    //         first "counter" input values
                    //     && No previous value of ch was SENTINEL_CHAR
```

```
            charList[counter] = ch;
            counter++;
            cin.get(ch);
        }
        length = counter;
    }


//***************************************************************

void ZeroFreqList( /* out */ int freqList[],     // Zeroed list
                   /* in */  int length      )   // Length of list

// Zeros out the first "length" positions of freqList

// Precondition:
//      length <= MAX_LENGTH
// Postcondition:
//      All freqList[0..length-1] == 0

{
    int index;   // Loop control and index variable

    for (index = 0; index < length; index++)

            // Invariant (prior to test):
            //      freqList[0..index-1] == 0
            //   && 0 <= index <= length

        freqList[index] = 0;
}

//***************************************************************
```

This is an example of a search (next chapter)

```
void ScanList(
          /* in */  const char charList[],   // List of chars
          /* in */  int         length,      // Length of char list
          /* in */  char        inputChar,   // Character to be checked
          /* out */ int&        index,       // Index of match
          /* out */ Boolean&    found    )   // False if no match

// Searches charList for inputChar, returning the index
// in charList if inputChar was found

// Precondition:
//      length <= MAX_LENGTH
//   && charList[0..length-1] are assigned  &&  inputChar is assigned
```

```
// Postcondition:
//     IF inputChar is in charList
//           found == TRUE  &&  charList[index] == inputChar
//     ELSE
//           found == FALSE  &&  index is undefined

{
    index = 0;
    while (index < length && inputChar != charList[index])

            // Invariant (prior to test):
            //     inputChar is not in charList[0..index-1]
            //  && 0 <= index <= length

        index++;

    // Assert:
    //     (index == length  &&  inputChar is not
    //                            in charList[0..length-1])
    //  OR (index < length  &&  inputChar == charList[index])

    found = (index < length);
}

//****************************************************************

void Print(
        /* in */ const int  freqList[],    // List of char counts
        /* in */ const char charList[],    // List of chars counted
        /* in */ int        length     )   // Length of lists

// Prints character list with associated frequencies

// Precondition:
//     length <= MAX_LENGTH
//  && freqList[0..length-1] are assigned
//  && charList[0..length-1] are assigned
// Postcondition:
//     charList[0..length-1] and freqList[0..length-1] have been
//     printed

{
    int index;   // Loop control and index variable
```

```
for (index = 0; index < length; index++)

        // Invariant (prior to test):
        //      charList[0..index-1] and freqList[0..index-1]
        //          have been printed
        //   && 0 <= index <= length

    cout << charList[index] << " occurred "
         << setw(3) << freqList[index] << " time(s)" << endl;
}
```

Let's do a partial code walk-through of this program with the following data. The characters to be counted are

    a e i o u

and the text is

    Roses are red,
    violets are blue.
    If I can learn C++,
    so can you.

Here are the contents of the arrays after functions `GetCharList` and `ZeroFreqList` are executed:

charList[0] is 'a'	freqList[0] is 0	length is 5
charList[1] is 'e'	freqList[1] is 0	
charList[2] is 'i'	freqList[2] is 0	
charList[3] is 'o'	freqList[3] is 0	
charList[4] is 'u'	freqList[4] is 0	

We assume that the control structure of the reading loop in the `main` function is correct and look at the three inner statements:

```
1. ScanList(charList, length, inputChar, index, found);
2. if (found)
        freqList[index]++;
3. dataFile.get(inputChar);
```

The following table shows the partial walk-through. The number to the left of the period refers to one of the three statements listed above, and the number to the right of the period refers to the number of times the statement has been executed.

Statement	Character	index	found	freqList
Priming read	R	?	?	
1.1	R	?	FALSE	
2.1	R	?	FALSE	
3.1	o	?	FALSE	
1.2	o	3	TRUE	
2.2	o	3	TRUE	freqList[3] is 1
3.2	s	3	TRUE	
1.3	s	?	FALSE	
2.3	s	?	FALSE	
3.3	e	?	FALSE	
1.4	e	1	TRUE	
2.4	e	1	TRUE	freqList[1] is 1
.				
.				
.				
3.8	e	?	FALSE	
1.9	e	1	TRUE	
2.9	e	1	TRUE	freqList[1] is 2

The output from the program using this data would be as follows:

```
a occurred  5 time(s)
e occurred  7 time(s)
i occurred  1 time(s)
o occurred  4 time(s)
u occurred  2 time(s)
```

At first glance, the output does not seem right. If you count the characters by hand, you come up with three occurrences of 'i'. Note, however, that two of these are of 'I', not 'i'. If we want to count uppercase letters and lowercase letters as the same, we have to convert one of them (using, for example, the tolower or toupper standard library functions).

Testing: The test data for this program should include cases in which (1) there are no characters to be counted and (2) there is no text to count.

PROBLEM-SOLVING CASE STUDY

Frequency of All Characters

Problem: Count the frequency of occurrence of *all* the characters in a sample of text.

Input: A file of text (`dataFile`).

Output: Each printable character in the character set, followed by the number of times it occurred.

Discussion: In the previous case study, the CharCount program implements an algorithm that not only uses parallel arrays and subarray processing, but parallels the way in which a human would do the problem. There is nothing wrong with this solution except that we are not taking advantage of all the information on hand. By changing the problem statement slightly, we can approach the solution from another angle, this time keeping in mind the features of C++.

In a sense, C++ already has a built-in list of all the characters—type `char`. C++ also allows us to use any integral type as an index type. So, instead of searching a list of characters and counting them in a parallel array, we let C++ do all that by using the characters themselves as the indices in the counting array. Here's how it works.

First, we define a named constant NUM_CHARS as the number of characters in the character set (128 for ASCII, 256 for EBCDIC). Focusing on ASCII, we use the following declarations:

```
const int NUM_CHARS = 128;    // Number of chars in ASCII char set

int freqCount[NUM_CHARS];     // Frequency counts
```

The indices for `freqCount` range from 0 through 127. This range corresponds to the internal representations of the 128 ASCII characters. (Recall from Chapter 10 that the character 'A' is stored internally as the integer 65, 'B' is stored as 66, and so forth.) If we input the character 'A' into the variable inputChar, the statement

```
freqCount[inputChar]++;
```

PROBLEM-SOLVING CASE STUDY cont'd.

increments the value in freqCount[65]. If we were to take a snapshot of the freqCount array while the program was executing, we might see the array contents shown in Figure 11-11. The interpretation is that our program has encountered three A's in the input file, no B's, two C's, and so on.

In Chapter 10, we mentioned that the ASCII and EBCDIC character sets have nonprinting characters. We want to count only those characters that are printable. Therefore, not all of the array elements in freqCount will be used. If we define the named constants MIN_CHAR and MAX_CHAR as the first and last printable characters in the character set, only freqCount[MIN_CHAR] through freqCount[MAX_CHAR] will be used.

	ASCII		*EBCDIC*	
	Character	*Internal Representation*	*Character*	*Internal Representation*
MIN_CHAR	' '	32	' '	64
MAX_CHAR	'~'	126	'9'	249

freqCount[MIN_CHAR] would be the counter for blanks in ASCII and EBCDIC.
freqCount[MAX_CHAR] would be the counter for '~'s in ASCII, and '9's in EBCDIC.
freqCount[inputChar] would be the counter for whatever character inputChar contained.

■ FIGURE 11-11
freqCount Array

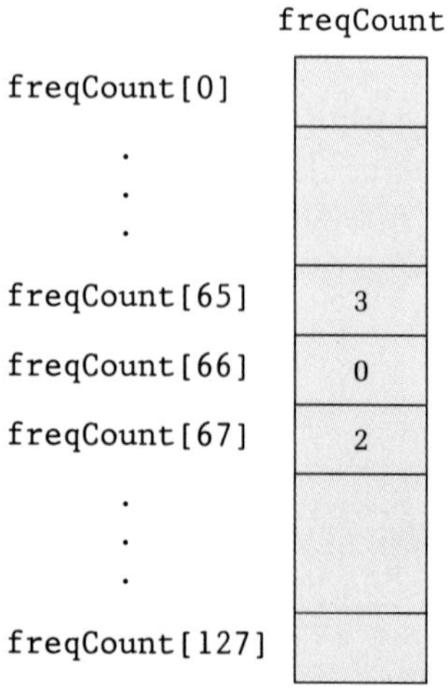

Let's look at how this problem is simplified by the fact that the index itself has meaning (semantic content).

Data Structures: An array of frequencies (freqCount) indexed by the characters being counted.

Main   *Level 0*

```
Open dataFile (and verify success)
Zero out freqCount
Read inputChar from dataFile
WHILE NOT EOF on dataFile
    IF inputChar is a printable character
        Increment freqCount[inputChar] by 1
    Read inputChar from dataFile
Print characters and frequencies
```

Zero FreqCount (Out: freqCount)   *Level 1*

```
FOR index going from MIN_CHAR through MAX_CHAR
    Set freqCount[index] = 0
```

Is Printable (In: inputChar)

```
Use the standard library function isprint
```

Print Characters and Frequencies (In: freqCount)

```
FOR index going from MIN_CHAR through MAX_CHAR
    Print index, " occurred ", freqCount[index], " time(s)"
```

The Is Printable module can be implemented as a call to the library function isprint (available through the header file ctype.h), so we code the function call directly in the main module.

PROBLEM-SOLVING CASE STUDY *cont'd.*

Module Structure Chart:

```
//**********************************************************************
// CountAll program
// This program counts the frequency of occurrence of all printable
// characters in a text file.
//
// The program assumes use of the ASCII character set.  If your
// machine uses the EBCDIC character set, the constant definitions
// for NUM_CHARS, MIN_CHAR, and MAX_CHAR must be modified as shown
// in the comments at that location
//**********************************************************************
#include <iostream.h>
#include <iomanip.h>      // For setw()
#include <fstream.h>      // For file I/O
#include <ctype.h>        // For isprint()
#include "bool.h"         // For Boolean type

const int  NUM_CHARS = 128;      // Number of chars in ASCII char set
const char MIN_CHAR = ' ';       // First printable char (ASCII)
const char MAX_CHAR = '~';       // Last printable char (ASCII)

// Substitute the following if your machine uses EBCDIC:
// const int  NUM_CHARS = 256;   // Number of chars in EBCDIC
// const char MIN_CHAR = ' ';    // First printable char (EBCDIC)
// const char MAX_CHAR = '9';    // Last printable char (EBCDIC)

void Print( const int[] );
void ZeroFreqCount( int[] );

int main()
{
    int      freqCount[NUM_CHARS];   // Frequency counts
    char     inputChar;              // Temporary character
    ifstream dataFile;               // Input file to be analyzed
```

```cpp
    dataFile.open("text.dat");
    if ( !dataFile )
    {
        cout << "** Can't open input file **" << endl;
        return 1;
    }

    ZeroFreqCount(freqCount);

    // Keep reading and counting until no more characters

    dataFile.get(inputChar);                    // Don't skip whitespace
    while (dataFile)                            // While not EOF...
    {
            // Invariant (prior to test):
            //      For all previous values of inputChar,
            //      freqCount contains the counts of printable chars

        if (isprint(inputChar))
            freqCount[inputChar]++;
        dataFile.get(inputChar);                // Don't skip whitespace
    }

    Print(freqCount);
    return 0;
}

//****************************************************************

void ZeroFreqCount( /* out */ int freqCount[] )    // Zeroed list

// Zeros out positions MIN_CHAR through MAX_CHAR of freqCount

// Postcondition:
//     freqCount[MIN_CHAR..MAX_CHAR] == 0

{
    char index;   // Loop control and index variable

    for (index = MIN_CHAR; index <= MAX_CHAR; index++)

            // Invariant (prior to test):
            //      freqCount[MIN_CHAR..index-1] == 0
            //   && MIN_CHAR <= index <= MAX_CHAR+1

        freqCount[index] = 0;
}
```

PROBLEM-SOLVING CASE STUDY cont'd.

```
//*********************************************************************

void Print( /* in */ const int freqCount[] )   // List of char counts

// Prints each character and its frequency (if nonzero)

// Precondition:
//      freqCount[MIN_CHAR..MAX_CHAR] are assigned
// Postcondition:
//      For all i, where MIN_CHAR <= i <= MAX_CHAR,
//          IF freqCount[i] > 0
//              freqCount[i] and the char equivalent of i
//              have been printed

{
    char index;   // Loop control and index variable

    for (index = MIN_CHAR; index <= MAX_CHAR; index++)

            // Invariant (prior to test):
            //      For all i, where MIN_CHAR <= i <= index-1,
            //          IF freqCount[i] > 0
            //              freqCount[i] and the char equivalent of i
            //              have been printed
            //   && MIN_CHAR <= index <= MAX_CHAR+1

        if (freqCount[index] > 0)
            cout << index << " occurred "
                << setw(3) << freqCount[index] << " time(s)"
                << endl;
}
```

See how much simpler the solution becomes when we take advantage of the fact that the character itself can be the index to its own frequency counter? In Case Study Follow-Up Question 3 at the end of this chapter, you are asked to modify this program to handle the case in which a specified subset of the characters is counted (as was done in the previous case study).

Using the same input file as was used in the previous problem,

```
Roses are red,
violets are blue.
If I can learn C++,
so can you.
```

we get the following output from the CountAll program:

```
  occurred  10 time(s)
+ occurred   2 time(s)
, occurred   2 time(s)
. occurred   2 time(s)
C occurred   1 time(s)
I occurred   2 time(s)
R occurred   1 time(s)
a occurred   5 time(s)
b occurred   1 time(s)
c occurred   2 time(s)
d occurred   1 time(s)
e occurred   7 time(s)
f occurred   1 time(s)
i occurred   1 time(s)
l occurred   3 time(s)
n occurred   3 time(s)
o occurred   4 time(s)
r occurred   4 time(s)
s occurred   4 time(s)
t occurred   1 time(s)
u occurred   2 time(s)
v occurred   1 time(s)
y occurred   1 time(s)
```

Testing: In order to test this program, we must verify that it counts characters correctly. To do so, we create a data file that contains all the printable characters at least once and some of them more than once.

TESTING AND DEBUGGING

We add a word of caution about the choice of looping structure to use when processing arrays. The most common error in processing arrays is an out-of-bounds array index. That is, the program attempts to access a component using an index that is either less than zero or greater than the array size minus one. For example, given the declarations

```
char line[100];
int  counter;
```

the following For statement would print the 100 elements of the line array and then print a 101st value—the value that resides in memory immediately beyond the end of the array.

```
for (counter = 0; counter <= 100; counter++)
    cout << line[counter];
```

This example is easy to debug; 101 characters get printed instead of 100. The loop test should be `counter < 100`. But you won't always use a simple For statement in accessing arrays. Suppose we read data into the `line` array in another part of the program. Let's use a While statement that reads to the newline character:

```
counter = 0;
cin.get(ch);
while (ch != '\n')
{
    line[counter] = ch;
    counter++;
    cin.get(ch);
}
```

This code seems reasonable enough, but what if the input contains a line with more than 100 characters? After the hundredth character is read and stored into the array, the loop continues to execute with the array index out of bounds. Characters are stored into memory locations past the end of the array, wiping out other data values (or even machine language instructions in the program!).

The moral is: When processing arrays, give special attention to the design of loop termination conditions. Always ask yourself if there is any possibility that the loop could keep running after the last array component has been processed.

Whenever an array index goes out of bounds, the first suspicion should be a loop that fails to terminate properly. The second thing to check is any array access involving an index that is based on input data or a calculation. When an array index is input as data, then a data validation check is an absolute necessity.

Testing and Debugging Hints

1. When an individual component of an array is accessed, the index must be within the range 0 through the array size minus one. Attempting to use an index value that is not within this range causes your program to access memory locations outside the array.
2. The individual components of an array are themselves variables of the component type. When values are stored into an array, they should either be of the component type or be explicitly converted to the component type; otherwise, implicit type coercion occurs.

3. C++ does not allow aggregate operations on arrays. There is no aggregate assignment, aggregate comparison, aggregate I/O, or aggregate arithmetic. You must write code to do all of these operations, one array element at a time.

4. Omitting the size of an array in its declaration is permitted only in two cases: (1) when an array is declared as a formal parameter and (2) when an array is initialized in its declaration. In all other declarations, you *must* specify the size of the array with a constant integer expression.

5. If an array parameter is incoming-only, declare the formal parameter as const to prevent the function from modifying the parameter accidentally.

6. Don't pass an individual array component as an actual parameter when the function expects to receive the base address of an entire array.

7. The size of an array is determined at compile time, but its actual length is determined at run time. This means that an array must be declared to be as large as it could ever be for the particular problem. Subarray processing is used to process only the components that have data in them.

8. Pass the length as well as the name of the array to functions when subarray processing is to take place.

SUMMARY

In addition to being able to create user-defined atomic data types, we can create structured data types. In a structured data type, a name is given to a group of components that have a specific arrangement. With many structured types, the group can be accessed as a whole, or each individual component can be accessed separately.

The one-dimensional array gives a name to a sequential group of components. Each component can be accessed by its relative position within the group, and each component is a variable of the component type. To access a particular component, we give the name of the array and an index that specifies which component of the group we want. The index can be an expression of any integral type, as long as it evaluates to an integer from 0 through the array size minus one. Array components can be accessed in random order directly, or they can be accessed sequentially by stepping through the index values one at a time.

QUICK CHECK

1. Declare an array named `quiz` that contains 12 components indexed by the integers 0 through 11. The component type is Boolean. (Assume that type `Boolean` has already been defined.) (pp. 594–596)
2. If an array is to hold the number of correct answers given by students to each question on a 20-question true/false quiz, what data type should be used for the components of the array? (pp. 594–596)
3. Given the declarations

   ```
   const int MAX_LENGTH = 30;

   char firstName[MAX_LENGTH];
   ```

   write an assignment statement that stores 'A' into the first component of array `firstName`. (pp. 596–599)
4. Given the declarations in Question 3, write an output statement that prints the value of the fourteenth component of array `firstName`. (pp. 596–599)
5. Given the declarations in Question 3, write a For statement that fills array `firstName` with blanks. (pp. 599–601)
6. Declare a five-element `int` array named `oddNums`, and initialize it (in its declaration) to contain the first five odd integers, starting with 1. (pp. 601–602)
7. Give the function heading for a void function named `SomeFunc`, where
   a. `SomeFunc` has a single parameter: a `float` array `x` that is an Inout parameter.
   b. `SomeFunc` has a single parameter: a `float` array `x` that is an In parameter.
   (pp. 608–610)
8. Given the declarations in Question 3 and the following program fragment, which reads characters into array `firstName` until a blank is encountered, write a For statement that prints out the portion of the array that is filled with input data. (pp. 610–613)

   ```
   length = 0;
   do
   {
       cin.get(letter);
       if (letter != ' ')
       {
           firstName[length] = letter;
           length++;
       }
   } while (letter != ' ');
   ```

9. Declare two parallel arrays indexed by the integers 0 through 99. One of the arrays will contain student ID numbers (type `long`); the other will consist of values of the enumeration type defined by

   ```
   enum GenderType {FEMALE, MALE};
   ```

   (pp. 610–613)
10. Define an enumeration type for the musical notes A through G (excluding sharps and flats). Then declare an array in which the index values represent musical

notes, and the component type is float. Finally, show an example of a For loop that prints out the contents of the array. (pp. 610–613)

Answers
1. `Boolean quiz[12];`
2. `int (or perhaps short)`
3. `firstName[0] = 'A';`
4. `cout << firstName[13];`
5. ```
for (index = 0; index < MAX_LENGTH; index++)
     firstName[index] = ' ';
```
6. `int oddNums[5] = {1, 3, 5, 7, 9};`
7. a. `void SomeFunc( float x[] )`
   b. `void SomeFunc( const float x[] )`
8. ```
for (index = 0; index < length; index++)
     cout << firstName[index];
```
9. ```
long number[100];   // Student numbers for 100 students
GenderType gender[100];   // Genders for the same 100 students
```
10. ```
enum NoteType {A, B, C, D, E, F, G};
float noteVal[7];
NoteType index;

for (index = A; index <= G; index = NoteType(index + 1))
     cout << noteVal[index] << endl;
```

EXAM PREPARATION EXERCISES

1. Every component in an array must have the same type, and the number of components is fixed at compile time. (True or False?)
2. The components of an array must be of an integral type. (True or False?)
3. Declare one-dimensional arrays according to the following descriptions.
   a. A 24-element float array
   b. A 500-element int array
   c. A 50-element double precision floating point array
   d. A 10-element char array
4. Write a code fragment to do the following tasks:
   a. Declare a constant named CLASS_SIZE representing the number of students in a class.
   b. Declare an array quizAvg of size CLASS_SIZE whose components will contain quiz score averages (floating point).
5. Write a code fragment to do the following tasks:
   a. Declare an enumeration type BirdType made up of bird names.
   b. Declare an int array sightings that is to be indexed by BirdType.
6. Given the declarations

```
const int MAX_LENGTH = 100;

enum Colors
{
     BLUE, GREEN, GOLD, ORANGE, PURPLE, RED, WHITE, BLACK
};
```

For practice

```
int      count[8];
Colors cIndex;                      // Index for count array
Colors rainbow[MAX_LENGTH];
int      rIndex;                    // Index for rainbow array
```

write code fragments to do the following tasks:
a. Set count to all zeros.
b. Set rainbow to all WHITE.
c. Count the number of times GREEN appears in rainbow.
d. Print the value in count indexed by BLUE.
e. Total the values in count.

7. What is the output of the following program? The data for the program is given below it.

```
#include <iostream.h>

int main()
{
    int a[100];
    int b[100];
    int j;
    int m;
    int sumA = 0;
    int sumB = 0;
    int sumDiff = 0;

    cin >> m;
    for (j = 0; j < m; j++)
    {
        cin >> a[j] >> b[j];
        sumA = sumA + a[j];
        sumB = sumB + b[j];
        sumDiff = sumDiff + (a[j] - b[j]);
    }
    for (j = m - 1; j >= 0; j--)
        cout << a[j] << ' ' << b[j] << ' '
             << a[j] - b[j] << endl;
    cout << endl;
    cout << sumA << ' ' << sumB << ' ' << sumDiff << endl;
    return 0;
}
```

Data:
```
    5
11 15
19 14
 4  2
17  6
 1  3
```

8. A person wrote the following code fragment, intending to print 10 20 30 40.

```
int arr[4] = {10, 20, 30, 40};
int index;
```

out of bounds ary [4]

```
for (index = 1; index <= 4; index++)
    cout << ' ' << arr[index];
```

Instead, the code printed 20 30 40 24835. Explain the reason for this output.

9. Given the declarations

```
int sample[8];
int i;
int k;
```

show the contents of the array `sample` after the following code segment is executed. Use a question mark to indicate any undefined values in the array.

```
for (k = 0; k < 8; k++)
    sample[k] = 10 - k;
```

10. Using the same declarations given for Exercise 9, show the contents of the array `sample` after the following code segment is executed.

```
for (i = 0; i < 8; i++)
    if (i <= 3)
        sample[i] = 1;
    else
        sample[i] = -1;
```

11. Using the same declarations given for Exercise 9, show the contents of the array `sample` after the following code segment is executed.

```
for (k = 0; k < 8; k++)
    if (k % 2 == 0)
        sample[k] = k;
    else
        sample[k] = k + 100;
```

PROGRAMMING WARM-UP EXERCISES

Use the following declarations in Exercises 1–8. Assume the data type `Boolean` already has been defined. You may declare any other variables that you need.

```
const int MAX_STUD = 100;   // Max. number of students

Boolean failing[MAX_STUD];
Boolean passing[MAX_STUD];
int      grade;
int      length;
int      score[MAX_STUD];
```

1. Write a C++ function that initializes all components of `failing` to FALSE. Pass `failing` and `length` as parameters.
2. Write a C++ function that has `failing`, `score`, and `length` as parameters. Set the components of `failing` to TRUE wherever the parallel value of `score` is less than 60.
3. Write a C++ function that has `passing`, `score`, and `length` as parameters. Set the components of `passing` to TRUE wherever the parallel value of `score` is greater than or equal to 60.
4. Write a C++ value-returning function `PassTally` that takes `passing` and `length` as parameters, and returns the count of components in `passing` that are TRUE.
5. Write a C++ value-returning function `Error` that takes `passing`, `failing`, and `length` as parameters. `Error` returns TRUE if any parallel components are the same.
6. Write a C++ function that takes `score`, `passing`, `grade`, and `length` as parameters. The function should set the components of `passing` to TRUE wherever the parallel value of `score` is greater than `grade`.
7. Write a C++ value-returning function that takes `grade`, `length`, and `score` as parameters. The function should return the count of values in `score` that are greater than or equal to `grade`.
8. Write a C++ function that takes `score` and `length` as parameters, and reverses the order of the components in `score`; that is, `score[0]` goes into `score[length-1]`, `score[1]` goes into `score[length-2]`, and so on.

PROGRAMMING PROBLEMS

1. The local baseball team is computerizing its records. You are to write a program that computes batting averages. There are 20 players on the team, identified by the numbers 1 through 20. Their batting records are coded in a file as follows. Each line contains four numbers: the player's identification number and the number of hits, walks, and outs he or she made in a particular game. Here is a sample:

   3 2 1 1

   The example above indicates that during a game, player number 3 was at bat four times and made 2 hits, 1 walk, and 1 out. For each player there are several records in the file. Each player's batting average is computed by adding the player's total number of hits and dividing by the total number of times at bat. A walk does not count as either a hit or a time at bat when the batting average is being calculated. Your program prints a table showing each player's identification number, batting average, and number of walks. (Be careful: The players' identification numbers are 1 through 20, but C++ array indices start at 0.)

2. An advertising company wants to send a letter to all its clients announcing a new fee schedule. The clients' names are on several different lists in the company. The various lists are merged to form one file, `clientNames`, but obviously, the company does not want to send a letter twice to anyone.

   Write a program that removes any names appearing on the list more than once. On each line of data, there is a four-digit code number, followed by a blank and then the client's name. For example, Amalgamated Steel is listed as

   0231 Amalgamated Steel

Your program should output each client's code and name, but no duplicates should be printed.

3. Write a program that calculates the mean and standard deviation of integers stored in a file. The output should be of type `float` and should be properly labeled and formatted to two decimal places. The formula for calculating the mean of a series of integers is to add all the numbers, then divide by the number of integers. Expressed in mathematical terms, the mean $\overline{X}$ of N numbers $X_1, X_2, \ldots X_N$ is

$$\overline{X} = \frac{\sum\limits_{i=1}^{N} X_i}{N}$$

To calculate the standard deviation of a series of integers, subtract the mean from each integer (you may get a negative number) and square the result, add all these squared differences, divide by the number of integers minus one, then take the square root of the result. Expressed in mathematical terms, the standard deviation S is

$$S = \sqrt{\frac{\sum\limits_{i=1}^{N} (X_i - \overline{X})^2}{N-1}}$$

4. One of the local banks is gearing up for a big advertising campaign and would like to see how long its customers are waiting for service at drive-up windows. Several employees have been asked to keep accurate records for the 24-hour drive-up service. The collected information, which is read from a file, consists of the time when the customer arrived in hours, minutes, and seconds; the time when the customer actually was served; and the ID number of the teller. Write a program that does the following:
   a. Reads in the wait data.
   b. Computes the wait time in seconds.
   c. Calculates the mean, standard deviation (defined in Programming Problem 3), and range.
   d. Prints a single-page summary showing the values calculated in part c.

Input:

The first data line contains a title.

The remaining lines each contain a teller ID, an arrival time, and a service time.
   The times are broken up into integer hours, minutes, and seconds according to a 24-hour clock.

Processing:

Calculate the mean and the standard deviation.

Locate the shortest wait time and the longest wait time for any number of records up to 100.

Output:

The input data (echo print).

The title.

The following values, all properly labeled: number of records, mean, standard deviation, and range (minimum and maximum).

5. Your history professor has so many students in her class that she has trouble determining how well the class does on exams. She has discovered that you are a computer whiz and has asked you to write a program to perform some simple statistical analyses on exam scores. Your program must work for any class size up to 100 ($0 < N \leq 100$). Write and test a computer program that does the following:

a. Reads the test grades from file inData.

b. Calculates the class mean, standard deviation (defined in Programming Problem 3), and percentage of the test scores falling in the ranges <10, 10–19, 20–29, 30–39, ... , 80–89, and ≥90.

c. Prints a summary showing the mean and the standard deviation, as well as a histogram showing the percentage distribution of test scores.

Input:

The first data line contains the number of exams to be analyzed and a title for the report.

The remaining lines have ten test scores on each line until the last, and one to ten scores on the last. The scores are all integers.

Output:

The input data as they are read.

A report consisting of the title that was read from data, the number of scores, the mean, the standard deviation (all clearly labeled), and the histogram.

6. A small postal system ships packages within your state. Acceptance of parcels is subject to the following constraints:

a. Parcels are not to exceed a weight of 50 pounds.

b. Parcels are not to exceed 3 feet in length, width, or depth, and may not have a combined length and girth exceeding 6 feet. (The girth of a package is the circumference of the package around its two smallest sides; the mathematical formula is

$$girth = 2 * (s1 + s2 + s3 - largest)$$

where *largest* is the largest of the three parcel dimensions, $s1$, $s2$, and $s3$.)

Your program should process a transaction file containing one entry for each box mailed during the week. Each entry contains a transaction number, followed by the weight of the box and its dimensions (the dimensions can be in any order). The program should print the transaction number, weight, and postal charge for all accepted packages, and the transaction number and weight for all rejected packages. At the end of the report, the program must print the number of packages processed and the number rejected.

Input:

Parcel post table—weight and cost (contains 25 pairs of values). This table should be stored in two one-dimensional arrays. You can determine the postal cost of each parcel by first searching the weight array and then using the corresponding element in the cost array. If a package weight falls between weight categories in the table, your program should use the cost for the higher weight.

Transaction file—transaction number, weight, and three dimensions for an arbitrary number of transactions. Assume that all weights are whole numbers, and that all dimensions are given to the nearest inch.

Output:

First line—appropriate headings.

Next *n* records—transaction number, whether accepted or rejected; weight; and cost.

Last line—number of packages processed, number of packages rejected.

7. The final exam in your psychology class consists of 30 multiple-choice questions. Your instructor says that if you write the program to grade the finals, you won't have to take the exam.

Input:

The first data line contains the key to the exam. The correct answers are the first 30 characters; they are followed by an integer number that says how many students took the exam (call it *n*).

The next *n* lines contain student answers in the first 30 character positions, followed by the student's name in the next 10 character positions.

Output:

For each student—the student's name; followed by the number of correct answers; followed by PASS if the number correct is 60 percent or better, or FAIL otherwise.

CASE STUDY FOLLOW-UP

1. For the Comparison of Two Lists case study, rewrite the program by eliminating the assumption that the two lists are of equal length. If one list is longer than the other, print a message indicating which is longer, and stop the comparison.

2. In the Frequency of Certain Characters case study, the GetCharList function declares a formal parameter charList. Would it be all right to prefix the declaration of charList with the word const? Explain.

3. Modify the CountAll program so that its output is the same as the CharCount program; that is, print the frequency of occurrence of a specified list of characters.

12

Applied Arrays: Lists and Strings

GOALS

- To be able to search a list for a component with a given value.
- To be able to sort the components of a list into ascending or descending order.
- To be able to insert a value into an ordered list.
- To be able to search an ordered list using the binary search algorithm.
- To be able to declare and use character strings.

Chapter 11 introduced the concept of a one-dimensional array, a data structure that is a collection of components of the same type given a single name. In general, a one-dimensional array is a structure used to represent a list of items. In this chapter, we examine some common algorithms that are applied again and again to data stored as a list in a one-dimensional array. These are implemented as general-purpose functions that can be modified easily to work with many kinds of lists.

We also consider the *string*, a special kind of one-dimensional array that is used to process character information like words or names. We use strings to rewrite the `GetMonth` function in the BirthdayReminder program, as promised in Chapter 10. We conclude with some case studies that make use of the algorithms developed in this chapter.

 # Lists and List Algorithms

As defined in Chapter 11, a one-dimensional array is a data structure that consists of a fixed number of homogeneous components. By *homogeneous* we mean that all the components are of the same data type. One use for an array is to store a list of values. We noted that a list may contain fewer values than the number of places reserved in the array. We used a variable `length` to keep track of the number of values currently stored in the array, and we employed subarray processing in the case studies to prevent processing array components that were not part of the list of values. That is, the number of places in the array is fixed, but the number of values in the list stored there may vary.

For a moment, let's think of the concept of a list not in terms of arrays but as a separate data type. We can define a **list** as a varying-length, linear collection of homogeneous components. That's quite a mouthful. By *linear* we mean that each component (except the first) has a unique component that comes before it and each component (except the last) has a unique component that comes after it. The **length** of a list—the number of values currently stored in the list—can vary during the execution of the program.

List   A variable-length, linear collection of homogeneous components.
Length   The actual number of values stored in the list.

Like any data type, a list must have associated with it a set of allowable operations. What kinds of operations would we want to define for a list? Here are some possibilities: create a list, add an item to a list, delete an item from a list, print a list, search a list for a particular value, sort a list into alphabetical or numerical order, and so on. When we define a data type formally—by specifying its properties and the operations that preserve those properties—we are creating an *abstract data type*. In this chapter, we focus on lists and—later—strings as abstract data types. In Chapter 15, we explore the concept of abstract data types in greater detail.

Defining an abstract data type is a paper-and-pencil activity. We conceive of the properties we want the data values to have, and we choose a useful set of operations that manipulate those data values. But to use an abstract data type in a computer program, we must *implement* the abstract data type by using existing data types. In this chapter, we implement lists by using arrays. But an array is not the only way to implement a list. In Chapter 15, we introduce a new C++ type—the class—which is a tool for implementing abstract data types, and in Chapter 18, we show yet another way to implement lists.

Using arrays to implement lists is a widely used technique. The remainder of this section is devoted to developing a set of general-purpose operations for creating and manipulating lists that are stored in arrays.

Sequential Search in an Unordered List

In the CharCount program (Chapter 11), we used a function ScanList that searched through an array of characters looking for a particular one. Scanning a list to find a particular value is part of many everyday tasks. We scan the television guide to see what time a program is aired. We scan a course syllabus to locate the current reading assignment.

The ScanList function assumes that the values in the list are unordered—that is, they are not arranged in any particular order in the list, such as ascending order or descending order of value. Therefore, ScanList uses a *sequential search*—an algorithm in which we start at the beginning of the list and look at each item in sequence. We stop the search as soon as we find the item we are looking for (or when we reach the end of the list, concluding that the desired item is not present in the list).

We recode the ScanList function as a general-purpose sequential search function that can be used in any program that uses a list. To make it more general, we replace the problem-dependent variable names with general ones. The following declarations are assumed to be global declarations.

```
const int MAX_LENGTH = [    ];    // Maximum possible number of
                                  //    components needed
typedef [    ] ItemType;          // Type of each component
                                  //    (some simple type)
```

The general-purpose search function needs five parameters:

1. The array containing the list to be searched
2. The length of the list

3. The item being searched for
4. A flag telling whether or not the search was successful
5. The index indicating where the item was located (if found)

The array containing the list is made up of components of type ItemType.

We call the array list and the item being searched for item. The variables length, found, and index serve the same purposes here as they did in the ScanList function; that is, length is the number of filled components in the list array, found tells whether the item is in list, and index gives the location of item if it is present in list.

Note that the two outgoing parameters, index and found, are redundant. The index parameter would be sufficient because the calling routine could check to see if index is greater than length–1. If it is, then item was not found. We keep this redundancy, however, for clarity.

```
#include "bool.h"    // For Boolean type
    :
    :
void Search(
        /* in */ const ItemType list[],    // List to be searched
        /* in */       ItemType item,       // Item to be found
        /* in */       int      length,     // Length of list
        /* out */      int&     index,      // Location of item if found
        /* out */      Boolean& found  )    // True if item is found

// Searches list for item, returning the index
// of item if item was found

// Precondition:
//     length <= MAX_LENGTH
//  && list[0..length-1] are assigned  &&  item is assigned
// Postcondition:
//     IF item is in list
//         found == TRUE  &&  list[index] == item
//     ELSE
//         found == FALSE  &&  index == length

{
    index = 0;
    while (index < length && item != list[index])

            // Invariant (prior to test):
            //     item is not in list[0..index-1]
            //  && 0 <= index <= length

        index++;

    found = (index < length);
}
```

To see how the While loop and the subsequent assignment statement work, let's look at the two possibilities: either item is in the list or it is not. If item is in the list, the loop terminates when the expression index < length is TRUE and the expression item != list[index] is FALSE. After loop exit, the variable found is therefore assigned the value of the expression index < length, which is TRUE. On the other hand, if item is not in the list, the loop terminates when the expression index < length is FALSE—that is, when index becomes equal to length. Subsequently, the value assigned to found is FALSE (see Figure 12-1).

We can use this sequential search function in any program requiring a list search. In the form shown, it searches a list of ItemType components, provided that ItemType is an integral type. When the function is used with a list of floating point values, it must be modified so that the While statement tests for near equality (for the reasons discussed in Chapter 10). In the following statement, it is assumed that EPSILON is defined as a global constant.

```
while (index < length && fabs(item - list[index]) >= EPSILON)
    index++;
```

The sequential search algorithm finds the first occurrence of the searched-for item. How would we modify it to find the last occurrence? We would initialize index to length–1 and decrement index each time through the loop, stopping when we found the item we wanted or when index became –1.

Before we leave this search algorithm, let's introduce a variation that makes the program more efficient, although a little more complex. The

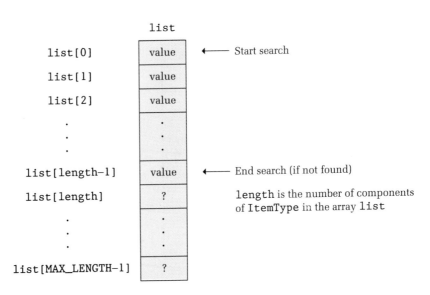

■ FIGURE 12-1

Generalized
Sequential Search

While loop contains a compound condition: it stops when it either finds `item` or reaches the end of the list. We can insert a copy of `item` into `list[length]`—that is, into the array component beyond the end of the list—as a sentinel. By doing so, we are guaranteed to find `item` in the list. The condition that checks for the end of the list (`index < length`) can then be eliminated (see Figure 12-2). Eliminating a condition saves the machine time that would be required to test it. In this case, we save time during every iteration of the loop, so the savings add up quickly. (The time saving comes at a cost, however. We sacrifice one array position for the sentinel.)

In storing a copy of `item` as a sentinel in `list[length]`, we assume that length is always less than `MAX_LENGTH`. We must document this assumption in the function precondition. Also, we must document the fact that `list[length]` is modified by the function (even though `list[length]` is assumed to contain meaningless data initially). As well, we remove the word `const` in the declaration of the `list` parameter so that the compiler lets us modify the array.

After the loop terminates, `found` can be set by checking to see if `index` is less than `length`. Function `Search2` incorporates all of these changes.

```
void Search2(
        /* inout */ ItemType  list[],     // List to be searched
        /* in */    ItemType  item,       // Item to be found
        /* in */    int       length,     // Length of list
        /* out */   int&      index,      // Location of item if found
        /* out */   Boolean&  found  )    // True if item is found
```

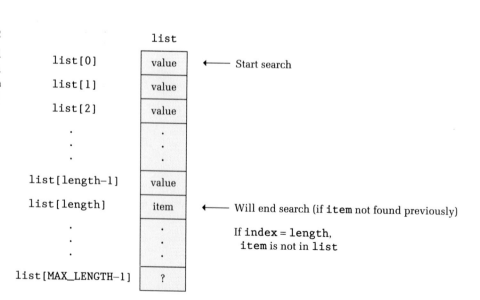

■ FIGURE 12-2

Generalized Sequential Search with Copy of `item` in `list[length]`

```
// Searches list for item, returning the index
// of item if item was found

// Precondition:
//      length < MAX_LENGTH
//   && list[0..length-1] are assigned  &&  item is assigned
// Postcondition:
//      list is the same as list@entry except that list[length] is
//         overwritten to aid in the search
//   && IF item is in list@entry
//           found == TRUE  &&  list[index] == item
//      ELSE
//           found == FALSE  &&  index == length

{
    index = 0;
    list[length] = item;             // Store item at position beyond
                                     //   end of list

    while (item != list[index])

            // Invariant (prior to test):
            //     item is not in list[0..index-1]

        index++;

    found = (index < length);
}
```

Sorting

The Search and Search2 algorithms both assume that the list to be searched is unordered. A drawback to searching an unordered list is that we must scan the entire list to discover that the search item is not there. Think what it would be like if your city telephone book contained people's names in random rather than alphabetical order. To look up Mary Anthony's phone number, you would have to start with the first name in the phone book and scan sequentially, page after page, until you found it. In the worst case, you might have to examine tens of thousands of names only to find out that Mary's name is not in the book.

Of course, telephone books *are* alphabetized, and the alphabetical ordering makes searching easier. If Mary Anthony's name is not in the book, you discover this fact quickly by starting with the A's and stopping the search as soon as you have passed the place where her name should be. In software development, arranging list items into order is a very common operation on lists. For example, we might want to put a list of stock numbers into either ascending or descending order, or we might want to put a list of words into alphabetical order. Arranging values into order is known as **sorting**.

Sorting   Arranging the components of a list into order (for instance, words into alphabetical order or numbers into ascending or descending order).

If you were given a sheet of paper with a column of twenty numbers on it and were asked to write the numbers in ascending order, you would probably:

1. Make a pass through the list, looking for the smallest number.
2. Write it on the paper in a second column.
3. Cross the number off the original list.
4. Repeat the process, always looking for the smallest number remaining in the original list.
5. Stop when all the numbers have been crossed off.

We can implement this algorithm directly in C++, but we need two arrays—one for the original list and a second for the ordered list. If the list is large, we might not have enough memory for two copies of it. Also, it is difficult to "cross off" an array component. We would have to simulate this with some dummy value like INT_MAX. We would set the value of the crossed-off variable to something that would not interfere with the processing of the rest of the components. A slight variation of this hand-done algorithm allows us to sort the components *in place*. This means that we do not have to use a second array; we can put a value into its proper place in the original list by having it swap places with the component that is there.

If our array is called list and contains length values, we can state the algorithm as follows:

FOR count going from 0 through length–2
   Find minimum value in list[count . . length–1]

   Swap minimum value with list[count]

Figure 12-3 illustrates how this algorithm works.

Observe that we make length–1 passes through the list, with count running from 0 through length–2. The loop does not need to be executed when count equals length–1 because the last value, list[length-1], is in its proper place after the preceding components have been sorted.

This sort, known as *straight selection*, belongs to a class of sorts called selection sorts. There are many types of sorting algorithms. Selection sorts are characterized by swapping one component into its proper place on each pass through the list. Swapping the contents of two variables—two components in an array—requires a temporary variable so that no values are lost (see Figure 12-4).

■ FIGURE 12-3   Straight Selection Sort

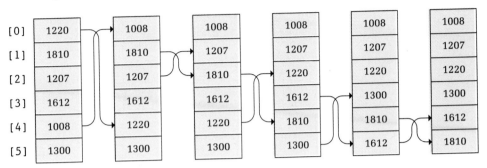

Two parameters are needed for the selection sort function: the array containing the list to be sorted and the length of the list. The code for this sorting algorithm is:

```
void SelSort( /* inout */ ItemType list[],    // List to be sorted
              /* in */    int      length )   // Length of list

// Sorts list into ascending order

// Precondition:
//      length <= MAX_LENGTH
//   && list[0..length-1] are assigned
// Postcondition:
//      list contains the same values as list@entry, rearranged
//      into ascending order

{
    ItemType temp;          // Temporary variable
    int      passCount;     // Loop control variable
```

■ FIGURE 12-4

Exchanging the
Contents of Two
Variables, x and y

x ⟶ ☐

1. Contents of x goes into temp

2. Contents of
   y goes into x

y ⟶ ☐   ☐ ⟵ temp

3. Contents of temp
   goes into y

```
int        placeCount;          // Loop control variable
int        minIndex;            // Index of minimum so far

for (passCount = 0; passCount < length - 1; passCount++)
{
    // Invariant (prior to test):
    //      list[0..passCount-1] are in ascending order
    //          and contain the passCount smallest items
    //  && 0 <= passCount <= length - 1

    minIndex = passCount;

    // Find the index of the smallest component
    // in list[passCount..length-1]

    for (placeCount = passCount + 1; placeCount < length;
                                               placeCount++)

        // Invariant (prior to test):
        //    list[minIndex] <= all list[passCount..placeCount-1]
        // && placeCount <= length

        if (list[placeCount] < list[minIndex])
            minIndex = placeCount;

    // Swap list[minIndex] and list[passCount]

    temp = list[minIndex];
    list[minIndex] = list[passCount];
    list[passCount] = temp;
}
}
```

Note that with each pass through the inner loop, we are looking for the minimum value in the rest of the list (list[passCount] through list[length-1]). Therefore, minIndex is initialized to passCount and the inner loop runs from placeCount equal to passCount+1 through length-1.

Note also that we may swap a component with itself, which occurs if no value in the remaining list is smaller than list[passCount]. We could avoid such an unnecessary swap by checking to see if minIndex is equal to passCount. Because this comparison would have to be made during each iteration of the loop, it is more efficient not to check for this possibility and just to swap something with itself occasionally. If the components we are sorting are much more complex than simple numbers, we might reconsider this decision.

This algorithm sorts the components into ascending order. To sort them into descending order, we need to scan for the maximum value instead of the minimum value. Simply changing the relational operator in the inner loop from "<" to ">" effects this change. Of course, `minIndex` would no longer be a meaningful identifier and should be changed to `maxIndex`.

Sequential Search in a Sorted List

When we search for an item in an unordered list, we won't discover that the item is missing until we reach the end of the list. If the list is ordered, we know that an item is missing when we pass its correct place in the list. For example, if a list contains the values

```
  7
 11
 13
 76
 98
102
```

and we are looking for 12, we need only compare 12 with 7, 11, and 13 to know that 12 is not in the list.

If the search item is greater than the current list component, we move on to the next component. If the item is equal to the current component, we have found what we are looking for. If the item is less than the current component, then we know that it is not in the list. In either of the last two cases, we stop looking. We can restate this algorithmically as follows.

Set current position to beginning of list
WHILE item > current component in list AND more places to look
   Increment current position
Set found = (item equals current component)

We can make this algorithm more efficient by removing the compound condition ("AND more places to look"), as we did in Search2. We store `item` as a sentinel into `list[length]`. On exit from the loop, we can set `found` to TRUE if `item` is equal to the current component and the current position does not equal `length`.

Store a copy of item beyond end of list
Set current position to beginning of list
WHILE item > current component in list
   Increment current position
Set found = (current position < length AND item equals current component)

This search function needs the same parameters as the previous one. To the function precondition we must add the requirement that the list is already sorted.

```
void SearchOrd(
        /* inout */ ItemType list[],       // List to be searched
        /* in */    ItemType item,         // Item to be found
        /* in */    int      length,       // Length of list
        /* out */   int&     index,        // Location of item if found
        /* out */   Boolean& found  )      // True if item is found

// Searches list for item, returning the index of item if item was
// found.  If item was not found, SearchOrd returns the index where
// item belongs.

// Precondition:
//      length < MAX_LENGTH
//   && list[0..length-1] are in ascending order
//   && item is assigned
// Postcondition:
//      list is the same as list@entry except that list[length] is
//          overwritten to aid in the search
//   && IF item is in list@entry
//          found == TRUE  &&  list[index] == item
//      ELSE
//          found == FALSE  &&  index is where item belongs

{
    index = 0;

    // Store item at position beyond end of list

    list[length] = item;

    // Exit loop when item is found, perhaps as sentinel

    while (item > list[index])

            // Invariant (prior to test):
            //      item is not in list[0..index-1]

        index++;

    // Determine whether item was found prior to sentinel

    found = (index < length && item == list[index]);
}
```

On average, searching an ordered list in this way takes the same number of iterations to find an item as searching an unordered list. The advantage of this new algorithm is that we find out sooner if an item is missing. Thus, it is slightly more efficient; however, it works only on a sorted list.

Inserting into an Ordered List

What if we want to add a new value to an already sorted list? We can store the new value at list[length], increment length, and sort the array again. However, such a solution is *not* an efficient way of solving the problem. Inserting five new items results in five separate sorting operations. Let's build another list operation, named Insert, that inserts a value into a sorted list.

If we were to insert a value by hand into a sorted list, we would write the new value out to the side and draw a line showing where it belongs. We do so by scanning the list until we find a value greater than the one we are inserting. The new value goes in the list just before that point.

We can do something similar in our function. We can find the proper place in the list using the by-hand algorithm. Instead of writing the value to the side, we have to shift all the values larger than the new one down one place to make room for it. The main algorithm is expressed as follows, where item is the value being inserted.

```
WHILE place not found AND more places to look
    IF item > current component in list
        increment current place
    ELSE
        place found
Shift remainder of list down
Insert item
Increment length
```

Assuming that index is the place where item is to be inserted, the algorithm for Shift List Down is

```
Set list[length]   = list[length−1]
Set list[length−1] = list[length−2]
              ⋮             ⋮
              ⋮             ⋮
Set list[index+1]  = list[index]
```

We can use a For loop that decrements the control variable to shift the components in the list down one position. We can code the modules Insert Item and Increment Length directly. This algorithm is illustrated in Figure 12-5. There is something familiar about the While loop in our algorithm: it is logically like the While loop in SearchOrd. In SearchOrd, we leave the loop either when we find item or when we pass the place in the list where item belongs.

We can simply use SearchOrd to find the insertion place for us. On return from SearchOrd, if found is FALSE, index is the place in list where item should be inserted. If found is TRUE, we can either insert a second copy or

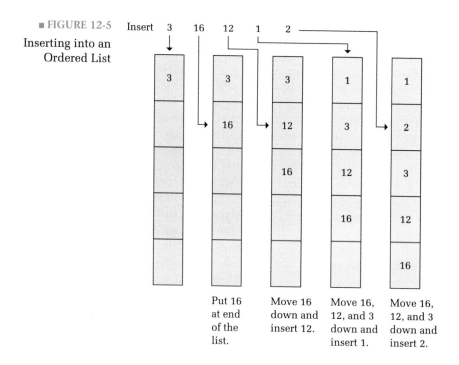

■ FIGURE 12-5

Inserting into an
Ordered List

skip the insertion, as we choose, as long as we clearly document what is done. Inserting a second copy seems more reasonable. Therefore, index is the insertion point, whether or not item already exists in the list.

This function needs three parameters: the array containing the list, the number of components in the list, and the item being inserted. Again, we use the variable names list, item, and length. This time, both list and length must be incoming/outgoing parameters because they are changed each time the function is invoked.

```
void Insert( /* inout */ ItemType list[],     // List to be changed
             /* inout */ int&       length,   // Length of list
             /* in */    ItemType item   )    // Item to be inserted

// Inserts item into its proper place in the sorted list

// Precondition:
//     length < MAX_LENGTH
//  && list[0..length-1] are in ascending order
//  && item is assigned
// Postcondition:
//     item is in list
//  && length == length@entry + 1
//  && list[0..length-1] are in ascending order
//  && IF item was already in list@entry
//         item has been inserted before the one that was there
```

```
{
    Boolean placeFound;      // True if item is already in the list
    int      index;          // Position where item belongs
    int      count;          // Loop control variable

    SearchOrd(list, item, length, index, placeFound);

    // Shift list[index..length-1] down one

    for (count = length - 1; count >= index; count--)

            // Invariant (prior to test):
            //     list[length-1..count+1] have been shifted down
            //  && length - 1 >= count >= index - 1

        list[count+1] = list[count];

    // Insert item

    list[index] = item;

    // Increment length of list

    length++;
}

//*************************************************************************

void SearchOrd(
        /* inout */ ItemType list[],      // List to be searched
        /* in */    ItemType item,        // Item to be found
        /* in */    int      length,      // Length of list
        /* out */   int&     index,       // Location of item if found
        /* out */   Boolean& found  )     // True if item is found
{
    .
    .     // Same as before
    .
}
```

Notice that the Insert function works even if the list is empty. SearchOrd stores item into list[0], where it is immediately found. On return from SearchOrd, index is 0. Because index is greater than the value of length–1 (which is –1), the body of the For loop is not executed. item is then stored into the first position in list, and length is set to 1. This algorithm also works if item is larger than any component in the list. When this happens, index equals length, and item is placed at the end of the list.

This algorithm is the basis for another sorting algorithm—an *insertion sort*. In an insertion sort, values are inserted one at a time into a list that was originally empty. An insertion sort is often used when input data must be sorted; each value is put into its proper place as it is read. We develop this sorting technique in the Exam Attendance case study at the end of this chapter.

Binary Search in an Ordered List

There is a second search algorithm on a sorted list that is considerably faster both for finding an item and for discovering that an item is missing. This algorithm is called a *binary search*. A binary search is based on the principle of successive approximation. The algorithm divides the list in half (divides by 2—that's why it's called *binary* search) and decides which half to look in next. Division of the selected portion of the list is repeated until the item is found or it is determined that the item is not in the list.

This method is analogous to the way in which we look up a word in a dictionary. We open the dictionary in the middle and compare the word with one on the page that we turned to. If the word we're looking for comes before this word, we continue our search in the left-hand section of the dictionary. Otherwise, we continue in the right-hand section of the dictionary. We repeat this process until we find the word. If it is not there, we realize that either we have misspelled the word or our dictionary isn't complete.

The algorithm for a binary search is given below. The list of values is called list, and the value being looked for is called item (see Figure 12-6).

1. Compare item to list[middle]. If item = list[middle], then we have found it. If item < list[middle], then look in the first half of list. If item > list[middle], then look in the second half of list.
2. Redefine list to be the half of list that we look in next, and repeat the process in Step 1.
3. Stop when we have found item or know it is missing. We know it's missing when there is nowhere else to look and we still have not found it.

This algorithm should make sense. With each comparison, at best, we find the item for which we are searching; at worst, we eliminate half of the remaining list from consideration.

■ FIGURE 12-6

Binary Search

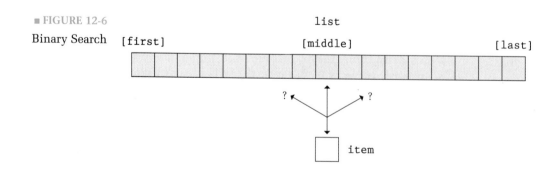

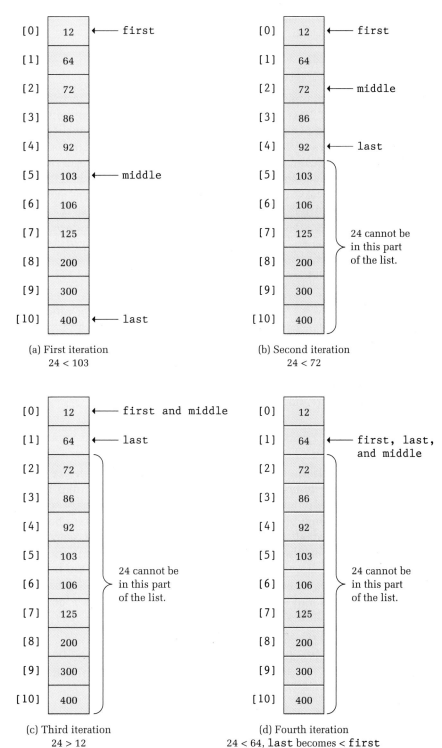

■ FIGURE 12-7

Code Walk-Through of `BinSearch` Function (Search Item Is 24)

The calculation

```
middle = (first + last) / 2;
```

explains why the function precondition restricts the value of `length` to `INT_MAX/2`. If the item being searched for happens to reside in the last position of the list (for example, when `item` equals 400 in our sample list), then `first + last` equals `length + length`. If `length` is greater than `INT_MAX/2`, the sum `length + length` would produce an integer overflow.

Notice in the table that whether we searched for 106, 400, or 406, the loop never executed more than four times. It never executes more than four times in a list of 11 components because the list is being cut in half each time through the loop. The table below compares a sequential search and a binary search in terms of the average number of iterations needed to find an item.

	Average Number of Iterations	
Length of List	*Sequential Search*	*Binary Search*
10	5.5	2.9
100	50.5	5.8
1,000	500.5	9.0
10,000	5000.5	12.4

If the binary search is so much faster, why not use it all the time? It certainly is faster in terms of the number of times through the loop, but more computations are performed within the binary search loop than in the other search algorithms. This means that if the number of components in the list is small (say, less than 20), the sequential search algorithms are faster because they do less work at each iteration. As the number of components in the list increases, the binary search algorithm becomes relatively more efficient. Remember, however, that the binary search requires the list to be sorted, and sorting itself takes time. Keep three factors in mind when you are deciding which search algorithm to use:

1. The length of the list to be searched
2. Whether or not the list already is ordered
3. The number of times the list is to be searched

THEORETICAL FOUNDATIONS

Complexity of Searching and Sorting

We introduced Big-O notation in Chapter 6 as a way of comparing the work done by different algorithms. Let's apply it to the algorithms that we've developed in this chapter and see how they compare with each other. In each algorithm, we start with a list containing some number of values. We'll refer to the number of values as N.

In the worst case, our original Search function scans all N values to locate an item. Thus, it requires N steps to execute. On average, Search takes roughly $N/2$ steps to find an item; however, recall that in Big-O notation, we ignore constant factors (as well as lower-order terms). Thus, function Search is an order N—that is, an $O(N)$—algorithm.

Search2 is also an $O(N)$ algorithm because, even though we saved a comparison on each loop iteration, the same number of iterations are performed. However, making the loop more efficient without changing the number of iterations decreases the constant (the number of steps) that N is multiplied by in the algorithm's work formula. Thus, function Search2 is said to be a constant factor faster than Search.

What about SearchOrd? The number of iterations is decreased for the case in which the item is missing from the list. However, all we have done is take a case that would require N steps and reduce its time, on average, to $N/2$ steps. Thus, SearchOrd is also $O(N)$.

Now consider BinSearch. In the worst case, it eliminates half of the remaining array components on each iteration. Thus, the worst-case number of iterations is equal to the number of times N must be divided by 2 to eliminate all but one value. This number is computed by taking the logarithm, base 2, of N (written $\log_2 N$). Here are some examples of $\log_2 N$ for different values of N:

N	$Log_2 N$
2	1
4	2
8	3
16	4
32	5
1,024	10
32,768	15
1,048,576	20
33,554,432	25
1,073,741,824	30

As you can see, for a list of over 1 billion values, `BinSearch` takes only 30 iterations. It is definitely the best choice for searching large lists. Algorithms such as `BinSearch` are said to be of *logarithmic order*.

Now let's turn to sorting. Function `SelSort` contains nested For loops. The total number of iterations is the product of the iterations performed by the two loops. The outer loop executes $N-1$ times. The inner loop also starts out executing $N-1$ times, but steadily decreases until it performs just one iteration: the inner loop executes $N/2$ iterations. The total number of iterations is thus

$$\frac{(N-1)*N}{2}$$

Ignoring the constant factor and lower-order term, this is N^2 iterations, and `SelSort` is an $O(N^2)$ algorithm. Consider that, whereas `BinSearch` takes only 30 iterations to search an ordered array of 1 billion values, putting the array into order takes `SelSort` approximately 1 billion times 1 billion iterations!

We mentioned that in a case study we would develop the technique of inserting values into an ordered list as they are input. In the meantime, we can consider the approach in the abstract. On average, `Insert` has to shift down half of the values ($N/2$) in the list; thus, it is an $O(N)$ algorithm. If `Insert` is called for each input value, we are executing an $O(N)$ algorithm N times; therefore, sorting with insertion is an $O(N^2)$ algorithm.

Is every sorting algorithm $O(N^2)$? Most of the simpler ones are, but $O(N * \log_2 N)$ sorting algorithms exist. Algorithms that are $O(N * \log_2 N)$ are much closer in performance to $O(N)$ algorithms than are $O(N^2)$ algorithms. For example, if N is one million, then an $O(N^2)$ algorithm takes a million times a million (one trillion) iterations, but an $O(N * \log_2 N)$ algorithm takes only 20 million iterations—that is, it is 20 times slower than the $O(N)$ algorithm but 50,000 times faster than the $O(N^2)$ algorithm.

Now let's turn our attention to a second application of arrays—a special kind of array that is useful when working with alphanumeric data.

 # Working with Character Strings

In Chapter 2, we introduced string constants. Syntactically, a string constant is a sequence of characters enclosed by double quotes:

```
"Hi"
```

A string constant is stored as a `char` array with enough components to hold each specified character plus one more—the *null character*. The null character, which is the first character in both the ASCII and EBCDIC character sets, has internal representation 0. In C++, the escape sequence \0 stands for the null character. When the compiler encounters the string "Hi" in a program, it stores the three characters 'H', 'i', and '\0' into a three-element, anonymous (unnamed) char array as follows:

Unnamed array

```
[0]     'H'

[1]     'i'

[2]     '\0'
```

The **string** is the only kind of C++ array for which there exists an aggregate constant—the string constant. Notice that in a C++ program, the symbols 'A' denote a single character, whereas the symbols "A" denote two: the character 'A' and the null character.

In addition to string constants, we can create string *variables*. To do so, we explicitly declare a char array and store into it whatever characters we want to, finishing with the null character. Here's an example:

```
char myStr[8];    // Room for 7 significant characters plus '\0'

myStr[0] = 'H';
myStr[1] = 'i';
myStr[2] = '\0';
```

String A collection of characters interpreted as a single item; in C++, a null-terminated sequence of characters stored in a char array.

In C++, all strings (constants or variables) are assumed to be null-terminated. This convention is agreed upon by all C++ programmers and standard library functions. The null character serves as a sentinel value; it allows algorithms to locate the end of the string. For example, here is a function that determines the length of any string, not counting the terminating null character:

```
int StrLength( /* in */ const char str[] )

// Precondition:
//      str is a null-terminated string
// Postcondition:
//      Function value == number of characters in str (excluding '\0')
```

```
{
    int i = 0;     // Index variable

    while (str[i] != '\0')

                    // Invariant (prior to test):
                    //     No character in str[0..i-1] is '\0'

        i++;
    return i;
}
```

The value of i is the correct value for this function to return. If the array being examined is

```
[0]    'B'
[1]    'y'
[2]    '\0'
[3]
        .
        .
        .
```

then i equals 2 at loop exit. The string length is therefore 2.

The actual parameter to the StrLength function can be a string variable, as in the function call

```
cout << StrLength(myStr);
```

or it can be a string constant:

```
cout << StrLength("Hello");
```

In the first case, the base address of the myStr array is sent to the function, as we discussed in Chapter 11. In the second case, a base address is also sent to the function—the base address of the unnamed array that the compiler set aside for the string constant.

There is one more thing we should say about our StrLength function. A C++ programmer would not actually write this function. The standard library supplies several string-processing functions, one of which is named strlen and does exactly what our StrLength function does. Later in the chapter, we look at strlen and other library functions.

Thinking of a string as an abstract data type, what kinds of operations might we find useful? Here are a few:

Create and initialize a string
Input a string
Output a string
Determine the length of a string
Compare two strings
Copy one string to another

We could come up with many other operations as well, but let's look at these particular ones.

Initializing Strings

In Chapter 11, we showed how to initialize an array in its declaration, by specifying a list of initial values within braces, like this:

```
int delta[5] = {25, -3, 7, 13, 4};
```

To initialize a string variable in its declaration, you could use the same technique:

```
char message[8] = {'W', 'h', 'o', 'o', 'p', 's', '!', '\0'};
```

However, C++ allows a more convenient way to initialize a string. You can simply initialize the array by using a string constant:

```
char message[8] = "Whoops!";
```

This shorthand notation is unique to strings because there is no other kind of array for which there are aggregate constants.

We said in Chapter 11 that you can omit the size of an array when you initialize it in its declaration (in which case, the compiler determines its size). This feature is often used with strings because it keeps you from having to count the number of characters. For example,

```
char promptMsg[] = "Enter a positive number:";
char errMsg[] = "Value must be positive.";
```

Be very careful about one thing: C++ treats initialization (in a declaration) and assignment (in an assignment statement) as two distinct operations. Different rules apply. Array initialization is legal, but aggregate array assignment is not.

```
char myStr[20] = "Hello";    // OK
   :
   :
myStr = "Howdy";             // Not allowed
```

String Input and Output

In Chapter 11, we emphasized that C++ does not provide aggregate operations on arrays. There is no aggregate assignment, aggregate comparison, or aggregate arithmetic on arrays. We also said that aggregate input/output of arrays is not possible, with one exception. Strings are that exception. Let's look first at output.

To output the contents of an array that is *not* a string, you aren't allowed to do this:

```
int alpha[100];
   :
   :
cout << alpha;    // No
```

Instead, you must write a loop and print the array elements one at a time. However, aggregate output of a null-terminated char array (that is, a string) is valid. The string can be a string constant (as we've been doing since Chapter 2):

```
cout << "Results are:";
```

or it can be a string variable:

```
char msg[8] = "Welcome";
   :
   :
cout << msg;
```

In both cases, the insertion operator (<<) outputs each character in the array until the null character is found. It is up to you to double-check that the terminating null character is present in the array. If not, the << operator will march through the array and into the rest of memory, printing out bytes until—just by chance—it encounters a byte whose integer value is 0.

To input strings, we have several options in C++. The first is to use the extraction operator (>>). When reading input characters into a string variable, the >> operator skips any leading whitespace characters such as blanks and newlines. It then reads successive characters into the array, stopping at the first *trailing* whitespace character (which is not consumed, but remains as the first character waiting in the input stream). The **>>** operator also takes care of adding the null character to the end of the string. For example, assume we have the following code:

```
char firstName[31];    // Room for 30 characters plus '\0'
char lastName[31];

cin >> firstName >> lastName;
```

Suppose that the input stream initially looks like this (where ☐ denotes a blank):

☐☐Mary☐Smith☐☐☐18

Then our input statement stores 'M', 'a', 'r', 'y', and '\0' into `firstName[0]` through `firstName[4]`; stores 'S', 'm', 'i', 't', 'h', and '\0' into `lastName[0]` through `lastName[5]`; and leaves the input stream as

☐☐☐18

Although the **>>** operator is widely used for string input, it has two potential drawbacks.

1. If your string variable isn't large enough to hold the sequence of input characters (and the '\0'), the **>>** operator will continue to store characters into memory past the end of the array.
2. The **>>** operator cannot be used to input a string that has blanks within it. (It stops reading as soon as it encounters the first whitespace character.)

To deal with these facts, we use a variation of the `get` function. We have used the `get` function to input a single character, even if it is a whitespace character:

```
cin.get(inputChar);
```

The `get` function also can be used to input string data, in which case the function call requires two parameters. The first is a string variable and the second is an `int` expression.

```
cin.get(myStr, charCount + 1);
```

The `get` function does not skip leading whitespace characters and continues until it either has read `charCount` characters or it reaches the newline character '\n', whichever comes first. It then appends the null character to the end of the string. With the statements

```
char oneLine[81];    // Room for 80 characters plus '\0'
    .
    .
    .
cin.get(oneLine, 81);
```

the get function reads and stores an entire input line (to a maximum of 80 characters), embedded blanks and all. If the line has fewer than 80 characters, reading stops at '\n' but does not consume it. The newline character is now the first one waiting in the input stream. To read two consecutive lines worth of strings, it is necessary to consume the newline character:

```
char dummy;
    .
    .
    .
cin.get(string1, 81);
cin.get(dummy);            // Eat newline before next "get"
cin.get(string2, 81);
```

The first function call reads characters up to, but not including, '\n'. If the input of dummy were omitted, then the input of string2 would read *no* characters because '\n' would immediately be the first character waiting in the stream.

Finally, the ignore function—introduced in Chapter 4—can be useful in conjunction with the get function. Recall that the statement

```
cin.ignore(200, '\n');
```

says to skip at most 200 input characters but stop if a newline was read. (The newline character *is* consumed by this function.) If a program inputs a long string from the user but only wants to retain the first four characters of the response, here is a way to do it:

```
char response[5];       // Room for 4 characters plus '\0'

cin.get(response, 5);   // Input at most 4 characters
cin.ignore(100, '\n');  // Skip remaining chars up to and
                        // including '\n'
```

The value 100 in the last statement is arbitrary. Any "large enough" number will do.

Here is a table that summarizes the differences between the >> operator and the get function when reading string data:

Statement	*Skips Leading Whitespace?*	*Stops Reading When?*
`cin >> inputStr;`	Yes	At the first trailing whitespace character (which is *not* consumed)
`cin.get(inputStr, 21);`	No	When either 20 characters are read or '\n' is encountered (which is *not* consumed)

Run-Time Input of File Names

Until now, our programs that have read from input files and written to output files have included code similar to this:

```
ifstream inFile;     // Input file to be analyzed

inFile.open("datafile.dat");
if ( !inFile )
{
    cout << "** Can't open input file **" << endl;
    return 1;
}
    .
    .
    .
```

The open function associated with the `ifstream` data type requires a string parameter that specifies the name of the actual data file on disk. By using a string constant, as in the above example, the file name is fixed at compile time. That is, the program works only for this one particular disk file.

We often want to make a program more flexible by allowing the file name to be determined at *run time*. A common technique is to prompt the user for the name of the file, read the user's response into a string variable, and pass the string variable as a parameter to the open function. The following code fragment, which is another example of the use of the `get` and `ignore` functions, demonstrates the run-time input of a file name.

```
ifstream inFile;        // Input file to be analyzed
char     fileName[51];  // Max. 50 characters plus '\0'

cout << "Enter the input file name: ";
cin.get(fileName, 51);          // Read at most 50 characters
cin.ignore(100, '\n');          // Skip rest of input line

inFile.open(fileName);
if ( !inFile )
{
```

```
                cout << "** Can't open input file **" << endl;
                return 1;
        }
        .
        .
        .
```

From now on, our end-of-chapter case studies use this technique of reading a file name at run time.

String Library Routines

Through the header file `string.h`, the C++ standard library provides a large assortment of string operations that people have found to be useful. In this section, we discuss three of these library functions: `strlen`, which returns the length of a string; `strcmp`, which compares two strings using the relations less-than, equal, and greater-than; and `strcpy`, which copies one string to another. Here is a summary of `strlen`, `strcmp`, and `strcpy`:

Header File	Function	Function Value	Effect
`<string.h>`	`strlen(str)`	Integer length of `str` (excluding '\0')	Computes length of `str`.
`<string.h>`	`strcmp(str1, str2)`	An integer < 0, if `str1` < `str2` The integer 0, if `str1` = `str2` An integer > 0, if `str1` > `str2`	Compares `str1` and `str2`.
`<string.h>`	`strcpy(toStr, fromStr)`	Base address of `toStr` (usually ignored)	Copies `fromStr` (including '\0') to `toStr`, overwriting what was there; `toStr` must be large enough to hold the result.

The `strlen` function is similar to the `StrLength` function we wrote earlier. It returns the number of characters in a string prior to the terminating '\0'. Here's an example of a call to the function:

```
#include <string.h>
        .
        .
        .
char subject[] = "Computer Science";

cout << strlen(subject);    // Prints 16
```

The strcpy routine is important because aggregate assignment with the = operator is not allowed. In the following code fragment, we show the wrong way and the right way to perform a string copy.

```
#include <string.h>
    .
    .
    .
char myStr[100];
    .
    .
    .
myStr = "Abracadabra";            // No
strcpy(myStr, "Abracadabra");     // Yes
```

In strcpy's parameter list, the destination string is the one on the left, just as an assignment operation transfers data from right to left. It is the caller's responsibility to make sure that the destination array is large enough to hold the result.

The strcpy function is technically a value-returning function; it not only copies one string to another, it also returns as a function value the base address of the destination array. The reason why the caller would want to use this function value is not at all obvious, and we don't discuss it here. Programmers nearly always ignore the function value and simply invoke strcpy as if it were a void function (as we did above). You may wish to review the Background Information box in Chapter 8 entitled "Ignoring a Function Value."

The strcmp function is used for comparing two strings. The function receives two strings as parameters and compares them in *lexicographic* order (the order in which they would appear in a dictionary). Specifically, corresponding characters in the strings are compared one by one, starting with the first. The first unequal pair of characters determines the order. For example, "Hello" compares less than "Helvetica". The first three characters are the same in both strings, but 'l' compares less than 'v' in both ASCII and EBCDIC. Given the function call strcmp(str1, str2), the function returns one of the following int values: a negative integer, if str1 < str2 lexicographically; the value 0, if str1 = str2; or a positive integer, if str1 > str2. The precise values of the negative integer and the positive integer are unspecified. You simply test to see if the result is less than zero, zero, or greater than zero. Here is an example:

```
if (strcmp(str1, str2) < 0)     // If str1 is less than str2 ...
    .
    .
    .
```

Given the declarations

```
char word1[6] = "Small";
char word2[6] = "Small";
```

the following function calls would return the results indicated.

Function Call	Function Value	
strcmp(word1, word2)	0	(They are equal.)
strcmp(word1, "Tree")	Negative number	('S' comes before 'T'.)
strcmp("Smile", word1)	Positive number	('i' comes after 'a'.)
strcmp("S", word1)	Negative number	('\0' comes before 'm'.)

The preceding results would be the same with any character set. Different character sets give different results, however, if an uppercase letter and a lowercase letter are compared. Uppercase letters come before lowercase letters in ASCII and after lowercase letters in EBCDIC. Also, special symbols, such as punctuation marks, are ordered differently with respect to each other in the two sets.

We have described only three of the string-handling routines provided by the standard library. These three are the most commonly needed, but there are many more. If you are designing programs that use strings extensively, you should read the documentation on strings for your C++ system.

Using Typedef with Arrays

In Chapter 10, we discussed the Typedef statement as a way of giving an additional name to an existing data type. The most familiar example is

```
typedef int Boolean;
```

We can also use Typedef to give a name to an array type. Here's an example:

```
typedef float FloatArr[100];
```

This statement says that the type `FloatArr` is the same as the type "100-element array of `float`." (Notice that the array size in brackets comes at the very end of the statement.) We can now declare variables to be of type `FloatArr`:

```
FloatArr angle;
FloatArr velocity;
```

The compiler essentially translates these declarations into

```
float angle[100];
float velocity[100];
```

Up to this point, we haven't used Typedef to give names to array types. We tend to picture an integer or floating point array as a group of individual, separate components. On the other hand, we often visualize a string as a complete unit, almost as if it were a simple data type. Using Typedef to give a name to a string type gives us some consistency in that vision:

```
typedef char String20[21];
       .
       .
       .
String20 firstName;
String20 lastName;

cin >> firstName >> lastName;
if (strcmp(lastName, "Jones") > 0)
       .
       .
       .
```

Notice how the identifier `String20` suggests a maximum of 20 significant characters, and the physical size we use is 21 to allow room for the terminating null character.

The two Problem-Solving Case Studies that follow use many of the concepts we have described in this section: string initialization, string I/O, string-handling library functions, and Typedef to define string types.

P ROBLEM-SOLVING CASE STUDY

Birthday Reminder Revisited

Problem: Rewrite the `GetMonth` function, from the Birthday Reminder case study in Chapter 10, so that it uses strings to convert the input month to a value of enumeration type `Months`. Rerun the program without making any other changes.

Discussion: The BirthdayReminder program inputs a month and prints the names and birthdays of friends who have birthdays that month. In the original program, the characters in the month's name are read one at a time until the program recognizes the month, and any remaining characters in the month are ignored. Now that we know how to use strings, we can read the entire name of the month into a string variable and process it as a whole word rather than decoding it character by character.

We use an array of strings containing the months of the year. A month is read into a string variable. The Search function is used to search the array for the input string. If it is found at location index, we use index to access a parallel array containing the values of the enumeration type Months. In other words, we convert a month in string form to the equivalent month in the enumeration type by using parallel arrays, one containing strings and the other containing the enumeration equivalents. If the string is not found, the program can issue an error message and prompt the user to reenter the month.

Data Structures:

An array of strings containing the months of the year.
An array containing enumeration type values for the months of the year.

The two arrays look like those in Figure 12-8. Although these two arrays look similar, they have quite different representations in the computer. One contains the months in character form; the other contains the months in the form of an enumeration type.

Let's call the string representation of a month strMonth and the enumeration version month, as it is called in the BirthdayReminder program. The array of strings can be called strMonthAry, and the parallel array can be called monthAry. The algorithm for GetMonth using this structure is as follows:

■ FIGURE 12-8

Data Structures for GetMonth Function

[0]	"January"
[1]	"February"
[2]	"March"
[3]	"April"
[4]	"May"
[5]	"June"
[6]	"July"
[7]	"August"
[8]	"September"
[9]	"October"
[10]	"November"
[11]	"December"

[0]	JANUARY
[1]	FEBRUARY
[2]	MARCH
[3]	APRIL
[4]	MAY
[5]	JUNE
[6]	JULY
[7]	AUGUST
[8]	SEPTEMBER
[9]	OCTOBER
[10]	NOVEMBER
[11]	DECEMBER

Get Month (Out: month) *Level 1*

```
DO
   Read strMonth
   Search(strMonthAry, strMonth, 12, index, found)
   IF found
       Set month = monthAry[index]
   ELSE
       Print error message
WHILE NOT found
```

Now we can code the new function GetMonth. We must remember to initialize the arrays strMonthAry and monthAry. We also need to modify the Search function to make it work on string data.

```
#include <string.h>         // For strcmp()
   .
   .
   .
typedef char String9[10];   // Room for 9 characters plus '\0'
   .
   .
   .


//*************************************************************************

void GetMonth( /* out */ Months& month )    // User's desired month

// Inputs a month after prompting the user

// Postcondition:
//     User has been prompted to enter a month
//   && On invalid input, the user has been repeatedly prompted to
//       type a correct month
//   && month == value of type Months corresponding to user's input

{
    String9 strMonth;                // Input month in string form
    Months  monthAry[12] =           // Table of months in enum form
    {
        JANUARY, FEBRUARY, MARCH, APRIL,
        MAY, JUNE, JULY, AUGUST,
        SEPTEMBER, OCTOBER, NOVEMBER, DECEMBER
    };
```

```
    String9 strMonthAry[12] =        // Parallel table in string form
    {
        "January", "February", "March", "April",
        "May", "June", "July", "August",
        "September", "October", "November", "December"
    };
    int     index;                   // Index of located month
    Boolean found;                   // True if month is valid

    do
    {
        cout << "Please enter month, capitalizing first letter."
            << endl;
        cin.get(strMonth, 10);        // Input at most 9 chars and
                                      //    leave room for '\0'
        cin.ignore(100, '\n');        // Consume '\n' because the
                                      //    "get" routine does not
        Search(strMonthAry, strMonth, 12, index, found);
        if (found)
            month = monthAry[index];
        else
            cout << "Month is misspelled." << endl << endl;

            // Invariant:
            //      All values of strMonth prior to current
            //          value were invalid
            //   && found == TRUE if and only if current
            //          strMonth is valid

    } while ( !found );
}

//**************************************************************

void Search(
    /* in */   const String9 strMonthAry[],  // List to be searched
    /* in */   const String9 strMonth,       // Search value
    /* in */   int           length,         // Length of list
    /* out */  int&          index,          // Location if found
    /* out */  Boolean&      found      )     // True if value found

// Searches strMonthAry for strMonth, returning the index
// of strMonth if strMonth was found

// Precondition:
//      length <= 12
//   && strMonthAry[0..length-1] are assigned
//   && strMonth is assigned
```

PROBLEM-SOLVING CASE STUDY *cont'd.*

```
// Postcondition:
//     IF strMonth is in strMonthAry
//         found == TRUE  &&  strMonthAry[index] contains strMonth
//     ELSE
//         found == FALSE  &&  index == length

{
    index = 0;
    while (index < length &&
           strcmp(strMonth, strMonthAry[index]) != 0)

           // Invariant (prior to test):
           //     strMonth is not in strMonthAry[0..index-1]
           // && 0 <= index <= length

        index++;
    found = (index < length);
}
```

Because the BirthdayReminder program is so long, it is not repeated here. However, we guarantee that this function GetMonth was substituted for the one in Chapter 10 and the program was rerun. Notice that strMonthAry is an array of arrays, making it a *two-dimensional array*. We return to this subject in Chapter 13.

PROBLEM-SOLVING CASE STUDY

Exam Attendance

Problem: You are the grader for a U.S. government class. The teacher has asked you to prepare two lists: students taking an exam and students who have missed it. The catch is that he wants the lists before the exam is over. You decide to write a program for your portable computer that takes each student's name as the student enters the exam room and prints the lists of absentees and attendees for your teacher.

Input:

A list of last names of the students in the class, ordered by social security number (file roster)

Each student's last name as he or she enters the room (standard input device)

Output:

A list of those students taking the exam
A list of those students who are absent

Discussion: How would you take attendance by hand? You would stand at the door with a class roster. As each student came in, you would check off his or her name. When all the students had entered, you would go through the roster, making a list of those present. Then you would do the same for those who are absent.

This by-hand algorithm can serve as a model for your program. As each student enters the room, you enter his or her name at the keyboard. Your program scans the list of students for that name and marks that the student is present. When the last student has entered, you can enter a special sentinel name, perhaps "EndData", to signal the program to print the lists.

You can simulate "Mark that the student is present" by having a parallel array made up of Boolean values. This array is initialized to all FALSE; when a name is found in the list of students, the corresponding position in the second array is set to TRUE.

You will have to prepare the list of students in advance from the class roster, which is ordered by social security number. If you enter the names directly from the roster, they will not be in alphabetical order. Does that matter? Yes, in this case it does matter. The size of the class is 200, and the students need to enter the exam room with minimum delay (because most arrive just before the exam starts).

The size of the list and the speed required suggest that a binary search is appropriate. A binary search requires that the list be in sorted form. The names in the input file are in order by social security number, so your program must sort them alphabetically. All the names can be input at once and sorted using function SelSort, or each name can be put into its proper place as it is read using function Insert. You decide to take the second approach.

Data Structures:

A one-dimensional array of strings representing student names (student)
A one-dimensional array of "checks" (isPresent)
A temporary string to read a name into (stuName)

Figure 12-9 pictures the data structures used in this program.

Problem-Solving Case Study cont'd.

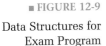

■ FIGURE 12-9

Data Structures for
Exam Program

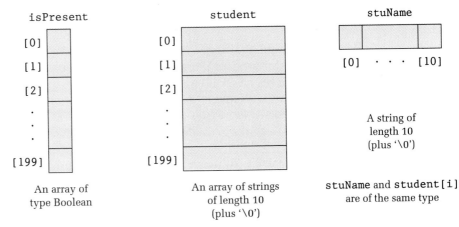

| isPresent | student | stuName |

An array of
type Boolean

An array of strings
of length 10
(plus '\0')

A string of
length 10
(plus '\0')

stuName and student[i]
are of the same type

Main   *Level 0*

> Open roster file for input
> IF file could not be opened
>   Terminate program
> Get class roster
> Check in students
> Print lists

To open the input file, we'll make our program more flexible by prompting the user for a file name and reading it in as a string.

Open For Input (Inout: someFile)   *Level 1*

> Prompt user for name of disk file
> Read fileName
> Associate fileName with stream someFile,
>   and try to open it
> IF file could not be opened
>   Print error message

Get Class Roster (Out: student, length; Inout: roster)

```
Set length = 0
Read stuName from roster file
WHILE NOT EOF on roster
    Insert stuName into student list, incrementing length
    Read stuName from roster file
```

The decision to use a sentinel string to end the data requires a priming read in the Check In Students module—stuName must have a value on entering the loop. A prompt to the user should also be included.

Check in Students (In: student, length; Inout: isPresent)

```
Print "Enter last name"
Read stuName
WHILE stuName isn't "EndData"
    Process stuName
    Print "Enter last name"
    Read stuName
```

Insert Name (Inout: list, length; In: item)

Level 2

```
(For Insert Name you can use functions Insert and
SearchOrd, which we wrote earlier.)
```

Process Name (In: student, length, stuName; Inout: isPresent)

```
Search student list for stuName (use BinSearch here)
IF found
    Set isPresent[index] = TRUE
ELSE
    Print "Name not on roster."
```

Problem-Solving Case Study cont'd.

Print (In: student, isPresent, length)   *Level 1*

> Print "The following students are taking the exam."
> FOR count going from 0 through length–1
>   IF isPresent[count]
>   Print student[count]
> Print "The following students have missed the exam."
> FOR count going from 0 through length–1
>   IF NOT isPresent[count]
>   Print student[count]

At this point, you need to go back over the top-down design and test it. Have you forgotten anything? Yes, you need to initialize the array `isPresent` to all FALSE.

Initialize Attendance (Out: isPresent)   *Level 1*

> FOR count going from 0 through max. number of students minus 1
>   Set isPresent[count] = FALSE

The design is now ready to be coded.

Module Structure Chart:

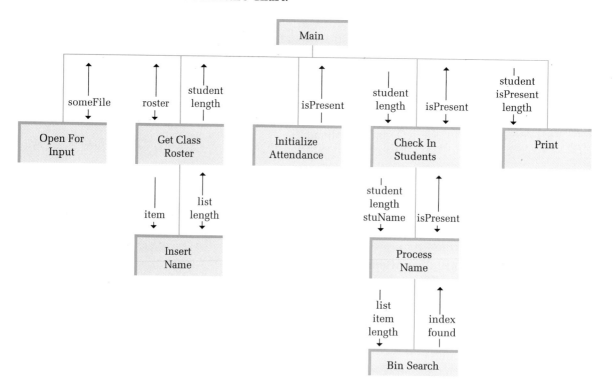

```
//****************************************************************
// Exam program
// This program compares students who come to take an exam against
// a class roster.  A list of students who took the exam and a list
// of students who missed the exam are printed.
// Assumption:  Student names are unique within the first 10
// characters
//****************************************************************
#include <iostream.h>
#include <fstream.h>          // For file I/O
#include <string.h>           // For strcpy(), strcmp()
#include "bool.h"             // For Boolean type

const int  MAX_LENGTH = 200;         // Maximum number of students
const char END_DATA[] = "EndData";   // Sentinel value for
                                     //   student name
typedef char String10[11];           // Room for 10 characters
                                     //   plus '\0'
```

```
    void BinSearch( const String10[], const String10, int, int&,
                 Boolean& );
    void CheckInStudents( const String10[], int, Boolean[] );
    void GetClassRoster( String10[], int&, ifstream& );
    void InitializeAttendance( Boolean[] );
    void Insert( String10[], int&, const String10 );
    void OpenForInput( ifstream& );
    void Print( const String10[], const Boolean[], int );
    void ProcessName( const String10[], int, const String10,
                 Boolean[] );
    void SearchOrd( String10[], const String10, int, int&, Boolean& );

    int main()
    {
        String10  student[MAX_LENGTH];    // Array of student names
        Boolean   isPresent[MAX_LENGTH];  // Array of 'check marks'
        int       length;                 // Number of students there
        ifstream  roster;                 // Input file to be analyzed

        OpenForInput(roster);
        if ( !roster )
            return 1;

        InitializeAttendance(isPresent);
        GetClassRoster(student, length, roster);
        CheckInStudents(student, length, isPresent);
        Print(student, isPresent, length);
        return 0;
    }

    //************************************************************

    void OpenForInput( /* inout */ ifstream& someFile )    // File to be
                                                           // opened

    // Prompts the user for the name of an input file
    // and attempts to open the file

    // Postcondition:
    //     The user has been prompted for a file name
    //  && IF the file could not be opened
    //         An error message has been printed
    // Note:
    //     Upon return from this function, the caller must test
    //     the stream state to see if the file was successfully opened

    {
        char fileName[51];    // User-specified file name (max. 50 chars)
```

```
        cout << "Input file name: ";
        cin.get(fileName, 51);
        cin.ignore(100, '\n');

        someFile.open(fileName);
        if ( !someFile )
            cout << "** Can't open " << fileName << " **" << endl;
}

//*************************************************************

void InitializeAttendance(
                /* out */ Boolean isPresent[] )    // Check mark list

// Initializes all components of the array isPresent to FALSE

// Postcondition:
//     isPresent[0..MAX_LENGTH-1] == FALSE

{
    int count;       // Loop control variable

    for (count = 0; count < MAX_LENGTH; count++)

            // Invariant (prior to test):
            //     isPresent[0..count-1] == FALSE
            //  && 0 <= count <= MAX_LENGTH

        isPresent[count] = FALSE;
}

//*************************************************************

void GetClassRoster(
                /* out */    String10  student[],    // List of students
                /* out */    int&      length,       // Length of list
                /* inout */ ifstream& roster    )    // Roster data file

// Reads the class roster from the data file

// Precondition:
//     The roster file has been successfully opened for input
//  && The no. of student names in the file <= MAX_LENGTH
// Postcondition:
//     length == number of student names in the file
//  && student[0..length-1] contain the student names read from
//     the file, truncated to 10 characters each
```

```
{
        String10 stuName;        // An input student name

        length = 0;
        roster.get(stuName, 11);                   // Input at most 10 chars and
                                                   //   leave room for '\0'
        while (roster)
        {
                // Invariant (prior to test):
                //      student[0..length-1] contain the
                //      first "length" input names

            roster.ignore(100, '\n');        // Consume chars through '\n'
            Insert(student, length, stuName);
            roster.get(stuName, 11);
        }
}

//**************************************************************

void Insert(
            /* inout */ String10        list[],     // List to be changed
            /* inout */ int&            length,     // Length of list
            /* in */    const String10 item    )    // Item to be inserted

// Inserts item into its proper place in the sorted list

// Precondition:
//      length < MAX_LENGTH
//   && list[0..length-1] are in ascending order
//   && item is assigned
// Postcondition:
//      item is in list
//   && length == length@entry + 1
//   && list[0..length-1] are in ascending order
//   && IF item was already in list@entry
//          item has been inserted before the one that was there

{
        Boolean placeFound;      // True if item is already in the list
        int     index;           // Position where item belongs
        int     count;           // Loop control variable

        SearchOrd(list, item, length, index, placeFound);

        // Shift list[index..length-1] down one

        for (count = length - 1; count >= index; count--)
```

```
                        // Invariant (prior to test):
                        //     list[length-1..count+1] have been shifted down
                        //  && length - 1 >= count >= index - 1

            strcpy(list[count+1], list[count]);

      // Insert item

      strcpy(list[index], item);

      // Increment length of list

      length++;
}

//*****************************************************************

void SearchOrd(
      /* inout */ String10     list[],    // List to be searched
      /* in */    const String10 item,    // Item to be found
      /* in */    int          length,    // Length of list
      /* out */   int&         index,     // Item location if found
      /* out */   Boolean&     found  )   // True if item is found

// Searches list for item, returning the index if item was found.
// If item was not found, SearchOrd returns the index where
// item belongs

// Precondition:
//      length < MAX_LENGTH
//   && list[0..length-1] are in ascending order
//   && item is assigned
// Postcondition:
//      list is the same as list@entry except that list[length] is
//         overwritten to aid in the search
//   && IF item is in list@entry
//          found == TRUE  &&  list[index] contains item
//      ELSE
//          found == FALSE  &&  index is where item belongs

{

      index = 0;

      // Store item at position beyond end of list

      strcpy(list[length],item);
```

```
    // Exit loop when item is found, perhaps as sentinel

    while (strcmp(item, list[index]) > 0)

            // Invariant (prior to test):
            //      item is not in list[0..index-1]

        index++;

    // Determine whether item was found prior to sentinel

    found = (index < length && strcmp(item, list[index]) == 0);
}

//*****************************************************************

void CheckInStudents(
        /* in */    const String10 student[],       // List of students
        /* in */    int             length,         // Length of list
        /* inout */ Boolean         isPresent[] )    // Check mark list

// Inputs student names from standard input,
// marking students present

// Precondition:
//     length <= MAX_LENGTH
//  && student[0..length-1] are in ascending order
//  && isPresent[0..length-1] are assigned
// Postcondition:
//     The user has been repeatedly prompted to enter student names
//  && For all i, where student[i] matches an input name,
//         isPresent[i] == TRUE
//  && For all input names not found in the student array,
//     an error message has been printed

{
    String10 stuName;        // Name of student who is checking in

    cout << "Enter last name: ";
    cin.get(stuName, 11);                     // At most 10 chars plus '\0'
    cin.ignore(100, '\n');
    while (strcmp(stuName, END_DATA) != 0)
    {
            // Invariant (prior to test):
            //      All students prior to current one
            //      have been checked in
```

```
                ProcessName(student, length, stuName, isPresent);
                cout << "Enter last name: ";
                cin.get(stuName, 11);
                cin.ignore(100, '\n');
        }
}

//*********************************************************************

void ProcessName(
        /* in */     const String10 student[],      // List of students
        /* in */     int            length,         // Length of list
        /* in */     const String10 stuName,        // Input student name
        /* inout */  Boolean        isPresent[] )   // Check mark list

// Searches for stuName in the student array.  If stuName
// is found, the corresponding position in the isPresent array
// is set to TRUE.  Otherwise, an error message is printed

// Precondition:
//     length <= MAX_LENGTH
//   && student[0..length-1] are in ascending order
//   && stuName is assigned
//   && isPresent[0..length-1] are assigned
// Postcondition:
//     IF there is some i for which student[i] contains stuName
//         isPresent[i] == TRUE
//     ELSE
//         An error message has been printed

{
    int     index;       // Location of student name if found
    Boolean found;       // True if student is on roster

    BinSearch(student, stuName, length, index, found);
    if (found)
        isPresent[index] = TRUE;
    else
        cout << "Name not on roster." << endl;
}

//*********************************************************************

void BinSearch(
        /* in */   const String10 list[],      // List to be searched
        /* in */   const String10 item,        // Item to be found
        /* in */   int            length,      // Length of list
        /* out */  int&           index,       // Item location if found
```

PROBLEM-SOLVING CASE STUDY cont'd.

```
        /* out */ Boolean&        found  )   // True if item is found

// Searches list for item, returning the index if item was found.

// Precondition:
//     length <= INT_MAX / 2
//  && list[0..length-1] are in ascending order
//  && item is assigned
// Postcondition:
//     IF item is in list
//         found == TRUE  &&  list[index] contains item
//     ELSE
//         found == FALSE  &&  index is undefined

{
    int first = 0;          // Lower bound on list
    int last = length - 1;  // Upper bound on list
    int middle;             // Middle index

    found = FALSE;
    while (last >= first && !found)
    {
        // Invariant (prior to test):
        //     If item is in list[0..length-1] then
        //     item is in list[first..last]

        middle = (first + last) / 2;
        if (strcmp(item, list[middle]) < 0)
            // Assert: item is not in list[middle..last]
            last = middle - 1;
        else if (strcmp(item, list[middle]) > 0)
            // Assert: item is not in list[first..middle]
            first = middle + 1;
        else
            // Assert: item is in list[middle]
            found = TRUE;
    }
    index = middle;
}

//****************************************************************

void Print(
        /* in */ const String10 student[],    // List of students
        /* in */ const Boolean  isPresent[],   // Check mark list
        /* in */ int            length      )  // Length of lists
```

```
// Prints the names of those taking the exam, then the names
// of those who are absent

// Precondition:
//     length <= MAX_LENGTH
//  && student[0..length-1] are assigned
//  && isPresent[0..length-1] are assigned
// Postcondition:
//     For every i such that isPresent[i] == TRUE,
//         student[i] has been printed
//     Then, for every i such that isPresent[i] == FALSE,
//         student[i] has been printed

{
    int count;      // Loop control variable

    cout << endl << "The following students are taking the exam."
        << endl;
    for (count = 0; count < length; count++)

            // Invariant (prior to test):
            //     For all i, where 0 <= i <= count - 1,
            //         IF isPresent[i]
            //             student[i] has been printed
            //  && 0 <= count <= length

        if (isPresent[count])
            cout << student[count] << endl;

    cout << endl << "The following students have missed the exam."
        << endl;
    for (count = 0; count < length; count++)

            // Invariant (prior to test):
            //     For all i, where 0 <= i <= count - 1,
            //         IF NOT isPresent[i]
            //             student[i] has been printed
            //  && 0 <= count <= length

        if ( !isPresent[count] )
            cout << student[count] << endl;
}
```

Testing: The program must be tested with names that are more than ten characters, exactly ten characters, and less than ten characters. Names read from the keyboard must be spelled incorrectly as well as correctly. The following data was used.

Roster File

```
Dale
MacDonald
Weems
Vitek
Westby
Smith
Jamison
Jones
Kirshen
NameLongerThanTenCharacters
Gleason
Thompson
Ripley
Lilly
Headington
```

Copy of the Screen During the Run

```
Input file name: roster.dat
Enter last name: Weems
Enter last name: Dale
Enter last name: McDonald
Name not on roster.
Enter last name: MacDonald
Enter last name: Vitek
Enter last name: Westby
Enter last name: NameLongerThanTenCharacters
Enter last name: Gleason
Enter last name: EndData

The following students are taking the exam.
Dale
Gleason
MacDonald
NameLonger
Vitek
Weems
Westby

The following students have missed the exam.
Headington
Jamison
Jones
Kirshen
Lilly
Ripley
Smith
Thompson
```

By assuming that all students have unique last names, we have simplified the problem considerably. Programming Problem 2 is similar, but you must account for both first and last names.

TESTING AND DEBUGGING

In this chapter, we have discussed and coded six general-purpose functions: three sequential searches, a binary search, a selection sort, and an insertion into an ordered list (which can also be used as a sort). We have used three of these functions in the Exam program that has been tested. We test the other three functions by embedding them in driver programs. The drivers should read in data, call the function, and print out the results. Following is the algorithm for a driver to test the Search2 function:

```
Get list of components
WHILE more items to be searched for
   Get item
   Search(list, item, length, index, found)
   IF found
      Print item, "found at position", index
   ELSE
      Print item, "not found in list"
```

The driver would have to be run with several sets of test data to test the Search2 function thoroughly. The minimum set of lists of components would be:

1. A list of no components
2. A list of one component
3. A list of MAX_LENGTH − 1 components
4. A list of more than one but less than MAX_LENGTH − 1 components

The minimum set of items being searched for would be:

1. item in list[0]
2. item in list[length-1]
3. item between list[0] and list[length-1]
4. item < list[0]
5. item > list[length-1]
6. item value between list[0] and list[length-1] but not there

Because ItemType can be any data type that the relational operators can be applied to, function Search2 should be tested with components of several different types.

We leave the coding of this driver program and the creation of the test data as an exercise (see Programming Problem 6). Functions `Search` and `SelSort` should be tested in a similar manner.

At the beginning of this section, we said that three of the functions used in this chapter had been tested in the Exam program. However, to make sure that they stand up as general-purpose functions, they should be subjected to the same rigorous testing proposed for Search, Search2, and SelSort.

In two of the search functions (Search2 and SearchOrd), we stored the value being searched for in `list[length]`. The assumption that `length` would be less than `MAX_LENGTH` (the number of places in the array) is written into the documentation. This could lead to a potential error if the calling module fails to check that `length` is less than `MAX_LENGTH`.

If the precondition listed in the function documentation is that `length <` `MAX_LENGTH`, then the calling module must make sure that the function is not called with `length ≥ MAX_LENGTH`. Another way of dealing with the case where `length ≥ MAX_LENGTH` is to add an error flag to the functions' formal parameter lists and have the functions themselves check for `length ≥` `MAX_LENGTH`. If `length ≥ MAX_LENGTH`, the error flag is set to `TRUE` and the search is terminated. This approach changes the preconditions of the functions so that they can be called even when `length ≥ MAX_LENGTH`.

Either way of handling the problem is acceptable. The important point is that it must be clearly stated whether the calling routine or the called function is to check for the error condition.

Testing and Debugging Hints

1. Review the Testing and Debugging Hints for Chapter 11. They apply to all one-dimensional arrays, including strings.
2. Make sure that every string is terminated with the null character. String constants are automatically null-terminated by the compiler. On input, the >> operator and the `get` function automatically add the null character. If you store characters into a string variable individually or manipulate the array in any way, be sure to account for the null character.
3. Remember that C++ treats string initialization (in a declaration) as different from string assignment. Initialization is allowed but assignment is not.
4. Aggregate input/output is allowed for strings but not for other array types.
5. If you use the >> operator to input into a string variable, be sure the array is large enough to hold the null character plus the longest sequence of (nonwhitespace) characters in the input stream.
6. With string input, the >> operator stops at, *but does not consume*, the first trailing whitespace character. Likewise, if the `get` function stops reading early because it encounters a newline character, the newline character is not consumed.
7. When you use the `strcpy` library function, ensure that the destination array is at least as large as the array from which you are copying.

8. General-purpose functions should be tested outside the context of a particular program, using a driver.
9. Test data should be chosen carefully to test all end conditions and some in the middle. End conditions are those that reach the limits of the structure used to store them. For example, in a one-dimensional array, there should be test data items in which the number of components is 0, 1, and MAX_LENGTH (MAX_LENGTH − 1 in the case of Search2 and SearchOrd), as well as between 1 and MAX_LENGTH.

SUMMARY

This chapter has provided practice in working with lists represented by one-dimensional arrays. We have examined algorithms that search and sort data stored in a list, and we have written functions to implement these algorithms. We can use these functions again and again in different contexts because we have written them in a general fashion.

In the searching and sorting functions, the components in the array are of type ItemType. ItemType can be defined as any simple data type, although slight modifications may be required to accommodate floating point types.

Strings are a special case of char arrays in C++. The last significant character must be followed by a null character to mark the end of the string. Strings are useful in working with character information. Because strings can be copied and compared using standard library functions, our general-purpose list operations can be adapted easily to work with arrays of strings.

QUICK CHECK

1. In a sequential search of an unordered array of 1000 values, what is the average number of loop iterations required to find a value? What is the maximum number of iterations that may be required to find a value? (pp. 667–668)
2. The following program fragment sorts a list into ascending order. Change it to sort into descending order. (pp. 653–657)

```
for (passCount = 0; passCount < length - 1; passCount++)
{
    minIndex = passCount;
    for (placeCount = passCount + 1; placeCount < length;
                                                placeCount++)
        if (list[placeCount] < list[minIndex])
            minIndex = placeCount;
    temp = list[minIndex];                  // Swap
    list[minIndex] = list[passCount];
    list[passCount] = temp;
}
```

3. Describe how the list insertion operation can be used to build a sorted list from unordered input data. (pp. 659–662)
4. Describe the basic principle behind the binary search algorithm. (pp. 662–666)
5. Using Typedef, define an array data type that holds a string of 15 characters plus the null character. Declare an array variable of this type, initializing it to your first name. Then use a library function to replace the contents of the variable with your last name. (pp. 668–679)

Answers   1. The average number is 500 iterations. The maximum is 1000 iterations.   2. The only required change is to replace the "<" symbol in the inner loop with a ">". As a matter of style, `minIndex` should be changed to `maxIndex`.   3. The list initially has a length of 0. Each time a data value is read, insertion adds the value to the list in its correct position. When all the data have been read, they are in the array in sorted order.   4. The binary search takes advantage of ordered list values, looking at a component in the middle of the list and deciding whether the search value precedes or follows the midpoint. The search is then repeated on the appropriate half, quarter, eighth, and so on, of the list until the value is located.

5. `typedef char String15[16];`

   `String15 name = "Anna";`

   `strcpy(name, "Rodriguez");`

EXAM PREPARATION EXERCISES

1. What three factors should you consider when you are deciding which search algorithm to use on a list?
2. The following values are stored in an array in ascending order.

   28 45 97 103 107 162 196 202 257

   Applying function `Search2` to this array, search for the following values and indicate how many comparisons are required to either find the number or find that it is not in the list.
   a. 28
   b. 32
   c. 196
   d. 194
3. Repeat Exercise 2 using the `SearchOrd` function.
4. The following values are stored in an array in ascending order.

   29 57 63 72 79 83 96 104 114 136

   Apply function `BinSearch` with `item` = 114 to this list, and trace the values of `first`, `last`, and `middle`. Indicate any undefined values with a *U*.
5. A binary search is always better to use than a sequential search. (True or False?)
6. a. Define a data type `NameType` to be a string of at most 40 characters plus the null character.
   b. Declare a variable `oneName` to be of type `NameType`.
   c. Declare `employeeName` to be a 100-element array variable whose elements are strings of type `NameType`.
7. Given the declarations

```
typedef char NameString[21];
typedef char WordString[11];

NameString firstName;
NameString lastName;
WordString word;
```

mark the following statements valid or invalid. (Assume the header file string.h has been included.)

a. `i = 0;`
```
   while (firstName[i] != '\0')
   {
       cout << firstName[i];
       i++;
   }
```
b. `cout << lastName;`
c. `if (firstName == lastName)`
```
       n = 1;
```
d. `if (strcmp(firstName, lastName) == 0)`
```
       m = 8;
```
e. `cin >> word;`
f. `lastName = word;`
g. `if (strcmp(NameString, "Hi") < 0)`
```
       n = 3;
```
h. `if (firstName[2] == word[5])`
```
       m = 4;
```

8. Given the declarations

```
typedef char String20[21];
typedef char String30[31];

String20 rodent;
String30 mammal;
```

write code fragments for the following tasks. (If the task is not possible, say so.)
a. Store the string "Moose" into `mammal`.
b. Copy whatever string is in `rodent` into `mammal`.
c. If the string in `mammal` is greater than "Opossum" lexicographically, increment a variable count.
d. If the string in `mammal` is less than or equal to "Jackal", decrement a variable count.
e. Store the string "Grey-tipped field shrew" into `rodent`.
f. Print the length of the string in `rodent`.
9. Given the declarations

```
const int NUMBER_OF_BOOKS = 200;

typedef char BookName[31];
typedef char PersonName[21];
```

```
BookName    bookOut[NUMBER_OF_BOOKS];
PersonName  borrower[NUMBER_OF_BOOKS];
BookName    bookIn;
PersonName  name;
```

mark the following statements valid or invalid. (Assume the header file string.h has been included.)

a. `cout << bookIn;`
b. `cout << bookOut;`
c. `for (i = 0; i < NUMBER_OF_BOOKS; i++)`
   `    cout << bookOut[i] << endl;`
d. `if (bookOut[3] > bookIn)`
   `    cout << bookIn;`
e. `for (i = 0; i < NUMBER_OF_BOOKS; i++)`
   `    if (strcmp(bookIn, bookOut[i]) == 0)`
   `        cout << bookIn << ' ' << borrower[i] << endl;`
f. `bookIn = "Don Quixote";`
g. `cout << name[2];`

10. Write code fragments to perform the following tasks, using the declarations given in Exercise 9. Assume that the books listed in bookOut have been borrowed by the person listed in the corresponding position of borrower.
    a. Write a code fragment to print each book borrowed by name.
    b. Write a code fragment to count the number of books borrowed by name.
    c. Write a code fragment to count the number of copies of bookIn that have been borrowed.
    d. Write a code fragment to count the number of copies of bookIn that have been borrowed by name.

PROGRAMMING WARM-UP EXERCISES

1. Write a C++ value-returning function Index that searches an int array list for a value item and returns its place in the array. There are length values in list. If item is not in the array, Index should return –1.
2. Write a C++ value-returning function Count that counts the occurrences of a value item, of simple type ItemType, in an unsorted array numList. There are length items in numList.
3. Write a C++ value-returning function that receives two int arrays (arr1 and arr2) of length length. This function should return the product of all components of arr2 for which the corresponding components of arr1 are negative.
4. Write a C++ value-returning function Found that searches a float array list for a float value greater than the value of item. If such a value is found, the function returns TRUE; otherwise, FALSE is returned. The number of components in list is passed as a parameter.
5. Rewrite SearchOrd to give it an additional formal parameter overflow. If length is greater than or equal to MAX_LENGTH, overflow is TRUE, an appropriate error message is printed, and the search is not made. Otherwise, overflow is FALSE. The constant MAX_LENGTH may be accessed globally. Change the function documentation to reflect this change.

6. Rewrite function `SearchOrd` so that it searches a text file instead of an array.

7. Write a C++ function that searches a list `list` of length `length` for `item`. If `item` is found, it is deleted and the list is compacted (that is, all the components below `item` are moved up one place). Adjust `length` appropriately. `item` is of simple type `ItemType`.

8. Repeat Exercise 7, assuming that `item` is of string type `StrType` and `list` contains components of type `StrType`.

9. Write a C++ function that removes all occurrences of `item` in a list `list` of length `length`. Adjust `length` appropriately. `item` is of simple type `ItemType`.

10. Write a C++ function that takes two parallel arrays, `isAbsent` (Boolean) and `score` (`float`), and `length` as parameters. This function should store a zero into each position of `score` for which `FALSE` is in the parallel position of `isAbsent`. The other components of `score` should be left alone.

11. Write a C++ value-returning function that returns the sum of the products of parallel components in two `int` arrays, `data` and `weight`. Pass `length` as a parameter.

12. Modify function `BinSearch` so that `index` is where `item` should be inserted when `found` is `FALSE`.

13. Modify function `Insert` so that it uses function `BinSearch` rather than function `SearchOrd` to find the insertion point. (Assume that `BinSearch` has been modified as in Exercise 12.)

14. Given the declarations

```
const int MAX_LEN = 200;
typedef int ItemType;

ItemType list1[MAX_LEN];
ItemType list2[MAX_LEN];
int        length1;        // Length of list1
int        length2;        // Length of list2
ItemType item;
```

and viewing a list as an abstract data type, implement the following operations on a list.

a. A function named `Empty` that returns `TRUE` if a given list is empty. (*Hint:* Pass the length of the list to the function.)

b. A function named `Full` that returns `TRUE` if no more space is left in the array containing the list.

c. A function named `Equal` that takes two lists as parameters and returns `TRUE` if they are of the same length and each element in one list equals the corresponding element in the second list.

d. A function named `Delete` that takes a list and an item and searches the list for an instance of the item. If the item is found, it is removed from the list, and succeeding items are moved up to fill the empty space.

e. A function named `DeleteAll` that removes all instances of an item from a list without leaving gaps in the array.

f. A function named `Component` that returns a component of the list if a given position number (index value) is in the range 0 through `length`–1. The function should also return a Boolean flag named `valid` that is `FALSE` if the index is outside this range.

PROGRAMMING PROBLEMS

1. A company wants to know the percentages of total sales and total expenses attributable to each salesperson. Each has a data line giving his or her last name (maximum of 20 characters), followed by a comma, followed by his or her first name (maximum of 10 characters). The next line contains his or her total sales (int) and expenses (float). Write a program that produces a report with a header line containing the total sales and total expenses. Following this header should be a table with each salesperson's first name, last name, percentage of total sales, and percentage of total expenses.

2. Only authorized shareholders are allowed to attend a stockholders' meeting. Write a program to read a person's name from the keyboard, check it against a list of shareholders, and print a message saying whether or not the person may attend the meeting. The list of shareholders is in a file inFile in the following format: first name (maximum 10 characters), blank, last name (maximum 20 characters). Use the end-of-file condition to stop reading the file. The maximum number of shareholders is 1000.

   The user should be prompted to enter his or her name in the same format as is used for the data in the file. If the name does not appear on the list, the program should repeat the instructions on how to enter the name and then tell the user to try again. A message saying that the person may not enter should be printed only after he or she has been given a second chance to enter the name. The prompt to the user should include the message that a *Q* should be entered to end the program.

3. Enhance the program in Problem 2 as follows:
   a. Print a report showing how many stockholders there were at the time of the meeting, how many were present at the meeting, and how many people who tried to enter were denied permission to attend.
   b. Follow this summary report with a list of the names of the stockholders, with either *Present* or *Absent* after each name.

4. A life insurance company has hired you to write a program to print a list of their customers and the premium that each customer pays. Premiums are based on the age the customer was when he or she became a customer. The following table is used to determine each customer's premium, but these rates are subject to change.

Age	Premium
25	$277.00
35	287.00
45	307.00
55	327.00
65	357.00

   Each age listed in this table is the upper limit for the premium. For example, if a customer signed up for a policy when she was 37, she would pay $307.00.

   Write a program that reads the table into parallel arrays, then reads in the customers' names and ages when they bought the policies into another pair of parallel arrays. The table and the customers' names and ages are stored in two files. Print out a formatted, labeled list showing each customer's name, his or her age when the policy was bought, and the customer's premium.

5. The local bank in Programming Problem 4, Chapter 11, was so successful with its advertising campaign that the parent bank decided to collect data on waiting times from banks all over the state and run a contest. However, this time they decided to assign frustration levels to wait times as follows:

Wait Time	Frustration Level
wait ≤ (mean − standardDev)	"Amazed"
(mean − standardDev) < wait < mean	"Pleased"
mean ≤ wait < (mean + standardDev)	"Calm"
(mean + standardDev) ≤ wait < (mean + 2 * standardDev)	"Irritated"
(mean + 2 * standardDev) ≤ wait	"Berserk"

where mean is the mean waiting time, wait is the wait time, and standardDev is the standard deviation of the waiting times. Calculate frustration levels for each recorded wait.

Input:

Same as in Programming Problem 4, Chapter 11, except that two digits have been added to the teller ID number to indicate at which bank the teller is located.

Output:

Same as for Programming Problem 4, Chapter 11, plus 1) a bar graph (histogram) showing frustration level distribution; and 2) a table sorted by three-digit ID numbers showing (a) ID number, (b) wait time, and (c) frustration level.

6. Complete the driver program described in the Testing and Debugging section. Use it to test the functions Search, Search2, SearchOrd, and BinSearch thoroughly. Choose your test data carefully, making sure that all cases are tested.

CASE STUDY FOLLOW-UP

1. In the Birthday Reminder Revisited case study, the GetMonth function declares and initializes two local arrays, monthAry and strMonthAry. These are automatic variables, so they are created and initialized every time the function is called, and they are destroyed each time the function returns. Improve the function by ensuring that the arrays are created and initialized only once and remain "alive" for the duration of the entire program. (*Hint:* Review the description in Chapter 8 of lifetimes of variables.)

2. The Exam Attendance case study uses an insertion sort, placing each student's name into its proper place in the list as it is input. Rewrite the program to input all the names at once and then sort them using SelSort.

3. The Exam Attendance case study uses a binary search to search the student list. Assuming a list of 200 students, how many loop iterations are required to determine that a student is absent? How many iterations would be required if we had used the Search function instead of BinSearch?

13

Multidimensional Arrays

GOALS

- To be able to declare a two-dimensional array.
- To be able to access a component of a two-dimensional array.
- To be able to perform fundamental operations on a two-dimensional array:

  Initialize the array

  Print the values in the array

  Process the array by rows

  Process the array by columns
- To be able to declare a two-dimensional array as a formal parameter.
- To be able to view a two-dimensional array as an array of arrays.
- To be able to declare and process a multidimensional array.
- To be able to choose an appropriate array data structure for a given problem.

Data structures play an important role in the design process. The choice of data structure directly affects the design, because it determines the algorithms used to process the data. We have discussed the one-dimensional array, which gives us the ability to reference a group of data objects by one name. This simplifies the design of many algorithms.

In many problems, however, the relationships between data items are more complex than a simple list. In this chapter, we begin by examining the two-dimensional array, which is useful when data is to be organized in the form of a table with rows and columns. Two-dimensional arrays are also useful for representing board games, like chess, tic-tac-toe, or Scrabble, and in computer graphics, where the screen is thought of as a two-dimensional array.

The definition of an array then is extended to allow arrays with any number of dimensions, called multidimensional arrays. Each dimension of such an array is used to represent a different feature of a component. For example, a three-dimensional array of sales figures might be indexed by (1) store number, (2) month, and (3) item number.

 ## Two-Dimensional Arrays

A one-dimensional array is used to represent a list. A **two-dimensional array** is used to represent a table with rows and columns, provided each item in the table is of the same data type. A component in a two-dimensional array is accessed by specifying the row and column indices of the item in a table. This is a familiar task. For example, if you want to find a street on a map, you look up the street name on the back of the map to find the coordinates of the street, usually a letter and a number. The letter specifies a column to look on, and the number specifies a row. You find the street where the row and column meet.

Two-Dimensional Array A collection of components, all of the same type, structured in two dimensions. Each component is accessed by a pair of indices that represent the component's position in each dimension.

Figure 13-1 shows a two-dimensional array that has 100 rows and 9 columns. The rows are accessed by an integer ranging from 0 through 99; the columns are accessed by an integer ranging from 0 through 8. Each component is accessed by a row-column pair—for example, 0, 5.

A two-dimensional array is declared in exactly the same way as a one-dimensional array, except that sizes must be specified for two dimensions. Below is the syntax template for declaring an array with more than one dimension, along with an example.

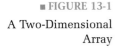

A Two-Dimensional Array

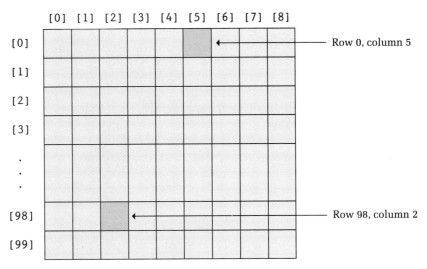

ArrayDeclaration

DataType ArrayName **[** ConstIntExpression **]** **[ConstIntExpression]** . . . **;**

```
const int NUM_ROWS = 100;
const int NUM_COLS = 9;
     .
     .
     .
float alpha[NUM_ROWS][NUM_COLS];
              ↑              ↑
            First        Second
         dimension    dimension
```

This example declares alpha to be a two-dimensional array, all of whose components are float values. The declaration creates the array that was pictured in Figure 13-1.

To access an individual component of the alpha array, two expressions (one for each dimension) are used to specify its position. Each expression is in its own pair of brackets next to the name of the array:

```
alpha[0][5] = 36.4;
        ↗    ↖
     Row    Column
   number   number
```

The syntax template for accessing an array component is

ArrayComponentAccess

> ArrayName [IndexExpression] [IndexExpression] . . .

As with one-dimensional arrays, each index expression must result in an integer value.

Let's look now at some examples. Here is the declaration of a two-dimensional array with 364 integer components:

```
int hiTemp[52][7];
```

We can think of hiTemp as a table with 52 rows and 7 columns. The contents of each place in the table (each component) can be any int value. Our intention is that the array contains high temperatures for each day in a year. Each row represents one of the 52 weeks in a year, and each column represents one of the 7 days in a week. (To keep the example simple, we ignore the fact that there are 365—and sometimes 366—days in a year.) The expression hiTemp[2][6] refers to the int value in the third row (row 2) and the seventh column (column 6). Semantically, hiTemp[2][6] is the temperature for the seventh day of the third week. The code fragment shown in Figure 13-2 would print the temperature values for the third week.

Another representation of the same data might be as follows:

```
enum DayType
{
    MONDAY, TUESDAY, WEDNESDAY, THURSDAY, FRIDAY, SATURDAY, SUNDAY
};

int hiTemp[52][7];
```

■ FIGURE 13-2

hiTemp Array

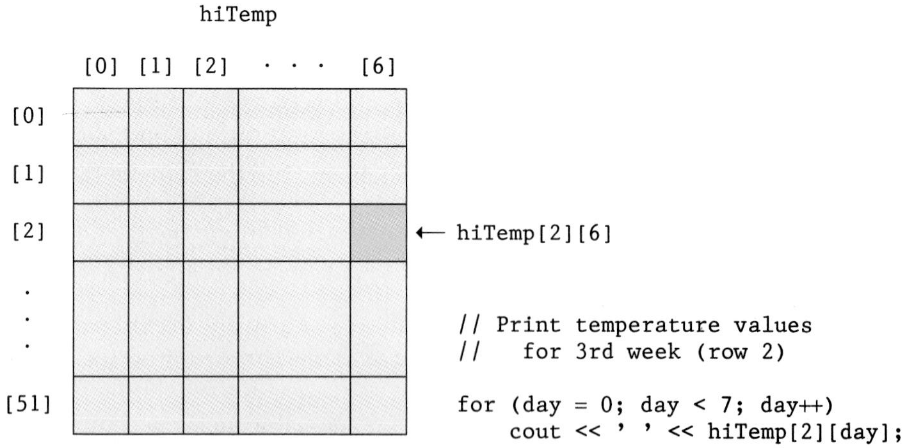

```
// Print temperature values
//    for 3rd week (row 2)

for (day = 0; day < 7; day++)
    cout << ' ' << hiTemp[2][day];
```

■ FIGURE 13-3   `hiTemp` Array (Alternate Form)

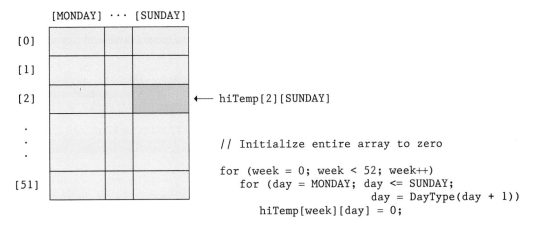

Here, `hiTemp` is declared the same as before, but we use an expression of type `DayType` for the column index. `hiTemp[2][SUNDAY]` corresponds to the same component as `hiTemp[2][6]` in the first example. (Recall that enumerators such as `MONDAY`, `TUESDAY`, . . . are represented internally as the integers 0, 1, 2, ...) If `day` were of type `DayType` and `week` of type `int`, the code fragment shown in Figure 13-3 would set the entire array to 0. (Notice that by using `DayType`, the temperature values in the array begin with the first Monday of the year, not necessarily with January 1.)

If the declaration of `hiTemp` listed the sizes of the two dimensions in reverse order, the rows and columns would be reversed; that is, the declaration

```
int hiTemp[7][52];
```

declares an array like that shown in Figure 13-4. Notice how the code fragment in this figure differs from the equivalent code in Figure 13-3: the two index expressions are reversed. The order in which we define the rows and columns doesn't matter to the computer as long as we're consistent. To help visualize a two-dimensional array, we always use the convention of letting the first dimension define the rows and the second dimension define the columns.

Another way of looking at a two-dimensional array is to see it as a structure in which each component has two features. For example, in the following code,

■ FIGURE 13-4   hiTemp Array (Third Variation)

hiTemp

```
[0] [1] [2]  · · ·  [51]
```

[MONDAY]

·
·
·

[SUNDAY]

hiTemp[SUNDAY][2]

```
// Initialize entire array to zero

for (week = 0; week < 52; week++)
    for (day = MONDAY; day <= SUNDAY;
                      day = DayType(day + 1))
        hiTemp[day][week] = 0;
```

```
enum Colors {RED, ORANGE, YELLOW, GREEN, BLUE, INDIGO, VIOLET};
enum Makes
{
    FORD, TOYOTA, HYUNDAI, JAGUAR, CITROEN, BMW, FIAT, SAAB
};
const int NUM_COLORS = 7;
const int NUM_MAKES = 8;

float crashRating[NUM_COLORS][NUM_MAKES];   // Array of crash
                                            // likelihoods by color
                                            // and make
     ⋮
     ⋮
crashRating[BLUE][JAGUAR] = 0.83;           // Blue Jaguars have a crash
                                            //    likelihood of 0.83
crashRating[RED][FORD] = 0.19;              // Red Fords have a crash
                                            //    likelihood of 0.19
```

the data structure uses one dimension to represent the color and the other to represent the make of automobile. In other words, both indices have semantic content—a concept we discussed in Chapter 11.

Processing Two-Dimensional Arrays

Processing data in a two-dimensional array generally means accessing the array in one of four patterns: randomly, along rows, along columns, or throughout the entire array. Each of these may also involve subarray processing.

The simplest way to access a component is to look in a given location. For example, a user enters map coordinates that we use as indices into an array of street names to access the sought-after name at those coordinates. This process is referred to as *random access* because the user may enter any set of coordinates at random.

There are many cases in which we might wish to perform an operation on all the elements of a particular row or column in a table. Look back at the hiTemp array pictured in Figure 13-3, where the rows represent weeks of the year and the columns represent days of the week. The data represents the high temperatures for each day in a year. If we wanted the average high temperature for a given week, we would sum the values in that row and divide by 7. If we wanted the average for a given day of the week, we would sum the values in that column and divide by 52. The former case is access along rows; the latter case is access along columns.

Now, suppose that we wish to determine the average for the year. We must access every element in the array, sum them, and divide by 364. In this case, the order of access—by row or by column—is not important. (The same is true when we initialize every element of an array to 0.) This is access throughout the array.

There are situations when we must access every element in an array in a particular order, either by rows or by columns. For example, if we wanted the average for every week, we would run through the entire array, taking each row in turn. However, if we wanted the average for each day of the week, we would run through the array a column at a time.

Let's take a closer look at these patterns of access by considering four common examples of array processing.

1. Sum the rows.
2. Sum the columns.
3. Initialize the table to all zeroes (or some special value).
4. Print the table.

First, let's define some constants and variables using general identifiers, such as row and col, rather than problem-dependent identifiers. Then let's look at each algorithm in terms of generalized table processing.

```
const int NUM_ROWS = 50;
const int NUM_COLS = 50;

int table[NUM_ROWS][NUM_COLS];   // A two-dimensional array
int rowLength;                   // Data is in 0..rowLength-1
int row;                         // A row index
int colLength;                   // Data is in 0..colLength-1
int col;                         // A column index
int total;                       // A variable for summing
```

Sum the Rows

Suppose we want to sum row number 3 (the fourth row) in array `table` and print the result. We can do this easily with a For loop:

```
total = 0;
for (col = 0; col < NUM_COLS; col++)

        // Invariant (prior to test):
        //    total == table[3][0] + ... + table[3][col-1]
        //    && 0 <= col <= NUM_COLS

    total = total + table[3][col];
cout << "Row sum: " << total << endl;
```

This For loop runs through each column of `table`, while keeping the row index equal to 3. Every value in row 3 is added to `total`. Suppose we wanted to sum and print two rows—row 2 and row 3. We could add a duplicate of the preceding code fragment, but with the index set to 2:

```
// Sum row 2 and print the sum

total = 0;
for (col = 0; col < NUM_COLS; col++)

        // Invariant (prior to test):
        //    total == table[2][0] + ... + table[2][col-1]
        //    && 0 <= col <= NUM_COLS

    total = total + table[2][col];
cout << "Row sum: " << total << endl;

// Sum row 3 and print the sum

total = 0;
for (col = 0; col < NUM_COLS; col++)

        // Invariant (prior to test):
        //    total == table[3][0] + ... + table[3][col-1]
        //    && 0 <= col <= NUM_COLS

    total = total + table[3][col];
cout << "Row sum: " << total << endl;
```

or we could use a nested loop and make the row index a variable:

```
for (row = 2; row < 4; row++)
{
        // Invariant (prior to test):
        //     Rows 2 through row-1 have been summed and printed
        //     && 2 <= row <= 4

    total = 0;
    for (col = 0; col < NUM_COLS; col++)

            // Invariant (prior to test):
            //     total == table[row][0] + ... + table[row][col-1]
            //     && 0 <= col <= NUM_COLS

        total = total + table[row][col];
    cout << "Row sum: " << total << endl;
}
```

The second approach is shorter, but its real advantage is that we can easily modify it to process any range of rows.

The outer loop controls the rows, and the inner loop controls the columns. For each value of row, every column is processed; then the outer loop moves to the next row. In the first iteration of the outer loop, row is held at 2 and col goes from 0 through NUM_COLS–1. Therefore, the array is accessed in the following order:

```
table[2][0]   [2][1]   [2][2]   [2][3]   . . .   [2][NUM_COLS-1]
```

In the second iteration of the outer loop, row is incremented to 3, and the array is accessed as follows:

```
table[3][0]   [3][1]   [3][2]   [3][3]   . . .   [3][NUM_COLS-1]
```

We can generalize this row processing to run through every row of the table by having the outer loop run from 0 through NUM_ROWS–1. However, if we want to access only part of the array (subarray processing), we write the code fragment as follows:

```
for (row = 0; row < rowLength; row++)
{
        // Invariant (prior to test):
        //     Rows 0 through row-1 have been summed and printed
        //     && 0 <= row <= rowLength
```

```
                    total = 0;
                    for (col = 0; col < colLength; col++)

                        // Invariant (prior to test):
                        //    total == table[row][0] + ... + table[row][col-1]
                        // && 0 <= col <= colLength

                    total = total + table[row][col];
                cout << "Row sum: " << total << endl;
            }
```

Figure 13-5 illustrates subarray processing by row.

Sum the Columns

Suppose we want to sum and print each column. The code to perform this task is given below. Again we have generalized the code to sum only the portion of the array that contains valid data.

```
for (col = 0; col < colLength; col++)
{

        // Invariant (prior to test):
        //    Columns 0 through col-1 have been summed and printed
        // && 0 <= col <= colLength
```

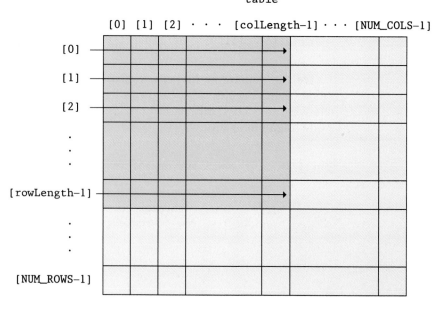

■ FIGURE 13-5

Partial Table
Processing by Row

```
      total = 0;
      for (row = 0; row < rowLength; row++)

            // Invariant (prior to test):
            //     total == table[0][col] + ... + table[row-1][col]
            //  && 0 <= row <= rowLength

         total = total + table[row][col];
      cout << "Column sum: " << total << endl;
}
```

In this case, the outer loop controls the column, and the inner loop controls the row. All the components in the first column are accessed and summed before the outer loop index changes and the components in the second column are accessed. Figure 13-6 illustrates subarray processing by column.

Initialize the Table

As with one-dimensional arrays, we can initialize a two-dimensional array either by initializing it in its declaration or by using assignment statements. If the array is small, it is simplest to initialize it in its declaration. To initialize a 2-row by 3-column table to look like this:

```
14    3  -5
 0   46   7
```

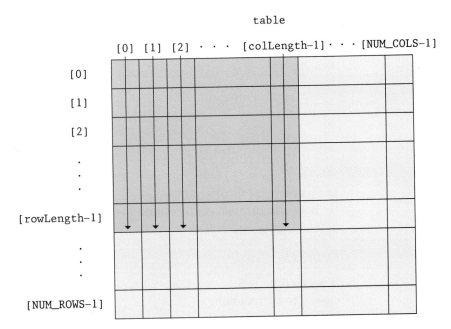

■ FIGURE 13-6

Partial Table
Processing by
Column

we can use the following declaration.

```
int table[2][3] =
{
    {14, 3, -5},
    {0, 46, 7}
};
```

In this declaration, the initializer list consists of two items, each of which is itself an initializer list. The first inner initializer list stores 14, 3, and –5 into row 0 of the table; the second stores 0, 46, and 7 into row 1. The use of two initializer lists makes sense if you think of each row of the table as a one-dimensional array of three ints. The first initializer list initializes the first array (the first row), and the second list initializes the second array (the second row). Later in the chapter, we revisit this notion of viewing a two-dimensional array as an array of arrays.

Initializing a table in its declaration is impractical if the table is large. For a 100-row by 100-column table, you don't want to list 10,000 values. If the values are all different, you should store them into a file and input them into the table at run time. If the values are all the same, the usual approach is to use nested For loops and an assignment statement. Here is a general-purpose code segment that zeroes out a table with NUM_ROWS rows and NUM_COLS columns:

```
for (row = 0; row < NUM_ROWS; row++)

        // Invariant (prior to test):
        //     table[0..row-1][0..NUM_COLS-1] == 0
        //  && 0 <= row <= NUM_ROWS

    for (col = 0; col < NUM_COLS; col++)

            // Invariant (prior to test):
            //     table[row][0..col-1] == 0
            //  && 0 <= col <= NUM_COLS

        table[row][col] = 0;
```

In this case, we initialized the table a row at a time, but we could just as easily have run through each column instead. The order doesn't matter as long as we access every element.

Print the Table

If we wish to print out a table with one row per line, then we have another case of row processing:

```
#include <iomanip.h>        // For setw()
    .
    .
    .

for (row = 0; row < NUM_ROWS; row++)
{
        // Invariant (prior to test):
        //      Rows 0 through row-1 of table have been output
        //   && 0 <= row <= NUM_ROWS

    for (col = 0; col < NUM_COLS; col++)

            // Invariant (prior to test):
            //      table[row][0..col-1] have been output
            //   && 0 <= col <= NUM_COLS

        cout << setw(15) << table[row][col];
    cout << endl;
}
```

This code fragment prints the values of the table in columns that are 15 characters wide. As a matter of proper style, this fragment should be preceded by code that prints headings over the columns to identify their contents.

There's no rule that we have to print each row on a line. We could turn the table sideways and print each column on one line simply by exchanging the two For loops. When you are printing a table, you must consider which order of presentation makes the most sense and how the table fits on the page. For example, a table with 6 columns and 100 rows would be best printed as 6 columns, 100 lines long.

Almost all processing of data stored in a two-dimensional array involves either processing by row or processing by column. In most of our examples the index type has been int, but the pattern of operation of the loops is the same no matter what types the indices are.

The looping patterns for row processing and column processing are so useful that they are summarized below. To make them more general, we use minRow for the first row number and minCol for the first column number. Remember that row processing has the row index in the outer loop, and column processing has the column index in the outer loop.

Row Processing

```
for (row = minRow; row < rowLength; row++)
    for (col = minCol; col < colLength; col++)
        .
        .                 // Whatever processing is required
        .
```

Column Processing

```
for (col = minCol; col < colLength; col++)
    for (row = minRow; row < rowLength; row++)
        .
        .
        .
                        // Whatever processing is required
```

 Passing Two-Dimensional Arrays as Parameters

In Chapter 11, we said that when one-dimensional arrays are declared as formal parameters in a function, the size of the array usually is omitted:

```
void SomeFunc( /* inout */ float list[],
               /* in */    int   size   )
{
    .
    .
    .
}
```

If you include a size in the square brackets, the compiler ignores it. As you learned, the base address of the actual parameter (the memory address of the first array element) is passed to the function. The function works for an actual parameter of any size. Because the function cannot know the size of the caller's actual array, we either pass the size as a parameter—as in SomeFunc above—or use a declared constant if the function always operates on an array of a certain size.

When a two-dimensional array is passed as a parameter, again the base address of the actual array is sent to the function. But you cannot leave off the sizes of both of the array dimensions. You can omit the size of the first dimension (the number of rows) but not the second (the number of columns). Here is the reason.

In the computer's memory, C++ stores two-dimensional arrays in row order. Thinking of memory as one long line of memory cells, the first row of the array is followed by the second row, which is followed by the third, and so on (see Figure 13-7). To locate table[1][0] in this figure, a function that receives table's base address must be able to know that there are four elements in each row—that is, that the table consists of four columns. Therefore, the declaration of a formal parameter must always state the number of columns:

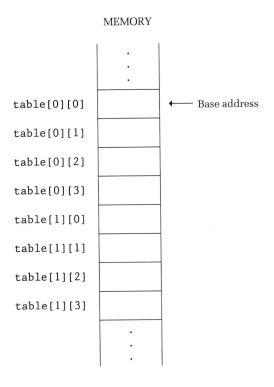

MEMORY

table[0][0]   ←——— Base address

table[0][1]

table[0][2]

table[0][3]

table[1][0]

table[1][1]

table[1][2]

table[1][3]

```
void AnotherFunc( /* inout */ int arr[][4] )
{
    .
    .
    .
}
```

Furthermore, the number of columns declared for the formal parameter must be *exactly* the same as the number of columns in the caller's actual array. As you can tell from Figure 13-7, if there is any discrepancy in the number of columns, the function will access the wrong array element in memory.

Our AnotherFunc function works for a two-dimensional array of any number of rows, as long as it has exactly four columns. In practice, we seldom write programs that use arrays with a varying number of rows but the same number of columns. To avoid problems with mismatches in formal and actual parameter sizes, it's practical to use a Typedef statement to define a two-dimensional array type and then declare both the actual and the formal parameters to be of that type. For example, we might make the declarations

```
const int NUM_ROWS = 10;
const int NUM_COLS = 20;
typedef int TableType[NUM_ROWS][NUM_COLS];
```

and then write the following general-purpose function that initializes all elements of an array to a specified value:

```
void Initialize( /* out */ TableType table,    // Array to initialize
                 /* in */   int       initVal) // Initial value

// Initializes each element of table to initVal


// Precondition:
//      initVal is assigned
// Postcondition:
//      table[0..NUM_ROWS-1][0..NUM_COLS-1] == initVal

{
    int row;
    int col;

    for (row = 0; row < NUM_ROWS; row++)

            // Invariant (prior to test):
            //      table[0..row-1][0..NUM_COLS-1] == initVal
            //   && 0 <= row <= NUM_ROWS

        for (col = 0; col < NUM_COLS; col++)

                // Invariant (prior to test):
                //      table[row][0..col-1] == initVal
                //   && 0 <= col <= NUM_COLS

            table[row][col] = initVal;
}
```

The calling code could then declare and initialize one or more arrays of type TableType by making calls to the Initialize function. For example,

```
TableType delta;
TableType gamma;

Initialize(delta, 0);
Initialize(gamma, -1);
    .
    .
    .
```

Another Way of Defining Two-Dimensional Arrays

We hinted earlier that a two-dimensional array can be viewed as an array of arrays. This view is supported by C++ in the sense that the components of a one-dimensional array do not have to be atomic; they can also be structured. For example, in the Exam program in Chapter 12, we slipped in the declaration of a two-dimensional array. The student array was declared as:

```
const int MAX_LENGTH = 200;
typedef char String10[11];       // Room for 10 characters plus '\0'

String10 student[MAX_LENGTH];    // Array of student names
```

With this declaration, the components of the array student are one-dimensional arrays of type String10. In other words, student has two dimensions. We can access each row as an entity: student[57] accesses the name of student number 57. We can also access each individual component of student by specifying both indices: student[57][0] accesses the first letter in the name of student 57.

Now that you know how to declare a two-dimensional array, student can be redeclared as follows:

```
char student[MAX_LENGTH][11];
```

Does it matter which way we declare a two-dimensional array? Not to C++. The choice should be based on readability and understandability. Sometimes the features of the data are shown more clearly if both indices are specified in a single declaration. At other times, the code is clearer if one dimension is defined first as a one-dimensional array type.

Here is an example of when it is advantageous to define a two-dimensional array as an array of arrays. If the rows have been defined first as a one-dimensional array type, each can be passed to a function expecting as a parameter a one-dimensional array of the same type. The following function reads a student name into a variable of type String10, returning both the name and its length.

```
#include <string.h>    // For strlen()
       .
       .
       .

void GetAName( /* out */ String10 stuName,    // Input name
               /* out */ int&     length  )   // Length of name

// Reads a name from input until either '\n' or the maximum
// length is reached. Also returns the length of the name
```

```
// Postcondition:
//      One input line has been read through '\n'
//   && stuName contains at most 10 of the input characters
//      encountered before '\n'
//   && length == length of stuName

{
    cin.get(stuName, 11);        // Read at most 10 characters
    cin.ignore(100, '\n');
    length = strlen(stuName);
}
```

We can call GetAName using a component of student as follows.

```
GetAName(student[2], nameLength);
```

Row 2 of student is passed to GetAName, which treats it like any other one-dimensional array of type String10 (see Figure 13-8). It makes sense to pass the row as a parameter because both it and the formal parameter are of the same named type, String10.

Declaring student as a one-dimensional array of strings is clearer than declaring it directly as a two-dimensional array. Whenever possible, we like to treat a string as a single item rather than as an array of individual characters.

 Multidimensional Arrays

C++ does not place a limit on the number of dimensions that an array can have. We can generalize our definition of an array to cover all cases.

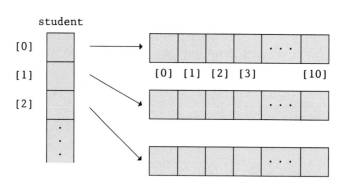

■ FIGURE 13-8

A One-Dimensional Array of One-Dimensional Arrays

The components of **student** are one-dimensional arrays of type **String10**.

Array A collection of components, all of the same type, ordered on N dimensions ($N \geq 1$). Each component is accessed by N indices, each of which represents the component's position within that dimension.

You should have guessed from the syntax templates that you can have as many dimensions as you want. How many should you have in a particular case? As many as there are features that describe the components in the array.

Take, for example, a chain of department stores. Monthly sales figures must be kept for each item by store. There are three important pieces of information about each item: the month in which it was sold, the store from which it was purchased, and the item number. We can define an array type to summarize these data as follows:

```
const int NUM_ITEMS = 100;
const int NUM_STORES = 10;

typedef int SalesType[NUM_STORES][12][NUM_ITEMS];

SalesType sales;      // Array of sales figures
int       item;
int       store;
int       month;
int       numberSold;
int       currentMonth;
```

A graphic representation of the array variable `sales` is shown in Figure 13-9.

The number of components in `sales` is 12,000 ($10 \times 12 \times 100$). If sales figures are available only for January through June, then half the array is empty. If we want to process the data in the array, we must use subarray processing. The following program fragment sums and prints the total number of each item sold this year to date by all stores.

```
for (item = 0; item < NUM_ITEMS; item++)
{
    numberSold = 0;
    for (store = 0; store < NUM_STORES; store++)
        for (month = 0; month <= currentMonth; month++)
            numberSold = numberSold + sales[store][month][item];
    cout << "Item #" << item << " Sales to date = " << numberSold
        << endl;
}
```

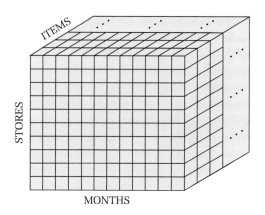

Because item controls the outer For loop, we are summing each item's sales by month and store. If we want to find the total sales for each store, we use store to control the outer For loop, summing its sales by month and item with the inner loops.

```
for (store = 0; store < NUM_STORES; store++)
{
    numberSold = 0;
    for (item = 0; item < NUM_ITEMS; item++)
        for (month = 0; month <= currentMonth; month++)
            numberSold = numberSold + sales[store][month][item];
    cout << "Store #" << store << " Sales to date = " << numberSold
        << endl;
}
```

It takes two loops to access each component in a two-dimensional array; it takes three loops to access each component in a three-dimensional array. The task to be accomplished determines which index controls the outer loop, the middle loop, and the inner loop. If we want to calculate monthly sales by store, month controls the outer loop and store controls the middle loop. If we want to calculate monthly sales by item, month controls the outer loop and item controls the middle loop.

If we want to keep track of the departments that sell each item, we can add a fourth dimension.

```
enum Departments {A, B, C, D, E, F, G};
const int NUM_DEPTS = 7;
typedef int SalesType[NUM_STORES][12][NUM_ITEMS][NUM_DEPTS];
```

How would we visualize this new structure? Not very easily! Fortunately, we do not have to visualize a structure in order to use it. If we want the number of sales in store 1, during June, for item number 4, in department C, we simply access the array element

```
sales[1][5][4][C]
```

When a multidimensional array is declared as a formal parameter in a function, C++ requires you to state the sizes of all dimensions except the first. For our four-dimensional version of SalesType, a function heading would look either like

```
void DoSomething( /* inout */ int arr[][12][NUM_ITEMS][NUM_DEPTS] )
```

or, better yet, like

```
void DoSomething( /* inout */ SalesType arr )
```

The second version is the safest (and the most uncluttered to look at). It ensures that the sizes of all dimensions of the formal parameter match those of the actual parameter exactly. With the first version, the reason why you must declare the sizes of all but the first dimension is the same as we discussed earlier for two-dimensional arrays. Because arrays are stored linearly in memory (one array element after another), the compiler must use this size information to locate correctly an element that lies in the middle of the array.

SOFTWARE ENGINEERING TIP

Choosing a Data Structure

We have now seen two different data structures that can be used to represent data arranged as a table: parallel arrays and two-dimensional arrays. We can always use parallel arrays instead of a two-dimensional array. How do we decide which is most appropriate?

Recall that, in an array, all the components are of the same type; they represent the same thing. But what if we want to process information on the number of items sold, the cost of each item, and the percent tax to be charged for each item? We can define a table with the following headings to hold this information:

Item Number   Number Sold   Cost per Item   Tax Rate

If we keep the item number and number sold as floating point numbers, we can define a two-dimensional array of type float with four columns, each corresponding to one of the headings; however, in this case, four parallel arrays are more appropriate.

Even though the components are all of the same data type, they represent different things. The components in the Item Number column represent an identifying number; those in the Number Sold column represent the quantity sold; the Cost per Item column contains prices; and the Tax Rate column holds percentages. Defining this structure as a set of four parallel arrays also allows us to represent Item Number and Number Sold with integers, which are a better choice for this type of information.

To decide whether to use parallel arrays or a multidimensional array, we can ask three questions:

1. Are all the components of the same data type?
2. Do all the components represent the same kinds of values?
3. Can a set of independent features be used as indices to select a component?

If the answer to all three questions is yes, a multidimensional array is appropriate. Otherwise, parallel arrays are a better choice.

In some cases, a single data structure is more appropriate than multiple arrays. In the next chapter, we look at a data structure called a *record*, a structure that allows us to group nonhomogeneous items. As we introduce more data structures, we provide additional guidelines on how to choose among them.

PROBLEM-SOLVING CASE STUDY

City Council Election

Problem: There has just been a hotly contested city council election. In four voting precincts, citizens have cast their ballots for four candidates. Let's do an analysis of the votes for the four candidates by precinct. We want to know how many votes each candidate received in each precinct, how many total votes each candidate received, and how many total votes were cast in each precinct.

Input: An arbitrary number of votes in a file voteFile, with each vote represented as a pair of numbers: a precinct number (1 through 4) and a candidate number (1 through 4); and candidate names, entered from the keyboard (to be used for printing the output).

Output: The following three items, written to a file reportFile: a table showing how many votes each candidate received in each precinct, the total number of votes for each candidate, and the total number of votes in each precinct.

PROBLEM-SOLVING CASE STUDY cont'd.

■ FIGURE 13-10

Precinct	Smith	Jones	Adams	Smiley
1	卌 //	//	卌 卌 //	卌
2	卌 卌	//	卌	///
3	//	卌 ///	卌 卌 卌	///
4	卌	卌 ///	卌 卌	//

Discussion: The data are available in the form of a pair of numbers for each vote. The first number is the precinct number; the second number is the candidate number.

If we were doing the analysis by hand, our first task would be to go through the data, counting how many people in each precinct voted for each candidate. We would probably create a table with precincts down the side and candidates across the top. Each vote would be recorded as a hash mark in the appropriate column and row (see Figure 13-10).

When all of the votes had been recorded, a sum of each column would tell us how many votes each candidate had received. A sum of each row would tell us how many people had voted in each precinct.

As is so often the case, this by-hand algorithm can be used directly in our program. A two-dimensional array can be created where each component is a counter for the number of votes for a particular candidate in each precinct; that is, the value indexed by [2][1] would be the counter for the votes for candidate 1 in precinct 2. Well, not quite. C++ arrays are indexed beginning at 0, so the correct array component would be indexed by [1][0]. When we input a precinct number and candidate number, we must remember to subtract 1 from each before indexing into the array. Likewise, we must add 1 to an array index that represents a precinct number or candidate number before printing it out.

Data Structures:

A two-dimensional array votes, where the rows represent precincts and the columns represent candidates

A one-dimensional array of strings containing the names of the candidates, to be used for printing (see Figure 13-11).

In the top-down design beginning on the following page, we use named constants NUM_PRECINCTS and NUM_CANDIDATES in place of the literal constants 4 and 4.

■ FIGURE 13-11

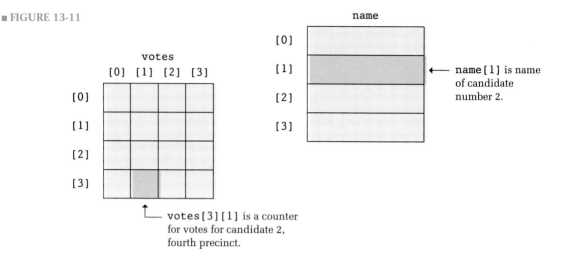

votes[3][1] is a counter for votes for candidate 2, fourth precinct.

name[1] is name of candidate number 2.

Main   *Level 0*

> Open file voteFile for input
> IF voteFile could not be opened
>   Terminate program
> Open file reportFile for output
> IF reportFile could not be opened
>   Terminate program
> Get candidate names
> Set votes array to zero
> Read precinct, candidate from voteFile
> WHILE NOT EOF on voteFile
>   Increment votes[precinct–1][candidate–1] by 1
>   Read precinct, candidate from voteFile
> Write table of votes to reportFile
> Write totals per candidate to reportFile
> Write totals per precinct to reportFile

Open For Input (Inout: someFile)   *Level 1*

> We can reuse the Open For Input module from the
> Exam program in Chapter 12.

Open For Output (Inout: someFile)

> We can modify the Open For Input module so that it
> opens an output file.

Get Candidate Names (Out: name)

> Print "Enter the names of the candidates, one per line,
>   in the order they appear on the ballot."
> FOR candidate going from 0 through NUM_CANDIDATES – 1
>   Read name[candidate]

Note that each candidate's name is stored in the slot in the name array corresponding to his or her candidate number (minus 1). These names are useful when the totals are printed.

Set Votes to Zero (Out: votes)

> FOR each precinct
>   FOR each candidate
>   Set votes[precinct][candidate] = 0

Write Table (In: votes, name; Inout: reportFile)

> // Set up headings
> FOR each candidate
>   Write name[candidate] to reportFile
> Write newline to reportFile
> // Print table by row
> FOR each precinct
>   FOR each candidate
>   Write votes[precinct][candidate] to reportFile
>   Write newline to reportFile

PROBLEM-SOLVING CASE STUDY *cont'd.*

Write Totals Per Candidate (In: votes, name; Inout: reportFile)

```
FOR each candidate
    Set total = 0
    // Compute column sum
    FOR each precinct
        Add votes[precinct][candidate] to total
Write "Total votes for", name[candidate], total to reportFile
```

Write Totals Per Precinct (In: votes; Inout: reportFile)

```
FOR each precinct
    Set total = 0
    // Compute row sum
    FOR each candidate
        Add votes[precinct][candidate] to total
Write "Total votes for precinct", precinct, ':', total to reportFile
```

Module Structure Chart:

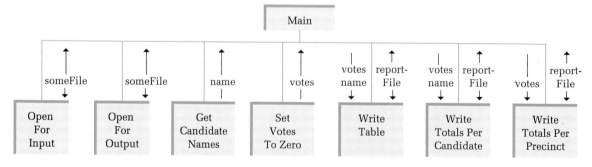

The program for this algorithm follows.

```
//*****************************************************************
// Election program
// This program reads votes represented by precinct number and
// ballot position from a data file, calculates the sums per
// precinct and per candidate, and writes all totals to an
// output file
//*****************************************************************
#include <iostream.h>
#include <iomanip.h>        // For setw()
#include <fstream.h>        // For file I/O
```

```
const int NUM_PRECINCTS = 4;
const int NUM_CANDIDATES = 4;

typedef char String10[11];        // Room for 10 characters plus '\0'

typedef int VoteTable[NUM_PRECINCTS][NUM_CANDIDATES];
                                  // 2-dimensional array type
                                  //    for votes
void GetNames( String10[] );
void OpenForInput( ifstream& );
void OpenForOutput( ofstream& );
void WritePerCandidate( const VoteTable, const String10[],
                        ofstream& );
void WritePerPrecinct( const VoteTable, ofstream& );
void WriteTable( const VoteTable, const String10[], ofstream& );
void ZeroVotes( VoteTable );

int main()
{
    VoteTable votes;          // Totals for precincts vs. candidates

    String10  name[NUM_CANDIDATES];  // Array of candidate names

    int       candidate;      // Candidate number input from voteFile
    int       precinct;       // Precinct number input from voteFile
    ifstream  voteFile;       // Input file of precincts, candidates
    ofstream  reportFile;     // Output file receiving summaries

    OpenForInput(voteFile);
    if ( !voteFile )
        return 1;
    OpenForOutput(reportFile);
    if ( !reportFile )
        return 1;

    GetNames(name);
    ZeroVotes(votes);

    // Read and tally votes

    voteFile >> precinct >> candidate;
    while (voteFile)
    {
            // Invariant (prior to test):
            //     For each pair (precinct, candidate) of input
            //     values prior to the current pair,
            //     votes[precinct-1][candidate-1] has been
            //     incremented by 1
```

```
                    votes[precinct-1][candidate-1]++;
                    voteFile >> precinct >> candidate;
            }

        // Write results to report file

        WriteTable(votes, name, reportFile);
        WritePerCandidate(votes, name, reportFile);
        WritePerPrecinct(votes, reportFile);

        return 0;
}

//********************************************************************

void OpenForInput( /* inout */ ifstream& someFile )    // File to be
                                                       // opened
// Prompts the user for the name of an input file
// and attempts to open the file

// Postcondition:
//      The user has been prompted for a file name
//   && IF the file could not be opened
//          An error message has been printed
// Note:
//      Upon return from this function, the caller must test
//      the stream state to see if the file was successfully opened

{
        char fileName[51];    // User-specified file name (max. 50 chars)

        cout << "Input file name: ";
        cin.get(fileName, 51);
        cin.ignore(100, '\n');

        someFile.open(fileName);
        if ( !someFile )
            cout << "** Can't open " << fileName << " **" << endl;
}

//********************************************************************

void OpenForOutput( /* inout */ ofstream& someFile )   // File to be
                                                       // opened
// Prompts the user for the name of an output file
// and attempts to open the file
```

PROBLEM-SOLVING CASE STUDY cont'd.

```
// Postcondition:
//      The user has been prompted for a file name
//   && IF the file could not be opened
//          An error message has been printed
// Note:
//      Upon return from this function, the caller must test
//      the stream state to see if the file was successfully opened

{
    char fileName[51];    // User-specified file name (max. 50 chars)

    cout << "Output file name: ";
    cin.get(fileName, 51);
    cin.ignore(100, '\n');

    someFile.open(fileName);
    if ( !someFile )
        cout << "** Can't open " << fileName << " **" << endl;
}

//***********************************************************************

void GetNames( /* out */ String10 name[] )    // Array of candidate
                                              //   names
// Reads the list of candidate names from standard input

// Postcondition:
//      The user has been prompted to enter the candidate names
//   && name[0..NUM_CANDIDATES-1] contain the input names,
//      truncated to 10 characters each

{
    int  candidate;       // Loop counter

    cout << "Enter the names of the candidates, one per line,"
         << endl << "in the order they appear on the ballot."
         << endl;

    for (candidate = 0; candidate < NUM_CANDIDATES; candidate++)
    {
            // Invariant (prior to test):
            //      name[0..candidate-1] have been read
            //   && 0 <= candidate <= NUM_CANDIDATES
```

```
            cin.get(name[candidate], 11);   // At most 10 chars plus '\0'
            cin.ignore(100, '\n');
        }
    }

    //*********************************************************************

    void ZeroVotes( /* out */ VoteTable votes )   // Array of vote totals

    // Zeroes out the votes array

    // Postcondition:
    //      All votes[0..NUM_PRECINCTS-1][0..NUM_CANDIDATES-1] == 0

    {
        int precinct;       // Loop counter
        int candidate;      // Loop counter

        for (precinct = 0; precinct < NUM_PRECINCTS; precinct++)

                // Invariant (prior to test):
                //     votes[0..precinct-1][0..NUM_CANDIDATES-1] == 0
                //  && 0 <= precinct <= NUM_PRECINCTS

            for (candidate = 0; candidate < NUM_CANDIDATES; candidate++)

                    // Invariant (prior to test):
                    //     votes[precinct][0..candidate-1] == 0
                    //  && 0 <= candidate <= NUM_CANDIDATES

                votes[precinct][candidate] = 0;
    }

    //*********************************************************************

    void WriteTable(
            /* in */    const VoteTable votes,      // Total votes
            /* in */    const String10  name[],     // Candidate names
            /* inout */ ofstream&       reportFile ) // Output file

    // Writes the vote totals in tabular form to the report file

    // Precondition:
    //      votes[0..NUM_PRECINCTS-1][0..NUM_CANDIDATES] are assigned
    //   && name[0..NUM_CANDIDATES-1] are assigned
    // Postcondition:
    //      The name array has been output across one line, followed by
    //      the votes array, one row per line
```

```cpp
{
    int precinct;        // Loop counter
    int candidate;       // Loop counter

    // Set up headings

    reportFile << "            ";
    for (candidate = 0; candidate < NUM_CANDIDATES; candidate++)

            // Invariant (prior to test):
            //     name[0..candidate-1] have been output
            //  && 0 <= candidate <= NUM_CANDIDATES

        reportFile << setw(12) << name[candidate];
    reportFile << endl;

    // Print table by row

    for (precinct = 0; precinct < NUM_PRECINCTS; precinct++)
    {
            // Invariant (prior to test):
            //     votes[0..precinct-1][0..NUM_CANDIDATES-1] have
            //     been output
            //  && 0 <= precinct <= NUM_PRECINCTS

        reportFile << "Precinct" << setw(4) << precinct + 1;
        for (candidate = 0; candidate < NUM_CANDIDATES; candidate++)

                // Invariant (prior to test):
                //     votes[precinct][0..candidate-1] have
                //     been output
                //  && 0 <= candidate <= NUM_CANDIDATES

            reportFile << setw(12) << votes[precinct][candidate];
        reportFile << endl;
    }
    reportFile << endl;
}

//****************************************************************
```

```
void WritePerCandidate(
      /* in */     const VoteTable votes,      // Total votes
      /* in */     const String10  name[],      // Candidate names
      /* inout */ ofstream&        reportFile )  // Output file

// Sums the votes per person and writes the totals to the
// report file

// Precondition:
//     votes[0..NUM_PRECINCTS-1][0..NUM_CANDIDATES] are assigned
//   && name[0..NUM_CANDIDATES-1] are assigned
// Postcondition:
//     For each person i, name[i] has been output,
//     followed by the sum
//     votes[0][i] + votes[1][i] + ... + votes[NUM_PRECINCTS-1][i]

{
    int precinct;      // Loop counter
    int candidate;      // Loop counter
    int total;          // Total votes for a candidate

    for (candidate = 0; candidate < NUM_CANDIDATES; candidate++)
    {
          // Invariant (prior to test):
          //     Votes for candidates 0 through (candidate-1) have
          //     been summed and output
          //   && 0 <= candidate <= NUM_CANDIDATES

        total = 0;

        // Compute column sum

        for (precinct = 0; precinct < NUM_PRECINCTS; precinct++)

              // Invariant (prior to test):
              //     total == votes[0][candidate] + ... +
              //              votes[precinct-1][candidate]
              //   && 0 <= precinct <= NUM_PRECINCTS

            total = total + votes[precinct][candidate];

        reportFile << "Total votes for"
                  << setw(10) << name[candidate] << ":"
                  << setw(3) << total << endl;
    }
    reportFile << endl;
}
```

```
//***************************************************************

void WritePerPrecinct(
            /* in */      const VoteTable  votes,        // Total votes
            /* inout */ ofstream&          reportFile )   // Output file

// Sums the votes per precinct and writes the totals to the
// report file

// Precondition:
//     votes[0..NUM_PRECINCTS-1][0..NUM_CANDIDATES] are assigned
// Postcondition:
//     For each precinct i, the value of i+1 has been output,
//     followed by the sum
//     votes[i][0] + votes[i][1] + ... + votes[i][NUM_CANDIDATES-1]

{
    int precinct;        // Loop counter
    int candidate;       // Loop counter
    int total;           // Total votes for a precinct

    for (precinct = 0; precinct < NUM_PRECINCTS; precinct++)
    {
            // Invariant (prior to test):
            //     Votes for precincts 0 through (precinct-1) have
            //     been summed and output
            //   && 0 <= precinct <= NUM_PRECINCTS

        total = 0;

        // Compute row sum

        for (candidate = 0; candidate < NUM_CANDIDATES; candidate++)

                // Invariant (prior to test):
                //     total == votes[precinct][0] + ... +
                //                 votes[precinct][candidate-1]
                //   && 0 <= candidate <= NUM_CANDIDATES

            total = total + votes[precinct][candidate];

        reportFile << "Total votes for precinct"
                   << setw(3) << precinct + 1 << ':'
                   << setw(3) << total << endl;
    }
}
```

Testing: This program was run with the data listed below. (We list the data in three columns to save space.) The names of the candidates entered from the keyboard were Smith, Jones, Adams, and Smiley. In this data set, there is at least one vote for each candidate in each precinct. Case Study Follow-Up Exercise 1 asks you to outline a complete testing strategy for this program.

Input Data

1 1	3 1	3 3
1 1	4 3	4 4
1 2	3 4	4 4
1 2	3 2	4 3
1 3	3 3	4 4
1 4	2 1	4 4
2 2	2 3	4 1
2 2	4 3	4 2
2 3	4 4	2 4
2 1	3 2	4 4

The output, which was written to file reportFile, is shown below.

		Jones	Smith	Adams	Smiley
Precinct	1	2	2	1	1
Precinct	2	2	2	2	1
Precinct	3	1	2	2	1
Precinct	4	1	1	3	6

```
Total votes for    Jones:   6
Total votes for    Smith:   7
Total votes for    Adams:   8
Total votes for    Smiley:  9

Total votes for precinct  1:  6
Total votes for precinct  2:  7
Total votes for precinct  3:  6
Total votes for precinct  4: 11
```

PROBLEM-SOLVING CASE STUDY

Absenteeism Pattern

Problem: Management wants to see the patterns in absenteeism across each department for a week. The absentee figures are kept in a file named `dataFile`. Each data line contains the daily figures for departments A through F.

The output must be in the form of a table showing the number of employees absent in each department each day and the percentage difference (+ or −) from each department's weekly average. In addition, they want a summary of absenteeism across the entire company for a week. This summary is to be in the form of a bar chart showing what percentage of the total absences occurred on each day of the week.

Input: Five lines of absentee data, each line containing the number of people out for each of six departments.

Output: A file `reportFile` containing two items: a table showing absentee figures and percentage differences from the average for each day of the week, by department, and a bar chart showing the percentage of total absenteeism that occurs on each day of the week.

Discussion: Each data line contains the daily absentee figures for every department. The figures must be read in and stored in a table. Once the table has been created, we can calculate the average absentee rate for each department. We can use the table and the averages to calculate the percentage difference.

The first step is to decide what the table that holds the input data should look like. We can make the departments the columns and the days the rows or vice versa. There are only six departments now but the company is growing, so it might be better to make the days of the week the columns and the departments the rows. Then we could alter the program to run with more departments simply by adding a row for each. It is easy to add rows to a table; adding columns can cause a problem with printing because the width of a print line or screen is fixed.

As the data are read, they are stored into an array having the structure shown in Figure 13-12.

Finding the average for each department requires row processing—summing the row components and dividing by 5. Comparing each day's

PROBLEM-SOLVING CASE STUDY *cont'd.*

■ FIGURE 13-12   Absentee Data

	[MONDAY]	[TUESDAY]	[WEDNESDAY]	[THURSDAY]	[FRIDAY]
[A]	2	1	0	1	2
[B]	1	0	0	0	0
[C]	1	1	0	1	0
[D]	3	3	2	1	2
[E]	4	0	0	2	1
[F]	1	0	0	0	2

Data line 1

Data line 2

Data line 3, etc.

figures to the average also requires row processing, as does printing the table. We can calculate the percentage differences while we print the table.

To compile the summary figures for the week, we must take the number of people absent on each day, divided by the total number of people absent during the entire week. A bar chart showing this information might look as follows, with each asterisk representing 10 percent:

```
        Monday    Tuesday  Wednesday   Thursday     Friday
100%
 90%
 80%
 70%
 60%
 50%
 40%     *
 30%     *
 20%     *          *                                *
 10%     *          *           *          *         *
```

This chart has the following interpretation: 40 percent of the total absences were on Monday, 20 percent were on Tuesday, and so on.

We can represent this chart as a two-dimensional array with ten rows and five columns. The rows represent the percentages to the nearest 10 percent.

■ FIGURE 13-13   absenteeData

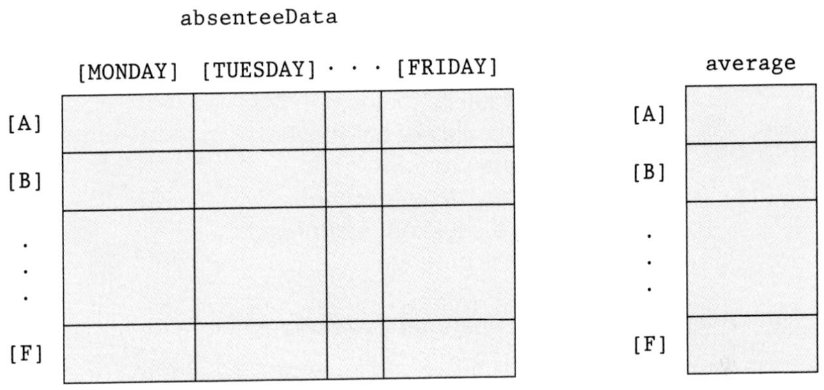

For each day, the percentage of employees absent is calculated and then rounded to the nearest 10 percent to determine how many asterisks are printed in each column.

Data Structures:

A two-dimensional array for holding the input (absenteeData)
A one-dimensional array (average) for holding the average daily absentee figures for each department (see Figure 13-13)
A two-dimensional array (barChart) for holding the asterisks to be printed in the bar chart (see Figure 13-14)

■ FIGURE 13-14   barChart

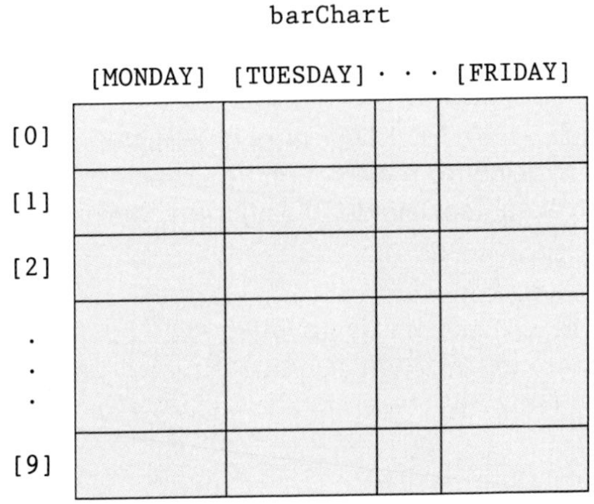

Main   *Level 0*

```
Open file dataFile for input
IF dataFile could not be opened
    Terminate program
Open file reportFile for output
IF reportFile could not be opened
    Terminate program
Get data
Compute departmental averages
Write table to reportFile
Calculate summary
Write bar chart to reportFile
```

Open For Input (Inout: someFile)   *Level 1*

```
We can reuse the Open For Input module from the
preceding Election program.
```

Open For Output (Inout: someFile)

```
We can reuse the Open For Output module from the
preceding Election program.
```

Get Data (Out: absenteeData; Inout: dataFile)

```
FOR day going from MONDAY through FRIDAY
    FOR dept going from A through F
        Read absenteeData[dept][day] from dataFile
```

Compute Averages (In: absenteeData; Out: average)

We can use the general algorithm we developed to sum the rows of a table. Each average is the row sum divided by 5.

Write Table (In: absenteeData, average; Inout: reportFile)

```
Write table headings to reportFile
// Process table by row
Set deptChar = 'A'
FOR dept going from A through F
    Write "Dept", deptChar to reportFile
    FOR day going from MONDAY through FRIDAY
        Write absenteeData[dept][day] to reportFile
    IF average[dept] > 0.0
        Set diffFromAvg = absenteeData[dept][day] − average[dept]
        Set percentDiff = diffFromAvg * 100.0 / average[dept]
    ELSE
        Set percentDiff = 0.0
    IF percentDiff >= 0.0
        Write int(percentDiff + 0.5) to reportFile
    ELSE
        Write int(percentDiff − 0.5) to reportFile
    Write newline to reportFile
    Increment deptChar to next character
```

Calculate Summary (In: absenteeData; Out: barChart)

First, we can use either row processing or column processing to sum the entire table (in module Total Absences, which follows). We can then use column processing to sum each column, dividing the column sum by the total sum to get the percent of the total absences for each day. Next, we must put the appropriate number of asterisks into the bar chart, which we'll do in module Set Asterisks.

Problem-Solving Case Study cont'd.

Total Absences (In: absenteeData)   *Level 2*
    Out: Function value

```
Set total = 0
FOR dept going from A through F
    FOR day going from MONDAY through FRIDAY
        Add absenteeData[dept][day] to total
Return total
```

Set Asterisks (In: day, percent; Out: barChart)

The number of asterisks needed in the bar chart can be used as an index to tell us how many blanks and how many asterisks to store in a column. For example, if Monday had 38 percent of the absences, we would fill the first column as shown in Figure 13-15. We show the array column upside down because we'll be printing it that way.

```
Set nearestTen = int(percent / 10.0 + 0.5)
FOR counter going from 9 down through nearestTen
    Set barChart[counter][day] = ' '
FOR counter going from nearestTen – 1 down through 0
    Set barChart[counter][day] = '*'
```

Write Bar Chart (In: barChart; Inout: reportFile)   *Level 1*

We can use row processing to print the bar chart with appropriate headings. Note, however, that the array `barChart` needs to be printed upside down. We have used the index to correspond to one less than the nearest 10 percent. Therefore, we have to print from row 9 down to row 0 to display the chart in the usual form.

```
Write chart headings to reportFile
FOR counter going from 9 down through 0
    Write counter + 1, "0%" to reportFile
    FOR day going from MONDAY through FRIDAY
        Write barChart[counter][day] to reportFile
    Write newline to reportFile
```

PROBLEM-SOLVING CASE STUDY cont'd.

■ FIGURE 13-15

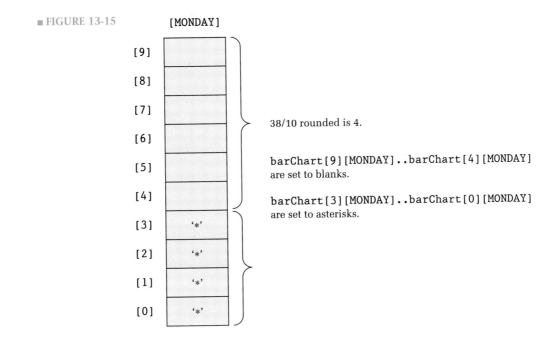

38/10 rounded is 4.

`barChart[9][MONDAY]..barChart[4][MONDAY]`
are set to blanks.

`barChart[3][MONDAY]..barChart[0][MONDAY]`
are set to asterisks.

Module Structure Chart:

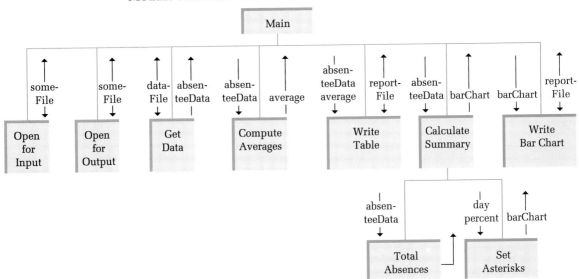

Here is the program that implements our design. To conserve space we have omitted the loop invariants.

```
//*****************************************************************
// Absentee program
// This program examines absentee data across departments for a
// week.  Percentage differences from the average per department
// are written to an output file, along with a summary bar chart
// showing percent of total absences on each day of the week
//*****************************************************************
#include <iostream.h>
#include <iomanip.h>      // For setw()
#include <fstream.h>      // For file I/O

const int NUM_DEPTS = 6;       // Number of departments in the company

enum DayType {MONDAY, TUESDAY, WEDNESDAY, THURSDAY, FRIDAY};
enum DeptType {A, B, C, D, E, F};

typedef int TableType[NUM_DEPTS][5]; // 2-dimensional array type for
                                     //   department vs. day of week
typedef char ChartType[10][5];       // 2-dimensional array type for
                                     //   percent vs. day of week

void ComputeAverages( const TableType, float[] );
void GetData( TableType, ifstream& );
void OpenForInput( ifstream& );
void OpenForOutput( ofstream& );
void SetAsterisks( ChartType, DayType, float );
void Summarize( const TableType, ChartType );
int  TotalAbsences( const TableType );
void WriteBarChart( const ChartType, ofstream& );
void WriteTable( const TableType, const float[], ofstream& );

int main()
{
    TableType absenteeData;         // Absences by dept. and day
    ChartType barChart;             // Summary chart of percentages
    float     average[NUM_DEPTS];   // Array of department averages
    ifstream  dataFile;             // Input file of absentee data
    ofstream  reportFile;           // Output file receiving report

    OpenForInput(dataFile);
    if ( !dataFile )
        return 1;
    OpenForOutput(reportFile);
    if ( !reportFile )
        return 1;
```

```
        GetData(absenteeData, dataFile);
        ComputeAverages(absenteeData, average);
        WriteTable(absenteeData, average, reportFile);
        Summarize(absenteeData, barChart);
        WriteBarChart(barChart, reportFile);
        return 0;
    }

    //*******************************************************************

    void OpenForInput( /* inout */ ifstream& someFile )    // File to be
                                                           // opened

    // Prompts the user for the name of an input file
    // and attempts to open the file

    // Postcondition:
    //     The user has been prompted for a file name
    //   && IF the file could not be opened
    //          An error message has been printed
    // Note:
    //     Upon return from this function, the caller must test
    //     the stream state to see if the file was successfully opened

    {
        char fileName[51];    // User-specified file name (max. 50 chars)

        cout << "Input file name: ";
        cin.get(fileName, 51);
        cin.ignore(100, '\n');

        someFile.open(fileName);
        if ( !someFile )
            cout << "** Can't open " << fileName << " **" << endl;
    }

    //*******************************************************************

    void OpenForOutput( /* inout */ ofstream& someFile )    // File to be
                                                            // opened

    // Prompts the user for the name of an output file
    // and attempts to open the file

    // Postcondition:
    //     The user has been prompted for a file name
    //   && IF the file could not be opened
    //          An error message has been printed
    // Note:
    //     Upon return from this function, the caller must test
    //     the stream state to see if the file was successfully opened
```

```
    {
        char fileName[51];    // User-specified file name (max. 50 chars)

        cout << "Output file name: ";
        cin.get(fileName, 51);
        cin.ignore(100, '\n');

        someFile.open(fileName);
        if ( !someFile )
            cout << "** Can't open " << fileName << " **" << endl;
    }

//*****************************************************************

void GetData(
        /* out */    TableType absenteeData,    // Table of absences
        /* inout */ ifstream& dataFile    )    // Input data file

// Reads the absentee data from the data file

// Precondition:
//     File dataFile has been successfully opened for input
//   && The file contains 5 * NUM_DEPTS integer values, arranged
//      in column order (all absences for Monday, then all absences
//      for Tuesday, etc.)
// Postcondition:
//      absenteeData[A..F][MONDAY..FRIDAY] contain the input values

    {
        DayType   day;       // Loop counter
        DeptType dept;       // Loop counter

        for (day = MONDAY; day <= FRIDAY; day = DayType(day + 1))
            for (dept = A; dept <= F; dept = DeptType(dept + 1))
                dataFile >> absenteeData[dept][day];
    }

//*****************************************************************

void ComputeAverages(
        /* in */   const TableType absenteeData,    // Table of absences
        /* out */  float               average[]    )    // Average per dept.

// Calculates averages across the rows of absenteeData
```

```
// Precondition:
//     absenteeData[A..F][MONDAY..FRIDAY] are assigned
// Postcondition:
//     For all i, where A <= i <= F,
//        average[i] == average of the values absenteeData[i][MONDAY]
//                      through absenteeData[i][FRIDAY]

{
    DayType   day;       // Loop counter
    DeptType  dept;      // Loop counter
    int       total;     // Total absences for a department

    for (dept = A; dept <= F; dept = DeptType(dept + 1))
    {
        total = 0;

        // Compute row sum

        for (day = MONDAY; day <= FRIDAY; day = DayType(day + 1))
            total = total + absenteeData[dept][day];

        average[dept] = float(total) / 5.0;
    }
}

//**********************************************************************

void WriteTable(
    /* in */      const TableType absenteeData,   // Table of absences
    /* in */      const float     average[],      // Average per dept.
    /* inout */   ofstream&       reportFile  )   // Output file

// Writes a table to the report file showing percentage differences
// from the averages and original data

// Precondition:
//     absenteeData[A..F][MONDAY..FRIDAY] are assigned
//  && average[A..F] are assigned
// Postcondition:
//     A table has been written to reportFile with one row per
//     department showing, for each day of the week, the number of
//     absences and the percentage difference from the department's
//     weekly average
```

```
{
    DayType   day;            // Loop counter
    DeptType  dept;           // Loop counter
    char      deptChar;       // Printable department letter
    float     diffFromAvg;    // Difference from average
    float     percentDiff;    // Percent difference from average

    // Set up headings

    reportFile << setw(49) << "ABSENTEE DATA" << endl
               << setw(20) << "Monday" << setw(13) << "Tuesday"
               << setw(13) << "Wednesday" << setw(13) << "Thursday"
               << setw(13) << "Friday" << endl;
    reportFile << setw(7) << " ";
    for (day = MONDAY; day <= FRIDAY; day = DayType(day + 1))
        reportFile << setw(13) << "Value    %";
    reportFile << endl;

    // Process table by row

    deptChar = 'A';
    for (dept = A; dept <= F; dept = DeptType(dept + 1))
    {
        reportFile << "Dept " << deptChar << ' ';
        for (day = MONDAY; day <= FRIDAY; day = DayType(day + 1))
        {
            reportFile << setw(6) << absenteeData[dept][day];
            if (average[dept] > 0.0)
            {
                diffFromAvg = float(absenteeData[dept][day]) -
                                  average[dept];
                percentDiff = diffFromAvg * 100.0 / average[dept];
            }
            else
                percentDiff = 0.0;

            if (percentDiff >= 0.0)
                reportFile << setw(7) << int(percentDiff + 0.5);
            else
                reportFile << setw(7) << int(percentDiff - 0.5);
        }
        reportFile << endl;
        deptChar++;
    }
}
```

PROBLEM-SOLVING CASE STUDY cont'd.

```
//***********************************************************

void Summarize(
  /* in */   const TableType absenteeData,    // Table of absences
  /* out */  ChartType        barChart    )   // Chart of percentages

// Calculates total percentages by day and represents
// the results in a bar chart

// Precondition:
//      absenteeData[A..F][MONDAY..FRIDAY] are assigned
// Postcondition:
//      For each day, the total number of absences over all
//      departments has been computed as a percentage of total
//      absences all week
//   && For all j, where MONDAY <= j <= FRIDAY,
//          column j of barChart has been filled with the number of
//          asterisks corresponding to day j's absence percentage,
//          rounded to the nearest 10 percent

{
    DayType   day;          // Loop counter
    DeptType  dept;         // Loop counter
    float     percent;      // Daily percentage
    int       dailyTotal;   // Total per day
    int       weeklyTotal;  // Total of entire table

    weeklyTotal = TotalAbsences(absenteeData);
    for (day = MONDAY; day <= FRIDAY; day = DayType(day + 1))
    {
        dailyTotal = 0;
        for (dept = A; dept <= F; dept = DeptType(dept + 1))
            dailyTotal = dailyTotal + absenteeData[dept][day];
        if (weeklyTotal > 0)
            percent = float(dailyTotal) / float(weeklyTotal) * 100.0;
        else
            percent = 0.0;
        SetAsterisks(barChart, day, percent);
    }
}

//***********************************************************
```

```
int TotalAbsences(
     /* in */ const TableType absenteeData )    // Table of absences

// Calculates total number of absences during the entire week

// Precondition:
//      absenteeData[A..F][MONDAY..FRIDAY] are assigned
// Postcondition:
//      Function value == sum of all
//                          absenteeData[A..F][MONDAY..FRIDAY]

{
    DayType  day;          // Loop counter
    DeptType dept;         // Loop counter
    int      total = 0;    // Total absences

    for (dept = A; dept <= F; dept = DeptType(dept + 1))
        for (day = MONDAY; day <= FRIDAY; day = DayType(day + 1))
            total = total + absenteeData[dept][day];
    return total;
}


//**********************************************************************

void SetAsterisks(
             /* out */ ChartType barChart,     // Chart of percentages
             /* in */  DayType   day,          // Chart index
             /* in */  float     percent )     // Percentage to chart

// Stores asterisks into column "day" of barChart to represent
// each 10 percent.  Blanks are stored in balance of column

// Precondition:
//      day is assigned  &&  0.0 <= percent <= 100.0
// Postcondition:
//      Suppose percent, rounded to the nearest 10, equals k.  Then
//         all barChart[0..k-1][day] == '*'
//       && all barChart[k..9][day] == ' '

{
    int nearestTen;    // Percent to the nearest ten
    int counter;       // Loop counter
```

```
        nearestTen = int(percent / 10.0 + 0.5);
        for (counter = 9; counter >= nearestTen; counter--)
            barChart[counter][day] = ' ';
        for (counter = nearestTen - 1; counter >= 0; counter--)
            barChart[counter][day] = '*';
}


//************************************************************

void WriteBarChart(
    /* in */    const ChartType barChart,      // Chart of percentages
    /* inout */ ofstream&       reportFile )    // Output file

// Writes the bar chart to the report file

// Precondition:
//     barChart[0..9][MONDAY..FRIDAY] are assigned
// Postcondition:
//     barChart has been output to the report file with
//     appropriate headings

{
    int      counter;   // Loop counter
    DayType  day;       // Loop counter

    reportFile << endl
               << setw(42) << "BAR CHART:  ABSENCES BY DAY" << endl
               << setw(11) << "Monday" << setw(11) << "Tuesday"
               << setw(11) << "Wednesday" << setw(11) << "Thursday"
               << setw(11) << "Friday" << endl;

    for (counter = 9; counter >= 0; counter--)
    {
        reportFile << setw(2) << counter + 1 << "0%";
        for (day = MONDAY; day <= FRIDAY; day = DayType(day + 1))
            reportFile << "   " << barChart[counter][day]
                       << "      ";
        reportFile << endl;
    }
}
```

PROBLEM-SOLVING CASE STUDY *cont'd.*

Testing: The program was executed with the following test data, which include at least one zero in each row and column. Case Study Follow-Up Exercise 2 asks you to outline a complete testing strategy for this program.

File dataFile

```
0  6  3  3  4  1
1  0  1  3  0  3
1  1  0  2  1  1
1  0  1  0  0  1
2  3  4  2  1  0
```

Listed below are the results written to file reportFile.

ABSENTEE DATA

	Monday		Tuesday		Wednesday		Thursday		Friday	
	Value	%	Value	%	Value	%	Value	%	Value	%
Dept A	0	-100	1	0	1	0	1	0	2	100
Dept B	6	200	0	-100	1	-50	0	-100	3	50
Dept C	3	67	1	-44	0	-100	1	-44	4	122
Dept D	3	50	3	50	2	0	0	-100	2	0
Dept E	4	233	0	-100	1	-17	0	-100	1	-17
Dept F	1	-17	3	150	1	-17	1	-17	0	-100

BAR CHART: ABSENCES BY DAY

```
       Monday    Tuesday  Wednesday   Thursday      Friday
100%
 90%
 80%
 70%
 60%
 50%
 40%     *
 30%     *                                            *
 20%     *          *                                 *
 10%     *          *          *          *           *
```

Something looks a little strange: the percentages in the bar chart add up to 110 percent. Remember that in Chapter 10 we mentioned that strange things can happen with floating point numbers. In the Absentee program, each percentage figure is changed to an integer for use as an index. To do so, the percentages are rounded to the nearest 10 percent. When we noticed that the percentages added up to 110 percent, we put a debugging output statement in the program to monitor what was happening. The percentages and rounded values are shown below.

Percent	Nearest 10 Percent
36.957	40
17.391	20
13.043	10
6.522	10
26.087	30
100.000	110

This is a classic example of round-off error. Case Study Follow-Up Exercise 3 asks you to rewrite the functions that create the bar chart using a smaller interval, so that an asterisk represents 5 percentage points instead of 10.

TESTING AND DEBUGGING

Errors with multidimensional arrays usually fall into two major categories: index expressions that are out of order and index range errors. In addition, undefined-value errors may result from trying to access uninitialized components.

As the number of dimensions increases, so does the likelihood of a subtle logic error. The syntax of your nested loop structure may be valid, but what you intended to have happen may not be what you coded. Using meaningful identifiers for your loop control variables will help. If you were to use `i`, `j`, and `k` as the loop control variables in the department store example, it would be easy to interchange them by mistake. If you use `item`, `store`, and `month`, you are less likely to confuse the indices. Even if you have the index expressions in the correct order following the array name, you can end up with index range errors if you use the wrong upper (or lower) limits for an index variable that is controlling a loop.

Suppose we were to expand the Election program to accommodate 10 candidates and four precincts. Let's declare the `votes` array as

```
int votes[4][10];
```

The first dimension represents the precincts, and the second represents the candidates. An example of the first kind of error—incorrect order of the index expressions—would be to print out the `votes` array as follows.

```
for (precinct = 0; precinct < 4; precinct++)
{
    for (candidate = 0; candidate < 10; candidate++)
        cout << setw(4) << votes[candidate][precinct];
    cout << endl;
}
```

In the output statement we have specified the array indices in the wrong order. The loops march through the array with the first index ranging from 0 through 9 (instead of 0 through 3) and the second index ranging from 0 through 3 (instead of 0 through 9). The effect of executing this code may vary from system to system. The program may output the wrong array components and continue executing, or the program may crash with a memory access error.

An example of the second kind of error—an incorrect index range in an otherwise correct loop—can be seen in this code:

```
for (precinct = 0; precinct < 10; precinct++)
{
    for (candidate = 0; candidate < 4; candidate++)
        cout << setw(4) << votes[precinct][candidate];
    cout << endl;
}
```

Here, the output statement correctly uses precinct for the first index and candidate for the second. However, the For statements use incorrect upper limits for the index variables. As with the preceding example, the effect of executing this code is undefined but is certainly wrong. A valuable way to prevent this kind of error is to use named constants instead of the literals 10 and 4. In the case study, we used NUM_PRECINCTS and NUM_CANDIDATES. You are much more likely to spot an error (or to avoid making an error in the first place) if you write something like this:

```
for (precinct = 0; precinct < NUM_PRECINCTS; precinct++)
```

than if you use a literal constant as the upper limit for the index variable.

Testing and Debugging Hints

1. Initialize all components of an array if there is any chance that you will attempt to access the entire array.
2. Use the proper number of indices with array names when referencing an array component, and make sure the indices are in the correct order.
3. Use meaningful identifiers for index variables.
4. In array-processing loops, double-check the upper and lower bounds on each index variable to be sure they are correct for that dimension of the array.

5. When declaring a multidimensional array as a formal parameter, you must state the sizes of all but the first dimension. Also, these sizes must agree exactly with the sizes of the caller's actual parameter.
6. To eliminate the chances of size mismatches referred to in item 5, use a Typedef statement to define a multidimensional array type. Declare both the actual parameter and the formal parameter to be of this type.

SUMMARY

Two-dimensional arrays are useful for processing information that is represented naturally in table form. Processing data in two-dimensional arrays usually takes one of two forms: processing by row or processing by column. An array of arrays, which is useful if rows of the array must be passed as parameters, is an alternative way of defining a two-dimensional array.

A multidimensional array is a collection of like components, ordered on more than one dimension. Each component is accessed by a set of indices, one for each dimension, that represents the component's position on the various dimensions. Each index may be thought of as describing a feature of a given array component.

Data structures should be selected to reflect accurately the relationships inherent in the data values themselves. Two-dimensional arrays and parallel arrays can be used to hold the same data. An analysis of what the data mean can help you make the appropriate choice.

QUICK CHECK

1. Declare a two-dimensional array, named `plan`, with 30 rows and 10 columns. The component type of the array is `float`. (pp. 708–712)
2. Assign the value 27.3 to the component in row 13, column 7 of the array `plan` from Question 1. (pp. 708–712)
3. Nested For loops can be used to sum the values in each row of array `plan`. What range of values would the outer For loop count through to do this? (pp. 714–716)
4. Nested For loops can be used to sum the values in each column of array `plan`. What range of values would the outer For loop count through to do this? (pp. 716–717)
5. Write a program fragment that initializes array `plan` from Question 1 to all zeros. (pp. 717–718)
6. Write a program fragment that prints the contents of array `plan`, one row per line of output. (pp. 718–720)
7. Suppose array `plan` is passed as a parameter to a function in which the corresponding formal parameter is named `someArray`. What would the declaration of `someArray` look like in the formal parameter list? (pp. 720–722)

8. Given the declarations

   ```
   typedef int OneDimType[100];

   OneDimType twoDim[40];
   ```

   rewrite the declaration of **twoDim** without referring to type **OneDimType**. (pp. 723–724)
9. How many components does the following data type contain? (pp. 724–727)

   ```
   const int SIZE = 10;
   typedef char FourDim[SIZE][SIZE][SIZE][SIZE-1];
   ```

10. Write a program fragment that fills a variable of type **FourDim**, named **quick**, with blanks. (pp. 724–727)
11. Suppose you are writing a program to process a table of employee numbers, names, and pay rates. Is a two-dimensional array an appropriate data structure for this problem? Explain. (pp. 727–728)

Answers   1. float plan[30][10];   2. plan[13][7] = 27.3;
 3. for (row = 0; row < 30; row++)   4. for (col = 0; col < 10; col++)
 5. for (row = 0; row < 30; row++)
        for (col = 0; col < 10; col++)
            plan[row][col] = 0.0;
 6. for (row = 0; row < 30; row++)
    {
        for (col = 0; col < 10; col++)
            cout << setw(8) << plan[row][col];
        cout << endl;
    }
 7. Either
        float someArray[30][10]
    or
        float someArray[][10]
 8. int twoDim[40][100];   9. Nine thousand (10 * 10 * 10 * 9)
10. for (dim1 = 0; dim1 < SIZE; dim1++)
        for (dim2 = 0; dim2 < SIZE; dim2++)
            for (dim3 = 0; dim3 < SIZE; dim3++)
                for (dim4 = 0; dim4 < SIZE - 1; dim4++)
                    quick[dim1][dim2][dim3][dim4] = ' ';
11. A two-dimensional array is inappropriate because the data types of the columns are not the same. Parallel arrays are appropriate in this case.

EXAM PREPARATION EXERCISES

1. Given the declarations

   ```
   const int NUM_WEEKS = 5;
   const int NUM_TEAMS = 6;

   int tickets[NUM_TEAMS][NUM_WEEKS];
   ```

answer the following questions:

a. What is the number of rows in `tickets`?

b. What is the number of columns in `tickets`?

c. How many components does `tickets` have?

d. What kind of processing (row or column) would be needed to total the ticket sales by weeks?

e. What kind of processing (row or column) would be needed to total the ticket sales by teams?

2. Given the declarations

```
const int NUM_SCHOOLS = 10;
const int NUM_SPORTS = 3;
enum SportType {FOOTBALL, BASKETBALL, VOLLEYBALL};

int    kidsInSports[NUM_SCHOOLS][NUM_SPORTS];
float costOfSports[NUM_SPORTS][NUM_SCHOOLS];
```

answer the following questions:

a. What is the number of rows in `kidsInSports`?

b. What is the number of columns in `kidsInSports`?

c. What is the number of rows in `costOfSports`?

d. What is the number of columns in `costOfSports`?

e. How many components does `kidsInSports` have?

f. How many components does `costOfSports` have?

g. What kind of processing (row or column) would be needed to total the amount of money spent on each sport?

h. What kind of processing (row or column) would be needed to total the number of children participating in sports at a particular school?

3. Given the following code segments, draw the arrays and their contents after the code is executed. Indicate any undefined values with the letter *U*.

a.
```
int exampleA[4][3];
int i, j;

for (i = 0; i < 4; i++)
    for (j = 0; j < 3; j++)
        exampleA[i][j] = i * j;
```

b.
```
int exampleB[4][3];
int i, j;

for (i = 0; i < 3; i++)
    for (j = 0; j < 3; j++)
        exampleB[i][j] = (i + j) % 3;
```

c.
```
int exampleC[8][2];
int i, j;

exampleC[7][0] = 4;
exampleC[7][1] = 5;
for (i = 0; i < 7; i++)
{
    exampleC[i][0] = 2;
    exampleC[i][1] = 3;
}
```

4. a. Define enumeration types for the following:

   TeamType made up of classes (freshman, sophomore, etc.) on your campus. ResultType made up of game results (won, lost, or tied)

   b. Using Typedef, declare an integer array type named Outcome, intended to be indexed by TeamType and ResultType.
   c. Declare an array variable standings to be of type Outcome.
   d. Give a C++ statement that increases the number of freshman wins by one.

5. The following code fragment includes a call to a function named DoSomething.

```
typedef float ArrType[100][20];

ArrType x;
    .
    .
    .
DoSomething(x);
```

   Indicate whether each of the following would be valid or invalid as the function heading for DoSomething.

   a. `void DoSomething( /* inout */ ArrType arr )`
   b. `void DoSomething( /* inout */ float arr[100][20] )`
   c. `void DoSomething( /* inout */ float arr[100][] )`
   d. `void DoSomething( /* inout */ float arr[][20] )`
   e. `void DoSomething( /* inout */ float arr[][] )`
   f. `void DoSomething( /* inout */ float arr[][10] )`

6. Given the following declarations

```
typedef char String20[21];

String20 oneName;
String20 nameList[50];
```

   indicate whether each of the following is valid or invalid.

a. `strcpy(nameList[3], oneName);`
b. `nameList[14][27] = 'z';`
c. `nameList[3][7] = 'y';`
d. `cin >> nameList;`
e. `cin >> nameList[0];`
f. `cin >> nameList[0][5];`

7. Declare the array variables described below. Use proper style.
   a. A table with five rows and six columns that contains Boolean values. (Assume the Boolean type has been defined previously.)
   b. A table, indexed from 0 through 39 and 0 through 199, that contains `float` values.
   c. A `char` table with rows indexed by a type

   ```
   enum FruitType {LEMON, PEAR, APPLE, ORANGE};
   ```

   and columns indexed by the integers 0 through 15.

8. A logging operation keeps records of 37 loggers' monthly production for purposes of analysis, using the following array structure:

   ```
   const int NUM_LOGGERS = 37;

   int logsCut[NUM_LOGGERS][12];   // Logs cut per logger per month
   int monthlyHigh;
   int monthlyTotal;
   int yearlyTotal;
   int high;
   int month;
   int bestMonth;
   int logger;
   int bestLogger;
   ```

   a. The following statement would assign the January log total for logger number 7 to `monthlyTotal`. (True or False?)

   ```
   monthlyTotal = logsCut[7][0];
   ```

   b. The following statements would compute the yearly total for logger number 11. (True or False?)

   ```
   yearlyTotal = 0;
   for (month = 0; month < NUM_LOGGERS; month++)
       yearlyTotal = yearlyTotal + logsCut[month][10];
   ```

   c. The following statements would find the best logger (most logs cut) in March. (True or False?)

```
monthlyHigh = 0;
for (logger = 0; logger < NUM_LOGGERS; logger++)
    if (logsCut[logger][2] > monthlyHigh)
    {
        bestLogger = logger;
        monthlyHigh = logsCut[logger][2];
    }
```

d. The following statements would find the logger with the highest monthly production and the logger's best month. (True or False?)

```
high = -1;
for (month = 0; month < 12; month++)
    for (logger = 0; logger < NUM_LOGGERS; logger++)
        if (logsCut[logger][month] > high)
        {
            high = logsCut[logger][month];
            bestLogger = logger;
            bestMonth = month;
        }
```

9. Declare the **float** array variables described below. Use proper style.
   a. A three-dimensional array where the first dimension is indexed from 0 through 9, the second dimension is indexed by an enumeration type representing the days of the week, and the third dimension is indexed from 0 through 20.
   b. A four-dimensional array where the first two dimensions are indexed from 0 through 49, and the third and fourth are indexed by any valid ASCII character.

PROGRAMMING WARM-UP EXERCISES

1. Write a C++ value-returning function that returns TRUE if all the values in a certain subarray of a two-dimensional array are positive, and returns FALSE otherwise. The array (of type **TableType**), the number of columns in the subarray, and the number of rows in the subarray should be passed as parameters.
2. A *square array* is a two-dimensional array in which the number of rows is the same as the number of columns. Write a C++ function to initialize the two diagonals of a square **char** array to a specified character. The array (named **data**, of type **DataType**), the row and column lengths of the array (**length**), and the specified character (**someChar**) should be passed as parameters.
3. Write a C++ function **Copy** that takes an array **data**, defined to be NUM_ROWS by NUM_COLS, and copies the values into a second array **data2**, defined the same way. **data** and **data2** are of type **DataType**. The constants NUM_ROWS and NUM_COLS may be accessed globally.
4. Write a C++ function that finds the largest value in a two-dimensional **float** array of 50 rows and 50 columns.
5. Using the declarations in Exam Preparation Exercise 1, write functions to do the following tasks. Use proper style. Only constants may be accessed globally.
   a. Determine the team that sold the most tickets during the first week of ticket sales.

b. Determine the week in which the second team sold the most tickets.

c. Determine the week in which the most tickets were sold.

d. Determine the team that sold the most tickets.

6. Using the declarations in Exam Preparation Exercise 2, write functions, in proper style, to do the following tasks. Only constants may be accessed globally.

a. Determine which school spent the most money on football.

b. Determine which sport the last school spent the most money on.

c. Determine which school had the most students playing basketball.

d. Determine in which sport the third school had the most students participating.

e. Determine the total amount spent by all the schools on volleyball.

f. Determine the total number of students who played any sport. (Assume that each student played only one sport.)

g. Determine which school had the most students participating in sports.

h. Determine which was the most popular sport in terms of money spent.

i. Determine which was the most popular sport in terms of student participation.

7. Given the following declarations

```
const int NUM_DEPTS = 100;
const int NUM_STORES = 10;
const int NUM_MONTHS = 12;

typedef int SalesType[NUM_STORES][NUM_MONTHS][NUM_DEPTS];
```

write a C++ function to initialize an array of type `SalesType` to 0. The constants `NUM_STORES`, `NUM_MONTHS`, and `NUM_DEPTS` may be accessed globally. The array should be passed as a parameter.

8. Sales figures are kept on items sold by store, by department, and by month. Write a C++ function to calculate and print the total number of items sold during the year by each department in each store. The data are stored in an array of type `SalesType` as defined in Programming Warm-Up Exercise 7. The array containing the data should be passed as a parameter. The constants `NUM_STORES`, `NUM_MONTHS`, and `NUM_DEPTS` may be accessed globally.

9. Write a C++ value-returning function that returns the sum of the elements in a specified row of an array. The array, the number of filled-in columns, and which row is to be totaled should be passed as parameters.

PROGRAMMING PROBLEMS

1. A group of playing cards can be represented as a two-dimensional array, where the first dimension is rank and the second dimension is suit. Read in a bridge hand (13 cards) and determine whether the player should pass or bid. Each card should be input on a line by itself, with the suit given first and the rank next.

The decision to pass or bid is based on the number of points the hand is worth. Points are counted as follows:

An ace is worth 4 points.
A king is worth 3 points.
A queen is worth 2 points.
A jack is worth 1 point.

Add up the points in the hand and print one of the following messages.

Below 13 points,   "Pass"
From 13 through 16 points,   "Bid one of a suit"
From 17 through 19 points,   "Bid one no trump"
From 20 through 22 points,   "Bid one of a suit"
Over 22 points,   "Bid two of a suit"

2. Write an interactive program that plays tic-tac-toe. Represent the board as a three-by-three character array. Initialize the array to blanks and ask each player in turn to input a position. The first player's position will be marked on the board with an *O*, and the second player's position will be marked with an *X*. Continue the process until a player wins or the game is a draw. To win, a player must have three marks in a row, in a column, or on a diagonal. A draw occurs when the board is full and no one has won.

Each player's position should be input as indices into the tic-tac-toe board—that is, a row number, a space, and a column number. Make the program user-friendly.

After each game, print out a diagram of the board showing the ending positions. Keep a count of the number of games each player has won and the number of draws. Before the beginning of each game, ask each player if he or she wishes to continue. If either player wishes to quit, print out the statistics and stop.

3. Write a C++ program to read in two 2-dimensional arrays, and then multiply one by the other. This is called matrix multiplication. For example, if `firstArray` (a 2-row by 2-column array) appears as

2   7
9   3

and `secondArray` (a 2-row by 1-column array) appears as

8
6

then the product matrix is

```
productMatrix[0][0] = 2 * 8 + 7 * 6
productMatrix[1][0] = 9 * 8 + 3 * 6
```

Matrix multiplication can be done only if the number of columns in the multiplicand (the first array) equals the number of rows in the multiplier (the second array).

The program should read in the two arrays, test to see if multiplication is possible, and then multiply them if it is. The output will be a printout of the two arrays and will either output the product array or print a message saying that multiplication is not possible.

4. Photos taken in space by the Galileo spacecraft are sent back to earth as a stream of numbers. Each number represents a level of brightness. A large number represents a high brightness level, and a small number represents a low level. Your job is to take a matrix (a two-dimensional array) of the numbers and print it as a picture.

One approach to generating a picture is to print a dark character (like a $) when the brightness level is low, and to print a light character (like a blank or a period) when the level is high. Unfortunately, errors in transmission sometimes occur. Thus, your program should first attempt to find and correct these errors. Assume a value is in error if it differs by more than one from each of its four neighboring values. Correct the erroneous value by giving it the average of its neighboring values, rounded to the nearest integer.

Example:

```
    5           The 2 would be regarded as an error and would be given
  4 2 5         a corrected value of 5.
    5
```

Note that values on the corners or boundaries of the matrix have to be processed differently than the values on the interior. Your program should print an image of the uncorrected picture and then an image of the corrected picture.

5. The following diagram represents an island surrounded by water (shaded area).

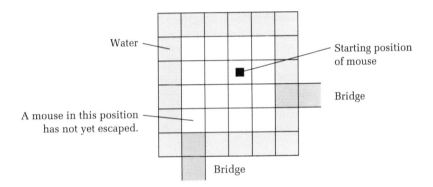

Two bridges lead out of the island. A mouse is placed on the black square. Write a program to make the mouse take a walk across the island. The mouse is allowed to travel one square at a time, either horizontally or vertically. A random number from 1 through 4 should be used to decide which direction the mouse is to take.* The mouse drowns when he hits the water; he escapes when he enters a bridge. You may generate a random number up to 100 times. If the mouse does not find his way by the hundredth try, he will die of starvation. Restart the mouse in a reinitialized array and go back and repeat the whole process. Count the number of times he escapes, drowns, and starves.

---

*Through the header file stdlib.h, the C++ standard library supplies a value-returning, parameterless function named rand. Each time it is called, rand returns a random int in the range 0 through RAND_MAX, a constant defined in stdlib.h (usually the same as INT_MAX). The following statement assigns to randNum a random integer in the range 1 through 4:

randNum = rand() % 4 + 1;

See Appendix C for further details.

Input:

First input line—the size of the array, including border of water and bridges (not
larger than 20 x 20)

Next *N* input lines—the rows of the two-dimensional array, where the positions
containing negative numbers represent the water, the positions in the edge containing a 0 represent the bridges, the position containing a 1 represents the
starting position of the mouse, and all other positions contain zeros

Output:

A line stating whether the mouse escaped, drowned, or starved

A line showing the mouse's starting position and the position of the two bridges

A map showing the frequency of the mouse's visits to each position

You should print the items above (double spaced between trips) for each trip by
the mouse.

6. In competitive diving, each diver makes three dives of varying degrees of difficulty. Nine judges score each dive from 0 through 10 in steps of 0.5. The total score
is obtained by discarding the lowest and highest of the judges' scores, adding the
remaining scores, and then multiplying the scores by the degree of difficulty. The
divers take turns, and when the competition is finished, they are ranked according to score. Write a program to do the above, using the following input and output specifications.

Input:

Number of divers

Diver's name (10 characters), difficulty (`float`), and judges' ratings (nine `floats`)

There is a line of data for each diver for each dive. All the data for Dive 1 are
grouped together, then all for Dive 2, then all for Dive 3.

Output:

The input data, echo-printed in tabular form with appropriate headings—for example, Name, Difficulty, judge's number (1–9)

A table that contains the following information, sorted by final total, in descending order (highest diver first):

Name   Dive 1   Dive 2   Dive 3   Total

where Name is the diver's name; Dive 1, Dive 2, and Dive 3 are the total points
received for a single dive, as described above; and Total is the overall total

7. You work for the Jet Propulsion Laboratory. They want you to write a program
that takes an array containing the digitized representation of a picture of the night
sky and locates the stars on it. Each element of the array represents the amount of
light hitting that portion of the image when the picture was taken. Intensities
range from 0 through 20.

14

Records
(C++ Structs)

- To be able to declare a record (struct) data type—that is, a data structure whose components may be nonhomogeneous.
- To be able to access a member of a record variable.
- To be able to use arrays of records to solve a given problem.
- To be able to define a hierarchical record structure.
- To be able to access values stored in a hierarchical record variable.
- To understand the general concept of a C++ union type.
- To be able to choose and design an appropriate array and/or record data structure for a given problem.

In the last three chapters, we looked in depth at a homogeneous structured data type called an array. We discussed common algorithms that are applied to arrays: sorting, linear searching, and binary searching. We added a data structures section to our top-down design. Clearly, how we choose to represent our data is an important aspect of the programming process.

Although the array is an extremely useful data structure, it can be used only when the components are all the same data type. In this chapter, we examine a *heterogeneous* (nonhomogeneous) structured data type called a **record**. The components of a record do not have to be of the same data type, and they are accessed by name rather than by relative position.

The last chapter closed with a discussion of how to choose a data structure. We continue this discussion at the end of this chapter, adding the record data type to our list of possible choices.

 Records

Records allow us to group related components together, regardless of their data types. Each component in a record is called a **field** of the record, and each field is given a name called the **field name.** C++ uses its own terminology with records. A record is called a **structure,** the fields of a record are called **members** of the structure, and each member has a **member name.**

Record (Structure, in C++)   A structured data type with a fixed number of components that are accessed by name, not by index. The components may be heterogeneous (of different types).

Field (Member, in C++)   A component of a record.

In C++, record data types are most commonly declared according to the following syntax:

StructDeclaration

```
struct TypeName
{
    MemberList
};
```

where TypeName is an identifier giving a name to the data type, and MemberList is defined as

MemberList

The reserved word `struct` is an abbreviation for *structure*, the C++ term for a record. Because the word *structure* has many other meanings in computer science, we'll use `struct` or *record* to avoid any possible confusion about what we are referring to.

You probably recognize the syntax of a member list as being nearly identical to a series of variable declarations. Be careful: a `struct` declaration is a type declaration, and we still must declare variables of this type for any memory locations to be associated with the member names. As an example, let's use a `struct` to describe a student in a class. We want to store the first and last names, the overall grade point average prior to this class, the grade on programming assignments, the grade on quizzes, the final exam grade, and the final course grade.

```
// Type declarations

enum GradeType {A, B, C, D, F};

typedef char NameString[16];    // Max. 15 characters plus '\0'

struct StudentRec
{
    NameString firstName;
    NameString lastName;
    float      gpa;             // Grade point average
    int        programGrade;    // Assume 0..400
    int        quizGrade;       // Assume 0..300
    int        finalExam;       // Assume 0..300
    GradeType  courseGrade;
};

// Variable declarations

StudentRec firstStudent;
StudentRec student;
int        index;
int        grade;
```

Notice, both in this example and in the syntax template, that a `struct` declaration ends with a semicolon. By now, you have learned not to put a semicolon after the right brace of a compound statement. However, the member list in a struct declaration is not considered to be a compound statement; the braces are simply required syntax in the declaration. A struct declaration, like all C++ declaration statements, must end with a semicolon.

firstName, lastName, gpa, programGrade, quizGrade, finalExam, and courseGrade are member names within the struct type StudentRec. These member names make up the member list. Note that each member name is given a type.

firstName and lastName are of type NameString, which is a char array type. gpa is a float member. programGrade, quizGrade, and finalExam are int members. courseGrade is of an enumeration data type made up of the grades A through D and F.

None of these struct members are associated with memory locations until we declare a variable of the StudentRec type. StudentRec is merely a pattern for a struct (see Figure 14-1). The variables firstStudent and student are variables of type StudentRec.

The members of a struct variable are accessed by giving the name of the variable, followed by a dot (period), and then the member name. This expression is called a **member selector**. The syntax template is

MemberSelector

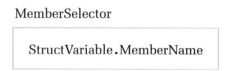

StructVariable.MemberName

Just as brackets ([ ]) are used to select individual components of an array, *dot notation* is used to select individual components of a struct. To access the grade point average of firstStudent, we would write

firstStudent.gpa

■ FIGURE 14-1

Pattern for a Struct

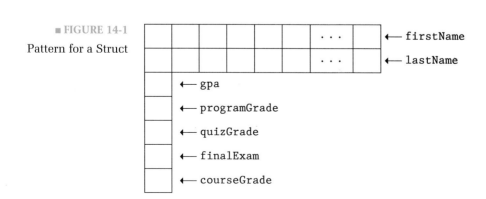

To access the final exam score of student, we would write

```
student.finalExam
```

Member Selector The expression used to access components of a struct variable. It is formed by using the struct variable name and the member name, separated by a dot (period).

The component of a struct accessed by the member selector is treated just like any other variable of the same type. It may be used in an assignment statement, passed as a parameter, and so on. Figure 14-2 shows the struct variable student with the member selector for each member. In this example, some processing has already taken place, so values are stored in some of the components.

Let's demonstrate the use of these member selectors. Using our student variable, the following code segment reads in a final exam grade; adds up the program grade, the quiz grade, and the final exam grade; and then assigns a letter grade to the result.

```
cin >> student.finalExam;
grade = student.finalExam + student.programGrade +
        student.quizGrade;
if (grade >= 900)
    student.courseGrade = A;
else if (grade >= 800)
    student.courseGrade = B;
else .
        .
        .
```

■ FIGURE 14-2

Struct Variable
student with
Member Selectors

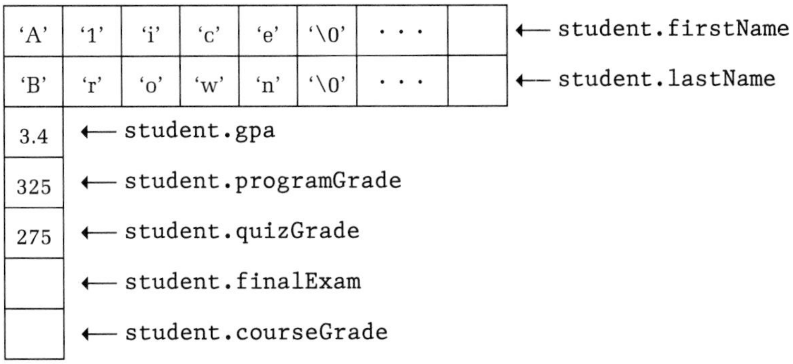

| 'A' | '1' | 'i' | 'c' | 'e' | '\0' | · · · | | ← student.firstName |
| 'B' | 'r' | 'o' | 'w' | 'n' | '\0' | · · · | | ← student.lastName |

3.4	← student.gpa
325	← student.programGrade
275	← student.quizGrade
	← student.finalExam
	← student.courseGrade

Just as we can read values into specific components of an array, we can read values into members of a struct. The statement

```
cin >> student.finalExam;
```

reads a value from the standard input device and stores the value into the finalExam member of student. As with arrays, we *cannot* read in an entire struct as an aggregate; we must read values into a struct one member at a time.

An alternative to reading in values is to initialize a struct in its declaration. The syntax is similar to the initialization of an array: you provide a list of initial values, separate the values with commas, and enclose the whole list within braces. Here's an example of declaring and initializing the variable student:

```
StudentRec student =
{
    "John",
    "Smith",
    3.24,
    320,
    290,
    95,
    B
};
```

We have formatted the initializer list vertically but could just as well have arranged it horizontally. Each value in the initializer list corresponds to one member of the struct. The two strings are stored into the firstName and lastName members, 3.24 is stored into the gpa member, 320 is stored into the programGrade member, and so forth.

The struct component student.lastName is an array. We can access the individual elements in this component just as we would access the elements of any other array: we give the name of the array followed by the index, which is enclosed in brackets.

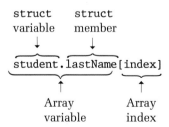

The expression student.lastName[0] would access the first letter in the last name, student.firstName[1] would access the second letter in the first name, and so on.

In addition to accessing individual components of a struct variable, we can in some cases manipulate structs as a whole. C++ is more permissive about aggregate operations on structs than on arrays, but there still are restrictions. The following table compares arrays and structs with respect to aggregate operations:

Aggregate Operation	Arrays	Structs
I/O	No (except strings)	No
Assignment	No	Yes
Arithmetic	No	No
Comparison	No	No
Parameter passage	By reference only	By value or by reference
Return as a function's return value	No	Yes

According to the table, one struct variable can be assigned to another. However, both variables must be declared to be of the same type. For example, if student and anotherStudent are both declared to be of type StudentRec, the statement

```
anotherStudent = student;
```

copies the entire contents of the struct variable student to the variable anotherStudent, member by member.

An entire struct can also be passed as a parameter, either by value or by reference, and a struct can be returned as the value of a value-returning function. Let's define a function that takes a StudentRec variable as a parameter.

The task of this function is to determine if a student's grade in a course is consistent with his or her overall grade point average (GPA). We define *consistent* to mean that the course grade is the same as the rounded GPA. The GPA is calculated on a 4-point scale, where A is 4, B is 3, C is 2, D is 1, and F is 0. If the rounded GPA is 4 and the course grade is A, then the function returns TRUE. If the rounded GPA is 4 and the course grade is not A, then the function returns FALSE. Each of the other grades is tested in the same way.

The Consistent function is coded below. The formal parameter aStudent, a struct of type StudentRec, is passed by value. (Assume that the data type Boolean has been defined previously.)

```
Boolean Consistent( /* in */ StudentRec aStudent )

// Precondition:
//      0.0 <= aStudent.gpa <= 4.0
// Postcondition:
//      Function value == TRUE, if the course grade is consistent
//                                  with the overall GPA
//                          == FALSE, otherwise

{
    int roundedGPA = int(aStudent.gpa + 0.5);

    switch (roundedGPA)
    {
        case 0: return (aStudent.courseGrade == F);
        case 1: return (aStudent.courseGrade == D);
        case 2: return (aStudent.courseGrade == C);
        case 3: return (aStudent.courseGrade == B);
        case 4: return (aStudent.courseGrade == A);
    }
}
```

Let's review the basic features of struct data types in the context of another example. A parts wholesaler wants to computerize her operation. Until now, she has kept the inventory on handwritten 8 × 10 cards. A typical inventory card contains the following data:

Part number: 1A3321
Description: Cotter pin
Cost: 0.012
Quantity on hand: 2100

A struct is a natural choice for describing a part. Each item on the inventory card can be a member of the struct. The relevant declarations look like this:

```
typedef char String6[7];
typedef char String20[21];

struct PartType
{
    String6    partNumber;
    String20   description;
    float      cost;
    int        quantity;
};

PartType part;
```

The left and right braces surround the member list, and a semicolon terminates the `struct` declaration. Each member name is preceded by the name of a data type, just like the declaration of any variable. Member names must be unique within a `struct` type, just as variable names must be unique within a block.

Once a `struct` variable has been declared, the member selectors of the `struct` variable are treated and used in the same way as any other declared variable. Member selectors can be used in expressions such as

```
part.quantity = part.quantity + 24;
if (part.cost <= 5.00)
    cout << part.description << ' ' << part.cost;
```

If the parts wholesaler supplies inventory data that look like

```
2B3310Ring, piston       2.95    15
```

then the following program segment would read and store the data into the appropriate members.

```
cin.get(part.partNumber, 7);
cin.get(part.description, 21);
cin >> part.cost >> part.quantity;
```

`part.partNumber`, `part.description`, `part.cost`, and `part.quantity` are the member selectors for the members of the `struct` variable part.

To complete our initial look at C++ structs, we give a more complete syntax template for a `struct` type declaration:

StructDeclaration

```
struct TypeName
{
    MemberList
} VariableList ;
```

As you can see in the syntax template, two items are optional: TypeName (the name of the `struct` type being declared), and a list of variable names between the right brace and the semicolon. Our examples thus far have declared a type name but have not included a variable list. The variable list allows you not only to declare a struct type but also to declare variables of that type, all in one statement. For example, you could write the declarations

```
struct StudentRec
{
    NameString firstName;
    NameString lastName;
        .
        .
        .
};

StudentRec firstStudent;
StudentRec student;
```

more compactly in the form

```
struct StudentRec
{
    NameString firstName;
    NameString lastName;
        .
        .
        .
} firstStudent, student;
```

In this book, we avoid combining variable declarations with type declarations, preferring to keep the two notions separate.

If you omit the type name but include the variable list, you create an anonymous type:

```
struct
{
    int   firstMember;
    float secondMember;
} someVar;
```

Here, someVar is a variable of an anonymous type. No other variables of that type can be declared because the type has no name. Therefore, someVar cannot participate in aggregate operations such as assignment or parameter passage. All the arguments given in Chapter 10 against anonymous typing of enumeration types apply to struct types as well.

Arrays of Records

Although single records can be useful, many applications require a collection of records. For example, a business needs a list of parts records, and a teacher needs a list of students in a class. Arrays are ideal for these applications. We simply define an array whose components are records.

Let's define a grade book to be a list of students as follows:

```
const int MAX_STUDENTS = 150;

enum GradeType {A, B, C, D, F};

typedef char NameString[16];

struct StudentRec
{
    NameString firstName;
    NameString lastName;
    float      gpa;
    int        programGrade;
    int        quizGrade;
    int        finalExam;
    GradeType  courseGrade;
};

StudentRec gradeBook[MAX_STUDENTS];
int        length;
int        count;
```

This data structure can be visualized as shown in Figure 14-3.

An element of gradeBook is selected by an index. For example, gradeBook[2] is the third component in the array variable gradeBook. Each component of gradeBook is a record of type StudentRec. To access the course grade of the third student, we use the following expression:

gradeBook[2].courseGrade

Specifies third record in array gradeBook

Specifies courseGrade member in record gradeBook[2]

To access the first character in the last name of the third student, we use the following expression:

■ FIGURE 14-3   Array `gradeBook` with Records as Elements

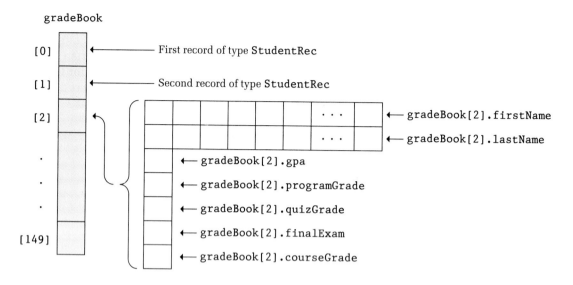

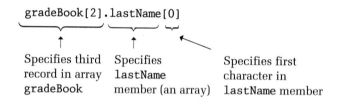

The following code fragment prints the first and last names of each student in the class:

```
for (count = 0; count < length; count++)
    cout << gradeBook[count].firstName << ' '
         << gradeBook[count].lastName << endl;
```

Hierarchical Records

We have seen examples where the components of a record are simple variables and arrays. A component of a record can also be another record. Records whose components are themselves records are called **hierarchical records.**

Hierarchical Records   Records in which at least one of the components is itself a record.

Let's look at an example where a hierarchical structure is appropriate. A
small machine shop keeps information about each of its machines. There is
descriptive information, such as the identification number, a description of
the machine, the purchase date, and the cost. Statistical information is also
kept, such as the number of down days, the failure rate, and the date of last
service. What is a reasonable way of representing all this information?
First, let's look at a flat (nonhierarchical) record structure that holds this
information.

```
typedef char String50[51];

struct MachineRec
{
    int       idNumber;
    String50  description;
    float     failRate;
    int       lastServicedMonth;   // Assume 1..12
    int       lastServicedDay;     // Assume 1..31
    int       lastServicedYear;    // Assume 1900..2050
    int       downDays;
    int       purchaseDateMonth;   // Assume 1..12
    int       purchaseDateDay;     // Assume 1..31
    int       purchaseDateYear;    // Assume 1900..2050
    float     cost;
};
```

Type `MachineRec` has 11 members. There is so much detailed information
here that it is difficult to quickly get a feeling for what the record represents.
Let's see if we can reorganize it into a hierarchical structure that makes more
sense. We can divide the information into two groups: information that
changes and information that does not. There are also two dates to be kept:
date of purchase and date of last service. These observations suggest use of a
record describing a date, a record describing the statistical data, and an
overall record containing the other two as components. The following type
declaration reflects this structure.

```
const int NUM_MACHINES = 25;

typedef char String50[51];
```

```
struct DateType
{
    int month;   // Assume 1..12
    int day;     // Assume 1..31
    int year;    // Assume 1900..2050
};
struct StatisticsType
{
    float     failRate;
    DateType  lastServiced;
    int       downDays;
};
struct MachineRec
{
    int            idNumber;
    String50       description;
    StatisticsType history;
    DateType       purchaseDate;
    float          cost;
};

MachineRec inventory[NUM_MACHINES];
MachineRec machine;
int        counter;
```

The contents of a machine record are now much more obvious. Two of the components of the struct type MachineRec are themselves structs: purchaseDate is of struct type DateType, and history is of struct type StatisticsType. One of the components of struct type StatisticsType is a struct of type DateType.

How do we access a hierarchical structure such as this one? We build the accessing expressions (member selectors) for the members of the embedded structs from left to right, beginning with the struct variable name. Following are some expressions and the components they access.

Expression	Component Accessed
machine.purchaseDate	DateType struct variable
machine.purchaseDate.month	month member of a DateType struct variable
machine.purchaseDate.year	year member of a DateType struct variable
machine.history.lastServiced.year	year member of a DateType struct variable contained in a struct of type StatisticsType

Figure 14-4 is a pictorial representation of machine with values. Look carefully at how each component is accessed.

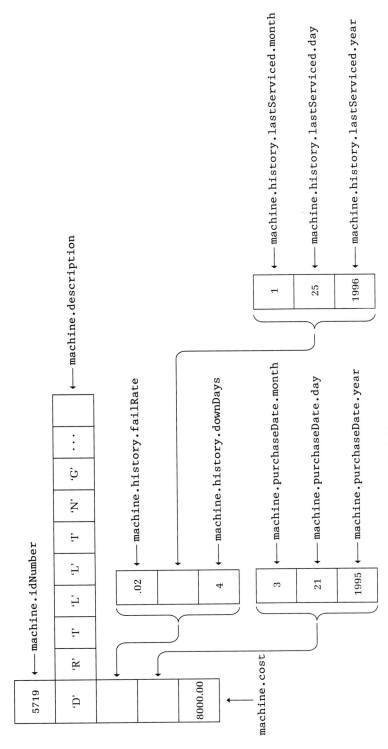

We can, of course, have an array of hierarchical records; `inventory` is such an array. We can access the year that the first machine was purchased using the following expression:

```
inventory[0].purchaseDate.year
```

And here is a code segment that prints out the ID number and the year of purchase of each machine that has a failure rate of more than 8 percent:

```
for (counter = 0; counter < NUM_MACHINES; counter++)
    if (inventory[counter].history.failRate > 0.08)
        cout << inventory[counter].idNumber << ' '
             << inventory[counter].purchaseDate.year << endl;
```

 Unions

In Chapter 11, we presented a diagram (Figure 11-2) showing the structured types available in C++. We repeat this diagram in Figure 14-5.

So far we have discussed two of the four structured types: arrays and structs. We now look briefly at *union* types. The fourth structured type—the class—is the topic of Chapter 15.

In C++, a union is defined to be a struct that holds only one of its members at a time during program execution. Here is a declaration of a union type and a union variable:

```
union WeightType
{
    long   wtInOunces;
    int    wtInPounds;
    float  wtInTons;
};
```

■ FIGURE 14-5

C++ Structured
Types

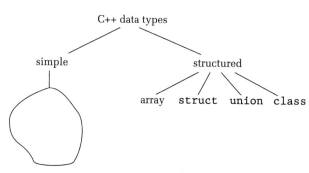

```
WeightType weight;
```

The syntax for declaring a union type is identical to that of a `struct` type, except that the word `union` is substituted for `struct`.

At run time, the memory space allocated to the variable `weight` does *not* include room for three distinct components. Instead, `weight` can contain only one of the following: *either* a `long` value *or* an `int` value *or* a `float` value. The assumption is that the program will never need a weight in ounces, a weight in pounds, and a weight in tons simultaneously while executing. The purpose of a union is to conserve memory by forcing several values to use the same memory space, one at a time. The following code shows how the `weight` variable might be used.

```
weight.wtInTons = 4.83;
        .
        .
        .
// Weight in tons is no longer needed. Reuse the memory space.

weight.wtInPounds = 35;
        .
        .
        .
```

After the last assignment statement, the previous `float` value 4.83 is gone, replaced by the `int` value 35.

It's quite reasonable to argue that a union is not a data structure at all. It does not represent a collection of values; it represents only a single value from among several *potential* values. On the other hand, unions are grouped together with the structured types because of their similarity to `struct`s.

There is much more to be said about unions, including subtle issues related to their declaration and usage. However, these issues are more appropriate in an advanced study of data structures and system programming. We have introduced unions only to present a complete picture of the structured types provided by C++ and to acquaint you with the general idea in case you encounter unions in other C++ programs.

 ## More on Choosing Data Structures

Representing Logical Entities with Hierarchical Records

We have demonstrated how to design algorithms and data structures in parallel. We progress from the logical or abstract data structure envisioned at the top level through the refinement process until we reach the concrete coding in C++. We have also shown two ways of representing the logical structure of a machine record in a shop inventory. The first used a record where all the components in an entry were defined (made concrete) at the same time. The second used a hierarchical record where the dates and statistics describing a machine's history were defined in lower-level records.

Let's look again at the two different ways in which we represented our logical data structure.

```cpp
typedef char String50[51];

// ** Version 1 **

struct MachineRec
{
    int      idNumber;
    String50 description;
    float    failRate;
    int      lastServicedMonth;  // Assume 1..12
    int      lastServicedDay;    // Assume 1..31
    int      lastServicedYear;   // Assume 1900..2050
    int      downDays;
    int      purchaseDateMonth;  // Assume 1..12
    int      purchaseDateDay;    // Assume 1..31
    int      purchaseDateYear;   // Assume 1900..2050
    float    cost;
};

// ** Version 2 **

struct DateType
{
    int month;  // Assume 1..12
    int day;    // Assume 1..31
    int year;   // Assume 1900..2050
};
struct StatisticsType
{
    float    failRate;
    DateType lastServiced;
    int      downDays;
};
struct MachineRec
{
    int            idNumber;
    String50       description;
    StatisticsType history;
    DateType       purchaseDate;
    float          cost;
};
```

Which of these two representations is better? The second one is better for two reasons.

First, it groups elements together logically. The statistics and the dates are entities within themselves. We may want to have a date or a machine history in another record structure. If we define the dates and statistics only within MachineRec (as in the first structure), we would have to define them again for every other data structure that needs them, giving us multiple definitions of the same logical entity.

Second, the details of the entities (statistics and dates) are pushed down to a lower level in the second structure. The principle of deferring details to as low a level as possible should be applied to designing data structures as well as to designing algorithms. How a machine history or a date is represented is not relevant to our concept of a machine record, so the details need not be specified until it is time to write the algorithms to manipulate those members.

Pushing the implementation details of a data type to a lower level separates the logical description from the implementation. This concept is analogous to control abstraction, which we discussed in Chapter 8. The separation of the logical properties of a data type from its implementation details is called **data abstraction,** which is a goal of effective programming and the foundation upon which abstract data types are built. (We introduced the concept of abstract data types briefly in Chapter 12 and explore them more fully in Chapter 15.)

Data Abstraction   The separation of a data type's logical properties from its implementation.

Eventually, all the logical properties have to be defined in terms of concrete data types and routines written to manipulate them. If the implementation is properly designed, we can use the same routines to manipulate the structure in a wide variety of applications. For example, if we have a routine to compare dates, that routine can be used to compare dates representing days on which equipment was bought or maintained, or dates representing people's birthdays. The concept of designing a low-level structure and writing routines to manipulate it is the basis for C++ class types, which we examine in Chapter 15.

Style Considerations in Choice of Data Structure

Just as there are style considerations in writing programs, there are also style considerations in choosing data structures. A program can produce a correct answer, but if it is difficult to debug, read, or modify, it can still be a poor program. A data structure can be used to solve a problem, and yet not accurately reflect the relationships within the problem. If the data structure does not reflect these relationships, it is not an effective structure for that program.

A data structure is a framework for holding data. This framework should be tailored to each particular problem by reflecting the relationships among data values, making it easy for readers to see how the data items are related and how they should be processed to produce the required output. Because each problem is different, it is impossible to give a set of rules by which to judge an effective data structure. Instead, we examine the choices within a specific context, discuss the issues involved, and make some generalizations.

The Absentee program in Chapter 13 analyzed absentee data, made up of the number of people who were absent from each of six departments of a company during a particular week. The data were broken down further by day of the week. The main data structure used was a two-dimensional array absenteeData, where the first dimension represented departments and the second dimension represented the days of the week. Each component was an integer value that represented the number of people who were absent. A parallel, one-dimensional array average held the average daily absentee figures for each department (see Figure 14-6).

Would a record structure be a better choice to represent this information? Let's look at two possible representations of this same information as an array of structs, and discuss the implications of each representation.

```
const int NUM_DEPTS = 6;

enum DeptType {A, B, C, D, E, F};
enum DayType {MONDAY, TUESDAY, WEDNESDAY, THURSDAY, FRIDAY};
```

■ FIGURE 14-6

Arrays absenteeData and average

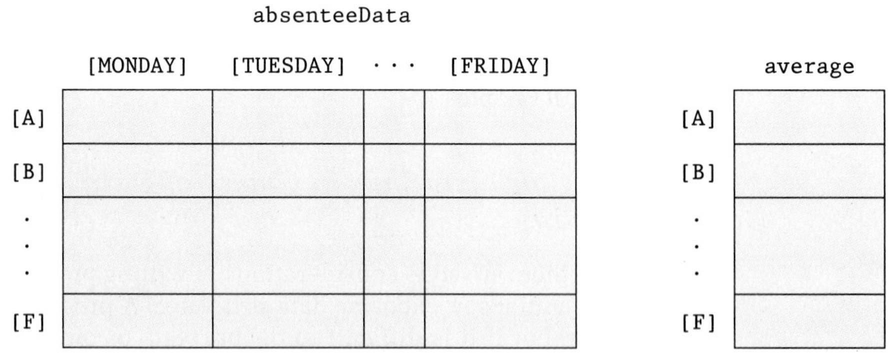

```
struct DailyAbsences
{
    int byDepartment[NUM_DEPTS];      // To be indexed by DeptType
};
struct DeptAbsences
{
    int byDay[5];                     // To be indexed by DayType
};

DailyAbsences table1[5];              // To be indexed by DayType
DeptAbsences  table2[NUM_DEPTS];      // To be indexed by DeptType
```

table1 represents the data by day of the week; table2 represents the data by department. The two representations are pictured in Figures 14-7 and 14-8.

table1 and table2 provide another example of data abstraction. In the first representation, the fact that the absences are recorded by day of the week is the important feature. The detail that the absences are further broken down by department is pushed to a lower level. Conversely, in the second representation, the fact that the absences are further broken down by day of the week is pushed to a lower level. In the two-dimensional array representation, both features—recording by department and recording by day of the week—are equally important (see Figure 14-9).

The best representation for a particular problem is the one that reflects the emphasis of the processing within the problem. We can determine this emphasis by looking at the questions that are being asked—that is, the results to be computed. If the primary processing involves absences by day of the week, the first structure is best. If the primary processing involves absences by department, the second representation is best. If both aspects of the processing are equally important, the two-dimensional array representation is best.

In this particular problem, management asks for absentee patterns across departments; therefore, the second record structure, table2, is a better choice. In fact, the parallel array average, which is used in the processing, can be incorporated into the struct type DeptAbsences.

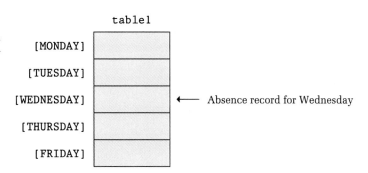

■ FIGURE 14-7

Absence Records by Day

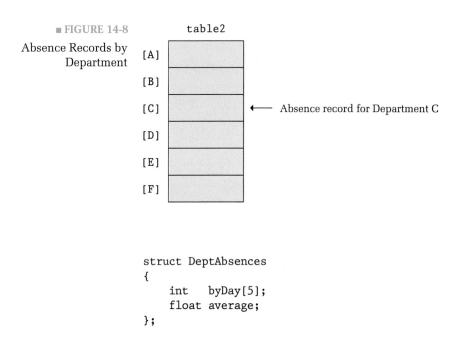

Absence Records by
Department

Absence record for Department C

```
struct DeptAbsences
{
    int    byDay[5];
    float  average;
};
```

Figure 14-10 depicts this structure. Notice that if all the processing on a two-dimensional array is *either* row processing *or* column processing, then an array of structs may reflect the problem and the processing better than a two-dimensional array.

Data structures that accurately reflect the relationships among the data values in a problem lead to effective programs. The logic of the program is easier to understand because the data structures mirror the problem. The code of the program is easier to maintain because the logic of the program is clearer. The program is easier to modify because the data structure accurately represents the problem.

Two-Dimensional
Array of Absentee
Data

absenteeData

[MONDAY] [TUESDAY] · · · [FRIDAY]

[A]

[B]

[F]

■ FIGURE 14-10

Absence Records,
Including Averages,
by Department

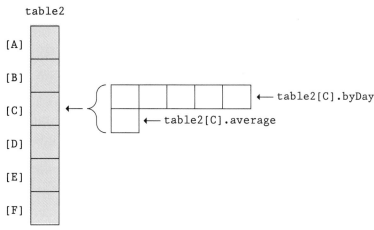

We should make one additional point here. The best structure is the *simplest* one that accurately reflects the problem and the processing. For example, don't use either an array or a `struct` if simple variables suffice.

When you are deciding whether or not to use a structured data type, ask yourself, "Can I process as I read, or must all the data be read in before I can begin processing?" For example, if you are finding the average of a set of test grades, each test grade can be added into the sum as it is read. All you need are simple variables—no structured data types are necessary.

What if you want to compare each grade to the average? Because the average cannot be calculated until all grades have been read, each individual grade must be kept in memory. Therefore, the test grades should be stored in an array.

This discussion presupposes that you know where to begin. What if you look at a problem and don't even know what the choices are? Go back and carefully examine the problem statement. Do you understand what is being asked? Can you do by hand what is being asked? If so, what sorts of forms would you use? Would you set up a table with rows and columns on a sheet of paper? Would you set up a column and make hash marks? More than likely, the appropriate data structure resembles the forms you would create to do the job by hand.

If you cannot do the job by hand, your problem is more fundamental than the choice of a data structure—you need to clarify the problem. Try writing down everything you know about the problem. Then write down what your output must be and what you must have as input in order to produce that output. If necessary, refer to the problem-solving heuristics in Chapter 2.

$P_{ROBLEM\text{-}SOLVING}$ CASE STUDY

Automated Address Book

Problem: You have a pocket address book that you have used for years, and it is now falling apart. Instead of copying all the items into a new book, you decide to automate your address book, including the following information for each entry:

Name _____

Address _____
      (street)

_____
(city)   (state)   (zip)

Telephone (___) _____ – _____

Birth Date _____ / _____ / _____

Input: A series of entries containing a first and a last name, a phone number, and a birth date. (We'll omit the address for this case study.) The exact form of an entry is to be determined.

Output: The entries in alphabetical order, written to a file `friendFile`.

Discussion: If we think of an address book as an abstract data type (Chapter 12), there are all kinds of interesting operations we might provide:

Enter a new person into the address book
Delete a person from the address book
Search for a name and print the person's phone number
Print all of the entries in the address book
Print a list of the people with birthdays each month
Print names and addresses in zip-code order to facilitate sending cards
    ⋮

Let's not be too ambitious. We should do the program in stages. In the first stage (this case study), we create the address book and save the information in a file. Because we want to enhance the program at a later time, we need to make the data structures as flexible as possible. As we do the top-down design, we pay particular attention to the development of the data structures. At first, we think of an address book as an abstraction and keep our algorithms general. As we refine our design, we make decisions about actual data structures to use and add more detail to the algorithms accordingly.

As we start our design phase for this problem, we call all the information about one person an entry. We want to keep our entries in order by last name so that we can use a binary search to locate specific people. We can either enter the entries in alphabetical order, or enter them in any order and then sort them. Because some last names have changed over the years and you have not bothered to copy them on the appropriate page, it is easier to let the program sort them rather than to enter them in alphabetical order.

Data Structures: To be determined.

Main   *Level 0*

```
Open friendFile for output (and verify success)
WHILE more entries
    Get entry
    Insert entry in alphabetical order
Write entries to file friendFile
```

Before we can write the Get Entry module, we have to decide what information we want to keep on each person. Because we use this address book mainly to look up telephone numbers, we need each person's name and phone number. We skip addresses in this case study, but include birth dates.

Get Entry (parameters to be determined)   *Level 1*

```
Get name
Get phone number
Get birth date
```

Write Entries (parameters to be determined)

```
FOR each entry
    Write firstName, lastName to friendFile
    Write areaCode, phoneNumber to friendFile
    Write month, day, year to friendFile
```

Get Name (parameters to be determined)   *Level 2*

```
Read firstName
Read lastName
```

Get Phone Number (parameters to be determined)

> Read areaCode
> Read phoneNumber

Get Birth Date (parameters to be determined)

> Read month, day, year

Now we must decide what data types to use. We began with the general concept of an entry. We refined it to include the items needed in the entry. To go any further, we must decide how we will represent these items in C++. And we must design specific algorithms for our data structure: reading in items, sorting items, and printing items.

Two of the items are names—that is, sequences of alphabetic characters. We can represent them as strings. The area code and phone number could be integer numbers, but we would like to store the hyphen that is between the third and fourth digits of the phone number. Therefore, the area code is an integer number but the phone number is a string. (We assume that an area code is 100 or greater so that we don't have to worry about how to print leading zeros in area codes such as 052. A Case Study Follow-Up exercise asks you to rethink this assumption.) We can represent birth dates as three integers: month, day, and year. Thus, an entry is represented by the seven components shown in Figure 14-11.

We can create a set of parallel arrays to hold these items for all of our friends. firstName, lastName, and phoneNumber are arrays of strings; areaCode, month, day, and year are one-dimensional arrays of integers. Each

■ FIGURE 14-11   Entry for Address Book

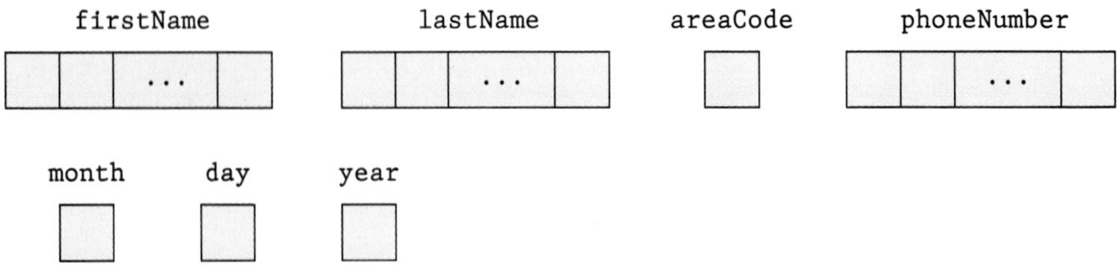

parallel row represents the information for one entry. This set of structures is shown in Figure 14-12.

A parallel organization of seven different arrays seems to be a clumsy way of representing this logical structure. Yet this is the structure that you have to use for this type of problem if your programming language does not have record data types—and some do not. However, in C++, it makes more sense to define an entry using a record (`struct`) data type.

Let's look now at a data structure in which an array of `struct`s is used to represent the address book. The following declarations describe this data structure.

```
const int MAX_FRIENDS = 150;     // Maximum number of friends

typedef char String8[9];         // Room for 8 characters plus '\0'
typedef char String15[16];       // Room for 15 characters plus '\0'

struct EntryType
{
    String15  firstName;
    String15  lastName;
    int       areaCode;          // Range 100..999
    String8   phoneNumber;
    int       month;             // Range 1..12
    int       day;               // Range 1..31
    int       year;              // Range 1900..2100
};

EntryType addressBook[MAX_FRIENDS];
```

`firstName`, `lastName`, `areaCode`, `phoneNumber`, `month`, `day`, and `year` are member names within the `struct` type `EntryType`. The members `firstName` and `lastName` are strings of type `String15`, `areaCode` is an integer, and `phoneNumber` is a string of type `String8`. Phone numbers have only seven digits, but we decided to include the hyphen between the first three digits and the last four digits because this is how phone numbers are usually printed. The members `month`, `day`, and `year` are integers. A complete entry with values stored in the `struct` variable `addressBook[0]` is shown in Figure 14-13.

Notice that `EntryType` is a flat (nonhierarchical) structure. For birth dates, we could have used a lower-level `DateType` `struct` as we did earlier in the `MachineRec` type. Also, the two pieces of a phone number—the area code and the number—might reasonably be defined in a lower-level `struct` type. The second Problem-Solving Case Study in this chapter uses just such a phone number type as part of a hierarchical record.

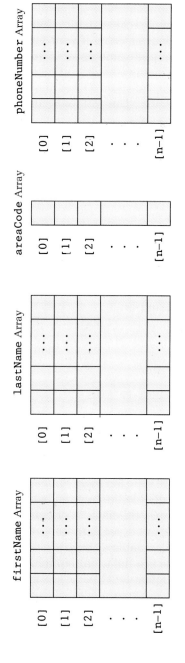

■ FIGURE 14-12 Parallel Arrays for Address Book

PROBLEM-SOLVING CASE STUDY cont'd.

■ FIGURE 14-13   Entry for Struct Variable `addressBook[0]`

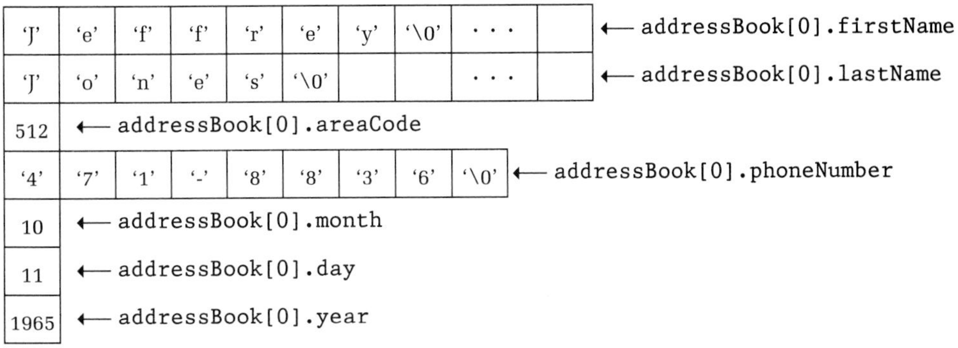

| 'J' | 'e' | 'f' | 'f' | 'r' | 'e' | 'y' | '\0' | · · · | | ← `addressBook[0].firstName` |

| 'J' | 'o' | 'n' | 'e' | 's' | '\0' | | | · · · | | ← `addressBook[0].lastName` |

| 512 | ← `addressBook[0].areaCode` |

| '4' | '7' | '1' | '-' | '8' | '8' | '3' | '6' | '\0' | ← `addressBook[0].phoneNumber` |

| 10 | ← `addressBook[0].month` |

| 11 | ← `addressBook[0].day` |

| 1965 | ← `addressBook[0].year` |

We have now defined a data structure to hold the information in our address book. Before we can finish the algorithms to read the data, we have to decide how we want to enter the data. Let's enter it interactively, prompting the user to enter each component. Here is a refined version of the Get Name module.

Get Name (Out: entry)   *Level 2*

> Prompt user for first name
> Read entry.firstName
> Prompt user for last name
> Read entry.lastName

We also redo the module for getting the phone number.

Get Phone Number (Inout: entry)

> Prompt user for area code, then a blank, then the number
> Read entry.areaCode
> Consume the blank
> Read entry.phoneNumber

Because the birth date can be read with a single statement, we incorporate Get Birth Date directly into Get Entry.

In Chapter 12, we wrote functions Insert and SearchOrd to insert an item into its proper place in a list. These functions were used in the Exam program to insert last names as they were read into an array of last names. We can use the same functions here with the following minor modification. The statement that compared the item being inserted with the components already in the list was:

```
while (strcmp(item, list[index]) > 0)
    index++;
```

Because our data structure is an array of structs, item and list[index] are structs, not strings. Therefore, the name of the member that is being compared must be added as follows:

```
while (strcmp(item.lastName, list[index].lastName) > 0)
    index++;
```

When coding the design, we need to write the prompts for the phone number and the birth date. Also, we haven't made any provision for keying errors, which is not realistic. After an entry has been read and before it is entered into the address book, let's ask the user whether or not the entry is correct. If the user says it is, the entry can be stored. If the user says it is not, the entry will not be saved.

We also have not determined how to end the reading process. After each entry, let's ask the user whether another entry is to be read. Regardless of the user's response, we must stop reading if the addressBook array becomes full. The main module now needs rewriting.

PROBLEM-SOLVING CASE STUDY cont'd.

Main   *Level 0*

> Open friendFile for output (and verify success)
> Set length = 0
> DO
>   Get entry
>   Print "Is this entry correct? (Y or N)"
>   Read response
>   IF response is 'Y' or 'y'
>   Insert entry into addressBook, updating length
>   Print "Do you wish to continue? (Y or N)"
>   Read response
> WHILE response is 'Y' or 'y' AND length < MAX_FRIENDS
> Write entries to file friendFile

Finally, we must redo the Get Entry and Write Entries modules, filling in the parameter lists and the details that depend on our chosen data structure.

Get Entry (Out: entry)   *Level 1*

> Get name
> Get phone number
> Prompt user for birth date
> Read entry.month, entry.day, entry.year

Write Entries (In: addressBook, length; Inout: friendFile)

> FOR counter going from 0 through length − 1
>   Write addressBook[counter].firstName, ' ',
>   addressBook[counter].lastName to friendFile
>   Write '(', addressBook[counter].areaCode, ')',
>   addressBook[counter].phoneNumber to friendFile
>   Write addressBook[counter].month, '/',
>   addressBook[counter].day, '/',
>   addressBook[counter].year to friendFile

Module Structure Chart:

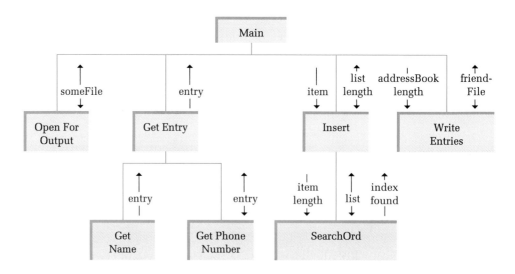

```
//*********************************************************************
// Friends program
// This program creates an address book by reading first names,
// last names, phone numbers, and birth dates from standard input
// and writing an alphabetical listing to an output file
//*********************************************************************
#include <iostream.h>
#include <iomanip.h>      // For setw()
#include <fstream.h>      // For file I/O
#include <string.h>       // For strcmp()
#include <ctype.h>        // For toupper()
#include "bool.h"         // For Boolean type

const int MAX_FRIENDS = 150;      // Maximum number of friends

typedef char String8[9];          // Room for 8 characters plus '\0'
typedef char String15[16];        // Room for 15 characters plus '\0'

struct EntryType
{
    String15 firstName;
    String15 lastName;
    int      areaCode;        // Range 100..999
    String8  phoneNumber;
    int      month;           // Range 1..12
    int      day;             // Range 1..31
    int      year;            // Range 1900..2100
};
```

```
void GetEntry( EntryType& );
void GetName( EntryType& );
void GetPhoneNumber( EntryType& );
void Insert( EntryType[], int&, EntryType );
void OpenForOutput( ofstream& );
void SearchOrd( EntryType[], EntryType, int, int&, Boolean& );
void WriteEntries( const EntryType[], int, ofstream& );

int main()
{
    EntryType addressBook[MAX_FRIENDS]; // Array of friends' records

    int       length = 0;       // Number of entries in addressBook
    EntryType entry;            // Current record being entered
    char      response;         // Response character from keyboard
    ofstream  friendFile;       // Output file of entries

    OpenForOutput(friendFile);
    if ( !friendFile )
        return 1;
    do
    {
        GetEntry(entry);
        cout << "Is this entry correct? (Y or N) ";
        cin >> response;
        if (toupper(response) == 'Y')
            Insert(addressBook, length, entry);
        cout << "Do you wish to continue? (Y or N) ";
        cin >> response;
        cin.ignore(100, '\n');

            // Invariant:
            //     addressBook[0..length-1] contain entries
            //     as input from the user
            //  && 0 <= length <= MAX_FRIENDS

    } while (toupper(response) == 'Y' && length < MAX_FRIENDS);

    if (length == MAX_FRIENDS)
        cout << "Address book is full." << endl;
    WriteEntries(addressBook, length, friendFile);
    return 0;
}

//****************************************************************
```

PROBLEM-SOLVING CASE STUDY cont'd.

```cpp
void OpenForOutput( /* inout */ ofstream& someFile )    // File to be
                                                        // opened

// Prompts the user for the name of an output file
// and attempts to open the file

// Postcondition:
//     The user has been prompted for a file name
//     && IF the file could not be opened
//           An error message has been printed
// Note:
//     Upon return from this function, the caller must test
//     the stream state to see if the file was successfully opened

{
    char fileName[51];    // User-specified file name (max. 50 chars)

    cout << "Output file name: ";
    cin.get(fileName, 51);
    cin.ignore(100, '\n');

    someFile.open(fileName);
    if ( !someFile )
        cout << "** Can't open " << fileName << " **" << endl;
}

//****************************************************************

void GetEntry( /* out */ EntryType& entry )    // Struct being built

// Builds and returns a complete address book entry

// Postcondition:
//     User has been prompted for a friend's first name, last name,
//     phone number, and birth date
//     && The input values are stored in the corresponding
//     members of entry

{
    GetName(entry);
    GetPhoneNumber(entry);
    cout << "Enter birth date as three integers, separated by"
         << " spaces: MM DD YYYY" << endl;
    cin >> entry.month >> entry.day >> entry.year;
}

//****************************************************************
```

```cpp
void GetName( /* out */ EntryType& entry )   // Struct receiving name

// Inputs friend's first and last name, storing them into entry

// Postcondition:
//     User has been prompted for a friend's first name and
//     last name
//   && entry.firstName == the input string for first name
//   && entry.lastName == the input string for last name

{
    cout << "Enter person's first name." << endl;
    cin.get(entry.firstName, 16);
    cin.ignore(100, '\n');

    cout << "Enter person's last name." << endl;
    cin.get(entry.lastName, 16);
    cin.ignore(100, '\n');

}

//****************************************************************

void GetPhoneNumber(
            /* inout */ EntryType& entry )   // Struct receiving number

// Inputs area code and phone number, storing them into entry

// Postcondition:
//     User has been prompted for the area code and phone number
//   && entry.areaCode == the input integer for the area code
//   && entry.phoneNumber == the input string for the phone number

{
    cout << "Enter area code, blank, and the number"
        << " (including '-')." << endl;
    cin >> entry.areaCode;
    cin.ignore(1, ' ');                        // Consume blank
    cin.get(entry.phoneNumber, 9);
    cin.ignore(100, '\n');
}

//****************************************************************

void Insert( /* inout */ EntryType list[],    // List to be changed
             /* inout */ int&       length,   // Length of list
             /* in */    EntryType item    )  // Item to be inserted
```

```
// Inserts item into its proper place in the sorted list

// Precondition:
//    length < MAX_FRIENDS
//    && list[0..length-1] are in ascending order
//    && item is assigned
// Postcondition:
//     item is in list
//    && length == length@entry + 1
//    && list[0..length-1] are in ascending order
//    && IF item was already in list@entry
//          item has been inserted before the one that was there

{
    Boolean placeFound;    // True if item is already in the list
    int     index;         // Position where item belongs
    int     count;         // Loop control variable

    SearchOrd(list, item, length, index, placeFound);

    // Shift list[index..length-1] down one

    for (count = length - 1; count >= index; count==)

            // Invariant (prior to test):
            //     list[length-1..count+1] have been shifted down
            //   && length - 1 >= count >= index - 1

        list[count+1] = list[count];

    // Insert item

    list[index] = item;

    // Increment length of list

    length++;
}

//**********************************************************************

void SearchOrd(
        /* inout */ EntryType list[],      // List to be searched
        /* in */    EntryType item,        // Item to be found
        /* in */    int       length,      // Length of list
        /* out */   int&      index,       // Item location if found
        /* out */   Boolean&  found  )     // True if item is found
```

```
// Searches list for item, returning the index if item was found.
// If item was not found, SearchOrd returns the index where
// item belongs

// Precondition:
//     length < MAX_FRIENDS
//     && list[0..length-1] are in ascending order
//     && item is assigned
// Postcondition:
//     list is the same as list@entry except that list[length] is
//       overwritten to aid in the search
//     && IF item is in list@entry
//           found == TRUE  &&  list[index] contains item
//        ELSE
//           found == FALSE  &&   index is where item belongs

{
    index = 0;

    // Store item at position beyond end of list

    list[length] = item;

    // Exit loop when item is found, perhaps as sentinel

    while (strcmp(item.lastName, list[index].lastName) > 0)

              // Invariant (prior to test):
              //     item is not in list[0..index-1]

        index++;

    // Determine whether item was found prior to sentinel

    found = (index < length &&
              strcmp(item.lastName, list[index].lastName) == 0);
}

//*****************************************************************

void WriteEntries(
    /* in */    const EntryType addressBook[],   // Array of entries
    /* in */    int             length,          // Number of entries
    /* inout */ ofstream&       friendFile   )   // File receiving
                                                 //   list
// Writes all entries to the file friendFile
```

```
// Precondition:
//      length <= MAX_FRIENDS
//   && addressBook[0..length-1] are assigned
// Postcondition:
//      Contents of addressBook[0..length-1] have been output
//      to friendFile

{
    int counter;          // Loop counter

    for (counter = 0; counter < length; counter++)
    {
            // Invariant (prior to test):
            //      Contents of addressBook[0..counter-1] have
            //      been output
            //   && 0 <= counter <= length

        friendFile << addressBook[counter].firstName << ' '
                   << addressBook[counter].lastName << endl;
        friendFile << '(' << addressBook[counter].areaCode << ") "
                   << addressBook[counter].phoneNumber << endl;
        friendFile << setw(2) << addressBook[counter].month << '/'
                   << setw(2) << addressBook[counter].day << '/'
                   << setw(4) << addressBook[counter].year << endl;
        friendFile << endl;
    }
}
```

Testing: This is an interactive program in which the user has a great deal of control. The user is prompted to enter data, then is asked if the data have been entered correctly. If the user indicates that there has been an error, the data are not saved. After the information about a person is entered, the user is asked whether he or she wishes to continue.

In testing this program, each of the two options must be selected by the user at least once. When testing an interactive program, you may be tempted to sit down and just enter data randomly. However, if you don't keep a record of the data entered, the saved file will show only the correct entries. You won't know whether or not the sections of code that allow the program to ignore an incorrect entry were tested.

Another thing to be tested is the alternate way in which the main reading loop can terminate: the address book becomes full. As MAX_FRIENDS is defined to be 150, you don't want to sit at the keyboard and type 150 entries to watch it become full! What you can do is "comment out" the const declaration by preceding it with //. Then insert a new declaration defining

PROBLEM-SOLVING CASE STUDY cont'd.

MAX_FRIENDS to be, say, 3. Now you can compile and run the program again, verifying that the loop terminates after three iterations. After this test, you can go back and remove the temporary const declaration and restore the original one by deleting the //.

*P*ROBLEM-SOLVING *CASE STUDY*

Campaigning for a Candidate

Problem: A friend is running for City Council. It's down to the wire, and we want to call all those people who showed an interest in our friend and remind them to vote on election day. We have three different lists of people we should call. We don't want to annoy people by calling them twice—or worse still, three times—so we decide to merge the three lists and remove any duplicates. Each list is already in alphabetical order by last name, and there are no duplicates within any one list. A dummy record with a last name of all Zs is appended at the end of each file.

Input: Three input files (file1, file2, and file3), each containing a sequence of lines in the form

```
Jones Arthur 612 374-6715
```

A person's last name (maximum 15 characters with no blanks), first name (maximum 15 characters with no blanks), area code (integer), and phone number (8 characters) are separated by one or more blanks. The people's records are in alphabetical order by last name. A sentinel record containing all Zs for the last name signals the end of each file. The values on the rest of this line can be anything:

```
ZZZZZZZZZZZZZZZ A 111 111-1111
```

Output: The records from file1, file2, and file3 merged onto file masterFile, which should have the same form as the three input files.

Discussion: One of our problem-solving heuristics is to solve simpler problems first. Let's solve the problem for two lists, and then expand the solution to three lists.

How would we do this process by hand if we had two stacks of index cards? We would probably take the top card from each stack and compare the names. If they were the same, we would put one in a new stack and throw the other one away. If they weren't the same, we would put the card with the name that came first alphabetically in the new stack and take a replacement card from the stack that the card came from. We would repeat this process until one of the stacks of index cards became empty. Then we would move the rest of the other stack to the new one. Of course, the lists might both end at the same time with a duplicate name.

We can employ this same process to solve the problem using two computer lists. Rather than having two stacks of index cards, we have two computer files. Examining the next person's record is the equivalent of "take a replacement card from that stack."

Now that we have solved the problem for two files, we can expand the solution to three files. We can merge the first two files and store the result into a temporary list, then merge that list with the records from the third file.

Data Structures: We use a struct type to represent one person's information:

```
typedef char String15[16];        // Room for 15 characters plus '\0'
struct PersonRec
{
    String15   lastName;
    String15   firstName;
    PhoneType  phone;
};
```

where PhoneType is itself a struct type.

```
typedef char String8[9];        // Room for 8 characters plus '\0'
struct PhoneType
{
    int      areaCode;        // Range 100..999
    String8  phoneNumber;
};
```

Notice that PersonRec is therefore a hierarchical record type.

To store the records from the input files and merge them, we use four one-dimensional arrays whose components are of type PersonRec:

```
const int MAX_RECS = 100;              // Max. no. of records in a file
                                       //   (including sentinel record)
PersonRec firstList[MAX_RECS];         // Records from an input file
PersonRec secondList[MAX_RECS];        // Records from an input file
PersonRec tempList[MAX_RECS*2];        // Temporary merged list
PersonRec masterList[MAX_RECS*3];      // Final merged list
```

Each of `firstList` and `secondList` holds the records from one input file. The `tempList` array must be large enough to hold the merged records from two input files, and `masterList` holds the merged records from all three files.

Main   *Level 0*

> Open file1, file2, and file3 for input (and verify success)
> Open masterFile for output (and verify success)
> Get records from file1 into firstList
> Get records from file2 into secondList
> Merge firstList and secondList into tempList
> Get records from file3 into firstList
> Merge firstList and tempList into masterList
> Write masterList to file masterFile

Get Records (Inout: inFile; Out: list)   *Level 1*

> Set index = 0
> DO
>   Read   list[index].lastName, list[index].firstName,
>   list[index].phone.areaCode, list[index].phone.phoneNumber from inFile
>   Increment index
> WHILE list[index−1] isn't the sentinel record

Merge (In: list1, list2; Out: mergedList)

```
Set index1 = 0
Set index2 = 0
Set index3 = 0
WHILE neither list1[index1] nor list2[index2] is the sentinel record
    Process components, using index3 to index mergedList
Append any records left over
```

Write (In: masterList; Inout: masterFile)

```
Set index = 0
DO
    Write masterList[index].lastName, ' ',
          masterList[index].firstName, ' ',
          masterList[index].phone.areaCode, ' ',
          masterList[index].phone.phoneNumber to masterFile
    Increment index
WHILE masterList[index−1] isn't the sentinel record
```

Process Components (In: list1, list2;   *Level 2*
Inout: mergedList, index1, index2, index3)

```
IF list1[index1].lastName < list2[index2].lastName alphabetically
    Set mergedList[index3] = list1[index1]
    Increment index1
ELSE IF list1[index1].lastName > list2[index2].lastName alphabetically
    Set mergedList[index3] = list2[index2]
    Increment index2
ELSE
    Set mergedList[index3] = list1[index1]
    Increment index1
    Increment index2     // Ignore duplicate record in list2
Increment index3
```

Because Process Components is fairly simple, we include it as part of the
Merge function in the program.

PROBLEM-SOLVING CASE STUDY cont'd.

Append (In: list1, list2; Inout: mergedList, index1, index2, index3)

```
WHILE list1[index1] isn't the sentinel record
    Set mergedList[index3] = list1[index1]
    Increment index1
    Increment index3
WHILE list2[index2] isn't the sentinel record
    Set mergedList[index3] = list2[index2]
    Increment index2
    Increment index3
Set mergedList[index3] = sentinel record
```

Notice that the Append module does *not* start with an If statement to determine which list is "empty." If one of the lists is "empty," the While condition for that list ensures that the loop body is skipped. If both lists are "empty," both loop bodies are skipped. An If statement is unnecessary and would simply be extra code.

Module Structure Chart:

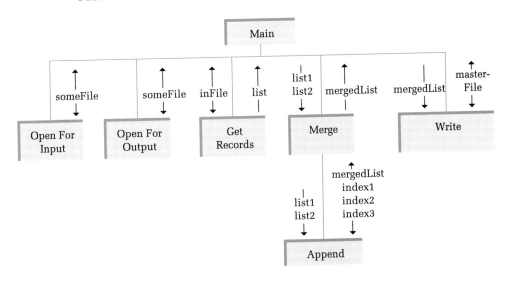

```
//****************************************************************
// MergeLists program
// This program merges sorted data from three files
// onto a master file with no duplicates.
```

```
//***********************************************************************
#include <iostream.h>
#include <fstream.h>      // For file I/O
#include <string.h>       // For strcmp()

const char SENTINEL[] = "ZZZZZZZZZZZZZZZ";
const int MAX_RECS = 100;      // Max. no. of records in a file
                               //    (including sentinel record)

typedef char String8[9];       // Room for 8 characters plus '\0'
typedef char String15[16];     // Room for 15 characters plus '\0'

struct PhoneType
{
    int      areaCode;      // Range 100..999
    String8 phoneNumber;
};
struct PersonRec
{
    String15  lastName;
    String15  firstName;
    PhoneType phone;
};

void Append( const PersonRec[], const PersonRec[], PersonRec[],
          int&, int&, int& );
void GetRecords( ifstream&, PersonRec[] );
void Merge( const PersonRec[], const PersonRec[], PersonRec[] );
void OpenForInput( ifstream& );
void OpenForOutput( ofstream& );
void Write( const PersonRec[], ofstream& );

int main()
{
    PersonRec firstList[MAX_RECS];      // Records from an input file
    PersonRec secondList[MAX_RECS];     // Records from an input file
    PersonRec tempList[MAX_RECS*2];     // Temporary merged list
    PersonRec masterList[MAX_RECS*3];   // Final merged list
    ifstream  file1;                    // Input file
    ifstream  file2;                    // Input file
    ifstream  file3;                    // Input file
    ofstream  masterFile;               // Output file

    OpenForInput(file1);
    if ( !file1 )
        return 1;
```

```
                OpenForInput(file2);
                if ( !file2 )
                    return 1;
                OpenForInput(file3);
                if ( !file3 )
                    return 1;
                OpenForOutput(masterFile);
                if ( !masterFile )
                    return 1;

                GetRecords(file1, firstList);
                GetRecords(file2, secondList);
                Merge(firstList, secondList, tempList);
                GetRecords(file3, firstList);
                Merge(firstList, tempList, masterList);
                Write(masterList, masterFile);
                return 0;
            }

//******************************************************************

void OpenForInput( /* inout */ ifstream& someFile )    // File to be
                                                       // opened

// Prompts the user for the name of an input file
// and attempts to open the file

// Postcondition:
//     The user has been prompted for a file name
//  && IF the file could not be opened
//         An error message has been printed
// Note:
//     Upon return from this function, the caller must test
//     the stream state to see if the file was successfully opened

{
    char fileName[51];    // User-specified file name (max. 50 chars)

    cout << "Input file name: ";
    cin.get(fileName, 51);
    cin.ignore(100, '\n');

    someFile.open(fileName);
    if ( !someFile )
        cout << "** Can't open " << fileName << " **" << endl;
}

//******************************************************************
```

```
void OpenForOutput( /* inout */ ofstream& someFile )      // File to be
                                                          // opened
// Prompts the user for the name of an output file
// and attempts to open the file

// Postcondition:
//     The user has been prompted for a file name
//  && IF the file could not be opened
//         An error message has been printed
// Note:
//     Upon return from this function, the caller must test
//     the stream state to see if the file was successfully opened

{
    char fileName[51];    // User-specified file name (max. 50 chars)

    cout << "Output file name: ";
    cin.get(fileName, 51);
    cin.ignore(100, '\n');

    someFile.open(fileName);
    if ( !someFile )
        cout << "** Can't open " << fileName << " **" << endl;
}


//*************************************************************************

void GetRecords( /* inout */ ifstream& inFile,    // Input file
                 /* out */   PersonRec list[] )    // List receiving
                                                   //    input records
// Reads people's records from inFile
// and stores them into array "list"

// Precondition:
//     inFile has been successfully opened for input
//  && inFile contains at least one record and at most MAX_RECS
//     records, including the sentinel record
//  && People's last names and first names are at most
//     15 characters each
// Postcondition:
//     Assuming inFile contains N records (including the
//     sentinel record), list[0..N-1] contain the input records

{
    int index = 0;    // Array index
```

QUICK CHECK

1. Write the type declaration for a struct data type named TimeType with three members: hour, minute, and second. The hour member is intended to store integer values from 0 through 23. The other two members store values from 0 through 59. (pp. 772–780)
2. Assume a variable named now, of type TimeType, has been declared. Write the assignment statements necessary to store the time 8:37:28 into now. (pp. 772–780)
3. Declare a hierarchical record type named Interval that consists of two members of type TimeType. The members are named past and present. (pp. 782–786)
4. Assume a variable named channelCrossing, of type Interval, has been declared. Write the assignment statements necessary to store the time 7:12:44 into the past member of channelCrossing. Write the assignment statement that stores the contents of variable now into the present member of channelCrossing. (pp. 782–786)
5. Declare a variable boatTimes that is an array of Interval values to be indexed by an enumeration type named BoatNames:

   enum BoatNames {LUCKY, MY_PRIDE, SWELL_STUFF};

   Then write a statement that stores the contents of variable now into the present member of the struct for the boat named "Swell Stuff." (pp. 781–782)
6. Decide what form of data structure is appropriate for the following problem. A single card in a library catalog system must contain the call number, author, title, and description of a single book. (pp. 787–793)
7. What is the primary purpose of C++ union types? (pp. 786–787)

Answers
1. struct TimeType
   {
       int hour;   // Range 0..23
       int minute;   // Range 0..59
       int second;   // Range 0..59
   };
2. now.hour = 8;
   now.minute = 37;
   now.second = 28;
3. struct Interval
   {
       TimeType past;
       TimeType present;
   };
4. channelCrossing.past.hour = 7;
   channelCrossing.past.minute = 12;
   channelCrossing.past.second = 44;
   channelCrossing.present = now;
5. Interval boatTimes[3];
   boatTimes[SWELL_STUFF].present = now;
6. A simple struct with four members is sufficient.   7. The primary purpose is to save memory by forcing different values to share the same memory space, one at a time.

EXAM PREPARATION EXERCISES

1. Define the following terms:

   record (struct in C++)
   member
   member selector
   hierarchical record
   data abstraction

2. Given the declarations

   ```cpp
   typedef char CodeString[26];     // Max. 25 characters plus '\0'

   enum StyleType {FORMAL, BRIEF};

   struct RefType
   {
       CodeString token[2000];
       CodeString symbol[20];
   };
   struct MapType
   {
       CodeString mapCode;
       StyleType  style;
       RefType    chart;
   };

   MapType     guide[200];
   MapType     aMap;
   RefType     aRef;
   int         count;
   CodeString  aCode;
   ```

   mark each of the following statements as valid or invalid. (Assume that all the valid variables have been assigned values.)

Statement	Valid	Invalid
a. `if (aMap.style == BRIEF)` `count++;`	_____	_____
b. `guide[1].chart.token[2] = aMap;`	_____	_____
c. `guide[6].chart = aRef;`	_____	_____
d. `strcpy(aMap.mapCode[0], aRef.token[0]);`	_____	_____
e. `guide[100].chart.token[1][2] = aCode[2];`	_____	_____
f. `guide[20].token[1] = aCode;`	_____	_____
g. `if (guide[20].style == FORMAL)` `guide[20].chart.token[0][0] = 'A';`	_____	_____
h. `aMap = guide[5];`	_____	_____
i. `aMap.chart = aRef;`	_____	_____

3. Using the declarations in Exercise 2, write a single statement to do each of the following:

   a. Assign the value of the `chart` member of the seventy-first element of `guide` to the variable aRef.
   b. Copy the first element of the `token` member of the `chart` member of the eighty-eighth element of `guide` to the variable aCode.
   c. Assign the value 'X' to the first element of the twenty-third element of the `token` member of the `chart` member of the ninety-fourth element of `guide`.
   d. Copy the fourth element of the `mapCode` member of `aMap` to the ninth element of the twentieth element of the `symbol` member of `aRef`.
4. What are the two basic differences between a record and an array?
5. A hierarchical record structure may not contain another hierarchical record structure as a member. (True or False?)
6. If the members of a record are all the same data type, an array data structure could be used instead. (True or False?)
7. For each of the following descriptions of data, determine which general type of data structure (array, record, array of records, or hierarchical record) is appropriate.
   a. A payroll entry with a name, address, and pay rate.
   b. A person's address.
   c. An inventory entry for a part.
   d. A list of addresses.
   e. A list of hourly temperatures.
   f. A list of passengers on an airliner, including names, addresses, fare class, and seat assignment.
   g. A departmental telephone directory with last name and extension number.
   h. A street name.
8. Given the declarations

```
typedef char String20[21];

struct DateType
{
    int month;
    int day;
    int year;
};
struct InfoType
{
    String20 firstName;
    String20 lastName;
    DateType birthDate;
};

DateType today;
String20 aName;
InfoType aFriend;
InfoType self;
```

show the value of each variable after the following program segment is executed.

```
strcpy(aName, " ");
strcpy(aFriend.firstName, aName);
strcpy(aFriend.lastName, aName);
today.month = 1;
today.day = 1;
today.year = 1996;
aFriend.birthDate = today;
self = aFriend;
```

9. Declare a `struct` type named `RecType` to contain two integer variables and one Boolean variable. (Assume a `Boolean` type has already been defined.)

10. Using the declarations in this chapter of the `MachineRec` type and the `inventory` array, the code below is supposed to count the number of machines that have not been serviced within the current year. The code has an error. Correct the error by using a proper member selector in the If statement.

```
DateType currentDate;
   .
   .
   .
machineCount = 0;
for (index = 0; index < NUM_MACHINES; index++)
    if (currentDate.year != lastServiced.year)
        machineCount++;
```

11. Given the declarations

```
typedef char String20[21];
typedef char String2[3];

struct NameType
{
    String20 first;
    String20 last;
};
struct PlaceType
{

    String20 city;
    String2  state;
    long     zipCode;
};
struct PersonType
{
    NameType   name;
    PlaceType  place;
};

PersonType person;
```

write C++ code that stores information about yourself into **person**.

PROGRAMMING WARM-UP EXERCISES

1. a. Write a `struct` declaration to contain the following information about a student:

   Name (string of characters)
   Social security number (string of characters)
   Year (freshman, sophomore, junior, senior)
   Grade point average (floating point)
   Sex (M, F)

   b. Declare a `struct` variable of the type in part (a), and write a program segment that prints the information in each member of the variable.

   c. Declare `roll` to be an array of 3000 `structs` of the type in part (a).

2. Write a program segment to read in a set of part numbers and associated unit costs. Keep the data sorted by part number as you read it in. Use an array of structs with two members, `number` and `cost`, to represent each pair of input values. Assume the end-of-file condition terminates the input.

3. Write a hierarchical C++ `struct` declaration to contain the following information about a student:

   Name (up to 30 characters)
   Student ID number
   Credit hours to date
   Number of courses taken
   Course grades (a list of up to 50 elements containing an integer course ID and
      the letter grade)
   Date first enrolled (month and year)
   Year (freshman, sophomore, junior, senior)
   Grade point average

   Each `struct` and enumeration type should have a separate type declaration.

4. a. Declare a `struct` type named `AptType` for an apartment locator service. The following information should be included:

   Landlord (a string of up to 20 characters)
   Address (a string of up to 20 characters)
   Bedrooms (integer)
   Price (floating point)

   b. Declare `available` to be an array of up to 200 `structs` of type `AptType`.

   c. Write a function to read values into the members of a variable of type `AptType`. (The `struct` variable should be passed as a parameter.) The order in which the data is read is the same as that of the items in the `struct`.

5. Using the declarations given in Exam Preparation Exercise 2, write statements to do the following:

   a. Assign the contents of the `chart` member of `aMap` to `aRef`.

   b. Assign `aMap` to the fourth element of `guide`.

   c. Copy `aCode` to the `mapCode` member of the tenth element of `guide`.

   d. Compare the first character in `aCode` and the first character in the `mapCode` member of the second element of `guide`. If they are equal, then output the `mapCode` member and the `style` member of the second element of `guide`.

e. Compare aMap.chart and aRef for equality. Show which elements (if any) are not equal by outputting the indices for the appropriate token members and/or symbol members. For example, if the second element of the token members of both structs were not equal, you would output "1," and so on, for the remaining nonequal elements.

6. You are designing an automated library catalog system. The library contains 50,000 books. For each book, there is a catalog entry consisting of the call number (up to 10 characters), the number of copies in the library (an integer), the author (up to 30 characters), the title (up to 100 characters), and a description of the contents (up to 300 characters).

   a. Write the type declarations necessary to represent this information.

   b. Estimate how many characters of memory space are required to hold all the catalog information for the library. (Assume that an integer value occupies the equivalent of four characters in memory.)

   c. How many book records can a computer with 650,000 characters of memory hold?

7. Write a function that reads the information for a book into a struct of the type defined in Exercise 6. Write another function that prints the information contained in a struct of the type defined in Exercise 6. The struct should be passed as a parameter to each of these functions.

8. You are writing the subscription renewal system for a magazine. For each subscriber, the system is to keep the following information:

   Name (first, last)
   Address (street, city, state, zip code)
   Expiration date (month, year)
   Date renewal notice was sent (month, day, year)
   Number of renewal notices sent so far
   Number of years for which subscription is being renewed (0 for renewal not yet received; otherwise, 1, 2, or 3 years)
   Whether or not the subscriber's name may be included in a mailing list for sale to other companies

   Write a hierarchical record type declaration to represent this information. Each subrecord should be declared separately as a named data type.

9. You are writing a program that keeps track of the terminals connected to a company computer. The computer may have up to 30 terminals connected to it. For each terminal, the following information must be kept:

   Brand and model (a string of up to 15 characters)
   Data rate (an integer representing 10 through 19,200 characters per second)
   Parity (an enumeration type representing Even, Odd, One, Zero, or None)
   Echoplex (an enumeration type representing Half or Full)
   Data bits (an integer representing 7 or 8)
   Stop bits (an integer representing 1 or 2)

   Design a data structure for this problem, and write the type declarations for all the data types that are needed to implement your design.

10. Write a struct declaration to contain a string of no more than 20 characters and the length of the string. Then write a value-returning function that returns the length of a string stored in this struct.

11. Write a function that concatenates (joins) two strings into a third string. Use the declaration you wrote in Exercise 10.

12. You are writing a program to keep track of a manufacturing company's inventory. For each part, the following information needs to be stored:

Part number
Part name
Cost
Quantity

Write a function and the necessary declarations to read in a variable of `struct` type `Inventory`.

PROGRAMMING PROBLEMS

1. The MergeLists program merges three lists by merging two lists, and then merging the third list with the result of the merger of the first two. Another way of solving the same problem is to merge three lists at the same time, storing the result into a fourth list. Design a solution to the problem using this second strategy. Code your design in C++. Test your program thoroughly.

2. The Emerging Manufacturing Company has just installed its first computer and hired you as a junior programmer. Your first program is to read employee pay data and produce two reports: 1) an error and control report, and 2) a report on pay amounts. The second report must contain a line for each employee and a line of totals at the end of the report.

Input:

Transaction File

Set of five job site number/name pairs
One line for each employee containing ID number, job site number, and number of hours worked

These data items have been presorted by ID number.

Master File

ID number
Name
Pay rate per hour
Number of dependents
Type of employee (1 is management, 0 is union)
Job site
Sex (M, F)

This file is ordered by ID number.

NOTE: 1) Union members, unlike management, get time and a half for hours over 40. 2) The tax formula for tax computation is as follows: If number of dependents is 1, tax rate is 15%. Otherwise, the tax rate is the greater of 2.5% and

$$\left[1 - \left(\frac{\text{No. of dep.}}{\text{No. of dep.} + 6} \right) \right] \times 15\%$$

Output:

Error and Control Report

Lists the input lines for which there is no corresponding master record, or where the employees' job site numbers do not agree with those in the master file. Continues processing with the next line of data

Gives the total number of employee records that were processed correctly during the run

Payroll Report (Labeled for Management)

Contains a line for each employee showing the name, ID number, job site name, gross pay, and net pay

Contains a total line showing the total amount of gross pay and total amount of net pay

3. The Emerging Manufacturing Company has decided to use its new computer for parts inventory control as well as payroll. You are writing a program that is to be run each night. It takes the stock tickets from the day's transactions, makes a list of the parts that need ordering, and prints an updated report that must be given to the five job site managers each morning. Note that you are not being asked to update the file.

Input:

Transaction File

Set of five job site number/name pairs

One line for each stock transaction containing part ID number, job site number, and number of parts bought or sold (a negative number indicates that it has been sold)

These data have been presorted by site number within part ID number.

Master File

Part ID number

Part name (no embedded blanks)

Quantity on hand

Order point (the minimum quantity on hand that will trigger a reorder of the part)

Job site

This file is also ordered by job site number within part ID number. If a part is not in the master file and the transaction is a sale, an error message should be printed. If the transaction is a purchase, the part should be listed in the proper place in the parts report. Note that there is a separate entry in the master file for parts at each job site.

Output:

Error and Control Report

Contains error messages

Lists the parts that need to be ordered (those for which quantity on hand is less than order point)

A Report for All the Parts in the Master File
Contains the part number
Contains the part name
Contains the job site name
Contains the number on hand

Remember, this report is for management. Be sure it is written so managers can read it.

4. You have taken a job with the IRS because you want to learn how to save on your income tax. They want you to write a toy tax computing program so that they can get an idea of your programming abilities. The program reads in the names of the members of families and each person's income, and computes the tax that the family owes. You may assume that people with the same last name who appear consecutively in the input are in the same family. The number of deductions that a family can count is equal to the number of people listed in that family in the input data. Tax is computed as follows:

adjusted income = income − (5000 * number of deductions)

$$\text{tax rate} \quad = \quad \begin{cases} \text{adjusted income}/100{,}000 \text{ if income} < 60{,}000 \\ .50, \text{ otherwise} \end{cases}$$

tax   = tax rate * adjusted income

There will be no refunds, so you must check for people whose tax would be negative and set it to zero.

Input entries are in the following form:

Last name First name Total income

Sample Data:
```
Jones Ralph 19765.43
Jones Mary 8532.00
Jones Francis 0
Atwell Humphrey 5678.12
Murphy Robert 13432.20
Murphy Ellen 0
Murphy Paddy 0
Murphy Eileen 0
Murphy Conan 0
Murphy Nora 0
```

Input:
The data as described above, with end-of-file indicating the end of the input data.

Output:
A table containing all the families, one family per line, with each line containing the last name of the family, their total income, and their computed tax.

5. Your assignment is to write a program for a computer dating service. Clients give you their names, phone numbers, and a list of interests. Your job is to maintain lists of men and women using the service and to match up the compatible couples.

Data Structures:

The problem requires you to maintain two lists, one for men and one for women. The lists must include the following information: name (20 characters), phone number (8 characters), number of interests (maximum number is 10), interests (10 characters each; must be in alphabetical order), and a variable that gives the position of the client's current match (–1 if not matched). When a new client is added to the list, his or her name is added to the bottom of the appropriate list. (You do not keep the names of the clients in alphabetical order.)

Input:

Number of current clients

Sex ('M' or 'F'), name (20 characters), phone number (8 characters), number of interests, list of interests (10 characters for each one, with no embedded blanks; interests are separated by blanks). There is a record like this for each of the current clients.

The rest of the file includes data lines that look like one of the following (all the lines start with a 10-character word as outlined below; □ indicates a blank):

NewClient □ sex ('M' or 'F'), name (20 characters), number of interests, interests (10 characters for each one; see above for description)

If the keyword NewClient occurs, you should add the client to the appropriate list by storing the required information. Match him or her with a member of the opposite sex. (A match occurs when at least three of the interests are the same. Interests are sorted, which makes the matching process easier. Use an insertion sort to sort interests.) Make sure you then designate both persons matched as described above. Print the name of the new client, his or her match, and both phone numbers. If no match is found, print an appropriate message.

OldClient □ name (20 characters)

Unmatch this name from its current match by setting the match variables for the name and its match to –1.

PrintMatch

Print a list of all matched pairs.

PrintNot□□

Print the names and phone numbers of clients who are not currently matched.

StopProg□□

This will be the last line in the file.

Output:

Information as described above, printed with appropriate titles.

6. A *sparse matrix* is a matrix (two-dimensional array) in which the great majority of elements are zero. It is inefficient to store these as two-dimensional arrays because most of the elements do not contain any useful information. Instead, the elements that are not equal to zero should be stored as an array of `struct`s where the first two members of the `struct` contain the row and column number and the third member contains the element. For example, this matrix

0.0	0.0	7.0	0.0	0.0
0.0	0.0	0.0	0.0	8.0
0.0	0.0	0.0	0.0	0.0

would be stored as follows:

1	3	7.0
2	5	8.0

Write a C++ program that reads a sparse matrix and converts it into an array of `struct`s of this form. The program should then output the `struct`s (properly labeled).

CASE STUDY FOLLOW-UP

1. In both case studies, we represented a person's area code as an `int` value. Printing an `int` area code works fine for North American phone numbers, where area codes are greater than 200. But international area codes may start with a zero. Our programs would print an area code of 052 as 52. Suggest two ways of accommodating international area codes so that leading zeros are printed.
2. Change the Campaigning for a Candidate case study so that the sentinel line consists of 15 Zs only—no first name, area code, or phone number. Specifically, rewrite the `GetRecords` function so that input of the first name, area code, and phone number are not attempted if the last name is all Zs.
3. Recode the MergeLists program so that the sentinel records are not stored in any arrays in memory. Function `GetRecords` should input data until the sentinel record is encountered, returning both the list and its length. Thereafter, whenever a list is passed as a parameter to a function, its length should be passed also.

15

Classes and Data Abstraction

GOALS

- To understand the difference between specification and implementation of an abstract data type.
- To be able to declare a C++ class type.
- To be able to declare class objects, given the declaration of a class type.
- To be able to write client code that invokes class member functions.
- To be able to implement class member functions.
- To understand how encapsulation and information hiding are enforced by the C++ compiler.
- To be able to organize the code for a C++ class into two files: the specification (.h) file and the implementation file.
- To be able to write a C++ class constructor.

At the end of the last chapter, we introduced the concept of data abstraction, the separation of a data type's logical properties from its implementation. Data abstraction is important because it allows us to create data types not otherwise available in a programming language. Another benefit of data abstraction is the ability to produce *off-the-shelf software*—pieces of software that can be used over and over again in different programs either by the creator of the software or by any programmer wishing to use them.

The primary tool for practicing data abstraction is the abstract data type, introduced briefly in Chapter 12. In this chapter, we examine abstract data types in depth and introduce the C++ language feature designed expressly for creating abstract data types: the *class*. We conclude with two case studies that demonstrate data abstraction, abstract data types, and C++ classes.

Abstract Data Types

We live in a complex world. Throughout the course of each day, we are constantly bombarded with information, facts, and details. Most government and business operations, legal regulations, and technical products are too complicated for one person to understand thoroughly. To cope with complexity, the human mind engages in *abstraction*—the act of separating the essential qualities of an idea or object from the details of how it works or is composed.

With abstraction, we focus on the *what*, not the *how*. For example, our understanding of automobiles is largely based on abstraction. Most of us know *what* the engine does (it propels the car), but fewer of us know—or want to know—precisely *how* the engine works internally. Abstraction allows us to discuss, think about, and use automobiles without having to know everything about how they work.

In the world of software design, it is now recognized that abstraction is an absolute necessity for managing immense, complex software projects. In introductory computer science courses, programs are usually small (perhaps 50 to 200 lines of code) and understandable in their entirety by one person. However, large commercial software products composed of hundreds of thousands—even millions—of lines of code cannot be designed, understood, or proven correct without using abstraction in various forms. To manage complexity, software developers regularly use two important abstraction techniques: control abstraction and data abstraction.

In Chapter 8, we defined control abstraction as the separation of the logical properties of an action from its implementation. We engage in control abstraction whenever we write a function that reduces a complicated algorithm to an abstract action performed by a function call. By invoking a library function, as in the expression

```
4.6 + sqrt(x)
```

we depend only on the function's *specification*, a written description of what it does. We can use the function without having to know its *implementation* (the algorithms that accomplish the result). By invoking the `sqrt` function, our program is less complex because all the details involved in computing square roots are absent.

Abstraction techniques also apply to data. Every data type consists of a set of values (the domain) along with a collection of allowable operations on those values. In Chapter 14, we described data abstraction as the separation of a data type's logical properties from its implementation details. Data abstraction comes into play when we need a data type that is not built into the programming language. We can define the new data type as an **abstract data type (ADT),** concentrating only on its logical properties and deferring the details of its implementation.

Abstract Data Type   A data type whose properties (domain and operations) are specified independently of any particular implementation.

As with control abstraction, an abstract data type has both a specification (the *what*) and an implementation (the *how*). The specification of an ADT describes the characteristics of the data values as well as the behavior of each of the operations on those values. The user of the ADT needs to understand only the specification, not the implementation, in order to use it. Here's a very informal specification of a list ADT:

TYPE
    IntList
DOMAIN
    Each IntList value is a collection of up to 100 separate integer numbers.
OPERATIONS
    Insert an item into the list.
    Delete an item from the list.
    Search the list for an item.
    Return the current length of the list.
    Sort the list into ascending order.
    Print the list.

Notice the complete absence of implementation details. We have not mentioned how the data might actually be stored in a program (for example, in an array) or how the operations might be implemented. Concealing the implementation details reduces complexity for the user and also shields the user from changes in the implementation.

Below is the specification of another ADT, one that might be useful for representing time in a program.

TYPE
> TimeType

DOMAIN
> Each TimeType value is a time of day in the form of hours, minutes, and seconds.

OPERATIONS
> Set the time.
> Print the time.
> Increment the time by one second.
> Compare two times for equality.
> Determine if one time is "less than" (comes before) another.

The specification of an ADT defines abstract data values and abstract operations for the user. Ultimately, of course, the ADT must be implemented in program code. To implement an ADT, the programmer must do two things:

1. Choose a concrete **data representation** of the abstract data, using data types that already exist.
2. Implement each of the allowable operations in terms of program instructions.

Data Representation   The concrete form of data used to represent the abstract values of an abstract data type.

To implement the IntList ADT, we could choose a concrete data representation consisting of two items: a 100-element `int` array and an `int` variable that keeps track of the current length of the list. To implement the IntList operations, we must create algorithms—such as the searching and sorting routines we wrote in Chapter 12—based on the chosen data representation.

To implement the TimeType ADT, we might use three `int` variables for the data representation—one for the hours, one for the minutes, and one for the seconds. Or we might use three strings (`char` arrays) as the data representation, or even a three-element `int` array. The specification of the ADT does not confine us to any particular data representation. As long as we satisfy the specification, we are free to choose among alternative data representations and their associated algorithms. Our choice may be based on time efficiency (the speed at which the algorithms execute), space efficiency (the economical use of memory space), or simplicity and readability of the algorithms. Over time, you will acquire knowledge and experience that help you decide which implementation is best for a particular context.

THEORETICAL FOUNDATIONS

Categories of Abstract Data Type Operations

In general, the basic operations that are performed on an abstract data type fall into three categories: **constructors, transformers,** and **observers.**

Constructor   An operation that creates a new instance (variable) of an ADT.

Transformer   An operation that builds a new value of the ADT, given one or more previous values of the type.

An operation that creates a new instance of an ADT (such as a list) is a constructor. Operations that insert an item into a list and delete an item from a list are transformers. An operation that takes one list and appends it to the end of a second list is also a transformer.

Observer   An operation that allows us to observe the state of an instance of an ADT without changing it.

A Boolean function that returns TRUE if a list is empty and FALSE if it contains any components is an example of an observer. A Boolean function that tests to see if a certain value is in the list is another observer.

Some operations are combinations of observers and constructors. An operation that takes two lists and merges them into a (new) third list is both an observer (of the two existing lists) and a constructor (of the third list).

In addition to the three basic categories of ADT operations, there is a fourth category that is less common: **iterators.**

Iterator   An operation that allows us to process—one at a time—all the components in an instance of an ADT.

An operation that returns the first item in a list when it is called initially and returns the next one with each successive call is an iterator.

 # C++ Classes

In previous chapters, we have treated data structures as passive quantities to be acted upon by functions. In Chapter 12, we viewed an integer list as an ADT, representing the list as an `int` array and implementing the list operations as functions that take an `int` array as a parameter. Similarly, in Chapter 14, we treated an address book as an ADT, using a `struct` as the data representation and implementing the operations as functions receiving a `struct` as a parameter (see Figure 15-1).

This separation of operations and data does not correspond very well with the notion of an abstract data type. After all, an ADT consists of *both* data values and operations on those values. It is preferable to view an ADT as defining an *active* data structure—one that combines both data and operations into a single, cohesive unit (see Figure 15-2). C++ supports this view by providing a built-in structured type known as a **class.**

In Chapter 14, we listed the four structured types available in the C++ language: the array, the `struct`, the union, and the class (Figure 14-5). A class is a structured type provided specifically for implementing abstract data types. A class is similar to a `struct` but is nearly always designed so that its components (**class members**) include not only data but also functions that manipulate that data. Here is a C++ class declaration corresponding to the TimeType ADT that we defined in the previous section:

■ FIGURE 15-1

Data and
Operations as
Separate Entities

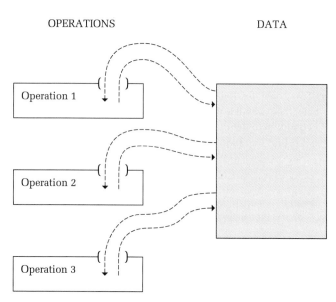

■ FIGURE 15-2

Data and
Operations Bound
into a Single Unit

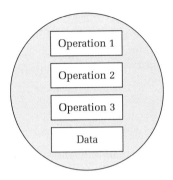

```
class TimeType
{
public:
    void    Set( int, int, int );
    void    Increment();
    void    Write() const;
    Boolean Equal( TimeType ) const;
    Boolean LessThan( TimeType ) const;
private:
    int hrs;
    int mins;
    int secs;
};
```

(For now, you should ignore the word const appearing in some of the function prototypes. We explain this use of const later in the chapter.)

The TimeType class has eight members—five member functions (Set, Increment, Write, Equal, LessThan) and three member variables (hrs, mins, secs). As you might guess, the three member variables form the concrete data representation for the TimeType ADT. The five member functions correspond to the operations we listed for the TimeType ADT: set the time (to the hours, minutes, and seconds passed as parameters to the Set function), increment the time by one second, print the time, compare two times for equality, and determine if one time is less than another. Although the Equal function compares two TimeType variables for equality, its parameter list has only one parameter—a TimeType variable. Similarly, the LessThan function has only one parameter, even though it compares two times. We'll see the reason later.

Like a struct declaration, the declaration of TimeType creates a data type but does not create variables of the type. Class variables (more often referred to as **class objects** or **class instances**) are created by using ordinary variable declarations:

```
TimeType startTime;
TimeType endTime;
```

Any software that declares and manipulates `TimeType` objects is called a **client** of the class.

Class   A structured type in a programming language that is used to represent an abstract data type.

Class Member   A component of a class. Class members may be either data or functions.

Class Object (Class Instance)   A variable of a class type.

Client   Software that declares and manipulates objects of a particular class.

As you look at the preceding declaration of the `TimeType` class, you can see the reserved words `public` and `private` (each followed by a colon). Data and/or functions declared between the words `public` and `private` constitute the public interface; clients can access these class members directly. Class members declared after the word `private` are considered private information and are inaccessible to clients. If client code attempts to access a private item, the compiler will signal an error.

Private class members can be accessed only by the class's member functions. In the `TimeType` class, the private variables `hrs`, `mins`, and `secs` can be accessed only by the member functions `Set`, `Increment`, `Write`, `Equal`, and `LessThan`, not by client code. This separation of class members into private and public parts is a hallmark of ADT design. To preserve correctly the properties of an ADT, an instance of the ADT should be manipulated *only* through the operations that form the public interface. We have more to say about this issue later in the chapter.

Matters of Style

Declaring Public and Private Class Members

C++ does not require you to declare public and private class members in a fixed order. Several variations are possible.

By default, class members are private; the word `public` must be used to "open up" any members for public access. Therefore, we could write the `TimeType` class declaration as follows:

```
class TimeType
{
    int hrs;
    int mins;
    int secs;
public:
    void    Set( int, int, int );
    void    Increment();
    void    Write() const;
    Boolean Equal( TimeType ) const;
    Boolean LessThan( TimeType ) const;
};
```

By default, the variables hrs, mins, and secs are private. The public part extends from the word public to the end of the class declaration.

Even with the private part located first, some programmers use the reserved word private to be as explicit as possible:

```
class TimeType
{
private:
    int hrs;
    int mins;
    int secs;
public:
    void    Set( int, int, int );
    void    Increment();
    void    Write() const;
    Boolean Equal( TimeType ) const;
    Boolean LessThan( TimeType ) const;
};
```

Our preference is to locate the public part first so as to focus attention on the public interface and deemphasize the private data representation:

```
class TimeType
{
public:
    void    Set( int, int, int );
    void    Increment();
    void    Write() const;
    Boolean Equal( TimeType ) const;
    Boolean LessThan( TimeType ) const;
private:
    int hrs;
    int mins;
    int secs;
};
```

We use this style throughout the remainder of the book.

Regarding public versus private accessibility, we can now describe more fully the difference between C++ structs and classes. C++ defines a struct to be a class whose members are all, by default, public. In contrast, members of a class are, by default, private. Furthermore, it is most common to use only data, not functions, as members of a struct. Note that you *can* declare struct members to be private and you *can* include member functions in a struct, but then you might as well use a class!

Classes, Class Objects, and Class Members

It is important to restate that a class is a type, not a data object. Like any type, a class is a pattern from which you create (or *instantiate*) many objects of that type. Think of a type as a cookie cutter and objects of that type as the cookies.

The declarations

```
TimeType time1;
TimeType time2;
```

create two objects of the TimeType class: time1 and time2. Each object has its own copies of hrs, mins, and secs, the private data members of the class. At a given moment during program execution, time1's copies of hrs, mins, and secs might contain the values 5, 30, and 10; and time2's copies might contain the values 17, 58, and 2. Figure 15-3 is a visual image of the class objects time1 and time2.

(In truth, the C++ compiler does not waste memory by placing duplicate copies of a member function—say, Increment—into both time1 and time2. The compiler generates just one physical copy of Increment, and any class object executes this one copy of the function. Nevertheless, the diagram in Figure 15-3 is a good mental picture of two different class objects.)

Be sure you are clear about the difference between the terms *class object* and *class member*. Figure 15-3 depicts two objects of the TimeType class, and each object has eight members.

Built-In Operations on Classes

In many ways, programmer-defined classes are like built-in types. You can declare as many objects of a class as you like. You can pass class objects as parameters to functions and return them as function values. You can declare arrays of class objects. Like any variable, a class object can be automatic (created each time control reaches its declaration and destroyed when con-

■ FIGURE 15-3   Conceptual View of Two Class Objects

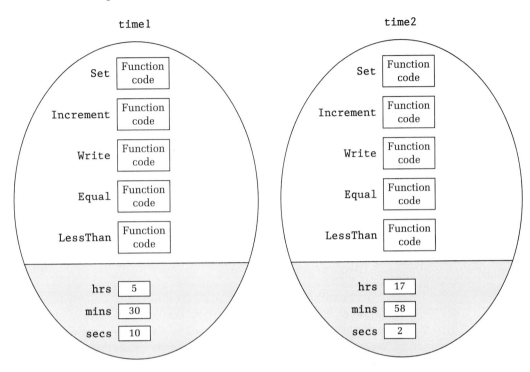

trol exits its surrounding block) or static (created once when control reaches its declaration and destroyed when the program terminates).

In other ways, C++ treats structs and classes differently from built-in types. Most of the built-in operations do not apply to structs or classes. You cannot use the + operator to add two TimeType objects, nor can you use the == operator to compare two TimeType objects for equality.

Two built-in operations that are valid for struct and class objects are member selection (.) and assignment (=). As with structs, you select an individual member of a class by writing the name of the class object, then a dot, then the member name. The statement

```
time1.Increment();
```

invokes the Increment function for the time1 object, presumably to add one second to the time stored in time1. The other built-in operation, assignment, performs aggregate assignment of one class object to another with the following semantics: If x and y are objects of the same class, then the assignment x = y copies the data members of y into x. Below is a fragment of client code that demonstrates member selection and assignment.

```
TimeType time1;
TimeType time2;
int       inputHrs;
int       inputMins;
int       inputSecs;

time1.Set(5, 20, 0);
// Assert: time1 corresponds to 5:20:0

cout << "Enter hours, minutes, seconds: ";
cin >> inputHrs >> inputMins >> inputSecs;
time2.Set(inputHrs, inputMins, inputSecs);

if (time1.LessThan(time2))
    DoSomething();

time2 = time1;                      // Member-by-member assignment
time2.Write();
// Assert: 5:20:0 is output
```

Earlier we remarked that the `Equal` and `LessThan` functions have only one parameter each, even though they are comparing two `TimeType` objects. In the If statement of the code segment above, we are comparing `time1` and `time2`. Because `LessThan` is a class member function, we invoke it by giving the name of a class object (`time1`), then a dot, then the function name (`LessThan`). Only one item remains unspecified: the class object that `time1` should be compared with (`time2`). Therefore, the `LessThan` function requires only one parameter, not two. Here is another way of explaining it: If a class member function represents a binary (two-operand) operation, the first operand appears to the left of the dot operator and the second operand is in the parameter list. (To generalize, an *n*-ary operation has *n*–1 operands in the parameter list. Thus, a unary operation—such as `Write` or `Increment` in the `TimeType` class—has an empty parameter list.)

In addition to member selection and assignment, a few other built-in operators are valid for classes. These operators are used for manipulating memory addresses, and we defer discussing them until later in the book. For now, think of **.** and = as the only valid built-in operators.

From the very beginning, you have been working with C++ classes in a particular context: input and output. The standard header file `iostream.h` contains the declarations of two classes—`istream` and `ostream`—that manage a program's I/O. The C++ standard library declares `cin` and `cout` to be objects of these classes:

```
istream cin;
ostream cout;
```

(The actual declarations are slightly different from these, but the differences are not important to this discussion.)

The `istream` class has many member functions, two of which—the `get` function and the `ignore` function—you have already seen in statements like these:

```
cin.get(someChar);
cin.ignore(200, '\n');
```

As with any C++ class object, we use dot notation to select a particular member function to invoke.

You also have used C++ classes when performing file I/O. The header file `fstream.h` contains declarations for the `ifstream` and `ofstream` classes. The client code

```
ifstream dataFile;

dataFile.open("input.dat");
```

declares an `ifstream` class object named `dataFile`, then invokes the class member function `open` to try to open a file `input.dat` for input.

We do not examine in detail the `istream`, `ostream`, `ifstream`, and `ofstream` classes and all of their member functions. To study these would be beyond the goals of this book. What is important to recognize is that classes and objects are fundamental to all I/O activity in a C++ program.

Class Scope

As with members of a `struct`, the name of a class member has class scope—that is, the name is local to the class. If the same identifier happens to be declared outside the class, the two identifiers are unrelated.

The `TimeType` class has a member function named `Write`. In the same program, another class (say, `SomeClass`) could also have a member function named `Write`. Furthermore, the program might have a global `Write` function that is completely unrelated to any classes. If the program has statements like

```
TimeType  checkInTime;
SomeClass someObject;
int       n;
   .
   .
   .
```

```
checkInTime.Write();
someObject.Write();
Write(n);
```

then the C++ compiler has no trouble distinguishing among the three `Write` functions. In the first two function calls, the dot notation denotes class member selection. The first statement invokes the `Write` function of the `TimeType` class, and the second statement invokes the `Write` function of the `SomeClass` class. The final statement does not use dot notation, so the compiler knows that the function being called is the global `Write` function.

Information Hiding

Conceptually, a class object has an invisible wall around it. This wall, called the **abstraction barrier,** protects private data and functions from being accessed by client code. The barrier also prohibits the class object from directly accessing data and functions outside the object. This barrier is a critical characteristic of classes and abstract data types.

For a class object to share information with the outside world (that is, with clients), there must be a gap in the abstraction barrier. This gap is the public interface—the class members declared to be `public`. The only way that a client can manipulate the internals of the class object is indirectly—through the operations in the public interface. Engineers have a similar concept called a **black box.** A black box is a module or device whose inner workings are hidden from view. The user of the black box depends only on the written specification of *what* it does, not on *how* it does it. The user connects wires to the interface and assumes that the module works correctly by satisfying the specification (see Figure 15-4).

In software design, the black box concept is referred to as **information hiding.** Information hiding protects the user of a class from having to know all the details of its implementation. Information hiding also assures the

■ FIGURE 15-4

A Black Box

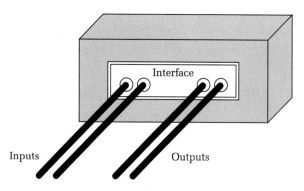

class's implementor that the user cannot directly access any private code or data and compromise the correct functioning of the implementation.

You have been introduced to encapsulation and information hiding before. In Chapter 7, we discussed the possibility of hiding a function's implementation in a separate file. In this chapter, you'll see how to hide the implementations of class member functions by placing them in files separate from the client code.

Abstraction Barrier   The invisible wall around a class object that encapsulates implementation details. The wall can be breached only through the public interface.

Black Box   An electrical or mechanical device whose inner workings are hidden from view.

Information Hiding   The encapsulation and hiding of implementation details to keep the user of an abstraction from depending on or incorrectly manipulating these details.

The creator of a C++ class is free to choose which members are private and which are public. However, making data members public allows the client to inspect and modify them directly. Because information hiding is so fundamental to data abstraction, most classes exhibit a typical pattern: the private part contains data, and the public part contains the functions that manipulate the data.

The TimeType class exemplifies this organization. The data members hrs, mins, and secs are private, so the compiler prohibits a client from accessing these members directly. The following client statement therefore results in a compile-time error:

```
checkInTime.hrs = 9;    // Prohibited
```

Because only the class's member functions can access the private data, the creator of the class can offer a reliable product, knowing that external access to the private data is impossible. If it is acceptable to let the client *inspect* (but not modify) private data members, a class might provide observer functions. The TimeType class has three such functions: Write, Equal, and LessThan. Because these observer functions are not intended to modify the private data, they are declared with the word const following the parameter list:

```
void    Write() const;
Boolean Equal( TimeType ) const;
Boolean LessThan( TimeType ) const;
```

C++ refers to these functions as *const member functions*. Within the body of a `const` member function, a compile-time error occurs if any statement tries to modify a private data member. Although not required by the language, it is good practice to declare as `const` those member functions that do not modify private data.

Specification and Implementation Files

An abstract data type consists of two parts: a specification and an implementation. The specification describes the behavior of the data type without reference to its implementation. The implementation creates an abstraction barrier by hiding the concrete data representation as well as the code for the operations.

The `TimeType` class declaration serves as the specification of `TimeType`. This declaration presents the public interface to the user in the form of function prototypes. To implement the `TimeType` class, we must provide function definitions (declarations with bodies) for all the member functions.

In C++, it is customary (though not required) to package the class declaration and the class implementation into separate files. One file—the *specification file*—is a header (.h) file containing only the class declaration. The second file—the *implementation file*—contains the function definitions for the class member functions. Let's look first at the specification file.

The Specification File

Below is the specification file for the `TimeType` class. On our computer system, we have named the file `timetype.h`. The class declaration is the same as we presented earlier, with one important exception: We include function preconditions and postconditions to specify the semantics of the member functions as unambiguously as possible for the user.

```
//****************************************************************
// SPECIFICATION FILE (timetype.h)
// This file gives the specification
// of a TimeType abstract data type
//****************************************************************
#include "bool.h"
```

```
class TimeType
{
public:
    void Set( /* in */ int hours,
              /* in */ int minutes,
              /* in */ int seconds );
        // Precondition:
        //     0 <= hours <= 23  &&  0 <= minutes <= 59
        //     && 0 <= seconds <= 59
        // Postcondition:
        //     Time is set according to the incoming parameters
        // NOTE:
        //     This function MUST be called prior to
        //     any of the other member functions

    void Increment();
        // Precondition:
        //     The Set function has been invoked at least once
        // Postcondition:
        //     Time has been advanced by one second, with
        //     23:59:59 wrapping around to 0:0:0

    void Write() const;
        // Precondition:
        //     The Set function has been invoked at least once
        // Postcondition:
        //     Time has been output in the form HH:MM:SS

    Boolean Equal( /* in */ TimeType otherTime ) const;
        // Precondition:
        //     The Set function has been invoked at least once
        //     for both this time and otherTime
        // Postcondition:
        //     Function value == TRUE, if this time equals otherTime
        //                    == FALSE, otherwise

    Boolean LessThan( /* in */ TimeType otherTime ) const;
        // Precondition:
        //     The Set function has been invoked at least once
        //     for both this time and otherTime
        //     && This time and otherTime represent times in the
        //     same day
        // Postcondition:
        //     Function value == TRUE, if this time is earlier
        //                            in the day than otherTime
        //                    == FALSE, otherwise
private:
    int hrs;
    int mins;
    int secs;
};
```

Notice the preconditions for the `Increment`, `Write`, `Equal`, and `LessThan` functions. It is the responsibility of the client to set the time before incrementing, printing, or testing it. If the client fails to set the time, the effect of each of these functions is undefined.

In principle, a specification file should not reveal any implementation details to the user of the class. The file should specify *what* each member function does without disclosing how it does it. However, as you can see in the class declaration, there is one implementation detail that is visible to the user: the concrete data representation of our ADT that is listed in the private part. However, the data representation is still considered hidden information in the sense that the compiler prohibits client code from accessing the data directly.

The Implementation File

The specification (`.h`) file for the `TimeType` class contains only the class declaration. The implementation file must provide the function definitions for all the class member functions. In the opening comments of the implementation file below, we document the file name as `timetype.cpp`. Your system may use a different file name suffix for source code files, perhaps `.c`, `.C`, or `.cxx`.

We recommend that you first skim the C++ code below, not being too concerned about the new language features such as prefixing the name of each function with the symbols

```
TimeType::
```

Immediately following the program code, we explain the new features.

```
//*******************************************************************
// IMPLEMENTATION FILE (timetype.cpp)
// This file implements the TimeType member functions
//*******************************************************************
#include "timetype.h"
#include <iostream.h>

// Private members of class:
//      int hrs;
//      int mins;
//      int secs;


//*******************************************************************

void TimeType::Set( /* in */ int hours,
                    /* in */ int minutes,
                    /* in */ int seconds )
```

```
// Precondition:
//      0 <= hours <= 23   &&   0 <= minutes <= 59
//   && 0 <= seconds <= 59
// Postcondition:
//      hrs == hours   &&   mins == minutes   &&   secs == seconds
// NOTE:
//      This function MUST be called prior to
//      any of the other member functions

{
    hrs = hours;
    mins = minutes;
    secs = seconds;
}


//******************************************************************

void TimeType::Increment()

// Precondition:
//      The Set function has been invoked at least once
// Postcondition:
//      Time has been advanced by one second, with
//      23:59:59 wrapping around to 0:0:0

{
    secs++;
    if (secs > 59)
    {
        secs = 0;
        mins++;
        if (mins > 59)
        {
            mins = 0;
            hrs++;
            if (hrs > 23)
                hrs = 0;
        }
    }
}


//******************************************************************

void TimeType::Write() const

// Precondition:
//      The Set function has been invoked at least once
// Postcondition:
//      Time has been output in the form HH:MM:SS
```

```
{
    if (hrs < 10)
        cout << '0';
    cout << hrs << ':';
    if (mins < 10)
        cout << '0';
    cout << mins << ':';
    if (secs < 10)
        cout << '0';
    cout << secs;
}


//*****************************************************************

Boolean TimeType::Equal( /* in */ TimeType otherTime ) const

// Precondition:
//      The Set function has been invoked at least once
//      for both this time and otherTime
// Postcondition:
//      Function value == TRUE, if this time equals otherTime
//                     == FALSE, otherwise

{
    return (hrs == otherTime.hrs && mins == otherTime.mins &&
            secs == otherTime.secs);
}


//*****************************************************************

Boolean TimeType::LessThan( /* in */ TimeType otherTime ) const

// Precondition:
//      The Set function has been invoked at least once
//      for both this time and otherTime
//   && This time and otherTime represent times in the
//      same day
// Postcondition:
//      Function value == TRUE, if this time is earlier
//                              in the day than otherTime
//                     == FALSE, otherwise

{
    return (hrs < otherTime.hrs ||
            hrs == otherTime.hrs && mins < otherTime.mins ||
            hrs == otherTime.hrs && mins == otherTime.mins
                            && secs < otherTime.secs);
}
```

■ FIGURE 15-5   Shared Access to a Specification File

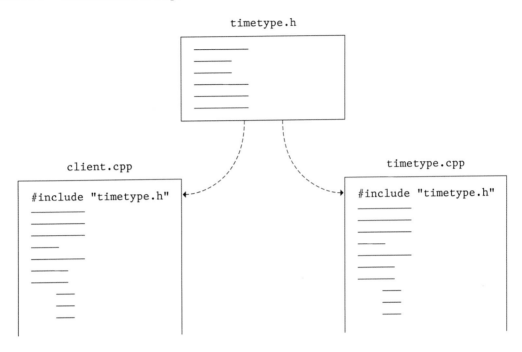

This implementation file demonstrates several important points.

1. The file begins with the preprocessor directive

   ```
   #include "timetype.h"
   ```

   Both the implementation file and the client code must #include the specification file. Figure 15-5 pictures this shared access to the specification file. This sharing guarantees that all declarations related to an abstraction are consistent. That is, both client.cpp and timetype.cpp must reference the same declaration of the TimeType class located in timetype.h.

2. Near the top of the implementation file we have included a comment that restates the private members of the TimeType class.

   ```
   // Private members of class:
   //      int hrs;
   //      int mins;
   //      int secs;
   ```

This comment reminds the reader that any references to these identifiers are references to the private class members.

3. In the heading of each function definition, the name of the member function is prefixed by the class name (TimeType) and the C++ *scope resolution operator* (::). As we discussed earlier, it is possible for several different classes to have member functions with the same name, say, Write. In addition, there may be a global Write function that is not a member of any class. The scope resolution operator eliminates any uncertainty about which particular function is being defined.

4. Although clients of a class must use the dot operator to refer to class members (for example, startTime.Write()), members of a class refer to each other directly without using dot notation. Looking at the bodies of the Set and Increment functions, you can see that the statements refer directly to the member variables hrs, mins, and secs without using the dot operator.

An exception to this rule occurs when a member function manipulates two or more class objects. Consider the Equal function. Suppose that the client code has two class objects, startTime and endTime, and uses the statement

```
if (startTime.Equal(endTime))
        .
        .
        .
```

At execution time, the startTime object is the object for whom the Equal function is invoked. In the body of the Equal function, the relational expression

```
hrs == otherTime.hrs
```

refers to class members of two different class objects. The unadorned identifier hrs refers to the hrs member of the class object for whom the function is invoked (that is, startTime). The expression otherTime.hrs refers to the hrs member of the class object that is passed as a function parameter: endTime.

5. Write, Equal, and LessThan are observer functions; they do not modify the private data of the class. Because we have declared these to be const member functions, the compiler will prevent them from assigning new values to the private data. The use of const is both an aid to the user of the class (as a visual signal that this function does not modify any private data) and an aid to the class implementor (as a way of preventing accidental modification of the data). Note that the word const must appear in both the function prototype (in the class declaration) and the heading of the function definition.

Compiling and Linking a Multifile Program

Now that we have created a specification file and an implementation file for our `TimeType` class, how do we (or any other programmer) make use of these files in our programs? Let's begin by looking at the notion of *separate compilation* of source code files.

We have referred several times in earlier chapters to the concept of a multifile program—a program divided up into several files containing source code. In C++, it is possible to compile each of these files separately. The compiler translates each source code file into an object code file. Figure 15-6 shows a multifile program consisting of the source code files `myprog.cpp`, `file2.cpp`, and `file3.cpp`. We can compile each of these files independently, yielding object code files `myprog.obj`, `file2.obj`, and `file3.obj`. Although each `.obj` file contains machine language code, it is not yet in executable form. The system's linker program brings the object code together to form an executable program file. (In Figure 15-6, we use the file name suffixes `.cpp`, `.obj`, and `.exe`. Your C++ system may use different file name conventions.)

Files such as `file2.cpp` and `file3.cpp` typically contain function definitions for functions that are called by the code in `myprog.cpp`. An important benefit of separate compilation is that modifying the code in just one file requires recompiling only that file. The new `.obj` file is then relinked with the other existing `.obj` files. Of course, if a modification to one file affects the code in another file—for example, changing a function's interface by altering the number or data types of the function parameters—then the affected files also need to be modified and recompiled.

■ FIGURE 15-6

Separate Compilation and Linking

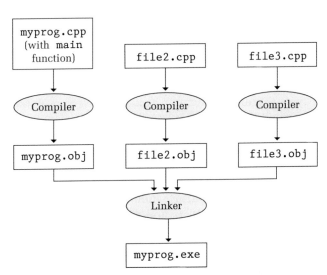

Returning to our `TimeType` class, let's assume we have used the system's editor to create the `timetype.h` and `timetype.cpp` files. Now we can compile `timetype.cpp` into object code. If we are working at the operating system's command line, we use a command similar to the following:

```
cc -c timetype.cpp
```

In this example, we assume that `cc` is the name of a command that invokes either the C++ compiler or the linker or both, depending on various options given on the command line. The command-line option `-c` means, on many systems, "compile but do not link." In other words, this command produces an object code file, say, `timetype.obj`, but does not attempt to link this file with any other file.

A programmer wishing to use the `TimeType` class will write code that #includes the file `timetype.h`, then declares and uses `TimeType` objects:

```
#include "timetype.h"
    .
    .
    .
TimeType appointment;

appointment.Set(15, 30, 0);
appointment.Write();
    .
    .
    .
```

If this client code is in a file named `diary.cpp`, an operating system command like

```
cc diary.cpp timetype.obj
```

compiles the client program into object code, links this object code with `timetype.obj`, and produces an executable program (see Figure 15-7).

The mechanics of compiling, linking, and executing vary from one computer system to another. The examples we gave using the `cc` command assume you are working at the operating system's command line. Some C++ systems provide an *integrated environment*—a program that bundles the editor, the compiler, and the linker into one package. Integrated environments put you back into the editor when a compile-time or link-time error occurs, pinpointing the location of the error. Some integrated environments also manage *project files*. Project files contain information about all the constituent files of a multifile program. With project files, the system automatically recompiles or relinks any files that have become out-of-date because of changes to other files of the program.

Whichever environment you use—the command-line environment or an integrated environment—the overall process is the same: you compile the individual source code files into object code, link the object files into an executable program, then execute the program.

Before leaving the topic of multifile programs, we stress an important point. Referring to Figure 15-7, the files timetype.h and timetype.obj must be available to users of the TimeType class. The user needs to examine timetype.h to see what TimeType objects do and how to use them. The user must also be able to link his or her program with timetype.obj to produce an executable program. But the user does *not* need to see timetype.cpp. The implementation of TimeType should be treated as a black box. The main purpose of abstraction is to simplify the programmer's job by reducing complexity. Users of an abstraction should not have to look at its implementation to see how to use it, nor should they write programs that depend on implementation details. In the latter case, any changes made to the implementation could "break" the user's programs. In Chapter 7, the Software Engineering Tip box entitled "Conceptual Versus Physical Hiding of a Function Implementation" discussed the hazards of writing code that relies on implementation details.

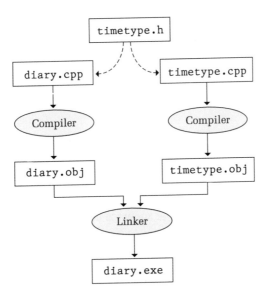

■ FIGURE 15-7

Linking with the
TimeType
Implementation
File

Matters of Style

Avoiding Multiple Inclusion of Header Files

The TimeType specification file contains the preprocessor directive #include "bool.h". To avoid typing the lines

```
typedef int Boolean;
const Boolean TRUE = 1;
const Boolean FALSE = 0;
```

in every file that uses Boolean data, we have said that it's useful to put these three lines into a file named bool.h and then #include the file whenever required. But think about what happens if a programmer using the TimeType class already has included bool.h for other purposes, overlooking the fact that timetype.h also includes it:

```
#include "bool.h"
#include "timetype.h"
```

The preprocessor inserts the file bool.h, then timetype.h, and then bool.h a second time (because timetype.h also includes bool.h). The result is a compile-time error, because the identifiers TRUE and FALSE are defined twice.

The widely used solution to this problem is to write bool.h this way:

```
#ifndef BOOL_H
#define BOOL_H
typedef int Boolean;
const Boolean TRUE = 1;
const Boolean FALSE = 0;
#endif
```

The lines beginning with "#" are directives to the preprocessor. BOOL_H (or any identifier you wish to use) is a preprocessor identifier, not a C++ program identifier. In effect, these directives say:

If the preprocessor identifier BOOL_H is not already defined, then:

1. define BOOL_H as an identifier known to the preprocessor,
   and
2. let the typedef and const declarations pass through to the compiler.

If a subsequent #include "bool.h" is encountered, the test #ifndef BOOL_H will fail. The typedef and const declarations will not pass through to the compiler a second time.

Guaranteed Initialization with Class Constructors

The `TimeType` class we have been discussing has a weakness. It depends on the client to invoke the `Set` function before calling any other member function. For example, the `Increment` function's precondition is

```
// Precondition:
//     The Set function has been invoked at least once
```

If the client fails to invoke the `Set` function first, this precondition is false and the contract between the client and the function implementation is broken. Because classes nearly always encapsulate data, the creator of a class should not rely on the user to initialize the data. If the user forgets to, unpleasant results may occur.

C++ provides a mechanism, called a *class constructor*, to guarantee the initialization of a class object. A constructor is a member function that is implicitly invoked whenever a class object is created.

A constructor function has an unusual name: the name of the class itself. Let's change the `TimeType` class by adding two class constructors:

```
class TimeType
{
public:
    void    Set( int, int, int );
    void    Increment();
    void    Write() const;
    Boolean Equal( TimeType ) const;
    Boolean LessThan( TimeType ) const;
    TimeType( int, int, int );          // Constructor
    TimeType();                         // Constructor
private:
    int hrs;
    int mins;
    int secs;
};
```

This class declaration includes two constructors, differentiated by their parameter lists. The first has three `int` parameters which, as we will see, are used to initialize the private data when a class object is created. The second constructor is parameterless and initializes the time to some default value, such as 0:0:0. A parameterless constructor is known in C++ as a *default constructor*.

Constructor declarations are unique in two ways. First, as we have mentioned, the name of the function is the same as the name of the class. Second, the data type of the function is omitted. The reason is that a constructor cannot return a function value. Its purpose is only to initialize a class object's private data.

In the implementation file, the function definitions for the two `TimeType` constructors might look like the following:

```
//****************************************************************

TimeType::TimeType( /* in */ int initHrs,
                    /* in */ int initMins,
                    /* in */ int initSecs )
// Constructor

// Precondition:
//      0 <= initHrs <= 23   &&   0 <= initMins <= 59
//   && 0 <= initSecs <= 59
// Postcondition:
//      hrs == initHrs   &&   mins == initMins   &&   secs == initSecs

{
    hrs = initHrs;
    mins = initMins;
    secs = initSecs;
}


//****************************************************************

TimeType::TimeType()

// Default constructor

// Postcondition:
//      hrs == 0   &&   mins == 0   &&   secs == 0

{
    hrs = 0;
    mins = 0;
    secs = 0;
}
```

Invoking a Constructor

Although a constructor is a member of a class, it is never invoked using dot notation. A constructor is automatically invoked whenever a class object is created. The declaration

```
TimeType lectureTime(10, 30, 0);
```

includes a parameter list to the right of the name of the class object being declared. When this declaration is encountered at execution time, the first (parameterized) constructor is automatically invoked, initializing the private data of `lectureTime` to the time 10:30:0. The declaration

```
TimeType startTime;
```

has no parameter list after the identifier `startTime`. The default (parameterless) constructor is implicitly invoked, initializing `startTime`'s private data to the time 0:0:0.

Remember that a declaration in C++ is a genuine statement and can appear anywhere among executable statements. Placing declarations among executable statements is extremely useful when creating class objects whose initial values are not known until execution time. Here's an example:

```
cout << "Enter appointment time in hours, minutes, and seconds: ";
cin >> hours >> minutes >> seconds;

TimeType appointmentTime(hours, minutes, seconds);

cout << "The appointment time is ";
appointmentTime.Write();
    .
    .
    .
```

Revised Specification and Implementation Files for TimeType

By including constructors for the `TimeType` class, we are sure that each class object is initialized before any subsequent calls to the class member functions. One of the constructors allows the client code to specify an initial time; the other creates an initial time of 0:0:0 if the client does not specify a time. Because of these constructors, it is *impossible* for a `TimeType` object to be in an uninitialized state after it is created. As a result, we can delete from the `TimeType` specification file the warning to call `Set` before calling any other member functions. Also, we can remove all of the function preconditions that require `Set` to be called previously. Here is the revised `TimeType` specification file:

```
//*************************************************************
// SPECIFICATION FILE (timetype.h)
// This file gives the specification
// of a TimeType abstract data type
//*************************************************************
```

```
#include "bool.h"

class TimeType
{
public:
    void Set( /* in */ int hours,
              /* in */ int minutes,
              /* in */ int seconds );
        // Precondition:
        //     0 <= hours <= 23  &&  0 <= minutes <= 59
        //     && 0 <= seconds <= 59
        // Postcondition:
        //     Time is set according to the incoming parameters

    void Increment();
        // Postcondition:
        //     Time has been advanced by one second, with
        //     23:59:59 wrapping around to 0:0:0

    void Write() const;
        // Postcondition:
        //     Time has been output in the form HH:MM:SS

    Boolean Equal( /* in */ TimeType otherTime ) const;
        // Postcondition:
        //     Function value == TRUE, if this time equals otherTime
        //                    == FALSE, otherwise

    Boolean LessThan( /* in */ TimeType otherTime ) const;
        // Precondition:
        //     This time and otherTime represent times in the
        //     same day
        // Postcondition:
        //     Function value == TRUE, if this time is earlier
        //                             in the day than otherTime
        //                    == FALSE, otherwise

    TimeType( /* in */ int initHrs,
              /* in */ int initMins,
              /* in */ int initSecs );
        // Precondition:
        //     0 <= initHrs <= 23  &&  0 <= initMins <= 59
        //     && 0 <= initSecs <= 59
        // Postcondition:
        //     Class object is constructed
        //     && Time is set according to the incoming parameters

    TimeType();
        // Postcondition:
        //     Class object is constructed  &&  Time is 0:0:0
```

```
private:
    int hrs;
    int mins;
    int secs;
};
```

To save space, we do not include the revised implementation file here. The only changes are

1. the inclusion of the function definitions for the two class constructors, which we presented earlier.
2. the deletion of all function preconditions stating that the Set function must be invoked previously.

At this point, you may wonder why we need the Set function at all. After all, both the Set function and the parameterized constructor seem to do the same thing—set the time according to values passed as parameters—and the implementations of the two functions are essentially identical. The difference is that Set can be invoked for a class object whenever and as often as we wish, whereas the parameterized constructor is invoked once only—at the moment a class object is created. Therefore, we retain the Set function to provide maximum flexibility to clients of the class.

Guidelines for Using Class Constructors

The class is an essential language feature for creating abstract data types in C++. The class mechanism is a powerful design tool, but along with this power come rules for using classes correctly.

C++ has some very intricate rules about using constructors, many of which relate to language features we have not yet discussed. Below are some guidelines that are pertinent at this point.

1. A constructor cannot return a function value, so the function is declared without a return value type.
2. A class may provide several constructors. When a class object is declared, the compiler chooses the appropriate constructor according to the number and data types of the parameters to the constructor.
3. Parameters to a constructor are passed by placing the actual parameter list immediately after the name of the class object being declared:

```
SomeClass anObject(param1, param2);
```

4. If a class object is declared without a parameter list, as in the statement

```
SomeClass anObject;
```

then the effect depends upon what constructors (if any) the class provides.

If the class has no constructors at all, memory is allocated for `anObject` but its private data members are in an uninitialized state.

If the class does have constructors, then the default (parameterless) constructor is invoked if there is one. If there is no default constructor, a syntax error occurs.

5. If a class has at least one constructor, and an array of class objects is declared:

```
SomeClass arr[10];
```

then one of the constructors must be the default (parameterless) constructor. This constructor is invoked for each element of the array. There is no way to pass parameters to a constructor when creating an array of class objects.

Before leaving the topic of constructors, we give you a brief preview of another special member function supported by C++: the *class destructor*. Just as a constructor is implicitly invoked when a class object is created, a destructor is implicitly invoked when a class object is destroyed—for example, when control leaves the block in which a local object is declared. A class destructor is named the same as a constructor except that the first character is a tilde (~):

```
class SomeClass
{
public:
    .
    .
    .
    SomeClass();     // Constructor
    ~SomeClass();    // Destructor
private:
    .
    .
    .
};
```

In this chapter and the next, we won't be using destructors; the kinds of classes we'll be writing have no need to perform special actions at the moment a class object is destroyed. In Chapter 17, we explore destructors in detail and describe the situations in which you need to use them.

***P*ROBLEM-*SOLVING** *CASE STUDY*

Manipulating Dates

Dates are often necessary pieces of information. Both the address book and the machine shop examples in Chapter 14 had a date as part of the data. In fact, the machine shop example had two dates: the date of purchase and the date of last service. Each time we needed a date, we defined it again.

Often our processing of dates calls for us to compare two dates, print out a date, or determine the date a certain number of days in the future. Let's stop this duplication of effort and do the job once and for all—let's write the code to support dates as an abstract data type.

The format for this case study needs to be a little different. Because we are developing only one software component—an ADT—and not a complete program, we omit the Input and Output sections. Instead, we include two sections entitled Specification of the ADT and Implementation of the ADT.

Problem: Design and implement an ADT to represent a date. Make the domain and operations general enough to be used in any program that needs to perform these operations on dates. The informal specification of the ADT is given below.

TYPE
 DateType
DOMAIN
 Each DateType value is a single date after the year 1582 A.D. in the form of month, day, and year.
OPERATIONS
 Construct a new DateType instance.
 Set the date.
 Inspect the date's month.
 Inspect the date's day.
 Inspect the date's year.
 Print the date.
 Compare two dates for "before," "equal," or "after."
 Increment the date by one day.

Discussion: We create the DateType ADT in two stages: specification, followed by implementation. The result of the first stage is a C++ specification (`.h`) file containing the declaration of a `DateType` class. This file must describe for the user the precise semantics of each of the ADT operations.

The informal specification given above would be unacceptable to the user of the ADT. The descriptions of the operations are too imprecise and ambiguous to be helpful to the user.

The second stage—implementation—requires us to (1) choose a concrete data representation for a date, and (2) implement each of the operations as a C++ function definition. The result is a C++ implementation file containing these function definitions.

Specification of the ADT: The domain of our ADT is the set of all dates after the year 1582 A.D. in the form of a month, a day, and a year. We restrict the year to be after 1582 A.D. in order to simplify the ADT operations (10 days were skipped in 1582 in switching from the Julian to the Gregorian calendar).

To represent the DateType ADT as program code we use a C++ class named `DateType`. The ADT operations become public member functions of the class. Let's now specify the operations more carefully.

Construct a new DateType instance: For this operation we use a C++ default constructor, initializing the date to January 1 of the year 1583. The client code can reset the date at any time using the "Set the date" operation.

Set the date: The client must supply three parameters for this operation: month, day, and year. Although we haven't yet determined a concrete data representation for a date, we must decide what data types the client should use for these parameters. We choose integers, where the month must be in the range 1 through 12, the day must be in the range 1 through the maximum number of days in the month, and the year must be greater than 1582. Notice that these range restrictions will be the precondition for invoking this operation.

Inspect the date's month, Inspect the date's day, Inspect the date's year: These three operations are all observer operations. They give the client access, indirectly, to the private data. In the `DateType` class, we represent these operations as value-returning member functions with the following prototypes.

```
int Month();
int Day();
int Year();
```

Why do we need these observer operations? Why not simply let the data representation of the month, day, and year be public instead of private so that the client can access the values directly? The answer is that the client should be allowed to inspect *but not modify* these values. If the data were public, a client could store incorrect values (such as January 35, 1956) into the public data, compromising the correct behavior of the ADT.

Print the date: This operation prints the date on the standard output device in the following form:

```
January 12, 1996
```

Compare two dates: This operation compares two dates and determines whether the first one comes before the second one, they are the same, or the first one comes after the second one. To indicate the result of the comparison we define an enumeration type with three values:

```
enum RelationType {BEFORE, SAME, AFTER};
```

Then we can code the comparison operation as a class member function that returns a value of type `RelationType`. Here is the function prototype:

```
RelationType ComparedTo( /* in */ DateType otherDate ) const;
```

Because this is a class member function, the date being compared to `otherDate` is the class object for which the member function is invoked. That is, the following client code tests to see whether `date1` comes before `date2`.

```
DateType date1;
DateType date2;
    .
    .
    .
if (date1.ComparedTo(date2) == BEFORE)
    DoSomething();
```

Increment the date by one day: This operation advances the date to the next day. For example, given the date March 31, 1997, this operation changes the date to April 1, 1997.

We are now almost ready to write the C++ specification file for our `DateType` class. However, the class declaration requires us to include the private part—the private variables that are the concrete data representation of the ADT. Choosing a concrete data representation properly belongs in the ADT implementation phase, not the specification phase. But to satisfy the

C++ class declaration requirement we now choose a data representation. The simplest representation for a date is three int values—one each for the month, day, and year. Here, then, is the specification file containing the DateType class declaration (along with the declaration of the RelationType enumeration type).

```
//****************************************************************
// SPECIFICATION FILE (datetype.h)
// This file gives the specification of a DateType abstract data
// type and provides an enumeration type for comparing dates
//****************************************************************

enum RelationType {BEFORE, SAME, AFTER};

class DateType
{
public:
    void Set( /* in */ int newMonth,
              /* in */ int newDay,
              /* in */ int newYear  );
        // Precondition:
        //      1 <= newMonth <= 12
        //   && 1 <= newDay <= maximum no. of days in month newMonth
        //   && 1582 < newYear
        // Postcondition:
        //      Date is set according to the incoming parameters

    int Month() const;
        // Postcondition:
        //      Function value == this date's month

    int Day() const;
        // Postcondition:
        //      Function value == this date's day

    int Year() const;
        // Postcondition:
        //      Function value == this date's year

    void Print() const;
        // Postcondition:
        //      Date has been output in the form
        //          month day, year
        //      where the name of the month is printed as a string
```

```
        RelationType ComparedTo( /* in */ DateType otherDate ) const;
            // Postcondition:
            //      Function value == BEFORE, if this date is
            //                              before otherDate
            //                       == SAME, if this date equals otherDate
            //                       == AFTER, if this date is
            //                              after otherDate

        void Increment();
            // Postcondition:
            //      Date has been advanced by one day

        DateType();
            // Postcondition:
            //      New DateType object is constructed with a
            //      month, day, and year of 1, 1, and 1583
    private:
        int mo;
        int day;
        int yr;
};
```

Implementation of the ADT: We have already chosen a concrete data representation for a date, shown in the specification file as the int variables mo, day, and yr. Now we must implement each class member function, placing the function definitions into a C++ implementation file named, say, datetype.cpp. As we implement the member functions, we also discuss testing strategies that can help to convince us that the implementations are correct.

The class constructor, Set, Month, Day, *and* Year *functions:* The implementations of these functions are so straightforward that no discussion is needed.

The class constructor DateType ( )

```
Set mo = 1
Set day = 1
Set yr = 1583
```

Set (In: newMonth, newDay, newYear)

```
Set mo = newMonth
Set day = newDay
Set yr = newYear
```

Month ( )
Out: Function value

```
Return mo
```

Day ( )
Out: Function value

```
Return day
```

Year ( )
Out: Function value

```
Return yr
```

Testing: The Month, Day, and Year observer functions can be used to verify that the class constructor and Set functions work correctly. The code

```
DateType someDate;

cout << someDate.Month() << ' ' << someDate.Day() << ' '
    << someDate.Year() << endl;
```

should print out 1 1 1583. To test the Set function, it is sufficient to set a DateType object to a few different values (obeying the precondition for the Set function), then print out the month, day, and year as above.

PROBLEM-SOLVING CASE STUDY cont'd.

The `Print` *function:* The date is to be printed in the form month, day, comma, and year. We need a blank to separate the month and the day, and a comma followed by a blank to separate the day and the year. The month is to be printed in word form rather than as an integer. We set up a local data structure to store the names of the months: a 12-element array of strings containing the names of the months. Remembering that arrays are indexed starting at 0 in C++, we select the appropriate string by using the index [mo-1].

Print ( )

> Declare monthString to be a 12-element array of strings and
>   initialize monthString[0] to "January", monthString[1]
>   to "February", and so forth
> Print monthString[mo–1], ' ', day, ", ", yr

When we implement the `Print` function in C++, we want to be sure to declare `monthString` to be `static`. By default, local variables in C++ are automatic variables—that is, memory is allocated for them when the function begins execution and is deallocated when the function returns. By declaring `monthString` to be `static`, the array is allocated once only, when the program begins execution, and remains allocated until the program terminates. From function call to function call, the computer does not waste time creating and destroying the array. The body of the `Print` function appears as follows.

```
{
    static char monthString[12][10] =
    {
        "January", "February", "March", "April", "May", "June",
        "July", "August", "September", "October", "November",
        "December"
    };

    cout << monthString[mo-1] << ' ' << day << ", " << yr;
}
```

Testing: In testing the `Print` function, we should print each month at least once. Both the year and the day should be tested at their end points and at several points between.

The `ComparedTo` *function:* If we were to compare two dates in our heads, we would look first at the years. If the years were different, we would immediately determine which date came first. If the years were the same, we would look at the months. If the months were the same, we would have to look at the days. As so often happens, we can use this algorithm directly in our function.

ComparedTo (In: otherDate)
  Out: Function value

```
IF yr < otherDate.yr
    Return BEFORE
IF yr > otherDate.yr
    Return AFTER

// Years are equal.  Compare months
IF mo < otherDate.mo
    Return BEFORE
IF mo > otherDate.mo
    Return AFTER

// Years and months are equal. Compare days
IF day < otherDate.day
    Return BEFORE
IF day > otherDate.day
    Return AFTER

// Years, months, and days are equal
Return SAME
```

Testing: In testing this function, each path must be taken at least once. Case Study Follow-Up Exercise 2 asks you to design test data for this function and to write a driver that does the testing.

The `Increment` *function:* The algorithm to increment the date is similar to our earlier algorithm for incrementing a `TimeType` value by one second. If the current date plus 1 is still within the same month, we are done. If the current date plus 1 is within the next month, then we must increment the month and reset the day to 1. Finally, we must not forget to increment the year when the month changes from December to January.

To determine whether the current date plus 1 is within the current month, we add 1 to the current day and compare this value with the maximum number of days in the current month. In this comparison, we must remember to check for leap year if the month is February.

Increment ( )

> Increment day by 1
> IF day > number of days in month "mo"
>   Set day = 1
>   Increment mo by 1
>   IF mo > 12
>   Set mo = 1
>   Increment yr by 1

We can code the algorithm for finding the number of days in a month as a separate function—an auxiliary ("helper") function that is not a member of the `DateType` class. In this function, we set up a local 12-element `int` array, `numDays`, containing the number of days in each month. That is, `numDays[0]` = 31, `numDays[1]` = 28, `numDays[2]` = 31, and so on, giving the number of days in January, February, March, ... The number of days in February might need to be adjusted for leap year, so this function must receive as parameters both a month and a year.

DaysInMonth (In: month, year)
Out: Function value

> Declare a 12-element integer array, numDays, and initialize numDays[0] to 31,
>   numDays[1] to 28, and so forth
> IF month isn't 2
>   Return numDays[month–1]
> // It's February. Check for leap year
> IF (year MOD 4 is 0 AND year MOD 100 isn't 0) OR year MOD 400 is 0
>   Return 29
> ELSE
>   Return 28

Testing: To test the `Increment` function, we need to create a driver that calls the function with different values for the date. Values that cause the month to change must be tested, as well as values that cause the year to change. Leap year must be tested, including a year with the last two digits 00. Case Study Follow-Up Exercise 3 asks you to carry out this testing.

Here is the implementation file that contains function definitions for all of the ADT operations:

```
//****************************************************************
// IMPLEMENTATION FILE (datetype.cpp)
// This file implements the DateType member functions
//****************************************************************
#include "datetype.h"
#include "bool.h"
#include <iostream.h>

// Private members of class:
//      int mo;
//      int day;
//      int yr;

int DaysInMonth( int, int );   // Prototype for auxiliary function

//****************************************************************

DateType::DateType()

// Constructor

// Postcondition:
//      mo == 1  &&  day == 1  &&  yr == 1583

{
    mo = 1;
    day = 1;
    yr = 1583;
}

//****************************************************************

void DateType::Set( /* in */ int newMonth,
                    /* in */ int newDay,
                    /* in */ int newYear  )

// Precondition:
//      1 <= newMonth <= 12
//   && 1 <= newDay <= maximum no. of days in month newMonth
//   && 1582 < newYear
// Postcondition:
//      mo == newMonth  &&  day == newDay  &&  yr == newYear

{
    mo = newMonth;
    day = newDay;
    yr = newYear;
}
```

```
//************************************************************

int DateType::Month() const

// Postcondition:
//      Function value == mo

{
    return mo;
}

//************************************************************

int DateType::Day() const

// Postcondition:
//      Function value == day

{
    return day;
}

//************************************************************

int DateType::Year() const

// Postcondition:
//      Function value == yr

{
    return yr;
}

//************************************************************

void DateType::Print() const

// Postcondition:
//      Date has been output in the form
//          month day, year
//      where the name of the month is printed as a string

{
    static char monthString[12][10] =
    {
        "January", "February", "March", "April", "May", "June",
```

```
              "July", "August", "September", "October", "November",
              "December"
          };

          cout << monthString[mo-1] << ' ' << day << ", " << yr;
      }

//*************************************************************

RelationType DateType::ComparedTo(
                      /* in */ DateType otherDate ) const

// Postcondition:
//      Function value == BEFORE, if this date is
//                                  before otherDate
//                      == SAME, if this date equals otherDate
//                      == AFTER, if this date is
//                                  after otherDate

{
      if (yr < otherDate.yr)            // Compare years
          return BEFORE;
      if (yr > otherDate.yr)
          return AFTER;

      if (mo < otherDate.mo)            // Years are equal. Compare
          return BEFORE;                //   months
      if (mo > otherDate.mo)
          return AFTER;

      if (day < otherDate.day)          // Years and months are equal.
          return BEFORE;                //   Compare days
      if (day > otherDate.day)
          return AFTER;

      return SAME;                      // Years, months, and days
}                                       //   are equal

//*************************************************************

void DateType::Increment()

// Postcondition:
//      Date has been advanced by one day

{
```

```cpp
        day++;
        if (day > DaysInMonth(mo, yr))
        {
            day = 1;
            mo++;
            if (mo > 12)
            {
                mo = 1;
                yr++;
            }
        }
    }

//****************************************************************

int DaysInMonth( /* in */ int month,
                 /* in */ int year  )

// Returns the number of days in month "month", taking
// leap year into account

// Precondition:
//      1 <= month <= 12  &&  year > 1582
// Postcondition:
//      Function value == number of days in month "month"

{
    static int numDays[12] =                 // No. of days per month
    {
        31, 28, 31, 30, 31, 30, 31, 31, 30, 31, 30, 31
    };

    if (month != 2)
        return numDays[month-1];

    // It's February.  Check for leap year

    if ((year % 4 == 0 && year % 100 != 0) ||
         year % 400 == 0)
        return 29;
    else
        return 28;
}
```

A date is a logical entity for which we now have developed an implementation. We have designed, implemented, and tested a date ADT that we (or any programmer) can use whenever we have a date as part of our program data. If we discover in the future that additional operations on a date would be useful, we can implement, test, and add them to our set of date operations.

We have said that data abstraction is an important principle of software design. What we have done here is an example of data abstraction. From now on, when a problem needs a date, we can stop our decomposition at the logical level. We do not need to worry about implementing a date each time.

PROBLEM-SOLVING CASE STUDY

Birthday Calls

Problem: In Chapter 10, we commented that everyone has at least one friend who never forgets important dates in the lives of his or her friends. Let's write a program to go through your address book and print the names and phone numbers of all the people who have birthdays within the next two weeks, so you can give them a call.

Input: Today's date (from the keyboard); and a list of names, phone numbers, and birth dates (file `friendFile`). The file `friendFile` is the address book created by running the Friends program in Chapter 14. Entries in this file are in the form

```
John Arbuthnot
(493) 384-2938
1/12/1970

Mary Smith
(123) 123-4567
10/12/1960
```

Output: The names, phone numbers, and birthdays of any friends whose birthdays are within the next two weeks. A sample of the output is

```
John Arbuthnot
(493) 384-2938
January 12, 1996
```

Note that the date printed is the friend's next birthday, not the friend's birth date.

Discussion: When looking for birthdays, we are interested in month and day only—the year is not important. If we were going through a conventional address book checking for birthdays by hand, we would write down the month and day of the date two weeks away and compare it to the month and day of each friend's birth date.

We can use the same algorithm in our program. Using the `DateType` class that we developed, the member function `Increment` can be used to calculate the date two weeks (14 days) from the current date. We can use the class member function `ComparedTo` to determine whether a friend's birthday lies between the current date and the date two weeks away, inclusive. How do we ignore the year? We set the year of each friend's birth date to the current year for the comparison. However, if the current date plus 14 days is in the next year, and the friend's birthday is in January, then we must set the year to the current year plus one for the comparison to work correctly.

Data Structures:

The `DateType` class, for manipulating dates.

A `struct` type `PhoneType` that stores an integer area code and an 8-character phone number.

A `struct` type `EntryType` that stores a 15-character first name, a 15-character last name, a telephone number of type `PhoneType`, and a birth date of type `DateType`.

Main   *Level 0*

```
Open friendFile for input (and verify success)
Get current date into class object currentDate
Set targetDate = currentDate
FOR count going from 1 through 14
    targetDate.Increment()

Get entry
WHILE NOT EOF on friendFile
    IF targetDate.Year() isn't currentDate.Year() AND
            entry.birthDate.Month() is 1
        Set birthdayYear = targetDate.Year()
    ELSE
        Set birthdayYear = currentDate.Year()
    birthday.Set(entry.birthDate.Month(), entry.birthDate.Day(), birthdayYear)
    IF birthday.ComparedTo(currentDate) ≥ SAME AND
            birthday.ComparedTo(targetDate) ≤ SAME
        Print entry
    Get entry
```

Get Current Date (Out: currentDate) *Level 1*

> Prompt user for current date
> Read month, day, year
> currentDate.Set(month, day, year)

Get Entry (Inout: friendFile; Out: entry)

> Read entry.firstName from friendFile
> IF EOF on friendFile
>   Return
> Read entry.lastName from friendFile
>
> // Below, dummy is a char variable to consume the '(' and ')'
> Read dummy, entry.phone.areaCode,
>   dummy, entry.phone.number from friendFile
>
> // Below, dummy consumes the '/' and '/'
> Read month, dummy, day, dummy, year from friendFile
>
> entry.birthDate.Set(month, day, year)

Print Entry (In: entry, birthday)

> Print entry.firstName, ' ', entry.lastName
> Print '(', entry.phone.areaCode, ')', entry.phone.number
> birthday.Print()

Because the `DateType` member functions (`Increment`, `ComparedTo`, and so on) already exist, no more decomposition is necessary.

The second example is the test

```
if (time1.LessThan(time2))
        .
        .
        .
```

where the programmer intends `time1` to be 11:00:00 on a Wednesday and `time2` to be 1:20:00 on a Thursday. (The result of the test is FALSE, not TRUE as the programmer expects.) Do you see the problem? In each example, the client has violated the function precondition. The precondition of `Set` requires the first parameter to have a value from 0 through 23. The precondition of `LessThan` requires the two times to be on the same day, not on two different days.

If a class has been well tested and there are bugs when client code uses the class, always check the member function preconditions. You can waste many hours trying to debug a class member function when, in fact, the function is correct. The bug may lie in the client code.

Testing and Debugging Hints

1. The declarations of `struct` and class types both end with semicolons.
2. Regarding semicolons, the declarations and definitions of class member functions are treated the same as any C++ function. The member function prototype, located in the class declaration, ends with a semicolon. The function heading—the part of the function definition preceding the body—does not end with a semicolon.
3. When implementing a class member function, don't forget to prefix the function name with the name of the class and the scope resolution operator (`::`).

   ```
   void TimeType::Increment()
   {
           .
           .
           .
   }
   ```

4. For now, the only built-in operations that apply to class objects are member selection (`.`) and assignment (`=`). To perform other operations, such as comparing two class objects, you must write class member functions.
5. If a class member function inspects but does not modify the private data, it is a good idea to make it a `const` member function.

6. A member function does not use dot notation to access private members of the class object for which the function is invoked. In contrast, a member function *must* use dot notation to access the private members of a class object that is passed to it as a parameter.

7. To avoid bugs caused by uninitialized data, it is good practice to always include a class constructor when designing a class.

8. A class constructor is declared without a return value type and cannot return a function value.

9. It is not possible to pass parameters to a class constructor when creating an array of class objects. The class either must have no constructors at all or must include a default (parameterless) constructor, which is then invoked for each element of the array.

10. If a client of a class has bugs that seem to be related to the class, start by checking the preconditions of the class member functions. The errors may be in the client, not the class.

SUMMARY

Data abstraction is a powerful technique for reducing the complexity and increasing the reliability of programs. Separating the properties of a data type from the details of its implementation frees the user of the type from having to write code that depends on a particular implementation of the type. This separation also assures the implementor of the type that client code cannot accidentally compromise a correct implementation.

An abstract data type (ADT) is a type whose specification is separate from its implementation. The specification announces the abstract properties of the type. The implementation consists of (a) a concrete data representation and (b) the implementations of the ADT operations. In C++, an ADT can be realized by using the class mechanism. A class is similar to a struct, but the members of a class are not only data but also functions. Class members can be designated as public or private. Most commonly, the private members are the concrete data representation of the ADT, and the public members are the functions corresponding to the ADT operations.

Among the public member functions of a class, the programmer often includes one or more class constructors—functions that are invoked automatically whenever a class object is created.

Separate compilation of program units is central to the separation of specification from implementation. The declaration of a C++ class is typically placed in a specification (.h) file, and the implementations of the class member functions reside in another file: the implementation file. The client code is compiled separately from the class implementation file, and the two resulting object code files are linked together to form an executable file. Through separate compilation, the user of an ADT can treat the ADT as an off-the-shelf component without ever seeing how it is implemented.

QUICK CHECK

1. The specification of an ADT describes only its properties (the domain and allowable operations). To implement the ADT, what two things must a programmer do? (pp. 838–840)
2. Write a C++ class declaration for the following Checkbook ADT. Do not implement the ADT other than to include in the private part a concrete data representation for the current balance. All monetary amounts are to be represented as floating point numbers.

    TYPE
       Checkbook
    DOMAIN
       Each instance of the Checkbook type is a value representing one customer's current checking account balance.
    OPERATIONS
       Open the checking account, specifying an initial balance.
       Write a check for a specified amount.
       Deposit a specified amount into the checking account.
       Return the current balance.

    (pp. 842–846)
3. Write a segment of client code that declares two Checkbook objects, one for a personal checkbook and one for a business account. (pp. 842–846)
4. For the personal checkbook in Question 3, write a segment of client code that opens the account with an initial balance of $300.00, writes two checks for $50.25 and $150.00, deposits $87.34 into the account, and prints out the resulting balance. (pp. 846–849)
5. Implement the following Checkbook member functions. (pp. 854–858)
    a. Open
    b. WriteCheck
    c. CurrentBalance
6. A compile-time error occurs if a client of Checkbook tries to access the private class members directly. Give an example of such a client statement. (pp. 850–851)
7. In which file—the specification file or the implementation file—would the solution to Question 2 be located? In which file would the solution to Question 5 be located? (pp. 852–858)
8. For the Checkbook class, replace the Open function with two C++ class constructors. One (the default constructor) initializes the account balance to zero. The other initializes the balance to an amount passed as a parameter. (pp. 863–868)
    a. Revise the class declaration.
    b. Implement the two class constructors.

Answers   1. a. Choose a concrete data representation of the abstract data, using data types that already exist. b. Implement each of the allowable operations in terms of program instructions.

2. ```
class Checkbook
{
public:
    void Open(/* in */ float initBalance);
    void WriteCheck(/* in */ float amount);
```
```

```
            void Deposit( /* in */ float amount );
            float CurrentBalance() const;
        private:
            float balance;
    };
```

3. `Checkbook personalAcct;`
   `Checkbook businessAcct;`
4. `personalAcct.Open(300.0);`
   `personalAcct.WriteCheck(50.25);`
   `personalAcct.WriteCheck(150.0);`
   `personalAcct.Deposit(87.34);`
   `cout << '$' << personalAcct.CurrentBalance() << endl;`

5. a. `void Checkbook::Open( /* in */ float initBalance )`
```
        {
            balance = initBalance;
        }
```

   b. `void Checkbook::WriteCheck( /* in */ float amount )`
```
        {
            balance = balance - amount;
        }
```

   c. `float Checkbook::CurrentBalance() const`
```
        {
            return balance;
        }
```

6. `personalAcct.balance = 10000.0;`

7. The C++ class declaration of Question 2 would be located in the specification file. The C++ function definitions of Question 5 would be located in the implementation file.

8. a. `class Checkbook`
```
        {
        public:
            void WriteCheck( /* in */ float amount );
            void Deposit( /* in */ float amount );
            float CurrentBalance() const;
            Checkbook();
            Checkbook( /* in */ float initBalance );
        private:
            float balance;
    };
```

   b. `Checkbook::Checkbook()`
```
        {
            balance = 0.0;
        }
```
   `Checkbook::Checkbook( /* in */ float initBalance )`
```
        {
            balance = initBalance;
        }
```

EXAM PREPARATION EXERCISES

1. The specification of an abstract data type (ADT) should not mention implementation details. (True or False?)
2. Below are some real-world objects you might want to represent in a program as ADTs. For each, give some abstract operations that might be appropriate. (Ignore the concrete data representation for each object.)
   a. A thesaurus
   b. An automatic dishwasher
   c. A radio-controlled model airplane

3. Consider the following C++ class declaration and client code:

Class declaration   *Client code*

```
class SomeClass              SomeClass object1;
{                            SomeClass object2;
public:                      int      m;
   void Func1( int n );
   int  Func2( int n ) const;   object1.Func1(3);
   void Func3();                m = object2.Func2(5);
private:
   int someInt;
};
```

   a. List all the identifiers that refer to data types (both built-in and programmer-defined).
   b. List all the identifiers that are names of class members.
   c. List all the identifiers that are names of class objects.
   d. List the names of all member functions that are allowed to inspect the private data.
   e. List the names of all member functions that are allowed to modify the private data.
   f. In the implementation of SomeClass, which one of the following would be the correct function definition for Func3?

   i. ```
       void Func3()
       {
          .
          .
          .
       }
       ```
   ii. ```
       void SomeClass::Func3()
       {
          .
          .
          .
       }
       ```
   iii. ```
        SomeClass::void Func3()
        {
           .
           .
           .
        }
        ```
        ```

4. If you do not use the reserved words `public` and `private`, all members of a C++ class are private and all members of a `struct` are public. (True or False?)

5. Define the following terms:

   instantiate
   `const` member function
   specification file
   implementation file

6. To the `TimeType` class we wish to add three observer operations: `CurrentHrs`, `CurrentMins`, and `CurrentSecs`. These operations simply return the current values of the private data to the client. We can amend the class declaration by inserting the following function prototypes into the public part:

```
int CurrentHrs() const;
    // Postcondition:
    //      Function value == hours part of the time of day

int CurrentMins() const;
    // Postcondition:
    //      Function value == minutes part of the time of day

int CurrentSecs() const;
    // Postcondition:
    //      Function value == seconds part of the time of day
```

   Write the function definitions for these three functions as they would appear in the implementation file.

7. Classify each of the seven member functions of the `TimeType` class (pages 866–867) as a constructor, a transformer, or an observer operation.

8. Answer the following questions about Figure 15-6, which illustrates the process of compiling and linking a multifile program.
   a. If only the file `myprog.cpp` is modified, which files must be recompiled?
   b. If only the file `myprog.cpp` is modified, which files must be relinked?
   c. If only the files `file2.cpp` and `file3.cpp` are modified, which files must be recompiled? (Assume that the modifications do not affect existing code in `myprog.cpp`.)
   d. If only the files `file2.cpp` and `file3.cpp` are modified, which files must be relinked? (Assume that the modifications do not affect existing code in `myprog.cpp`.)

9. Define the following terms:

   scope resolution operator
   separate compilation
   C++ class constructor
   default constructor

10. The following class has two constructors among its public member functions:

```
class SomeClass
{
public:
    float Func1() const;
        .
        .
        .
    SomeClass( /* in */ float f );
        // Precondition:
        //     f is assigned
        // Postcondition:
        //     Private data is initialized to f
    SomeClass();
        // Postcondition:
        //     Private data is initialized to 8.6
private:
    float someFloat;
};
```

Write declarations for the following class objects.
a. An object obj1, initialized to 0.0.
b. An object obj2, initialized to 8.6.
c. An array arr1 of class objects, each initialized to 8.6. (If it cannot be done, explain why.)
d. An array arr2 of class objects, each initialized to 24.7. (If it cannot be done, explain why.)

11. The C++ compiler will signal a syntax error in the following class declaration. What is the error?

```
class SomeClass
{
public:
    void Func1( int n );
    int  Func2();
    int  SomeClass();
private:
    int privateInt;
};
```

PROGRAMMING WARM-UP EXERCISES

1. The TimeType class supplies two member functions, Equal and LessThan, that correspond to the relational operators == and <. Show how *client code* can simulate the other four relational operators (!=, <=, >, and >=) using only the Equal and LessThan functions. Specifically, express each of the following pseudocode statements in C++, where time1 and time2 are objects of type TimeType.

a. IF time1 ≠ time2
     Set n = 1

b. IF time1 ≤ time2
    Set n = 5
c. IF time1 > time2
    Set n = 8
d. IF time1 ≥ time2
    Set n = 5

2. In reference to Programming Warm-Up Exercise 1, make life easier for the user of the `TimeType` class by adding new member functions `NotEqual`, `LessOrEqual`, `GreaterThan`, and `GreaterOrEqual` to the class.
   a. Show the function specifications (prototypes and preconditions and postconditions) as they would appear in the new class declaration.
   b. Write the function definitions as they would appear in the implementation file. (*Hint:* Instead of writing the algorithms from scratch, simply have the function bodies invoke the existing functions `Equal` and `LessThan`. And remember: Class members can refer to each other directly without using dot notation.)
3. Enhance the `TimeType` class by adding a new member function `WriteAmPm`. This function prints the time in 12-hour rather than 24-hour form, adding AM or PM at the end. Show the function specification (prototype and precondition and postcondition) as it would appear in the new class declaration. Then write the function definition as it would appear in the implementation file.
4. Add a member function named `Minus` to the `TimeType` class. This value-returning function yields the difference in seconds between the times represented by two class objects. Show the function specification (prototype and precondition and postcondition) as it would appear in the new class declaration. Then write the function definition as it would appear in the implementation file.
5. a. Design the data sets necessary to thoroughly test the `LessThan` function of the `TimeType` class.
   b. Write a driver and test the `LessThan` function using your test data.
6. a. Design the data sets necessary to thoroughly test the `Write` function of the `TimeType` class.
   b. Write a driver and test the `Write` function using your test data.
7. a. Design the data sets necessary to thoroughly test the `WriteAmPm` function of Programming Warm-Up Exercise 3.
   b. Write a driver and test the `WriteAmPm` function using your test data.
8. Reimplement the `TimeType` class so that the private data representation is a single variable:

```
long secs;
```

This variable represents time as the number of seconds since midnight. *Do not change the public interface in any way.* The user's view is still hours, minutes, and seconds, but the class's view is seconds since midnight.

Notice how this data representation simplifies the `Equal` and `LessThan` functions but makes the other operations more complicated by converting seconds back and forth to hours, minutes, and seconds. Use auxiliary functions, hidden inside the implementation file, to perform these conversions instead of duplicating the algorithms in several places.

9. The Friends program of Chapter 14 creates an address book with people's names, telephone numbers, and birth dates. A birth date is represented as three separate components of a `struct` type named `EntryType`. Modify the Friends program so that friends' birth dates are represented using the `DateType` class developed in this chapter.

10. Below is the specification of a "safe array" class, which halts the program if an array index goes out of bounds. (Recall that C++ does not check for out-of-bounds indices when you use built-in arrays.)

```
const int MAX_SIZE = 200;

class IntArray
{
public:
    int ValueAt( /* in */ int i ) const;
        // Precondition:
        //      i is assigned
        // Postcondition:
        //      IF i >= 0  &&  i < declared size of array
        //          Function value == value of array element
        //                              at index i
        //      ELSE
        //          Program has halted with error message

    void Store( /* in */ int val,
                /* in */ int i   );
        // Precondition:
        //      val and i are assigned
        // Postcondition:
        //      IF i >= 0  &&  i < declared size of array
        //          val is stored in array element i
        //      ELSE
        //          Program has halted with error message

    IntArray( /* in */ int arrSize );
        // Precondition:
        //      arrSize is assigned
        // Postcondition:
        //      IF arrSize >= 1  &&  arrSize <= MAX_SIZE
        //          Array created with all array elements == 0
        //      ELSE
        //          Program has halted with error message
private:
    int arr[MAX_SIZE];
    int size;
};
```

Implement each member function as it would appear in the implementation file. To halt the program, use the **exit** function supplied by the C++ standard library through the header file **stdlib.h** (see Appendix C).

11. a. Design the data sets necessary to thoroughly test the **IntArray** class of Programming Warm-Up Exercise 10.

  b. Write a driver and test the **IntArray** class using your test data.

PROGRAMMING PROBLEMS

1. A rational number is a number that can be expressed as a fraction whose numerator and denominator are integers. Examples of rational numbers are 0.75 (which is ¾) and 1.125 (which is ⁹⁄₈). The value π is not a rational number; it cannot be expressed as the ratio of two integers.

   Working with rational numbers on a computer is often a problem. Inaccuracies in floating point representation can yield imprecise results. For example, the result of the C++ expression

```
1.0 / 3.0 * 3.0
```

is likely to be a value like 0.999999 rather than 1.0.

   Design, implement, and test a **Rational** class that represents a rational number as a pair of integers instead of a single floating point number. The **Rational** class should have two class constructors. The first one lets the client specify an initial numerator and denominator. The other—the default constructor—creates the rational number 0, represented as a numerator of 0 and a denominator of 1. The segment of client code

```
Rational num1(1, 3);
Rational num2(3, 1);
Rational result;

cout << "The product of ";
num1.Write();
cout << " and ";
num2.Write();
cout << " is ";
result = num1.MultipliedBy(num2);
result.Write();
```

would produce the output

```
The product of 1/3 and 3/1 is 1/1
```

   At the very least, you should provide the following operations:

• constructors for explicit as well as default initialization of **Rational** objects
• arithmetic operations that add, subtract, multiply, and divide two **Rational** objects. These should be implemented as value-returning functions, each returning a **Rational** object.

- a Boolean operation that compares two `Rational` objects for equality
- an output operation that displays the value of a `Rational` object in the form numerator/denominator

Include any additional operations that you think would be useful for a rational number class.

2. A complex ("imaginary") number has the form $a + bi$, where i is the square root of -1. Here, a is called the real part and b is called the imaginary part. Alternatively, $a + bi$ can be expressed as the ordered pair of real numbers (a, b).

   Arithmetic operations on two complex numbers (a, b) and (c, d) are as follows:

   $$(a,b) + (c,d) = (a + c, b + d)$$
   $$(a,b) - (c,d) = (a - c, b - d)$$
   $$(a,b) * (c,d) = (a * c - b * d, a * d + b * c)$$
   $$(a,b) / (c,d) = (\frac{a*c + b*d}{c^2 + d^2}, \frac{b*c - a*d}{c^2 + d^2})$$

   Also, the absolute value (or magnitude) of a complex number is defined as

   $$|(a,b)| = \sqrt{a^2 + b^2}$$

   Design, implement, and test a complex number class that represents the real and imaginary parts as double precision values (data type `double`) and provides at least the following operations:

   - constructors for explicit as well as default initialization. The default initial value should be (0.0, 0.0).
   - arithmetic operations that add, subtract, multiply, and divide two complex numbers. These should be implemented as value-returning functions, each returning a class object.
   - a complex absolute value operation
   - two observer operations, `RealPart` and `ImagPart`, that return the real and imaginary parts of a complex number

3. Design, implement, and test a countdown timer class named `Timer`. This class mimics a real-world timer by counting off seconds, starting from an initial value. When the timer reaches zero, it beeps (by sending the alert character, `'\a'`, to the standard output device). Some appropriate operations might be the following:

   - Create a timer, initializing it to a specified number of seconds.
   - Start the timer.
   - Reset the timer to some value.

   When the `Start` operation is invoked, it should repeatedly decrement and output the current value of the timer approximately every second. To delay the program for one second, use a For loop whose body does absolutely nothing; that is, its body is the null statement. Experiment with the number of loop iterations to achieve as close to a one-second delay as you can.

   If your C++ standard library provides functions to clear the screen and to position the cursor anywhere on the screen, you might want to do the following. Begin by clearing the screen. Then, always display the timer value at the same position in the center of the screen. Each output should overwrite the previous value displayed, just like a real-world timer.

4. In Chapter 12, we introduced the list informally as an abstract data type. Design, implement, and test a class named `IntList`. Each `IntList` object is an unordered list of up to 100 `int` values. (Recall that an unordered list is one whose components are not assumed to be arranged in order of value.) Include at least the following operations:

- Create an initially empty list.
- Report whether the list is empty (TRUE or FALSE).
- Report whether the list is full (TRUE or FALSE).
- Insert a specified integer into the list.
- Delete a specified integer from the list.
- Search for a specified integer, returning TRUE or FALSE according to whether the item is present in the list.
- Sort the list into ascending order.
- Output all the items in the list.

Think carefully as you choose a precondition for each operation. For example, the precondition for the `Delete` operation should be that the list is not empty. Fortunately, the client can check this precondition by first invoking the operation that reports whether the list is empty. You should also decide whether it is allowed to delete a nonexistent integer from the list. If it is allowed, the `Delete` operation should silently have no effect (and the postcondition should make this clear to the user). If it is not allowed, you should say so in the precondition. The burden of error checking is then on the caller, not on the `Delete` operation.

For the concrete data representation of `IntList`, you might consider using two items: a 100-element `int` array to hold the list items, and a simple variable that stores the current length of the list.

5. Modify Programming Problem 4 by creating an *ordered* integer list class, `OrdIntList`. Keep the list in ascending order at all times when inserting and deleting items. Remove the `Sort` operation; it is no longer necessary. Notice that the algorithms for inserting, deleting, and searching are now different from those in Programming Problem 4. You may want to review the discussions of these operations in Chapter 12.

CASE STUDY FOLLOW-UP

1. Classify each of the eight member functions of the `DateType` class as a constructor, a transformer, or an observer operation.
2. a. Design the data sets necessary to thoroughly test the `ComparedTo` function of the `DateType` class.
   b. Write a driver and test the `ComparedTo` function using your test data.
3. a. Design the data sets necessary to thoroughly test the `Increment` function of the `DateType` class.
   b. Write a driver and test the `Increment` function using your test data.

16

Object-Oriented
Software Development

GOALS

- To be able to distinguish between structured (procedural) programming and object-oriented programming.
- To be able to define the characteristics of an object-oriented programming language.
- To be able to create a new C++ class from an existing class by using inheritance.
- To be able to create a new C++ class from an existing class by using composition.
- To be able to distinguish between static and dynamic binding of operations to objects.
- To be able to apply the object-oriented design methodology to solve a problem.
- To be able to take an object-oriented design and code it in C++.

When we examined `struct` data types in Chapter 14, we explained that the components combine to describe an object or an entity of some kind. We also introduced the concept of data abstraction—the separation of the logical properties of data and actions from the implementation details.

In Chapter 15, we expanded on these concepts by defining the notion of an abstract data type (ADT) and by using the C++ class mechanism to incorporate both data and operations into a single data type. We described how each object of a given class maintains its own private data and is manipulated by calling its public member functions.

In this chapter, we examine how classes and objects can be used to guide the entire software development process. Although the design phase precedes the implementation phase in the development of software, we reverse the order of presentation in this chapter. We begin with *object-oriented programming*, a topic that includes design but is more about implementation issues. We describe the basic principles, terminology, and programming language features associated with the object-oriented approach. After presenting these fundamental concepts, we look more closely at the design phase—*object-oriented design*.

Object-Oriented Programming

Throughout this text we have used top-down design (also called *structured design*) to develop algorithmic problem solutions. Top-down design decomposes a problem into modules, where each module is a self-contained collection of steps that solves one part of the overall problem. The process of implementing a top-down design is often called **structured** (or **procedural**) **programming**. Some modules are translated directly into a few programming language instructions, whereas others are coded as functions with or without parameters. The end result is a program that is a collection of interacting functions (see Figure 16-1). Throughout structured design and structured programming, data are considered passive quantities to be acted upon by control structures and functions.

Structured design is satisfactory for programming in the small (a concept we discussed in Chapter 4) but often does not "scale up" well for programming in the large. In building large software systems, structured design has two important limitations. First, the technique yields an inflexible structure. If the top-level algorithm requires modification, the changes may force many lower level algorithms to be modified as well. Second, the technique does not lend itself easily to code reuse. By *code reuse* we mean the ability to use pieces of code—either as they are or adapted slightly—in other sections of the program or in other programs. It is rare to be able to take a complicated C++ function and reuse it easily in a different context.

■ FIGURE 16-1

Program Resulting
from Structured
(Procedural)
Programming

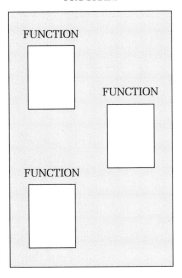

■ FIGURE 16-1

Program Resulting
from Structured
(Procedural)
Programming

A methodology that often works better for creating large software systems is object-oriented design (OOD), which we introduced briefly in Chapter 4. OOD decomposes a problem into objects—self-contained entities composed of data and operations on the data. The process of implementing an object-oriented design is called **object-oriented programming (OOP).** The end result is a program that is a collection of interacting objects (see Figure 16-2). In OOD and OOP, data plays a leading role; the primary contribution of algorithms is to implement the operations on objects. In this chapter, we'll see why OOD tends to result in programs that are more flexible and conducive to code reuse than programs produced by structured design.

Several programming languages have been created specifically to support OOD and OOP: C++, Smalltalk, Simula, CLOS, Objective-C, Eiffel, Actor, Object-Pascal, recent versions of Turbo Pascal, and others. These languages, called *object-oriented programming languages*, have facilities for

1. data abstraction
2. inheritance
3. dynamic binding

You have already seen that C++ supports data abstraction through the class mechanism. Some non-OOP languages also have facilities for data abstraction. But only OOP languages support the other two concepts—*inheritance* and *dynamic binding*. Before we define these two concepts, we discuss some of the fundamental ideas and terminology of object-oriented programming.

■ FIGURE 16-2

Program Resulting
from Object-
Oriented
Programming

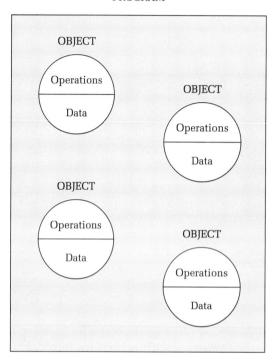

■ FIGURE 16-2

Program Resulting from Object-Oriented Programming

Structured (Procedural) Programming   The construction of programs that are collections of interacting functions or procedures.

Object-Oriented Programming (OOP)   The use of data abstraction, inheritance, and dynamic binding to construct programs that are collections of interacting objects.

 Objects

The major principles of OOP originated as far back as the mid-1960s with a language called Simula. However, much of the current terminology of OOP is due to Smalltalk, a language developed in the late 1970s at Xerox's Palo Alto Research Center. In OOP, the term *object* has a very specific meaning: it is a self-contained entity encapsulating data and operations on the data. In other words, an object represents an instance of an ADT. More specifically, an object has an internal *state* (the current values of its private data, called *instance variables*), and it has a set of *methods* (public operations). Methods are the only means by which an object's state can be inspected or modified by another object. An object-oriented program consists of a collection of objects, communicating with one another by *message passing*. If object *A* wants object *B* to perform some task, object *A* sends a message containing the name of the object (*B*, in this case) and the name of the particular method to execute. *B* responds by executing this method in its own way, possibly changing its state and sending messages to other objects as well.

As you can tell, an object is quite different from a traditional data structure. A C++ struct is a passive data structure that contains only data and is acted upon by a program. In contrast, an object is an active data structure; the data and the code that manipulates the data are bound together within the object. In OOP jargon, an object knows how to manipulate itself.

The vocabulary of Smalltalk has influenced the vocabulary of OOP. The literature of OOP is full of phrases such as "methods," "instance variables," and "sending a message to." But don't be put off by the vocabulary. Here are some OOP terms and their C++ equivalents:

OOP	C++
Object	Class object or class instance
Instance variable	Private data member
Method	Public member function
Message passing	Function call (to a public member function)

In C++, we define the properties and behavior of objects by using the class mechanism. Within a program, classes can be related to each other in various ways. The three most common relationships are:

1. Two classes are independent of each other and have nothing in common.
2. Two classes are related by *inheritance*.
3. Two classes are related by *composition*.

The first relationship—none—is not very "interesting." Let's look at the other two—inheritance and composition.

 Inheritance

In the world at large, it is often possible to arrange concepts into an *inheritance hierarchy*—a hierarchy in which each concept inherits the properties of the concept immediately above it in the hierarchy. For example, we might classify different kinds of vehicles according to the inheritance hierarchy in Figure 16-3. Moving down the hierarchy, each kind of vehicle is more specialized than its *parent* (and all of its *ancestors*) and is more general than its

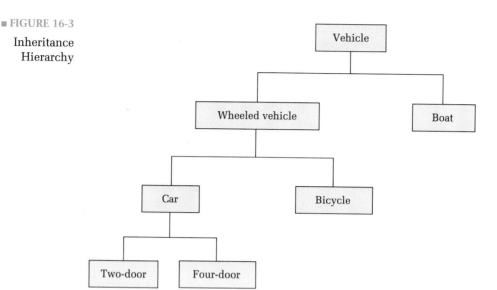

child (and all of its *descendants*). A wheeled vehicle inherits properties common to all vehicles (it holds one or more people and carries them from place to place) but has an additional property that makes it more specialized (it has wheels). A car inherits properties common to all wheeled vehicles but also has additional, more specialized properties (four wheels, an engine, a body, and so forth).

The inheritance relationship can be viewed as an *is-a relationship*. Every two-door car is a car, every car is a wheeled vehicle, and every wheeled vehicle is a vehicle.

OOP languages provide a way of creating inheritance relationships among classes. In these languages, **inheritance** is the mechanism by which one class acquires the properties of another class. You can take an existing class *A* (called the **base class** or **superclass**) and create from it a new class *B* (called the **derived class** or **subclass**). The derived class *B* inherits all the properties of its base class *A*. In particular, the data and operations defined for *A* are now also defined for *B*. (Notice the is-a relationship—every *B* is also an *A*.) The idea, next, is to specialize class *B*, usually by adding specific properties to those already inherited from *A*. Let's look at an example in C++.

Inheritance A mechanism by which one class acquires the properties—the data and operations—of another class.

Base Class (Superclass) The class being inherited from.

Derived Class (Subclass) The class that inherits.

Deriving One Class from Another

Suppose that someone has already written a `Time` class with the following specification, abbreviated by omitting the preconditions and postconditions:

```
class Time
{
public:
    void Set( /* in */ int hours,
              /* in */ int minutes,
              /* in */ int seconds );
    void Increment();
    void Write() const;
    Time( /* in */ int initHrs,          // Constructor
          /* in */ int initMins,
          /* in */ int initSecs );
    Time();                              // Default constructor,
private:                                 //   setting time to 0:0:0
    int hrs;
    int mins;
    int secs;
};
```

This class is the same as our `TimeType` class of Chapter 15, simplified by omitting the `Equal` and `LessThan` member functions. Figure 16-4 displays a *class interface diagram* for the `Time` class. The public interface, shown as ovals in the side of the large circle, consists of the operations available to client code. The private data items shown in the interior are inaccessible to clients.

Suppose we want to modify the `Time` class by adding, as private data, a variable of an enumeration type indicating the (American) time zone—EST for Eastern Standard Time, CST for Central Standard Time, MST for Mountain Standard Time, PST for Pacific Standard Time, EDT for Eastern Daylight Time, CDT for Central Daylight Time, MDT for Mountain Daylight Time, or PDT for Pacific Daylight Time. We'll need to modify the `Set` function and the class constructors to accommodate a time zone value. And the `Write` function should print the time in the form

```
12:34:10 CST
```

The `Increment` function, which advances the time by one second, does not need to be changed.

To add these time-zone features to the `Time` class, the conventional approach would be to obtain the source code found in the `time.cpp` implementation file, analyze in detail how the class is implemented, then modify and recompile the source code. This process has several drawbacks. If `Time` is an

■ FIGURE 16-4

Class Interface
Diagram for
Time Class

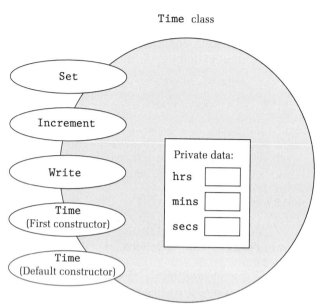

off-the-shelf class on a system, the source code for the implementation is probably unavailable. Even if it is available, modifying it may introduce bugs into a previously debugged solution. Access to the source code also violates a principal benefit of abstraction: users of an abstraction should not need to know how it is implemented.

In C++, as in other OOP languages, there is a far quicker and safer way in which to add time-zone features: use inheritance. Let's derive a new class from the Time class and then specialize it. This new, extended time class— call it ExtTime—inherits the members of its base class, Time. Here is the declaration of ExtTime:

```
enum ZoneType {EST, CST, MST, PST, EDT, CDT, MDT, PDT};

class ExtTime : public Time
{
public:
    void Set( /* in */ int       hours,
              /* in */ int       minutes,
              /* in */ int       seconds,
              /* in */ ZoneType  timeZone );
    void Write() const;
    ExtTime( /* in */ int       initHrs,        // Constructor
             /* in */ int       initMins,
             /* in */ int       initSecs,
             /* in */ ZoneType  initZone );
```

```
    ExtTime();                          // Default constructor,
                                        //   setting time to
private:                                //   0:0:0 EST
    ZoneType zone;
};
```

The opening line

```
class ExtTime : public Time
```

states that `ExtTime` is derived from `Time`. The reserved word `public` declares `Time` to be a *public base class* of `ExtTime`. This means that all public members of `Time` (except constructors) are also public members of `ExtTime`. In other words, `Time`'s member functions `Set`, `Increment`, and `Write` can also be invoked for `ExtTime` objects.* However, the public part of `ExtTime` specializes the base class by reimplementing (**overriding**) the inherited functions `Set` and `Write` and by providing its own constructors.

Overriding Reimplementing a member function inherited from a parent class.

The private part of `ExtTime` declares that a new private member is added: zone. The private members of `ExtTime` are therefore `hrs`, `mins`, `secs` (all inherited from `Time`), and `zone`. Figure 16-5 pictures the relationship between the `ExtTime` and `Time` classes.

This diagram shows that each `ExtTime` object has a `Time` object as a *subobject*. Every `ExtTime` is a `Time`, and more. C++ uses the terms base class and derived class instead of superclass and subclass. The terms superclass and

---

*If a class declaration omits the word `public` and begins as

```
class DerivedClass : BaseClass
```

or if it explicitly uses the word private,

```
class DerivedClass : private BaseClass
```

then `BaseClass` is called a *private base class* of `DerivedClass`. Public members of `BaseClass` are *not* public members of `DerivedClass`. That is, clients of `DerivedClass` cannot invoke `BaseClass` operations on `DerivedClass` objects. We do not work with private base classes in this book.

■ FIGURE 16-5   Class Interface Diagram for ExtTime Class

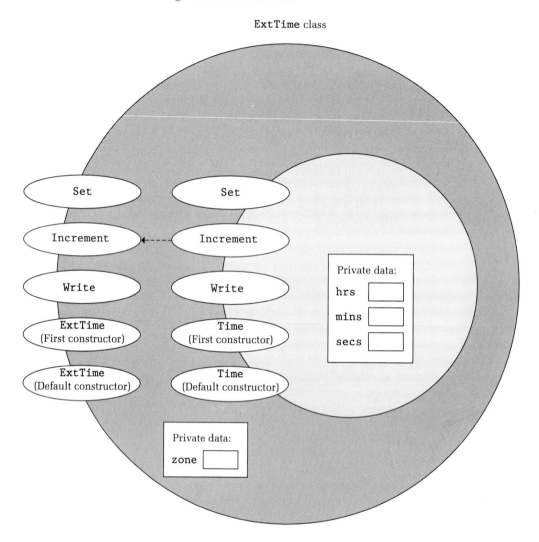

subclass can be confusing because the prefix *sub-* usually implies something smaller than the original (for example, subset of a mathematical set). In contrast, a subclass is often "bigger" than its superclass—that is, it has more data and/or functions.

In Figure 16-5, you see an arrow between the two ovals labeled Increment. Because Time is a public base class of ExtTime, and because Increment is not overridden by ExtTime, the Increment function available to clients of ExtTime is the same as the one inherited from Time. We use the arrow between the corresponding ovals to indicate this fact. (Notice in the diagram that Time's constructors are operations on Time, not on ExtTime. The ExtTime class must have its own constructors.)

SOFTWARE ENGINEERING TIP

Inheritance and Accessibility

With C++, it is important to understand that inheritance does not imply accessibility. Although a derived class inherits the members of its base class, both private and public, it cannot access the private members of the base class. Figure 16-5 shows the variables hrs, mins, and secs to be encapsulated within the Time class. Neither external client code nor ExtTime member functions can refer to these three variables directly. If a derived class were able to access the private members of its base class, any programmer could derive a class from another and then write code to directly inspect or modify the private data, defeating the benefits of encapsulation and information hiding.

Specification of the ExtTime Class

Below is the fully documented specification of the ExtTime class. Notice that the preprocessor directive

```
#include "time.h"
```

is necessary for the compiler to verify the consistency of the derived class with its base class.

```
//****************************************************************
// SPECIFICATION FILE (exttime.h)
// This file gives the specification of an ExtTime abstract data
// type.  The Time class is a public base class of ExtTime, so
// public operations of Time are also public operations of ExtTime.
//****************************************************************
#include "time.h"

enum ZoneType {EST, CST, MST, PST, EDT, CDT, MDT, PDT};
```

```
class ExtTime : public Time
{
public:
    void Set( /* in */ int        hours,
              /* in */ int        minutes,
              /* in */ int        seconds,
              /* in */ ZoneType timeZone );
        // Precondition:
        //      0 <= hours <= 23  &&  0 <= minutes <= 59
        //   && 0 <= seconds <= 59  &&  timeZone is assigned
        // Postcondition:
        //      Time is set according to the incoming parameters

    void Write() const;
        // Postcondition:
        //      Time has been output in the form HH:MM:SS ZZZ
        //      where ZZZ is the time zone

    ExtTime( /* in */ int        initHrs,
             /* in */ int        initMins,
             /* in */ int        initSecs,
             /* in */ ZoneType initZone );
        // Precondition:
        //      0 <= initHrs <= 23  &&  0 <= initMins <= 59
        //   && 0 <= initSecs <= 59  &&  initZone is assigned
        // Postcondition:
        //      Class object is constructed
        //   && Time is set according to the incoming parameters

    ExtTime();
        // Postcondition:
        //      Class object is constructed
        //   && Time is 0:0:0 Eastern Standard Time
private:
    ZoneType zone;
};
```

With this new class, the programmer can set the time with a time zone (via a class constructor or the overridden Set function), output the time with its time zone (via the overridden Write function), and increment the time by one second (via the inherited Increment function):

```
#include "exttime.h"
    .
    .
    .
ExtTime time1(8, 35, 0, PST);
ExtTime time2;                        // Default constructor called
```

```
time2.Write();                    // Outputs 0:0:0 EST
cout << endl;

time2.Set(16, 49, 23, CDT);
time2.Write();                    // Outputs 16:49:23 CDT
cout << endl;

time1.Increment();
time1.Increment();
time1.Write();                    // Outputs 08:35:02 PST
cout << endl;
    .
    .
    .
```

Implementation of the ExtTime Class

The implementation of the ExtTime class needs to deal only with the new features that are different from Time. Specifically, we must write code to override the Set and Write functions and we must write the two constructors.

With derived classes, constructors are subject to special rules. At run time, the base class constructor is implicitly called first, before the body of the derived class's constructor executes. Additionally, if the base class constructor requires parameters, these parameters must be passed by the derived class's constructor. To see how these rules pertain, let's examine the implementation file exttime.cpp (see Figure 16-6).

■ FIGURE 16-6

ExtTime
Implementation
File

```
//*************************************************************
// IMPLEMENTATION FILE (exttime.cpp)
// This file implements the ExtTime member functions.
// The Time class is a public base class of ExtTime
//*************************************************************
#include "exttime.h"
#include <iostream.h>

// Additional private members of class:
//     ZoneType zone;


//*************************************************************

ExtTime::ExtTime( /* in */ int      initHrs,
                  /* in */ int      initMins,
                  /* in */ int      initSecs,
                  /* in */ ZoneType initZone )

    : Time(initHrs, initMins, initSecs)

// Constructor
```

■ FIGURE 16-6

(continued)

```
// Precondition:
//     0 <= initHrs <= 23   &&   0 <= initMins <= 59
//   && 0 <= initSecs <= 59   &&   initZone is assigned
// Postcondition:
//     Time is set according to initHrs, initMins, and initSecs
//     (via call to base class constructor)
//   && zone == initZone

{
    zone = initZone;
}

//*****************************************************************

ExtTime::ExtTime()

// Default constructor

// Postcondition:
//     Time is 0:0:0 (via implicit call to base class's
//     default constructor)
//   && zone == EST

{
    zone = EST;
}

//*****************************************************************

void ExtTime::Set( /* in */ int       hours,
                   /* in */ int       minutes,
                   /* in */ int       seconds,
                   /* in */ ZoneType timeZone )

// Precondition:
//     0 <= hours <= 23   &&   0 <= minutes <= 59
//   && 0 <= seconds <= 59   &&   timeZone is assigned
// Postcondition:
//     Time is set according to hours, minutes, and seconds
//   && zone == timeZone

{
    Time::Set(hours, minutes, seconds);
    zone = timeZone;
}

//*****************************************************************
```

■ FIGURE 16-6

(continued)

```
void ExtTime::Write() const

// Postcondition:
//     Time has been output in the form HH:MM:SS ZZZ
//     where ZZZ is the time zone

{
    static char zoneString[8][4] =
    {
        "EST", "CST", "MST", "PST", "EDT", "CDT", "MDT", "PDT"
    };

    Time::Write();
    cout << ' ' << zoneString[zone];
}
```

In the first constructor in Figure 16-6, notice the syntax by which a constructor passes parameters to its base class constructor:

```
ExtTime::ExtTime( /* in */ int      initHrs,
                  /* in */ int      initMins,
                  /* in */ int      initSecs,
                  /* in */ ZoneType initZone )

    : Time(initHrs, initMins, initSecs)   ← Constructor initializer

{
    zone = initZone;
}
```

After the parameter list to the `ExtTime` constructor (but before its body), you insert what is called a *constructor initializer*—a colon and then the name of the base class along with the actual parameters to *its* constructor. When an `ExtTime` object is created with a declaration such as

```
ExtTime time1(8, 35, 0, PST);
```

the `ExtTime` constructor receives four parameters. The first three are simply passed along to the `Time` class constructor by means of the constructor initializer. After the `Time` class constructor has executed (creating the base class subobject as shown in Figure 16-5), the body of the `ExtTime` constructor executes, setting `zone` equal to the fourth parameter.

The second constructor in Figure 16-6 (the default constructor) does not need a constructor initializer; there are no parameters to pass to the base class's default constructor. When an `ExtTime` object is created with the declaration

```
ExtTime time2;
```

the `ExtTime` class's default constructor first implicitly calls `Time`'s default constructor, after which its body executes, setting `zone` to `EST`.

Next, look at the `Set` function in Figure 16-6. This function overrides the `Set` function inherited from the base class. Consequently, there are two distinct `Set` functions, one a public member of the `Time` class, the other a public member of the `ExtTime` class. Their full names are `Time::Set` and `ExtTime::Set`. In Figure 16-6, the `ExtTime::Set` function begins by "reaching up" into its base class and calling `Time::Set` to set the hours, minutes, and seconds. (Remember that a class derived from `Time` cannot access the private data `hrs`, `mins`, and `secs` directly; these variables are private to the `Time` class.) The function then finishes by assigning a value to `ExtTime`'s private data, the `zone` variable.

The `Write` function in Figure 16-6 uses a similar strategy. It reaches up into its base class and invokes `Time::Write` to output the hours, minutes, and seconds. Then it outputs a string corresponding to the time zone. (Recall that a value of enumeration type cannot be output directly in C++. If we were to print the value of `zone` directly, the output would be an integer from 0 through 7—the internal representations of the `ZoneType` values. The `Write` function establishes an array of eight strings and selects the correct string by using `zone` to index into the array.)

Now we can compile the file `exttime.cpp` into an object code file, say, `exttime.obj`. After writing a test driver and compiling it into `test.obj`, we can obtain an executable file by linking three object files:

1. `test.obj`
2. `exttime.obj`
3. `time.obj`

We can then test the resulting program.

The remarkable thing about derived classes and inheritance is that modification of the base class is unnecessary. The source code for the implementation of the `Time` class may be unavailable. Yet variations of this ADT can continue to be created without that source code, in ways the creator never even considered. Through classes and inheritance, OOP languages facilitate code reuse. A class such as `Time` can be used as-is in many different contexts, or it can be adapted to a particular context by using inheritance. Inheritance allows us to create *extensible* data abstractions—a derived class typically extends the base class by including additional private data or public operations or both.

Composition

Earlier we said that two classes typically exhibit one of the following relationships: they are independent of each other, they are related by inheritance, or they are related by **composition.** Composition (or **containment**) is the relationship in which the internal data of one class *A* includes an object of another class *B*. Stated another way, a *B* object is contained within an *A* object.

Composition (Containment) A mechanism by which the internal data (the state) of one class includes an object of another class.

C++ does not have (or need) any special language notation for composition. You simply declare an object of one class to be one of the data members of another class. Let's look at an example.

Design of a `TimeCard` Class

You are developing a program to manage a factory's payroll. Employees are issued time cards containing their ID numbers. When reporting for work, an employee "punches in" by inserting the card into a clock, which punches the current time onto the card. When leaving work, the employee takes a new card and "punches out" to record the departure time. For your program, you decide that you need a `TimeCard` ADT to represent an employee's time card. The abstract data consist of an ID number and a time. The abstract operations include Punch the Time, Print the Time Card Data, constructor operations, and others. To implement the ADT, you must choose a concrete data representation for the abstract data and you must implement the operations. Assuming an employee ID number is a large integer value, you choose the `long` data type to represent the ID number. To represent time, you remember that one of your friends has already written and debugged a `Time` class (we'll use the one from earlier in this chapter). At this point, you create a `TimeCard` class declaration as follows:

```
#include "time.h"
    :
    :
class TimeCard
{
```

```
public:
    void Punch( /* in */  int hours,
                /* in */  int minutes,
                /* in */  int seconds );
    void Print() const;
        .
        .
        .
    TimeCard( /* in */  long idNum,
              /* in */  int  initHrs,
              /* in */  int  initMins,
              /* in */  int  initSecs );
    TimeCard();
private:
    long id;
    Time timeStamp;
};
```

In designing the `TimeCard` class, you have used composition; a `TimeCard` object is composed of a `Time` object (and a `long` variable). Composition creates a *has-a relationship*—a `TimeCard` object *has a* `Time` object as a subobject (see Figure 16-7).

Implementation of the TimeCard *Class*

The private data of `TimeCard` consists of a `long` variable named `id` and a `Time` object named `timeStamp`. The `TimeCard` member functions can manipulate `id` by using ordinary built-in operations, but they must manipulate `timeStamp` through the member functions defined for the `Time` class. For example, you could implement the `Print` and `Punch` functions as follows:

```
void TimeCard::Print() const
{
    cout << "ID: " << id << " Time: ";
    timeStamp.Write();
}

void TimeCard::Punch( /* in */  int hours,
                      /* in */  int minutes,
                      /* in */  int seconds )
{
    timeStamp.Set(hours, minutes, seconds);
}
```

Implementing the class constructors is a bit more complicated to describe. Let's start with an implementation of the first constructor shown in the `TimeCard` class declaration:

■ FIGURE 16-7   Class Interface Diagram for `TimeCard` Class

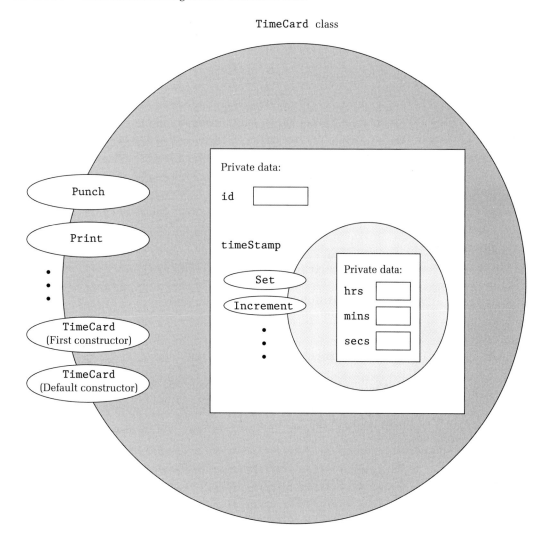

```
TimeCard::TimeCard( /* in */ long idNum,
                    /* in */ int  initHrs,
                    /* in */ int  initMins,
                    /* in */ int  initSecs )

    : timeStamp(initHrs, initMins, initSecs) ←  Constructor initializer

{
    id = idNum;
}
```

This is the second time we've seen the unusual notation—the constructor initializer—inserted between the formal parameter list and the body of a constructor. The first time was when we implemented the parameterized ExtTime class constructor (Figure 16-6). There, we used the constructor initializer to pass some of the incoming parameters to the base class constructor. Here, we use a constructor initializer to pass some of the parameters to a member object's (timeStamp's) constructor. Whether you are using inheritance or composition, the purpose of a constructor initializer is the same: to pass parameters to another constructor. The only difference is the following: With inheritance, you specify the name of the *base class* prior to the actual parameter list:

```
ExtTime::ExtTime( /* in */ int      initHrs,
                  /* in */ int      initMins,
                  /* in */ int      initSecs,
                  /* in */ ZoneType initZone )

    : Time(initHrs, initMins, initSecs)
```

With composition, you specify the name of the *member object* prior to the actual parameter list:

```
TimeCard::TimeCard( /* in */ long idNum,
                    /* in */ int  initHrs,
                    /* in */ int  initMins,
                    /* in */ int  initSecs )

    : timeStamp(initHrs, initMins, initSecs)
```

Furthermore, if a class has several members that are objects of classes with parameterized constructors, you form a list of constructor initializers separated by commas:

```
SomeClass::SomeClass( ... )

    : memberObject1(param1, param2), memberObject2(param3)
```

Having discussed both inheritance and composition, we can give a complete description of the order in which constructors are executed:

Given a class X, if X is a derived class, its base class constructor is executed first. Next, constructors for member objects (if any) are executed. Finally, the body of X's constructor is executed.

The Slicing Problem

Our `Print` function uses pass-by-value for the formal parameter `someTime`. Pass-by-value sends a copy of the actual parameter to the formal parameter. Whenever you pass an object of a child class to an object of its parent class using pass-by-value, only the data members they have in common are copied. Remember that a child class is often "larger" than its parent—that is, it contains additional data members. For example, a `Time` object has three data members (`hrs`, `mins`, and `secs`), but an `ExtTime` object has four data members (`hrs`, `mins`, `secs`, and `zone`). When the larger class object is copied to the smaller formal parameter using pass-by-value, the extra data members are discarded or "sliced off." This situation is called the *slicing problem* (see Figure 16-8).

(The slicing problem also occurs with assignment operations. In the statement

```
parentClassObject = childClassObject;
```

only the data members that the two objects have in common are copied. Additional data members contained in `childClassObject` are not copied.)

With pass-by-reference, the slicing problem does not occur because the *address* of the actual parameter is sent to the function. Let's change the heading of our `Print` function so that `someTime` is a reference parameter:

```
void Print( /* in */ Time& someTime )
```

Now when we pass `endTime` as the actual parameter, its address is sent to the function. Its time zone member is not sliced off because no copying takes place. But to our dismay, the `Print` function *still* prints only three of `endTime`'s data members—hours, minutes, and seconds. Within the `Print` function, the difficulty is that static binding is used in the statement

```
someTime.Write();
```

The compiler must generate machine language code for the `Print` function at compile time, but the type of the actual parameter (`Time` or `ExtTime`) isn't known until run time. How can the compiler know which `Write` function to use—`Time::Write` or `ExtTime::Write`? The compiler cannot know, so it uses `Time::Write` because the formal parameter `someTime` is of type `Time`. Therefore, the `Print` function always prints just three values—hours, minutes, and seconds—regardless of the type of the actual parameter. Fortunately, C++ provides a very simple solution to our problem: *virtual functions*.

■ FIGURE 16-8   The Slicing Problem Resulting from Pass-by-Value

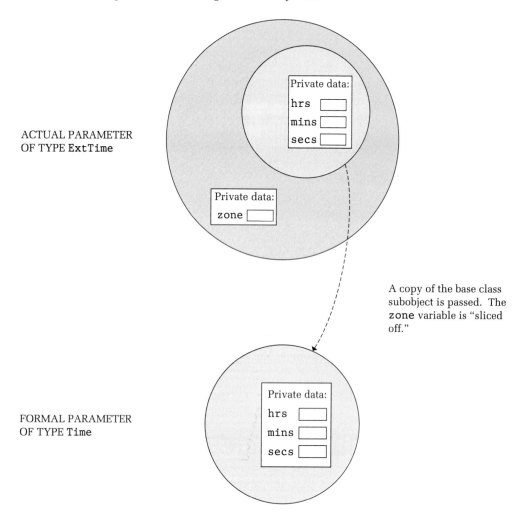

ACTUAL PARAMETER
OF TYPE ExtTime

A copy of the base class
subobject is passed. The
zone variable is "sliced
off."

FORMAL PARAMETER
OF TYPE Time

Virtual Functions

Suppose we make one small change to our `Time` class declaration: we begin
the declaration of the `Write` function with the reserved word `virtual`.

```
class Time
{
public:
    .
    .
    .
    virtual void Write() const;
    .
    .
    .
```

```
private:
    ⋮
};
```

Declaring a member function to be `virtual` instructs the compiler to generate code that guarantees **dynamic** (run-time) **binding** of a function to an object. That is, the determination of which function to call is postponed until run time. (Note that to make `Write` a virtual function, the word `virtual` appears in one place only—the `Time` class declaration. It does not appear in the `Write` function definition that is located in the `time.cpp` file, nor does it appear in any descendant class—such as `ExtTime`—that overrides the `Write` function.)

Dynamic Binding   The run-time determination of which function to call for a particular object.

Virtual functions work in the following way. If a class object is passed *by reference* to some function, and if the body of that function contains a statement

```
formalParam.MemberFunc( ... );
```

then

1. If `MemberFunc` is not a virtual function, the type of the *formal parameter* determines which function to call. (Static binding is used.)
2. If `MemberFunc` is a virtual function, the type of the *actual parameter* determines which function to call. (Dynamic binding is used.)

With just one word—`virtual`—the difficulties we encountered with our `Print` function disappear entirely. If we declare `Write` to be a virtual function in the `Time` class, the function

```
void Print( /* in */ Time& someTime )
{
    ⋮
    someTime.Write();
    ⋮
}
```

works correctly for actual parameters either of type `Time` or of type `ExtTime`. The correct `Write` function (`Time::Write` or `ExtTime::Write`) is invoked because the actual parameter carries the information necessary at run time to choose the appropriate function. Deriving a new and unanticipated class from `Time` presents no complications. If this new class overrides the `Write` function, then our `Print` function still works correctly. Dynamic binding ensures that each object knows how to print itself, and the appropriate version will be invoked. In OOP terminology, `Write` is a **polymorphic operation**—an operation that has multiple meanings depending on the type of the object that responds to it at run time.

Polymorphic Operation   An operation that has multiple meanings depending on the type of the object to which it is bound at run time.

Here are some things to know about using virtual functions in C++:

1. To obtain dynamic binding, you must use pass-by-reference when passing a class object to a function. If you use pass-by-value, the compiler does not use the `virtual` mechanism; instead, member slicing and static binding occur.
2. In the declaration of a virtual function, the word `virtual` appears only in the base class, not in any derived class.
3. If a base class declares a virtual function, it *must* implement that function, even if the body is empty.
4. A derived class is not required to provide its own reimplementation of a virtual function. In this case, the base class's version is used by default.
5. A derived class cannot redefine the function return type of a virtual function.

 Object-Oriented Design

We have looked at language features that let us implement an object-oriented design. Now let's turn to the phase that precedes implementation—OOD itself.

A computer program usually models some real-life activity or concept. A banking program models the real-life activities associated with a bank. A spreadsheet program models a real spreadsheet, a large paper form used by accountants and financial planners. A robotics program models human perception and human motion.

Nearly always, the aspect of the world that we are modeling (the *application domain* or *problem domain*) consists of objects—checking accounts, bank tellers, spreadsheet rows, spreadsheet columns, robot arms, robot legs. The computer program that solves the real-life problem also includes objects (the *solution domain*)—counters, lists, menus, windows, and so forth. OOD is based on the philosophy that programs are easier to write and understand if the major objects in a program correspond closely to the objects in the problem domain.

There are many ways in which to perform object-oriented design. Different authors advocate different techniques. Our purpose is not to choose one particular technique or to present a summary of all the techniques. It is to describe a three-step process that captures the essence of OOD:

1. Identify the objects and operations.
2. Determine the relationships among objects.
3. Design the driver.

In this section, we do not show a complete example of an object-oriented design of a problem solution—we save that for the Problem-Solving Case Study at the end of the chapter. Instead, we describe the important issues involved in each of the three steps.

Step 1: Identify the Objects and Operations

Recall that structured (top-down) design begins with identification of the major actions the program is to perform. In contrast, OOD begins by identifying the major objects and the associated operations on those objects. In both design methods, it is often difficult to see where to start.

A good way to start to identify solution-domain objects is to look at the problem domain. More specifically, go to the problem definition and look for important nouns and verbs. The nouns (and noun phrases) may suggest objects; the verbs (and verb phrases) may suggest operations. For example, the problem definition for a banking program might include the following sentences:

. . . The program must handle a customer's savings account. The customer is allowed to deposit funds into the account and withdraw funds from the account, and the bank must pay interest on a quarterly basis. . . .

In these sentences, the key nouns are

Savings account
Customer

and the key verb phrases are

Deposit funds
Withdraw funds
Pay interest

Although we are working with a very small portion of the entire problem definition, the list of nouns suggests two potential objects: `savingsAccount` and `customer`. The operations on a `savingsAccount` object are suggested by the list of verb phrases—namely, `Deposit`, `Withdraw`, and `PayInterest`. What are the operations on a `customer` object? We would need more information from the rest of the problem definition in order to answer this question. In fact, `customer` may not turn out to be a useful object at all. The nouns-and-verbs technique is only a starting point—it points us to *potential* objects and operations.

Determining which nouns and verbs are significant is one of the most difficult aspects of OOD. There are no cookbook formulas for doing so, and there probably never will be. Not all nouns become objects, and not all verbs become operations. The nouns-and-verbs technique is imperfect, but it does give us a first approximation to a solution.

The solution domain includes not only objects drawn from the problem domain but also *implementation-level* objects. These are objects that do not model the problem domain but are used in building the program itself. In systems with graphical user interfaces—Microsoft Windows or the Macintosh operating system, for example—a program may need several kinds of implementation-level objects: window objects, menu objects, objects that respond to mouse clicks, and so on. Objects such as these are often available in class libraries so that we don't need to design and implement them from scratch each time we need them in different programs.

Step 2: Determine the Relationships Among Objects

After selecting potential objects and operations, the next step is to examine the relationships among the objects. In particular, we want to see whether certain objects might be related either by inheritance or by composition. Inheritance and composition relationships not only pave the way for code reuse—as we emphasized in our discussion of OOP—they also simplify the design and allow us to model the problem domain more accurately. For example, the banking problem may require several kinds of savings accounts—one for general customers, another for preferred customers, and another for children under the age of 12. If these are all variations on a basic savings account, the is-a relationship (and, therefore, inheritance) is probably appropriate. Starting with a `SavingsAccount` class that provides operations common to any savings account, we could design each of the other accounts as a child class of `SavingsAccount`, concentrating our efforts only on the properties that make each one different from the parent class.

Sometimes the choice between inheritance and composition is not immediately clear. Earlier we wrote a `TimeCard` class to represent an employee's time card. Given an existing `Time` class, we used composition to relate `TimeCard` and `Time`—the private part of the `TimeCard` class is composed of a `Time` object (and an ID number). We could also have used inheritance. We could have derived class `TimeCard` from `Time` (inheriting the hours, minutes, and seconds members) and then specialized it by adding an extra data member (the ID number) and the extra operations of Punch, Print, and so forth. Both inheritance and composition give us four private data members: hours, minutes, seconds, and ID number. However, the use of inheritance means that all of the Time operations are also valid for TimeCard objects. A user of the TimeCard class could—either intentionally or accidentally—invoke operations such as Set and Increment, which are not appropriate operations on a time card. Furthermore, inheritance leads to a confused design in this example. It is not true that a TimeCard *is a* Time; rather, a TimeCard *has a* Time (and an ID number). In general, the best design strategy is to use inheritance for is-a relationships and composition for has-a relationships.

Step 3: Design the Driver

The final step is to design the driver—the top-level algorithm. In OOD, the driver is the glue that puts the objects (along with their operations) together. When implementing the design in C++, the driver becomes the main function.

Notice that structured design *begins* with the design of the top-level algorithm, whereas OOD *ends* with the top-level algorithm. In OOD, most of the control flow has already been designed in steps 1 and 2; the algorithms are located within the operations on objects. As a result, the driver often has very little to do but process user commands or input some data and then delegate tasks to various objects.

SOFTWARE ENGINEERING TIP

The Iterative Nature of Object-Oriented Design

Software developers, researchers, and authors have proposed many different strategies for performing OOD. Common to nearly all of these strategies are three fundamental steps:

1. Identify the objects and operations.
2. Determine the relationships among objects.
3. Design the driver.

Experience with large software projects has shown that these three steps are not necessarily sequential—Step 1, Step 2, Step 3, then we are done. In practice, Step 1 occurs first, but only as a first approximation. During Steps 2 and 3, new objects or operations may be discovered, leading us back to Step 1 again. It is realistic to think of Steps 1 through 3 not as a sequence but as a loop.

Furthermore, each step is an iterative process within itself. Step 1 may entail working and reworking our view of the objects and operations. Similarly, Steps 2 and 3 often involve experimentation and revision. In any step, we may conclude that a potential object is not useful after all. Or we might decide to add or eliminate operations on a particular object.

There is always more than one way to solve a problem. Iterating and reiterating through the design phase leads to insights that produce a better solution.

 Implementing the Design

In OOD, when we first identify an object, it is an *abstract object*. We do not immediately choose an exact data representation for that object. Similarly, the operations on objects begin as *abstract operations*, because there is no initial attempt to provide algorithms for these operations.

Eventually, we have to implement the objects and operations. For each abstract object, we must

- choose a suitable data representation.
- create algorithms for the abstract operations.

To select a data representation for an object, the C++ programmer has three options:

1. Use a built-in data type.
2. Use an existing ADT.
3. Create a new ADT.

For a given object, a good rule of thumb is to consider these three options in the order listed. A built-in type is the most straightforward to use and understand, and operations on these types are already defined by the language. If a built-in type is not adequate to represent an object, you should survey available ADTs in a class library (either the system's or your own) to see if any are a good match for the abstract object. If no suitable ADT exists, you must design and implement a new ADT to represent the object.

Fortunately, even if you must resort to option 3, the mechanisms of inheritance and composition allow you to combine options 2 and 3. When we needed an ExtTime class earlier in the chapter, we used inheritance to build on an existing Time class. And when we created a TimeCard class, we used composition to include a Time object in the private data.

In addition to choosing a data representation for the abstract object, we must implement the abstract operations. With OOD, the algorithms that implement the abstract operations are often short and straightforward. We have seen numerous examples in this chapter and Chapter 15 in which the code for ADT operations is only a few lines long. But this is not always the case. If an operation is extremely complex, it may be best to treat the operation as a new problem and use top-down design on the control flow. In this situation, it is appropriate to apply both top-down and object-oriented method-

ologies together. Experienced programmers are familiar with both methodologies and use them either independently or in combination with each
other. However, the software development community is becoming increasingly convinced that, although top-down design is important for designing
low-level algorithms and operations on ADTs, the future in developing huge
software systems lies in OOD and OOP.

*P*ROBLEM-SOLVING *CASE STUDY*

Time Card Lookup

Problem: In this chapter, we talked about a factory that is computerizing
its employee time card information. Work on the software has already
begun, and you have been hired to join the effort. Each morning after the
employees have punched in, the time card data (ID number and time stamp)
for all employees are written to a file named punchInFile. Your task is to
write a program that inputs the data from this file and allows the user to
look up the time stamp (punch-in time) for any employee. The program is
to prompt the user for an ID number, look up that employee's time card information, and print it out. This interactive lookup process is repeated until
the user types a negative number for the employee ID. The factory has, at
most, 500 employees. If punchInFile contains more than 500 time cards, the
excess time cards should be ignored and a warning message printed.

Input: Employee time card information (file punchInFile) and a sequence of employee ID numbers to be looked up (standard input device).

Each line in file punchInFile contains an employee's ID number (long integer) and the time he or she punched in (three integers—hours, minutes,
and seconds):

```
246308 7 45 50
129336 8 15 29
```

The end-of-file condition signals the end of the input data.

Interactive input from the user consists of employee ID numbers, entered
one at a time in response to a prompt. A negative ID number signals the end
of the interactive input.

Output: For each employee ID that is input from the user, the corresponding time at which the employee punched in (or a message if the program cannot find a time card for the employee).

Below is a sample of the run-time dialogue. The user's input is highlighted.

```
Enter an employee ID (negative to quit): 129336
ID: 129336 Time: 08:15:29

Enter an employee ID (negative to quit): 222000
222000 has not punched in yet.

Enter an employee ID (negative to quit): -3
```

Discussion: Using structured (top-down) design, we would begin by thinking about the overall flow of control and the major actions to be performed. With object-oriented design, we consider the overall flow of control *last.*

We begin our design by identifying objects and their associated operations. The best place to start is by examining the problem domain. In object-oriented fashion, we search for important nouns and noun phrases in the problem definition. Here is a list of candidate objects (potential objects):

Factory
Employee
File punchInFile
ID number
Time card
Time stamp (punch-in time)
User

Reviewing this list, we conclude that the first two candidates—factory and employee—are probably not objects in the solution domain. In the problem we are to solve, a factory and an employee have no useful properties or interesting operations. Also, we can eliminate the last candidate listed—a user. *User* is merely a noun appearing in the problem definition; it has nothing to do with the problem domain. At this point, we can pare down our list of potential objects to the following:

File punchInFile
ID number
Time card
Time stamp

To determine operations on these objects, we look for significant verb phrases in the problem definition. Here are some possibilities:

Punch a time card
Input data from the file
Look up time card information
Print out time card information
Input an employee ID

To associate these operations with the appropriate objects, let's make an *object table* as follows:

Object	Operation
File `punchInFile`	Input data from the file
ID number	Input an employee ID
Time card	Punch a time card
	Look up time card information
	Print out time card information
Time stamp	—

Analyzing the object table, we see that something is not quite right. For one thing, "Look up time card information" is not an operation on a single time card—it's more properly an operation that applies to a *collection* of time cards. What we're missing is an object that represents a list of time cards. That is, the program should read all the time cards from the data file and store them into a list. From this list, our program can look up the time card that matches a particular employee ID. Notice that this new object—the time card list—is an implementation-level object rather than a problem-domain object. This object is not readily apparent in the problem domain, yet we need it in order to design and implement the program.

Another thing we notice in the object table is the absence of any operations on the time stamp object. A little thought should convince us that this object simply represents the time of day. As with the `Time` class we discussed in this chapter, suitable operations might be to set the time and to print the time.

Here is a revised object table that includes the time card list object and refines the operations that might be suitable for each object:

Object	Operation
File `punchInFile`	Open the file
	Input data from the file
ID number	Input an employee ID
	Print an employee ID
Time card	Set the ID number on a time card
	Inspect the ID number on a time card
	Punch the time stamp on a time card
	Inspect the time stamp on a time card
	Print the time card information
Time card list	Read all time cards into the list
	Look up time card information
Time stamp	Set the time of day
	Print the time

The second major step in OOD is to determine the relationships among the objects. Specifically, we're looking for inheritance and composition relationships. Our object table does not reveal any inheritance relationships. Using *is-a* as a guide, we cannot say that a time card is a kind of time stamp or vice versa, that a time card list is a kind of time card or vice versa, and so on. However, we find several composition relationships. Using *has-a* as a guide, we see that a time card has a time stamp as part of its state, a time card has an ID number as part of its state, and a time card list has several time cards as part of its state (see Figure 16-9). Discovery of these relationships helps us to further refine the design (and implementation) of the objects.

Now that we have determined a reasonable set of objects and operations, let's look at each object in detail. Keep in mind that the decisions we have made are not necessarily final. We may change our minds as we proceed, perhaps adding and deleting objects and operations as we focus in on a solution. Remember that OOD is an iterative process, characterized by experimentation and revision.

The punchInFile Object: This object represents an ordinary kind of input file with the ordinary operations of opening the file and reading from the file. No further design of this object is necessary. To implement the object, the obvious choice for a data representation is the ifstream class supplied by the C++ standard library. The ifstream class provides operations for opening and reading from a file, so we don't need to implement these operations ourselves.

The ID Number Object: This object merely represents an integer number (possibly large), and the only abstract operations we have identified are

■ FIGURE 16-9

Composition Relationships Among Objects

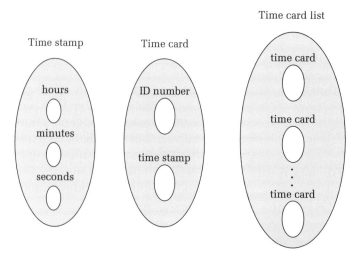

input and output. Therefore, the built-in `long` type is the most straightforward data representation. To implement the abstract operations of input and output we can simply use the `<<` and `>>` operators.

The Time Stamp Object: The time stamp object represents a time of day. There is no built-in type we can use as a data representation, but we can use an existing class—the `Time` class we worked with earlier in the chapter. The complete specification of the `Time` class appears below.

```
//**********************************************************************
// SPECIFICATION FILE (time.h)
// This file gives the specification of a Time abstract data type
//**********************************************************************
#ifndef TIME_H
#define TIME_H

#include "bool.h"

class Time
{
public:
    void Set( /* in */ int hours,
              /* in */ int minutes,
              /* in */ int seconds );
        // Precondition:
        //     0 <= hours <= 23  &&  0 <= minutes <= 59
        //   && 0 <= seconds <= 59
        // Postcondition:
        //     Time is set according to the incoming parameters

    void Increment();
        // Postcondition:
        //     Time has been advanced by one second, with
        //     23:59:59 wrapping around to 0:0:0

    void Write() const;
        // Postcondition:
        //     Time has been output in the form HH:MM:SS

    Time( /* in */ int initHrs,
          /* in */ int initMins,
          /* in */ int initSecs );
        // Precondition:
        //     0 <= initHrs <= 23  &&  0 <= initMins <= 59
        //   && 0 <= initSecs <= 59
```

```
                        // Postcondition:
                        //      Class object is constructed
                        //   && Time is set according to the incoming parameters

          Time();
                        // Postcondition:
                        //      Class object is constructed  &&  Time is 0:0:0
private:
    int hrs;
    int mins;
    int secs;
};
#endif
```

(We surround the specification file with the preprocessor directives

```
#ifndef TIME_H
#define TIME_H
    .
    .
    .
#endif
```

to prevent multiple inclusion of the `Time` class declaration in cases where a new class is created from `Time` by inheritance or composition. Later in the case study, we discuss this issue further. Meanwhile, you may want to review the Matters of Style box entitled "Avoiding Multiple Inclusion of Header Files" in Chapter 15.)

You have already seen the implementations of the `Time` class member functions. They are the same as in the `TimeType` class of Chapter 15.

By declaring a time stamp object to be of type `Time`, we can simply implement our time stamp operations as calls to the `Time` class member functions:

```
Time timeStamp;

timeStamp.Set(hours, minutes, seconds);
timeStamp.Write();
```

Notice that the abstract operations we listed for a time stamp do not include an increment operation. Should we rewrite the `Time` class to eliminate the `Increment` function? No. Wherever possible, we want to reuse existing code. Let's use the `Time` class as it exists. The presence of the `Increment` function does no harm. We simply have no need to invoke it on behalf of a time stamp object.

PROBLEM-SOLVING CASE STUDY cont'd.

Testing: Testing the `Time` class amounts to testing each of its member functions. In the Testing and Debugging section of Chapter 15, we described at length how to test a similar class, `TimeType`. `Time` is identical to `TimeType` except for the absence of two member functions, `Equal` and `LessThan`.

The Time Card Object: A time card object represents a pair of values: an employee ID number and a time stamp. The abstract operations are those we listed in our object table. There is no built-in type or existing C++ class that we can use directly to represent a time card, so we'll have to design a new class. (We sketched a `TimeCard` class earlier in the chapter, but it was not complete.)

Here is a possible specification of the class. Notice that we have added a new operation that did not appear in our object table: a class constructor.

```
//************************************************************
// SPECIFICATION FILE (timecard.h)
// This file gives the specification of a TimeCard ADT
//************************************************************
#ifndef TIMECARD_H
#define TIMECARD_H

#include "time.h"

class TimeCard
{
public:
    void Punch( /* in */ int hours,
                /* in */ int minutes,
                /* in */ int seconds );
        // Precondition:
        //     0 <= hours <= 23  &&  0 <= minutes <= 59
        //  && 0 <= seconds <= 59
        // Postcondition:
        //     Time is punched according to the incoming parameters

    void SetID( /* in */ long idNum );
        // Precondition:
        //     idNum is assigned
        // Postcondition:
        //     ID number on the time card is idNum

    long IDPart() const;
        // Postcondition:
        //     Function value == ID number on the time card
```

```
        Time TimePart() const;
            // Postcondition:
            //     Function value == time stamp on the time card

        void Print() const;
            // Postcondition:
            //     Time card has been output in the form
            //         ID: 235658 Time: 08:14:25

        TimeCard();
            // Postcondition:
            //     Class object is constructed with an ID number of 0
            //     and a time of 0:0:0
    private:
        long id;
        Time timeStamp;
};
#endif
```

The private part of this class declaration shows very clearly the composition relationship we proposed earlier—namely, that a time card object is composed of an ID number object and a time stamp object.

To implement the abstract operations on a time stamp, we must implement the TimeCard class member functions. Earlier in the chapter, we showed how to implement the constructor, Punch, and Print functions, so we do not repeat the discussion here. Now we must implement SetID, IDPart, and TimePart. These are easy. The body of SetID merely sets the private variable id equal to the incoming parameter, idNum:

```
id = idNum;
```

The body of IDPart needs only to return the current value of id, and the body of TimePart simply returns the current value of the private object timeStamp. Here is the implementation file containing the definitions of all the TimeCard member functions:

```
//**************************************************************
// IMPLEMENTATION FILE (timecard.cpp)
// This file implements the TimeCard class member functions
//**************************************************************
#include "timecard.h"
#include <iostream.h>
```

```
// Private members of class:
//     long id;
//     Time timeStamp;

//***********************************************************

TimeCard::TimeCard()

// Default constructor

// Postcondition:
//     Time is 0:0:0 (via implicit call to timeStamp object's
//     default constructor)
//   && id == 0

{
    id = 0;
}

//***********************************************************

void TimeCard::Punch( /* in */ int hours,
                      /* in */ int minutes,
                      /* in */ int seconds )
// Precondition:
//     0 <= hours <= 23  &&  0 <= minutes <= 59
//   && 0 <= seconds <= 59
// Postcondition:
//     Time is punched according to hours, minutes, and seconds

{
    timeStamp.Set(hours, minutes, seconds);
}

//***********************************************************

void TimeCard::SetID( /* in */ long idNum )

// Precondition:
//     idNum is assigned
// Postcondition:
//     id == idNum

{
    id = idNum;
}
```

```
//******************************************************************

long TimeCard::IDPart() const

// Postcondition:
//      Function value == id

{
    return id;
}

//******************************************************************

Time TimeCard::TimePart() const

// Postcondition:
//      Function value == timeStamp

{
    return timeStamp;
}

//******************************************************************

void TimeCard::Print() const

// Postcondition:
//      Time card has been output in the form
//          ID: 235658 Time: 08:14:25

{
    cout << "ID: " << id << " Time: ";
    timeStamp.Write();
}
```

Testing: These functions are all very easy to test. Because the `Time` class has already been tested and debugged, the `Punch` function (which calls `Time::Set`) and the `Print` function (which calls `Time::Write`) should work correctly. Also, none of the `TimeCard` member functions use loops or branching, so it is sufficient to write a single test driver that calls each of the member functions, supplying parameter values that satisfy the preconditions.

The Time Card List Object: This object represents a list of time cards. Once again, we'll have to write a new C++ class for this list because no built-in type or existing class will do.

In Chapter 12, we introduced the notion of a list as an ADT. At various times, we have talked about typical list operations: insert an item into the list, delete an item, report whether the list is full, report whether the list is empty, search for a particular item, sort the list items into order, print the entire list, and so forth. Shouldn't we include all these operations when designing our list of time cards? Probably not. It's unlikely that a list of time cards would be considered general-purpose enough to warrant the effort. Let's stick to the operations we listed in the object table:

Read all time cards into the list
Look up time card information

To choose a data representation for the list, let's review the relationships among the objects in our program. We said that the time card list object is composed of time card objects. Therefore, we can use a 500-element array of `TimeCard` class objects to represent the list. Because we'll be searching the array for time card information, the data representation should also include an integer variable indicating the length of the list (the number of array elements that are actually in use).

Before we write the specification of the `TimeCardList` class, let's review the operations once more. The lookup operation must search the array for a particular time card. Because the array is potentially very large (500 elements), a binary search is better than a sequential search. However, a binary search requires the array elements to be in sorted order. We must either insert each time card into its proper place as it is read from the data file or sort the time cards after they have been read. Let's take the latter approach and add another operation—a sorting operation. (We'll use the selection sort we developed in Chapter 12.) Finally, we need one more operation to initialize the private data: a class constructor. Here is the resulting class specification:

```
//****************************************************************
// SPECIFICATION FILE (tclist.h)
// This file gives the specification of TimeCardList, an ADT for a
// list of TimeCard objects.
//****************************************************************
#ifndef TCLIST_H
#define TCLIST_H

#include "timecard.h"
#include "bool.h"
#include <fstream.h>

const int MAX_LENGTH = 500;    // Maximum number of time cards
```

```
class TimeCardList
{
public:
    void ReadAll( /* inout */ ifstream& inFile );
        // Precondition:
        //      inFile has been opened for input
        // Postcondition:
        //      List contains at most MAX_LENGTH employee time cards
        //      as read from inFile. (Excess time cards are ignored
        //      and a warning message is printed)

    void SelSort();
        // Postcondition:
        //      List components are in ascending order of employee ID

    void BinSearch( /* in */   long       idNum,
                    /* out */ TimeCard&  card,
                    /* out */ Boolean&   found ) const;
        // Precondition:
        //      List components are in ascending order of employee ID
        //   && idNum is assigned
        // Postcondition:
        //      IF time card for employee idNum is in list
        //          found == TRUE  &&  card == time card for idNum
        //      ELSE
        //          found == FALSE  &&  value of card is undefined

    TimeCardList();
        // Postcondition:
        //      Empty list created
private:
    TimeCard list[MAX_LENGTH];
    int      length;
};
#endif
```

The BinSearch function is a little different from the one we presented in
Chapter 12. There, we returned the index of the array element where the
item was found. Here, an array index would be useless to a client of
TimeCardList. The array of time cards is encapsulated within the private
part of the class and is inaccessible to clients. This version of BinSearch,
therefore, returns the entire time card to the client.

Now we implement the TimeCardList member functions. Let's begin with
the class constructor. Remember that when a class *X* is composed of objects
of other classes, the constructors for those objects are executed before the
body of *X*'s constructor is executed. When the TimeCardList constructor is

called, all 500 `TimeCard` objects in the private `list` array are first constructed. These objects are constructed via implicit calls to the `TimeCard` class's
default constructor. (Recall from Chapter 15 that an array of class objects is
constructed using the class's default constructor, not a parameterized constructor.) After the `list` array elements are constructed, there is nothing left
to do but to set the private variable `length` equal to zero:

```
TimeCardList::TimeCardList()

// Postcondition:
//      Each element of list array has an ID number of 0
//      and a time of 0:0:0 (via implicit call to each array
//      element's default constructor)
//   && length == 0

{
    length = 0;
}
```

To implement the `ReadAll` member function, we use a loop that reads
each employee's data (ID number and hours, minutes, and seconds of the
punch-in time) and stores the data into the next unused element of the `list`
array. The loop terminates either when end-of-file occurs or when the length
of the array reaches `MAX_LENGTH`. After exiting the loop, we are to print a
warning message if more data exist in the file (that is, if end-of-file has not
occurred).

ReadAll (Inout: inFile)

```
Read idNum, hours, minutes, seconds from inFile
WHILE NOT EOF on inFile AND length < MAX_LENGTH
    list[length].SetID(idNum)
    list[length].Punch(hours, minutes, seconds)
    Increment length by 1
    Read idNum, hours, minutes, seconds from inFile
IF NOT EOF on inFile
    Print warning that remaining time cards will be ignored
```

The implementation of the `SelSort` member function has to be slightly
different from the one we developed in Chapter 12. Remember that `SelSort`
finds the minimum value in the list and swaps it with the value in the first
place in the list. Then the next smallest value in the list is swapped with the
value in the second place. This process continues until all the values are in

order. The location in this algorithm that we must change is where the minimum value is determined. Instead of comparing two time cards in the list (which doesn't make any sense), we compare the *ID numbers* on the time cards. To inspect the ID number on a time card, we use the observer function IDPart provided by the TimeCard class. The statement that did the comparison in the original SelSort function must be changed from

```
if (list[placeCount] < list[minIndex])
```

to

```
if (list[placeCount].IDPart() < list[minIndex].IDPart())
```

We must make a similar change in the BinSearch function. The original version in Chapter 12 compared the search item with list components directly. Here, we cannot compare the search item (an ID number of type long) with a list component (an object of type TimeCard). Again, we must use the IDPart observer function to inspect the ID number on a time card.

Below is the implementation file for the TimeCardList class.

```
//******************************************************************
// IMPLEMENTATION FILE (tclist.cpp)
// This file implements the TimeCardList class member functions.
// List representation: an array of TimeCard objects and an
// integer variable giving the current length of the list
//******************************************************************
#include "tclist.h"
#include <iostream.h>

// Private members of class:
//    TimeCard list[MAX_LENGTH];   Array of TimeCard objects
//    int      length;             Current length of list


//******************************************************************

TimeCardList::TimeCardList()

// Default constructor

// Postcondition:
//    Each element of list array has an ID number of 0
//    and a time of 0:0:0 (via implicit call to each array
//    element's default constructor)
```

Testing: To test this program, we begin by preparing an input file that contains time card information for, say, five employees. The data should be in random order of employee ID to make sure that the sorting routine works properly. Using this input file, we run the program and supply the following interactive input: the ID numbers of all five employees in the data file (the program should print their punch-in times), a few ID numbers that are not in the data file (the program should print the message that these employees have not checked in yet), and a negative ID number (the program should quit). If the program tells us that one of the five employees in the data file has not checked in yet or prints a punch-in time for one of the employees not in the data file, the fault clearly lies with the punchInList object—the object responsible for reading the file, sorting, and searching. Using a hand trace, debug output statements, or the system debugger, we should check the TimeCardList member functions in the following order: ReadAll (to verify that the file data was read into the list correctly), SelSort (to confirm that the time card information ends up in ascending order of ID number), then BinSearch (to ensure that items in the list are indeed found and that items not in the list are reported as not there).

One more thing needs to be tested. If the data file contains more than MAX_LENGTH time cards, the ReadAll function should print a warning message and ignore the excess time cards. To test this feature, we obviously don't want to create an input file with over 500 time cards. Instead, we go into tclist.h and change the const definition of MAX_LENGTH from 500 to a more manageable value—3, for example. We then recompile only tclist.cpp and relink all four object code files. When we run the program, it should read only the first three time cards from the file, print a warning message, and work with a list of only three time cards. Here is a sample run of the program using 3 as the value of MAX_LENGTH:

Input File

```
398405 7 45 04
290387 7 48 10
193847 7 53 20
938473 7 55 14
837485 8 00 00
385473 8 05 45
573920 8 12 13
483948 8 14 45
```

Copy of the Screen During the Run

```
Input file name: punchin.dat
More than 3 time cards in input file.  Remainder are ignored.
```

```
Enter an employee ID (negative to quit): 398405
ID: 398405 Time: 07:45:04
Enter an employee ID (negative to quit): 193847
ID: 193847 Time: 07:53:20
Enter an employee ID (negative to quit): 290387
ID: 290387 Time: 07:48:10
Enter an employee ID (negative to quit): 938473
938473 has not punched in yet.
Enter an employee ID (negative to quit): 111111
111111 has not punched in yet.
Enter an employee ID (negative to quit): -5
```

After testing this aspect of the program, we must not forget to change the value of MAX_LENGTH back to 500, recompile tclist.cpp, and relink the object code files.

TESTING AND DEBUGGING

Testing and debugging an object-oriented program is largely a process of testing and debugging the C++ classes on which the program is built. The top-level driver also needs testing, but this testing is usually uncomplicated—OOD tends to result in a simple driver.

To review how to test a C++ class, you should refer back to the Testing and Debugging section of Chapter 15. There we walked through the process of testing each member function of a class. We made the observation that you could write a separate test driver for each member function or you could write just one test driver that tests all of the member functions. The latter approach is recommended only for classes that have a few simple member functions.

When an object-oriented program uses inheritance and composition, the order in which you test the classes is, in a sense, predetermined. If class *X* is derived from class *Y* or contains an object of class *Y*, you cannot test *X* until you have designed and implemented *Y*. Thus, it makes sense to test and debug the lower level class (class *Y*) before testing class *X*. This chapter's Problem-Solving Case Study demonstrated this sequence of testing. We tested the lowest level class—the Time class—first. Next, we tested the TimeCard class, which contains a Time object. Finally, we tested the TimeCardList class, which contains an array of TimeCard objects. The general principle is that if class *X* is built on class *Y* (through inheritance or composition), the testing of *X* is simplified if *Y* is already tested and is known to behave correctly.

Testing and Debugging Hints

1. Review the Testing and Debugging Hints for Chapter 15. They apply to the design and testing of C++ classes, which are at the heart of OOP.
2. When using inheritance, don't forget to include the word `public` when declaring the derived class:

```
class DerivedClass : public BaseClass
{
    .
    .
    .
};
```

   The word `public` makes `BaseClass` a public base class of `DerivedClass`. That is, clients of `DerivedClass` can apply any public `BaseClass` operation (except constructors) to a `DerivedClass` object.
3. The header file containing the declaration of a derived class must `#include` the header file containing the declaration of the base class.
4. Although a derived class inherits the private and public members of its base class, it cannot directly access the inherited private members.
5. If a base class has a constructor, it is invoked before the derived class's constructor is executed. If the base class constructor requires parameters, you must pass these parameters using a constructor initializer:

```
DerivedClass::DerivedClass( ... )
    : BaseClass(param1, param2)
{
    .
    .
    .
}
```

   If you do not include a constructor initializer, the base class's default constructor is invoked.
6. If a class has a member that is an object of another class and this member object's constructor requires parameters, you must pass these parameters using a constructor initializer:

```
SomeClass::SomeClass( ... )
    : memberObject(param1, param2)
{
    .
    .
    .
}
```

If there is no constructor initializer, the member object's default constructor is invoked.

7. To obtain dynamic binding of an operation to an object when passing class objects as parameters, you must

- pass the object using pass-by-reference.
- declare the operation to be `virtual` in the class declaration.

8. If a base class declares a virtual function, it *must* implement that function even if the body is empty.

9. A derived class cannot redefine the function return type of a virtual function.

SUMMARY

Object-oriented design (OOD) decomposes a problem into objects—self-contained entities in which data and operations are bound together. In OOD, data is treated as an active, rather than passive, quantity. Each object is responsible for one part of the solution, and the objects communicate by invoking one another's operations.

OOD begins by identifying potential objects and their operations. Examining objects in the problem domain is a good way to begin the process. The next step is to determine the relationships among the objects using inheritance (to express is-a relationships) and composition (to express has-a relationships). Finally, a driver algorithm is designed to coordinate the overall flow of control.

Object-oriented programming (OOP) is the process of implementing an object-oriented design by using language mechanisms for data abstraction, inheritance, and dynamic binding. Inheritance allows any programmer to take an existing class (the base class) and create a new class (the derived class) that inherits the data and operations of the base class. The derived class then specializes the base class by adding new private data, adding new operations, or overriding inherited operations—all without analyzing and modifying the implementation of the base class in any way. Dynamic binding of operations to objects allows objects of many different derived types to respond to a single function name, each in its own way. Together, inheritance and dynamic binding have been shown to reduce dramatically the time and effort required to customize existing ADTs. The result is truly reusable software components whose applications and lifetimes extend beyond those conceived of by the original creator.

Quick Check

1. Fill in the blanks: Structured (procedural) programming results in a program that is a collection of interacting _____ , whereas OOP results in a program that is a collection of interacting _____. (pp. 906–909)
2. Name the three language features that characterize object-oriented programming languages. (pp. 906–909)
3. Given the class declaration

```
class Point
{
public:
    int X_Coord() const;        // Return the x-coordinate
    int Y_Coord() const;        // Return the y-coordinate
    Point( /* in */ int initX,  // Constructor
           /* in */ int initY );
private:
    int x;
    int y;
};
```

and the type declaration

```
enum StatusType {ON, OFF};
```

declare a class `Pixel` that inherits from class `Point`. Class `Pixel` has an additional data member of type `StatusType` named status; it has an additional member function `CurrentStatus` that returns the value of status; and it supplies its own constructor that receives three parameters. (pp. 909–917)

4. Write a client statement that creates a `Pixel` object named `onePixel` with an initial (x, y) position of (3, 8) and a status of OFF. (pp. 909–917)
5. Assuming `somePixel` is an object of type `Pixel`, write client code that prints out the current x- and y-coordinates and status of `somePixel`. (pp. 909–917)
6. Write the function definitions for the `Pixel` class constructor and the `CurrentStatus` function. (pp. 917–920)
7. Fill in the private part of the following class declaration, which uses composition to define a `Line` object in terms of two `Point` objects. (pp. 921–922)

```
class Line
{
public:
    Point StartingPoint() const;   // Return line's starting point
    Point EndingPoint() const;     // Return line's ending point
    float Length() const;          // Return length of the line
    Line( /* in */ int startX,     // Constructor
          /* in */ int startY,
```

```
                         /* in */  int endX,
                         /* in */  int endY  );
        private:
```

```
        ┌─────────────────────────────────────┐
        │                                     │
        │                                     │
        │                                     │
        └─────────────────────────────────────┘
```

```
        };
```

8. Write the function definition for the `Line` class constructor. (pp. 922–925)
9. What is the difference between static and dynamic binding of an operation to an object? (pp. 925–930)
10. Although there are many specific techniques for performing OOD, this chapter uses a three-step process. What are these three steps? (pp. 930–934)
11. When selecting a data representation for an abstract object, what three choices does the C++ programmer have? (pp. 934–935)

Answers 1. functions, objects 2. Data abstraction, inheritance, dynamic binding

```
3. class Pixel : public Point
   {
   public:
       StatusType CurrentStatus() const;
       Pixel( /* in */ int          initX,
              /* in */ int          initY,
              /* in */ StatusType initStatus );
   private:
       StatusType status;
   };
```

```
4. Pixel onePixel(3, 8, OFF);
```

```
5. cout << "x-coordinate: " << somePixel.X_Coord() << endl;
   cout << "y-coordinate: " << somePixel.Y_Coord() << endl;
   if (somePixel.CurrentStatus() == ON)
       cout << "Status: on" << endl;
   else
       cout << "Status: off" << endl;
```

```
6. Pixel::Pixel( /* in */ int          initX,
                 /* in */ int          initY,
                 /* in */ StatusType initStatus )

       : Point(initX, initY)              // Constructor initializer
   {
       status = initStatus;
   }
```

```
7. Point startPt;
   Point endPt;
```

```
8. Line::Line( /* in */ int startX,
               /* in */ int startY,
               /* in */ int endX,
               /* in */ int endY     )

       : startPt(startX, startY), endPt(endX, endY)
   {
```

```
        // Empty body--nothing more to do
    }
```

9. With static binding, the determination of which function to call for an object occurs at compile time. With dynamic binding, the determination of which function to call for an object occurs at run time.   10. Identify the objects and operations, determine the relationships among the objects, and design the driver.   11. Use a built-in data type, use an existing ADT, or create a new ADT.

EXAM PREPARATION EXERCISES

1. Define the following terms:

structured design	method (of an object)
code reuse	is-a relationship
state (of an object)	has-a relationship
instance variable (of an object)	

2. In C++, inheritance allows a derived class to access directly all of the functions and data of its base class. (True or False?)   True.

3. Given an existing class declaration

```
class Sigma
{
public:
    void Write() const;
        .
        .
        .
private:
    int n;
};
```

a programmer derives a new class Epsilon as follows:

                    Public
```
class Epsilon : Sigma
{
public:
    void Twist();
    Epsilon( /* in */ float initVal );
private:
    float x;
};
```

Then the following client code results in a compile-time error:

```
Epsilon someObject(4.8);

someObject.Write();    // Error
```

a. Why is the call to the Write function erroneous?
b. How would you fix the problem?

4. Consider the following two class declarations:

```
class Abc
{
public:
    void DoThis();
private:
    void DoThat();
    int   alpha;
    int   beta;
};
```

```
class Xyz : public Abc
{
public:
    void TryIt();
private:
    int gamma;
};
```

For *each* class, do the following:

a. List all private data members.

b. List all private data members that the class's member functions can reference directly.

c. List all functions that the class's member functions can invoke.

d. List all member functions that a client of the class may legally invoke.

5. A class *X* uses both inheritance and composition as follows. *X* is derived from class *Y* and has a member that is an object of class *Z*. When an object of class *X* is created, in what order are the constructors for classes *X*, *Y*, and *Z* executed?

6. With parameter passage in C++, you can pass an object of an ancestor class to a formal parameter that is an object of a descendant class. (True or False?)

7. Consider the following two class declarations:

```
class A
{
public:
    virtual void Write() const;
    A( /* in */ char ch );
private:
    char c;
};
```

```
class B : public A
{
public:
    void Write() const;
    B( /* in */ char ch1,
       /* in */ char ch2 );
private:
    char d;
};
```

Let the implementations of the constructors and `Write` functions be as follows:

```
A::A( /* in */ char ch )                    // constructor
{
    c = ch;
}

void A::Write() const
{
    cout << c;
}

B::B( /* in */ char ch1,                    // constructor with argu.
      /* in */ char ch2 )

      : A(ch1)
{
    d = ch2;
}
void B::Write() const
{
    A::Write();
    cout << d;
}
```

Suppose that we declare two class objects, objectA and objectB:

```
A objectA('x');
B objectB('y', 'z');
```

a. If we write a global function PrintIt, defined as

```
void PrintIt( /* in */ A someObject )
{
    someObject.Write();
}
```

then what is printed by the following code segment?

```
PrintIt(objectA);
cout << endl;
PrintIt(objectB);
```

b. Repeat part (a), assuming that PrintIt uses pass-by-reference instead of pass-by-value:

```
void PrintIt( /* in */ A& someObject )
{
    someObject.Write();
}
```

c. Repeat part (b), assuming that Write is *not* a virtual function.

8. Define the following terms associated with object-oriented design:

   problem domain
   solution domain
   implementation-level object

9. Mark each of the following statements as True or False.
   a. Every noun and noun phrase in a problem definition becomes an object in the solution domain.
   b. For a given problem, there are usually more objects in the solution domain than in the problem domain.
   c. In the three-step process for performing object-oriented design, all decisions made during each step are final.

10. For each of the following design methodologies, at what general time (beginning, middle, end) is the driver—the top-level algorithm—designed?
    a. Object-oriented design
    b. Structured (top-down) design

11. Fill in each blank below with either *is-a* or *has-a*.
    In general, the best strategy in object-oriented design is to use inheritance for _____ relationships and composition for _____ relationships.

PROGRAMMING WARM-UP EXERCISES

1. For the `Line` class of Quick Check Question 7, implement the `StartingPoint` and `EndingPoint` member functions.
2. For the `Line` class of Quick Check Question 7, implement the `Length` member function. *Hint:* The distance between two points (x_1, y_1) and (x_2, y_2) is

   $$\sqrt{(x_1 - x_2)^2 + (y_1 - y_2)^2}$$

3. The following class represents a person's mailing address in the United States.

   ```
   typedef char String20[21];

   class Address
   {
   public:
       void Write() const;
       Address( /* in */ const String20 newStreet,
                /* in */ const String20 newCity,
                /* in */ const String20 newState,
                /* in */ const String20 newZip   );
   private:
       String20 street;
       String20 city;
       String20 state;
       String20 zipCode;
   };
   ```

   Using inheritance, we want to derive an international address class, `InterAddress`, from the `Address` class. For this exercise, an international address has all the attributes of a U.S. address plus a country code (a string indicat-

> **Pointer Type**   A simple data type consisting of an unbounded set of values, each of which addresses or otherwise indicates the location of a variable of a given type. Among the operations defined on pointer variables are assignment and test for equality.

Let's begin this discussion by looking at how pointer variables are declared in C++.

Pointer Variables

Surprisingly, the word *pointer* isn't used in declaring pointer variables; the symbol * is used instead. The declaration

```
int* intPtr;
```

states that `intPtr` is a variable that can point to (that is, contain the address of) an `int` variable. Here is the syntax template for declaring pointer variables:

PointerVariableDeclaration

> DataType* Variable ;
> DataType *Variable , *Variable . . . ;

The syntax template shows two forms, one for declaring a single variable and the other for declaring several variables. In the first form, the compiler does not care where the asterisk is placed. Both of the following declarations are equivalent:

```
int* intPtr;
int *intPtr;
```

Although C++ programmers use both styles, we prefer the first. Attaching the asterisk to the data type name instead of the variable name readily suggests that `intPtr` is of type "pointer to `int`."

According to the syntax template, if you declare several variables in one statement you must precede each variable name with an asterisk. Otherwise, only the first variable is taken to be a pointer variable. The compiler interprets the statement

```
int* p, q;
```

as if it were written

```
int* p;
int  q;
```

To avoid unintended errors when declaring pointer variables, it is safest to declare each variable in a separate statement.

Given the declarations

```
int  beta;
int* intPtr;
```

we can make `intPtr` point to beta by using the unary & operator, which is called the *address-of* operator. At run time, the assignment statement

```
intPtr = &beta;
```

takes the memory address of beta and stores it into `intPtr`. Alternatively, we could initialize `intPtr` in its declaration as follows:

```
int  beta;
int* intPtr = &beta;
```

Suppose that `intPtr` and beta happen to be located at memory addresses 5000 and 5008, respectively. Then storing the address of beta into `intPtr` results in the relationship pictured in Figure 17-2.

Because actual numeric addresses are generally unknown to the C++ programmer, it is more common to display the relationship between a pointer and a pointed-to variable by using rectangles and arrows as in Figure 17-3.

To access a variable that a pointer points to, we use the unary * operator—the *dereference* or *indirection* operator. The expression

```
*intPtr
```

denotes the variable pointed to by `intPtr`. In our example, `intPtr` currently points to beta, so the statement

```
*intPtr = 28;
```

■ FIGURE 17-2

Machine-Level
View of a Pointer
Variable

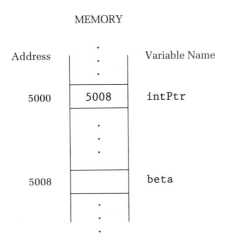

dereferences `intPtr` and stores the value 28 into `beta`. This statement represents **indirect addressing** of `beta`; the machine first accesses `intPtr`, then uses its contents to locate `beta`. In contrast, the statement

```
beta = 28;
```

represents **direct addressing** of `beta`. Direct addressing is like opening a post office box (P.O. Box 15, for instance) and finding a package, whereas indirect addressing is like opening P.O. Box 15 and finding a note that says your package is sitting in P.O. Box 23.

Direct Addressing Accessing a variable in one step by using the variable name.

Indirect Addressing Accessing a variable in two steps by first using a pointer that gives the location of the variable.

Continuing with our example, if we execute the statements

■ FIGURE 17-3

Abstract Diagram of
a Pointer Variable

```
*intPtr = 28;
cout << intPtr << endl;
cout << *intPtr << endl;
```

then the output is

```
5008
28
```

The first output statement prints the contents of `intPtr` (5008); the second prints the contents of the variable pointed to by `intPtr` (28).

Let's look at a more involved example of declaring pointers, taking addresses, and dereferencing pointers. The following program fragment declares several types and variables. In this code, the `TimeType` class is the C++ class we developed in Chapter 15 with member functions `Set`, `Increment`, `Write`, `Equal`, and `LessThan`.

```
#include "timetype.h"    // For TimeType class
    :
    :
enum ColorType {RED, GREEN, BLUE};
struct PatientRec
{
    int idNum;
    int height;
    int weight;
};

int        alpha;
ColorType  color;
PatientRec patient;
TimeType   startTime(8, 30, 0);

int*        intPtr = &alpha;
ColorType*  colorPtr = &color;
PatientRec* patientPtr = &patient;
TimeType*   timePtr = &startTime;
```

The variables `intPtr`, `colorPtr`, `patientPtr`, and `timePtr` are all pointer variables. `intPtr` points to (contains the address of) a variable of type `int`; `colorPtr` points to a variable of type `Color`; `patientPtr` points to a `struct` variable of type `PatientRec`; and `timePtr` points to a class object of type `TimeType`.

The expression `*intPtr` denotes the variable pointed to by `intPtr`. The pointed-to variable can contain any `int` value. The expression `*colorPtr` denotes a variable of type `ColorType`. It can contain `RED`, `GREEN`, or `BLUE`. The expression *patientPtr denotes a struct variable of type PatientRec. Furthermore, the expressions (*patientPtr).idNum, (*patientPtr).height, and (*patientPtr).weight denote the idNum, height, and weight members of *patientPtr. Notice how the accessing expression is built.

patientPtr	A pointer variable of type "pointer to PatientRec."
*patientPtr	A struct variable of type PatientRec.
(*patientPtr).weight	The weight member of a struct variable of type PatientRec.

The expression (*patientPtr).weight is a mixture of pointer dereferencing and struct member selection. The parentheses are necessary because the dot operator has higher precedence than the dereference operator (see Appendix B for C++ operator precedence). Without the parentheses, the expression *patientPtr.weight would be interpreted wrongly as *(patientPtr.weight).

When a pointer points to a struct (or a class or a union) variable, enclosing the pointer dereference within parentheses can become tedious. In addition to the dot operator, C++ provides another member selection operator: ->. This *arrow operator* consists of two consecutive symbols: a hyphen and a greater-than symbol. By definition,

PointerExpression -> MemberName

is equivalent to

(*PointerExpression).MemberName

Therefore, we can write (*patientPtr).weight as patientPtr->weight. The general guideline for choosing between the two member selection operators (dot and arrow) is the following:

Use the dot operator if the first operand denotes a struct, class, or union variable; use the arrow operator if the first operand denotes a *pointer* to a struct, class, or union variable.

If we want to increment and print the TimeType class object pointed to by timePtr, we could use either the statements

```
(*timePtr).Increment();
(*timePtr).Write();
```

or the statements

```
timePtr->Increment();
timePtr->Write();
```

And if we had declared an array of pointers

```
PatientRec* patPtrArray[20];
```

and initialized the array elements, then we could access the idNum member of the fourth patient as follows:

```
patPtrArray[3]->idNum
```

Pointed-to variables can be used in the same way as any other variable. The following statements are all valid:

```
*intPtr = 250;
*colorPtr = RED;
patientPtr->idNum = 3245;
patientPtr->height = 64;
patientPtr->weight = 114;
patPtrArray[3]->idNum = 6356;
patPtrArray[3]->height = 73;
patPtrArray[3]->weight = 185;
```

Figure 17-4 shows the results of these assignments.

At this point, you may be wondering why we should use pointers at all. Instead of making intPtr point to alpha and storing 250 into *intPtr, why not just store 250 directly into alpha? The truth is that there is no good reason to program this way; on the contrary, the examples we have shown would make a program more roundabout and confusing. The major use of pointers in C++ is to manipulate *dynamic variables*—variables that come into existence at execution time only as they are needed. Later in the chapter, we show how to use pointers to create dynamic variables. In the meantime, let's continue with some of the basic aspects of pointers themselves.

Pointer Expressions

You learned in the early chapters that an arithmetic expression is made up of variables, constants, operator symbols, and parentheses. Similarly, pointer expressions are composed of pointer variables, pointer constants, certain allowable operators, and parentheses. We have already discussed pointer variables—variables that hold addresses of other variables. Let's look now at pointer constants.

In C++, there is only one literal pointer constant: the value 0. The pointer constant 0, called the *null pointer*, points to absolutely nothing. The statement

```
intPtr = 0;
```

■ FIGURE 17-4

Results of
Assignment
Statements

POINTER   POINTED-TO VARIABLE

```
intPtr                      *intPtr

┌──────────┐          ┌──────────┐
│    •─────┼────────▶ │   250    │
└──────────┘          └──────────┘


colorPtr                    *colorPtr

┌──────────┐          ┌──────────┐
│    •─────┼────────▶ │   RED    │
└──────────┘          └──────────┘


patientPtr                  *patientPtr

┌──────────┐          ┌──────────┐
│    •─────┼────────▶ │   3245   │
└──────────┘          ├──────────┤
                      │    64    │
                      ├──────────┤
                      │   114    │
                      └──────────┘


patPtrArray                 *patPtrArray[3]

      ┌──────────┐          ┌──────────┐
  [0] │          │       ┌▶ │   6356   │
      ├──────────┤       │  ├──────────┤
  [1] │          │       │  │    73    │
      ├──────────┤       │  ├──────────┤
  [2] │          │       │  │   185    │
      ├──────────┤       │  └──────────┘
  [3] │    •─────┼───────┘
      ├──────────┤
      │     .    │
      │     .    │
      │     .    │
      └──────────┘
```

stores the null pointer into intPtr. This statement does *not* cause intPtr to point to memory location zero; the null pointer is guaranteed to be distinct from any actual memory address. Because the null pointer does not point to anything, we diagram the null pointer as follows, instead of using an arrow to point somewhere:

intPtr

Instead of using the constant 0, many programmers prefer to use the named constant NULL that is supplied by the standard header file stddef.h:

```
#include <stddef.h>
    .
    .
    .
intPtr = NULL;
```

As with any named constant, the identifier NULL makes a program more self-documenting. Its use also reduces the chance of confusing the null pointer with the integer constant 0.

It is an error to dereference the null pointer, as it does not point to anything. The null pointer is used only as a special value that a program can test for:

```
if (intPtr == NULL)
    DoSomething();
```

We'll see examples of using the null pointer later in this chapter and in Chapter 18.

Although 0 is the only literal constant of pointer type, there is another pointer expression that is considered to be a constant pointer expression: an array name without any index brackets. The value of this expression is the base address (the address of the first element) of the array. Given the declarations

```
int  arr[100];
int* ptr;
```

the assignment statement

```
ptr = arr;
```

has exactly the same effect as

```
ptr = &arr[0];
```

Both of these statements store the base address of arr into ptr.

Although we did not explain it at the time, you have already used the fact that an array name without brackets is a pointer expression. Consider the following code, which calls a ZeroOut function to zero out an array whose size is given as the second parameter:

```
int main()
{
```

```
float velocity[30];
     .
     .
     .
ZeroOut(velocity, 30);
     .
     .
     .
}
```

In the function call, the first parameter—an array name without index brackets—is a pointer expression. The value of this expression is the base address of the `velocity` array. This base address is passed to the function. We can write the `ZeroOut` function in one of two ways. The first approach—one that you have seen many times—declares the first formal parameter to be an array of unspecified size.

```
void ZeroOut( /* out */ float arr[],
              /* in */  int   size  )
{
    int i;

    for (i = 0; i < size; i++)
        arr[i] = 0.0;
}
```

Alternatively, we can declare the formal parameter to be of type `float*`, because the parameter simply holds the address of a `float` variable (the address of the first array element).

```
void ZeroOut( /* out */ float* arr,
              /* in */  int    size )
{
    .
    .   // Function body is unchanged
    .
}
```

Whether we declare the formal parameter as `float arr[]` or as `float* arr`, the result is exactly the same to the C++ compiler: within the `ZeroOut` function, `arr` is a simple variable that points to the beginning of the caller's actual array (see Figure 17-5).

Even though `arr` is a pointer variable within the `ZeroOut` function, we are still allowed to attach an index expression to the name `arr`:

```
arr[i] = 0.0;
```

■ FIGURE 17-5

Formal Parameter
Pointing to an
Actual Parameter

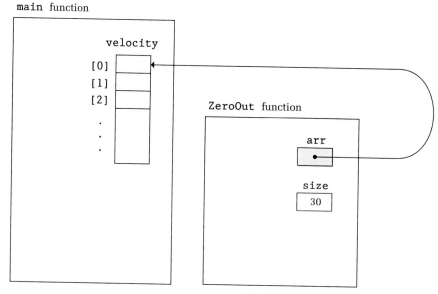

Indexing a pointer variable is made possible by the following rule in C++:

Indexing is valid for *any* pointer expression, not only an array name. (Indexing a pointer only makes sense, though, if the pointer points to an array.)

We have now seen four C++ operators that are valid for pointers: `=`, `*`, `->`, and `[]`. The following table lists the most common operations that may be applied to pointers.

Operator	Meaning	Example	Remarks
`=`	Assignment	`ptr = &someVar;` `ptr1 = ptr2;` `ptr = 0;`	Except for the null pointer, both operands must be of the same data type.
`*`	Dereference	`*ptr`	
`==, !=, <, <=, >, and >=`	Relational operators	`ptr1 == ptr2`	The two operands must be of the same data type.
`!`	Logical NOT	`!ptr`	The result is 1 if the operand is 0 (the null pointer), else the result is 0.
`[]`	Index (or subscript)	`ptr[4]`	The indexed pointer should point to an array.
`->`	Member selection	`ptr->height`	Selects a member of the class, `struct`, or union variable that is pointed to.

Notice that the logical NOT operator can be used to test for the null pointer:

```
if ( !ptr )
    DoSomething();
```

Some people find this notation confusing because `ptr` is a pointer expression, not a Boolean expression. We prefer to phrase the test this way for clarity:

```
if (ptr == NULL)
    DoSomething();
```

When looking at the table above, it is important to keep in mind that the operations listed are operations on pointers, *not* on the pointed-to variables. For example, if `intPtr1` and `intPtr2` are variables of type `int*`, the test

```
if (intPtr1 == intPtr2)
```

compares the pointers, not what they point to. In other words, we are comparing memory addresses, not ints. To compare the integers that `intPtr1` and `intPtr2` point to, we would need to write

```
if (*intPtr1 == *intPtr2)
```

In addition to the operators we have listed in the table, the following C++ operators may be applied to pointers: `++`, `--`, `+`, `-`, `+=`, and `-=`. These operators perform arithmetic on pointers that point to arrays. For example, the expression `ptr++` causes `ptr` to point to the next element of the array, regardless of the size in bytes of each array element. And the expression `ptr + 5` accesses the array element that is five elements beyond the one currently pointed to by `ptr`. We'll say no more about these operators or about pointer arithmetic; the topic of pointer arithmetic is off the main track of what we want to emphasize in this chapter. Instead, we proceed now to explore one of the most important uses of pointers: the creation of dynamic data.

 ## Dynamic Data

In Chapter 8, we described two categories of program data in C++: static data and automatic data. Any global variable is static, as is any local variable explicitly declared as `static`. The lifetime of a static variable is the lifetime of

the entire program. In contrast, an automatic variable—a local variable not declared as static—is allocated (created) when control reaches its declaration and deallocated (destroyed) when control exits the block in which the variable is declared.

With the aid of pointers, C++ provides a third category of program data: **dynamic data**. Dynamic variables are not declared with ordinary variable declarations; they are explicitly allocated and deallocated at execution time by means of two special operators, new and delete. When a program requires an additional variable, it uses new to allocate the variable. When the program no longer needs the variable, it uses delete to deallocate it. The lifetime of a dynamic variable is therefore the time between the execution of new and the execution of delete. The advantage of being able to create new variables at execution time is that we don't need to create any more of them than we need.

Dynamic Data   Variables created during execution of a program by means of special operations. In C++, these operations are new and delete.

The new operation has two forms, one for allocating a single variable and one for allocating an array. Here is the syntax template:

AllocationExpression

> **new** DataType
> **new** DataType [IntExpression]

The first form is used for creating a single variable of type DataType. The second form creates an array whose elements are of type DataType; the desired number of array elements is given by IntExpression. Here is an example that demonstrates both forms of the new operation:

```
int*  intPtr;
char* nameStr;
```

`intPtr = new int;`	Creates a variable of type int and stores its address into intPtr.
`nameStr = new char[6];`	Creates a 6-element char array and stores the base address of the array into nameStr.

Normally, the new operator does two things: it creates an uninitialized variable (or array) of the designated type, and it returns a pointer to this variable (or the base address of an array). However, if the computer system has run out of space available for dynamic data, the new operator returns the null pointer.

Variables created by new are said to be on the **free store** (or **heap**), a region of memory set aside for dynamic variables. The new operator obtains a chunk of memory from the free store and, as we will see, the delete operator returns it to the free store.

Free Store (Heap)   A pool of memory locations reserved for allocation and deallocation of dynamic data.

A dynamic variable is unnamed and cannot be directly addressed. It must be indirectly addressed through the pointer returned by the new operator. Below is an example of creating dynamic data and then accessing the data through pointers. The code begins by initializing the pointer variables in their declarations.

```
#include <string.h>    // For strcpy()
   .
   .
   .
int*  intPtr = new int;
char* nameStr = new char[6];

*intPtr = 357;
strcpy(nameStr, "Ben");
```

Recall from Chapter 12 that the strcpy library function requires two parameters, each being the base address of a char array. For the first parameter, we are passing the base address of the dynamic array on the free store. For the second parameter, the compiler passes the base address of the anonymous array where the string "Ben" (including the terminating null character) is located. Figures 17-6a and 17-6b picture the effect of executing this code segment.

Dynamic data can be destroyed at any time during the execution of a program when it is no longer needed. The built-in operator delete is used to destroy a dynamic variable. The delete operation has two forms, one for deleting a single variable, the other for deleting an array:

DeallocationExpression

```
{ delete Pointer
{ delete [] Pointer
```

■ FIGURE 17-6

Allocating Dynamic
Data on the Free
Store

a. `int*  intPtr = new int;`
   `char* nameStr = new char[6];`

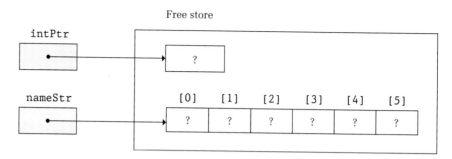

b. `*intPtr = 357;`
   `strcpy(nameStr, "Ben");`

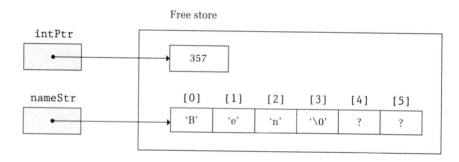

Using the previous example, we can deallocate the dynamic data pointed to by `intPtr` and `nameStr` with the following statements.

`delete intPtr;` Returns the variable pointed to by `intPtr` to the free store to be used again. The value of `intPtr` is then undefined.

`delete [] nameStr;` Returns the array pointed to by `nameStr` to the free store to be used again. The value of `nameStr` is then undefined.*

After execution of these statements, the values of `intPtr` and `nameStr` are undefined; they may or may not still point to the deallocated data. Before using these pointers again, you must assign new values to them (that is, store new memory addresses into them).

---

*The syntax for deallocating an array, `delete [] nameStr`, may not be accepted by some compilers. Early versions of the C++ language required the array size to be included within the brackets: `delete [6] nameStr`. If your compiler complains about the empty brackets, include the array size.

Until you gain experience with the new and delete operators, it is important to pronounce the statement

```
delete intPtr;
```

accurately. Instead of saying "Delete intPtr," it is better to say "Delete the variable *pointed to* by intPtr." The delete operation does not delete the pointer; it deletes the pointed-to variable.

When using the delete operator, you should keep two rules in mind.

1. Applying delete to the null pointer does no harm; the operation simply has no effect.
2. Excepting rule 1, the delete operator must only be applied to a pointer value that was obtained previously from the new operator.

The second rule is important to remember. If you apply delete to an arbitrary memory address that is not in the free store, the result is undefined and could prove to be very unpleasant.

Finally, remember that a major reason for using dynamic data is to economize on memory space. The new operator lets you create variables only as they are needed. When you are finished using a dynamic variable, you should delete it. It is counterproductive to keep dynamic variables when they are no longer needed—a situation known as a **memory leak.** If this is done too often, you may run out of memory.

Memory Leak   The loss of available memory space that occurs when dynamic data is allocated but never deallocated.

Let's look at another example of using dynamic data.

```
int* ptr1 = new int;      // Create a dynamic variable
int* ptr2 = new int;      // Create a dynamic variable

*ptr2 = 44;               // Assign a value to a dynamic variable
*ptr1 = *ptr2;            // Copy one dynamic variable to another
ptr1 = ptr2;              // Copy one pointer to another
delete ptr2;              // Destroy a dynamic variable
```

Here is a more detailed description of the effect of each statement:

```
int* ptr1 = new int;      Creates a pair of dynamic variables of type int
                          and stores their locations into ptr1 and ptr2.
int* ptr2 = new int;      The values of the dynamic variables are unde-
```

	fined even though the pointer variables now have values (see Figure 17-7a).
`*ptr2 = 44;`	Stores the value 44 into the dynamic variable pointed to by `ptr2` (see Figure 17-7b).
`*ptr1 = *ptr2;`	Copies the contents of the dynamic variable `*ptr2` to the dynamic variable `*ptr1` (see Figure 17-7c).
`ptr1 = ptr2;`	Copies the contents of the pointer variable `ptr2` to the pointer variable `ptr1` (see Figure 17-7d).
`delete ptr2;`	Returns the dynamic variable `*ptr2` back to the free store to be used again. The value of `ptr2` is undefined (see Figure 17-7e).

In Figure 17-7d, notice that the variable pointed to by `ptr1` before the assignment statement is still there. It cannot be accessed, however, because no pointer is pointing to it. This isolated variable is called an **inaccessible object.** Leaving inaccessible objects on the free store should be considered a logic error and is a cause of memory leaks.

Notice also that in Figure 17-7e `ptr1` is now pointing to a variable that, in principle, no longer exists. We call `ptr1` a **dangling pointer.** If the program later dereferences `ptr1`, the result is unpredictable. The pointed-to value might still be the original one (44), or it might be a different value stored there as a result of reusing that space on the free store.

Inaccessible Object   A dynamic variable on the free store without any pointer pointing to it.

Dangling Pointer   A pointer that points to a variable that has been deallocated.

Both situations shown in Figure 17-7e—an inaccessible object and a dangling pointer—can be avoided by deallocating `*ptr1` before assigning `ptr2` to `ptr1`, and by setting `ptr1` to NULL after deallocating `*ptr2`.

```
#include <stddef.h>    // For NULL
     .
     .
     .
int* ptr1 = new int;
int* ptr2 = new int;

*ptr2 = 44;
*ptr1 = *ptr2;
delete ptr1;           // Avoid an inaccessible object
ptr1 = ptr2;
delete ptr2;
ptr1 = NULL;           // Avoid a dangling pointer
```

Figure 17-8 shows the results of executing this revised code segment.

■ FIGURE 17-7   Results from Sample Code Segment

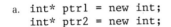

INITIAL CONDITIONS

a. ```
   int* ptr1 = new int;
   int* ptr2 = new int;
   ```

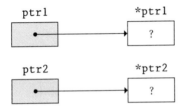

d. `ptr1 = ptr2;`

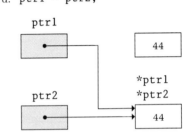

b. `*ptr2 = 44;`

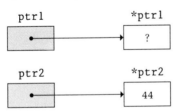

e. `delete ptr2;`

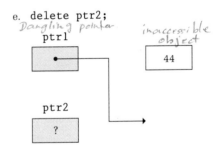

c. `*ptr1 = *ptr2;`

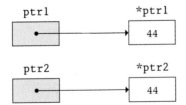
   ```

■ FIGURE 17-8   Results from Sample Code Segment After It Was Modified

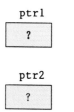

ptr1
ptr2

INITIAL CONDITIONS

a. ```
    int* ptr1 = new int;
    int* ptr2 = new int;
    ```

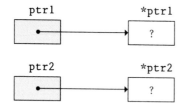

b.  `*ptr2 = 44;`

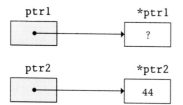

c.  `*ptr1 = *ptr2;`

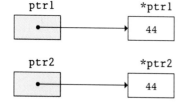

d.  `delete ptr1;`

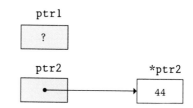

e.  `ptr1 = ptr2;`

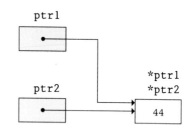

f.  `delete ptr2;`

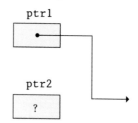

g.  `ptr1 = NULL;`

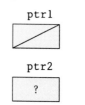
    ```

Reference Types

According to Figure 17-1, there is only one built-in type remaining: the **reference type.** Like pointer variables, reference variables contain the addresses of other variables. The statement

```
int& intRef;
```

declares that `intRef` is a variable that can contain the address of an `int` variable. Here is the syntax template for declaring reference variables:

ReferenceVariableDeclaration

```
{ DataType&  Variable ;
{ DataType  &Variable  , &Variable ... ;
```

Although reference variables and pointer variables both contain addresses of data objects, there are two fundamental differences. First, the dereferencing and address-of operators (* and &) are not used with reference variables. After a reference variable has been declared, the compiler *invisibly* dereferences every single appearance of that reference variable. This difference is illustrated below:

Using a reference variable

```
int  gamma = 26;
int& intRef = gamma;
// Assert: intRef points
//          to gamma

intRef = 35;
// Assert: gamma == 35

intRef = intRef + 3;
// Assert: gamma == 38
```

Using a pointer variable

```
int  gamma = 26;
int* intPtr = &gamma;
// Assert: intPtr points
//          to gamma

*intPtr = 35;
// Assert: gamma == 35

*intPtr = *intPtr + 3;
// Assert: gamma == 38
```

Some programmers like to think of a reference variable as an *alias* for another variable. In the preceding code, we can think of `intRef` as an alias for `gamma`. After `intRef` is initialized in its declaration, everything we do to `intRef` is actually happening to `gamma`.

The second difference between reference and pointer variables is that the compiler treats a reference variable as if it were a *constant* pointer. It cannot be reassigned after being initialized. In fact, absolutely no operations apply directly to a reference variable except initialization. (In this context, C++ defines initialization to mean (a) explicit initialization in a declaration, (b) implicit initialization by passing an actual parameter to a formal parameter, or (c) implicit initialization by returning a function value.) For example, the statement

```
intRef++;
```

does not increment `intRef`; it increments the variable to which `intRef` points. Why? Because the compiler implicitly dereferences each appearance of the name `intRef`.

The principal advantage of reference variables, then, is notational convenience. Unlike pointer variables, reference variables do not require the programmer to continually prefix the variable with an asterisk in order to access the pointed-to variable.

Reference Type A simple data type consisting of an unbounded set of values, each of which is the address of a variable of a given type. The only operation defined on a reference variable is initialization, after which every appearance of the variable is implicitly dereferenced.

A common use of reference variables is to pass nonarray parameters by reference instead of by value (as we have been doing ever since Chapter 7). Suppose the programmer wants to exchange the contents of two `float` variables with the function call

```
Swap(alpha, beta);
```

Because C++ normally passes simple variables by value, the following code fails:

```
void Swap( float x, float y )
// Caution: This routine does not work
{
    float temp = x;

    x = y;
```

```
        y = temp;
}
```

By default, C++ passes the two parameters by value. That is, *copies* of alpha's and beta's values are sent to the function. The local contents of **x** and **y** are exchanged within the function, but the actual parameters `alpha` and `beta` remain unchanged. To correct this situation, we have two options. The first is to send the addresses of `alpha` and `beta` explicitly by using the address-of operator (&):

```
Swap(&alpha, &beta);
```

The function must then declare the formal parameters to be pointer variables:

```
void Swap( float* px, float* py )
{
    float temp = *px;

    *px = *py;
    *py = temp;
}
```

This approach is necessary in the C language, which has pointer variables but not reference variables.

The other option is to use reference variables to eliminate the need for explicit dereferencing:

```
void Swap( float& x, float& y )
{
    float temp = x;

    x = y;
    y = temp;
}
```

In this case, the function call does not require the address-of operator (&) for the actual parameters:

```
Swap(alpha, beta);
```

The compiler implicitly generates code to pass the addresses, not the contents, of `alpha` and `beta`. This method of passing nonarray parameters by reference is the one that we have been using all along and continue to use throughout the book.

By now, you have probably noticed that the ampersand (&) has several meanings in the C++ language. To avoid errors, it pays to keep these meanings distinct from each other. Below is a table that summarizes the different uses of the ampersand. Note that a *prefix* operator is one that precedes its operand(s), an *infix* operator lies between its operands, and a *postfix* operator comes after its operand(s).

Position	Usage	Meaning
Prefix	&Variable	Address-of operation
Infix	Expression & Expression	Bitwise AND operation (mentioned, but not explored, in Chapter 10)
Infix	Expression && Expression	Logical AND operation
Postfix	DataType&	Data type (specifically, a reference type) *Exception:* To declare two variables of reference type, the & is attached to the variable name: `int &var1, &var2;`

Classes and Dynamic Data

When programmers use C++ classes, it is often useful for class objects to create dynamic data on the free store. Let's consider writing a variation of the `DateType` class of Chapter 15. In addition to a month, day, and year, we want each class object to store a message string such as "My birthday" or "Meet Al." When a client program prints a date, this message string will be printed next to the date. To keep the example simple, we'll supply only a bare minimum of public member functions. We begin with the class declaration for a Date class, abbreviated by leaving out the function preconditions and postconditions.

```
class Date
{
public:
    void Print() const;                         // Output operation
    Date( /* in */ int         initMo,          // Constructor
          /* in */ int         initDay,
          /* in */ int         initYr,
          /* in */ const char* msgStr );
private:
    int    mo;
    int    day;
```

```
      int    yr;
      char* msg;
};
```

In the class constructor's parameter list, we could just as well have declared msgStr as

```
const char[] msgStr
```

instead of

```
const char* msgStr
```

Remember that both of these declarations are equivalent as far as the C++ compiler is concerned. They both mean that the parameter being passed is the base address of a string.

As you can see in the private part of the class declaration, the private variable msg is a pointer, not a char array. If we declared msg to be an array of fixed size, say, 30, the array might be either too large or too small to hold the msgStr string that the client passes through the constructor's parameter list. Instead, the class constructor will dynamically allocate a char array of just the right size on the free store and make msg point to this array. Here is the implementation of the class constructor as it would appear in the implementation file:

```
#include <string.h>    // For strcpy() and strlen()
   .
   .
   .
Date::Date( /* in */ int        initMo,
            /* in */ int        initDay,
            /* in */ int        initYr,
            /* in */ const char* msgStr  )
{
    mo = initMo;
    day = initDay;
    yr = initYr;
    msg = new char[strlen(msgStr) + 1];
    // Assert:
    //      Storage for dynamic string is now on free store
    //      and its base address is in msg
    strcpy(msg, msgStr);
    // Assert:
    //      Incoming string has been copied to free store
}
```

The constructor begins by copying the first three incoming parameters into the appropriate private variables. Next, we use the `new` operator to allocate a `char` array on the free store. (We add 1 to the length of the incoming string to leave room for the terminating `'\0'` character.) Finally, we use `strcpy` to copy all the characters from the `msgStr` array to the new dynamic array. If the client code declares two class objects with the statements

```
Date date1(4, 15, 1997, "My birthday");
Date date2(5, 12, 1997, "Meet Al");
    .
    .
    .
```

then the two class objects point to dynamic `char` arrays as shown in Figure 17-9.

Figure 17-9 illustrates an important concept: a `Date` class object does not encapsulate an array—it only encapsulates *access* to the array. The array itself is located externally (on the free store), not within the protective abstraction barrier of the class object. This arrangement does not violate the principle of information hiding, however. The only access to the array is through the pointer variable `msg`, which is a private class member and is therefore inaccessible to clients.

Notice that the `Date` class allocates dynamic data, but we have made no provision for deallocating the dynamic data. To deal adequately with class objects that point to dynamic data, we need more than just a class constructor. We need an entire group of class member functions: a class constructor, a *class destructor*, a *deep copy operation*, and a *class copy-constructor*. One by one, we will explain each of these new functions. But first, here is the overall picture of what our new class declaration looks like:

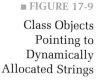

■ FIGURE 17-9

Class Objects
Pointing to
Dynamically
Allocated Strings

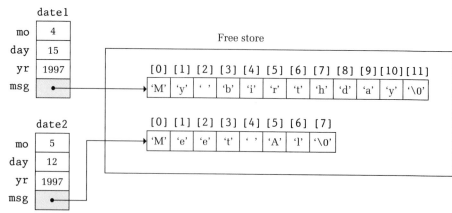

```
class Date
{
public:
    void Print() const;                          // Output operation
    void CopyFrom( /* in */ Date otherDate );   // Deep copy operation
    Date( /* in */ int        initMo,           // Constructor
          /* in */ int        initDay,
          /* in */ int        initYr,
          /* in */ const char* msgStr );
    Date( const Date& otherDate );               // Copy-constructor
    ~Date();                                     // Destructor
private:
    int    mo;
    int    day;
    int    yr;
    char*  msg;
};
```

This class declaration includes function prototypes for all four of the member functions we said we are going to need: constructor, destructor, deep copy operation, and copy-constructor. Before proceeding, let's define more precisely the semantics of each member function by furnishing the function preconditions and postconditions. We have placed the complete specification of the Date class in its own figure—Figure 17-10—so that we can refer to it later.

■ FIGURE 17-10

Specification of the
Date Class

```
//****************************************************************
// SPECIFICATION FILE (date.h)
// This file gives the specification of a Date abstract data
// type representing a date and an associated message
//****************************************************************

class Date
{
public:
    void Print() const;
        // Postcondition:
        //     Date and message have been output in the form
        //         month day, year    message
        //     where the name of the month is printed as a string

    void CopyFrom( /* in */ Date otherDate );
        // Postcondition:
        //     This date is a copy of otherDate, including
        //     the message string
```

■ FIGURE 17-10

(continued)

```
Date( /* in */ int         initMo,
      /* in */ int         initDay,
      /* in */ int         initYr,
      /* in */ const char* msgStr  );
    // Constructor
    // Precondition:
    //      1 <= initMo <= 12
    //   && 1 <= initDay <= maximum number of days in initMo
    //   && 1582 < initYr
    //   && msgStr is assigned
    // Postcondition:
    //      New class object is constructed with a date of
    //      initMo, initDay, initYr and a message string msgStr

Date( const Date& otherDate );
    // Copy-constructor
    // Postcondition:
    //      New class object is constructed with date and
    //      message string the same as otherDate's
    // Note:
    //      This constructor is implicitly invoked whenever a
    //      Date object is passed by value, is returned as a
    //      function value, or is initialized by another
    //      Date object in a declaration

~Date();
    // Destructor
    // Postcondition:
    //      Message string is destroyed
private:
    int   mo;
    int   day;
    int   yr;
    char* msg;

};
```

Class Destructors

The Date class of Figure 17-10 provides a destructor function named ~Date. A class destructor, identified by a tilde (~) preceding the name of the class, can be thought of as the opposite of a constructor. Just as a constructor is implicitly invoked when control reaches the declaration of a class object, a destructor is implicitly invoked when the class object is destroyed. A class object is destroyed when it "goes out of scope." (An automatic object goes out of scope when control leaves the block in which it is declared. A static object goes out of scope when program execution terminates.) The following block—which might be a function body, for example—includes remarks at the locations where the constructor and destructor are invoked:

```
{
    Date conf(1, 30, 1998, "Conference");        ← Constructor is invoked
                                                    here
        .
        .
        .
}              ← Destructor is invoked here because  conf  goes out of scope
```

In the implementation file `date.cpp`, the implementation of the class destructor is very simple:

```
Date::~Date()

// Destructor

// Postcondition:
//     Array pointed to by msg is no longer on the free store
{
    delete [] msg;
}
```

You cannot pass parameters to a destructor and, as with a class constructor, you must not declare the data type of the function.

Until now, we have not needed class destructors. In all previous examples of classes, the private data have been enclosed entirely within the abstraction barrier of the class. For example, in Chapter 15, a `TimeType` class object encapsulates all of its data:

```
         startTime
hrs    |    8    |
mins   |   30    |
secs   |   20    |
```

When `startTime` goes out of scope, destruction of `startTime` implies destruction of all of its component data.

With the `Date` class, some of the data are enclosed within the abstraction barrier and some of the data are not (Figure 17-9). Without the destructor function `~Date`, destruction of a class object would deallocate the *pointer* to the dynamic array, but would not deallocate the array itself. The result would be a memory leak; the dynamic array would remain allocated but no longer accessible.

Shallow Versus Deep Copying

Next, let's look at the `CopyFrom` function of the `Date` class (Figure 17-10). This function is designed to copy one class object to another, *including the dynamic message array*. With the built-in assignment operator (=), assignment of one class object to another copies only the class members; it does *not* copy any data pointed to by the class members. For example, given the `date1` and `date2` objects of Figure 17-9, the effect of the assignment statement

```
date1 = date2;
```

is shown in Figure 17-11. The result is called a **shallow copy** operation. The pointer is copied, but the pointed-to data are not.

Shallow copying is perfectly fine if none of the class members are pointers. But if one or more members are pointers, then shallow copying may be erroneous. In Figure 17-11, the dynamic array originally pointed to by the `date1` object has been left inaccessible.

What we want is a **deep copy** operation—one that duplicates not only the class members but also the pointed-to data. The `CopyFrom` function of the `Date` class performs a deep copy. Here is the function implementation:

```
void Date::CopyFrom( /* in */ Date otherDate )

// Postcondition:
//     mo == otherDate.mo
//  && day == otherDate.day
//  && yr == otherDate.yr
//  && msg points to a duplicate of otherDate's message string
//     on the free store
```

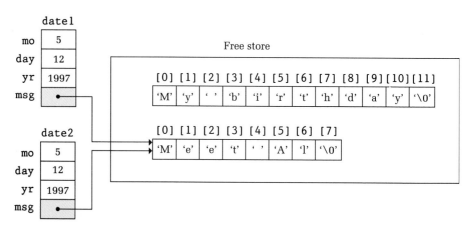

■ FIGURE 17-11

A Shallow Copy Caused by the Assignment date1 = date2

```
{
    mo = otherDate.mo;
    day = otherDate.day;
    yr = otherDate.yr;
    delete [] msg;                                    // Deallocate the
                                                      //   original array
    msg = new char[strlen(otherDate.msg) + 1];        // Allocate a new
                                                      //   array
    strcpy(msg, otherDate.msg);                       // Copy the chars
}
```

First, the function copies the month, day, and year from the otherDate object into the current object. Next, the function deallocates the current object's dynamic array from the free store, allocates a new dynamic array, and copies all elements of otherDate's array into the new array. The result is therefore a deep copy—two identical class objects pointing to two identical (but *separate*) dynamic arrays. Given our date1 and date2 objects of Figure 17-9, the statement

```
date1.CopyFrom(date2);
```

yields the result shown in Figure 17-12. Compare this figure with the shallow copy pictured in Figure 17-11.

Shallow Copy   An operation that copies one class object to another without copying any pointed-to data.

Deep Copy   An operation that not only copies one class object to another but also makes copies of any pointed-to data.

■ FIGURE 17-12

A Deep Copy

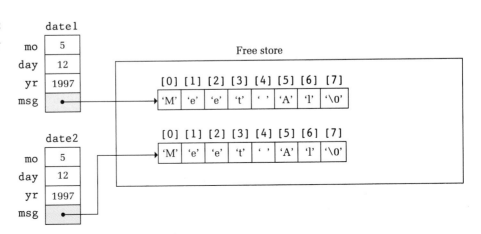

Class Copy-Constructors

As we have discussed, the built-in assignment operator (=) leads to a shallow copy when class objects point to dynamic data. The issue of deep versus shallow copying can also appear in another context: initialization of one class object by another. C++ defines initialization to mean

1. initialization in a variable declaration

```
Date date1 = date2;
```

2. passing a copy of an actual parameter to a formal parameter (that is, pass-by-value)
3. returning an object as the value of a function

```
return someObject;
```

By default, C++ performs such initializations using shallow copy semantics. In other words, the newly created class object is initialized via a member-by-member copy of the old object without regard for any data to which the class members may point. For our Date class, the result would again be two class objects pointing to the same dynamic data.

To handle this situation, C++ has a special kind of constructor known as a *copy-constructor*. In a class declaration, its prototype has the following form:

```
class SomeClass
{
public:
    .
    .
    .
    SomeClass( const SomeClass& someObject );    // Copy-constructor
    .
    .
    .
};
```

Notice that the function prototype does not use any special words to suggest that this is a copy-constructor. You simply have to recognize the pattern of symbols: the class name followed by a parameter list, which contains a single parameter of type

```
const SomeClass&
```

For example, our Date class declaration in Figure 17-10 shows the prototype of the copy-constructor to be

```
Date( const Date& otherDate );
```

If a copy-constructor is present, the default method of initialization (member-by-member copying) is inhibited. Instead, the copy-constructor is implicitly invoked whenever one class object is initialized by another. The following implementation of the Date class copy-constructor shows the steps that are involved:

```
Date::Date( const Date& otherDate )

// Copy-constructor

// Postcondition:
//      mo == otherDate.mo
//   && day == otherDate.day
//   && yr == otherDate.yr
//   && msg points to a duplicate of otherDate's message string
//      on the free store

{
    mo = otherDate.mo;
    day = otherDate.day;
    yr = otherDate.yr;
    msg = new char[strlen(otherDate.msg) + 1];
    strcpy(msg, otherDate.msg);
}
```

The body of the copy-constructor function differs from the body of the CopyFrom function in only one line of code: the CopyFrom function executes

```
delete [] msg;
```

before allocating a new array. The difference between these two functions is that CopyFrom is copying to an *existing* class object (which is already pointing to a dynamic array that must be deallocated), whereas the copy-constructor is creating a new class object that doesn't already exist.

Notice the use of the reserved word const in the parameter list of the copy-constructor. The word const ensures that the function cannot alter otherDate, even though otherDate is passed by reference.

As with any nonarray variable in C++, a class object can be passed to a function either by value or by reference. Because C++ defines initialization to include pass-by-value, copy-constructors are vitally important when class objects point to dynamic data. Assume that we did not include a copy-constructor for the Date class, and assume that the following call to the DoSomething function uses pass-by-value:

```
int main()
{
    Date quizDate(2, 18, 1998, "Geography quiz");
        .
        .
        .
    DoSomething(quizDate);
        .
        .
        .
```

Without a copy-constructor, quizDate would be copied to the DoSomething function's formal parameter using a shallow copy. A copy of quizDate's dynamic array would *not* be created for use within DoSomething. Both quizDate and the formal parameter within DoSomething would point to the same dynamic array (see Figure 17-13). If the DoSomething function were to modify the dynamic array (thinking it is working on a *copy* of the original), then after the function returns, quizDate would point to a corrupted dynamic array.

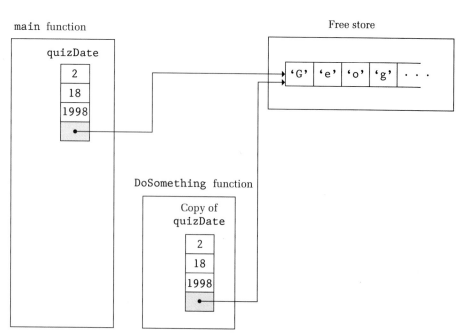

■ FIGURE 17-13

Shallow Copy Caused by Pass-by-Value without a Copy-Constructor

In summary, the default operations of assignment and initialization may be dangerous when class objects point to dynamic data on the free store. Member-by-member assignment and initialization cause only pointers to be copied, not the pointed-to data. If a class allocates and deallocates data on the free store, it almost certainly needs the following suite of member functions to ensure deep copying of dynamic data:

```
class SomeClass
{
public:
       .
       .
       .
    void CopyFrom( SomeClass anotherObject );
        // A deep copy operation

    SomeClass( ... );
        // Constructor, to create data on the free store

    SomeClass( const SomeClass& anotherObject );
        // Copy-constructor, for deep copying in initializations

    ~SomeClass();
        // Destructor, to clean up the free store
private:
       .
       .
       .
};
```

At the beginning of this chapter, we said that pointers are used for two reasons: to make a program more efficient—either in speed or in memory usage—and to create complex data structures called linked structures. We give examples of the use of pointers to make a program more efficient in the case studies in this chapter. Linked structures are covered in Chapter 18.

PROBLEM-SOLVING CASE STUDY

Personnel Records

Problem: We have a file of personnel records, and there is a great deal of data associated with each person. The task is to read in these records, sort them alphabetically by last name, and print out the sorted records.

Input: A file of personnel records (`masterFile`), where each record corresponds to the data type `PersonnelData` in the declarations below.

```
typedef char String20[21];        // Room for 20 characters plus '\0'
typedef char String100[101];      // Room for 100 characters plus '\0'
typedef char String200[201];      // Room for 200 characters plus '\0'

struct AddressType
{
    String20 street;
    String20 city;
    String20 state;
};
struct PersonnelData
{
    String20    lastName;
    String20    firstName;
    AddressType address;
    String200   workHistory;
    String100   education;
    String200   payrollData;
};
```

Each of the eight character strings (last name, first name, street address, city, state, work history, education, and payroll data) is on a separate line in the file masterFile, and each string may contain embedded blanks.

The number of records in the file is unknown. The maximum number of employees that the company has ever had is 1000.

Output: The contents of the file masterFile with the records in alphabetical order by last name.

Discussion: Using object-oriented design (OOD) to solve this problem, we begin by identifying potential objects and their operations. Recall that a good way to start is to examine the problem definition, looking for important nouns and noun phrases (to find objects) and important verbs and verb phrases (to find operations). Additionally, implementation-level objects usually are necessary in the solution. Here is an object table for this problem:

Object	Operation
File masterFile	Open the file
	Input data from the file
Personnel record	Read a record
	Print a record
Record list	Read all personnel records into the list
	Sort
	Print all records in the list

Notice that the record list object is an implementation-level object. This object is not readily apparent in the problem domain, yet we need it in order for the operation of sorting to make any sense. ("Sort" is not an operation on an individual personnel record; it is an operation on a *list* of records.)

The second major step in OOD is to determine if there are any inheritance or composition relationships among the objects. Using *is-a* as a guide, we do not find any inheritance relationships. However, the record list object and the personnel record object clearly are related by composition. That is, a record list *has-a* personnel record within it (in fact, it probably contains many personnel records). Discovery of this relationship helps us as we proceed to design and implement each object.

The `masterFile` Object: For the concrete representation of this object, we can use the `ifstream` class supplied by the standard library. Then the abstract operations of opening a file and reading data are naturally implemented by using the operations already provided by the `ifstream` class.

The Personnel Record Object: We could implement this object by using a C++ class, hiding the data members as private data and supplying public operations for reading and writing the members. (Also, we might need to provide observer and transformer operations that retrieve and store the values of individual members.) Instead, let's treat this particular object as passive data (in the form of a `struct` with all members public) rather than as an active object with associated operations. We'll use the `struct` declarations shown earlier (`AddressType` and `PersonnelData`), and we can implement the reading and writing operations by using the `>>` and `<<` operators to input and output individual members of the `struct`.

The Record List Object: This object represents a list of personnel records. Thinking of a list as an ADT, we can use a C++ class to conceal the private data representation and provide public operations to read records into the list, sort the list, and print the list.

To choose a concrete data representation for the list, we remember the composition relationship we proposed—namely, that a record list is composed of one or more personnel record objects. Therefore, we could use a 1000-element array of `PersonnelData` structs, along with an integer variable to keep track of the length of the list. But there are two disadvantages to using an array of `struct`s in this particular problem.

First, the `PersonnelData` structs are quite large (600 bytes each). If we declare a 1000-element array of these `struct`s, the compiler reserves 600,000 bytes of memory even though the input file may contain only a few records!

Second, the act of sorting an array of `struct`s can take a lot of time. Consider the selection sort we introduced in Chapter 12. In the `SelSort` function, the contents of two variables are swapped during each iteration. Swapping two simple variables is a fast operation. If large `struct`s are being sorted, however, swapping two of them can be time-consuming. The C++ code to swap two `structs` is the same, regardless of the size of the `structs`— an ordinary assignment statement will do. But the length of time to make the swap varies greatly depending on the size of the `structs`. For example, it may take 10 times as long to swap `structs` with 20 members as it does to swap `structs` with 2 members.

If we are dealing with large `structs`, we can make the sorting operation more efficient and save memory by making the `structs` dynamic variables, and by sorting pointers to the `structs` rather than sorting the `structs` themselves. This way, only simple pointer variables are swapped on each iteration, rather than whole `structs`.

The `SelSort` function has to be modified somewhat to sort large `structs` rather than simple variables. The `structs` themselves are dynamically allocated, and a pointer to each is stored in an array. It is these pointers that are swapped when the algorithm calls for exchanging two values.

We have to declare an array `ptrList`, which holds pointers to the personnel records, to be the maximum size we might need. However, we create each `PersonnelData` variable only when we need it. Therefore, room for 1000 pointers is set aside in memory for the `ptrList` array, but at run time there are only as many `PersonnelData` variables in memory as there are records in the file (see Figure 17-14).

The `ptrList` array before and after sorting is shown in Figure 17-15. Note that when the algorithm wants to swap the contents of two `structs`, we swap the pointers instead.

Now that we have chosen a concrete data representation for the personnel record list, we should review the ADT operations once more. We identified

■ FIGURE 17-14   Array of Pointers to `PersonnelData` Structs

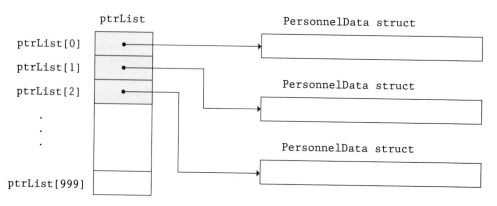

■ FIGURE 17-15   `ptrList` Array Before and After Sorting

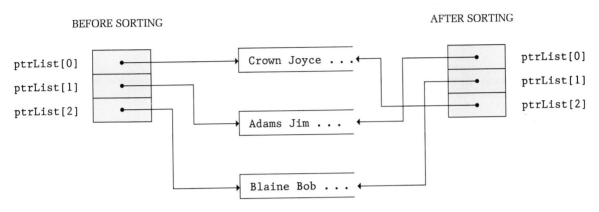

three operations: read all the records into the list, sort the list, and print all the records in the list. Because our data representation uses dynamically allocated data, we must consider supplying additional operations: a class constructor, a class destructor, a class copy-constructor, and a deep copy operation. At a minimum, we need a constructor to initialize the private data and a destructor to deallocate all the `PersonnelData` variables from the free store. (Case Study Follow-Up Exercise 3 asks you to write the copy-constructor and deep copy operations.)

Below is the specification of the `RecordList` class. Notice that we use a Typedef statement to define the identifier `PersonPtr` as a synonym for the type `PersonnelData*`. Thereafter, we can declare the `ptrList` array as

```
PersonPtr ptrList[MAX_EMPL];
```

instead of

```
PersonnelData* ptrList[MAX_EMPL];
```

```
//*************************************************************
// SPECIFICATION FILE (reclist.h)
// This file gives the specification of RecordList, an ADT for a
// list of personnel records.
//*************************************************************
```

```
#ifndef RECLIST_H
#define RECLIST_H

#include "bool.h"
#include <fstream.h>    // For file I/O

const int MAX_EMPL = 1000;      // Maximum number of employees

typedef char String20[21];      // Room for 20 characters plus '\0'
typedef char String100[101];    // Room for 100 characters plus '\0'
typedef char String200[201];    // Room for 200 characters plus '\0'

struct AddressType
{
    String20 street;
    String20 city;
    String20 state;
};
struct PersonnelData
{
    String20    lastName;
    String20    firstName;
    AddressType address;
    String200   workHistory;
    String100   education;
    String200   payrollData;
};

typedef PersonnelData* PersonPtr;

class RecordList
{
public:
    void ReadAll( /* inout */ ifstream& inFile,
                  /* out */   Boolean&  outOfMem );
        // Precondition:
        //     inFile has been opened for input
        //  && inFile contains at most MAX_EMPL records
        // Postcondition:
        //     List contains employee records as read from inFile
        //  && IF there was not enough memory for all input records
        //          outOfMem == TRUE
        //          && A warning message is printed
        //     ELSE
        //          outOfMem == FALSE
```

```
        void SelSort();
            // Postcondition:
            //     List is in ascending order of employee last name

        void PrintAll();
            // Postcondition:
            //     All employee records have been written to
            //     standard output

        RecordList();
            // Postcondition:
            //     Empty list created

        ~RecordList();
            // Postcondition:
            //     List destroyed
    private:
        PersonPtr ptrList[MAX_EMPL];
        int       length;
};
#endif
```

Now we are ready to implement the RecordList member functions. We begin with the class constructor, whose sole task is to initialize the private variable length to zero.

The class constructor RecordList ( )

```
Set length = 0
```

To implement the ReadAll member function, we use a loop that repeatedly does the following: allocates a dynamic PersonnelData struct, reads an employee record into that struct, and stores the pointer to that struct into the next unused element of the ptrList array. We must keep in mind that we might need as many as 1000 dynamic structs on the free store. When allocating large data structures dynamically, it is good to get into the habit of checking each allocation attempt to see if it was successful. Remember that the C++ new operator returns the null pointer instead of a pointer to dynamic data if the allocation failed. In the ReadAll function, if the allocation attempt fails, we report this fact to the caller through a Boolean parameter outOfMem.

ReadAll (Inout: inFile; Out: outOfMem)

```
Set outOfMem = FALSE
Set aPerson = new PersonnelData        // Allocate a dynamic struct
Get a record from inFile into
    the struct pointed to by aPerson
WHILE NOT EOF on inFile AND NOT outOfMem
    Set ptrList[length] = aPerson          // Store pointer into array
    Increment length
    Set aPerson = new PersonnelData  // Allocate a dynamic struct
    IF aPerson is NULL
        Print warning message
        Set outOfMem = TRUE
    ELSE
        Get a record from inFile into
            the struct pointed to by aPerson
```

The pseudocode step "Get a record from inFile ... " appears twice in ReadAll. This step breaks down into several substeps: read the last name, check for end-of-file, read the first name, and so on. To avoid physically writing down the substeps twice, let's write a separate "helper" function named GetRecord. In GetRecord's parameter list, aPerson is a pointer to a PersonnelData struct.

GetRecord (Inout: inFile; In: aPerson)

```
Read aPerson–>lastName from inFile
IF EOF on inFile
    Return
Read aPerson–>firstName from inFile
Read aPerson–>address.street from inFile
Read aPerson–>address.city from inFile
Read aPerson–>address.state from inFile
Read aPerson–>workHistory from inFile
Read aPerson–>education from inFile
Read aPerson–>payrollData from inFile
```

The SelSort function is nearly the same as in Chapter 12. The original SelSort finds the minimum value in the list and swaps it with the value in the first place in the list. Then the next smallest value in the list is swapped with the value in the second place. This process continues until all the values are in order. The location in this algorithm that we must change is where the minimum value is determined. Instead of comparing two components in the list, we compare the last name members in the structs to which these components point. The statement that did the comparison in the original SelSort function must be changed from

```
if (list[placeCount] < list[minIndex])
```

to

```
if (strcmp(ptrList[placeCount]->lastName,
          ptrList[minIndex]->lastName) < 0)
```

The remaining member functions—PrintAll and the class destructor—are straightforward to implement.

PrintAll ( )

```
FOR index going from 0 through length −1
    Print ptrList[index]->lastName, ", ", ptrList[index]->firstName
    Print ptrList[index]->address.street
    Print ptrList[index]->address.city, ", ", ptrList[index]->address.state
    Print ptrList[index]->workHistory
    Print ptrList[index]->education
    Print ptrList[index]->payrollData
```

The class destructor ~RecordList ( )

```
FOR index going from 0 through length −1
    Deallocate the struct pointed to by ptrList[index]
```

Below is the implementation file for the RecordList class. In the code, there are two C++ issues you should observe. First, GetRecord is a *helper function*—a function that is not a member of the class but is physically located in the implementation file to help a member function accomplish its task. Because GetRecord is not a class member, its name is not preceded by RecordList:: as are the names of the other functions. Second, the input description for this case study says that the input strings (last name, first name, street address, and so on) can contain embedded blanks. Therefore, in the `GetRecord` function, we cannot use the extraction operator (`>>`), which stops reading as soon as a whitespace character is found. For each string we must call the `get` function, followed by a call to the `ignore` function to consume the newline character.

```cpp
//*************************************************************
// IMPLEMENTATION FILE (reclist.cpp)
// This file implements the RecordList class member functions.
// List representation: an array of pointers to PersonnelData
// structs and an integer variable giving the current length
// of the list
//*************************************************************
#include "reclist.h"
#include <iostream.h>
#include <string.h>      // For strcmp()
#include <stddef.h>      // For NULL

// Private members of class:
//     PersonPtr ptrList[MAX_EMPL];    Array of pointers
//     int       length;              Number of valid pointers
//                                        in ptrList

void GetRecord( ifstream&, PersonPtr );    // Prototype for "helper"
                                           //    function


//*************************************************************

RecordList::RecordList()

// Default constructor

// Postcondition:
//     length == 0

{
    length = 0;
}

//*************************************************************

RecordList::~RecordList()

// Destructor

// Postcondition:
//     Structs pointed to by ptrList[0..length-1]
//     are no longer on the free store
```

```
{
    int index;    // Loop control variable

    for (index = 0; index < length; index++)

            // Invariant (prior to test):
            //     Structs pointed to by ptrList[0..index-1]
            //     are no longer on the free store
            //  && 0 <= index <= length

        delete ptrList[index];
}

//***************************************************************

void GetRecord( /* inout */ ifstream& inFile,
                /* in */    PersonPtr aPerson )

// Reads one record from file inFile

// Precondition:
//     inFile is open for input
//  && aPerson points to a valid PersonnelData struct
// Postcondition:
//     IF input of the lastName member failed due to end-of-file
//         The contents of *aPerson are undefined
//     ELSE
//         All members of *aPerson are filled with the values
//         for one person read from inFile

{
    inFile.get(aPerson->lastName, 21);
    if ( !inFile )
        return;
    inFile.ignore(100, '\n');

    inFile.get(aPerson->firstName, 21);
    inFile.ignore(100, '\n');

    inFile.get(aPerson->address.street, 21);
    inFile.ignore(100, '\n');

    inFile.get(aPerson->address.city, 21);
    inFile.ignore(100, '\n');

    inFile.get(aPerson->address.state, 21);
    inFile.ignore(100, '\n');
```

```
            inFile.get(aPerson->workHistory, 201);
            inFile.ignore(100, '\n');

            inFile.get(aPerson->education, 101);
            inFile.ignore(100, '\n');

            inFile.get(aPerson->payrollData, 101);
            inFile.ignore(100, '\n');
    }

    //****************************************************************

    void RecordList::ReadAll( /* inout */ ifstream&  inFile,
                              /* out */    Boolean&   outOfMem )

    // Precondition:
    //     inFile has been opened for input
    //  && inFile contains at most MAX_EMPL records
    // Postcondition:
    //     ptrList[0..length-1] point to dynamic structs
    //     containing values read from inFile
    //  && IF there was not enough free store for all input records
    //          outOfMem == TRUE
    //       && A warning message is printed
    //     ELSE
    //          outOfMem == FALSE

    {
        PersonPtr aPerson;    // Pointer to newly input record

        outOfMem = FALSE;
        aPerson = new PersonnelData;
        GetRecord(inFile, aPerson);
        while (inFile && !outOfMem)
        {
                // Invariant (prior to test):
                //     ptrList[0..length-1] point to dynamic structs
                //     containing values read from inFile
                //  && 0 <= length <= MAX_EMPL

            ptrList[length] = aPerson;      // Store pointer into array
            length++;
            aPerson = new PersonnelData;
            if (aPerson == NULL)
            {
                cout << "** Out of memory after " << length
                    << " records have been input **" << endl;
                outOfMem = TRUE;
```

```
            }
            else
                GetRecord(inFile, aPerson);
        }
    }

    //**********************************************************************

    void RecordList::SelSort()

    // Sorts ptrList so that the pointed-to structs are in
    // ascending order of last name

    // Precondition:
    //      ptrList[0..length-1] point to valid PersonnelData structs
    // Postcondition:
    //      ptrList contains the same values as ptrList@entry, rearranged
    //      so that consecutive elements of ptrList point to structs in
    //      ascending order of last name

    {
        PersonPtr  tempPtr;        // Used for swapping
        int        passCount;      // Loop control variable
        int        placeCount;     // Loop control variable
        int        minIndex;       // Index of minimum so far

        for (passCount = 0; passCount < length - 1; passCount++)
        {
            // Invariant (prior to test):
            //      ptrList[0..passCount-1] point to structs in
            //      ascending order of last name
            //  && 0 <= passCount <= length - 1

            minIndex = passCount;

            // Find the index of the pointer to the alphabetically first
            // last name remaining in ptrList[passCount..length-1]

            for (placeCount = passCount + 1; placeCount < length;
                                                        placeCount++)
                // Invariant (prior to test):
                //     ptrList[minIndex]->lastName is less than or equal
                //     to all ptrList[passCount]->lastName through
                //     ptrList[placeCount-1]->lastName
                // && placeCount <= length
```

```
            if (strcmp(ptrList[placeCount]->lastName,
                    ptrList[minIndex]->lastName) < 0)
                minIndex = placeCount;

        // Swap ptrList[minIndex] and ptrList[passCount]

        tempPtr = ptrList[minIndex];
        ptrList[minIndex] = ptrList[passCount];
        ptrList[passCount] = tempPtr;
    }
}

//*******************************************************************

void RecordList::PrintAll()

// Precondition:
//      ptrList[0..length-1] point to valid PersonnelData structs
// Postcondition:
//      Contents of the structs pointed to by ptrList[0..length-1]
//      have been written to standard output

{
    int index;    // Loop control variable

    for (index = 0; index < length; index++)
    {
            // Invariant (prior to test):
            //      Contents of the structs pointed to by
            //      ptrList[0..index-1] have been printed
            //  && 0 <= index <= length

        cout << ptrList[index]->lastName << ", "
            << ptrList[index]->firstName << endl;
        cout << ptrList[index]->address.street << endl;
        cout << ptrList[index]->address.city << ", "
            << ptrList[index]->address.state << endl;
        cout << ptrList[index]->workHistory << endl;
        cout << ptrList[index]->education << endl;
        cout << ptrList[index]->payrollData << endl << endl;
    }
}
```

Testing: As with any C++ class, testing RecordList amounts to testing each of its member functions. To test the ReadAll function, a test driver that invokes only ReadAll would not be useful; we would also need to invoke PrintAll to check the results. Likewise, a test driver cannot invoke only

PROBLEM-SOLVING CASE STUDY cont'd.

`PrintAll` without first putting something into the list (by invoking `ReadAll`). Thus, a minimal test driver must open a data file, call `ReadAll`, then call `PrintAll`. But now the test driver is almost identical to the main driver for the entire program, the only difference being that the main driver calls `SelSort` after calling `ReadAll`. Therefore, we postpone a detailed discussion of testing until we have written the main driver.

The Driver: The third step in OOD is to design the driver—the top-level algorithm. In this program, all the driver has to do is invoke the operations of the `masterFile` object and the record list object.

Main   *Level 0*

```
Create empty list of personnel records named list
Open masterFile for input and verify success
list.ReadAll(masterFile, outOfMem)
IF outOfMem
      Halt the program
list.SelSort()
list.PrintAll()
```

Assumption: File `masterFile` contains no more than 1000 personnel records.

Module Structure Chart:

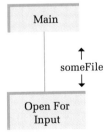

Below is the SortWithPointers program that implements our design. To run the program, we compile the source code files `reclist.cpp` and `sortwithpointers.cpp` into object code files `reclist.obj` and `sortwithpointers.obj`, then link the object code files to produce an executable file.

```
//****************************************************************
// SortWithPointers program
// This program reads personnel records from a data file,
// sorts the records alphabetically by last name,
// and writes them to the standard output device
// Assumption: The input file contains at most 1000 records
//****************************************************************
#include <iostream.h>
#include <fstream.h>      // For file I/O
#include "reclist.h"      // For RecordList class
#include "bool.h"

void OpenForInput( ifstream& );

int main()
{
    RecordList list;          // List of personnel records
    ifstream    masterFile;   // Input file of personnel records
    Boolean     outOfMem;     // True if not enough memory for
                              //    all input records

    OpenForInput(masterFile);
    if ( !masterFile )
        return 1;

    list.ReadAll(masterFile, outOfMem);
    if (outOfMem)
        return 1;

    list.SelSort();
    list.PrintAll();
    return 0;
}

//****************************************************************

void OpenForInput( /* inout */ ifstream& someFile )     // File to be
                                                        // opened

// Prompts the user for the name of an input file
// and attempts to open the file

{
    .
    .         (Same as in previous case studies)
    .
}
```

Testing: To test this program, we begin by preparing an input file that contains personnel information for, say, 10 employees. The data should be in random order by employee last name to make sure that the sorting routine works properly. Given this input data, we expect the program to output the personnel records in ascending order by last name.

File Data   *Expected Output*

Adams   Adams

⋮ } Remainder of Adams's data   ⋮ } Remainder of Adams's data

Gordon   Cava

⋮ } Remainder of Gordon's data   ⋮ } Remainder of Cava's data

Cava   Gleason

⋮   ⋮

Sheehan   Gordon

⋮   ⋮

McCorkle   Kirshen

⋮   ⋮

Pinard   McCorkle

⋮   ⋮

Ripley   Pinard

⋮   ⋮

Kirshen   Ripley

⋮   ⋮

Gleason   Sheehan

⋮   ⋮

Thompson   Thompson

If we run the program and find too many or too few employee records printed out, or if the records are not in alphabetical order, the problem lies in the record list object—the object responsible for reading the file, sorting, and printing. Using a hand trace, debug output statements, or the system debugger, we should check the RecordList member functions in the following order: ReadAll (to verify that the file data was read into the list correctly), SelSort (to confirm that the records are ordered by employee last name), then PrintAll (to ensure that all records are output properly).

After the program works correctly for the file of test data, we should also run the program against the following files: a nonexistent file and an empty file. With a nonexistent file, the program should halt after the OpenForInput function prints its error message. With an empty file, the program should terminate successfully but produce no output at all. (Look at the loops in the ReadAll, SelSort, and PrintAll functions to see why.)

Are we required to test the program with a file of more than 1000 employee records? No. Clearly, the program would misbehave if the index into the ptrList array exceeds 999. However, our program correctly satisfies the problem definition, which states a precondition for the entire program— namely, that the input file contains at most 1000 records. The user of the program must be informed of this precondition and is expected to comply. If the problem definition were changed to eliminate this precondition, then, of course, we would have to modify the program to deal with an input file that is too long.

One final remark: Regarding the SelSort function, what we have tested is that the program correctly sorts the data using pointers to dynamic variables of type PersonnelData. But the output may still be slightly wrong. Because SelSort compares the strings that make up the last names, it is ordering the names according to the machine's particular character set. As we mentioned in Chapter 12, such comparisons can lead to problems when uppercase and lowercase characters are mixed. For example, in the ASCII set, Macartney would come *after* MacDonald. Case Study Follow-Up Exercise 1 asks you to modify SelSort so that it orders names regardless of the case of the individual characters.

PROBLEM-SOLVING CASE STUDY

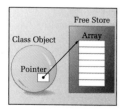

Dynamic Arrays

Problem: In Chapter 15, Programming Warm-Up Exercise 10 described a "safe array" class (IntArray) that prevents array indices from going out of bounds. The public member functions were: a class constructor, to create an array of up to MAX_SIZE elements and initialize all elements to zero; a Store function, to store a value into a particular array element; and a ValueAt function, to retrieve the value of an array element. We want to enhance the IntArray class so that a client of the class can create an array of *any* size—a size that is not bounded by a constant MAX_SIZE. Furthermore, the client should be able to specify the array size at execution time rather than at compile time.

In this case study, we omit the Input and Output sections because we are developing only a C++ class, not a complete program. Instead, we include two sections entitled Specification of the Class and Implementation of the Class.

Discussion: In Chapter 15's IntArray class, the private data include a fixed-size array of MAX_SIZE (which is 200) elements:

```cpp
class IntArray
{
    .
    .
    .
private:
    int arr[MAX_SIZE];
    int size;
};
```

Each class object contains an array of exactly 200 elements, whether the client needs that many or not. If the client requires fewer than 200 elements, then memory is wasted. If more than 200 elements are needed, the class cannot be used.

The disadvantage of any built-in array, such as arr in the IntArray class, is that its size must be known *statically* (at compile time). In this case study, we want to be able to specify the array size *dynamically* (at execution time). Therefore, we must design and implement a class (call it DynArray) that allocates dynamic data on the free store—specifically, an integer array of any size specified by the client code. The private part of our class will no longer include an entire array; rather, it will include a pointer to a dynamically allocated array:

```cpp
class DynArray
{
    .
    .
    .
private:
    int* arr;
    int  size;
};
```

Figure 17-9 depicted exactly the same strategy of keeping a pointer within a class object and letting it point to a dynamic array on the free store.

Specification of the Class: In choosing public operations for the DynArray class, we will retain the three operations from the IntArray class: ValueAt, Store, and a class constructor. The job of the constructor, when it receives a parameter arrSize, will be to allocate a dynamic array of exactly arrSize elements—no more, and no less. Because DynArray class objects point to dynamic data on the free store, we also need a deep copy operation, a class copy-constructor, and a class destructor. Here is the specification of DynArray, complete with preconditions and postconditions for the member functions.

```
//********************************************************************
// SPECIFICATION FILE (dynarray.h)
// This file gives the specification of an integer array class
// that allows:
//     1. Run-time specification of array size
//     2. Trapping of invalid array indices
//     3. Aggregate copying of one array to another
//     4. Aggregate array initialization (for parameter passage by
//        value, function value return, and initialization in a
//        declaration)
//********************************************************************

class DynArray
{
public:
    int ValueAt( /* in */ int i ) const;
        // Precondition:
        //     i is assigned
        // Postcondition:
        //     IF i >= 0  &&  i < declared size of array
        //         Function value == value of array element
        //                          at index i
        //     ELSE
        //         Program has halted with error message

    void Store( /* in */ int val,
                /* in */ int i   );
        // Precondition:
        //     val and i are assigned
        // Postcondition:
        //     IF i >= 0  &&  i < declared size of array
        //         val is stored in array element i
```

```
//      ELSE
//           Program has halted with error message

void CopyFrom( /* in */ DynArray array2 );
   // Postcondition:
   //      IF there is enough memory for a deep copy of array2
   //           This object is a copy of array2 (deep copy)
   //      ELSE
   //           Program has halted with error message

DynArray( /* in */ int arrSize );
   // Constructor
   // Precondition:
   //      arrSize is assigned
   // Postcondition:
   //      IF arrSize >= 1  &&  There is enough memory
   //           Array of size arrSize is created with all
   //           array elements == 0
   //      ELSE
   //           Program has halted with error message

DynArray( const DynArray& array2 );
   // Copy-constructor
   // Postcondition:
   //      IF there is enough memory
   //           New array is created with size and contents
   //           the same as array2 (deep copy)
   //      ELSE
   //           Program has halted with error message
   // Note:
   //      This constructor is implicitly invoked whenever a
   //      DynArray object is passed by value, is returned as
   //      a function value, or is initialized by another
   //      DynArray object in a declaration

~DynArray();
   // Destructor
   // Postcondition:
   //      Array is destroyed
private:
   int* arr;
   int  size;
};
```

Below is a simple client program that creates two class objects, **x** and **y**, stores the values 100, 101, 102, . . . into **x**, copies object **x** to object **y**, and prints out the contents of **y**.

```cpp
#include "dynarray.h"
#include <iostream.h>

int main()
{
    int numElements;    // Array size
    int index;          // Array index

    cout << "Enter the array size: ";
    cin >> numElements;

    DynArray x(numElements);
    DynArray y(numElements);

    for (index = 0; index < numElements; index++)
        x.Store(index + 100, index);
    y.CopyFrom(x);
    for (index = 0; index < numElements; index++)
        cout << y.ValueAt(index);
    return 0;
}
```

If the input value for numElements is 20, the class constructor creates a 20-element array for x and initializes all elements to zero. Similarly, y is created with all 20 elements initialized to zero. After using the Store function to store 20 new values into x, the program does an aggregate copy of x to y using the CopyFrom operation. Then the program outputs the 20 elements of y, which should be the same as the values contained in x. Finally, both class objects go out of scope (because control exits the block in which they are declared), causing the class destructor to be executed for each object. Each call to the destructor deallocates a dynamic array from the free store, as we will see when we look at the implementations of the class member functions.

Implementation of the Class: Next, we implement each class member function, placing the function definitions into a C++ implementation file dynarray.cpp. As we implement the member functions, we also discuss appropriate testing strategies.

The class constructor and destructor: According to the specification file, the class constructor should allocate an array of size arrSize, and the destructor should deallocate the array. The constructor must also do some error checking; it must verify that arrSize is at least 1, and that allocating the dynamic data succeeded. If both of these conditions are met, the constructor sets each array element to zero.

The class constructor DynArray (In: arrSize)

```
IF arrSize < 1
    Print error message
    Halt the program
Set size = arrSize
Set arr = new int[size]      // Allocate a dynamic array
IF arr is NULL
    Print error message
    Halt the program
FOR i going from 0 through size –1
    Set arr[i] = 0
```

The class destructor ~DynArray ( )

```
Deallocate the array pointed to by arr
```

In the constructor, we allocate an integer array of `arrSize` elements and store its base address into the pointer variable `arr`. Remember that in C++ any pointer can be indexed by attaching an index expression in brackets. Therefore, the assignment statement

```
arr[i] = 0;
```

does exactly what we want it to: it stores zero into element `i` of the array pointed to by `arr`.

Testing: Three things should be tested in the constructor: the two If statements and the initialization loop. To test the first If statement, we should try different values of the parameter `arrSize`: negative, zero, and positive. Negative and zero values should cause the program to halt. Testing the second If statement may or may not prove fruitful, depending on a particular compiler and machine. On some machines, passing a huge value of `arrSize` may cause the `new` operator to return NULL if there is not enough room on the free store. Other machines use a concept called *virtual memory*, which lets the machine "borrow" space on a disk device as if the disk were memory. In this case, the size of the free store is essentially unbounded, so the If test will always succeed. To test the initialization loop, it would suffice to create a class object, use the ValueAt function to output the array elements, and verify that the elements are all zero:

```
DynArray testArr(50);

for (index = 0; index < 50; index++)
    cout << testArr.ValueAt(index) << endl;
```

Regarding the class destructor, there is nothing to test. The function simply deallocates the dynamic array from the free store.

The ValueAt *and* Store *functions:* The essence of each of these functions is simple: the Store function stores a value into the array, and ValueAt retrieves a value. Additionally, the function postconditions require each function to halt the program if the index is out of bounds.

ValueAt (In: i)
    Out: Function value

```
IF i < 0 OR i ≥ size
    Print error message
    Halt the program
Return arr[i]
```

Store (In: val, i)

```
IF i < 0 OR i ≥ size
    Print error message
    Halt the program
Set arr[i] = val
```

Testing: To test these functions, valid indices (0 through size−1) as well as invalid indices should be passed as parameters. Programming Warm-Up Exercises 11 and 12 ask you to design test data for these functions and to write drivers that do the testing.

The class copy-constructor: This function is called whenever a new class object is created *and* initialized to be a copy of an existing class object. As with the basic class constructor, the function attempts to allocate a new dynamic array on the free store and must check the resulting pointer to see if the allocation succeeded.

The class copy-constructor DynArray (In: array2)

```
Set size = array2.size
Set arr = new int[size]    // Allocate a dynamic array
IF arr is NULL
    Print error message
    Halt the program
FOR i going from 0 through size – 1
    Set arr[i] = array2.arr[i]
```

Testing: A copy-constructor is implicitly invoked whenever a class object is passed by value as a parameter, is returned as a function value, or is initialized by another class object in a declaration. To test the copy-constructor, you could write a function that receives a DynArray object by value, outputs the contents (to confirm that the values of the array elements are the same as in the caller's actual parameter), and modifies some of the array elements. On return from the function, the calling code should print out the contents of the original array, which should be unchanged from the time before the function call. In other words, you want to verify that when the function modified some array elements, it was working on a *copy* of the actual parameter, not on the actual parameter itself.

The CopyFrom *function:* This function is nearly the same as the copy-constructor; it performs a deep copy of one class object to another. The important difference is that, whereas the copy-constructor creates a *new* class object to copy to, the CopyFrom function is applied to an *existing* class object. The only difference in the two algorithms, then, is that CopyFrom must begin by deallocating the dynamic array that is currently pointed to.

CopyFrom (In: array2)

```
Deallocate the dynamic array pointed to by arr
Set size = array2.size
Set arr = new int[size]          // Allocate a new dynamic array
IF arr is NULL
    Print error message
    Halt the program
FOR i going from 0 through size − 1
    Set arr[i] = array2.arr[i]
```

Testing: To test the CopyFrom function, we could use the client code we presented earlier:

```
for (index = 0; index < numElements; index++)
    x.Store(index + 100, index);
y.CopyFrom(x);
for (index = 0; index < numElements; index++)
    cout << y.ValueAt(index);
```

If the value of numElements is 20, the output should be the values 100 through 119, demonstrating that y is a copy of x.

Translating all of these pseudocode algorithms into C++, we obtain the following implementation file for the DynArray class.

```
//***********************************************************************
// IMPLEMENTATION FILE (dynarray.cpp)
// This file implements the DynArray class member functions
//***********************************************************************
#include "dynarray.h"
#include <iostream.h>
#include <stddef.h>        // For NULL
#include <stdlib.h>        // For exit()

// Private members of class:
//      int* arr;               Pointer to array on free store
//      int  size;              Size of array

//***********************************************************************

DynArray::DynArray( /* in */ int arrSize )

// Constructor
```

```
// Precondition:
//     arrSize is assigned
// Postcondition:
//     IF arrSize >= 1  &&  There is room on free store
//          New array of size arrSize is created on free store
//        && arr == base address of new array
//        && size == arrSize
//        && arr[0..size-1] == 0
//     ELSE
//          Program has halted with error message

{
    int i;    // Array index

    if (arrSize < 1)
    {
        cout << "** In DynArray constructor, invalid size: "
            << arrSize << " **" << endl;
        exit(1);
    }
    size = arrSize;
    arr = new int[size];
    if (arr == NULL)
    {
        cout << "** In DynArray constructor, not enough memory for "
            << size << " elements **" << endl;
        exit(1);
    }
    for (i = 0; i < size; i++)
        arr[i] = 0;
}

//*************************************************************

DynArray::DynArray( const DynArray& array2 )

// Copy-constructor

// Postcondition:
//     IF there is room on free store
//          New array of size array2.size is created on free store
//        && arr == base address of new array
//        && size == array2.size
//        && arr[0..size-1] == array2.arr[0..size-1]
//     ELSE
//          Program has halted with error message
```

```
{
    int i;      // Array index

    size = array2.size;
    arr = new int[size];
    if (arr == NULL)
    {
        cout << "** In DynArray copy-constructor, not enough memory"
            << " for " << size << " elements **" << endl;
        exit(1);
    }
    for (i = 0; i < size; i++)
        arr[i] = array2.arr[i];
}

//*****************************************************************

DynArray::~DynArray()

// Destructor

// Postcondition:
//      Array pointed to by arr is no longer on the free store

{
    delete [] arr;
}

//*****************************************************************

int DynArray::ValueAt( /* in */ int i ) const

// Precondition:
//      i is assigned
// Postcondition:
//      IF i >= 0  &&  i < size
//          Function value == arr[i]
//      ELSE
//          Program has halted with error message

{
    if (i < 0 || i >= size)
    {
        cout << "** In ValueAt function, invalid index: "
            << i << " **" << endl;
        exit(1);
    }
```

```cpp
        return arr[i];
}

//*****************************************************************

void DynArray::Store( /* in */ int val,
                      /* in */ int i   )

// Precondition:
//      val and i are assigned
// Postcondition:
//      IF i >= 0  &&  i < size
//          arr[i] == val
//      ELSE
//          Program has halted with error message

{
    if (i < 0 || i >= size)
    {
        cout << "** In Store function, invalid index: "
            << i << " **" << endl;
        exit(1);
    }
    arr[i] = val;
}

//*****************************************************************

void DynArray::CopyFrom( /* in */ DynArray array2 )

// Postcondition:
//      Array pointed to by arr@entry is no longer on free store
//      && IF free store has room for an array of size array2.size
//              New array of size array2.size is created on free store
//          && arr == base address of new array
//          && size == array2.size
//          && arr[0..size-1] == array2.arr[0..size-1]
//      ELSE
//          Program has halted with error message

{
    int i;      // Array index

    delete [] arr;
    size = array2.size;
    arr = new int[size];
    if (arr == NULL)
    {
```

```
                    cout << "** In CopyFrom function, not enough memory"
                         << " for " << size << " elements **" << endl;
                    exit(1);
                }
                for (i = 0; i < size; i++)
                    arr[i] = array2.arr[i];
            }
```

TESTING AND DEBUGGING

Programs that use pointers are more difficult to write and debug than programs without pointers. Indirect addressing never seems quite as "normal" as direct addressing when you want to get at the contents of a variable.

The most common errors associated with the use of pointer variables are

1. confusing the pointer variable with the variable it points to
2. trying to dereference the null pointer or an uninitialized pointer
3. inaccessible objects
4. dangling pointers

Let's look at each of these in turn.

If `ptr` is a pointer variable, care must be taken not to confuse the expressions `ptr` and `*ptr`. The expression

```
ptr
```

accesses the variable `ptr` (which contains a memory address). The expression

```
*ptr
```

accesses the variable that `ptr` points to.

`ptr1 = ptr2`	Copies the contents of `ptr2` into `ptr1`.
`*ptr1 = *ptr2`	Copies the contents of the variable pointed to by `ptr2` into the variable pointed to by `ptr1`.
`*ptr1 = ptr2`	Illegal—one is a pointer and one is a variable being pointed to.
`ptr1 = *ptr2`	Illegal—one is a pointer and one is a variable being pointed to.

The second common error is to dereference the null pointer or an uninitialized pointer. On many systems, an attempt to dereference the null pointer produces a run-time error message such as "NULL POINTER DEREFERENCE," followed immediately by termination of the program. When this event occurs, you have at least some notion of what went wrong with the program. The situation is worse, though, if your program dereferences an uninitialized pointer. In the code fragment

```
int   num;
int* intPtr;

num = *intPtr;
```

the variable `intPtr` has not been assigned any value before we dereference it. Initially, it contains some meaningless value such as 315987, but the computer does not know that it is meaningless. The machine simply accesses memory location 315987 and copies whatever it finds there into `num`. There is no way to test whether a pointer variable contains an undefined value. The only advice we can give is to check the code carefully to make sure that every pointer variable is assigned a value before being dereferenced.

The third error—leaving inaccessible objects on the free store—usually results from either a shallow copy operation or incorrect use of the new operator. In Figure 17-11, we showed how the built-in assignment operator causes a shallow copy; the dynamic data object originally pointed to by one pointer variable remains allocated but inaccessible. Misuse of the new operator also can leave dynamic data inaccessible. Execution of the code fragment

```
float* floatPtr;

floatPtr = new float;
*floatPtr = 38.5;
floatPtr = new float;
```

creates an inaccessible object: the dynamic variable containing 38.5. The problem is that we assigned a new value to `floatPtr` in the last statement without first deallocating the variable it pointed to. To guard against this kind of error, examine every use of the new operator in your code. If the associated variable currently points to data, `delete` the pointed-to data before executing the new operation.

Finally, dangling pointers are a source of bugs and can be difficult to detect. One cause of dangling pointers is deallocating a dynamic data object that is pointed to by more than one pointer. Figures 17-7d and 17-7e pictured this situation. A second cause of dangling pointers is returning a pointer to an automatic variable from a function. The following function, which returns a function value of type `int*`, is erroneous.

```
int* Func()
{
    int n;
        .
        .
        .
    return &n;
}
```

Remember that automatic variables are implicitly created at block entry and implicitly destroyed at block exit. The above function returns a pointer to the local variable n, but n disappears as soon as control exits the function. The caller of the function therefore receives a dangling pointer. Dangling pointers are hazardous for the same reason that uninitialized pointers are hazardous: when your program dereferences incorrect pointer values, it will access memory locations whose contents are unknown.

Testing and Debugging Hints

1. To declare two pointer variables in the same statement, you must use

    ```
    int *p, *q;
    ```

    You cannot use

    ```
    int* p, q;
    ```

    Similarly, you must use

    ```
    int &m, &n;
    ```

    to declare two reference variables in the same statement.
2. Do not confuse a pointer with the variable it points to.
3. Before dereferencing a pointer variable, be sure it has been assigned a meaningful value other than NULL.
4. Pointer variables must be of the same data type to be compared or assigned to one another.
5. In an expression, an array name without any index brackets is a pointer expression; its value is the base address of the array. The array name is considered a *constant* expression, so it cannot be assigned to. The following code shows correct and incorrect assignments.

```
int  arrA[5] = {10, 20, 30, 40, 50};
int  arrB[5] = {60, 70, 80, 90, 100};
int* ptr;

ptr = arrB;     // OK--you can assign to a variable
arrA = arrB;    // Wrong--you cannot assign to a constant
```

6. If ptr points to a struct, union, or class variable that has an int member named age, the expression

   ```
   *ptr.age
   ```

   is incorrect. You must either enclose the dereference operation in parentheses

   ```
   (*ptr).age
   ```

   or use the arrow operator:

   ```
   ptr->age
   ```

7. The delete operator must be applied to a pointer whose value was previously returned by new. Also, the delete operation leaves the value of the pointer variable undefined; do not use the variable again until you have assigned it a new value.
8. A function must not return a pointer to automatic local data, or else a dangling pointer will result.
9. If ptrA and ptrB point to the same dynamic data object, the statement

   ```
   delete ptrA;
   ```

   makes ptrB a dangling pointer. You should now assign ptrB the value NULL rather than leave it dangling.
10. Deallocate dynamic data when it is no longer needed. Memory leaks can cause you to run out of memory space.
11. Inaccessible objects—another cause of memory leaks—are caused by
    a. shallow copying of pointers that point to dynamic data. When designing C++ classes whose objects point to dynamic data, be sure to provide a deep copy operation and a copy-constructor.
    b. using the new operation when the associated variable already points to dynamic data. Before executing new, use delete to deallocate the data that is currently pointed to.

SUMMARY

Pointer types and reference types are simple data types for storing memory addresses. Variables of these types do not contain data; rather, they contain the addresses of other variables or data structures. Pointer variables require explicit dereferencing using the * operator. Reference variables are dereferenced implicitly and are commonly used to pass nonarray parameters by reference.

A powerful use of pointers is to create dynamic variables. The pointer is created at compile time, but the data to which the pointer points is created at run time. The built-in operator new creates a variable on the free store (heap) and returns a pointer to that variable. A dynamic variable is not given a name, but rather is accessed through a pointer variable.

The use of dynamic data saves memory space because a variable is created only when it is needed at run time. When a dynamic variable is no longer needed, it can be deallocated (using delete) and the memory space can be used again. The use of dynamic data can also save machine time when large structures are being sorted. The pointers to the large structures, rather than the large structures themselves, can be rearranged.

When C++ class objects point to data on the free store, it is important to distinguish between shallow and deep copy operations. A shallow copy of one class object to another copies only the pointers and results in two class objects pointing to the same dynamic variable. A deep copy results in two distinct copies of the pointed-to data. Therefore, classes that manipulate dynamic data usually require a complete collection of support routines: one or more constructors, a destructor (for cleaning up the free store), a deep copy operation, and a copy-constructor (for deep copying during initialization of one class object by another).

QUICK CHECK

1. How would you declare each of the following pointer variables? (pp. 968–979)
   a. A variable intPtr that can point to a single int variable.
   b. A variable arrPtr that can point to a float array.
   c. A variable recPtr that can point to a structure of the following type.

   ```
   struct RecType
   {
       int    age;
       float height;
       float weight;
   };
   ```

2. Given the declarations

```
int    someVal;
float velocity[10];
```

and the declarations in Question 1,
  a. how would you make intPtr point to someVal and then use intPtr to store 25 into someVal?
  b. how would you make arrPtr point to velocity and then use arrPtr to store 6.43 into the third element of velocity? (pp. 968–979)
3. Given the declaration

```
RecType oneRec;
```

and the declarations in Question 1,
  a. how would you make recPtr point to oneRec?
  b. what are two different expressions using recPtr that will store 120.5 into the weight member of oneRec? (pp. 968–979)
4. a. In a single statement, declare a pointer variable named dblPtr and initialize it to the address of a newly created dynamic variable of type double. Then, in a second statement, store 98.32586728 into the dynamic variable.
  b. In a single statement, declare a pointer variable named list and initialize it to the base address of a newly created dynamic array of 50 int elements. Then give a section of code that will zero out the array. (pp. 979–986)
5. Given the variables dblPtr and list of Question 4, show how to deallocate the dynamic data pointed to by dblPtr and list. (pp. 979–986)
6. Given the declaration and initialization

```
float delta = -42.7;
```

how would you declare a variable gamma to be of type "reference to float" and initialize it to contain the memory address of delta? (pp. 987–990)
7. Using the variable gamma of Question 6, how would you store the value 12.9 into delta? (pp. 987–990)
8. Which kind of copy operation—deep or shallow—copies one pointer to another without copying any pointed-to data? (pp. 990–997)
9. As defined by C++, assignment (using an assignment expression) and initialization are two different things. What are the three ways in which one C++ class object is initialized by another? (p. 998)
10. In designing a C++ class whose class objects point to dynamic data, what are the four member functions you should provide? (p. 1001)
11. What are two ways in which pointers may be used to improve program efficiency? (pp. 1001, 1034)

Answers
1. int*   intPtr;
   float* arrPtr;
   RecType* recPtr;
2. a. intPtr = &someVal;
      *intPtr = 25;
   b. arrPtr = velocity;   (or arrPtr = &velocity[0];)
      arrPtr[2] = 6.43;

3. a. `recPtr = &oneRec;`
   b. `(*recPtr).weight = 120.5;`
      `recPtr->weight = 120.5;`
4. a. `double* dblPtr = new double;`
      `*dblPtr = 98.32586728;`
   b. `int* list = new int[50];`
      `for (i = 0; i < 50; i++)`
          `list[i] = 0;`
5. `delete dblPtr;`
   `delete [] list;`
6. `float& gamma = delta;` 7. `gamma = 12.9;` (Remember that once a reference variable is initialized, each appearance of the variable is *implicitly* dereferenced.) 8. Shallow copying copies one pointer to another without copying any pointed-to data. 9. (a.) Passing a class object as a parameter using pass-by-value. (b.) Initializing a class object in its declaration. (c.) Returning a class object as a function value. 10. The class needs one or more constructors (to create the dynamic data), a destructor (to clean up the free store), a deep copy operation, and a copy-constructor (for deep copying during initializations). 11. Pointers, when used with dynamic data, improve memory efficiency because we create only as many dynamic variables as are needed. With respect to time efficiency, it is faster to move pointers than to move large data structures, as in the case of sorting large `structs`.

EXAM PREPARATION EXERCISES

1. How does a variable of type `float*` differ from a variable of type `float`?
2. Show what is output by the following C++ code. If an unknown value gets printed, write a *U*.

```
int main()
{
    int  m;
    int  n;
    int* p = &m;
    int* q;

    *p = 27;
    cout << *p << ' ' << *q << endl;
    q = &n;
    n = 54;
    cout << *p << ' ' << *q << endl;
    p = &n;
    *p = 6;
    cout << *p << ' ' << n << endl;
    return 0;
}
```

3. Given the declarations

```
struct PersonType
{
    char lastName[31];
    char firstInitial;
};
```

```
typedef PersonType* PtrType;

PersonType onePerson;
PtrType    ptr = &onePerson;
```

tell whether each statement below is valid or invalid.

a. `strcpy(ptr.lastName, "Alvarez");` *invalid*
b. `strcpy((*ptr).lastName, "Alvarez");` *valid*
c. `strcpy(*ptr.lastName, "Alvarez");` *invalid*
d. `strcpy(ptr->lastName, "Alvarez");` *valid*
e. `strcpy(*ptr->lastName, "Alvarez");` *invalid. cannot use star & -> together.*

4. What C++ built-in operation releases the space reserved for a dynamic variable back to the system?

5. Given the declarations

```
int* ptrA;
int* ptrB;
```

tell whether each code segment below results in an inaccessible object, a dangling pointer, or neither.

inaccessible object

a.
```
ptrA = new int;
ptrB = new int;
*ptrA = 345;
ptrB = ptrA;
```

d.
```
ptrA = new int;
ptrB = new int;
*ptrA = 345;
*ptrB = *ptrA;
```
neither

dangling pointer

b.
```
ptrA = new int;
*ptrA = 345;
ptrB = ptrA;
delete ptrA;
```

e.
```
ptrA = new int;
ptrB = new int;
*ptrA = 345;
ptrB = new int;
*ptrB = *ptrA;
```
inaccessible object.

c.
```
ptrA = LocationOfAge();
```
where function LocationOfAge is defined as

dangling pointer

```
int* LocationOfAge()
{
    int age;

    cout << "Enter your age: ";
    cin >> age;
    return &age;
}
```

6. The only operation that affects the contents of a reference variable is initialization. (True or False?)

7. Given the declarations

```
int n;
int& r = n;
```

what does the following statement do?

```
r = 2 * r;
```

a. It doubles the contents of n.
b. It doubles the contents of r.
c. It doubles the contents of the variable that n points to.
d. It doubles the contents of both r and n.
e. Nothing—it results in a compile-time error.

8. Define the following terms:

    deep copy
    shallow copy
    class destructor
    class copy-constructor

9. By default, C++ performs both assignment and initialization of class objects using shallow copying. (True or False?) *True*

10. Given the class declaration

```
class TestClass
{
public:
    void Write();
    TestClass( /* in */ int initValue );
    ~TestClass();
private:
    int privateData;
};
```

suppose that the member functions are implemented as follows:

```
void TestClass::Write()
{
    cout << "Private data is " << privateData << endl;
}


TestClass::TestClass( /* in */ int initValue )
{
    privateData = initValue;
    cout << "Constructor executing" << endl;
}


TestClass::~TestClass()
{
    cout << "Destructor executing" << endl;
}
```

What is the output of the following program?

```
#include "testclass.h"
#include <iostream.h>

int main()
{
    int      count;
    TestClass anObject(5);

    for (count = 1; count <= 3; count++)
        anObject.Write();
    return 0;
}
```

Private data is 5
" " "
" " " "
" " " "
" " " "
)
Destructor executing
" "
" "
" "

11. Given the TestClass class of Exercise 10, what is the output of the following program?

```
#include "testclass.h"
#include <iostream.h>

int main()
{
    int count;

    for (count = 1; count <= 3; count++)
    {
        TestClass anObject(count);
        anObject.Write();
    }
    return 0;
}
```

Private data is 1
Destructor executing
Private data is 2
Destructor executing
Private data is 3
Destructor is executing.

value

12. Let x and y be class objects of the DynArray class developed in this chapter.

```
DynArray x(100);
DynArray y(100);
```

What is the output of each of the following code segments?

```
a. x.Store(425, 10);
   y.CopyFrom(x);
   x.Store(250, 10);
   cout << x.ValueAt(10) << endl;
   cout << y.ValueAt(10) << endl;
b. x.Store(425, 10);
   y = x;
   x.Store(250, 10);
   cout << x.ValueAt(10) << endl;
   cout << y.ValueAt(10) << endl;
```

13. Given a class named `IntList`, which of the following is the correct function prototype for the class copy-constructor?

    a. `void IntList( IntList otherList );`
    b. `IntList( IntList& otherList );`
    c. `IntList( const IntList otherList );`
    d. `void IntList( const IntList& otherList );`
    e. `IntList( const IntList& otherList );`

14. How can the use of pointers make a program run faster?

Programming Warm-Up Exercises

1. a. Declare a pointer variable p and initialize it to point to a `char` variable named ch.
   b. Declare a pointer variable q and initialize it to point to the first element of a `long` array named `arr`.
   c. Declare a pointer variable r and initialize it to point to a variable named `box` of type

   ```
   struct BoxType
   {
       int length;
       int width;
       int height;
   };
   ```

2. Using the variables p, q, and r of Exercise 1, write code to do the following:
   a. Store '@' into the variable pointed to by p.
   b. Store 959263 into the first element of the array pointed to by q.
   c. Store a length, width, and height of 12, 14, and 5 into the variable pointed to by r.

3. Write a Boolean value-returning function that takes two pointer variables—ptr1 and ptr2—as parameters. Both variables point to `float` data. The function should return TRUE if the two pointers point to the same variable, and FALSE otherwise.

4. Write a Boolean value-returning function that takes two pointer variables—ptr1 and ptr2—as parameters. Both variables point to `float` data. The function should return TRUE if the values in the pointed-to variables are identical, and FALSE otherwise.

5. Given the code segment

   ```
   struct GradeType
   {
       int  score;
       char grade;
   };
   typedef GradeType* PtrType;
   ```

```
PtrType p1;
PtrType p2;
PtrType p3;
PtrType p4;
        ⋮
        ⋮
p4 = PtrToMax(p1, p2, p3);
```

the `PtrToMax` function returns a pointer: the value of p1, p2, or p3, whichever points to the struct with the highest value of score. Implement the `PtrToMax` function.

6. Write an If statement that compares the two dynamic int variables pointed to by variables p and q, puts the smaller into an int variable named `smaller`, and destroys the original two dynamic variables.

7. Declare all variables used in Exercise 6.

8. Given the declarations

```
int    numLetters;  // No. of letters in user's last name
int    i;           // Index variable
char* list;         // Pointer to array of letters in
                    //   user's last name
```

write a section of code that prompts the user for the number of letters in his or her last name, dynamically creates a char array of exactly the right size to hold the letters, inputs the letters, prints out the letters in reverse order (last through first), and deallocates the array.

9. Pretend that C++ provides pointer types but not reference types. Rewrite the following function using pointer variables instead of reference variables.

```
void AddAndIncr( /* in */     int  int1,
                 /* inout */ int& int2,
                 /* out */    int& sum  )
{
    sum = int1 + int2;
    int2++;
}
```

10. For the function of Exercise 9, change the function call

```
AddAndIncr(m, n, theirSum);
```

so that it corresponds to the new version of the function.

11. a. Design the data sets necessary to thoroughly test the `ValueAt` function of the DynArray class (pages 1020–1030).
    b. Write a driver and test the `ValueAt` function using your test data.

12. a. Design the data sets necessary to thoroughly test the `Store` function of the DynArray class (pages 1020–1030).
    b. Write a driver and test the `Store` function using your test data.

PROGRAMMING PROBLEMS

1. In Chapter 12, the Exam program printed the names of those students taking an exam and the names of those students missing an exam. Parallel arrays were used because the struct data type had not yet been introduced. Rewrite the Exam program combining student and isPresent into a struct (type StudentType) with two members: name and isPresent. Make these structs dynamic variables rather than named variables; that is, student should be an array of pointers to structs of type StudentType.

   As in the SortWithPointers program of this chapter, the use of dynamically allocated structs along with an array of pointers can save both execution time and memory space.

2. In Chapter 14, the MergeLists program merged the records from three input files onto a single master file containing no duplicate records. The program uses four arrays of structs. The array sizes are fixed statically (at compile time), so memory is wasted when the input files are very small. Also, the program merges the data by copying entire structs from one array to another, which requires considerable execution time when a great amount of copying occurs.

   Rewrite the MergeLists program so that the input records are stored into dynamically allocated structs. The four arrays should be arrays of pointers to structs. The benefits of this approach are increased memory efficiency (space is allocated only for as many structs as there are records in the files) and increased time efficiency (copying pointers during the merge operation is faster than copying entire structs).

3. Given two arrays a and b, we can define the relation a < b to mean a[0] < b[0] *and* a[1] < b[1] *and* a[2] < b[2], and so forth. (If the two arrays are of different sizes, the relation is defined only through the size of the smaller array.) We can define the other relational operators likewise. Enhance this chapter's DynArray class by adding two Boolean member functions, LessThan and Equal.

   These functions can be thought of as *deep comparison* operations because the dynamic arrays on the free store are to be compared element by element. In other words, the function call

   ```
   arr1.LessThan(arr2)
   ```

   returns TRUE if arr1's array elements are pairwise less than arr2's elements.
   Test your two new functions with suitable test drivers and comprehensive sets of test data.

4. Referring to Programming Problem 3, the client code can simulate the other four relational operators (!=, <=, >, and >=) using only the Equal and LessThan functions. However, you could make the class easier to use by supplying additional member functions NotEqual, LessOrEqual, GreaterThan, and GreaterOrEqual. Add these functions to the DynArray class in addition to Equal and LessThan. (*Hint:* Instead of writing each of the algorithms from scratch, simply have the function bodies invoke the existing functions Equal and LessThan. And remember: Class members can refer to each other directly without using dot notation.)
   Test your new functions with suitable test drivers and comprehensive sets of test data.

5. The size of a built-in array is fixed statically (at compile time). The size of a dynamic array can be specified dynamically (at run time). In both cases, however,

once memory has been allocated for the array, the array size cannot change while the program is executing. In this problem, you are to design and test a C++ class that represents an *expandable array*—one that can grow in size at run time.

Using this chapter's `DynArray` class as a starting point, create a class named `ExpArray`. This class has all of `DynArray`'s member functions plus one more:

```
void ExpandBy( /* in */ int n );
    // Precondition:
    //     n > 0
    // Postcondition:
    //     Size of array has increased by n elements
    //     && All of the additional n elements equal zero
```

Here is an example of client code:

```
ExpArray myArray(100);
// Assert: Class object created with array size 100
    .
    .
    .
myArray.ExpandBy(50);
// Assert: Array size is now 150
```

(*Hint:* To expand the array, you should allocate a new, larger dynamic array on the free store, copy the values from the old dynamic array to the new, and deallocate the old array.)

Test your class with a suitable test driver and a comprehensive set of test data. Note that your test driver should exercise the other class member functions to be sure they still work correctly.

CASE STUDY FOLLOW-UP

1. Rewrite the `RecordList::SelSort` function from the SortWithPointers program so that it correctly orders the `struct`s regardless of whether characters in the last names are uppercase or lowercase. (*Hint:* Temporarily convert all the characters in both strings to uppercase before making the comparison.)
2. Rewrite the `RecordList::SelSort` function from the SortWithPointers program so that it orders the `struct`s by last name, then first name (in case two or more people have the same last name).
3. We want to add two member functions to the `RecordList` class of the SortWith-Pointers program: a copy-constructor and a deep copy operation.
   a. Give the specification of the copy-constructor (as it would appear in the class declaration), then give the implementation of the function.
   b. Give the specification of a `CopyFrom` function (as it would appear in the class declaration), then give the implementation of the function.
4. In the Dynamic Arrays case study, suppose that the `DynArray` class had been written to store `float` rather than `int` values:

```
class DynArray
{
```

```
public:
    float ValueAt( /* in */ int i ) const;
    void Store( /* in */ float val,
                /* in */ int   i  );
    void CopyFrom( /* in */ DynArray array2 );
    DynArray( /* in */ int arrSize );
    DynArray( const DynArray& array2 );
    ~DynArray();
private:
    float* arr;
    int    size;
};
```

Indicate precisely how the implementation of each of the six member functions would differ from the code presented in the case study.

18

Linked Structures

GOALS

- To understand the concept of a linked data structure.
- To be able to declare the data types and variables needed for a dynamic linked list.
- To be able to print the contents of a linked list.
- To be able to insert new items into a linked list.
- To be able to delete items from a linked list.

In the last chapter, we saw that C++ has a mechanism for creating dynamic variables. These dynamic variables, which can be of any simple or structured type, can be created or destroyed at any time during execution of the program using the operators new and delete. A dynamic variable is referenced not by a name but through a pointer that contains its address (location). Every dynamic variable has an associated pointer by which it can be accessed. We used dynamic variables to save space and machine time. In this chapter, we see how to use them to build data structures that can grow and shrink as the program executes.

 ## Sequential Versus Linked Structures

As we have pointed out in previous chapters, many problems in computing involve lists of items. A list is an abstract data type (ADT) with certain allowable operations: searching the list, sorting it, printing it, and so forth. The structure we have used as the concrete data representation of a list is the array, a sequential structure. By sequential structure we mean that successive components of the array are located next to each other in memory.

If the list we are implementing is an *ordered list*—one whose components must be kept in ascending or descending order—certain operations are efficiently carried out using an array representation. For example, searching an ordered list for a particular value is quickly done by using a binary search. However, inserting and deleting items from an ordered list are inefficient with an array representation. To insert a new item into its proper place in the list, we must shift array elements down to make room for the new item (see Figure 18-1). Similarly, deleting an item from the list requires that we shift up all the array elements following the one to be deleted.

■ FIGURE 18-1

Inserting into a
Sequential
Representation of a
List

a. Array before inserting the value 25

list[0]	4
list[1]	16
list[2]	39
list[3]	46
list[4]	58
·	
·	
·	

b. Array after inserting the value 25

list[0]	4
list[1]	16
list[2]	25
list[3]	39
list[4]	46
list[5]	58
·	
·	
·	

When insertions and deletions are frequent, there is a better data representation for a list: the **linked list.** A linked list is a collection of items, called *nodes*, that can be scattered about in memory, not necessarily in consecutive memory locations. Each node, typically implemented as a `struct`, consists of two members:

1. A component member, which contains one of the data values in the list
2. A link member, which gives the location of the next node in the list

Component	Link
(Data)	(Location of next node)

Figure 18-2 shows an abstract diagram of a linked list. An arrow is used in the link member of each node to indicate the location of the next node. The slash (/) in the link member of the last node signifies the end of the list. The separate variable `head` is not a node in the linked list; its purpose is to give the location of the first node.

Accessing the items in a linked list is a little like playing the children's game of treasure hunt—each child is given a clue to the hiding place of the next clue, and the chain of clues eventually leads to the treasure.

As you look at Figure 18-2, you should observe two things. First, we have deliberately arranged the nodes in random positions. We have done this to emphasize the fact that the items in a linked list are not necessarily in adjacent memory locations (as they are in the array representation of Figure 18-1a). Second, you may already be thinking of pointers when you see the arrows in the figure because we drew pointer variables this way in Chapter 17. But so far, we have carefully avoided using the word *pointer*; we said only that the link member of a node gives the location of the next node. As we will see, there are two ways in which to implement a linked list. One way is to store it in an array of `struct`s, a technique that does not use pointers at all. The second way is to use dynamic data and pointers. Let's begin with the first of these two techniques.

■ FIGURE 18-2

A Linked List

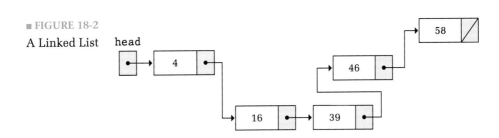

Linked List   A list in which the order of the components is determined by an explicit link member in each node, rather than by the sequential order of the components in memory.

 ## Array Representation of a Linked List

A linked list can be represented as an array of structs. For a linked list of int components, we use the following declarations:

```
struct NodeType
{
    int component;
    int link;
};

NodeType list[1000];    // Max. 1000 nodes
int       head;
```

The nodes all reside in an array named list. Each node has two members: component (in this example, an int data value) and link, which contains the *array index* of the next node in the list. The last node in the list will have a link member of –1. Because –1 is not a valid array index in C++, it is suitable as a special "end-of-list" value. The variable head contains the array index of the first node in the list. Figure 18-3 illustrates an array representation of the linked list of Figure 18-2.

Compare Figures 18-1 and 18-3. Figure 18-1 shows a list represented directly as an array. Figure 18-3 shows a list represented as a linked list, which, in turn, is represented as an array (of structs). We said that when insertions and deletions occur frequently, it is better to use a linked list to represent a list than it is to use an array directly. Let's see why.

Figure 18-1 showed the effect of inserting 25 into the list; we had to shift array elements 2, 3, 4, . . . down to insert the value 25 into element 2. If the list is long, we might have to move hundreds or thousands of numbers. In contrast, inserting the value 25 into the linked list of Figure 18-3 requires *no* movement of existing data. We simply find an unused slot in the array, store 25 into the component member, and adjust the link member of the node containing 16 (see Figure 18-4).

Before we introduce the second technique for implementing a linked list—the use of dynamic data and pointers—let's step back and look at the big picture. We are interested in the list as an ADT. Because it is an ADT, we

■ FIGURE 18-3

Array
Representation of a
Linked List

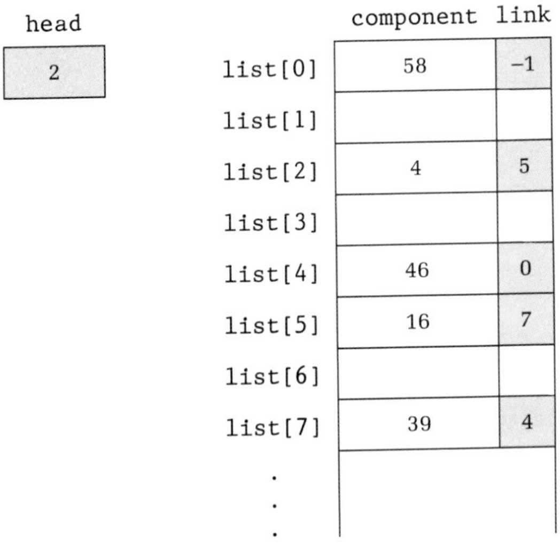

head

list[0]	58	−1
list[1]		
list[2]	4	5
list[3]		
list[4]	46	0
list[5]	16	7
list[6]		
list[7]	39	4

head box: 2

component link

.
.
.

must implement it using some existing data representation. One data representation is the built-in array, a sequential structure. Another data representation is the linked list, a linked structure. But a linked list is, itself, an ADT and requires a concrete data representation—an array of `structs`, for example. To help visualize all these relationships, we use an *implementation hierarchy diagram*, such as the one shown in Figure 18-5. In this diagram, each data type is implemented by using the data type(s) directly below it in the hierarchy.

■ FIGURE 18-4

Array
Representation of
Linked List After 25
Was Inserted

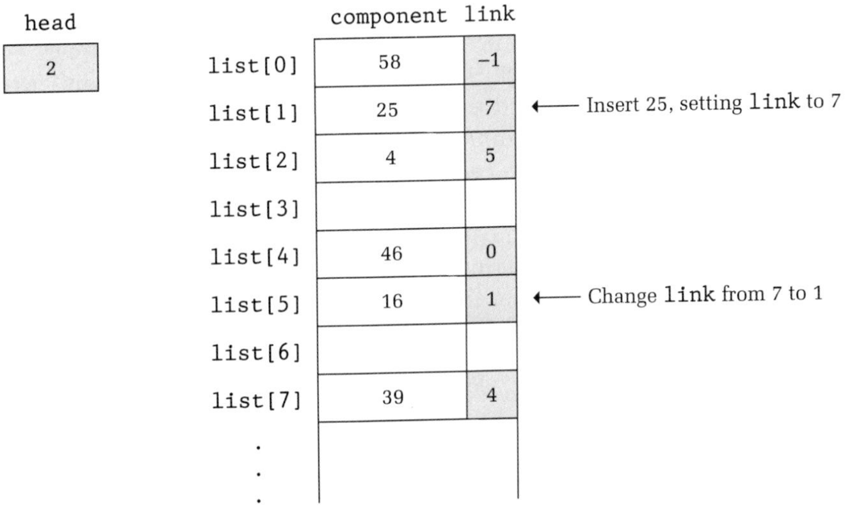

head

head box: 2

component link

list[0]	58	−1	
list[1]	25	7	←—— Insert 25, setting `link` to 7
list[2]	4	5	
list[3]			
list[4]	46	0	
list[5]	16	1	←—— Change `link` from 7 to 1
list[6]			
list[7]	39	4	

.
.
.

■ FIGURE 18-5

Implementation
Hierarchy for a List
ADT

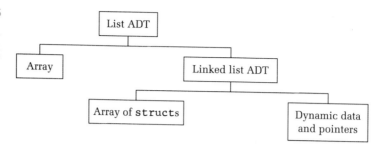

Dynamic Data Representation of a Linked List

Representing a list either as an array or as a linked list stored in an array of structs has a disadvantage: the size of the array is fixed and cannot change while the program is executing. Yet when we are working with lists, we often have no idea of the number of components we will have. The usual approach in this situation is to declare an array large enough to hold the maximum amount of data we can logically expect. Because we usually have less data than the maximum, memory space is wasted on the unused array elements.

There is another technique for representing a list in which the list components are dynamic variables that are created only as they are needed. We represent the list as a linked list whose nodes are dynamically allocated on the free store, and the link member of each node contains the memory address of the next dynamic node. In this data representation, called a **dynamic linked list,** the arrows in the diagram of Figure 18-2 really do represent pointers (and the slash in the last node is the null pointer). We access the list with a pointer variable that holds the address of the first node in the list. The pointer variable, named head in Figure 18-2, is called the **external pointer** or **head pointer.** Every node after the first node is accessed by using the link member in the node before it.

Such a list can expand or contract as the program executes. To insert a new item into the list, we allocate more space on the free store. To delete an item, we deallocate the memory assigned to it. We don't have to know in advance how long the list will be. The only limitation is the amount of available memory space. Data structures built using this technique are called **dynamic data structures.**

Dynamic Data Structure   A data structure that can expand and contract during execution.

Dynamic Linked List   A linked list composed of dynamically allocated nodes that are linked together by pointers.

External (Head) Pointer   A pointer variable that points to the first node in a dynamic linked list.

To create a dynamic linked list, we begin by allocating the first node and saving the pointer to it in the external pointer. We then allocate a second node and store the pointer to it into the link member of the first node. We continue this process—allocating a new node and storing the pointer to it into the link member of the previous node—until we have finished adding nodes to the list.

Let's look at how we can use C++ pointer variables to create a dynamic linked list of float values. We begin with the declarations

```
typedef float ComponentType;

struct NodeType
{
    ComponentType  component;
    NodeType*      link;
};
typedef NodeType* NodePtr;

NodePtr head;              // External pointer to list
NodePtr currPtr;           // Pointer to current node
NodePtr newNodePtr;        // Pointer to newest node
```

The order of these declarations is important. The Typedef for NodePtr refers to the identifier NodeType, so the declaration of NodeType must come first. (Remember that C++ requires every identifier to be declared before it is used.) Within the declaration of NodeType, we would like to declare link to be of type NodePtr, but we can't because the identifier NodePtr hasn't been declared yet. However, C++ allows *forward* (or *incomplete*) *declarations* of structs, classes, and unions:

```
typedef float ComponentType;

struct  NodeType;            // Forward (incomplete) declaration
typedef NodeType* NodePtr;
```

```
struct NodeType                    // Complete declaration
{
    ComponentType  component;
    NodePtr        link;
};
```

The advantage of using a forward declaration is that we can declare the type of link to be NodePtr just as we declare head, currPtr, and newNodePtr to be of type NodePtr.

Given the declarations above, the following code fragment creates a dynamic linked list with the values 12.8, 45.2, and 70.1 as the components in the list.

```
#include <stddef.h>       // For NULL
       .
       .
       .
head = new NodeType;
head->component = 12.8;
newNodePtr = new NodeType;
newNodePtr->component = 45.2;
head->link = newNodePtr;
currPtr = newNodePtr;
newNodePtr = new NodeType;
newNodePtr->component = 70.1;
currPtr->link = newNodePtr;
newNodePtr->link = NULL;
currPtr = newNodePtr;
```

Let's go through each of these statements, describing in words what is happening and showing the linked list as it appears after the execution of the statement.

head = new NodeType;   A dynamic variable of type NodeType is created. The pointer to this new node is stored into head. Variable head is the external pointer to the list we are building.

`head->component = 12.8;`   The value 12.8 is stored into the component member of the first node.

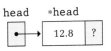

`newNodePtr = new NodeType;`   A dynamic variable of type `NodeType` is created. The pointer to this new node is stored into `newNodePtr`.

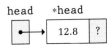   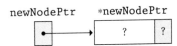

`newNodePtr->component = 45.2;`   The value 45.2 is stored into the component member of the new node.

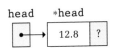   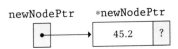

`head->link = newNodePtr;`   The pointer to the new node containing 45.2 in its component member is copied into the `link` member of `*head`. Variable `newNodePtr` still points to this new node. The node can be accessed either as `*newNodePtr` or as `*(head->link)`.

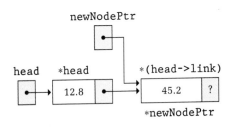

`currPtr = newNodePtr;`

The pointer to the new node is copied into `currPtr`. Now `currPtr`, `newNodePtr`, and `head->link` all point to the node containing 45.2 as its component.

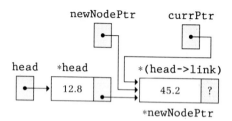

`newNodePtr = new NodeType;`

A dynamic variable of type `NodeType` is created. The pointer to this new node is stored into `newNodePtr`.

`newNodePtr->component = 70.1;`

The value 70.1 is stored into the component member of the new node.

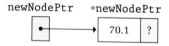

`currPtr->link = newNodePtr;`   The pointer to the new node containing 70.1 in the `component` member is copied into the `link` member of the node that contains 45.2.

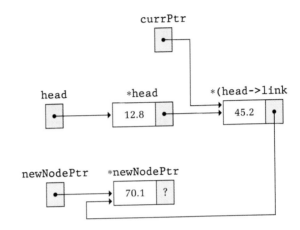

`newNodePtr->link = NULL;`   The special pointer constant `NULL` is stored into the `link` member of the last node in the list. When used in the `link` member of a node, `NULL` means the end of the list. `NULL` is shown in the diagram as a / in the `link` member.

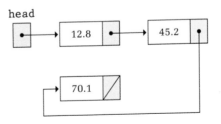

`currPtr = newNodePtr;`   `currPtr` is updated.

We would like to generalize this algorithm so that we can use a loop to create a dynamic linked list of any length. In the algorithm, we used three pointers:

1. `head`, which was used in creating the first node in the list and became the external pointer to the list.
2. `newNodePtr`, which was used in creating a new node when it was needed.
3. `currPtr`, which was updated to always point to the last node in the linked list.

When building any dynamic linked list by adding each new node to the end of the list, we always need three pointers to perform these functions. The algorithm that we used is generalized below to build a linked list of `int` numbers read from the standard input device. It is assumed that the user types in at least one number.

```
Set head = new NodeType
Read head->component
Set currPtr = head

Read inputVal
WHILE NOT EOF
    Set newNodePtr = new NodeType
    Set newNodePtr->component = inputVal
    Set currPtr->link = newNodePtr
    Set currPtr = newNodePtr
    Read inputVal
Set currPtr->link = NULL
```

The following code segment implements this algorithm. Notice how the first Typedef statement defines the component type to be `int` rather than `float`.

```
typedef int ComponentType;

struct  NodeType;                 // Forward declaration
typedef NodeType* NodePtr;

struct NodeType
{
    ComponentType  component;
    NodePtr        link;
};
```

```
NodePtr       head;              // External pointer to list
NodePtr       newNodePtr;        // Pointer to newest node
NodePtr       currPtr;           // Pointer to last node
ComponentType inputVal;

head = new NodeType;
cin >> head->component;
currPtr = head;

cin >> inputVal;
while (cin)
{
        // Invariant (prior to test):
        //     All previous values of inputVal have been placed
        //     into linked list pointed to by head
        //  && currPtr points to last node in list

    newNodePtr = new NodeType;       // Create new node
    newNodePtr->component = inputVal; // Set its component value
    currPtr->link = newNodePtr;      // Link node into list
    currPtr = newNodePtr;            // Set currPtr to last node
    cin >> inputVal;
}
currPtr->link = NULL;                // Mark end of list
```

Let's do a code walk-through and see just how this algorithm works.

`head = new NodeType;` A variable of type `NodeType` is created. The pointer is stored into head. Variable `head` will remain unchanged as the pointer to the first node (that is, `head` is the external pointer to the list).

`cin >> head->component;` The first number is read into the `component` member of the first node in the list.

`currPtr = head;` `currPtr` now points to the last node (the only node) in the list.

`cin >> inputVal;` The next number (if there is one) is read into variable `inputVal`.

`while (cin)`
`{` An event-controlled loop is used to read input values until end-of-file occurs.

`newNodePtr = new NodeType;` Another variable of type `NodeType` is created, with `newNodePtr` pointing to it.

`newNodePtr->component = inputVal;`	The current input value is stored into the `component` member of the newly created node.
`currPtr->link = newNodePtr;`	The pointer to the new node is stored into the `link` member of the last node in the list.
`currPtr = newNodePtr;`	`currPtr` is again pointing to the last node in the list.
`cin >> inputVal;`	The next input value (if there is one) is read in. The loop body repeats again.
`}`	
`currPtr->link = NULL;`	The `link` member of the last node is assigned the special end-of-list value `NULL`.

Following is the linked list that results when the program is run with the numbers 32, 78, 99, and 21 as data. The final values are shown for the auxiliary variables.

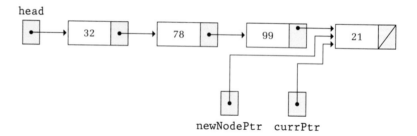

Algorithms on Dynamic Linked Lists

Now that we have looked at two examples of creating a dynamic linked list, let's look at algorithms that process nodes in a linked list. We need to be able to insert a node into a list, delete a node from a list, print the data values in a list, and so forth. For each of these operations, we make use of the fact that NULL is in the link member of the last node. NULL can be assigned to any pointer variable. It means that the pointer points to nothing. Its importance lies in the fact that we can compare the link member of each node to NULL to see when we have reached the end of the list.

As we develop these algorithms, we do so in the following context. We want to write a C++ class for a list (not linked list) ADT. As emphasized in Figure 18-5, a list ADT can be implemented in several ways. We choose a dynamic linked list as the data representation for a list, and we create the OrdList class whose specification is shown in Figure 18-6.

■ FIGURE 18-6

Specification of the
OrdList Class

```
//****************************************************************
// SPECIFICATION FILE (ordlist.h)
// This file gives the specification of an ordered list
// abstract data type. The list components are in ascending order
//****************************************************************
#include "bool.h"

typedef int ComponentType;

struct NodeType;                    // Forward declaration
                                    // (Complete declaration is
                                    // hidden in implementation file)

class OrdList
{
public:
    Boolean IsEmpty() const;
        // Postcondition:
        //      Function value == TRUE, if list is empty
        //                     == FALSE, otherwise

    void Print() const;
        // Postcondition:
        //      All components (if any) in list have been output

    void InsertTop( /* in */ ComponentType item );
        // Precondition:
        //      List components are in ascending order
        //   && item < first component in list
        // Postcondition:
        //      item is inserted as first component in list
        //   && List components are in ascending order

    void Insert( /* in */ ComponentType item );
        // Precondition:
        //      List components are in ascending order
        //   && item is assigned
        // Postcondition:
        //      item is inserted in list
        //   && List components are in ascending order

    void DeleteTop( /* out */ ComponentType& item );
        // Precondition:
        //      List is not empty
        //   && List components are in ascending order
        // Postcondition:
        //      item == first component in list at entry
        //   && item is no longer in list
        //   && List components are in ascending order
```

```
                   void Delete( /* in */ ComponentType item );
                      // Precondition:
                      //     item is somewhere in list
                      //  && List components are in ascending order
                      // Postcondition:
                      //     item is no longer in list
                      //  && List components are in ascending order

                   OrdList();
                      // Constructor
                      // Postcondition:
                      //     Empty list is created

                   OrdList( const OrdList& otherList );
                      // Copy-constructor
                      // Postcondition:
                      //     List is created as a duplicate of otherList

                   ~OrdList();
                      // Destructor
                      // Postcondition:
                      //     List is destroyed
                private:
                    NodeType* head;
                };
```

In Chapter 15, we classified ADT operations as constructors, transformers, observers, and iterators. IsEmpty and Print are observers. InsertTop, Insert, DeleteTop, and Delete are transformers. The class constructor and copy-constructor are ADT constructor operations.

In the class declaration, notice that the preconditions and postconditions of the member functions mention nothing about linked lists. The abstraction is a list, not a linked list. The user of the class is interested only in manipulating ordered lists of items and does not care how we implement a list. If we want to change to a different implementation—an array, for example—neither the public interface nor the client code would need to be changed.

The private data of the OrdList class consists of a single item: a pointer variable head. This variable is the external pointer to a dynamic linked list. As with any C++ class, different class objects have their own copies of the private data. For example, if the client code declares and manipulates two class objects like this:

```
OrdList list1;
OrdList list2;
```

```
list1.Insert(352);
list1.Insert(48);
list2.Insert(12);
     .
     .
     .
if ( !list2.IsEmpty() )
    list2.DeleteTop(item);
```

then each of the two objects list1 and list2 has its own private head variable and maintains its own dynamic linked list on the free store.

In Figure 18-6, the specification file ordlist.h declares a type NodeType, but only as a forward declaration. The only reason we need to declare the identifier NodeType in the specification file is so that the data type of the private variable head can be specified. In the spirit of information hiding, we place the complete declaration of NodeType into the implementation file ordlist.cpp. The complete declaration is an implementation detail that the user does not need to know about. Here's how ordlist.cpp starts out:

```
//*********************************************************************
// IMPLEMENTATION FILE (ordlist.cpp)
// This file implements the OrdList class member functions
// List representation: a linked list of dynamic nodes.
//*********************************************************************
#include "ordlist.h"
#include <iostream.h>
#include <stddef.h>        // For NULL

typedef NodeType* NodePtr;
struct NodeType
{
    ComponentType component;
    NodePtr        link;
};

// Private members of class:
//      NodePtr head;              External pointer to linked list
     .
     .
     .
```

To illustrate some commonly used algorithms on dynamic linked lists, let's look at the implementations of the OrdList member functions. Creating an empty linked list is the easiest of the algorithms, so we begin there.

Creating an Empty Linked List   To create a linked list with no nodes, all that is necessary is to assign the external pointer the value NULL. For the OrdList class, the appropriate place to do this is in the class constructor:

```
OrdList::OrdList()

// Constructor

// Postcondition:
//     head == NULL

{
    head = NULL;
}
```

One thing you will notice as we go through the OrdList member functions is that the *implementation assertions* (the preconditions and postconditions appearing in the implementation file) are often stated differently from the *abstract assertions* (those located in the specification file). Abstract assertions are written in terms that are meaningful to the user of the ADT; implementation details should not be mentioned. In contrast, implementation assertions can be made more precise by referring directly to variables and algorithms in the implementation code. In the case of the OrdList class constructor, the abstract postcondition is simply that an empty list (not a linked list) has been created. On the other hand, the implementation postcondition

```
// Postcondition:
//     head == NULL
```

is phrased in terms of our private data (head) and our particular list implementation (a dynamic linked list).

Testing for an Empty Linked List   The OrdList member function IsEmpty returns TRUE if the list is empty and FALSE if the list is not empty. Using a dynamic linked list representation, we return TRUE if head contains the value NULL, and FALSE otherwise:

```
Boolean OrdList::IsEmpty() const

// Postcondition:
//     Function value == TRUE, if head == NULL
//                    == FALSE, otherwise

{
    return (head == NULL);
}
```

Printing a Linked List   To print the components of a linked list, we need to access the nodes one at a time. This requirement implies an event-controlled loop where the event that stops the loop is reaching the end of the list. The loop control variable is a pointer that is initialized to the external pointer and is advanced from node to node by setting it equal to the link member of the current node. When the loop control pointer equals NULL, the last node has been accessed.

Print ( )

```
Set currPtr = head
WHILE currPtr doesn't equal NULL
    Print component member of *currPtr
    Set currPtr = link member of *currPtr
```

Note that this algorithm works correctly even if the list is empty (head equals NULL).

```
void OrdList::Print() const

// Postcondition:
//      component members of all nodes (if any) in linked list
//      have been output

{
    NodePtr currPtr = head;      // Loop control pointer

    while (currPtr != NULL)
    {
        // Invariant (prior to test):
        //      component members of all nodes before *currPtr
        //      have been output
        //   && currPtr points to a list node or == NULL

        cout << currPtr->component << ' ';
        currPtr = currPtr->link;
    }
}
```

Let's do a code walk-through using the following list.

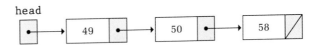

```
currPtr = head;
```
currPtr and head both point to the first node in the list.

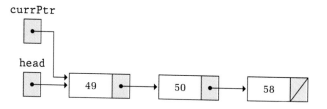

```
while (currPtr != NULL)
```
The loop body is entered because currPtr is not NULL.
```
cout << currPtr->component << ' ';
currPtr = currPtr->link;
```
The number 49 is printed.
currPtr now points to the second node in the list.

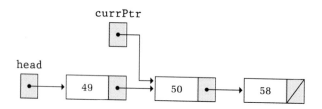

```
while (currPtr != NULL)
```
The loop body repeats because currPtr is not NULL.
```
cout << currPtr->component << ' ';
currPtr = currPtr->link;
```
The number 50 is printed.
currPtr now points to the third node in the list.

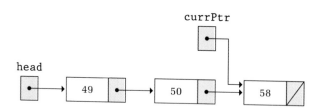

```
while (currPtr != NULL)                    The loop body repeats because
                                              currPtr is not NULL.

cout << currPtr->component << ' ';         The number 58 is printed.
currPtr = currPtr->link;                   currPtr is now NULL.
```

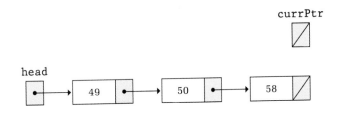

```
while (currPtr != NULL)                    The loop body is not repeated be-
                                              cause currPtr is NULL.
```

Inserting into a Linked List   A function for inserting a component into a linked list must have a parameter: the item to be inserted. The phrase *inserting into a linked list* could mean either inserting the component at the top of the list (as the first node) or inserting the component into its proper place according to some ordering (alphabetic or numeric). Let's examine these two situations separately.

Inserting a component at the top of a list is easy because we don't have to search the list to find where the item belongs.

InsertTop (In: item)

```
Set newNodePtr = new NodeType
Set component member of *newNodePtr = item
Set link member of *newNodePtr = head
Set head = newNodePtr
```

This algorithm is coded in the following function.

```
void OrdList::InsertTop( /* in */ ComponentType item )

// Precondition:
//      component members of list nodes are in ascending order
//   && item < component member of first list node
// Postcondition:
//      New node containing item is inserted at top of linked list
//   && component members of list nodes are in ascending order

{
    NodePtr newNodePtr = new NodeType;      // Temporary pointer

    newNodePtr->component = item;
    newNodePtr->link = head;
    head = newNodePtr;
}
```

The function precondition states that item must be smaller than the value in the first node. This precondition is not a requirement of linked lists in general. However, the OrdList abstraction we are implementing is an ordered list. The precondition/postcondition contract states that *if* the client sends a value smaller than the first one in the list, then the function guarantees to preserve the ascending order. If the client violates the precondition, the contract is broken.

The following code walk-through shows the steps in inserting a component with the value 20 as the first node in the linked list that was printed in the last section.

```
newNodePtr = new NodeType;           A new node is created.
newNodePtr->component = item;        The number 20 is stored into the
                                     component member of the new node.
```

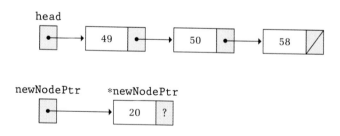

`newNodePtr->link = head;`

The `link` member of `*newNodePtr` now points to the first node in the list.

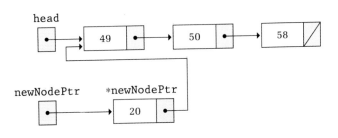

`head = newNodePtr;`

The external pointer to the list now points to the node containing the new component.

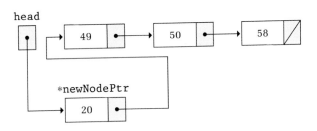

To insert a component into its proper place in an ordered list, we have to loop through the nodes until we find where the component belongs. Because the `OrdList` class keeps components in ascending order, we can recognize where a component belongs by finding the node that contains a value greater than the one being inserted. Our new node should be inserted directly before the node with that value; therefore, we must keep track of the node before the current one in order to insert our new node. We use a pointer `prevPtr` to point to this previous node. This method leads to the following algorithm:

Insert (In: item)

> Set newNodePtr = new NodeType
> Set component member of *newNodePtr = item
> Set prevPtr = NULL
> Set currPtr = head
> WHILE item > component member of *currPtr
>   Set prevPtr = currPtr
>   Set currPtr = link member of *currPtr
> Insert *newNodePtr between *prevPtr and *currPtr

This algorithm is basically sound, but there are problems with it in special cases. If the new component is larger than all other components in the list, the event that stops the loop (finding a node whose component is larger than the one being inserted) does not occur. When the end of the list is reached, the While condition tries to dereference currPtr, which now contains NULL. On some systems, the program will crash. We can take care of this case by using the following expression to control the While loop:

currPtr isn't NULL AND item > component member of *currPtr

This expression keeps us from dereferencing the null pointer because C++ uses short-circuit evaluation of logical expressions. If the first part evaluates to FALSE—that is, if currPtr equals NULL—the second part of the expression, which dereferences currPtr, is not evaluated.

There is one more point to consider in our algorithm: the special case when the list is empty or the new value is less than the first component in the list. Variable prevPtr remains NULL in this case, and *newNodePtr must be inserted at the top instead of between *prevPtr and *currPtr.

The following function implements our algorithm with these changes incorporated.

```
void OrdList::Insert( /* in */ ComponentType item )

// Precondition:
//      component members of list nodes are in ascending order
//   && item is assigned
// Postcondition:
//      New node containing item is inserted into its proper place
//      in linked list
//   && component members of list nodes are in ascending order

{
```

```
NodePtr currPtr;        // Moving pointer
NodePtr prevPtr;        // Pointer to node before *currPtr
NodePtr newNodePtr;     // Pointer to new node

// Set up node to be inserted

newNodePtr = new NodeType;
newNodePtr->component = item;

// Find previous insertion point

prevPtr = NULL;
currPtr = head;
while (currPtr != NULL && item > currPtr->component)
{
        // Invariant (prior to test):
        //      item > component member of each list node
        //      before *currPtr
        //   && currPtr points to a list node or == NULL
        //   && prevPtr points to node before *currPtr or == NULL

    prevPtr = currPtr;
    currPtr = currPtr->link;
}

// Insert new node

newNodePtr->link = currPtr;
if (prevPtr == NULL)
    head = newNodePtr;
else
    prevPtr->link = newNodePtr;
}
```

Let's go through this code for each of the three cases: inserting at the top (item is 20), inserting in the middle (item is 60), and inserting at the end (item is 100). Each insertion begins with the list below.

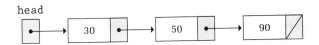

Insert(20)

```
newNodePtr = new NodeType;
newNodePtr->component = item;
prevPtr = NULL;
currPtr = head;
```

These four statements initialize the variables used in the searching process. The variables and their contents are shown below.

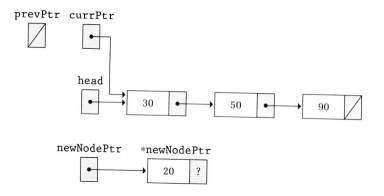

```
while (currPtr != NULL &&
       item > currPtr->component)

newNodePtr->link = currPtr;

if (prevPtr == NULL)
head = newNodePtr;
```

Because 20 is less than 30, the expression is FALSE and the loop body is not entered. link member of *newNodePtr now points to *currPtr. Because prevPtr is NULL, the then-clause is executed and 20 is inserted at the top of the list.

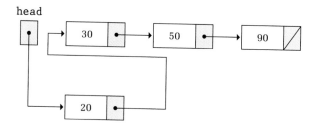

Insert(60)

```
newNodePtr = new NodeType;
newNodePtr->component = item;
prevPtr = NULL;
currPtr = head;
```

These four statements initialize the variables used in the searching process. The variables and their contents are shown below.

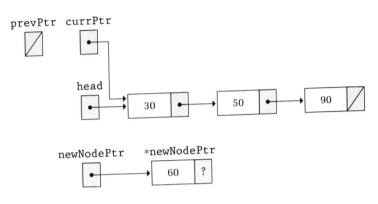

```
while (currPtr != NULL &&
       item > currPtr->component)

prevPtr = currPtr;
currPtr = currPtr->link;
```

Because 60 is greater than 30, this expression is TRUE and the loop body is entered. Pointer variables are advanced.

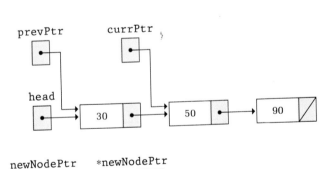

```
while (currPtr != NULL &&
        item > currPtr->component)

prevPtr = currPtr;
currPtr = currPtr->link;
```

Because 60 is greater than 50, this expression is TRUE and the loop body is repeated. Pointer variables are advanced.

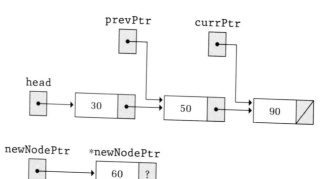

```
while (currPtr != NULL &&
        item > currPtr->component)


newNodePtr->link = currPtr;
```

Because 60 is not greater than 90, the expression is FALSE and the loop body is not repeated. link member of *newNodePtr now points to *currPtr.

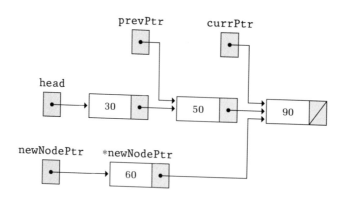

```
if (prevPtr == NULL)
prevPtr->link = newNodePtr;
```

Because `prevPtr` does not equal NULL, the else-clause is executed. The completed list is shown with the auxiliary variables removed.

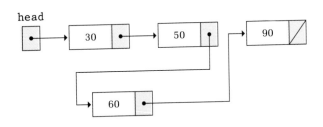

Insert(100)

We do not repeat the first part of the search, but pick up the walk-through where `prevPtr` is pointing to the node whose component is 50, and `currPtr` is pointing to the node whose component is 90.

```
while (currPtr != NULL &&
        item > currPtr->component)

prevPtr = currPtr;
currPtr = currPtr->link;
```

Because 100 is greater than 90, this expression is TRUE and the loop body is repeated. The pointer variables are advanced.

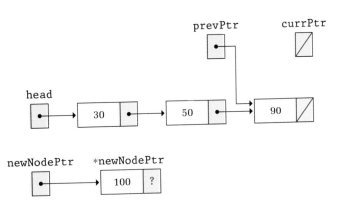

```
while (currPtr != NULL &&
        item > currPtr->component)

newNodePtr->link = currPtr;
if (prevPtr == NULL)
prevPtr->link = newNodePtr;
```

Because currPtr equals NULL,
the expression is FALSE and
the loop body is not repeated.
NULL is copied into link member of *newNodePtr.
Because prevPtr does not equal
NULL, the else-clause is executed. Node *newNodePtr is inserted after *prevPtr. The list
is shown with auxiliary variables removed.

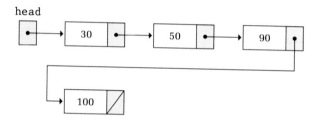

You may have noticed in both the InsertTop and the Insert functions
that we allocate a new dynamic node without checking to see whether the
allocation succeeded. It is possible for the client code to insert so many
items that the free store becomes full. On most systems, the free store is very
large, but it is risky to assume that the new operation will always succeed.
Programming Warm-Up Exercise 5 asks you to address this issue.

Deleting from a Linked List   To delete an existing node from a linked list,
we have to loop through the nodes until we find the node we want to delete.
We look at the mirror image of our insertions: deleting the top node and
deleting a node whose component is equal to an incoming parameter.
    To delete the first node, we just change the external pointer to point to the
second node (or to contain NULL if we are deleting the only node in a one-
node list). The value in the node being deleted can be returned as an outgoing parameter. Notice the precondition for the following function: the client
must not call the function if the list is empty.

```
void OrdList::DeleteTop( /* out */ ComponentType& item )

// Precondition:
//     Linked list is not empty (head != NULL)
//  && component members of list nodes are in ascending order
```

```
// Postcondition:
//      item == component member of first list node at entry
//   && Node containing item is removed from linked list
//   && component members of list nodes are in ascending order

{
    NodePtr tempPtr = head;      // Temporary pointer

    item = head->component;
    head = head->link;
    delete tempPtr;
}
```

We don't show a complete code walk-through because the code is so straightforward. Instead, we show the state of the data structure in two stages: after the first two statements and at the end. We use one of our previous lists. Following is the data structure after the execution of the first two statements in the function.

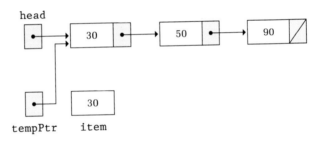

After the execution of the function, the structure is as follows:

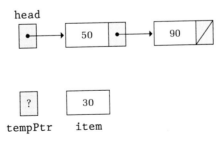

The function for deleting a node whose component contains a certain value is similar to the Insert function. The difference is that we are looking for a match, not a component member greater than our item. If we use a precondition that the component we are looking for is definitely in the list, our loop control is simple. We don't have to worry about dereferencing the null pointer.

As in the Insert function, we need the node before the one that is to be deleted so we can change its link member. In the following function, we demonstrate another technique for keeping track of the previous node. Instead of comparing item with the component member of *currPtr, we compare it with the component member of the node pointed to by currPtr->link; that is, we compare item with currPtr->link->component. When currPtr->link->component is equal to item, *currPtr is the previous node.

```
void OrdList::Delete( /* in */ ComponentType item )

// Precondition:
//     item == component member of some list node
//  && List components are in ascending order
// Postcondition:
//     Node containing item is removed from linked list
//  && component members of list nodes are in ascending order

{
    NodePtr delPtr;       // Pointer to node to be deleted
    NodePtr currPtr;      // Loop control pointer

    // Check if item is in first node

    if (item == head->component)
    {
        // Delete first node

        delPtr = head;
        head = head->link;
    }
    else
    {
        // Search for node in rest of list

        currPtr = head;
        while (currPtr->link->component != item)

                    // Invariant (prior to test):
                    //     item != component member of any list node
                    //     before *(currPtr->link)

            currPtr = currPtr->link;
```

```
        // Delete currPtr->link

        delPtr = currPtr->link;
        currPtr->link = currPtr->link->link;
    }
    delete delPtr;
}
```

Let's delete the node whose component is 90. The structure is shown below, with the nodes labeled as they are when the While statement is reached.

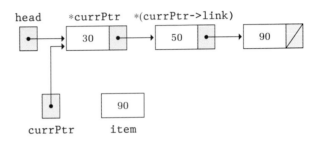

while (currPtr->link->component != item)   Because 50 is not equal to
                                             90, the loop body is
                                             entered.
currPtr = currPtr->link;   Pointer is advanced.

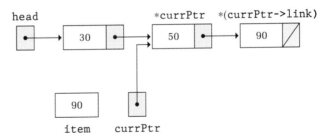

```
while (currPtr->link->component != item)
```
Because 90 is equal to 90, the loop is exited.

```
delPtr = currPtr->link;
currPtr->link = currPtr->link->link;
```
The `link` member of the node whose component is 90 is copied into the `link` member of the node whose component is 50. The `link` member equals `NULL` in this case.

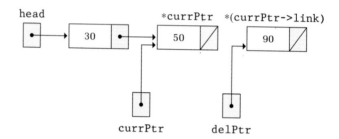

```
delete delPtr;
```
Memory allocated to `*delPtr` (the node that was deleted) is returned to the free store. The value of `delPtr` is undefined.

Note that `NULL` was stored into `currPtr->link` only because the node whose component was 90 was the last one in the list. If there had been more nodes beyond this one, a pointer to the next node would have been stored into `currPtr->link`.

Pointer Expressions

As you can see from the `OrdList::Delete` function, pointer expressions can be quite complex. Let's look at some examples.

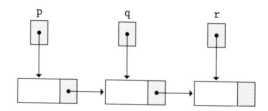

p, q, and r point to nodes in a dynamic linked list. The nodes themselves are *p, *q, and *r. Use the preceding diagram to convince yourself that the following relations are true.

```
p->link == q
*(p->link) == *q
p->link->link == r
*(p->link->link) == *r
q->link == r
*(q->link) == *r
```

And remember the semantics of assignment statements for pointers.

p = q;   Assigns the contents of pointer q to pointer p.

*p = *q;   Assigns the contents of the variable pointed to by q to the variable pointed to by p.

Classes and Dynamic Linked Lists

In Chapter 17, we said that classes whose objects manipulate dynamic data on the free store should provide not only a class constructor but also a destructor, a deep copy operation, and a copy-constructor. The OrdList class includes all of these except (to keep the example simpler) a deep copy operation. Let's look at the class destructor.

The purpose of the destructor is to deallocate the dynamic linked list when an OrdList class object is destroyed. Without a destructor, the linked list would be left behind on the free store, still allocated but inaccessible. The code for the destructor is easy to write. Using the existing member functions IsEmpty and DeleteTop, we simply march through the list and delete each node:

```
OrdList::~OrdList()

// Destructor

// Postcondition:
//     All linked list nodes have been deallocated from free store

{
    ComponentType temp;     // Temporary variable
```

```
    while ( !IsEmpty() )

        // Invariant (prior to test):
        //     All nodes before current first node in list
        //     have been deallocated

        DeleteTop(temp);
}
```

The copy-constructor is harder to write. Before we look at it, we must stress the importance of providing a copy-constructor whenever we also provide a destructor. Pretend that OrdList doesn't have a copy-constructor, and suppose that a client passes a class object to a function using pass-by-value. (Remember that passing a parameter by value sends a *copy* of the value of the actual parameter to the function.) Within the function, the formal parameter is initialized to be a copy of the caller's class object, including the caller's value of the private variable head. At this point, both the actual parameter and the formal parameter are pointing to the same dynamic linked list. When the client function returns, the class destructor is invoked for the formal parameter, destroying the only copy of the linked list. Upon return from the function, the caller's linked list has disappeared!

By providing a copy-constructor, we ensure deep copying of an actual parameter to a formal parameter whenever pass-by-value occurs. The implementation of the copy-constructor, shown below, employs a commonly used algorithm for creating a new linked list as a copy of another.

```
OrdList::OrdList( const OrdList& otherList )

// Copy-constructor

// Postcondition:
//     IF otherList.head == NULL  (i.e., the other list is empty)
//         head == NULL
//     ELSE
//         head points to a new linked list that is a copy of
//         the linked list pointed to by otherList.head

{
    NodePtr fromPtr;     // Pointer into list being copied from
    NodePtr toPtr;       // Pointer into new list being built

    if (otherList.head == NULL)
    {
        head = NULL;
        return;
    }
```

```
// Copy first node

fromPtr = otherList.head;
head = new NodeType;
head->component = fromPtr->component;

// Copy remaining nodes

toPtr = head;
fromPtr = fromPtr->link;
while (fromPtr != NULL)
{
        // Invariant (prior to test):
        //      The list from *head through *toPtr is a copy of
        //      the list from *(otherList.head) through the node
        //      preceding *fromPtr

    toPtr->link = new NodeType;
    toPtr = toPtr->link;
    toPtr->component = fromPtr->component;
    fromPtr = fromPtr->link;
}
toPtr->link = NULL;
}
```

Choice of Data Representation

We have looked in detail at two ways of representing lists of components: one where the components are physically next to each other (a direct array representation, as in Figure 18-1), and one where the components are logically next to each other (a linked list). Furthermore, a linked list is an abstraction that can be implemented either by using an array of structs or by using dynamically allocated structs and pointers (a dynamic linked list).

Let's compare the array representation with the dynamic linked list representation. (Throughout this discussion, we use *array* to mean a direct array representation, not an array of structs forming a linked list.) We look at common operations on lists and examine the advantages and disadvantages of each representation on each operation.

Common Operations

1. Read the components into an initially empty list.
2. Access all the components in the list in sequence.
3. Insert or delete the first component in a list.
4. Insert or delete the last component in a list.

5. Insert or delete the *n*th component in a list.
6. Access the *n*th component in a list.
7. Sort the components in a list.
8. Search the list for a specific component.

Reading components into a list is faster with an array representation than with a dynamic linked list because the new operation doesn't have to be executed for each component. Accessing the components in sequence takes approximately the same time with both structures.

Inserting or deleting the first component is much faster using a linked representation. Remember that with an array, all the other list items have to be shifted down (for an insertion) or up (for a deletion). Conversely, inserting or deleting the last component is much more efficient with an array; there is direct access to the last component, and no shifting is required. In a linked representation, the entire list must be searched to find the last component.

On average, the time spent inserting or deleting the *n*th component is about equal for the two types of lists. A linked representation would be better for small values of *n*, and an array representation would be better for values of *n* near the end of the list.

Accessing the *n*th element is *much* faster in an array representation. We can access it directly by using $n - 1$ as the index into the array. In a linked representation, we have to access the first $n - 1$ components sequentially to reach the *n*th one.

For many sorting algorithms, including the selection sort, the two representations are approximately equal in efficiency. However, there are some sophisticated, very fast sorting algorithms that rely on direct access to array elements by using array indices. These algorithms are not suitable for a linked representation, which requires sequential access to the components.

In general, searching an ordered list for a specific component is much faster in an array representation because a binary search can be used. When the components in the list to be searched are not ordered, the two representations are about the same.

When you are trying to decide whether to use an array representation or a linked representation, determine which of these common operations are likely to be applied most frequently. Use your analysis to determine which structure would be better in the context of your particular problem.

There is one additional point to consider when deciding whether to use an array or a dynamic linked list. How accurately can you predict the maximum number of components in the list? Does the number of components in the list fluctuate widely? If you know the maximum and it remains fairly constant, an array representation is fine in terms of memory usage. Otherwise, it is better to choose a dynamic linked representation, in order to use memory more efficiently.

PROBLEM-SOLVING CASE STUDY

Simulated Playing Cards

Problem: As an avid card player, you plan to write a program to play solitaire once you have become thoroughly comfortable with dynamic data structures. As a prelude to that program, you decide to design a C++ class that models a pile of playing cards. The pile could be a discard pile, a pile of cards face up on the table, or even a full deck of unshuffled cards. The card pile will be structured as a dynamic linked list.

In this case study, we omit the Input and Output sections because we are developing only a C++ class, not a complete program. Instead, we include two sections entitled Specification of the Class and Implementation of the Class.

Discussion: Thinking of a card pile as an ADT, what kinds of operations would we like to perform on this ADT? You might have come up with a different list, but here are some operations we have chosen:

Create an empty pile
Put a new card onto the pile
Take a card from the pile
Determine the current length of the pile
Inspect the nth card in the pile

We can base our design roughly on the OrdList class of this chapter, but there are some differences. First, we should consider a card pile to be an unordered list, not an ordered list, because the cards can be in random order in the pile. Second, the last two operations listed above were not present in OrdList. These operations allow more flexibility in asking questions about the list. If we use a private variable to keep track of the current length of the list, we can ask at any time how many cards there are in a pile. We also can simulate looking at a face-up pile of cards by using the last operation to inspect any card in the pile without removing it.

Before we write the class specification, we must decide how to represent an individual playing card. The suit of a card can be represented using an enumeration type. Rank can be represented using the numbers 1 through 13, with the ace as a 1 and the king as a 13. Each card is then represented as a struct with two members, suit and rank:

```
enum Suits {CLUB, DIAMOND, HEART, SPADE};

struct CardType
{
    Suits suit;
    int   rank;      // Range 1 (ace) through 13 (king)
};
```

Below is the specification file `cardpile.h`, which provides the client with declarations for the `CardType` type and the `CardPile` class.

```
//*****************************************************************
// SPECIFICATION FILE (cardpile.h)
// This file gives the specifications of
//    1. CardType--a data type representing an ordinary playing card
//    2. CardPile--an unordered list ADT representing a pile
//       of playing cards
//*****************************************************************
#ifndef CARDPILE_H
#define CARDPILE_H

enum Suits {CLUB, DIAMOND, HEART, SPADE};

struct CardType
{
    Suits suit;
    int   rank;      // Range 1 (ace) through 13 (king)
};

struct NodeType;       // Forward declaration (Complete declaration
                       // is hidden in implementation file)
class CardPile
{
public:
    int Length() const;
        // Postcondition:
        //      Function value == number of cards in pile

    CardType CardAt( /* in */ int n ) const;
        // Precondition:
        //      n >= 1  &&  n <= length of card pile
        // Postcondition:
        //      Function value == card at position n in pile
```

```
void InsertTop( /* in */ CardType newCard );
    // Precondition:
    //     newCard is assigned
    // Postcondition:
    //     newCard is inserted at top of pile

void RemoveTop( /* out */ CardType& topCard );
    // Precondition:
    //     Length of card pile > 0
    // Postcondition:
    //     topCard == value of first component in pile at entry
    //  && topCard is no longer in pile

CardPile();
    // Postcondition:
    //     Empty pile is created

CardPile( const CardPile& otherPile );
    // Postcondition:
    //     Pile is created as a duplicate of otherPile

~CardPile();
    // Postcondition:
    //     Pile is destroyed
private:
    NodeType* head;
    int       listLength;
};

#endif
```

Implementation of the Class For the data representation of a card pile, we use a linked list. Furthermore, we implement the linked list using dynamic data and pointers. Each node is of type NodeType, whose complete declaration (hidden in the implementation file) is as follows:

```
typedef NodeType* NodePtr;
struct NodeType
{
    CardType card;
    NodePtr  link;
};
```

The private variable head is the external pointer to the linked list, and the private variable listLength keeps track of the current length of the list.

The class constructor, copy-constructor, and destructor: These functions are essentially identical to those in the OrdList class. The only significant difference is in the constructor. In addition to setting head to NULL, the constructor must set listLength to zero.

The InsertTop *and* RemoveTop *functions:* These functions are the same as InsertTop and DeleteTop in the OrdList class, with the following differences. After inserting a new node, InsertTop must increment listLength; and after deleting a node, RemoveTop must decrement listLength.

The Length *function:* Because the private variable listLength always indicates the current length of the list, no looping and counting are required. The function body is a single statement:

```
return listLength;
```

The CardAt *function:* To access the card at position n in the pile, we must start at the front of the list and sequence our way through the first $n - 1$ nodes. When we get to the desired node, we return the card member of the node as the function return value.

CardAt (In: n)

```
Set currPtr = head
FOR count going from 1 through n -1
    Set currPtr = link member of *currPtr
Return card member of *currPtr
```

Here is the implementation file containing the definitions of the CardPile member functions:

```
//********************************************************************
// IMPLEMENTATION FILE (cardpile.cpp)
// This file implements the CardPile class member functions
// List representation: a linked list of dynamic nodes
//********************************************************************
#include "cardpile.h"
#include <stddef.h>        // For NULL
```

```
typedef NodeType* NodePtr;
struct NodeType
{
    CardType card;
    NodePtr  link;
};

// Private members of class:
//    NodePtr head;              External pointer to linked list
//    int     listLength;        Current length of list


//********************************************************************

CardPile::CardPile()

// Constructor

// Postcondition:
//    head == NULL  &&  listLength == 0

{
    head = NULL;
    listLength = 0;
}

//********************************************************************

CardPile::CardPile( const CardPile& otherPile )

// Copy-constructor

// Postcondition:
//    listLength == otherPile.listLength
//  && IF otherPile.head == NULL
//        head == NULL
//    ELSE
//        head points to a new linked list that is a copy of
//        the linked list pointed to by otherPile.head

{
    NodePtr toPtr;       // Pointer into new list being built
    NodePtr fromPtr;     // Pointer into list being copied from
```

```
        listLength = otherPile.listLength;
        if (otherPile.head == NULL)
        {
            head = NULL;
            return;
        }

        // Copy first node

        fromPtr = otherPile.head;
        head = new NodeType;
        head->card = fromPtr->card;

        // Copy remaining nodes

        toPtr = head;
        fromPtr = fromPtr->link;
        while (fromPtr != NULL)
        {
                // Invariant (prior to test):
                //     The list from *head through *toPtr is a copy of
                //     the list from *(otherPile.head) through the node
                //     preceding *fromPtr

            toPtr->link = new NodeType;
            toPtr = toPtr->link;
            toPtr->card = fromPtr->card;
            fromPtr = fromPtr->link;
        }
        toPtr->link = NULL;
    }


//**************************************************************

CardPile::~CardPile()

// Destructor

// Postcondition:
//     All linked list nodes have been deallocated from free store

{
    CardType temp;     // Temporary variable

    while (listLength > 0)

            // Invariant (prior to test):
```

```
                        //      All nodes before current first node in list
                        //      have been deallocated

            RemoveTop(temp);
        }

        //******************************************************************

        int CardPile::Length() const

        // Postcondition:
        //      Function value == listLength

        {
            return listLength;
        }

        //******************************************************************

        CardType CardPile::CardAt( /* in */ int n ) const

        // Precondition:
        //      1 <= n <= listLength
        // Postcondition:
        //      Function value == card member of list node at position n

        {
            int     count;          // Loop control variable
            NodePtr currPtr = head;     // Moving pointer variable

            for (count = 1; count < n; count++)

                    // Invariant (prior to test):
                    //      1 <= count <= n
                    //   && currPtr points to the list node at
                    //      position "count"

                currPtr = currPtr->link;
            return currPtr->card;
        }

        //******************************************************************

        void CardPile::InsertTop( /* in */ CardType newCard )

        // Precondition:
        //      newCard is assigned
```

```
// Postcondition:
//     New node containing newCard is inserted at top of linked list
//  && listLength == listLength@entry + 1

{
    NodePtr newNodePtr = new NodeType;    // Temporary pointer

    newNodePtr->card = newCard;
    newNodePtr->link = head;
    head = newNodePtr;
    listLength++;
}


//*****************************************************************

void CardPile::RemoveTop( /* out */ CardType& topCard )

// Precondition:
//     listLength > 0
// Postcondition:
//     topCard == card member of first list node at entry
//  && Node containing topCard is removed from linked list
//  && listLength == listLength@entry - 1

{
    NodePtr tempPtr = head;    // Temporary pointer

    topCard = head->card;
    head = head->link;
    delete tempPtr;
    listLength--;
}
```

PROBLEM-SOLVING CASE STUDY

Solitaire Simulation

Problem: There is a solitaire game that is quite simple but seems difficult to win. Let's write a program to play the game, then run it a number of times to see if it really is that difficult to win or if we have just been unlucky.

Although this card game is played with a regular poker or bridge deck, the rules deal with suits only; the face values (ranks) are ignored. The rules are listed below. Rules 1 and 2 are initialization.

1. Take a deck of playing cards and shuffle it.
2. Place four cards side by side, left to right, face up on the table.
3. If the four cards (or the rightmost four if there are more than four on the table) are of the same suit, move them to a discard pile. Otherwise, if the first one and the fourth one (of the rightmost four cards) are of the same suit, move the other two cards (second and third) to a discard pile. Repeat until no cards can be removed.
4. Take the next card from the shuffled deck and place it face up to the right of those already there. Repeat this step if there are fewer than four cards face up (assuming there are more cards in the deck).
5. Repeat Steps 3 and 4 until there are no more cards in the deck. You win if all the cards are on the discard pile.

Figure 18-7 walks us through the beginning of a typical game to demonstrate how the rules operate. Remember that the game deals with suits only. There must be at least four cards face up on the table before the rules can be applied.

Input: The number of times the simulation is to be run (numberOfGames), the number of times the deck is to be shuffled between games (numberOfShuffles), and an initial seed value for a random number generator (seed). We discuss the seed variable later.

Output: The number of games played, and the number of games won.

Discussion: A program that plays a game is an example of a *simulation program*. The program simulates what a human does when playing the game. Programs that simulate games or real-world processes are very common in computing.

In developing a simulation, object-oriented design helps us decide how to represent the physical items being simulated. In a card game, the basic item is, of course, a card. A deck of cards becomes a list of 52 cards in the program. We can use a variation of the CardPile class developed in the previous case study to represent the deck.

Cards face up on the table and the discard pile must also be simulated in this program. Putting a card face up on the table means that a card is being taken from the deck and put onto the table where the player can see it. The cards on the table can be represented by a CardPile class object. The rules that determine whether or not cards can be moved to the discard pile are applied to the top four cards in this list—that is, the last four cards put into the list.

The discard pile is also a list of cards and can be represented as a CardPile class object. If no cards remain on the table (they are all on the discard pile) at the end of the game, then the player has won. If any cards remain on the table face up, the player has lost.

PROBLEM-SOLVING CASE STUDY *cont'd.*

■ FIGURE 18-7

Solitaire Game

Initialize with the first 4 cards.

Remove the 2 inner cards.
Add 2 cards (need at least 4 cards to play).

Remove all 4 cards.
Add 4 more cards.

Remove the 2 inner cards.
Add 2 cards until another match.

Remove the 2 inner cards from group of last 4.

Remove the last 4 cards.
Add cards until another match.

Remove the 2 inner cards from group of last 4.
Add cards until another match.

Remove all 4 cards.

.
.
.

A linked list is a good choice for representing these three lists (the deck, the cards face up on the table, and the discard pile). The simulation requires a lot of deleting from one list and inserting into another list, and these operations are quite efficient with a linked list.

Using dynamic variables to represent our lists instead of a direct array representation saves memory space. If an array representation were used, three arrays of 52 components each would have to be used. In a dynamic linked representation, we use only 52 components in all, because a card can be in only one list at a time.

In our object-oriented design, we have now identified three objects: a card deck, an on-table pile, and a discard pile. A fourth object we'll use is a player object. This object can be thought of as a manager—it is responsible for coordinating the three card pile objects and playing the game according to the rules.

To determine the relationships among these four objects, we observe that the three card pile objects are independent of each other and are not related by inheritance or composition. However, the player object is composed of the other three objects—it *has-a* deck, an on-table pile, and a discard pile as part or all of its internal data. This relationship is seen more clearly when we design and implement the player object.

The On-Table Pile and Discard Pile Objects   We can represent these objects directly using the CardPile class from the previous case study.

The Card Deck Object   We could represent this object using the CardPile class, but a full deck of cards is more specialized than an ordinary card pile. For example, the CardPile class constructor creates an empty pile, whereas we would like a new card deck to be created as a list of all 52 cards, arranged in order by suit and rank. Also, we would like to include two more operations that are appropriate for a card deck—one to shuffle the deck, the other to recreate the deck at the end of each game by gathering together all 52 cards from the on-table pile and the discard pile.

The easiest way to add these new operations to the CardPile class is to use inheritance. From the CardPile class we can derive a new CardDeck class that inherits the CardPile class members and adds the new functions. Inheritance is appropriate here because a card deck *is-a* card pile (and more). Here is the class specification:

```
//*****************************************************************
// SPECIFICATION FILE (carddeck.h)
// This file gives the specification of a CardDeck class, derived
// from the CardPile class using inheritance
//*****************************************************************
#ifndef CARDDECK_H
#define CARDDECK_H

#include "cardpile.h"

const int DECK_SIZE = 52;

class CardDeck : public CardPile
{
public:
    void Shuffle( /* in */ int numberOfShuffles);
        // Precondition:
        //      Length of deck == DECK_SIZE
        //   && numberOfShuffles is assigned
        // Postcondition:
        //      The order of components in the deck has been
        //      rearranged numberOfShuffles times, randomly

    void Recreate( /* inout */ CardPile& pile1,
                   /* inout */ CardPile& pile2 );
        // Gathers cards from two piles and puts them back into deck
        // Precondition:
        //      Length of deck == 0
        //   && (Length of pile1 + length of pile2) == DECK_SIZE
        // Postcondition:
        //      Deck is the list consisting of all cards from
        //      pile1@entry followed by all cards from pile2@entry
        //   && Length of deck == DECK_SIZE
        //   && Length of pile1 == 0  &&  Length of pile2 == 0

    CardDeck();
        // Postcondition:
        //      List of DECK_SIZE components is created
        //      representing a standard deck of playing cards
        //   && Cards are in order by suit and by rank
private:
    void Merge( CardPile&, CardPile& );
};

#endif
```

Notice in the CardDeck class declaration that the private part does not include any additional data members. The only private data are the data inherited from the `CardPile` class. However, the private part declares a member function named `Merge`. This function is not accessible to clients of `Card-Deck`. As we see shortly, the `Merge` function is a "helper" function that is used by the `Shuffle` member function.

Now we implement the `CardDeck` member functions. We begin with the class constructor.

The class constructor CardDeck ( )

When a `CardDeck` class object is created, the constructor for its base class (`CardPile`) is implicitly executed first, creating an empty list. Starting with the empty list, we can generate the first card—the ace of clubs—and insert it into the list. The balance of the 52 cards can be generated in a loop. After every 13th card, we increment the suit and reset the rank to one.

```
Set tempCard.suit = CLUB
Set tempCard.rank = 1
InsertTop(tempCard)                        // Insert into deck
FOR count going from 2 through 52
    Increment tempCard.rank
    IF tempCard.rank > 13
        Increment tempCard.suit
        Set tempCard.rank = 1
    InsertTop(tempCard)                    // Insert into deck
```

Although we don't use the rank of a card, we leave it there because we may want to print out the contents of the list during debugging. Also, the `CardDeck` class may be used in other simulations. The class should be tested with a complete representation of a deck of cards.

Shuffle (In: numberOfShuffles)

When a human shuffles a deck of cards, he or she divides the deck into two nearly equal parts and then merges the two parts again. This process can be simulated directly (a simulation within a simulation). The list representing the deck can be divided into two lists, `halfA` and `halfB`. Then these two lists can be merged again. We use a random number generator to determine how many cards go into `halfA`. The rest go into `halfB`.

Through the header file `stdlib.h`, the C++ standard library provides two functions for producing random numbers. The first, named `rand`, has the following prototype:

```
int rand();
```

Each time this function is called, it returns a random integer in the range 0 through RAND_MAX, a constant defined in stdlib.h. (RAND_MAX is typically the same as INT_MAX.) Because we want our random number to be in the range 1 through 52, we use the conversion formula

Set sizeOfCut = rand( ) MOD 52 + 1

or, in C++,

```
sizeOfCut = rand() % 52 + 1;
```

Random number generators use an initial *seed* value from which to start the sequence of random numbers. The C++ library function srand lets you specify an initial seed before calling rand. The prototype for srand is

```
void srand( unsigned int );
```

If you do not call srand before the first call to rand, an initial seed of 1 is assumed. As you'll see in the initialization portion of our main function, we input an initial seed value from the user and pass it as a parameter to srand.

```
FOR count1 going from 1 through numberOfShuffles
    Create empty list halfA
    Create empty list halfB
    Set sizeOfCut = rand( ) MOD 52 + 1
    Move sizeOfCut cards from deck to halfA
    Move remaining 52–sizeOfCut cards from deck to halfB
    IF sizeOfCut <= 26
        Merge(halfA, halfB)
    ELSE
        Merge(halfB, halfA)
```

Merge (Inout: shorterList, longerList)

The merge algorithm is much simpler than the one developed in Chapter 14 because a component is taken alternately from each list without regard to the contents of the component. Also, we know the exact length of each list.

We call the `Merge` function with two parameters: the shorter list and the longer list.

```
WHILE more cards in shorterList
    shorterList.RemoveTop(tempCard)
    InsertTop(tempCard)                    // Insert into deck
    longerList.RemoveTop(tempCard)
    InsertTop(tempCard)
WHILE more cards in longerList
    longerList.RemoveTop(tempCard)
    InsertTop(tempCard)
```

Recreate (Inout: pile1, pile2)

The `Recreate` function takes an empty deck (an empty list) and gathers cards from two piles, putting them back into the deck.

```
WHILE more cards in pile1
    pile1.RemoveTop(tempCard)
    InsertTop(tempCard)                    // Insert into deck
WHILE more cards in pile2
    pile2.RemoveTop(tempCard)
    Deck.InsertTop(tempCard)
```

Below is the implementation file for the `CardDeck` member functions.

```
//*****************************************************************
// IMPLEMENTATION FILE (carddeck.cpp)
// This file implements the CardDeck class member functions.
// The CardPile class is a public base class of CardDeck
//*****************************************************************
#include "carddeck.h"
#include <stdlib.h>      // For rand()

const int HALF_DECK = 26;
```

```
// Additional private members of class (beyond those
// inherited from CardPile):
//     void Merge( CardPile&, CardPile& );     Used by the Shuffle
//                                             function


//*******************************************************************

CardDeck::CardDeck()

// Constructor--creates a list of DECK_SIZE components representing
// a standard deck of playing cards

// Postcondition:
//     After empty linked list created (via implicit call to base
//     class constructor), all DECK_SIZE playing cards have been
//     inserted into deck in order by suit and by rank

{
    int      count;       // Loop counter
    CardType tempCard;    // Temporary card

    tempCard.suit = CLUB;
    tempCard.rank = 1;
    InsertTop(tempCard);

    // Loop to create balance of deck

    for (count = 2; count <= DECK_SIZE; count++)
    {
        // Increment rank

        tempCard.rank++;

        // Test for change of suit

        if (tempCard.rank > 13)
        {
            tempCard.suit = Suits(tempCard.suit + 1);
            tempCard.rank = 1;
        }
        InsertTop(tempCard);
    }
}


//*******************************************************************
```

```
void CardDeck::Shuffle( /* in */ int numberOfShuffles )

// Rearranges the deck (the list of DECK_SIZE components) into a
// different order.  The list is divided into two parts, which are
// then merged.  The process is repeated numberOfShuffles times

// Precondition:
//     Length of deck == DECK_SIZE
//   && numberOfShuffles is assigned
// Postcondition:
//     The order of components in the deck has been rearranged
//     numberOfShuffles times, randomly

{
    CardType tempCard;      // Temporary card
    int      count1;        // Loop counter
    int      count2;        // Loop counter
    int      sizeOfCut;     // Size of simulated cut

    for (count1 = 1; count1 <= numberOfShuffles; count1++)
    {
        CardPile halfA;     // Half of the list, initially empty
        CardPile halfB;     // Half of the list, initially empty

        sizeOfCut = rand() % DECK_SIZE + 1;

        // Divide deck into two parts

        for (count2 = 1; count2 <= sizeOfCut; count2++)
        {
            RemoveTop(tempCard);
            halfA.InsertTop(tempCard);
        }
        for (count2 = sizeOfCut+1; count2 <= DECK_SIZE; count2++)
        {
            RemoveTop(tempCard);
            halfB.InsertTop(tempCard);
        }
        if (sizeOfCut <= HALF_DECK)
            Merge(halfA, halfB);
        else
            Merge(halfB, halfA);
    }
}
```

```
//**************************************************************

void CardDeck::Merge( /* inout */ CardPile& shorterList,
                      /* inout */ CardPile& longerList  )

// Merges shorterList and longerList into deck

// Precondition:
//     Length of shorterList > 0  &&  Length of longerList > 0
//   && Length of deck == 0
// Postcondition:
//     Deck is the list of cards obtained by merging
//       shorterList@entry and longerList@entry into one list
//   && Length of shorterList == 0
//   && Length of longerList == 0

{
    CardType tempCard;      // Temporary card

    // Take one card from each list alternately

    while (shorterList.Length() > 0)
    {
        shorterList.RemoveTop(tempCard);
        InsertTop(tempCard);
        longerList.RemoveTop(tempCard);
        InsertTop(tempCard);
    }

    // Copy remainder of longer list to deck

    while (longerList.Length() > 0)
    {
        longerList.RemoveTop(tempCard);
        InsertTop(tempCard);
    }
}

//**************************************************************
```

```
void CardDeck::Recreate( /* inout */ CardPile& pile1,
                         /* inout */ CardPile& pile2 )

// Gathers cards from two piles and puts them back into deck

// Precondition:
//     Length of deck == 0
//  && (Length of pile1 + length of pile2) == DECK_SIZE
// Postcondition:
//     Deck is the list consisting of all cards from pile1@entry
//     followed by all cards from pile2@entry
//  && Length of deck == DECK_SIZE
//  && Length of pile1 == 0  &&  Length of pile2 == 0

{
    CardType tempCard;      // Temporary card

    while (pile1.Length() > 0)
    {
        pile1.RemoveTop(tempCard);
        InsertTop(tempCard);
    }
    while (pile2.Length() > 0)
    {
        pile2.RemoveTop(tempCard);
        InsertTop(tempCard);
    }
}
```

The Player Object   This object manages the playing of the solitaire game. It encapsulates the card deck, on-table pile, and discard pile objects and is responsible for moving cards from one pile to another according to the rules of the game.

To represent the player object, we design a Player class with the following specification:

```
//*************************************************************
// SPECIFICATION FILE (player.h)
// This file gives the specification of a Player class that manages
// the playing of a solitaire game
//*************************************************************
#ifndef PLAYER_H
#define PLAYER_H
```

```
#include "cardpile.h"
#include "carddeck.h"
#include "bool.h"

class Player
{
public:
    void PlayGame( /* in */   int        numberOfShuffles,
                   /* out */ Boolean& won                 );
        // Precondition:
        //      numberOfShuffles is assigned
        // Postcondition:
        //      After deck has been shuffled numberOfShuffles times,
        //      one game of solitaire has been played
        //  && won == TRUE, if the game was won
        //            == FALSE, otherwise
private:
    CardDeck deck;
    CardPile onTable;
    CardPile discardPile;

    void TryRemove();
    void MoveFour();
    void MoveTwo();
};

#endif
```

The Player class has one public operation, PlayGame, that plays one game of solitaire and reports whether the game was won or lost. The private part of the class consists of three class objects—deck, onTable, and discardPile—and three private member functions. These "helper" functions are used in the playing of the game and are not accessible to clients of the class.

PlayGame (In: numberOfShuffles; Out: won)

```
deck.Shuffle(numberOfShuffles)
WHILE more cards in deck
    // Turn up a card
    deck.RemoveTop(tempCard)
    onTable.InsertTop(tempCard)
    // Try to remove it
    TryRemove()
Set won = (onTable.Length() equals 0)
deck.Recreate(onTable, discardPile)
```

TryRemove ( )

To remove cards, we first need to check the first and fourth cards. If these do not match, we can't move any cards. If they do match, we check to see how many can be moved. This process continues until there are fewer than four cards face up on the table, or until no move can be made.

```
Set moveMade = TRUE
WHILE onTable.Length() >= 4 AND moveMade
    IF suit of onTable.CardAt(1) matches suit of onTable.CardAt(4)
        IF suit of onTable.CardAt(1) matches suit of onTable.CardAt(2) AND
                suit of onTable.CardAt(1) matches suit of onTable.CardAt(3)
            Move four cards from onTable to discardPile
        ELSE
            Move two cards—the second and third—from onTable to discardPile
    ELSE
        Set moveMade = FALSE
```

MoveFour ( )

```
FOR count going from 1 through 4
    onTable.RemoveTop(tempCard)
    discardPile.InsertTop(tempCard)
```

MoveTwo ( )

```
Save top card from onTable
Move top card from onTable to discardPile
Move top card from onTable to discardPile
Restore original top card to onTable
```

The implementations of the `Player` class member functions are shown in the `player.cpp` file below.

```cpp
//******************************************************************
// IMPLEMENTATION FILE (player.cpp)
// This file implements the Player class member functions
//******************************************************************
#include "player.h"

// Private members of class
//     CardDeck deck;              Deck of cards
//     CardPile onTable;           Cards face up on the table
//     CardPile discardPile;       Cards on discard pile
//
//     void TryRemove( CardPile&, CardPile& );
//     void MoveFour( CardPile&, CardPile& );
//     void MoveTwo( CardPile&, CardPile& );

//******************************************************************

void Player::PlayGame( /* in */  int       numberOfShuffles,
                       /* out */ Boolean& won                 )

// Places each card in the deck face up on the table
// and applies rules for moving
```

PROBLEM-SOLVING CASE STUDY cont'd.

```
// Precondition:
//     numberOfShuffles is assigned
// Postcondition:
//     After deck has been shuffled numberOfShuffles times,
//     all cards have been moved one at a time from deck to onTable
//  && Cards have (possibly) been moved from onTable to discardPile
//     according to the rules of the game
//  && won == TRUE, if the game was won
//         == FALSE, otherwise

{
    CardType tempCard;     // Temporary card

    deck.Shuffle(numberOfShuffles);
    while (deck.Length() > 0)
    {
        deck.RemoveTop(tempCard);
        onTable.InsertTop(tempCard);
        TryRemove();
    }
    won = (onTable.Length() == 0);
    deck.Recreate(onTable, discardPile);
}

//**********************************************************************

void Player::TryRemove()

// If the first (top) four cards in onTable are the same suit,
// they are moved to discardPile.  If the first card and the fourth
// card are the same suit, the second and third cards are moved from
// onTable to discardPile.  This process continues until no further
// moves can be made

// Precondition:
//     Length of onTable > 0
// Postcondition:
//     Cards have (possibly) been moved from onTable to discardPile
//     according to the above rules

{
    Boolean moveMade = TRUE;     // True if a move has been made

    while (onTable.Length() >= 4 && moveMade)
        if (onTable.CardAt(1).suit == onTable.CardAt(4).suit)

            // A move will be made
```

```
            if (onTable.CardAt(1).suit == onTable.CardAt(2).suit &&
                onTable.CardAt(1).suit == onTable.CardAt(3).suit)
                MoveFour();  // Four alike
            else
                MoveTwo();   // 1st and 4th alike
        else
            moveMade = FALSE;
}

//**************************************************************

void Player::MoveFour()

// Moves the first four cards from onTable to discardPile

// Precondition:
//     Length of onTable >= 4
// Postcondition:
//     The first four cards have been removed from onTable and
//     placed at the front of discardPile

{
    CardType tempCard;    // Temporary card
    int      count;       // Loop counter

    for (count = 1; count <= 4; count++)
    {
        onTable.RemoveTop(tempCard);
        discardPile.InsertTop(tempCard);
    }
}

//**************************************************************

void Player::MoveTwo()

// Moves the second and third cards from onTable to discardPile

// Precondition:
//     Length of onTable >= 4
// Postcondition:
//     The second and third cards have been removed from onTable and
//     placed at the front of discardPile
//  && The first card in onTable at entry is still the first card
//     in onTable

{
```

```
CardType tempCard;      // Temporary card
CardType firstCard;     // First card in onTable

// Remove and save first card

onTable.RemoveTop(firstCard);

// Move second card

onTable.RemoveTop(tempCard);
discardPile.InsertTop(tempCard);

// Move third card

onTable.RemoveTop(tempCard);
discardPile.InsertTop(tempCard);

// Restore first card

onTable.InsertTop(firstCard);
}
```

The Driver We have now designed and implemented all the objects responsible for playing the solitaire game. All that remains is to write the top-level algorithm (the driver).

Main   *Level 0*

```
Create player—an object of type Player
Set gamesWon = 0
Prompt for number of games to be played
Read numberOfGames
Prompt for number of shuffles
Read numberOfShuffles
Prompt for random number seed
Read seed
Use seed to initialize the random number generator

FOR gamesPlayed going from 1 through numberOfGames
    player.PlayGame(numberOfShuffles, won)
    IF won
        Increment gamesWon
Print numberOfGames
Print gamesWon
```

Problem-Solving Case Study cont'd.

Module Structure Chart:

```
┌──────────────┐
│    Main      │
└──────────────┘
```

```cpp
//****************************************************************
// Solitaire program
// This program is a simulation of a card game.
// See text for rules of the game
//****************************************************************
#include "bool.h"
#include "player.h"        // For Player class
#include <iostream.h>
#include <stdlib.h>        // For srand()

int main()
{
    Player  player;              // Card-playing manager
    int     numberOfShuffles;    // Number of shuffles per game
    int     numberOfGames;       // Number of games to play
    int     gamesPlayed;         // Number of games played
    int     gamesWon;            // Number of games won
    int     seed;                // Used with random no. generator
    Boolean won;                 // True if a game has been won

    gamesWon = 0;
    cout << "Enter number of games to play: ";
    cin >> numberOfGames;
    cout << "Enter number of shuffles per game: ";
    cin >> numberOfShuffles;
    cout << "Enter integer seed for random no. generator: ";
    cin >> seed;
    srand(seed);                         // Seed the random no. generator

    for (gamesPlayed=1; gamesPlayed <= numberOfGames; gamesPlayed++)
    {
        player.PlayGame(numberOfShuffles, won);
        if (won)
            gamesWon++;
    }
    cout << endl;
    cout << "Number of games played: " << numberOfGames << endl;
    cout << "Number of games won: " << gamesWon << endl;
    return 0;
}
```

Testing: To exhaustively test this program, all possible configurations of a deck of 52 cards have to be generated. Although this is theoretically possible, it is not realistic. There are 52! (52 factorial) possible arrangements of a deck of cards, and 52! equals

52 * 51 * 50 * ... 2 * 1

This is a large number. Try multiplying it out.

Therefore, another method of testing is required. At a minimum, the questions to be examined are:

1. Does the program recognize a winning hand?
2. Does the program recognize a losing hand?

To answer these questions, we must examine at least one hand declared to be a winner and several hands declared to be losers. Specifying 20 as the number of games to play, we ran the program to see if there were any winning hands. There were none.

From past experience, we know this solitaire game is difficult. We let the simulation run, specifying 100 games and an initial seed of 3. There were two winning hands. Intermediate output statements were put in to examine the winning hands. They were correct. Several losing hands were also printed; they were indeed losing hands. Satisfied that the program was working correctly, we set up runs that varied in length, number of shuffles, and seed for the random number generator. The results are listed below. There is no strategy behind the particular choices of parameters; they are random.

Number of Games	Number of Shuffles	Seed	Games Won
100	1	3	2
100	2	4	0
500	3	4	3
1,000	6	3	6
5,000	10	327	11
10,000	4	4	40
10,000	4	3	45
10,000	4	120	44

TESTING AND DEBUGGING

In this chapter, all the functions that deleted a value from a data structure assumed that an item was there to be deleted (DeleteTop and RemoveTop) or that the specific item to be deleted was in the list (Delete). The calling code was responsible for guaranteeing this precondition.

When deleting from a data structure, the function can easily detect that the component is not there or that there is no component to remove. Should these functions have been written to guard against trying to delete a component that is not there? It depends on the interface between the calling code and the function. Either the caller is responsible for ensuring that the value is there to be deleted (guarantees the precondition), or the function should test for the case in which there is no value to delete or the specific value is not there. If the function does the testing, a flag should be returned to the caller showing whether or not the value was deleted successfully.

Following is a version of the `DeleteTop` function in which error checking is included within the function itself. Notice that there is an additional parameter named `failed`. Notice also that part of the original precondition—that the list must not be empty—has been eliminated.

```
void OrdList::DeleteTop(
        /* out */ ComponentType& item,      // Item removed from list
        /* out */ Boolean&        failed )   // Error flag

//  Precondition:
//        component members of list nodes are in ascending order
//  Postcondition:
//        IF list at entry is empty
//            failed == TRUE  &&  Value of item is undefined
//        ELSE
//                failed == FALSE
//            && item == component member of first list node at entry
//            && Node containing item is removed from linked list
//            && component members of list nodes are in ascending order

{
    if (head == NULL)
        failed = TRUE;
    else
    {
        NodePtr tempPtr = head;      // Temporary pointer
        item = head->component;
        head = head->link;
        delete tempPtr;
        failed = FALSE;
    }
}
```

Whenever it is possible for an error condition to occur in a function, you must decide where to check for the condition. If the caller is responsible for seeing that the situation does not occur, the assumption that the condition will not occur must be stated in the precondition of the function. If the function is to check for the error condition, your documentation of the function must state how the error will be handled if it occurs. Commonly, a function tests for the error condition and simply sets a flag to return if the error occurs, leaving the determination of what to do about the error to the calling code. The key point about error detection is that the interface between the calling code and a function must make it absolutely clear which party is responsible for the error checking.

Testing and Debugging Hints

1. Review the Testing and Debugging Hints for Chapter 17. They apply to the pointers and dynamic data that are used in dynamic linked lists.
2. Be sure that the link member in the last node of a dynamic linked list has been set to NULL.
3. When visiting the components in a dynamic linked list, be sure that you test for the end of the list in such a way that you don't try to dereference the null pointer. On many systems, dereferencing the null pointer causes a run-time error.
4. Be sure to initialize the external pointer to each dynamic data structure.
5. Do not use

```
currPtr++;
```

to make currPtr point to the next node in a dynamic linked list. The list nodes are not necessarily in consecutive memory locations on the free store.
6. Keep close track of pointers. Changing pointer values prematurely may cause problems when you try to get back to the pointed-to variable.
7. If a C++ class that points to dynamic data has a class destructor but not a copy-constructor, do not pass a class object to a function using pass-by-value. A shallow copy occurs, and both the formal parameter and the actual parameter point to the same dynamic data. When the function returns, the formal parameter's destructor is executed, destroying the actual parameter's dynamic data.
8. Be sure to test for possible error conditions when working with linked lists. There are two ways to handle error checking. The calling routine can check for the error condition and not call the function if the error occurs, or the function can test for the error condition. The documentation of the called function should state clearly how error checking is done.

SUMMARY

Dynamic data structures grow and contract during run time. They are made up of nodes that contain two kinds of members: the component, and one or more pointers to nodes of the same type. The pointer to the first node is saved in a variable called the external pointer to the structure.

A linked list is a data structure in which the components are logically next to each other rather than physically next to each other as they are in an array. A linked list can be represented either as an array of structs or as a collection of dynamic nodes, linked together by pointers. The end of a dynamic linked list is indicated by the special pointer constant NULL. Common operations on linked lists include inserting a node, deleting a node, and traversing the list (visiting each node from first to last).

In this chapter, we used linked lists to implement lists. But linked lists are also used to implement many data structures other than lists. The study of data structures forms a major topic in computer science. Entire books and courses are developed to cover the subject. A solid understanding of the fundamentals of linked lists is a prerequisite to creating more complex structures.

QUICK CHECK

1. What distinguishes a linked list from an array? (pp. 1046–1047)
2. Nodes in a linked list structure must contain a link member. (True or False?) (pp. 1050–1052)
3. The number of elements in a dynamic data structure must be determined before the program is compiled. (True or False?) (pp. 1050–1051)
4. When printing the contents of a dynamically allocated linked list, what operation advances the current node pointer to the next node? (pp. 1063–1065)
5. What is the difference between the operations of inserting a new item at the top of a linked list, and inserting the new item into its proper position in an ordered list? (pp. 1065–1074)
6. In deleting an item from a linked list, why do we need to keep track of the previous node (the node before the one to be deleted)? (pp. 1074–1078)

Answers   1. Arrays are data structures whose components are located next to each other in memory. Linked lists are data structures in which the locations of the components are defined by an explicit link member in each node.   2. True; every node (except the first) is accessed by using the link member in the node before it.   3. False; we do not have to know in advance how large it has to be. (In fact, we rarely know.) The only limitation is the amount of memory space available on the free store.   4. The current node pointer is set equal to the link member of the current node.   5. When inserting an item into position, the list must first be searched to find the proper place. We don't have to search the list when inserting at the top.   6. Because we must set the link member of the previous node equal to the link member of the current node as part of the deletion operation.

EXAM PREPARATION EXERCISES

1. Given the OrdList class of this chapter and a client's declaration

   OrdList myList;

   what is the output of each of the following code segments?

a. `myList.InsertTop(30);`
   `myList.InsertTop(20);`
   `myList.InsertTop(10);`
   `myList.Print();`

b. `myList.Insert(10);`
   `myList.Insert(20);`
   `myList.Insert(30);`
   `myList.Print();`

2. In a linked list, components are only logically next to each other, whereas in an array they are also physically next to each other. (True or False?)

3. Which of the following can be used to implement a list ADT?

   a. An array of the component type
   b. A linked list implemented using an array of `structs`
   c. A linked list implemented using dynamic `structs` and pointers

4. The following declarations for a node of a linked list are not acceptable to the C++ compiler:

```
typedef T* P;
struct T
{
    float x;
    P      link;
};
```

   Correct the problem by inserting another declaration before the Typedef statement.

5. What is the primary benefit of dynamic data structures?

6. This chapter's `OrdList` class represents an ordered list ADT. To make an *unordered* list ADT, which of the following member functions could be removed: `IsEmpty`, `Print`, `InsertTop`, `Insert`, `DeleteTop`, and `Delete`?

7. Use the C++ code below to identify the values of the variables and Boolean comparisons that follow. The value may be undefined, or the expression may be invalid.

```
struct NodeType;
typedef NodeType* NodePtr;

struct NodeType
{
    int      number;
    char     character;
    NodePtr link;
};

NodePtr currPtr = NULL;
NodePtr firstPtr = NULL;
NodePtr lastPtr = NULL;

currPtr = new NodeType;
currPtr->number = 13;
currPtr->character = 'z';
currPtr->link = new NodeType;
lastPtr = currPtr->link;
```

```
lastPtr->number = 9;
firstPtr = new NodeType;
lastPtr->link = firstPtr;
firstPtr->number = 9;
firstPtr->character = 'h';
firstPtr->link = currPtr;
    .
    .
    .
```

	Expression	*Value*
a.	`firstPtr->link->number`	_____
b.	`firstPtr->link->link->character`	_____
c.	`firstPtr->link == lastPtr`	_____
d.	`currPtr->link->number`	_____
e.	`currPtr->link == *lastPtr`	_____
f.	`firstPtr == lastPtr->link`	_____
g.	`firstPtr->number < firstPtr->link->number`	_____

8. Choose the best data structure (array or dynamic linked list) for each of the following situations. Assume unlimited memory but limited time.
   a. A list of the abbreviations for the 50 states.
   b. A fixed list of 1000 to 4000 (usually 1500) elements that has elements printed according to position requests that are input to the program.
   c. A list of an unknown number of elements that is read, then printed in reverse order.

9. Choose the best data structure (array or dynamic linked list) for each of the following situations. Assume limited memory but unlimited time.
   a. A list of the abbreviations for the 50 states.
   b. A fixed list of 1000 to 4000 (usually 1500) elements that has elements printed according to position requests that are input to the program.
   c. A list of an unknown number of elements that is read, then printed in reverse order.

10. What is the output of the following C++ code, given the input data 5, 6, 3, and 1?

```cpp
struct PersonNode;
typedef PersonNode* PtrType;

struct PersonNode
{
    int     ssNum;
    PtrType next;
};

int     ssNumber;
PtrType ptr;
PtrType head = NULL;
```

```
cin >> ssNumber;
while (cin)
{
    ptr = new PersonNode;
    ptr->ssNum = ssNumber;
    ptr->next = head;
    head = ptr;
    cin >> ssNumber;
}
ptr = head;
while (ptr != NULL)
{
    cout << ptr->ssNum;
    ptr = ptr->next;
}
```

PROGRAMMING WARM-UP EXERCISES

1. To the OrdList class of this chapter, add a value-returning member function named Length that counts and returns the number of nodes in a list.
2. To the OrdList class, add a value-returning member function named Sum that returns the sum of all the data values in a list.
3. To the OrdList class, add a Boolean member function named IsPresent that searches a list for a particular value (passed as a parameter) and returns TRUE if the value is found.
4. To the OrdList class, add a Boolean member function named Equal that compares two class objects and returns TRUE if the two lists they represent are identical.
5. Rewrite the InsertTop and Insert functions of the OrdList class so that the program prints an error message and halts if the new operator fails to obtain space on the free store. (To halt the program, use the exit function supplied by the C++ standard library.) Be sure to revise the function postconditions for the new versions.
6. Redo Exercise 5 as follows. Instead of halting the program if the new operation fails, each function should return (as a parameter) a Boolean flag indicating that the insertion failed.
7. The OrdList class provides a copy-constructor but not a deep copy operation. Add a CopyFrom function to the OrdList class that performs a deep copy of one class object to another.
8. To avoid special handling of empty linked lists for insertion and deletion routines, some programmers prefer to keep a dummy node permanently in the list. (The list is considered empty if it contains only the dummy node.) Rewrite the OrdList class to use a dummy node whose component value is equal to a constant named DUMMY. Do not keep any unnecessary code. (*Hint:* The first element of the list follows the dummy node.)
9. Given the declarations

```
struct NodeType;
typedef NodeType* NodePtr;
```

```
struct NodeType
{
    int     number;
    NodePtr link;
};
```

and the function prototype

```
void Exchange( /* in */ NodePtr head,
               /* in */ int     key );
```

implement the Exchange function. The function searches a linked list for the value given by key and exchanges it with the number preceding it in the list. If key is the first value in the list or if key is not found, then no exchange occurs.

10. Using the type declarations given in Exercise 9, write a function that reorganizes the items in a linked list so that the last item is first, the second to last is second, and so forth. (*Hint:* Use a temporary list.)

PROGRAMMING PROBLEMS

1. In the Solitaire program in this chapter, all insertions into a linked list are made using the function InsertTop, and all the deletions are made using RemoveTop. In some cases, this is inefficient. For example, function CardDeck::Recreate takes the cards from onTable and moves them one by one to the deck. Then the cards on discardPile are moved one by one to the deck. It would be more efficient simply to concatenate (join) the deck list and the onTable list, then concatenate the resulting list and the discardPile list.

   To the CardPile class, add a member function whose specification is the following:

```
void Concat( /* inout */ CardPile& otherList );
    // Postcondition:
    //      This list and otherList are concatenated (the front
    //      of otherList is joined to the rear of this list)
    //   && otherList is empty
```

Implement and test the Concat member function. Use it in the CardDeck::Recreate function of the Solitaire program to make the program more efficient.

2. In Chapter 15, the BirthdayCalls program uses a DateType class to process address book information found in a file friendFile. Entries in friendFile are in the form

```
John Arbuthnot
(493) 384-2938
1/12/1970

Mary Smith
(123) 123-4567
10/12/1960
```

Write a program to read in the entries from `friendFile` and store them into a dynamic linked list ordered by birth date. The output should consist of a listing by month of the names and telephone numbers of the people who have birthdays each month.

3. In Chapter 17, the Personnel Records case study reads a file of personnel records, sorts the records alphabetically, and prints out the sorted records. Rewrite the program so that it reads each record and stores it into its proper position in an ordered list. Implement the ordered list as a dynamic linked list using this chapter's `OrdList` class as a model. Note that the limit of 1000 employee records is no longer relevant because you are using a dynamic data structure.

4. This chapter's `OrdList` class implements an ordered list ADT by using a linked list. In turn, the linked list is implemented by using dynamic data and pointers. Reimplement the linked list using an array of `struct`s. You will have to manage a "free store" within the array—the collection of currently unused array elements. To mimic the `new` and `delete` operations, your implementation will need two auxiliary functions that obtain and release space on the "free store."

CASE STUDY FOLLOW-UP

1. The `CardDeck` class is derived from the `CardPile` class using inheritance.
   a. List the names of all the public members of the `CardDeck` class.
   b. List the names of all the private members of the `CardDeck` class.

2. In the `Shuffle` function of the `CardDeck` class, why are the declarations of `halfA` and `halfB` located inside the body of the For loop? What would happen if the declarations were placed outside the loop at the top of the function?

3. Give the `Player` class more responsibility by making it prompt for and input the number of shuffles and the random number seed. Encapsulate the `numberOfShuffles` and `seed` variables within the `Player` class, and add two member functions named `GetNumShuffles` and `GetSeed`. Show the new class declaration and the implementations of the two new functions. Also, rewrite the `main` function, given these changes.

19

Recursion

- To be able to identify the base case(s) and the general case in a recursive definition.
- To be able to write a recursive algorithm for a problem involving only simple variables.
- To be able to write a recursive algorithm for a problem involving structured variables.
- To be able to write a recursive algorithm for a problem involving linked lists.

In C++, any function can call another function. A function can even call it-self! When a function calls itself, it is making a **recursive call.** The word *re-cursive* means "having the characteristic of coming up again, or repeating." In this case, a function call is being repeated by the function itself. Recur-sion is a powerful technique that can be used in place of iteration (looping).

Recursive solutions are generally less efficient than iterative solutions to the same problem. However, some problems lend themselves to simple, ele-gant, recursive solutions and are exceedingly cumbersome to solve iterative-ly. Some programming languages, like early versions of FORTRAN, BASIC, and COBOL, do not allow recursion. Other languages are especially oriented to recursive algorithms—LISP is one of these. C++ lets us take our choice: we can implement both iterative and recursive algorithms in C++.

Our examples are broken into two groups: problems that use only simple variables and problems that use structured variables. If you are studying re-cursion before reading Chapter 11 on structured data types, then cover only the first set of examples and leave the rest until you have completed the chapters on structured data types.

What Is Recursion?

You may have seen a set of gaily painted Russian dolls that fit inside one an-other. Inside the first doll is a smaller doll, inside of which is an even small-er doll, inside of which is yet a smaller doll, and so on. A recursive algorithm is like such a set of Russian dolls. It reproduces itself with smaller and smaller examples of itself until a solution is found—that is, until there are no more dolls. The recursive algorithm is implemented by using a func-tion that makes recursive calls to itself.

Recursive Call A function call in which the function being called is the same as the one making the call.

In Chapter 8, we wrote a function named Power, which calculates the re-sult of raising an integer to a positive power. If X is an integer and N is a pos-itive integer, the formula for X^N is

$$X^N = \underbrace{X * X * X * X * \ldots * X}_{N \text{ times}}$$

We could also write this formula as

$$X^N = X * \underbrace{(X * X * \ldots * X)}_{(N-1) \text{ times}}$$

or even as

$$X^N = X * X * \underbrace{(X * X * \ldots * X)}_{(N-2) \text{ times}}$$

In fact, we can write the formula most concisely as

$$X^N = X * X^{N-1}$$

This definition of X^N is a classic **recursive definition**—that is, a definition given in terms of a smaller version of itself.

Recursive Definition   A definition in which something is defined in terms of smaller versions of itself.

X^N is defined in terms of multiplying X times X^{N-1}. How is X^{N-1} defined? Why, as $X * X^{N-2}$, of course! And X^{N-2} is $X * X^{N-3}$; X^{N-3} is $X * X^{N-4}$; and so on. In this example, "in terms of smaller versions of itself" means that the exponent is decremented each time.

When does the process stop? When we have reached a case where we know the answer without resorting to a recursive definition. In this example, it is the case where N equals 1: X^1 is X. The case (or cases) for which an answer is explicitly known is called the **base case**. The case for which the solution is expressed in terms of a smaller version of itself is called the **recursive** or **general case**. A **recursive algorithm** is an algorithm that expresses the solution in terms of a call to itself, a recursive call. A recursive algorithm must terminate; that is, it must have a base case.

Base Case   The case for which the solution can be stated nonrecursively.

General Case   The case for which the solution is expressed in terms of a smaller version of itself; also known as *recursive case*.

Recursive Algorithm   A solution that is expressed in terms of (a) smaller instances of itself and (b) a base case.

Figure 19-1 shows a recursive version of the Power function with the base case and the recursive call marked. The function is embedded in a program that reads in a number and an exponent and prints the result.

```
//***********************************************************
// Exponentiation program
//***********************************************************
#include <iostream.h>

int Power( int, int );

int main()
{
    int number;           // Number that is being raised to power
    int exponent;         // Power the number is being raised to

    cin >> number >> exponent;
    cout << Power(number, exponent);  ←————  // Nonrecursive call
    return 0;
}

//***********************************************************

int Power( /* in */ int x,    // Number that is being raised to power
           /* in */ int n )   // Power the number is being raised to

// Computes x to the n power by multiplying x times the result of
// computing x to the n - 1 power.

// Precondition:
//      x is assigned  &&  n > 0
// Postcondition:
//      Function value == x raised to the power n
// Note:
//      Large exponents may result in integer overflow

{
    if (n == 1)
        return x;  ←————————————————  // Base case
    else
        return x * Power(x, n - 1);  ←————  // Recursive call
}
```

Each recursive call to Power can be thought of as creating a completely new copy of the function, each with its own copies of the parameters x and n. The value of x remains the same for each version of Power, but the value of n decreases by one for each call until it becomes 1.

Let's trace the execution of this recursive function, with number equal to 2 and exponent equal to 3. We use a new format to trace recursive routines: we number the calls and then discuss what is happening in paragraph form.

Call 1: Power is called by main, with number equal to 2 and exponent equal to 3. Within Power, the formal parameters x and n are initialized to 2 and 3, respectively. Because n is not equal to 1, Power is called recursively with x and n − 1 as parameters. Execution of Call 1 pauses until an answer is sent back from this recursive call.

Call 2: x is equal to 2 and n is equal to 2. Because n is not equal to 1, the function Power is called again, this time with x and n − 1 as parameters. Execution of Call 2 pauses until an answer is sent back from this recursive call.

Call 3: x is equal to 2 and n is equal to 1. Because n equals 1, the value of x is to be returned. This call to the function has finished executing, and the function return value (which is 2) is passed back to the place in the statement from which the call was made.

Call 2: This call to the function can now complete the statement that contained the recursive call because the recursive call has returned. Call 3's return value (which is 2) is multiplied by x. This call to the function has finished executing, and the function return value (which is 4) is passed back to the place in the statement from which the call was made.

Call 1: This call to the function can now complete the statement that contained the recursive call because the recursive call has returned. Call 2's return value (which is 4) is multiplied by x. This call to the function has finished executing, and the function return value (which is 8) is passed back to the place in the statement from which the call was made. Because the first call (the nonrecursive call in main) has now completed, this is the final value of the function Power.

This trace is summarized in Figure 19-2. Each box represents a call to the Power function. The values for the parameters for that call are shown in each box.

What happens if there is no base case? We have **infinite recursion,** the recursive equivalent of an infinite loop. For example, if the statement

```
if (n == 1)
```

were omitted, Power would be called over and over again. Infinite recursion also occurs if Power is called with n less than or equal to zero.

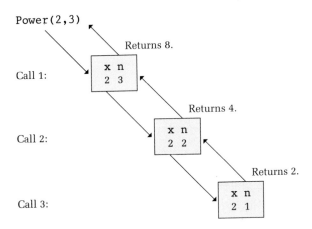

■ FIGURE 19-2

Execution of
Power(2, 3)

Infinite Recursion   The situation in which a function calls itself over and over endlessly.

In actuality, recursive calls can't go on forever. Here's the reason. When a function is called, either recursively or nonrecursively, the computer system creates temporary storage for the actual parameters and the function's (automatic) local variables. This temporary storage is a region of memory called the *run-time stack*. When the function returns, its parameters and local variables are released from the run-time stack. With infinite recursion, the recursive function calls never return. Each time the function calls itself, a little more of the run-time stack is used to store the new copies of the variables. Eventually, all the memory space on the stack is used. At that point, the program crashes with an error message such as "RUN-TIME STACK OVERFLOW" (or the computer may simply "hang").

 ## Recursive Algorithms with Simple Variables

Let's look at another example: calculating a factorial. The factorial of a number N (written $N!$) is N multiplied by $N - 1$, $N - 2$, $N - 3$, and so on. Another way of expressing factorial is

$$N! = N * (N - 1)!$$

This expression looks like a recursive definition. $(N - 1)!$ is a smaller instance of $N!$—that is, it takes one less multiplication to calculate $(N - 1)!$ than it does to calculate $N!$ If we can find a base case, we can write a recursive algorithm. Fortunately, we don't have to look too far: $0!$ is defined in mathematics to be 1.

Factorial (In: n)

```
IF n is 0
   Return 1
ELSE
   Return n * Factorial(n − 1)
```

This algorithm can be coded directly as follows.

```
int Factorial ( /* in */ int n )

// Precondition:
//      n >= 0
// Postcondition:
//      Function value == n!
// Note:
//      Large values of n may cause integer overflow

{
    if (n == 0)
        return 1;                           // Base case
    else
        return n * Factorial(n - 1);        // General case
}
```

Let's trace this function with an original n of 4.

Call 1: n is 4. Because n is not 0, the else branch is taken. The return statement cannot be completed until the recursive call to Factorial with n − 1 as the actual parameter has been completed.

Call 2: n is 3. Because n is not 0, the else branch is taken. The return statement cannot be completed until the recursive call to Factorial with n − 1 as the actual parameter has been completed.

Call 3: n is 2. Because n is not 0, the else branch is taken. The return statement cannot be completed until the recursive call to Factorial with n − 1 as the actual parameter has been completed.

Call 4: n is 1. Because n is not 0, the else branch is taken. The return statement cannot be completed until the recursive call to Factorial with n − 1 as the actual parameter has been completed.

Call 5: n is 0. Because n equals 0, this call to the function returns, sending back 1 as the result.

Call 4: The return statement in this copy can now be completed. The value to be returned is n (which is 1) times 1. This call to the function returns, sending back 1 as the result.

Call 3: The return statement in this copy can now be completed. The value to be returned is n (which is 2) times 1. This call to the function returns, sending back 2 as the result.

Call 2: The return statement in this copy can now be completed. The value to be returned is n (which is 3) times 2. This call to the function returns, sending back 6 as the result.

Call 1: The return statement in this copy can now be completed. The value to be returned is n (which is 4) times 6. This call to the function returns, sending back 24 as the result. Because this is the last of the calls to Factorial, the recursive process is over. The value 24 is returned as the final value of the call to Factorial with an actual parameter of 4. Figure 19-3

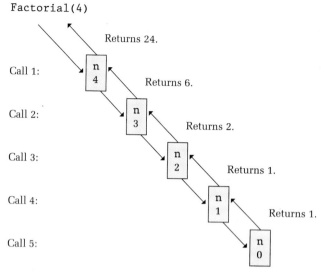

Factorial(4)

Returns 24.

Call 1:

Returns 6.

Call 2:

Returns 2.

Call 3:

Returns 1.

Call 4:

Returns 1.

Call 5:

summarizes the execution of the `Factorial` function with an actual parameter of 4.

Let's organize what we have done in these two solutions into an outline for writing recursive algorithms.

1. Understand the problem. (We threw this in for good measure; it is always the first step.)
2. Determine the base case(s).
3. Determine the recursive case(s).

We have used the factorial and the power algorithms to demonstrate recursion because they are easy to visualize. In practice, one would never want to calculate either of these functions using the recursive solution. In both cases, the iterative solutions are simpler and much more efficient because starting a new iteration of a loop is a faster operation than calling a function. Let's compare the code for the iterative and recursive versions of the factorial problem.

Iterative solution

```
int Factorial ( /* in */ int n )
{
    int factor;
    int count;

    factor = 1;
    for (count = 2; count <= n; count++)
        factor = factor * count;
    return factor;
}
```

Recursive solution

```
int Factorial ( /* in */ int n )
{
    if (n == 0)
        return 1;
    else
        return n * Factorial(n - 1);
}
```

The iterative version has two local variables, whereas the recursive version has none. There are usually fewer local variables in a recursive routine than in an iterative routine. Also, the iterative version always has a loop, while the recursive version always has a selection statement—either an If or a Switch. A branching structure is the main control structure in a recursive routine. A looping structure is the main control structure in an iterative routine.

In the next section, we examine a more complicated problem—one in which the recursive solution is not immediately apparent.

 Towers of Hanoi

One of your first toys may have been three pegs with colored circles of different diameters. If so, you probably spent countless hours moving the circles from one peg to another. If we put some constraints on how the circles or disks can be moved, we have an adult game called the Towers of Hanoi. When the game begins, all the circles are on the first peg in order by size, with the smallest on the top. The object of the game is to move the circles, one at a time, to the third peg. The catch is that a circle cannot be placed on top of one that is smaller in diameter. The middle peg can be used as an auxiliary peg, but it must be empty at the beginning and at the end of the game.

To get a feel for how this might be done, let's look at some sketches of what the configuration must be at certain points if a solution is possible. We use four circles or disks. The beginning configuration is:

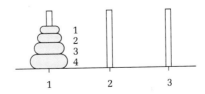

To move the largest circle (circle 4) to peg 3, we must move the three smaller circles to peg 2. Then circle 4 can be moved into its final place:

Let's assume we can do this. Now, to move the next largest circle (circle 3) into place, we must move the two circles on top of it onto an auxiliary peg (peg 1 in this case):

To get circle 2 into place, we must move circle 1 to another peg, freeing circle 2 to be moved to its place on peg 3:

The last circle (circle 1) can now be moved into its final place, and we are finished:

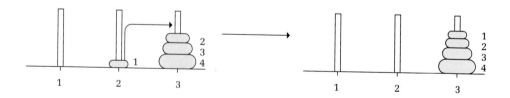

Notice that to free circle 4, we had to move three circles to another peg. To free circle 3, we had to move two circles to another peg. To free circle 2, we had to move one circle to another peg. This sounds like a recursive algorithm: to free the *n*th circle, we have to move *n* − 1 circles. Each stage can be thought of as beginning again with three pegs, but with one less circle each time. Let's see if we can summarize this process, using *n* instead of an actual number.

Get N Circles Moved from Peg 1 to Peg 3

> Get n − 1 circles moved from peg 1 to peg 2
> Move nth circle from peg 1 to peg 3
> Get n − 1 circles moved from peg 2 to peg 3

This algorithm certainly sounds simple; surely there must be more. But this really is all there is to it.

Let's write a recursive function that implements this algorithm. We can't actually move disks, of course, but we can print out a message to do so. Notice that the beginning peg, the ending peg, and the auxiliary peg keep changing during the algorithm. To make the algorithm easier to follow, we call the pegs beginPeg, endPeg, and auxPeg. These three pegs, along with the number of circles on the beginning peg, are the parameters of the function.

We have the recursive or general case, but what about a base case? How do we know when to stop the recursive process? The clue is in the expression "Get *n* circles moved." If we don't have any circles to move, we don't have anything to do. We are finished with that stage. Therefore, when the number of circles equals 0, we do nothing (that is, we return).

```
void DoTowers(
    /* in */ int circleCount,      // Number of circles to move
    /* in */ int beginPeg,         // Peg containing circles to move
    /* in */ int auxPeg,           // Peg holding circles temporarily
    /* in */ int endPeg     )      // Peg receiving circles being moved
{
    if (circleCount > 0)
    {
        // Move n - 1 circles from beginning peg to auxiliary peg

        DoTowers(circleCount - 1, beginPeg, endPeg, auxPeg);
        cout << "Move circle from peg " << beginPeg
            << " to peg " << endPeg << endl;

        // Move n - 1 circles from auxiliary peg to ending peg

        DoTowers(circleCount - 1, auxPeg, beginPeg, endPeg);
    }
}
```

It's hard to believe that such a simple algorithm actually works, but we'll prove it to you. Following is a driver program that calls the DoTowers function. Output statements have been added so you can see the values of the actual parameters with each recursive call. Because there are two recursive calls within the function, we have indicated which recursive statement issued the call.

```cpp
//*********************************************************************
// TestTowers program
// This program, a test driver for the DoTowers function, reads in
// a value from standard input and passes this value to DoTowers
//*********************************************************************
#include <iostream.h>
#include <iomanip.h>      // For setw()

void DoTowers( int, int, int, int );

int main()
{
    int circleCount;      // Number of circles on starting peg

    cout << "Input number of circles: ";
    cin >> circleCount;
    cout << "OUTPUT WITH " << circleCount << " CIRCLES" << endl
         << endl;
    cout << "CALLED FROM  #CIRCLES" << setw(8) << "BEGIN"
         << setw(8) << "AUXIL." << setw(5) << "END"
         << "     INSTRUCTIONS" << endl
         << endl;
    cout << "Original   :";
    DoTowers(circleCount, 1, 2, 3);
    return 0;
}


//*********************************************************************

void DoTowers(
    /* in */ int circleCount,      // Number of circles to move
    /* in */ int beginPeg,         // Peg containing circles to move
    /* in */ int auxPeg,           // Peg holding circles temporarily
    /* in */ int endPeg      )     // Peg receiving circles being moved

// This recursive function moves circleCount circles from beginPeg
// to endPeg.  All but one of the circles are moved from beginPeg
// to auxPeg, then the last circle is moved from beginPeg to endPeg,
// and then the circles are moved from auxPeg to endPeg.
// The subgoals of moving circles to and from auxPeg are what
// involve recursion
```

```
// Precondition:
//     All parameters are assigned  && circleCount >= 0
// Postcondition:
//     The values of all parameters have been printed
//  && IF circleCount > 0
//         circleCount circles have been moved from beginPeg to
//         endPeg in the manner detailed above
//     ELSE
//         No further actions have taken place

{
    cout << setw(6) << circleCount << setw(9) << beginPeg
         << setw(7) << auxPeg << setw(7) << endPeg << endl;
    if (circleCount > 0)
    {
        cout << "From  first:";
        DoTowers(circleCount - 1, beginPeg, endPeg, auxPeg);
        cout << setw(58) << "Move circle " << circleCount
             << " from " << beginPeg << " to " << endPeg << endl;
        cout << "From second:";
        DoTowers(circleCount - 1, auxPeg, beginPeg, endPeg);
    }
}
```

The output from a run with three circles follows. "Original" means that the parameters listed beside it are from the nonrecursive call, which is the first call to DoTowers. "From first:" means that the parameters listed are for a call issued from the first recursive statement. "From second:" means that the parameters listed are for a call issued from the second recursive statement. Notice that a call cannot be issued from the second recursive statement until the preceding call from the first recursive statement has completed execution.

OUTPUT WITH 3 CIRCLES

CALLED FROM	#CIRCLES	BEGIN	AUXIL.	END	INSTRUCTIONS
Original :	3	1	2	3	
From first:	2	1	3	2	
From first:	1	1	2	3	
From first:	0	1	3	2	
					Move circle 1 from 1 to 3
From second:	0	2	1	3	
					Move circle 2 from 1 to 2
From second:	1	3	1	2	
From first:	0	3	2	1	
					Move circle 1 from 3 to 2
From second:	0	1	3	2	

					Move circle 3 from 1 to 3
From second:	2	2	1	3	
From first:	1	2	3	1	
From first:	0	2	1	3	
					Move circle 1 from 2 to 1
From second:	0	3	2	1	
					Move circle 2 from 2 to 3
From second:	1	1	2	3	
From first:	0	1	3	2	
					Move circle 1 from 1 to 3
From second:	0	2	1	3	

 # Recursive Algorithms with Structured Variables

In our definition of a recursive algorithm, we said there were two cases: the recursive or general case, and the base case for which an answer can be expressed nonrecursively. In the general case for all our algorithms so far, a parameter was expressed in terms of a smaller value each time. When structured variables are used, the recursive case is often in terms of a smaller structure rather than a smaller value; the base case occurs when there are no values left to process in the structure.

We examine a recursive algorithm for printing the contents of a one-dimensional array of *n* elements to show what we mean.

Print Array

> IF more elements
>   Print the value of the first element
>   Print Array of n − 1 elements

The recursive case is to print the values in an array that is one element "smaller"; that is, the length of the array decreases by 1 with each recursive call. The base case is when the length of the array becomes 0—that is, when there are no more elements to print.

Our parameters must include the index of the first element (the one to be printed). How do we know when there are no more elements to print (that is, when the length of the array to be printed is 0)? We know we have printed the last element in the array when the index of the next element to be printed is beyond the index of the last element in the array. Therefore, the index of the last array element must be passed as a parameter. We call the indices first and last. When first is greater than last, we are finished. The name of the array is list.

```
void Print( /* in */ const int list[],      // Array to be printed
            /* in */           int first,   // Index of first element
            /* in */           int last  )  // Index of last element
{
        if (first <= last)                               // Recursive case
        {
            cout << list[first] << endl;
            Print(list, first + 1, last);
        }
        // Empty else-clause is the base case
}
```

Here is a code walk-through of the function call

```
Print(list, 0, 4);
```

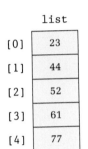

list

[0]	23
[1]	44
[2]	52
[3]	61
[4]	77

using the array shown at the left.

Call 1: first is 0 and last is 4. Because first is less than last, the value in list[first] (which is 23) is printed. Execution of this call pauses while the array from first + 1 through last is printed.

Call 2: first is 1 and last is 4. Because first is less than last, the value in list[first] (which is 44) is printed. Execution of this call pauses while the array from first + 1 through last is printed.

Call 3: first is 2 and last is 4. Because first is less than last, the value in list[first] (which is 52) is printed. Execution of this call pauses while the array from first + 1 through last is printed.

Call 4: first is 3 and last is 4. Because first is less than last, the value in list[first] (which is 61) is printed. Execution of this call pauses while the array from first + 1 through last is printed.

Call 5: first is 4 and last is 4. Because first is equal to last, the value in list[first] (which is 77) is printed. Execution of this call pauses while the array from first + 1 through last is printed.

Call 6: first is 5 and last is 4. Because first is greater than last, the execution of this call is complete. Control returns to the preceding call.

Call 5: Execution of this call is complete. Control returns to the preceding call.

Calls 4, 3, 2, and 1: Each execution is completed in turn, and control returns to the preceding call.

Notice that once the deepest call (the call with the highest number) was reached, each of the calls before it returned without doing anything. When no statements are executed after the return from the recursive call to the function, the recursion is known as **tail recursion**. Tail recursion often indicates that the problem could be solved more easily using iteration. We used the array example because it made the recursive process easy to visualize; in practice, an array should be printed iteratively.

Tail Recursion   A recursive algorithm in which no statements are executed after the return from the recursive call.

Figure 19-4 shows the execution of the `Print` function with the values of the actual parameters for each call. Notice that the array gets smaller with each recursive call (`list[first]` ... `list[last]`). If we want to print the array elements in reverse order recursively, all we have to do is interchange the two statements within the If statement.

■ FIGURE 19-4   Execution of `Print(list, 0, 4)`

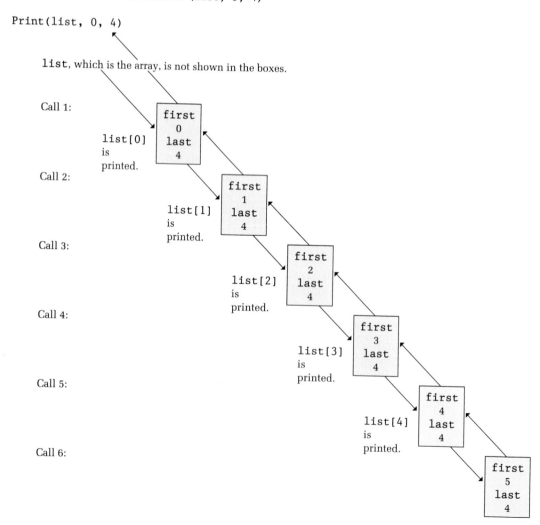

We imposed recursive solutions on these problems only to demonstrate how recursion works. As a rule of thumb, if an iterative solution is more obvious or easier to understand, use it; it will be more efficient. However, there are problems for which the recursive solution is more obvious or easier to devise, such as the Towers of Hanoi problem. (It turns out that Towers of Hanoi is surprisingly difficult to solve using iteration.) Computer science students should be aware of the power of recursion. If the definition of a problem is inherently recursive, then a recursive solution should certainly be considered.

P ROBLEM-SOLVING CASE STUDY

Converting Decimal Integers to Binary Integers

Problem: Convert a decimal (base 10) integer to a binary (base 2) integer.

Discussion: The algorithm for this conversion is as follows:

1. Take the decimal number and divide it by 2.
2. Make the remainder the rightmost digit in the answer.
3. Replace the original dividend with the quotient.
4. Repeat, placing each new remainder to the left of the previous one.
5. Stop when the quotient is 0.

This is clearly an algorithm for a calculator and paper and pencil. Expressions such as "to the left of" certainly cannot be implemented in C++ as yet. Let's do an example—convert 42 from base 10 to base 2—to get a feel for the algorithm before we try to write a computer solution. Remember, the quotient in one step becomes the dividend in the next.

Step 1	*Step 2*
$\underline{21}$ ←Quotient	$\underline{10}$ ←Quotient
2)42	2)21
$\underline{4}$	$\underline{2}$
2	1
$\underline{2}$	$\underline{0}$
0 ←Remainder	1 ←Remainder

Step 3	*Step 4*
$\underline{5}$ ←Quotient	$\underline{2}$ ←Quotient
2)10	2)5
$\underline{10}$	$\underline{4}$
0 ←Remainder	1 ←Remainder

Step 5   Step 6

1 ← Quotient   0 ← Quotient
2)2   2)1

2   0
0 ← Remainder   1 ← Remainder

The answer is the sequence of remainders from last to first. Therefore, the decimal number 42 is 101010 in binary.

It looks as though the problem can be implemented with a straightforward iterative algorithm. Each remainder is obtained from the MOD operation (% in C++), and each quotient is the result of the / operation.

```
WHILE number > 0
    Set remainder = number MOD 2
    Print remainder
    Set number = number / 2
```

Let's do a walk-through to test this algorithm.

Number	Remainder
42	0
21	1
10	0
5	1
2	0
1	1

Answer: 0 1 0 1 0 1
(remainder from step   1 2 3 4 5 6)

The answer is backwards! An iterative solution (using only simple variables) doesn't work. We need to print the last remainder first. The first remainder should be printed only after the rest of the remainders have been calculated and printed.

In our example, we should print 42 MOD 2 after (42 / 2) MOD 2 has been printed. But this, in turn, means that we should print (42 / 2) MOD 2 after ((42 / 2) / 2) MOD 2 has been printed. Now this begins to look like a recursive definition. We can summarize by saying that, for any given number, we should print number MOD 2 after (number / 2) MOD 2 has been printed. This becomes the following algorithm:

Convert (In: number)

```
IF number > 0
    Convert(number / 2)
    Print number MOD 2
```

If `number` is 0, we have called `Convert` as many times as we need to and can begin printing the answer. The base case is simply when we stop making recursive calls. The recursive solution to this problem is encoded in the `Convert` function.

```cpp
void Convert( /* in */ int number )      // Number being converted
                                         //    to binary
// Precondition:
//      number >= 0
// Postcondition:
//      IF number > 0
//          number has been printed in binary (base 2) form
//      ELSE
//          No action has taken place

{
    if (number > 0)
    {
        Convert(number / 2);                     // Recursive call
        cout << number % 2;
    }
    // Empty else-clause is the base case
}
```

Let's do a code walk-through of `Convert(10)`. We pick up our original example at step 3, where the dividend is 10.

Call 1: `Convert` is called with an actual parameter of 10. Because `number` is not equal to 0, the then-clause is executed. Execution pauses until the recursive call to `Convert` with an actual parameter of (`number` / 2) has completed.

Call 2: `number` is 5. Because `number` is not equal to 0, execution of this call pauses until the recursive call with an actual parameter of (`number` / 2) has completed.

Call 3: `number` is 2. Because `number` is not equal to 0, execution of this call pauses until the recursive call with an actual parameter of (`number` / 2) has completed.

Call 4: number is 1. Because number is not equal to 0, execution of this call pauses until the recursive call with an actual parameter of (number / 2) has completed.

Call 5: number is 0. Execution of this call to Convert is complete. Control returns to the preceding call.

Call 4: Execution of this call resumes with the statement following the recursive call to Convert. The value of number % 2 (which is 1) is printed. Execution of this call is complete.

Call 3: Execution of this call resumes with the statement following the recursive call to Convert. The value of number % 2 (which is 0) is printed. Execution of this call is complete.

Call 2: Execution of this call resumes with the statement following the recursive call to Convert. The value of number % 2 (which is 1) is printed. Execution of this call is complete.

Call 1: Execution of this call resumes with the statement following the recursive call to Convert. The value of number % 2 (which is 0) is printed. Execution of this call is complete. Because this is the nonrecursive call, execution resumes with the statement immediately following the original call.

Figure 19-6 shows the execution of the Convert function with the values of the actual parameters.

■ FIGURE 19-6

Execution of
Convert(10)

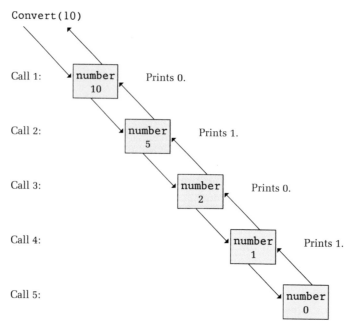

PROBLEM-SOLVING *CASE STUDY*

Minimum Value in an Integer Array

Problem: Find the minimum value in an integer array indexed from 0 through length − 1.

Discussion: This problem is easy to solve iteratively, but the objective here is to think recursively. The problem has to be stated in terms of a smaller case of itself. Because this is a problem using an array, a smaller case involves a smaller array. The minimum value in an array of length length is the smaller of list[length−1] and the smallest value in the array from list[0] ... list[length−2].

Minimum (In: list, length)

```
Set minSoFar = Minimum(list, length−1)
IF list[length−1] < minSoFar
    Return list[length−1]
ELSE
    Return minSoFar
```

This algorithm looks reasonable. All we need is a base case. Because each recursive call reduces the length of the array by one, our base case occurs when length is 1. We know the minimum value for this call: it is the only value in the array.

```cpp
int Minimum(
        /* in */ const int list[],     // Array of integers to examine
        /* in */ int        length )    // One greater than index of
                                        //    last number in array
// Precondition:
//     list[0..length-1] are assigned
//  && length >= 1
// Postcondition:
//     Function value == smallest number in list[0..length-1]

{
    int minSoFar;        // Minimum returned from recursive call

    if (length == 1)
        return list[0];                          // Base case
```

```
      else
      {                                                // Recursive case
          minSoFar = Minimum(list, length-1);
          if (list[length-1] < minSoFar)
              return list[length-1];
          else
              return minSoFar;
      }
}
```

We do not provide a code walk-through for this function. A diagram showing the actual parameters for each call appears in Figure 19-7.

Testing: To test this function, we need a driver program that reads values into an array, calls the function, and prints the result. The cases to be tested are the end cases (the minimum value is the first in the list, and the minimum value is the last in the list) and several cases between.

■ FIGURE 19-7

Execution of
Minimum(list, 5)

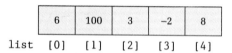

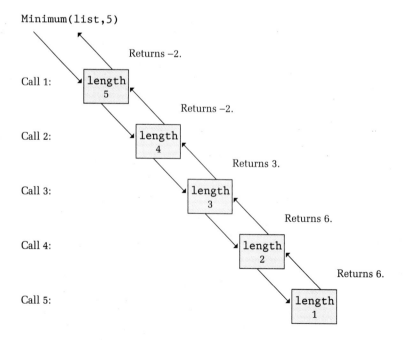

TESTING AND DEBUGGING

Recursion is a powerful technique when used correctly. Improperly used, recursion can cause errors that are difficult to diagnose. The best way to debug a recursive algorithm is to construct it correctly in the first place. To be realistic, however, we give a few hints about where to look if an error occurs.

Testing and Debugging Hints

1. Be sure there is a base case. If there is no base case, the algorithm continues to issue recursive calls until all of memory has been used. Each time the function is called, either recursively or nonrecursively, stack space is allocated for the parameters and automatic local variables. If there is no base case to end the recursive calls, the run-time stack eventually overflows. An error message such as "STACK OVERFLOW" indicates that the base case is missing.

2. Be sure you have not used a While structure. The basic structure in a recursive algorithm is the If-Then-Else. There must be at least two cases: the recursive case and the base case. If the base case does nothing, the else-clause is not present. The selection structure, however, must be there. If a While statement is used in a recursive algorithm, the While statement usually should not contain a recursive call.

3. As with nonrecursive functions, do not reference global variables directly within a recursive function unless you have justification for doing so.

4. Formal parameters that relate to the size of the problem must be value parameters, not reference parameters. The actual parameters that relate to the size of the problem are usually expressions. Arbitrary expressions can be passed only to value parameters.

5. Use your system's debugger program (or use debug output statements) to trace a series of recursive calls. Inspecting the values of parameters and local variables often helps to locate errors in a recursive algorithm.

SUMMARY

A recursive algorithm is expressed in terms of a smaller instance of itself. It must include a recursive case, for which the algorithm is expressed in terms of itself, and a base case, for which the algorithm is expressed in nonrecursive terms.

In many recursive problems, the smaller instance refers to a numeric parameter that is being reduced with each call. In other problems, the smaller instance refers to the size of the data structure being manipulated. The base case is the one in which the size of the problem (value or structure) reaches a point where an explicit answer is known.

In the example for finding the minimum using recursion, the size of the problem was the length of the array being searched. When the array length became 1, the solution was known. If there is only one array element, it is clearly the minimum (as well as the maximum).

In the Towers of Hanoi game, the size of the problem was the number of disks to be moved. When there was only one left on the beginning peg, it could be moved to its final destination.

QUICK CHECK

1. What distinguishes the base case from the recursive case in a recursive algorithm? (pp. 1120–1121)
2. What is the base case in the Towers of Hanoi algorithm? (pp. 1127–1132)
3. In working with simple variables, the recursive case is often stated in terms of a smaller value. What is typical of the recursive case in working with structured variables? (pp. 1132–1142)
4. In printing a linked list in reverse order recursively, what is the base case? (pp. 1135–1137)

Answers   1. The base case is the simplest case, the case where the solution can be stated non-recursively.   2. When there are no more circles left to move.   3. It is often stated in terms of a smaller structure.   4. When the value of the current node pointer is NULL.

EXAM PREPARATION EXERCISES

1. Recursion is an example of:
   a. selection
   b. a data structure
   ✓ c. repetition
   d. data-flow programming
2. A void function can be recursive, but a value-returning function cannot. (True or ✓False?)
3. When a function is called recursively, the actual parameters and automatic local variables of the calling version are saved until its execution is resumed. (True or False?)
4. Given the recursive formula $F(N) = -F(N-2)$, with base case $F(0) = 1$, what are the values of $F(4)$, $F(6)$, and $F(5)$? (If any of the values are undefined, say so.)
5. What algorithm error(s) lead to infinite recursion?
6. What control structure appears most commonly in a recursive function?
7. If you develop a recursive algorithm that employs tail recursion, what should you consider?
8. A recursive algorithm depends on making something smaller. When the algorithm works on a data structure, what may become smaller?
   a. Distance from a position in the structure.
   b. The data structure.
   c. The number of variables in the recursive function.
9. What is the name of the memory area used by the computer system to save information for pending recursive calls of a function?

[handwritten margin note next to item 5: "no base case" ; next to item 6: "or no progress towards base case."]

10. Given the following input data (where \n denotes the newline character):

    ABCDE\n

    what is the output of the following program?

    ```cpp
    #include <iostream.h>

    void Rev();

    int main()
    {
        Rev();
        cout << endl;
        return 0;
    }

    //**************************************

    void Rev()
    {
        char ch;

        cin.get(ch);
        if (ch != '\n')
        {
            Rev();
            cout << ch;
        }
    }
    ```

11. Repeat Exercise 10, replacing the Rev function with the following version:

    ```cpp
    void Rev()
    {
        char ch;

        cin.get(ch);
        if (ch != '\n')
        {
            cout << ch;
            Rev();
        }
    }
    ```

12. Given the following input:

    15
    23
    21
    19

what is the output of the following program?

```
#include <iostream.h>

void PrintNums();

int main()
{
    PrintNums();
    cout << endl;
    return 0;
}


//*************************************

void PrintNums()
{
    int n;

    cin >> n;
    if (cin)                // If not EOF ...
    {
        cout << n << ' ';
        PrintNums();
        cout << n << ' ';
    }
}
```

PROGRAMMING WARM-UP EXERCISES

1. Write a C++ value-returning function that implements the recursive formula $F(N) = F(N–1) + F(N–2)$ with base cases $F(0) = 1$ and $F(1) = 1$.
2. Add whatever is necessary to fix the following function so that Func(3) equals 10.

```
int Func( /* in */ int n )
{
    return Func(n - 1) + 3;
}
```

3. Rewrite the following DoubleSpace function without using recursion.

```
void DoubleSpace( /* inout */ ifstream& inFile )
{
    char ch;

    inFile.get(ch);
    if (inFile)            // If not EOF ...
    {
```

```
            cout << ch;
            if (ch == '\n')
                cout << endl;
            DoubleSpace();
        }
    }
```

4. Rewrite the following PrintSquares function using recursion.

```
void PrintSquares()
{
    int count;

    for (count = 1; count <= 10; count++)
        cout << count << ' ' << count * count;
}
```

5. Modify the Factorial function of this chapter to print its parameter and returned value indented two spaces for each level of call to the function. The call
Factorial(3) should produce the following output:

```
3
  2
    1
      0
      1
    1
  2
6
```

6. Write a recursive value-returning function that sums the integers from 1 through N.
7. Rewrite the following function so that it is recursive.

```
void PrintSqRoots( /* in */ int n )
{
    int i;

    for (i = n; i > 0; i--)
        cout << i << ' ' << sqrt(double(i)) << endl;
}
```

8. The RevPrint function of this chapter prints the contents of a dynamic linked
list in reverse order. Write a recursive function that prints the contents in forward order.
9. The Print function of this chapter prints the contents of an array from first element to last. Write a recursive function that prints from last element to first.
10. Given the following declarations:

```
struct NodeType;
typedef NodeType* PtrType;
```

```
struct NodeType
{
    int     info;
    PtrType link;
};

PtrType head;
int     key;
```

write a recursive value-returning function that searches a dynamic linked list for the integer value `key`. If the value is in the list, the function should return a pointer to the node where it was found. If the value is not in the list, the function should return `NULL`.

PROGRAMMING PROBLEMS

1. Use recursion to solve the following problem.

    A *palindrome* is a string of characters that reads the same forward and backward. Write a program that reads in strings of characters and determines if each string is a palindrome. Each string is on a separate input line. Echo-print each string, followed by "Is a palindrome" if the string is a palindrome or "Is not a palindrome" if the string is not a palindrome. For example, given the input string

    ```
    Able was I, ere I saw Elba.
    ```

    the program would print "Is a palindrome." In determining whether a string is a palindrome, consider uppercase and lowercase letters to be the same and ignore punctuation characters.

2. Write a program to place eight queens on a chessboard in such a way that no queen is attacking any other queen. This is a classic problem that lends itself to a recursive solution. The chessboard should be represented as an 8 × 8 Boolean array. If a square is occupied by a queen, the value is TRUE; otherwise, the value is FALSE. The status of the chessboard when all eight queens have been placed is the solution.

3. A maze is to be represented by a 10 × 10 array of an enumeration type composed of three values: PATH, HEDGE, and EXIT. There is one exit from the maze. Write a program to determine if it is possible to exit the maze from a given starting point. You may move vertically or horizontally in any direction that contains PATH; you may not move to a square that contains HEDGE. If you move into a square that contains EXIT, you have exited.

    The input data consists of two parts: the maze and a series of starting points. The maze is entered as ten lines of ten characters (P, H, and E). Each succeeding line contains a pair of integers that represents a starting point (that is, row and column numbers). Continue processing entry points until end-of-file occurs.

4. A group of soldiers is overwhelmed by an enemy force. Only one person can go for help because they have only one horse. To decide which soldier should go for help, they put their names in a helmet and put one slip of paper for each soldier with a number on it in another helmet. For example, if there are five soldiers, then the second helmet contains five pieces of paper with the numbers 1 through 5 each written on a separate slip.

circle and pull a name and a number
on whose name was pulled, they count
ach the number that was pulled. When
d from the circle. This continues until
ides for help.

ames are stored in a file, and the last
STOP. Use a circular linked list to repre-
ne in which the link member of the last
of containing NULL). Use recursive func-
nate the soldiers. Output the total num-
the soldiers who were eliminated, and
lp.

ert function?

s the first array index to be evaluated?

he list of integers is implemented as a

APPENDIXES

APPENDIX A   *Reserved Words*

The following identifiers are *reserved words*—identifiers with predefined meanings in the C++ language. The programmer cannot declare them for other uses (for example, variable names) in a C++ program.

asm	double	new	switch
auto	else	operator	template
break	enum	private	this
case	extern	protected	throw
catch	float	public	try
char	for	register	typedef
class	friend	return	union
const	goto	short	unsigned
continue	if	signed	virtual
default	inline	sizeof	void
delete	int	static	volatile
do	long	struct	while

APPENDIX B   *Operator Precedence*

Precedence (highest to lowest)

	Operator	Associativity
	::	Left to right
	() [] -> .	Left to right
Unary:	++ -- ~ ! + - & * new delete (cast) sizeof	Right to left
	->* .*	Left to right
	* / %	Left to right
	+ -	Left to right
	<< >>	Left to right
	< <= > >=	Left to right
	== !=	Left to right
	&	Left to right
	^	Left to right
	|	Left to right
	&&	Left to right

(continued on next page)

Precedence (continued)

Operator	Associativity
||	Left to right
?:	Right to left
= += -= etc.	Right to left
, (the operator, not the separator)	Left to right

Note

This book does not discuss the comma operator listed at the bottom of the chart or the ->* and .* operators (pointer-to-member selection operators). For a description, see Stroustrup's *The C++ Programming Language* (Addison-Wesley, 1991).

APPENDIX C   *C++ Library Routines*

The C++ standard library provides a wealth of functions, named constants, and specialized data types. This appendix details only some of the most widely used library routines (and several named constants). It is a good idea to consult the manual for your particular system to see what other routines the standard library provides.

This appendix is organized according to the header files your program must #include before accessing the listed items. For example, to use a mathematics routine such as sqrt, you would #include the header file math.h as follows:

```
#include <math.h>
   .
   .
   .
y = sqrt(x);
```

The Header File assert.h

assert(booleanExpr)

Parameter:	An int expression booleanExpr, usually written as a logical (Boolean) expression
Effect:	If booleanExpr is nonzero (TRUE), execution of the program simply continues. If booleanExpr equals 0 (FALSE), execution terminates immediately with a message stating the Boolean expression, the name of the file containing the source code, and the line number in the source code.

Function return value: None (a void function)

Note: If the preprocessor directive #define NDEBUG is placed before the directive #include <assert.h>, all assert statements are ignored.

The Header File ctype.h

isalnum(ch)

Parameter: A char value ch

Function return value: An int value that is

- nonzero (TRUE), if ch is a letter or a digit character ('A'–'Z', 'a'–'z', '0'–'9')
- 0 (FALSE), otherwise

isalpha(ch)

Parameter: A char value ch

Function return value: An int value that is

- nonzero (TRUE), if ch is a letter ('A'–'Z', 'a'–'z')
- 0 (FALSE), otherwise

iscntrl(ch)

Parameter: A char value ch

Function return value: An int value that is

- nonzero (TRUE), if ch is a control character (in ASCII, a character with the value 0–31 or 127)
- 0 (FALSE), otherwise

isdigit(ch)

Parameter: A char value ch

Function return value: An int value that is

- nonzero (TRUE), if ch is a digit character ('0'–'9')
- 0 (FALSE), otherwise

isgraph(ch)

Parameter: A char value ch

Function return value: An int value that is

- nonzero (TRUE), if ch is a nonblank printable character (in ASCII, '!' through '~')
- 0 (FALSE), otherwise

`islower(ch)`

Parameter: A char value ch

Function return value: An int value that is

- nonzero (TRUE), if ch is a lowercase letter ('a'–'z')
- 0 (FALSE), otherwise

`isprint(ch)`

Parameter: A char value ch

Function return value: An int value that is

- nonzero (TRUE), if ch is a printable character, including the blank (in ASCII, ' ' through '~')
- 0 (FALSE), otherwise

`ispunct(ch)`

Parameter: A char value ch

Function return value: An int value that is

- nonzero (TRUE), if ch is a punctuation character (equivalent to `isgraph(ch)` `&&` `!isalnum(ch)`)
- 0 (FALSE), otherwise

`isspace(ch)`

Parameter: A char value ch

Function return value: An int value that is

- nonzero (TRUE), if ch is a whitespace character (blank, newline, tab, carriage return, form feed)
- 0 (FALSE), otherwise

`isupper(ch)`

Parameter: A char value ch

Function return value: An int value that is

- nonzero (TRUE), if ch is an uppercase letter ('A'–'Z')
- 0 (FALSE), otherwise

`isxdigit(ch)`

Parameter: A char value ch

Function return value: An int value that is

- nonzero (TRUE), if ch is a hexadecimal digit ('0'–'9', 'A'–'F', 'a'–'f')
- 0 (FALSE), otherwise

```
tolower(ch)
```

Parameter: A char value ch

Function return value: A character that is

- the lowercase equivalent of ch, if ch is an uppercase letter
- ch, otherwise

```
toupper(ch)
```

Parameter: A char value ch

Function return value: A character that is

- the uppercase equivalent of ch, if ch is a lowercase letter
- ch, otherwise

The Header File `float.h`

This header file supplies named constants that define the characteristics of floating point numbers on your particular machine. Among these constants are the following:

FLT_DIG	Approximate number of significant digits in a `float` value on your machine
FLT_MAX	Maximum positive `float` value on your machine
FLT_MIN	Minimum positive `float` value on your machine
DBL_DIG	Approximate number of significant digits in a `double` value on your machine
DBL_MAX	Maximum positive `double` value on your machine
DBL_MIN	Minimum positive `double` value on your machine
LDBL_DIG	Approximate number of significant digits in a `long double` value on your machine
LDBL_MAX	Maximum positive `long double` value on your machine
LDBL_MIN	Minimum positive `long double` value on your machine

The Header File `limits.h`

This header file supplies named constants that define the limits of integer values on your particular machine. Among these constants are the following:

CHAR_BITS	Number of bits in a byte on your machine (8, for example)
CHAR_MAX	Maximum `char` value on your machine
CHAR_MIN	Minimum `char` value on your machine
SHRT_MAX	Maximum `short` value on your machine
SHRT_MIN	Minimum `short` value on your machine
INT_MAX	Maximum `int` value on your machine
INT_MIN	Minimum `int` value on your machine
LONG_MAX	Maximum `long` value on your machine

LONG_MIN	Minimum `long` value on your machine
UCHAR_MAX	Maximum `unsigned char` value on your machine
USHRT_MAX	Maximum `unsigned short` value on your machine
UINT_MAX	Maximum `unsigned int` value on your machine
ULONG_MAX	Maximum `unsigned long` value on your machine

The Header File `math.h`

In the following `math` routines,

1. Error handling for incalculable or out-of-range results is system-dependent.
2. All parameters and function return values are technically of type `double` (double-precision floating point). However, single-precision (`float`) values may be passed to the functions.

`acos(x)`

Parameter: A floating point expression x, where $-1.0 \le x \le 1.0$

Function return value: Arc cosine of x, in the range 0.0 through π

`asin(x)`

Parameter: A floating point expression x, where $-1.0 \le x \le 1.0$

Function return value: Arc sine of x, in the range $-\pi/2$ through $\pi/2$

`atan(x)`

Parameter: A floating point expression x

Function return value: Arc tangent of x, in the range $-\pi/2$ through $\pi/2$

`ceil(x)`

Parameter: A floating point expression x

Function return value: "Ceiling" of x (the smallest whole number $\ge$ x)

`cos(angle)`

Parameter: A floating point expression `angle`, measured in radians

Function return value: Trigonometric cosine of `angle`

`cosh(x)`

Parameter: A floating point expression x

Function return value: Hyperbolic cosine of x

`exp(x)`

Parameter: A floating point expression x

Function return value: The value e (2.718 . . .) raised to the power x `fabs(x)`

Parameter:	A floating point expression x
Function return value:	Absolute value of x

`floor(x)`

Parameter:	A floating point expression x
Function return value:	"Floor" of x (the largest whole number $\leq$ x)

`log(x)`

Parameter:	A floating point expression x, where x > 0.0
Function return value:	Natural logarithm (base *e*) of x

`log10(x)`

Parameter:	A floating point expression x, where x > 0.0
Function return value:	Common logarithm (base 10) of x

`pow(x, y)`

Parameters:	Floating point expressions x and y. If x = 0.0, y must be positive; if x $\leq$ 0.0, y must be a whole number
Function return value:	x raised to the power y

`sin(angle)`

Parameter:	A floating point expression `angle`, measured in radians
Function return value:	Trigonometric sine of `angle`

`sinh(x)`

Parameter:	A floating point expression x
Function return value:	Hyperbolic sine of x

`sqrt(x)`

Parameter:	A floating point expression x, where x $\geq$ 0.0
Function return value:	Square root of x

`tan(angle)`

Parameter:	A floating point expression `angle`, measured in radians
Function return value:	Trigonometric tangent of `angle`

`tanh(x)`

Parameter:	A floating point expression x
Function return value:	Hyperbolic tangent of x

The Header File `stddef.h`

This header file defines a few system-dependent constants and data types. From this header file, the only item we use in this book is the following symbolic constant:

NULL   The system-dependent null pointer constant (usually 0)

The Header File `stdlib.h`

`abs(i)`

Parameter:	An `int` expression `i`
Function return value:	An `int` value that is the absolute value of `i`

`atof(str)`

Parameter:	A string (null-terminated `char` array) `str` representing a floating point number, possibly preceded by whitespace characters and a '+' or '−'
Function return value:	A `double` value that is the floating point equivalent of the characters in `str`
Note:	Conversion stops at the first character in `str` that is inappropriate for a floating point number. If no appropriate characters were found, the return value is system-dependent.

`atoi(str)`

Parameter:	A string (null-terminated `char` array) `str` representing an integer number, possibly preceded by whitespace characters and a '+' or '−'
Function return value:	An `int` value that is the integer equivalent of the characters in `str`
Note:	Conversion stops at the first character in `str` that is inappropriate for an integer number. If no appropriate characters were found, the return value is system-dependent.

`atol(str)`

Parameter:	A string (null-terminated `char` array) `str` representing a long integer, possibly preceded by whitespace characters and a '+' or '−'
Function return value:	A `long` value that is the long integer equivalent of the characters in `str`
Note:	Conversion stops at the first character in `str` that is inappropriate for a long integer number. If no appropriate characters were found, the return value is system-dependent.

`exit(exitStatus)`

Parameter:	An int expression `exitStatus`
Effect:	Program execution terminates immediately with all files properly closed
Function return value:	None (a void function)
Note:	By convention, `exitStatus` is 0 to indicate normal program completion and is nonzero to indicate an abnormal termination.

`labs(i)`

Parameter:	A long expression `i`
Function return value:	A long value that is the absolute value of `i`

`rand()`

Parameter:	None
Function return value:	A random int value in the range 0 through `RAND_MAX`, a constant defined in `stdlib.h` (`RAND_MAX` is usually the same as `INT_MAX`)
Note:	See srand below.

`srand(seed)`

Parameter:	An int expression seed, where seed $\geq$ 0
Effect:	Using seed, the random number generator is initialized in preparation for subsequent calls to the rand function.
Function return value:	None (a void function)
Note:	If srand is not called before the first call to `rand`, a seed value of 1 is assumed.

`system(str)`

Parameter:	A string (null-terminated `char` array) `str` representing an operating system command, exactly as it would be typed by a user on the operating system command line
Effect:	The operating system command represented by `str` is executed.
Function return value:	An int value that is system-dependent
Note:	Programmers often ignore the function return value, using the syntax of a void function call rather than a value-returning function call.

The Header File `string.h`

`strcat(toStr, fromStr)`

Parameters:	Strings (null-terminated `char` arrays) `toStr` and `fromStr`, where `toStr` must be large enough to hold the result

Effect:	fromStr, including the null character '\0', is concatenated (joined) to the end of toStr.
Function return value:	The base address of toStr
Note:	Programmers usually ignore the function return value, using the syntax of a void function call rather than a value-returning function call.

strcmp(str1, str2)

Parameters:	Strings (null-terminated char arrays) str1 and str2
Function return value:	An int value < 0, if str1 < str2 lexicographically The int value 0, if str1 = str2 lexicographically An int value > 0, if str1 > str2 lexicographically

strcpy(toStr, fromStr)

Parameters:	toStr is a char array and fromStr is a string (null-terminated char array), and toStr must be large enough to hold the result.
Effect:	fromStr, including the null character '\0', is copied to toStr, overwriting what was there.
Function return value:	The base address of toStr
Note:	Programmers usually ignore the function return value, using the syntax of a void function call rather than a value-returning function call.

strlen(str)

Parameters:	A string (null-terminated char array) str
Function return value:	An int value ≥ 0 that is the length of str (excluding the '\0')

APPENDIX D *Syntax Templates*

The syntax templates in this appendix describe most, but not all, of the C++ language. To save space, some language features that are not discussed in this book have been omitted.

Each syntax template is labeled with a name. Within a syntax template, boldface words and symbols are literal symbols in the C++ language, and each nonboldface word can be replaced by another syntax template. Items that are shaded are optional. Three dots (. . .) mean that the preceding symbol or shaded block can be repeated. A (nonboldface) brace indicates a list of items from which any one can be chosen.

Table of Syntax Templates

Program

> SourceFile ...

SourceFile

> $\begin{cases} \text{Declaration} \\ \text{Function Definition} \end{cases}$ ...

FunctionDefinition

> DeclSpecifiers Declarator CtorInitializer
> Block

Block

> {
>   Statement
>   ⋮
> }

Statement

> Declaration
> Block
> ;
> Expr ;
> **if** (Expr) Statement **else** Statement
> **while** (Expr) Statement
> **do** Statement **while** (Expr) ;
> **for** (Expr ; Expr ; Expr) Statement
> **for** (Declaration Expr ; Expr) Statement
> **switch** (Expr) Statement
> **case** ConstantExpr : Statement
> **default** : Statement
> **break** ;
> **continue** ;
> **return** Expr ;
> **goto** Identifier ;
> Identifier : Statement

Identifier

LetterOrUnderscore
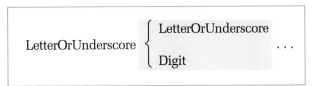

LetterOrUnderscore

> Any uppercase or lowercase alphabetic character or
> the underscore (_) character

Declaration

$$\left\{ \begin{array}{l} \text{DeclSpecifiers DeclaratorList ;} \\ \text{FunctionDefinition} \\ \text{LinkageSpec} \end{array} \right.$$

DeclSpecifiers

$$\left\{ \begin{array}{l} \text{StorageClassSpecifier} \\ \text{TypeSpecifier} \\ \text{FctSpecifier} \qquad \ldots \\ \textbf{friend} \\ \textbf{typedef} \end{array} \right.$$

StorageClassSpecifier

$$\left\{ \begin{array}{l} \textbf{auto} \\ \textbf{extern} \\ \textbf{register} \\ \textbf{static} \end{array} \right.$$

FctSpecifier

$$\left\{ \begin{array}{l} \textbf{inline} \\ \textbf{virtual} \end{array} \right.$$

TypeSpecifier

$$\left\{ \begin{array}{l} \text{SimpleTypeName} \\ \text{ClassSpecifier} \\ \text{EnumSpecifier} \\ \text{ElaboratedTypeSpecifier} \\ \text{ConstOrVol} \end{array} \right.$$

SimpleTypeName

> ⎰ ClassName
> ⎱ TypedefName
> char
> short
> int
> long
> signed
> unsigned
> float
> double
> void

ClassName

> An identifier declared as the name of a class,
> struct, or union

TypedefName

> An identifier introduced in a typedef statement

ElaboratedTypeSpecifier

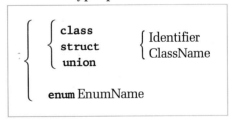

EnumName

> An identifier declared as the name of an enum type

EnumSpecifier

> **enum** Identifier { Enumerator , Enumerator ... }

Enumerator

> Identifier = ConstantExpr

ConstantExpr

> ConditionalExpr

LinkageSpec

> ⎧ **extern** String Declaration
> ⎨
> ⎩ **extern** String { Declaration ; Declaration ... }

DeclaratorList

> Declarator Initializer , Declarator Initializer ...

Declarator

> ⎧ Dname
> ⎪ (Declarator)
> ⎨ PtrOperator Declarator
> ⎪ Declarator (FormalParameterList)
> ⎩ Declarator [ConstantExpr]

PtrOperator

> ⎧ *
> ⎨ &   ConstOrVol ...
> ⎩ ClassName :: *

ConstOrVol

$$\left\{ \begin{array}{l} \texttt{const} \\ \texttt{volatile} \end{array} \right.$$

Dname

$$\left\{ \begin{array}{l} \text{Name} \\ \text{TypedefName} \\ \sim \text{ClassName} \end{array} \right.$$

Name

$$\left\{ \begin{array}{l} \text{Identifier} \\ \text{OperatorFunctionName} \\ \text{QualifiedName} \end{array} \right.$$

OperatorFunctionName

operator Operator

Operator

$$\left\{ \begin{array}{l} \text{UnaryOperator} \\ \text{BinaryOperator} \\ \texttt{()} \\ \texttt{[]} \\ \texttt{new} \\ \texttt{delete} \end{array} \right.$$

BinaryOperator

AssignmentOperator
+
-
*
/
%
<<
>>
<
>
<=
>=
==
!=
&
^
|
&&
||
,
->
->*
.*

QualifiedName

ClassName ::
$\begin{cases} \text{Identifier} \\ \text{OperatorFunctionName} \\ \sim \text{ClassName} \end{cases}$

FormalParameterList

FormalParamDeclaration , FormalParamDeclaration ...

FormalParamDeclaration

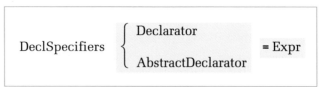

DeclSpecifiers $\begin{cases} \text{Declarator} \\ \text{AbstractDeclarator} \end{cases}$ = Expr

AbstractDeclarator

$$\begin{cases} \text{PtrOperator AbstractDeclarator} \\ \text{AbstractDeclarator (FormalParameterList) ConstOrVol} \dots \\ \text{AbstractDeclarator [ConstantExpr]} \\ \text{(AbstractDeclarator)} \end{cases}$$

Initializer

$$\begin{cases} \text{= AssignmentExpr} \\ \text{= \{ InitializerList , \}} \\ \text{(ExpressionList)} \end{cases}$$

InitializerList

$$\begin{cases} \text{AssignmentExpr} \\ \text{InitializerList , AssignmentExpr} \\ \text{\{ InitializerList , \}} \end{cases}$$

ClassSpecifier

ClassHead **{** MemberList **}**

ClassHead

$$\begin{cases} \textbf{class} \\ \textbf{struct} \\ \textbf{union} \end{cases} \begin{cases} \text{Identifier} \\ \\ \text{ClassName} \end{cases} \text{: BaseSpecifier , BaseSpecifier} \dots$$

BaseSpecifier

$$\begin{cases} \text{ClassName} \\ \textbf{virtual} \text{ AccessSpec ClassName} \\ \text{AccessSpec } \textbf{virtual} \text{ ClassName} \end{cases}$$

AccessSpec

$$\left\{ \begin{array}{l} \texttt{public} \\ \texttt{private} \\ \texttt{protected} \end{array} \right.$$

MemberList

$$\left\{ \begin{array}{l} \text{MemberDeclaration} \\ \\ \text{AccessSpec :} \end{array} \right. \quad \text{MemberList}$$

MemberDeclaration

$$\left\{ \begin{array}{l} \text{DeclSpecifiers MemberDeclarator , MemberDeclarator ... ;} \\ \text{FunctionDefinition ;} \\ \text{QualifiedName} \end{array} \right.$$

MemberDeclarator

$$\left\{ \begin{array}{l} \text{Declarator PureSpecifier} \\ \\ \text{Identifier : ConstantExpr} \end{array} \right.$$

PureSpecifier

$$\boxed{\texttt{= 0}}$$

CtorInitializer

: MemberInitializer , MemberInitializer ...

MemberInitializer

$$\left\{ \begin{array}{l} \text{Class Name} \\ \qquad\qquad \text{(ActualParameterList)} \\ \text{Identifier} \end{array} \right.$$

ActualParameterList

> ExpressionList

ExpressionList

> AssignmentExpr **,** AssignmentExpr . . .

Expr

> $\begin{cases} \text{AssignmentExpr , AssignmentExpr ...} \\ \text{Expr , AssignmentExpr} \end{cases}$

AssignmentExpr

> $\begin{cases} \text{ConditionalExpr} \\ \text{UnaryExpr AssignmentOperator AssignmentExpr} \end{cases}$

AssignmentOperator

> $\begin{cases} \text{=} \\ \text{+=} \\ \text{-=} \\ \text{*=} \\ \text{/=} \\ \text{\%=} \\ \text{\^{}=} \\ \text{\&=} \\ \text{|=} \\ \text{>>=} \\ \text{<<=} \end{cases}$

ConditionalExpr

$$\begin{cases} \text{LogicalORExpr} \\ \text{LogicalORExpr } \textbf{?} \text{ Expr } \textbf{:} \text{ ConditionalExpr} \end{cases}$$

LogicalORExpr

$$\begin{cases} \text{LogicalANDExpr} \\ \text{LogicalORExpr } \textbf{||} \text{ LogicalANDExpr} \end{cases}$$

LogicalANDExpr

$$\begin{cases} \text{InclusiveORExpr} \\ \text{LogicalANDExpr } \textbf{\&\&} \text{ InclusiveORExpr} \end{cases}$$

InclusiveORExpr

$$\begin{cases} \text{ExclusiveORExpr} \\ \text{InclusiveORExpr } \textbf{|} \text{ ExclusiveORExpr} \end{cases}$$

ExclusiveORExpr

$$\begin{cases} \text{ANDExpr} \\ \text{ExclusiveORExpr } \textbf{\^{}} \text{ ANDExpr} \end{cases}$$

ANDExpr

$$\begin{cases} \text{EqualityExpr} \\ \text{ANDExpr } \textbf{\&} \text{ EqualityExpr} \end{cases}$$

EqualityExpr

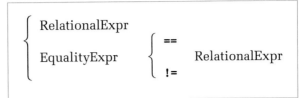

RelationalExpr

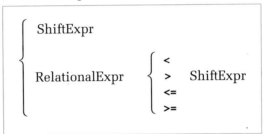

ShiftExpr

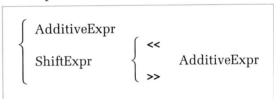

AdditiveExpr

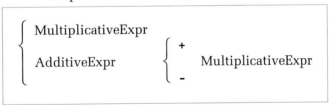

MultiplicativeExpr

PtrToMemberExpr

$$\left\{\begin{array}{l} \text{CastExpr} \\ \text{PtrToMemberExpr} \end{array}\right. \left\{\begin{array}{l} \text{.*} \\ \text{->*} \end{array}\right. \text{CastExpr}$$

CastExpr

$$\left\{\begin{array}{l} \text{UnaryExpr} \\ \text{(TypeName) CastExpr} \end{array}\right.$$

TypeName

TypeSpecifier . . . **AbstractDeclarator**

UnaryExpr

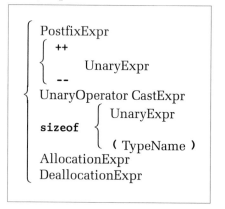

$$\left\{\begin{array}{l} \text{PostfixExpr} \\ \left\{\begin{array}{l} \text{++} \\ \text{--} \end{array}\right. \text{UnaryExpr} \\ \text{UnaryOperator CastExpr} \\ \textbf{sizeof} \left\{\begin{array}{l} \text{UnaryExpr} \\ \text{(TypeName)} \end{array}\right. \\ \text{AllocationExpr} \\ \text{DeallocationExpr} \end{array}\right.$$

UnaryOperator

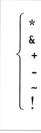

$$\left\{\begin{array}{l} * \\ \& \\ + \\ - \\ \sim \\ ! \end{array}\right.$$

Left Digit(s)	Right Digit	EBCDIC									
		0	1	2	3	4	5	6	7	8	9
6						□					
7						¢		.	<	(	+	|
8		&										
9		!	$	*	)	;	¬		—	/		
10								^		,	%	_
11		>	?									
12			`	:	#	@	'	=	"		a
13		b	c	d	e	f	g	h	i		
14								j	k	l	m	n
15		o	p	q	r						
16			~	s	t	u	v	w	x	y	z
17									\	{	}
18		[	]								
19						A	B	C	D	E	F	G
20		H	I								J
21		K	L	M	N	O	P	Q	R		
22								S	T	U	V
23		W	X	Y	Z						
24		0	1	2	3	4	5	6	7	8	9

Nonprintable control characters—codes 00–63, 250–255, and those for which empty spaces appear in the chart—are not shown.

APPENDIX F *Program Style, Formatting, and Documentation*

Throughout this text we encourage the use of good programming style and documentation. Although the programs you write for class assignments may not be looked at by anyone except the person grading your work, outside of class you will write programs that will be used by others.

Useful programs have very long lifetimes, during which they must be modified and updated. When maintenance work must be done, either you or another programmer will have to do it. Good style and documentation are essential if another programmer is to understand and work with your program. You also will discover that, after not working with your own program for a few months, you'll be amazed at how many of the details you've forgotten.

General Guidelines

The style used in the programs and fragments throughout this text provide a good starting point for developing your own style. Our goals in creating this style were to make it simple, consistent, and easy to read.

Style is of benefit only for a human reader of your program—differences in style make no difference to the computer. Good style includes the use of meaningful variable names, comments, and indentation of control structures, all of which help others to understand and work with your program. Perhaps the most important aspect of program style is consistency. If the style within a program is not consistent, then it becomes misleading and confusing.

Sometimes, a particular style is specified for you by your instructor or by the company you work for. When you are modifying someone else's code, you should use his or her style in order to maintain consistency within the program. However, you will also develop your own, personal programming style based on what you've been taught, your own experience, and your personal taste.

Comments

Comments are extra information included to make a program easier to understand. You should include a comment anywhere the code is difficult to understand. However, don't overcomment. Too many comments in a program can obscure the code and be a source of distraction.

In our style, there are four basic types of comments: headers, declarations, in-line, and sidebar.

1. *Header comments* appear at the top of the program and should include your name, the date that the program was written, and its purpose. It is also useful to include sections describing input, output, and assumptions. Think of the header comments as the reader's introduction to your program. Here is an example:

```
// This program computes the sidereal time for a given date and
// solar time.
//
// Written By: Your Name
//
// Date Completed: 4/8/96
//
// Input: A date and time in the form MM DD YY HH MM SS
//
// Output: Sidereal time in the form HH MM SS
//
```

```
// Assumptions: Solar time is specified for a longitude of 0
//      degrees (GMT, UT, or Z time zone)
```

Header comments should also be included for all user-defined functions. (See Chapters 7 and 8.)

2. *Declaration comments* accompany the constant and variable declarations in the program. Anywhere that an identifier is declared, it is helpful to include a comment that explains its purpose. In programs in the text, declaration comments appear to the right of the identifier being declared. For example:

```
const float E = 2.71828;     // The base of the natural logarithms

float deltaX;                // The difference in the x direction
float deltaY;                // The difference in the y direction
```

Notice that aligning the comments gives the code a neater appearance and is less distracting.

3. *In-line comments* are used to break long sections of code into shorter, more comprehensible fragments. These are often the names of modules in your algorithm design, although you may occasionally choose to include other information. It is generally a good idea to surround in-line comments with blank lines to make them stand out. For example:

```
// Prepare file for reading

scoreFile.open("scores.dat");

// Get data

scoreFile >> test1 >> weight1;
scoreFile >> test2 >> weight2;
scoreFile >> test3 >> weight3;

// Print heading

cout << "Test Score  Weight" << endl;
```

Even if comments are not used, blank lines can be inserted wherever there is a logical break in the code that you would like to emphasize.

4. *Sidebar comments* appear to the right of executable statements and are used to shed light on the purpose of the statement. Sidebar comments are often just pseudocode statements from the lowest levels of your design. If a

complicated C++ statement requires some explanation, the pseudocode statement should be written to the right of the C++ statement. For example:

```
while (file1 && file2)     // While neither file is empty...
{
    .
    .
    .
```

In addition to the four main types of comments that we have discussed, there are some miscellaneous comments that we should mention. (1) After the main function, we recommend using a row of asterisks (or dashes or equal signs or . . .) in a comment before and after each function to help it to stand out. For example:

```
//********************************************************************

void PrintSecondHeading()
{
    .
    .
    .
}

//********************************************************************
```

(2) In this text, we use C++'s alternative comment form

```
/* Some comment */
```

to document the flow of information for each formal parameter of a function:

```
void GetData( /* out */ int age,      // Patient's age
              /* out */ int weight )  // Patient's weight
{
    .
    .
    .
}

void Print( /* in */    float val,    // Value to be printed
            /* inout */ int&  count ) // Number of lines printed
{                                     //    so far
    .
    .
    .
}
```

(Chapter 7 describes the purpose of labeling each parameter as /* in */, /* out */, or /* inout */.)

(3) Programmers sometimes place a comment after the right brace of a block (compound statement) to indicate which control structure the block belongs to:

```
while (num >= 0)
{
    .
    .
    .
    if (num == 25)
    {
        .
        .
        .
    } // if
} // while
```

Attaching comments in this fashion can help to clarify the code and to aid in debugging mismatched braces.

Identifiers

The most important consideration in choosing a name for a data item or function in a program is that the name convey as much information as possible about what the data item is or what the function does. The name should also be readable in the context in which it is used. For example, the following names convey the same information but one is more readable than the other:

```
datOfInvc      invoiceDate
```

Identifiers for types, constants, and variables should be nouns, whereas names of void functions (non-value-returning functions) should be imperative verbs or phrases containing imperative verbs. Because of the way that value-returning functions are invoked, their names should be nouns or occasionally adjectives. Here are some examples:

Variables	`address, price, radius, monthNumber`
Constants	`PI, TAX_RATE, STRING_LENGTH, ARRAY_SIZE`
Data types	`NameType, CarMakes, RoomLists, Hours`
Void functions	`GetData, ClearTable, PrintBarChart`
Value-returning functions	`CubeRoot, Greatest, Color, AreaOf, IsEmpty`

Although an identifier may be a series of words, very long identifiers can become quite tedious and can make the program difficult to read. The best approach to designing an identifier is to try writing out different names until you reach an acceptable compromise—and then write an especially informative declaration comment next to the declaration.

Capitalization is another consideration when choosing an identifier. C++ is a case-sensitive language; that is, uppercase and lowercase letters are distinct. Different programmers use different conventions for capitalizing identifiers. In this text, we begin each variable name with a lowercase letter and capitalize the beginning of each successive English word. We begin each function name and data type name with a capital letter and, again, capitalize the beginning of each successive English word. For named constants, we capitalize the entire identifier, separating successive English words with underscore (_) characters. Keep in mind, however, that C++ reserved words such as `main`, `if`, and `while` are always lowercase letters, and the compiler will not recognize them if you capitalize them differently.

Formatting Lines and Expressions

C++ allows you to break a long statement in the middle and continue onto the next line. (However, you cannot split a line in the middle of an identifier, a literal constant, or a string.) When you must split a line, it's important to choose a breaking point that is logical and readable. Compare the readability of the following code fragments.

```
cout << "For a radius of " << radius << " the diameter of the cir"
    << "cle is " << diameter << endl;

cout << "For a radius of " << radius
    << " the diameter of the circle is " << diameter << endl;
```

When you must split an expression across multiple lines, try to end each line with an operator. Also, try to take advantage of any repeating patterns in the expression. For example,

```
meanOfMaxima = (Maximum(set1Value1, set1Value2, set1Value3) +
                Maximum(set2Value1, set2Value2, set2Value3) +
                Maximum(set3Value1, set3Value2, set3Value3)) / 3.0;
```

When writing expressions, also keep in mind that spaces improve readability. Usually you should include one space on either side of the = operator and most other operators. Occasionally, spaces are left out to emphasize the order in which operations are performed. Here are some examples:

```
if (x+y > y+z)
    maximum = x + y;
else
    maximum = y + z;
```

```
hypotenuse = sqrt(a*a + b*b);
```

Indentation

The purpose of indenting statements in a program is to provide visual cues to the reader and to make the program easier to debug. When a program is properly indented, the way the statements are grouped is immediately obvious. Compare the following two program fragments:

```
while (count <= 10)          while (count <= 10)
{                            {
cin >> num;                      cin >> num;
if (num == 0)                    if (num == 0)
{                                {
count++;                             count++;
num = 1;                             num = 1;
}                                }
cout << num << endl;             cout << num << endl;
cout << count << endl;           cout << count << endl;
}                            }
```

As a basic rule in this text, each nested or lower-level item is indented by four spaces. Exceptions to this rule are formal parameters and statements that are split across two or more lines. Indenting by four spaces is a matter of personal preference. Some people prefer to indent by three, five, or even more than five spaces.

In this book, we indent the entire body of a function. Also, in general, any statement that is part of another statement is indented. For example, the If-Then-Else contains two parts, the then-clause and the else-clause. The statements within both clauses are indented four spaces beyond the beginning of the If-Then-Else statement. The If-Then statement is indented like the If-Then-Else, except that there is no else-clause. Here are examples of the If-Then-Else and the If-Then:

```
if (sex == MALE)
{
    maleSalary = maleSalary + salary;
    maleCount++;
}
else
    femaleSalary = femaleSalary + salary;

if (count > 0)
    average = total / count;
```

For nested If-Then-Else statements that form a generalized multi-way branch (the If-Then-Else-If, described in Chapter 5), a special style of indentation is used in the text. Here is an example:

```
if (month == JANUARY)
    monthNumber = 1;
else if (month == FEBRUARY)
    monthNumber = 2;
else if (month == MARCH)
    monthNumber = 3;
else if (month == APRIL)
    .
    .
    .
else
    monthNumber = 12;
```

The remaining C++ statements all follow the basic indentation guideline mentioned previously. For reference purposes, here are examples of each.

```
while (count <= 10)
{
    cin >> value;
    sum = sum + value;
    count++;
}

do
{
    GetAnswer(letter);
    PutAnswer(letter);
} while (letter != 'N');

for (count = 1; count <= numSales; count++)
    cout << '*';

for (count = 10; count >= 1; count--)
{
    inFile >> dataItem;
    outFile << dataItem << ' ' << count << endl;
}
```

```
switch (color)
{
    RED     : cout << "Red";
              break;
    ORANGE  : cout << "Orange";
              break;
    YELLOW  : cout << "Yellow";
              break;
    GREEN   :
    BLUE    :
    INDIGO  :
    VIOLET  : cout << "Short visible wavelengths";
              break;
    WHITE   :
    BLACK   : cout << "Not valid colors";
              color = NONE;
}
```

GLOSSARY

abstract data type (ADT) a data type whose properties (domain and operations) are specified independently of any particular implementation

abstract step a step for which some implementation details remain unspecified

abstraction barrier the invisible wall around a class object that encapsulates implementation details. The wall can be breached only through the public interface

actual parameter a variable or expression listed in a call to a function

aggregate operation an operation on a data structure as a whole, as opposed to an operation on an individual component of the data structure

algorithm a step-by-step procedure for solving a problem in a finite amount of time

anonymous type a type that does not have an associated type identifier

arithmetic/logic unit (ALU) the component of the central processing unit that performs arithmetic and logical operations

array a collection of components, all of the same type, ordered on N dimensions ($N \geq 1$). Each component is accessed by N indices, each of which represents the component's position within that dimension.

assembler a program that translates an assembly language program into machine code

assembly language a low-level programming language in which a mnemonic is used to represent each of the machine language instructions for a particular computer

assignment expression a C++ expression with (1) a value and (2) the side effect of storing the expression value into a memory location

assignment statement a statement that stores the value of an expression into a variable

automatic variable a variable for which memory is allocated and deallocated when control enters and exits the block in which it is declared

auxiliary storage device a device that stores data in encoded form outside the computer's main memory

base address the memory address of the first element of an array

base case the case for which the solution can be stated nonrecursively

base class (superclass) the class being inherited from

binary operator an operator that has two operands

black box an electrical or mechanical device whose inner workings are hidden from view

central processing unit (CPU) the part of the computer that executes the instructions (program) stored in memory; made up of the arithmetic/logic unit and the control unit

class a structured type in a programming language that is used to represent an abstract data type

class member a component of a class. Class members may be either data or functions.

class object (class instance) a variable of a class type

client software that declares and manipulates objects of a particular class

communication complexity a measure of the quantity of information passing through a module's interface

compiler a program that translates a high-level language into machine code

composition (containment) a mechanism by which the internal data (the state) of one class includes an object of another class

computer a programmable device that can store, retrieve, and process data

computer program a list of instructions to be performed by a computer

computer programming the process of planning a sequence of steps for a computer to follow

concrete step a step for which the implementation details are fully specified

constructor an operation that creates a new instance (variable) of an ADT

control abstraction the separation of the logical properties of an action from its implementation

control structure a statement used to alter the normally sequential flow of control

control unit the component of the central processing unit that controls the actions of the other components so that instructions (the program) are executed in the correct sequence

count-controlled loop a loop that executes a specified number of times

dangling pointer a pointer that points to a variable that has been deallocated

data information that has been put into a form a computer can use

data abstraction the separation of a data type's logical properties from its implementation

data flow the flow of information from the calling code to a function and from the function back to the calling code

data representation the concrete form of data used to represent the abstract values of an abstract data type

data type a specific set of data values along with a set of operations on those values

declaration a statement that associates an identifier with a data object, a function, or a data type so that the programmer can refer to that item by name

deep copy an operation that not only copies one class object to another but also makes copies of any pointed-to data

demotion (narrowing) the conversion of a value from a "higher" type to a "lower" type according to a programming language's precedence of data types. Demotion may cause loss of information.

derived class (subclass) the class that inherits

direct addressing accessing a variable in one step by using the variable name

documentation the written text and comments that make a program easier for others to understand, use, and modify

driver a simple `main` function that is used to call a function being tested. The use of a driver permits direct control of the testing process.

dynamic binding the run-time determination of which function to call for a particular object

dynamic data variables created during execution of a program by means of special operations. In C++, these operations are `new` and `delete`.

dynamic data structure a data structure that can expand and contract during execution

dynamic linked list a linked list composed of dynamically allocated nodes that are linked together by pointers

editor an interactive program used to create and modify source programs or data

encapsulation hiding a module implementation in a separate block with a formally specified interface

enumeration type a user-defined data type whose domain is an ordered set of literal values expressed as identifiers

enumerator one of the values in the domain of an enumeration type

event counter a variable that is incremented each time a particular event occurs

event-controlled loop a loop that terminates when something happens inside the loop body to signal that the loop should be exited

expression statement a statement formed by appending a semicolon to an expression

external (head) pointer a pointer variable that points to the first node in a dynamic linked list

external representation the printable (character) form of a data value

field (member, in C++) a component of a record

file a named area in secondary storage that is used to hold a collection of data; the collection of data itself

flow of control the order in which the computer executes statements in a program

formal parameter a variable declared in a function heading

free store (heap) a pool of memory locations reserved for allocation and deallocation of dynamic data

function a subprogram in C++

function call (function invocation) the mechanism that transfers control to a function

function call (to a void function) a statement that transfers control to a void function. In C++, this statement is the name of the function, followed by a list of actual parameters.

function definition a function declaration that includes the body of the function

function prototype a function declaration without the body of the function

function value type the data type of the result value returned by a function

functional cohesion a property of a module in which all concrete steps are directed toward solving just one problem, and any significant subproblems are written as abstract steps. The principle that a module should perform exactly one abstract action

functional equivalence a property of a module that performs exactly the same operation as the abstract step it defines. A pair of modules are also functionally equivalent to each other when they perform exactly the same operation.

general case the case for which the solution is expressed in terms of a smaller version of itself; also known as *recursive case*

hardware the physical components of a computer

hierarchical records records in which at least one of the components is itself a record

identifier a name associated with a function or data object and used to refer to that function or data object

inaccessible object a dynamic variable on the free store without any pointer pointing to it

indirect addressing accessing a variable in two steps by first using a pointer that gives the location of the variable

infinite recursion the situation in which a function calls itself over and over endlessly

information any knowledge that can be communicated

information hiding the encapsulation and hiding of implementation details to keep the user of an abstraction from depending on or incorrectly manipulating these details

inheritance a mechanism by which one class acquires the properties—the data and operations—of another class

input/output (I/O) devices the parts of the computer that accept data to be processed (input) and present the results of that processing (output)

interactive system a system that allows direct communication between user and computer

interface a connecting link at a shared boundary that allows independent systems to meet and act on or communicate with each other. Also, the formal description of the purpose of a subprogram and the mechanism for communicating with it

internal representation the form in which a data value is stored inside the memory unit

iteration an individual pass through, or repetition of, the body of a loop

iteration counter a counter variable that is incremented with each iteration of a loop

iterator an operation that allows us to process—one at a time—all the components in an instance of an ADT

length the actual number of values stored in a list

lifetime the period of time during program execution when an identifier has memory allocated to it

linked list a list in which the order of the components is determined by an explicit link member in each node, rather than by the sequential order of the components in memory

list a variable-length, linear collection of homogeneous components

literal value any constant value written in a program

local variable a variable declared within a block and not accessible outside of that block

loop a control structure that causes a sequence of statements to be executed repeatedly

loop entry the point at which the flow of control reaches the first statement inside a loop

loop exit the point at which the repetition of the loop body ends and control passes to the first statement following the loop

loop test the point at which the While expression is evaluated and the decision is made either to begin a new iteration or skip to the statement immediately following the loop

loop invariant an assertion about the characteristics of a loop that must always be true for a loop to execute properly. The invariant is true on loop entry, at the start of each loop iteration, and on exit from the loop. It is not necessarily true at each point in the body of the loop.

machine language the language, made up of binary-coded instructions, that is used directly by the computer

member selector the expression used to access components of a `struct` or `class` variable. It is formed by using the `struct` or `class` variable name and the member name, separated by a dot (period).

memory leak the loss of available memory space that occurs when dynamic data is allocated but never deallocated

memory unit internal data storage in a computer

metalanguage a language that is used to write the syntax rules for another language

mixed type (mixed mode) expression an expression that contains operands of different data types; also called *mixed mode expression*

module a self-contained collection of steps that solves a problem or subproblem; can contain both concrete and abstract steps

name precedence the precedence that a local identifier in a block has over a nonlocal identifier with the same name in any references that the block makes to that identifier; also called *name hiding*

named constant a location in memory, referenced by an identifier, where a data value that cannot be changed is stored

named type a user-defined type whose declaration includes a type identifier that gives a name to the type

nonlocal identifier any identifier declared outside a given block is said to be nonlocal with respect to that block

object-oriented design (OOD) a technique for developing a program in which the solution is expressed in terms of objects—self-contained entities composed of data and operations on that data

object-oriented programming (OOP) the use of data abstraction, inheritance, and dynamic binding to construct programs that are collections of interacting objects

object program   the machine language version of a source program

observer   an operation that allows us to observe the state of an instance of an ADT without changing it

one-dimensional array   a structured collection of components, all of the same type, that is given a single name. Each component (array element) is accessed by an index that indicates the component's position within the collection.

operating system   a set of programs that manages all of the computer's resources

out-of-bounds array index   an index value that, in C++, is either less than zero or is greater than the array size minus one

overriding   reimplementing a member function inherited from a parent class

parameter list   a mechanism by which functions communicate with each other

peripheral device   an input, output, or auxiliary storage device attached to a computer

pointer type   a simple data type consisting of an unbounded set of values, each of which addresses or otherwise indicates the location of a variable of a given type. Among the operations defined on pointer variables are assignment and test for equality.

polymorphic operation   an operation that has multiple meanings depending on the type of the object to which it is bound at run time

postcondition   an assertion that should be true after a module has executed

precision   the maximum number of significant digits

precondition   an assertion that must be true before a module begins executing

programming   planning, scheduling, or performing a task or an event

programming language   a set of rules, symbols, and special words used to construct a program

promotion (widening)   the conversion of a value from a "lower" type to a "higher" type according to a programming language's precedence of data types

range of values   the interval within which values of a numeric type must fall, specified in terms of the largest and smallest allowable values

record (structure, in C++)   a structured data type with a fixed number of components that are accessed by name, not by index. The components may be heterogeneous (of different types).

recursive algorithm   a solution that is expressed in terms of (1) smaller instances of itself and (2) a base case

recursive call   a function call in which the function being called is the same as the one making the call

recursive definition   a definition in which something is defined in terms of smaller versions of itself

reference parameter   a formal parameter that receives the location (memory address) of the caller's actual parameter

reference type   a simple data type consisting of an unbounded set of values, each of which is the address of a variable of a given type. The only operation defined on a reference variable is initialization, after which every appearance of the variable is implicitly dereferenced.

representational error   arithmetic error that occurs when the precision of the true result of an arithmetic operation is greater than the precision of the machine

reserved word   a word that has special meaning in C++; it cannot be used as a programmer-defined identifier

scope   the region of program code where it is legal to reference (use) an identifier

scope rules   the rules that determine where in the program an identifier may be accessed, given the point where that identifier is declared

self-documenting code program code containing meaningful identifiers as well as judiciously used clarifying comments

semantics the set of rules that determines the meaning of instructions written in a programming language

shallow copy an operation that copies one class object to another without copying any pointed-to data

short-circuit (conditional) evaluation evaluation of a logical expression in left-to-right order with evaluation stopping as soon as the final truth value can be determined

side effect any effect of one function on another that is not a part of the explicitly defined interface between them

significant digits those digits from the first nonzero digit on the left to the last nonzero digit on the right (plus any zero digits that are exact)

simple (atomic) data type a data type in which each value is atomic (indivisible)

software computer programs; the set of all programs available on a computer

sorting arranging the components of a list into order (for instance, words into alphabetical order or numbers into ascending or descending order)

source program a program written in a high-level programming language

static binding the compile-time determination of which function to call for a particular object

static variable a variable for which memory remains allocated throughout the execution of the entire program

string a collection of characters interpreted as a single item; in C++, a null-terminated sequence of characters stored in a `char` array

structured data type a collection of components whose organization is characterized by the method used to access

individual components. The allowable operations on a structured data type include the storage and retrieval of individual components.

structured (procedural) programming the construction of programs that are collections of interacting functions or procedures

stub a dummy function that assists in testing part of a program. A stub has the same name and interface as a function that actually would be called by the part of the program being tested, but it is usually much simpler.

switch expression the expression whose value determines which switch label is selected. It cannot be a floating point expression.

syntax the formal rules governing how valid instructions are written in a programming language

tail recursion a recursive algorithm in which no statements are executed after the return from the recursive call

termination condition the condition that causes a loop to be exited

testing the state of a stream the act of using a C++ stream variable in a logical expression as if it were a Boolean variable; the result is nonzero (TRUE) if the last I/O operation on that stream succeeded, and zero (FALSE) otherwise

top-down design a technique for developing a program in which the problem is divided into more easily handled subproblems, the solutions of which create a solution to the overall problem

transformer an operation that builds a new value of the ADT, given one or more previous values of the type

two-dimensional array a collection of components, all of the same type, structured in two dimensions. Each component is accessed by a pair of indices that represent the component's position in each dimension.

type casting   the explicit conversion of a value from one data type to another; also called type conversion

type coercion   the implicit (automatic) conversion of a value from one data type to another

unary operator   an operator that has just one operand

value parameter   a formal parameter that receives a copy of the contents of the corresponding actual parameter

value-returning function   a function that returns a single value to its caller and is invoked from within an expression

variable   a location in memory, referenced by an identifier, in which a data value that can be changed is stored

void function (procedure)   a function that does not return a function value to its caller and is invoked as a separate statement

work   a measure of the effort expended by the computer in performing a computation

ANSWERS TO SELECTED EXERCISES

CHAPTER 1   **Exam Preparation Exercises**

2. Input: Source code file (program in a high-level language such as C++)
   Output: Object code file (machine-language program). Some compilers also
   output a listing (a copy of the program with error messages and other
   information inserted).
4. The following are peripheral devices: disk drive, magnetic tape drive, printer,
   CD-ROM drive, auxiliary storage, terminal, and mouse. The arithmetic/logic unit,
   the memory, and the control unit are not peripherals.

CHAPTER 1   **Case Study Follow-Up**

1. There are many valid solutions to this question. Here is one way of dividing the
   problem:

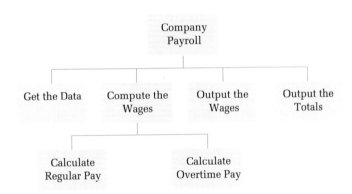

CHAPTER 2   **Exam Preparation Exercises**

1. a. invalid   b. valid   c. valid   d. invalid   e. valid
   f. invalid   g. valid   h. invalid
4. program—15; algorithm—14; compiler—3; identifier—1; compilation
   phase—12; execution phase—10; variable—11; constant—2; memory—
   13; syntax—6; semantics—8; block—7
5. a. Integer: 13   b. Floating point: −15.6   c. Floating point: 3.33333
   d. Integer: 3   e. Integer: 1   f. Illegal: Both operands of the % operator
   must be of integer type.   g. Integer: 0
7. a. reserved   b. programmer-defined   c. programmer-defined
   d. reserved   e. programmer-defined

A47

11. Cost is
    300
    Price is 30Cost is 300
    Grade A costs
    300

CHAPTER 2   Programming Warm-Up Exercises

1. Only one line needs to be changed. In the constant declaration

   ```
   const int LBS = 10;
   ```

   change 10 to 15.

3. ```
   cout << "The moon" << endl;
   cout << "is" << endl;
   cout << "blue." << endl;
   ```

CHAPTER 2   Case Study Follow-Up

1. The named constants make the program easier to read and understand. Also, to change one of the constants, you only need to change one line (the constant declaration) instead of changing every occurrence of the literal constant throughout the program.

CHAPTER 3   Exam Preparation Exercises

1. a. Floating point: 13.3333   b. Integer: 2   c. Integer: 5
   d. Floating point: 13.75   e. Integer: −4   f. Integer: 1
   g. Illegal: 10.0 / 3.0 is a floating point expression, but the % operator requires integer operands.

5. a. `iostream.h`   b. `stdlib.h`   c. `math.h`   d. `iostream.h`
   e. `iostream.h` and `iomanip.h`

9. ```
   A rolling
   stone
   ```
                  ← One blank line
   ```
   gathers
   ```
                  ← Three blank lines
   ```
   nomoss
   ```

11. False

CHAPTER 3   Programming Warm-Up Exercises

1. ```
   sum = n * (n + 1) / 2;
   ```
   ```

```
4. discriminant = sqrt(b * b - 4.0 * a * c);
   denominator = 2.0 * a;
   solution1 = (-b + discriminant) / denominator;
   solution2 = (-b - discriminant) / denominator;
```

CHAPTER 3   Case Study Follow-Up

1. Declare a constant ROUND_FACTOR (defined to be equal to the desired rounding factor, such as 100.0 for hundredths) and replace every occurrence of 10.0 with ROUND_FACTOR.

CHAPTER 4   Exam Preparation Exercises

2. a. int1 contains 17, int2 contains 13, and int3 contains 7.
   b. The leftover values remain waiting in the input stream. These values will be read by subsequent input statements (or they will be ignored if no more input statements are executed).

6. True

8. 123 147

11. Errors in the program are as follows:
    • The declaration of outData is missing:

      ofstream outData;

    • The opening of the input file is missing:

      inData.open("myfile.dat");

    • The statement

      cin >> n;

    does not read from the input file. Change cin to inData.

12. With the corrected version of the program in Exercise 11, file inData will still contain the 144 after the program is executed. File outData will contain 144, followed by a newline character.

CHAPTER 4   Programming Warm-Up Exercises

1. cin >> ch1 >> ch2 >> ch3;

3. cin >> length1 >> height1 >> length2 >> height2;

4. In the following, the value 100 is arbitrary. Any value greater than 4 will work.

```
cin.get(chr1);
cin.ignore(100, '\n');
cin.get(chr2);
```

```
       cin.ignore(100, '\n');
       cin.get(chr3);
       cin.ignore(100, '\n');
  8. #include <iostream.h>
     #include <fstream.h>

     int main()
     {
         int      val1;
         int      val2;
         int      val3;
         int      val4;
         ifstream dataIn;
         ofstream resultsOut;

         dataIn.open("myinput.dat");
         resultsOut.open("myoutput.dat");
         dataIn >> val1 >> val2 >> val3 >> val4;
         resultsOut << val1 << val2 << val3 << val4 << endl;
         return 0;
     }
```

9. Note that the problem statement said nothing about getting into the car, adjusting seatbelts, checking the mirror, or driving away. Presumably those tasks, along with starting the car, are subtasks of a larger design such as "Go to the store." Here we are concerned only with starting the car itself.

Main Module

Ensure car won't roll.
Disengage gears.
Attempt ignition.

Ensure car won't roll

Engage parking brake.
Turn wheels into curb.

Disengage gears

Push in clutch with left foot.
Move gearshift to neutral.
Release clutch.

Attempt ignition

Insert key into ignition slot.
Turn key to ON position.
Pump accelerator once.
Turn key to START position.
Release after engine catches or 5 seconds, whichever comes first.

CHAPTER 4   Case Study Follow-Up

1. Prepare File for Reading, Get Data, Find Weighted Average, Print Weighted Average, and Print Heading are concrete modules. Print Data is an abstract module because it has a submodule below it.

CHAPTER 5   Exam Preparation Exercises

2. a. No parentheses are needed.   b. No parentheses are needed.
   c. No parentheses are needed.   d. !(q && q)

6. a. 4   b. 2   c. 5   d. 3   e. 1

9. a. If-Then-Else   b. If-Then   c. If-Then   d. If-Then-Else

10. The error message is printed because there is a semicolon after the right brace of a block (compound statement).

13. Yes

CHAPTER 5   Programming Warm-Up Exercises

2. In the following statement, the outer parentheses are not required but are included for readability.

```
available = (numberOrdered <= (numberOnHand - numberReserved));
```

4. In the following statement, the parentheses are not required but are included for readability.

```
leftPage = (pageNumber % 2 == 0);
```

6.
```
if (year % 4 == 0)
    cout << year << " is a leap year." << endl;
else
{
    year = year + 4 - year % 4;
    cout << year << " is the next leap year." << endl;
}
```

7.
```
if (age > 64)
    cout << "Senior voter";
else if (age < 18)
    cout << "Under age";
else
    cout << "Regular voter";
```

9.
```
// This is a nonsense program
if (a > 0)
    if (a < 20)
    {
        cout << "A is in range." << endl;
        b = 5;
    }
```

```
            else
            {
                cout << "A is too large." << endl;
                b = 3;
            }
        else
            cout << "A is too small." << endl;
        cout << "All done." << endl;
```

CHAPTER 5   Case Study Follow-Up

```
1. if (temperature > 85)
        cout << "swimming.";
   else if (temperature > 70)
        cout << "tennis.";
   else if (temperature > 32)
        cout << "golf.";
   else if (temperature > 0)
        cout << "skiing.";
   else
        cout << "dancing.";
   cout << endl;
```

5. Use a nested If structure to eliminate the redundant testing.

```
   if ( ! (code == 'L' || code == 'P') )
        cout << "The item code is invalid." << endl;
   else if (code == 'L')
   {
        // Calculate lumber amount
        .
        .
        .
   }
   else
   {
        // Calculate plywood amount
        .
        .
        .
   }
```

CHAPTER 6   Exam Preparation Exercises

```
3. number = 1;
   while (number < 11)
   {
        cout << number << endl;
        number++;
   }
```

4. Six iterations are performed.

9. (sum contains the sum of the integers from 0 through count − 1) AND (0 ≤ count ≤ 22)

10. Telephone numbers read in as integers have many different values that could be used as sentinels. In the United States, a standard telephone number is a positive seven-digit integer (ignoring area codes) and cannot start with 0, 1, 411, or 911. Therefore, a reasonable sentinel may be negative, greater than 9999999, or less than 2000000.

13. a. (1) Change < to <=. (2) Change 1 to 0. (3) Change 20 to 21.

 b. Changes (1) and (3) make count range from 1 through 21. Change (2) makes count range from 0 through 20.

CHAPTER 6   Programming Warm-Up Exercises

```
1. dangerous = FALSE;
   while ( !dangerous )
   {
       cin >> pressure;
       if (pressure > 510.0)
           dangerous = TRUE;
   }
```

or

```
   dangerous = FALSE;
   while ( !dangerous )
   {
       cin >> pressure;
       dangerous = (pressure > 510.0);
   }
```

```
2. count28 = 0;
   loopCount = 1;
   while (loopCount <= 100)
   {
       inputFile >> number;
       if (number == 28)
           count28++;
       loopCount++;
   }
```

```
6. positives = 0;
   negatives = 0;
   cin >> number;
   while (cin)          // While NOT EOF...
   {
```

```
        if (number > 0)
            positives++;
        else if (number < 0)
            negatives++;
        cin >> number;
    }
    cout << "Number of positive numbers: " << positives << endl;
    cout << "Number of negative numbers: " << negatives << endl;

7. sum = 0;
   evenInt = 16;
   while (evenInt <= 26)
   {
       sum = sum + evenInt;
       evenInt = evenInt + 2;
   }

9. hour = 1;
   minute = 0;
   am = TRUE;
   done = FALSE;
   while ( !done )
   {
       cout << hour << ':';
       if (minute < 10)
           cout << '0';
       cout << minute;
       if (am)
           cout << " A.M." << endl;
       else
           cout << " P.M." << endl;

       minute++;
       if (minute > 59)
       {
           minute = 0;
           hour++;
           if (hour == 13)
               hour = 1;
           else if (hour == 12)
               am = !am;
       }
       if (hour == 1 && minute == 0 && am)
           done = TRUE;
   }
```

CHAPTER 6 Case Study Follow-Up

```
1. // Initialize ending condition

   cin >> temperature;
```

```
while (temperature != -999)
{
    // Update process

    cout << temperature << endl;
    if (temperature < low)          // Lowest temperature so far?
        low = temperature;
    if (temperature > high)         // Highest temperature so far?
        high = temperature;

    // Update loop ending condition

    cin >> temperature;
}
```

This is a sentinel-controlled loop.

CHAPTER 7   Exam Preparation Exercises

4. 5 3 13
   3 3 9
   9 12 30

7. For pass-by-value, parts (a) through (g) are all valid. For pass-by-reference, only parts (a) and (c) are valid.

8. 13571 (the memory address of the variable widgets).

10. The answers are 12 10 3

11. Variables in main just before Change is called: a = 10 and b = 7. Variables in Change at the moment control enters the function (before any statements are executed): x = 10, y = 7, and the value of b is undefined. Variables in main after return from Change: a = 10 (x in Change is a value parameter, so the actual parameter is not modified) and b = 17.

CHAPTER 7   Programming Warm-Up Exercises

2.
```
void RocketSimulation( /* in */      float      thrust,
                       /* inout */ float&    weight,
                       /* in */      int        timeStep,
                       /* in */      int        totalTime,
                       /* out */    float&    velocity,
                       /* out */    Boolean& outOfFuel )
```

5.
```
void Halve( /* inout */ int& firstNumber,
            /* inout */ int& secondNumber )

// Precondition:
//     firstNumber and secondNumber are assigned
```

```
// Postcondition:
//     firstNumber == firstNumber@entry / 2
//  && secondNumber == secondNumber@entry / 2

{
    .
    .
    .
}
```

7. a. Function definition:

```
void ScanHeart( /* out */ Boolean& normal )

// Postcondition:
//     normal == TRUE, if a normal heart rate (60–80) was input
//                      before EOF occurred
//            == FALSE, otherwise

{
    int heartRate;

    cin >> heartRate;
    while ((heartRate < 60 || heartRate > 80) && cin)
        cin >> heartRate;

    // At loop exit, either (heartRate >= 60 && heartRate <= 80)
    // or EOF occurred

    normal = (heartRate >= 60 && heartRate <= 80);
}
```

b. Function invocation:

```
ScanHeart(normal);
```

8. a. Function definition:

```
void Rotate( /* inout */ int& firstValue,
             /* inout */ int& secondValue,
             /* inout */ int& thirdValue  )

// This function takes three parameters and returns their values
// in a shifted order

// Precondition:
//     firstValue, secondValue, and thirdValue are assigned
// Postcondition:
//     firstValue == secondValue@entry
//  && secondValue == thirdValue@entry
//  && thirdValue == firstValue@entry
```

```
{
    int temp;      // Temporary holding variable

    // Save value of first parameter

    temp = firstValue;

    // Shift values of next two parameters

    firstValue = secondValue;
    secondValue = thirdValue;

    // Replace value of final parameter with saved value

    thirdValue = temp;
}
```

b. Test program:

```
#include <iostream.h>

void Rotate( int&, int&, int& );

int main()
{
    int int1;      // First input value
    int int2;      // Second input value
    int int3;      // Third input value

    cout << "Enter three values: ";
    cin >> int1 >> int2 >> int3;

    cout << "Before: " << int1 << ' ' << int2 << ' '
        << int3 << endl;
    Rotate(int1, int2, int3);
    cout << "After: " << int1 << ' ' << int2 << ' '
        << int3 << endl;
    return 0;
}

// The Rotate function, as above, goes here
```

CHAPTER 7   Case Study Follow-Up

```
2. void PrintData( /* in */ int    deptID,
                   /* in */ int    storeNum,
                   /* in */ float deptSales )
   {
       cout << setw(12) << "Dept " << deptID << endl;
```

```
                cout << setw(3) << storeNum << "      ";
                PrintBarGraph(deptSales);
                cout << endl;
        }
```

CHAPTER 8   Exam Preparation Exercises

1. True

5. 1 1
   1 2
   1 3

7. Yes

11. It is risky to use a reference parameter as a formal parameter of a value-returning function because it provides a mechanism for side effects to escape from the function. A value-returning function usually is designed to return a single result (the function value), which is then used in the expression that called the function. If a value-returning function declares a reference parameter and modifies the parameter, that function is returning more than one result, which is not obvious from the way the function is invoked. (However, an I/O stream variable *must* be declared as a reference parameter, even in a value-returning function.)

CHAPTER 8   Programming Warm-Up Exercises

3. Boolean NearlyEqual(/* in */ float num1,
                          /* in */ float num2,
                          /* in */ float difference)

5. float CompassHeading(/* in */ float trueCourse,
                           /* in */ float windCorrAngle,
                           /* in */ float variance,
                           /* in */ float deviation   )

```
    // Precondition:
    //      All parameters are assigned
    // Postcondition:
    //      Function value == trueCourse + windCorrAngle +
    //                          variance + deviation

    {
        return trueCourse + windCorrAngle + variance + deviation;
    }
```

8. Function body for Hypotenuse function (assuming the header file math.h has been included in order to access the sqrt function):

```
{
    return sqrt(side1*side1 + side2*side2);
}
```

13. Below, the type of `costPerOunce` and the function return type are `float` so that cost can be expressed in terms of dollars and cents (e.g., 1.23 means $1.23). These types could be integer if cost is expressed in terms of cents only (e.g., 123 means $1.23).

```
float Postage( /* in */ int   pounds,
               /* in */ int   ounces,
               /* in */ float costPerOunce )

// Precondition:
//     pounds >= 0  &&  ounces >= 0  &&  costPerOunce >= 0.0
// Postcondition:
//     Function value == (pounds * 16 + ounces) * costPerOunce

{
    return (pounds * 16 + ounces) * costPerOunce;
}
```

CHAPTER 8   Case Study Follow-Up

3. Change the body of `GetData` so that it begins as follows:

```
{
    Boolean badData;    // True if an input value is invalid

    badData = TRUE;
    while (badData)
    {
        cout << "Enter the number of crew (1 or 2)." << endl;
        cin >> crew;
        badData = (crew < 1 || crew > 2);
        if (badData)
            cout << "Invalid number of crew members." << endl;
    }

    badData = TRUE;
    while (badData)
    {
        cout << "Enter the number of passengers (0 through 8)."
            << endl;
        cin >> passengers;
        badData = (passengers < 0 || passengers > 8);
        if (badData)
            cout << "Invalid number of passengers." << endl;
    }
```

Continue in this manner to validate the closet weight (0–160 pounds), baggage weight (0–525 pounds), and amount of fuel loaded (10–565 gallons).

CHAPTER 9 **Exam Preparation Exercises**

2. False

4. False

6. MaryJoeAnneWhoops!

9. 1

13. False

CHAPTER 9 **Programming Warm-Up Exercises**

1.
```
switch (grade)
{
    case 'A' : sum = sum + 4;
               break;
    case 'B' : sum = sum + 3;
               break;
    case 'C' : sum = sum + 2;
               break;
    case 'D' : sum++;
               break;
    case 'F' : cout << "Student is on probation" << endl;
               break;    // Not required
}
```

2.
```
switch (grade)
{
    case 'A' : sum = sum + 4;
               break;
    case 'B' : sum = sum + 3;
               break;
    case 'C' : sum = sum + 2;
               break;
    case 'D' : sum++;
               break;
    case 'F' : cout << "Student is on probation" << endl;
               break;
    default  : cout << "Invalid letter grade" << endl;
               break;    // Not required
}
```

5.
```
do
{
    cout << "Enter 1, 2, or 3: ";
    cin >> response;
} while (response != 1 && response != 2 && response != 3);
```

6. ```cpp
cin >> ch;
while (cin)
{
    cout << ch;
    cin >> ch;
}
```

10. This solution returns proper results only if the precondition shown in the comments is true. Note that it returns the correct result for base$^0$, which is 1.

```cpp
int Power( /* in */ int base,
           /* in */ int exponent )

// Precondition:
//      base is assigned  &&  exponent >= 0
//   && (base to the exponent power) <= INT_MAX
// Postcondition:
//      Function value == base to the exponent power

{
    int result = 1;     // Holds intermediate powers of base
    int count;          // Loop control variable

    for (count = 1; count <= exponent; count++)
        result = result * base;
    return result;
}
```

CHAPTER 9   Case Study Follow-Up

1. Change the body of the function to the following:

```cpp
{
    if (isupper(ch))
        upperCount++;
    else if (islower(ch))
        lowerCount++;
    else if (isdigit(ch))
        digitCount++;
    else if (ch == ' ')
        blankCount++;
    else if (ch == '.' || ch == '?' || ch == '!')
        puncCount++;
    else
        leftOverCount++;
}
```
```

CHAPTER 10   Exam Preparation Exercises

3. a. `sumOfSquares += x * x;`
   b. `count--;`
      or
      `--count;`
   c. `k = (n > 8) ? 32 : 15 * n;`
5. Notice that
   the character \ is a backslash.
6. a. 1.4E+12 (to 10 digits)   b. 100.0 (to 10 digits)   c. 3.2E+5 (to 10 digits)
9. a. valid   b. invalid   c. invalid   d. valid
12. False. The angle brackets (< >) should be quotation marks.

CHAPTER 10   Programming Warm-Up Exercises

2. `cout << "Hello\tThere\n\n\n\"Ace\"";`

6. `enum CourseType {CS101, CS200, CS210, CS350, CS375, CS441};`

8. `enum DayType {MONDAY, TUESDAY, WEDNESDAY, THURSDAY, FRIDAY};`

9.
```
DayType CharToDay( /* in */ char ch1,
                   /* in */ char ch2 )
// Precondition:
//     ch1=='M' OR ch1=='W' OR ch1=='F' OR
//     (ch1=='T' && ch2=='U') OR (ch1=='T' && ch2=='H')
// Postcondition:
//     Function value == MONDAY, if ch1=='M'
//                    == TUESDAY, if (ch1=='T' && ch2=='U')
//                    == WEDNESDAY, if ch1=='W'
//                    == THURSDAY, if (ch1=='T' && ch2=='H')
//                    == FRIDAY, if ch1=='F'

{
    switch (ch1)
    {
        case 'M' : return MONDAY;
        case 'T' : if (ch2 == 'U')
                        return TUESDAY;
                   else
                        return THURSDAY;
        case 'W' : return WEDNESDAY;
        case 'F' : return FRIDAY;
    }
}
```

Case Study Follow-Up

2. The readability of the program is enhanced because we are using the actual values rather than char codes for the plays.

3. A sample might be

```
void PrintJanuary()
{
    cout << "Tracy Anderson: 1/14" << endl;
    cout << "Dallas Lightfoot: 1/27" << endl;
}
```

Exam Preparation Exercises

1. True

5. a. enum BirdType {CARDINAL, BLUEJAY, HUMMINGBIRD, ROBIN};
   b. int sightings[4];

7. 1 3 -2
   17 6 11
   4 2 2
   19 14 5
   11 15 -4

   52 40 12

9. sample [0][1][2][3][4][5][6][7]

10	9	8	7	6	5	4	3

Programming Warm-Up Exercises

```
1. void Initialize( /* out */ Boolean failing[],
                    /* in */  int      length    )

// Precondition:
//     length <= MAX_STUD
// Postcondition:
//     failing[0..length-1] == FALSE

{
    int index;   // Loop control and index variable
```

```
      for (index = 0; index < length; index++)

              // Invariant (prior to test):
              //     failing[0..index-1] == FALSE
              //  && 0 <= index <= length

          failing[index] = FALSE;
  }
```

3. void SetPassing(/* inout */   Boolean passing[],
                    /* in */   const int   score[],
                    /* in */   int   length   )

```
  // Precondition:
  //     length <= MAX_STUD
  //  && score[0..length-1] are assigned
  // Postcondition:
  //     For all i, where 0 <= i <= length-1,
  //         IF score[i] >= 60, THEN passing[i] == TRUE

  {
      int index;   // Loop control and index variable

      for (index = 0; index < length; index++)

              // Invariant (prior to test):
              //     For all i, where 0 <= i <= index-1,
              //         IF score[i] >= 60, THEN passing[i] == TRUE
              //  && 0 <= index <= length

          if (score[index] >= 60)
              passing[index] = TRUE;
  }
```

6. void SetPassing2(/* inout */   Boolean passing[],
                     /* in */   const int   score[],
                     /* in */   int   length,
                     /* in */   int   grade   )

```
  // Precondition:
  //     length <= MAX_STUD
  //  && score[0..length-1] are assigned
  // Postcondition:
  //     For all i, where 0 <= i <= length-1,
  //         IF score[i] > grade, THEN passing[i] == TRUE

  {
      int index;   // Loop control and index variable
```

```
                    for (index = 0; index < length; index++)

                        // Invariant (prior to test):
                        //      For all i, where 0 <= i <= index-1,
                        //          IF score[i] > grade, THEN passing[i] == TRUE
                        //      && 0 <= index <= length

                    if (score[index] > grade)
                        passing[index] = TRUE;
                }
```

CHAPTER 11   Case Study Follow-Up

2. No. If charList were declared to be a const formal parameter, the compiler would not allow the function body to modify the array. Specifically, the statement

```
charList[counter] = ch;
```

would generate a compile-time error.

CHAPTER 12   Exam Preparation Exercises

6. a. typedef char NameType[41];
   b. NameType oneName;
   c. NameType employeeName[100];

7. a. valid   b. valid   c. invalid   d. valid   e. valid   f. invalid
   g. invalid   h. valid
9. a. valid   b. invalid   c. valid   d. invalid   e. valid   f. invalid
   g. valid

CHAPTER 12   Programming Warm-Up Exercises

```
2. int Count( /* in */ const ItemType numList[],
              /* in */       ItemType item,
              /* in */       int      length    )

    // Precondition:
    //      length <= MAX_LENGTH
    //   && numList[0..length-1] are assigned  &&  item is assigned
    // Postcondition:
    //      Function value == number of occurrences of value "item"
    //                        in numList[0..length-1]

    {
        int index;        // Loop control and index variable
        int counter = 0;  // Number of occurrences of item
```

```
            for (index = 0; index < length; index++)

                    // Invariant (prior to test):
                    //     counter == number of occurrences of value
                    //                    "item" in numList[0..index-1]
                    //     && 0 <= index <= length

                if (numList[index] == item)
                        counter++;
            return counter;
        }
```

12. The BinSearch function remains the same until the last assignment statement. This statement should be replaced with the following code segment:

```
if (found)
    index = middle;
else
    index = first;
```

Also, the function postcondition should read:

```
//      IF item is in list
//          found == TRUE  &&  list[index] == item
//      ELSE
//          found == FALSE  &&  index is where item belongs
```

13. Assuming that BinSearch has been modified as in Exercise 12, simply replace the call to SearchOrd with a call to BinSearch.

CHAPTER 12   Case Study Follow-Up

3. Using a binary search, the number of loop iterations for an unsuccessful search of 200 items is eight (because $\log_2 128 = 7$ and $\log_2 256 = 8$). Using a sequential search, the number of loop iterations is 200.

CHAPTER 13   Exam Preparation Exercises

1. a. 6   b. 5   c. 30   d. column   e. row
5. a. valid   b. valid   c. invalid   d. valid   e. invalid   f. invalid
8. a. True   b. False   c. True   d. True

CHAPTER 13   Programming Warm-Up Exercises

```
2. void SetDiagonals( /* inout */ DataType data,
                      /* in */      int      length,
                      /* in */      char     someChar )
```

```
// Precondition:
//      length <= MAX_LENGTH  &&  someChar is assigned
// Postcondition:
//      All elements on both diagonals of the "data" array
//      contain someChar

{
    int i;          // Loop control and index variable

    for (i = 0; i < length; i++)
    {
            // Invariant (prior to test):
            //      For all k, where 0 <= k <= i-1,
            //          data[k][k] == someChar
            //       && data[k][length-k-1] == someChar
            //  && 0 <= i <= length

        data[i][i] = someChar;
        data[i][length-i-1] = someChar;
    }
}

9. int RowSum( /* in */ const TableType table,
              /* in */      int        whichRow,
              /* in */      int        colLength )

// Precondition:
//      colLength <= NUM_COLS  &&  whichRow < NUM_ROWS
//   && table[whichRow][0..colLength-1] are assigned
// Postcondition:
//      Function value == table[whichRow][0] + ...
//                          + table[whichRow][colLength-1]

{
    int col;        // Loop control and index variable
    int sum = 0;    // Accumulating sum

    for (col = 0; col < colLength; col++)

            // Invariant (prior to test):
            //      sum == table[whichRow][0] + ...
            //              + table[whichRow][col-1]
            //  && 0 <= col <= colLength

        sum = sum + table[whichRow][col];
    return sum;
}
```

CHAPTER 14   **Exam Preparation Exercises**

2. a. valid   b. invalid   c. valid   d. invalid   e. valid   f. invalid
   g. valid   h. valid   i. valid

3. a. aRef = guide[70].chart;
   b. strcpy(aCode, guide[87].chart.token[0]);
   c. guide[93].chart.token[22][0] = 'X';
   d. aRef.symbol[19][8] = aMap.mapCode[3];

5. False

7. a. hierarchical record   b. record   c. record   d. array of records
   e. array   f. array of hierarchical records   g. array of records
   h. array (string)

CHAPTER 14   **Programming Warm-Up Exercises**

1. a.

```
const int NAME_LENGTH = 21;

typedef char NameStr[NAME_LENGTH];
typedef char SSStr[12];

enum YearType {FRESHMAN, SOPHOMORE, JUNIOR, SENIOR};
enum SexType {M, F};

struct PersonType
{
    NameStr  name;
    SSStr    ssNumber;
    YearType year;
    float    gpa;
    SexType  sex;
};
```

b.

```
PersonType person;

cout << person.name << endl;
cout << person.ssNumber << endl;
switch (person.year)
{
    FRESHMAN  : cout << "Freshman" << endl;
                break;
    SOPHOMORE : cout << "Sophomore" << endl;
                break;
    JUNIOR    : cout << "Junior" << endl;
                break;
```

```
              SENIOR    : cout << "Senior" << endl;
      }
      cout << person.gpa << endl;
      if (person.sex == M)
          cout << "Male" << endl;
      else
          cout << "Female" << endl;
   c. PersonType roll[3000];


3. const int NAME_LENGTH = 31;
   const int MAX_COURSES = 50;

   enum YearType {FRESHMAN, SOPHOMORE, JUNIOR, SENIOR};
   enum GradeType {A, B, C, D, F, INCOMPLETE};
   struct DateType
   {
       int month;
       int year;
   };
   struct GradeRec
   {
       int       courseID;
       GradeType grade;
   };
   typedef GradeRec GradeArray[MAX_COURSES];
   typedef char NameStr[NAME_LENGTH];

   struct StudentType
   {
       NameStr    name;
       long       studentID;
       int        hoursToDate;
       int        coursesToDate;
       GradeArray courseGrades;
       DateType   firstEnrolled;
       YearType   year;
       float      gpa;
   };


10. struct String
    {
        char str[21];
        int  length;
    };
       .
       .
       .

    int StrLength( /* in */ String aString )
    {
        return aString.length;
    }
```

CHAPTER 14   Case Study Follow-Up

1. Assuming a variable `areaCode` is of type `int`, one solution is to print a leading zero if the area code is less than 100:

```
if (areaCode < 100)
    cout << '0';
cout << areaCode;
```

Another solution is to declare an area code to be a string rather than an `int`, thereby reading or printing exactly three characters each time I/O takes place.

CHAPTER 15   Exam Preparation Exercises

3. a. `SomeClass` and `int`   b. `Func1`, `Func2`, `Func3`, and `someInt`
   c. `object1` and `object2`   d. `Func1`, `Func2`, and `Func3`   e. `Func1` and `Func3`
   f. part (ii)
4. True
8. a. Only `myprog.cpp` must be recompiled.   b. All of the object (`.obj`) files must be relinked.   c. Only `file2.cpp` and `file3.cpp` must be recompiled.
   d. All of the object (`.obj`) files must be relinked.

CHAPTER 15   Programming Warm-Up Exercises

1. a. `if ( !time1.Equal(time2) )`
      `n = 1;`

   b. `if (time1.LessThan(time2) || time1.Equal(time2))`
      `n = 5;`

   c. `if (time2.LessThan(time1))`
      `n = 8;`

   d. `if ( !time1.LessThan(time2) )`
      `n = 5;`

   or

   `if (time2.LessThan(time1) || time2.Equal(time1))`
   `n = 5;`

3. Function specification (within the `TimeType` class declaration):

```
void WriteAmPm() const;
    // Postcondition:
    //      Time has been output in 12-hour form
    //          HH:MM:SS AM   or   HH:MM:SS PM
```

Function definition (omitting the postcondition to save space):

```
void TimeType::WriteAmPm() const
{
    Boolean am;         // True if AM should be printed
    int     tempHrs;    // Value of hours to be printed

    am = (hrs <= 11);
    if (hrs == 0)
        tempHrs = 12;
    else if (hrs >= 13)
        tempHrs = hrs - 12;
    else
        tempHrs = hrs;

    if (tempHrs < 10)
        cout << '0';
    cout << tempHrs << ':';
    if (mins < 10)
        cout << '0';
    cout << mins << ':';
    if (secs < 10)
        cout << '0';
    cout << secs;
    if (am)
        cout << " AM";
    else
        cout << " PM";
}
```

4. Function specification (within the TimeType class declaration):

```
long Minus( /* in */ TimeType time2 ) const;
    // Precondition:
    //     This time and time2 represent times in the same day
    // Postcondition:
    //     Function value == (this time) - time2, in seconds
```

Function definition (omitting the precondition and postcondition to save space):

```
long TimeType::Minus( /* in */ TimeType time2 ) const
{
    long thisTimeInSecs;    // This time in seconds since midnight
    long time2InSecs;       // time2 in seconds since midnight

    // Using 3600 seconds per hour and 60 seconds per minute...

    thisTimeInSecs = long(hrs)*3600 + long(mins)*60 + long(secs);
    time2InSecs = long(time2.hrs)*3600 + long(time2.mins)*60 +
                  long(time2.secs);
    return thisTimeInSecs - time2InSecs;
}
```

CHAPTER 15 Case Study Follow-Up

1. The class constructor `DateType()` is a constructor operation. `Set` and `Increment` are transformers. `Month`, `Day`, `Year`, `Print`, and `ComparedTo` are observers.

CHAPTER 16 Exam Preparation Exercises

2. False
4. *Class Abc:*
   a. The private data members are `alpha` and `beta`.
   b. Functions `DoThis` and `DoThat` can reference `alpha` and `beta` directly.
   c. Functions `DoThis` and `DoThat` can invoke each other directly.
   d. Clients can invoke `DoThis`.
   Class Xyz:
   a. The private data members are `alpha`, `beta`, and `gamma`.
   b. Function `TryIt` can reference only `gamma` directly.
   c. Function `TryIt` can invoke the parent class's `DoThis` function directly. The syntax for the function call is `Abc::DoThis()`.
   d. Clients can invoke `DoThis` and `TryIt`.
7. a. Member slicing occurs, and static binding is used. The output is

   x
   y

   b. Member slicing does not occur, and dynamic binding is used. The output is

   x
   yz

   c. Member slicing does not occur, but static binding is used. The output is

   x
   y

9. a. False   b. True   c. False

CHAPTER 16 Programming Warm-Up Exercises

2. ```
   #include <math.h>     // For sqrt()
       :
       :

   float Line::Length() const

   // Postcondition:
   //      Function value == length of this line

   {
   ```
   ```

```
        float diffX;    // Difference in x coordinates
        float diffY;    // Difference in y coordinates

        diffX = startPt.X_Coord() - endPt.X_Coord();
        diffY = startPt.Y_Coord() - endPt.Y_Coord();
        return sqrt(diffX*diffX + diffY*diffY);
    }
```

3. ```
   class InterAddress : public Address
   {
   public:
       void Write() const;
           // Postcondition:
           //     Address has been output

       InterAddress( /* in */ const String20 newStreet,
                     /* in */ const String20 newCity,
                     /* in */ const String20 newState,
                     /* in */ const String20 newZip,
                     /* in */ const String20 newCountry );
           // Precondition:
           //     All parameters are assigned
           // Postcondition:
           //     Class object is constructed with private data
           //     initialized by the incoming parameters
   private:
       String20 country;
   };
   ```

7. ```
   class TimeAndDay
   {
   public:
       void Set( /* in */ int hours,
                 /* in */ int minutes,
                 /* in */ int seconds,
                 /* in */ int month,
                 /* in */ int day,
                 /* in */ int year     );
           // Precondition:
           //     0 <= hours <= 23  &&  0 <= minutes <= 59
           //  && 0 <= seconds <= 59  &&  1 <= month <= 12
           //  && 1 <= day <= maximum no. of days in month
           //  && 1582 < year
           // Postcondition:
           //     Time and date are set according to the
           //     incoming parameters

       void Increment();
           // Postcondition:
           //     Time has been advanced by one second, with
   ```

```
//       23:59:59 wrapping around to 0:0:0
//    && IF new time is 0:0:0
//          Date has been advanced to the next day

    void Write() const;
    // Postcondition:
    //     Time and date have been output in the form
    //          HH:MM:SS  month day, year

    TimeAndDay();
    // Postcondition:
    //     Class object is constructed with a time of 0:0:0
    //     and a date of January 1, 1583
private:
    TimeType time;
    DateType date;
};
```

CHAPTER 17   Exam Preparation Exercises

4. The `delete` operation releases the space reserved for a dynamic variable back to the system.

5. a. inaccessible object   b. dangling pointer   c. dangling pointer
   d. neither   e. inaccessible object

7. The correct answer is (a).

11.
```
Constructor executing
Private data is 1
Destructor executing
Constructor executing
Private data is 2
Destructor executing
Constructor executing
Private data is 3
Destructor executing
```

13. The correct answer is (e).

CHAPTER 17   Programming Warm-Up Exercises

1. a. `char* p = &ch;`
   b. `long* q = arr;`

   or

   `long* q = &arr[0];`
   c. `BoxType* r = &box;`

2. a. `*p = '@';`

   b. `*q = 959263;`

   c.
```
r->length = 12;        (*r).length = 12;
r->width = 14;    or   (*r).width = 14;
r->height = 5;         (*r).height = 5;
```

6.
```
if (*p < *q)
    smaller = *p;
else
    smaller = *q;
delete p;
delete q;
```

10. `AddAndIncr(m, &n, &theirSum);`

CHAPTER 17   Case Study Follow-Up

4. Change the function headings for `ValueAt` and `Store` so that the data types match those in the function prototypes. The bodies of `ValueAt`, `Store`, and the destructor do not need to be changed. Change the bodies of the constructor, copy-constructor, and `CopyFrom` functions by replacing

```
arr = new int[size];
```

with

```
arr = new float[size];
```

CHAPTER 18   Exam Preparation Exercises

2. True
5. Dynamic data structures can expand and contract during program execution.
8. a. array   b. array   c. dynamic linked list

CHAPTER 18   Programming Warm-Up Exercises

1. Function specification (within the `OrdList` class declaration):

```
int Length() const;
    // Postcondition:
    //      Function value == number of components in list
```

Function definition:

```
int OrdList::Length() const
{
    NodePtr currPtr = head;      // Loop control pointer
    int     count = 0;           // Number of nodes in list

    while (currPtr != NULL)
    {
            // Invariant (prior to test):
            //     count == number of nodes preceding *currPtr
            //   && currPtr points to a list node or == NULL

        count++;
        currPtr = currPtr->link;
    }
    return count;
}
```

5. In each function, after the statement

```
newNodePtr = new NodeType;
```

insert the following:

```
if (newNodePtr == NULL)
{
    cout << "Not enough memory to insert " << item << endl;
    exit(1);
}
```

Change the postcondition for InsertTop to the following:

```
// IF not enough memory to add item to list
//     Program has halted with an error message
// ELSE
//     New node containing item is inserted at top of linked list
//   && component members of list nodes are in ascending order
```

Change the postcondition for Insert to the following:

```
// IF not enough memory to add item to list
//     Program has halted with an error message
// ELSE
//     New node containing item is inserted into its proper place
//     in linked list
//   && component members of list nodes are in ascending order
```

CHAPTER 18   Case Study Follow-Up

1. a. The functions Length, CardAt, InsertTop, RemoveTop, Shuffle, Recreate, and
      the class constructor are public members of the CardDeck class.

   b. The variables head and listLength and the function Merge are private
      members of the CardDeck class.

CHAPTER 19   Exam Preparation Exercises

2. False. Both void functions and value-returning functions can be recursive.

4. $F(4) = 1$, $F(6) = -1$, and $F(5)$ is undefined.

6. A selection control structure—either an If or a Switch statement

9. The run-time stack

CHAPTER 19   Programming Warm-Up Exercises

```
1. int F( /* in */ int n )
   {
       if (n == 0 || n == 1)
           return 1;
       else
           return F(n - 1) + F(n - 2);
   }
```

```
3. void DoubleSpace( /* inout */ ifstream& inFile )
   {
       char ch;

       inFile.get(ch);
       while (inFile)                      // While not EOF...
       {
           cout << ch;
           if (ch == '\n')
               cout << endl;
           inFile.get(ch);
       }
   }
```

8. In the If statement of the RevPrint function, change the sequence

```
   RevPrint(head->link);                 // Recursive call
   cout << head->component << endl;
```

to

```
cout << head->component << endl;
RevPrint(head->link);                              // Recursive call
```

and reword the function postcondition accordingly.

CHAPTER 19   Case Study Follow-Up

2. 0, the index of the first array element. The recursive algorithm starts at the fifth element but recursively calls itself until it reaches the first element, which is stored into minSoFar; then it compares minSoFar to the second element, and so on.

INDEX

A79